WRITING COACH

WELCOME TO Writing COACH

Seven Great Reasons to Learn to Write Well

Acknowledgments appear on page R55, which constitute an extension of this copyright page.

PEARSON

0-13-253145-3
978-0-13-253145-0
7 8 9 10 V063 14 13

PRENTICE HALL
WRITING COACH

PEARSON

Upper Saddle River, New Jersey
Boston, Massachusetts
Chandler, Arizona
Glenview, Illinois

1 Writing is hard, but hard is **rewarding**.

2 Writing helps you **sort things out**.

3 Writing helps you **persuade** others.

4 Writing makes you a **better reader**.

5 Writing makes you **smarter**.

6 Writing helps you get into and through **college**.

7 Writing **prepares you** for the world of work.

AUTHORS

The contributing authors guided the direction and philosophy of *Prentice Hall Writing Coach*. Working with the development team, they helped to build the pedagogical integrity of the program and to ensure its relevance for today's teachers and students.

Program Authors

Jeff Anderson

Jeff Anderson has worked with struggling writers and readers for almost 20 years. His works integrate grammar and editing instruction into the processes of reading and writing. Anderson has written articles in NCTE's *Voices from the Middle, English Journal*, and *Educational Leadership.* Anderson won the NCTE Paul and Kate Farmer Award for his *English Journal* article on teaching grammar in context. He has published two books, *Mechanically Inclined: Building Grammar, Usage, and Style into Writer's Workshop* and *Everyday Editing: Inviting Students to Develop Skill and Craft in Writer's Workshop* as well as a DVD, *The Craft of Grammar.*

> Grammar gives me a powerful lens through which to look at my writing. It gives me the freedom to say things exactly the way I want to say them.

Kelly Gallagher

Kelly Gallagher is a full-time English teacher at Magnolia High School in Anaheim, California. He is the former co-director of the South Basin Writing Project at California State University, Long Beach. Gallagher is the author of *Reading Reasons: Motivational Mini-Lessons for the Middle and High School, Deeper Reading: Comprehending Challenging Texts 4–12, Teaching Adolescent Writers,* and *Readicide.* He is also featured in the video series, *Building Adolescent Readers.* With a focus on adolescent literacy, Gallagher provides training to educators on a local, national and international level. Gallagher was awarded the Secondary Award of Classroom Excellence from the California Association of Teachers of English—the state's top English teacher honor.

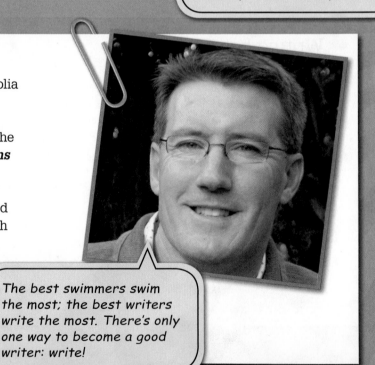

> The best swimmers swim the most; the best writers write the most. There's only one way to become a good writer: write!

Contributing Authors

Evelyn Arroyo

Evelyn Arroyo is the author of **A+RISE**, Research-based Instructional Strategies for ELLs (English Language Learners). Her work focuses on closing the achievement gap for minority students and English language learners. Through her publications and presentations, Arroyo provides advice, encouragement, and practical success strategies to help teachers reach their ELL students.

Your rich, colorful cultural life experiences are unique and can easily be painted through words. These experiences define who you are today, and writing is one way to begin capturing your history. Become a risk-taker and fall in love with yourself through your own words.

When you're learning a new language, writing in that language takes effort. The effort pays off big time, though. Writing helps us generate ideas, solve problems, figure out how the language works, and, above all, allows us to express ourselves.

Jim Cummins, Ph.D.

Jim Cummins is a Professor in the Modern Language Centre at the University of Toronto. A well-known educator, lecturer, and author, Cummins focuses his research on bilingual education and the academic achievement of culturally diverse students. He is the author of numerous publications, including **Negotiating Identities: Education for Empowerment in a Diverse Society**.

Grant Wiggins, Ed.D.

Grant Wiggins is the President of Authentic Education. He earned his Ed.D. from Harvard University. Grant consults with schools, districts, and state education departments; organizes conferences and workshops; and develops resources on curricular change. He is the co-author, with Jay McTighe, of **Understanding By Design,** the award-winning text published by ASCD.

I hated writing as a student—and my grades showed it. I grew up to be a writer, though. What changed? I began to think I had something to say. That's ultimately why you write: to find out what you are really thinking, really feeling, really believing.

Concepts of grammar can sharpen your reading, communication, and even your reasoning, so I have championed its practice in my classes and in my businesses. Even adults are quick to recognize that a refresher in grammar makes them keener—and more marketable.

Gary Forlini

Gary Forlini is managing partner of the School Growth initiative **Brinkman—Forlini—Williams,** which trains school administrators and teachers in Classroom Instruction and Management. His recent works include the book **Help Teachers Engage Students** and the data system **ObserverTab** for district administrators, **Class Acts: Every Teacher's Guide To Activate Learning**, and the initiative's workshop **Grammar for Teachers**.

CONTENTS IN BRIEF
WRITING

WRITING GAME PLAN

1 You, the Writer

2 Types of Writing

3 The Writing Process

4 Sentences, Paragraphs, and Compositions

Writing without grammar only goes so far. Grammar and writing work together. To write well, grammar skills give me great tools.

CORE WRITING CHAPTERS

5 Nonfiction Narration
Memoir
Memoir Storyboard
Script for a Documentary
Writing for Assessment

6 Fiction Narration
Historical Fiction
Script Conveying Historical Themes
Pitch for a Historical Fiction Screenplay
Writing for Assessment

7 Poetry and Description
Ballad or Free Verse Poem
Poetry Collage
Definition Essay
Writing for Assessment

8 Exposition
Pro-Con Essay
Pro-Con Analysis Television Report
Summary of a Feature Article
Writing for Assessment

9 Persuasion
Speech
Speech to Persuade
Proposal
Writing for Assessment

10 Response to Literature
Response to Literature Essay
Movie Trailer Ad for a Favorite Story
Script Adaptation
Writing for Assessment

11 Research
Informational Research Report
Script Based on a Research Report
Television Interview Script
Writing for Assessment

12 Workplace Writing
College Application Essay
Cover Letter
Proposal
Research Report for College Day
Request for a Letter of Recommendation
Writing for Assessment

WRITING COACH
Online

Interactive Writing Coach™

Interactive Graphic Organizer

Interactive Model

Online Journal

Resources

Video

GRAMMAR

GRAMMAR GAME PLAN

 Find It FIX IT  **20** **Major Grammatical Errors and How to Fix Them**

> *Grammar without writing is only a collection of rules, but when these rules are put into action as I write, the puzzle comes together.*

CORE GRAMMAR CHAPTERS

STUDENT RESOURCES

Handbooks
Glossaries

WRITING COACH

Online

www.phwritingcoach.com

- **Grammar Tutorials**
- **Grammar Practice**
- **Grammar Games**

Writing COACH : How to Use This Program

This program is organized into two distinct sections: one for WRITING and one for GRAMMAR.

In the **WRITING** section, you'll learn strategies, traits, and skills that will help you become a better writer.

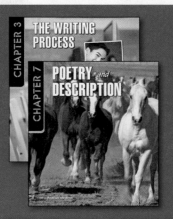
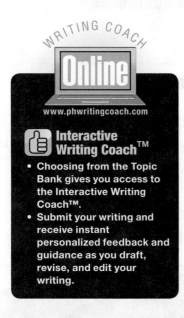

In the **GRAMMAR** section, you'll learn the rules and conventions of grammar, usage, and mechanics.

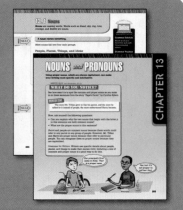

What DIGITAL writing and grammar resources are available?

The Writing Coach Online boxes will indicate opportunities to use online tools.

In **Writing,** use the **Interactive Writing Coach™** in two ways to get personalized guidance and support for your writing.

- Paragraph Feedback and
- Essay Scorer

WRITING COACH
Online
www.phwritingcoach.com

Interactive Writing Coach™

- **Choosing from the Topic Bank** gives you access to the Interactive Writing Coach™.
- **Submit your writing** and receive instant personalized feedback and guidance as you draft, revise, and edit your writing.

WRITING COACH
Online
www.phwritingcoach.com

Grammar Tutorials
Brush up on your grammar skills with these animated videos.

Grammar Practice
Practice your grammar skills with Writing Coach Online.

Grammar Games
Test your knowledge of grammar in this fast-paced interactive video game.

In **Grammar,** view grammar tutorials, practice your grammar skills, and play grammar video games.

What will you find in the WRITING section?

Writing Genre

Each chapter introduces a different **writing genre.**

Learn about the key characteristics of the **genre** before you start writing.

Focus on a single form of the genre with the **Feature Assignment**.

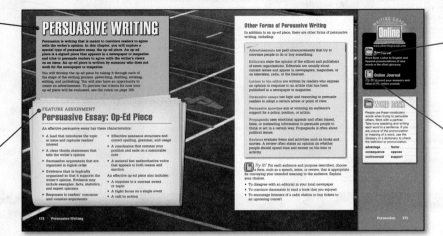

Writing Coach Online

- View the **Word Bank** words in the eText glossary, and hear them pronounced in both English and Spanish.

- Use your **Online Journal** to record your answers and ideas as you respond to *Try It!* activities.

Mentor Text and Student Model

The **Mentor Text** and **Student Model** provide examples of the genre featured in each chapter.

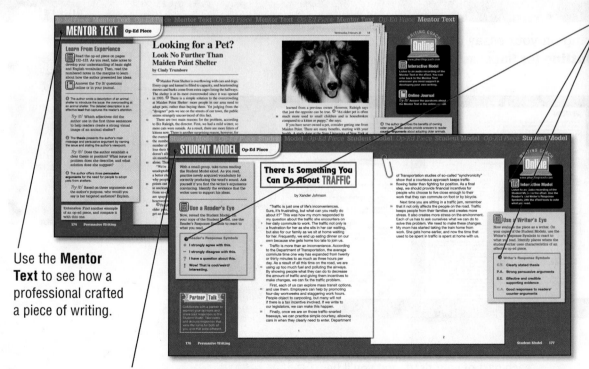

Writing Coach Online

- Use the **Interactive Model** to mark the text with Reader's and Writer's Response Symbols.

- Listen to an audio recording of the **Mentor Text** or **Student Model.**

Use the **Mentor Text** to see how a professional crafted a piece of writing.

Review the **Student Model** as a guide for composing your own piece.

The **Topic Bank** provides prompts for the **Feature Assignment**.

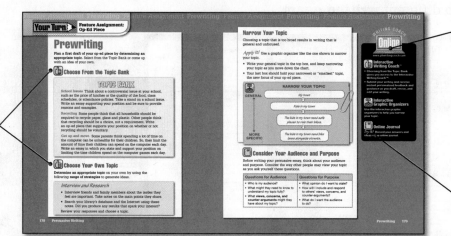

Choose from a bank of topics, or follow steps to find an idea of your own.

Whether you are working on your essay drafts online or with a pen and paper, an **Outline for Success** can get you started.

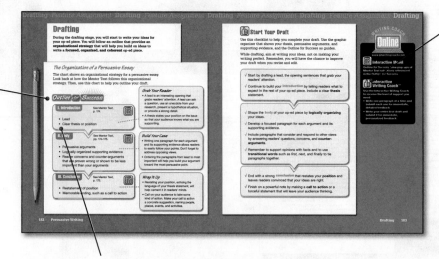

Consult this **outline** for a quick visual specific to the writing task assigned in each chapter.

Follow the bulleted suggestions for each part of your draft, and you'll be on your way to success.

Revision RADaR

You can use the **Revision RADaR** strategy as a guide for making changes to improve your draft.

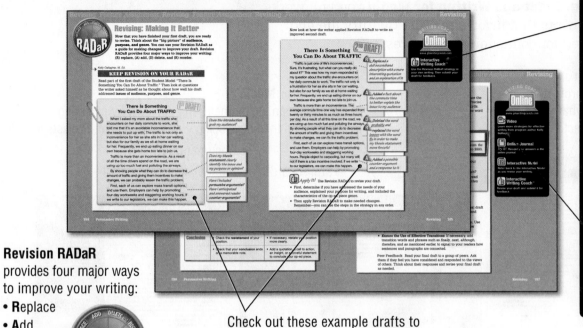

Revision RADaR

provides four major ways to improve your writing:

- **R**eplace
- **A**dd
- **D**elete
- **R**eorder

Check out these example drafts to see how to apply **Revision RADaR.**

What Do You Notice?

In the editing stage, **What Do You Notice?** and **Mentor Text** help you zoom in on powerful sentences.

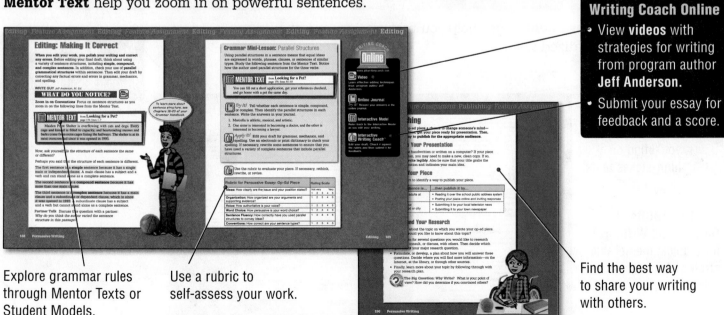

Explore grammar rules through Mentor Texts or Student Models.

Use a rubric to self-assess your work.

Find the best way to share your writing with others.

How do end-of-chapter features help you apply what you've learned?

21st Century Learning

In **Make Your Writing Count** and **Writing for Media** you will work on innovative assignments that involve the 21st Century life and career skills you'll need for communicating successfully.

Make Your Writing Count
Work collaboratively on project-based assignments and share what you have learned with others. Projects include:

- Debates
- TV Talk Shows
- News Reports

Writing for Media
Complete an assignment on your own by exploring media forms, and then developing your own content. Projects include:

- Blogs
- Storyboards
- Documentary Scripts
- Multimedia Presentations

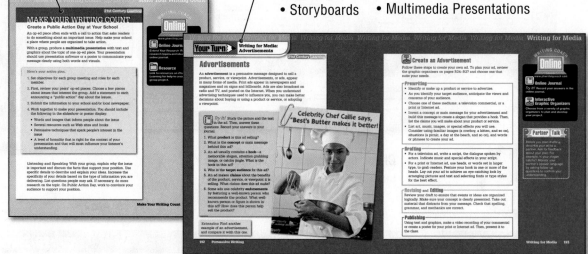

Test Prep

The **Writing for Assessment** pages help you prepare for important standardized tests.

Notice these icons that emphasize the types of writing you'll find on high-stakes tests.

Use **The ABCDs of On-Demand Writing** for a quick, memorable strategy for success.

Writing Coach Online
Submit your essay for feedback and a score.

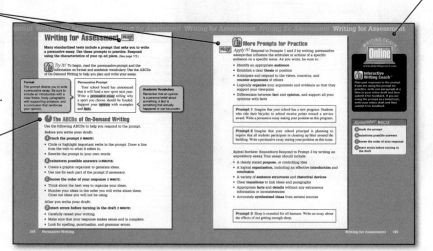

What will you find in the GRAMMAR section?

Grammar Game Plan

The **Find It/Fix It** reference guide helps you fix the **20** most common errors in student writing.

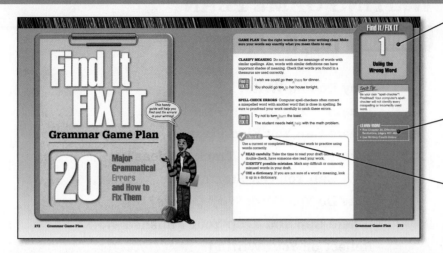

Study each of the 20 common errors and their corrections, which are clearly explained on each page.

Follow cross-references to more instruction in the grammar chapters.

Review the **Check It** features for strategies to help you avoid these errors.

Grammar Chapters

Each grammar chapter begins with a **What Do You Notice?** feature and **Mentor Text.**

Use the **Mentor Text** to help you zoom in on powerful sentences. It showcases the correct use of written language conventions.

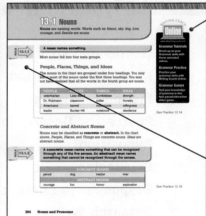

Writing Coach Online
The **Writing Coach Online** digital experience for Grammar helps you focus on just the lessons and practice you need.

Use the grammar section as a quick reference handbook. Each **grammar rule** is highlighted and numbered.

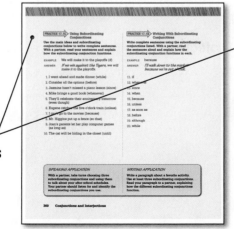

Try **Practice** pages and **Test Warm-Ups** to help you check your progress.

WRITING

WRITING GAME PLAN

CONTENTS

WRITING COACH

Online

www.phwritingcoach.com

All content available online

- Interactive Writing Coach™
- Interactive Graphic Organizer
- Interactive Models
- Online Journal
- Resources
- Video

WRITING

Connect to the Big Questions

- **What do you think?**
  What stories do sports tell best?

- **Why write?**
  What should we put in and leave out to be accurate and honest?

Connect to the Big Questions

- **What do you think?**
  Do we adapt our environment or adapt to it?

- **Why write?**
  What can fiction do better than nonfiction?

WRITING COACH

Online

www.phwritingcoach.com

All content available online

- Interactive Writing Coach™
- Interactive Graphic Organizer
- Interactive Models
- Online Journal
- Resources
- Video

WRITING

Connect to the Big Questions

- **What do you think?**
  What do music, art, and poetry best communicate?

- **Why write?**
  How do we best convey feelings through words on a page?

WRITING

Connect to the Big Questions

- **What do you think?**
  In team sports, how important is the individual?

- **Why write?**
  What is your point of view? How will you know if you've convinced others?

WRITING

Connect to the Big Questions

- **What do you think?**
  How important is it to explore the unknown?

- **Why write?**
  Do you understand a subject well enough to write about it? How will you find out what the facts are?

Connect to the Big Questions

• **What do you think?**
Which is more important—expertise or collaboration?

• **Why write?**
What do daily workplace communications require of format, content, and style?

WRITING COACH

Online

www.phwritingcoach.com

All content available online

• Interactive Writing Coach™
• Interactive Graphic Organizer
• Interactive Models
• Online Journal
• Resources
• Video

GRAMMAR

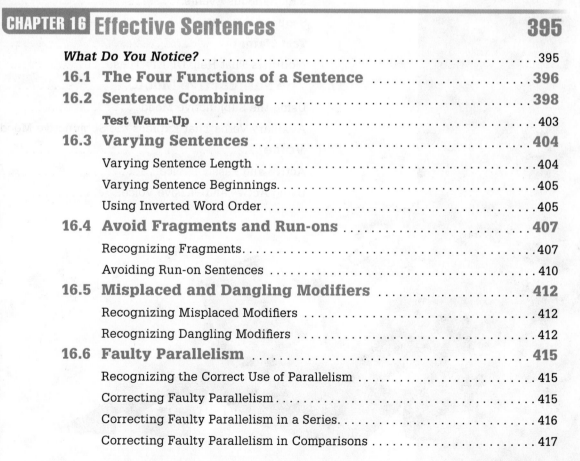

WRITING COACH

Online

www.phwritingcoach.com

All content available online
- Grammar Tutorials
- Grammar Practice
- Grammar Games

GRAMMAR

USAGE

WRITING COACH

Online

www.phwritingcoach.com

All content available online
- Grammar Tutorials
- Grammar Practice
- Grammar Games

GRAMMAR

MECHANICS

CHAPTER 23 Punctuation 563

WRITING COACH

Online

www.phwritingcoach.com

All content available online

- **Grammar Tutorials**
- **Grammar Practice**
- **Grammar Games**

GRAMMAR

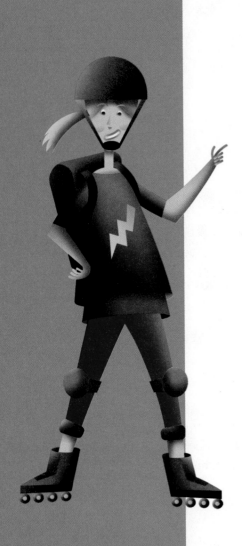

WRITING COACH

Online

www.phwritingcoach.com

All content available online
- **Grammar Tutorials**
- **Grammar Practice**
- **Grammar Games**

STUDENT RESOURCES

NONFICTION NARRATION *Memoir* FICTION NARRATION *Historical Fict*

peech RESPONSE TO LITERATURE *Response to Literature Essay* RESEAR

over Letter, Proposal NONFICTION NARRATION *Memoir* FICTION NAR

ssay PERSUASION *Speech* RESPONSE TO LITERATURE *Response to Liter*

pplication Essay, Cover Letter, Proposal NONFICTION NARRATION *Mem*

OSITION Pro-Con Essay PERSUASION *Speech* RESPONSE TO LITERATUR

RITING College Application Essay, Cover Letter, Proposal NONFICTION N

ree Verse Poem EXPOSITION *Pro-Con Essay* PERSUASION *Speech* RESPO

eport WORKPLACE WRITING *College Application Essay, Cover Letter, Prope*

Writing

CHAPTER 1

YOU, THE WRITER

Why Do You Write?

Writing well is one of the most important life skills you can develop. Being a good writer can help you achieve success in school and beyond. Most likely, you write for many reasons. You write:

To Share

You probably often write to **share** your experiences with others. Writing can be an easy way to **reach out** to people and connect with them.

To Persuade People

Writing can also be an effective way to **persuade** people to consider your opinions. For example, you may find it's easier to convince someone of your point of view when you've effectively organized your thoughts in an essay or a letter.

To Inform

Another reason to write is to **inform.** Perhaps you want to tell an audience how you built your computer network or how you finally got your e-mail to function properly.

To Enjoy

Personal fullfillment is another important motivation for writing, since writing enables you **to express** your thoughts and feelings. In addition, writing can also help you recall an event, or let you escape from everyday life.

Fortunately, writing well is a skill you can learn and one that you can continue to improve and polish. This program will help you improve your writing skills and give you useful information about the many types of writing.

What Do You Write?

Writing is already an important part of your everyday life. Each day is full of opportunities to write, allowing you to capture, express, think through, and share your thoughts and feelings, and demonstrate what you know. Here are some ways you might write.

- Recording thoughts in a journal
- Texting friends or posting on social networking sites
- E-mailing thank-you notes to relatives
- Creating lists of things to do or things you like
- Writing research reports, nonfiction accounts, fiction stories, and essays in school

How Can You Find Ideas?

The good news is that ideas are all around you. You just need to be aware of the rich resources that are available.

By Observing

Observing is a good way to start to find ideas. Did you see anything interesting on your way to school? Was there something unusual about the video game you played last night?

By Reading

Reading is another useful option—look through newspaper articles and editorials, magazines, blogs, and Web sites. Perhaps you read something that surprised you or really made you feel concerned. Those are exactly the subjects that can lead to the ideas you want to write about.

By Watching

Watching is another way to get ideas— watch online videos or television programs, for example.

" Writer to Writer "

I write when I want to be heard or connect. Writing lets me be a vital part of my community and reach outside it as well. All the while, I get to be me—my unique self.

—Jeff Anderson

How Can You Keep Track of Ideas?

You may sometimes think of great writing ideas in the middle of the night or on the way to math class. These strategies can help you remember those ideas.

Start an Idea Notebook or a Digital Idea File

Reserving a small **notebook** to record ideas can be very valuable. Just writing the essence of an idea, as it comes to you, can later help you develop a topic or essay. A **digital idea file** is exactly the same thing—but it's recorded on your computer, cell phone, or other electronic device.

Keep a Personal Journal

Many people find that keeping a **journal** of their thoughts is helpful. Then, when it's time to select an idea, they can flip through their journal and pick up on the best gems they wrote—sometimes from long ago.

Maintain a Learning Log

A **learning log** is just what it sounds like—a place to record information you have learned, which could be anything from methods of solving equations to computer shortcuts. Writing about something in a learning log might later inspire you to conduct further research on the same topic.

Free Write

Some individuals find that if they just let go and write whatever comes to mind, they eventually produce excellent ideas. **Free writing** requires being relaxed and unstructured. This kind of writing does not require complete sentences, correct spelling, or proper grammar. Whatever ends up on the paper or on the computer screen is fine. Later, the writer can go back and tease out the best ideas.

How Can You Get Started?

Every writer is different, so it makes sense that all writers should try out techniques that might work well for them. Regardless of your personal writing style, these suggestions should help you get started.

Get Comfortable

It's important to find and create an environment that encourages your writing process. Choose a spot where interruptions will be minimal and where you'll find it easy to concentrate. Some writers prefer a quiet library. Others prefer to work in a room with music playing softly on their computer.

Have Your Materials Ready

Before starting to write, gather all the background materials you need to get started, including your notes, free writing, reader's journal, and portfolio. Make sure you also have writing tools, such as a pen and paper or a computer.

Spend Time Wisely

Budgeting your available writing time is a wise strategy. Depending on your writing goal, you may want to sketch out your time on a calendar, estimating how long to devote to each stage of the writing process. Then, you can assign deadlines to each part. If you find a particular stage takes longer than you estimated, simply adjust your schedule to ensure that you finish on time.

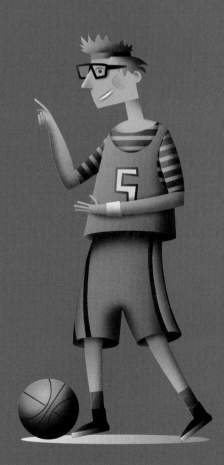

◀	October	▶				
SUNDAY	MONDAY	TUESDAY	WEDNESDAY	THURSDAY	FRIDAY	SATURDAY
		1 Start Research	2 Finish Research	3 Write Outline	4	5
6	7	8 Finish First Draft	9 Finish Revising	10 Finish Proofreading	11	12
13	14 DUE DATE	15	16	17	18	19
20	21	22	23	24	25	26
27	28	29	30	31		

How Do You Work With Others?

If you think of writing as a solitary activity, think again. Working with others can be a key part of the writing process.

Brainstorming

Brainstorming works when everyone in a group feels free to suggest ideas, whether they seem commonplace or brilliant.

Cooperative Writing

Cooperative writing is a process in which each member of a group concentrates on a different part of an assignment. Then, the group members come together to discuss their ideas and write drafts.

Peer Feedback

Peer feedback comes from classmates who have read your writing and offered suggestions for improvements. When commenting on a classmate's work, it's important to provide constructive, or helpful, criticism.

21st Century Learning

Collaborate and Discuss

In **collaborative writing,** each group member takes an assigned role on a writing project. A collaborative group may decide on such possible roles as leader, facilitator, recorder, and listener. The roles may change as the group discusses and works through the writing process. The goal, however, is to work and rework the writing until all members feel they have produced the best result.

Possible Roles in a Collaborative Writing Project

LEADER	**FACILITATOR**	**COMPROMISER**	**LISTENER**
Initiates the discussion by clearly expressing group goals and moderates discussions	Works to move the discussion forward and clarify ideas	Works to find practical solutions to differences of opinion	Actively listens and serves to recall details that were discussed

Using Technology

Technology allows collaboration to occur in ways that were previously unthinkable.

- By working together on the Internet, students around the world have infinite opportunities to collaborate online on a wide range of projects.

- Collaboration can range from projects that foster community cooperation, such as how to improve debates during local elections, to those that increase global awareness, such as focusing on how to encourage more recycling.

- Being able to log in and to contribute to media, such as journals, blogs, and social networks, allows you to connect globally, express your views in writing, and join a world-wide conversation.

Where Can You Keep Your Finished Work?

A **portfolio,** or growing collection of your work, is valuable for many reasons. It can serve as a research bank of ideas and as a record of how your writing is improving. You can create a portfolio on a computer or in a folder or notebook. You'll learn more about managing a portfolio in chapter 3.

A **Reader's Journal,** in which you record quotes and ideas from your reading, can also be used to store original ideas. Your journal can be housed on a computer or in a notebook.

Reflect on Your Writing

Analyzing, making inferences, and drawing conclusions about how you find ideas can help you become a better, more effective writer. Find out more about how you write by asking yourself questions like these:

- Which strategies have I found most effective for finding good ideas for writing?

- What pieces of writing represent my best work and my weakest work? What do the pieces in each group have in common?

Partner Talk

With a partner, talk about your collaborative writing experiences. Be sure to share your responses to such questions as these: What project did you work on as a collaborative effort? What did you learn that you might not have discovered if you were developing a writing project by yourself?

CHAPTER 2

TYPES *of* WRITING

Genres and Forms

Genres are types, or categories, of writing.

- Each genre has a specific **purpose,** or goal. For example, the purpose of persuasive writing is to convince readers to agree with the writer's point of view.

- Each genre has specific **characteristics**. Short stories, for example, have characters, a setting, and a plot.

In this chapter, you will be introduced to several genres: nonfiction narratives, fiction narratives, poetry and descriptive writing, expository writing, persuasive writing, responses to literature, and workplace writing.

Forms are subcategories of genres that contain all the characteristics of the genre plus some unique characteristics of their own. For example, a mystery is a form of short story. In addition to plot, characters, and setting, it has a mystery to be solved.

Selecting Genres

In some writing situations, you may need to select the correct genre for conveying your intended meaning.

- To **entertain,** you may choose to write a short story or a humorous essay.
- To **describe** an emotion, writing a poem may be best.
- To **persuade** someone to your point of view, you may want to write a persuasive essay or editorial.

Each genre has unique strengths and weaknesses, and your specific goals will help you decide which is best.

Nonfiction Narration

Nonfiction narratives are any kind of literary text that tells a story about real people, events, and ideas. This genre of writing can take a number of different forms but includes well-developed conflict and resolution, interesting and believable characters, and a range of literary strategies, such as dialogue and suspense. Examples include William Bradford's "Of Plymouth Plantation" and Sandra Cisneros's "Straw Into Gold: The Metamorphosis of the Everyday."

Personal Narratives

Personal narratives tell true stories about events in a writer's life. These types of writing are also called **autobiographical essays.** The stories may tell about an experience or relationship that is important to the writer, who is the main character. They have a clearly defined focus and communicate the reasons for actions and consequences.

Biographical Narratives

In a **biographical narrative,** the writer shares facts about someone else's life. The writer may describe an important period, experience, or relationship in that other person's life, but presents the information from his or her own perspective.

Blogs

Blogs are online journals that may include autobiographical narratives, reflections, opinions, and other types of comments. They may also reflect genres other than nonfiction such as expository writing, and they may include other media, such as photos, music, or video.

Diary and Journal Entries

Writers record their personal thoughts, feelings, and experiences in **diaries** or **journals.** Writers sometimes keep diaries and journals for many years and then analyze how they reacted to various events over time.

Eyewitness Accounts

Eyewitness accounts are nonfiction writing that focus on historical or other important events. The writer is the narrator and shares his or her thoughts about the event. However, the writer is not the main focus of the writing.

Memoirs

Memoirs usually focus on meaningful scenes from writers' lives. These scenes often reflect on moments of a significant decision or personal discovery. For example, many modern U.S. presidents have written memoirs after they have left office. These memoirs help the public gain a better understanding of the decisions they made while in office.

Reflective Essays

Reflective essays present personal experiences, either events that happened to the writers themselves or that they learned about from others. They generally focus on sharing observations and insights they had while thinking about those experiences. Reflective essays often appear as features in magazines and newspapers.

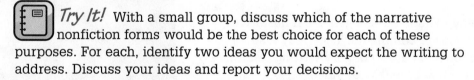 *Try It!* With a small group, discuss which of the narrative nonfiction forms would be the best choice for each of these purposes. For each, identify two ideas you would expect the writing to address. Discuss your ideas and report your decisions.

- To tell about seeing a championship kite-flying tournament
- To write about one of the first astronauts to walk in space
- To record personal thoughts about a favorite teacher

Fiction Narration

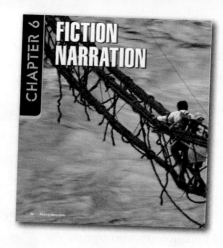

Fiction narratives are literary texts that tell a story about imagined people, events, and ideas. They contain elements such as characters, a setting, a sequence of events, and often, a theme. As with nonfiction narratives, this genre can take many different forms, but most forms include well-developed **conflict** and **resolution.** They also include **interesting and believable elements** and a range of **literary strategies,** such as dialogue and suspense. Examples include Washington Irving's "The Devil and Tom Walker" or Joyce Carol Oates's "Where Is Here?"

Realistic Fiction

Realistic fiction portrays invented characters and events in everyday situations that most readers would find familiar. Although characters may be imaginary, writers sometimes use real individuals in their own lives as a basis for the fictional ones. Because the focus is on everyday life, realistic fiction often presents problems that many people face and solutions they devise to solve them.

Fantasy Stories

Fantasy stories stretch the imagination and take readers to unreal worlds. Animals may talk, people may fly, or characters may have superhuman powers. Good fantasy stories have the elements of narrative fiction and manage to keep the fantastic elements believable.

Historical Fiction

Historical fiction is about imaginary people living in real places and times in history. Usually, the main characters are fictional people who know and interact with famous people and participate in important historical events.

Mystery Stories

Mystery stories present unexplained or strange events that characters try to solve. These stories are popular, probably because they are often packed full of suspense and surprises. Some characters in mystery stories, such as Sherlock Holmes, have become so famous that many people think of them as real people.

Myths and Legends

Myths and **legends** are traditional stories, told in cultures around the world. They were created to explain natural events that people could not otherwise explain or understand. They may, for example, tell about the origin of fire or thunder. Many myths and legends include gods, goddesses, and heroes who perform superhuman actions.

Science Fiction

Science fiction stories tell about real and imagined developments in science and technology and their effects on the way people think and live. Space travel, robots, and life in the future are popular topics in science fiction.

Tall Tales

You can tell a **tall tale** from other story types because it tells about larger-than-life characters in realistic settings. These characters can perform amazing acts of strength and bravery. One very famous hero of tall tales is Pecos Bill, who could ride just about anything—even a tornado!

Try It! Think about what you've read about narrative fiction and narrative nonfiction genres. Then, discuss in a group which **genre** would be best if you were planning a first draft and had these purposes in mind. **Select the correct genre** for conveying your intended meaning to your audiences. Then, identify two or three ideas that you would expect to include in a first draft. Be sure to explain your choices.

- To tell about a Texas rancher who can lasso lightning
- To share a true story about a famous person
- To tell the story of your most exciting day at school

Poetry and Description

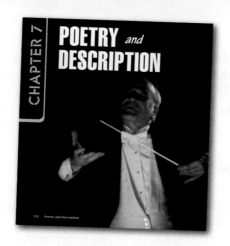

Poetry and other kinds of descriptive literature express ideas and feelings about real or imagined people, events, and ideas. They use rhythm, rhyme, precise language, and sensory details—words that appeal to the senses—to create vivid images. In addition, they use figurative language—writing that means something beyond what the words actually say—to express ideas in new, fresh, and interesting ways.

Structural elements, such as line length and stanzas, also help the poet express ideas and set a mood. Some examples of poetry include Edgar Allan Poe's "The Raven" and Walt Whitman's "I Hear America Singing."

Ballad

A **ballad** is a form of lyric poetry that expresses the poet's emotions toward someone or something. Ballads rhyme, and some have refrains that repeat after each stanza, which makes them easy to translate into songs.

In many places, traditional folk ballads were passed down as oral poems or songs and then later written. Some ballads tell about cultural heroes. Other ballads tell sad stories or make fun of certain events.

Free Verse

Free verse is poetry that has no regular rhyme, rhythm, or form. Instead, a free verse poem captures the patterns of natural speech. The poet writes in whatever form seems to fit the ideas best. A free verse poem can have almost anything as its subject.

" Writer to Writer "

Writing fiction and poetry sharpens your creativity—a skill valued by universities and employers.

—Kelly Gallagher

Partner Talk

Think about an example of fiction that you've especially enjoyed reading. Then, choose a partner and report your choices to each other. Be sure to explain what made the fiction piece so enjoyable, interesting, or exciting.

Prose Poem

A **prose poem** shares many of the features of other poetry, since it has rhythm, repetition, and vivid imagery. However, it is different from other poetry in one important way: it takes the form of prose or non-verse writing. Therefore, a prose poem may look like a short story on a page.

Sonnet

The **sonnet** is a form of rhyming lyric poetry with set rules. It is 14 lines long and usually follows a rhythm scheme called iambic pentameter. Each line has ten syllables and every other syllable is accented.

Haiku

Haiku is a form of non-rhyming poetry that was first developed in Japan hundreds of years ago. Many poets who write haiku in English write the poems in three lines. The first line has seven syllables, the second line has five syllables, and the third line has seven syllables. Haiku poets often write about nature and use vivid visual images.

Other Descriptive Writing

Descriptive writing includes descriptive essays, travel writing, and definition essays.

- **Descriptive essays** often use words that involve the senses to create a clear picture of a subject. For example, a descriptive essay about a freshly grilled hamburger might use adjectives such as *juicy*, *spicy*, *steamy*, *fragrant*, *hot*, and *glistening* to paint a word picture.
- A **travel essay** uses sensory words to describe a place.
- A **definition essay** can draw on a writer's emotional experience to describe something abstract, like friendship or happiness.

  The qualities of description can also be used in other types of writing. For example, a short story can be more realistic or compelling when it includes strong description.

Try It! Now that you've learned more about poetry and description, discuss which specific **genre** would be best for each of these purposes. **Select the correct genre** for conveying your intended meaning to your audiences. Then, identify two or three types of information that you would want to include in a first draft. Be ready to explain your thinking.

- To tell about a trip to a beach in Mexico
- To describe a drop of rain
- To tell the story of a character who lives in the wilderness

Exposition

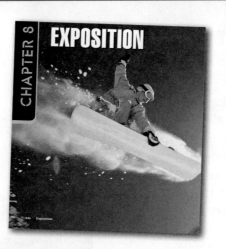

Exposition is writing that seeks to communicate ideas and information to specific audiences and for specific purposes. It relies on facts to inform or explain.

- Effective expository writing reflects an organization that is well planned—with effective introductory paragraphs, body paragraphs, and concluding paragraphs.

- In addition, good expository writing uses a variety of sentence structures and rhetorical devices—deliberate uses of language for specific effects.

Examples of expository writing include William Safire's "Onomatopoeia" and William L. Andrews's "American Begins With a Promise and a Paradox."

Analytical Essay

An **analytical essay** explores a topic by supplying relevant information in the form of facts, examples, reasons, and valid inferences to support the writer's claims.

- An **introductory paragraph** presents a thesis statement, the main point to be developed.

- The **body of the essay** provides facts about the topic, using a variety of sentence structures and transitions to help the writing flow.

- The **concluding paragraph** sums up ideas, helping readers understand why the topic is important.

Compare-and-Contrast Essay

A **compare-and-contrast** essay explores similarities and differences between two or more things for a specific purpose. As with other expository essays, the compare-and-contrast essay offers clear, factual details about the subject.

Cause-and-Effect Essay

A **cause-and-effect essay** traces the results of an event or describes the reasons an event happened. It is clearly organized and gives precise examples that support the relationship between the cause and effect.

" Writer to Writer "

Expository forms can shape my thinking and help my writing gel. I find the expository patterns clarifying my thoughts and filling in gaps that I may have otherwise missed.

—Jeff Anderson

Partner Talk

Choose a different partner this time. Discuss a poem that you've read in class. Share your thoughts about the poem and describe what made the piece successful.

Classification Essay

In a **classification essay,** a writer organizes a subject into categories and explains the category into which an item falls.

- An effective classification essay **sorts** its subjects—things or ideas—into several categories.
- It then offers **examples** that fall into each category. For example, a classification essay about video games might discuss three types of video games—action, adventure, and arcade.
- The essay might conclude with a statement about how the items classified are different or about how they are similar.

Problem-Solution Essay

A **problem-solution essay** presents a problem and then offers solutions to that problem. This type of essay may contain opinions, like a persuasive essay, but it is meant to explain rather than persuade.

- An effective problem-solution essay presents a clear statement of the problem, including a summary of its causes and effects.
- Then, it proposes at least one realistic solution and uses facts, statistics, or expert testimony to support the solution.
- The essay should be clearly organized, so that the relationship between the problem and the solution is obvious.

Pro-Con Essay

A **pro-con essay** examines arguments for and against an idea or topic.

- It has a topic that has two sides or points of view. For example, you might choose the following as a topic: Is it right to keep animals in zoos?
- Then, you would develop an essay that tells why it's good to keep animals in zoos, as well as why it's harmful to keep animals in zoos.
- It's important to be sure to give a clear analysis of the topic.

Newspaper and Magazine Articles

Newspaper and **magazine articles** offer information about news and events. They are typically factual and do not include the writer's opinions. They often provide an analysis of events and give readers background information on a topic. Some articles may also reflect genres other than the analytical essay, such as an editorial that aims to persuade.

Internet Articles

Articles on the **Internet** can supply relevant information about a topic.

- They are often like newspaper or magazine articles but may include shorter sentences and paragraphs. In addition, they include more visuals, such as charts and bulleted lists. They may also reflect genres other than analytical essays.

- It's always wise to consider the source when reading Internet articles because only the most reputable sources should be trusted to present correct facts.

On-Demand Writing

Because essay questions often appear on school tests, knowing how to write to **test prompts**, especially under time limits, is an important skill.

Test prompts provide a clear topic with directions about what should be addressed. The effective response to an essay demonstrates not only an understanding of academic content but also good writing skills.

 *Try It!* Think about what you've learned about expository writing and consider the other genres you've discussed. Then, discuss in a group which **genre** would be best if you were planning a first draft with these purposes in mind. **Select the correct genre** for conveying your intended meaning to your audiences. Then, identify two or three key ideas that you would want to include in a first draft. Be sure to explain your choices.

- To weigh the benefits of two kinds of pets
- To imagine what life would be like on the moon

Persuasion

Persuasive writing aims to influence the attitudes or actions of a specific audience on specific issues. A strong persuasive text is logically organized and clearly describes the issue. It also provides precise and relevant evidence that supports a clear thesis statement. Persuasive writing may contain diagrams, graphs, or charts. These visuals can help to convince the reader. Examples include John Jay's "The Federalist, No. 2" or Benjamin Franklin's "Speech in the Convention."

CHAPTER 9 PERSUASION

Persuasive Essays or Argumentative Essays

A **persuasive essay** or **argumentative essay** uses logic and reasoning to persuade readers to adopt a certain point of view or to take action. A strong persuasive essay starts with a clear thesis statement and provides supporting arguments based on evidence. It also anticipates readers' counter-arguments and responds to them as well.

Persuasive Speeches

Persuasive speeches are presented aloud and aim to win an audience's support for a policy, position, or action. These speeches often appeal to emotion and reason to convince an audience. Speakers sometimes change their script in order to address each specific audience's concerns.

Editorials

Editorials, which appear in newspapers, in magazines, or on television, radio, or the Internet, state the opinion of the editors and publishers of news organizations. Editorials usually present an opinion about a current issue, starting with a clear thesis statement and then offering strong supporting evidence.

Op-Ed Pieces

An **op-ed, piece** is an essay that tries to convince the readers of a publication to agree with the writer's views on an issue. The writer may not work for the publication and is often an expert on the issue or has an interesting point of view. The writer is identified so that people can judge his or her qualifications.

Letters to the Editor

Readers write **letters to editors** at print and Internet publications to express opinions in response to previously published articles. A good letter to the editor gives an accurate and honest representation of the writer's views.

Reviews

Reviews evaluate items and activities, such as books, movies, plays, and music, from the writer's point of view. A review often states opinions on the quality of an item or activity and supports those opinions with examples, facts, and other evidence.

Advertisements

Advertisements in all media—from print to online sites to highway billboards—are paid announcements that try to convince people to buy something or do something. Good advertisements use a hook to grab your attention and support their claims. They contain vivid, persuasive language and multimedia techniques, such as music, to appeal to a specific audience.

Propaganda

Propaganda uses emotional appeals and often biased, false, or misleading information to persuade people to think or act in a certain way. Propaganda may tap into people's strongest emotions by generating fear or attacking their ideas of loyalty or patriotism. Because propaganda appears to be objective, it is wise to be aware of the ways it can manipulate people's opinions and actions.

Try It! Think about what you have learned about exposition, description, and persuasion. Form a group to discuss and draw conclusions about which **genres** would be best if you were planning a first draft with each of these intentions in mind. **Select the correct genre** for conveying your intended meaning to your audiences. Then, identify two or three types of information that you would want to include in a first draft.

- To explain how an event happened
- To describe a beautiful landscape
- To encourage teens to buy teeth-whitening toothpaste

Partner Talk

Share your experiences with various types of persuasive texts with a partner. Talk about the types of persuasive text that you think are most effective, honest, and fair. Be sure to explain your thinking.

Responses to Literature

CHAPTER 10 · RESPONSE *to* LITERATURE

Responses to literature analyze and interpret an author's work. They use clear **thesis statements** and **evidence from the text using embedded quotations to support the writer's ideas.** They also evaluate how well authors have accomplished their goals. Effective responses to literature extend beyond literal analysis to evaluate and discuss how and why the text is effective or not effective. Examples include William L. Andrews's "Benjamin Franklin: America's Everyman" or Charles Johnson's "On Ralph Waldo Emerson."

Critical Reviews

Critical reviews evaluate books, plays, poetry, and other literary works. Reviews present the writer's opinions and support them with specific examples. The responses may analyze the aesthetic effects of an author's use of language in addition to responding to the content of the writing.

Compare-and-Contrast Essays

Compare-and-contrast essays explore similarities and differences between two or more works of literature. These essays provide relevant evidence to support the writer's opinions.

Letters to Authors

Readers write **letters to authors** to share their feelings and thoughts about a work of literature directly.

Blog Comments

Blog comments on an author's Web site or book retailer vlet readers share their ideas about a work. Readers express their opinions and give interpretations of what an author's work means.

Try It! As a group, decide which **genre** would be most appropriate if you were planning a first draft for each of these purposes. **Select the correct genre** for conveying your intended meaning to your audiences. Then, identify two or three key questions that you would want to answer in a first draft.

- To tell an author why you think her book is excellent
- To write an opinion about a newspaper article
- To imagine how a certain landform came to be

> **Partner Talk**
>
> Interview your partner about his or her experiences writing interpretative responses. Be sure to ask questions such as these:
>
> - How did you support your opinion of the author's work?
> - How did you choose evidence, such as quotes, to support your analysis or opinion?

Research Writing

Research writing is based on factual information from outside sources. Research reports organize and present ideas and information to achieve a particular purpose and reach a specific audience. They present evidence in support of a clear thesis statement.

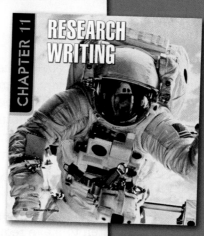

Research Reports and Documented Essays

Research reports and **documented essays** present information and analysis about a topic that the writer has studied. Start with a clear thesis statement. Research reports often include graphics and illustrations to clarify concepts. Documented essays are less formal research writings that show the source of every fact, quote, or borrowed idea in parentheses.

Experiment Journals and Lab Reports

Experiment journals and **lab reports** focus on the purposes, procedures, and results of a lab experiment. They often follow a strict format that includes dates and specific observation notes.

Statistical Analysis Reports

A **statistical analysis report** presents numerical data. Writers of this type of report must explain how they gathered their information, analyze their data, tell what significance the findings may have, and explain how these findings support their thesis statement.

Annotated Bibliographies

An **annotated bibliography** lists the research sources a writer used. It includes the title, author, publication date, publisher, and brief notes that describe and evaluate the source.

Partner Talk

Share with a partner the kinds of research writing you've done in school. Explain which projects you've enjoyed and why.

Try It! Discuss which kinds of reports you might write if you were planning a first draft for these purposes. **Select the correct form** for conveying your intended meaning to your audiences. Then, identify two or three key questions that you would want to answer in a first draft. Explain your choices.

- To accompany a project you plan to enter in a science fair
- To write about a poll taken to predict the results of a local election

Workplace Writing

Workplace writing is writing done on the job or as part of a job, often in an office setting. It usually communicates details about a particular job or work project. This type of writing features organized and accurately conveyed information and should include reader-friendly formatting techniques, such as clearly defined sections and enough blank space for easy reading.

Business Letters and Friendly Letters

A **business letter** is a formal letter written to, from, or within a business. It can be written to make requests or to express concerns or approval. For example, you might write to a company to ask about job opportunities. Business letters follow a specific format that includes an address, date, formal greeting, and closing.

In contrast, a **friendly letter** is a form of correspondence written to communicate between family, friends, or acquaintances. For example, you might write a thank-you note for a gift.

Memos

Memos are short documents usually written from one member of an organization to another or to a group. They are an important means of communicating information within an organization.

E-mails

E-mail is an abbreviation for "electronic mail" and is a form of electronic memo. Because it can be transmitted quickly allowing for instant long-distance communication, e-mail is a very common form of communication that uses a computer and software to send messages.

Forms

Forms are types of workplace writing that ask for specific information to be completed in a particular format. Examples include applications, emergency contact information forms, and tax forms.

Instructions

Instructions are used to explain how to complete a task or procedure. They provide clear, step-by-step guidelines. For example, recipes and user manuals are forms of instructions.

Project Plans

Project plans are short documents usually written from one member of an organization to another. They outline a project's goals and objectives and may include specific details about how certain steps of a project should be achieved.

Résumés

A **résumé** is an overview of a person's experience and qualifications for a job. This document lists a person's job skills and work history. Résumés can also feature information about a person's education.

College Applications

College applications are documents that ask for personal information and details about someone's educational background. College administrators use this information to decide whether or not to accept a student.

Job Applications

Job applications are similar to résumés in that they require a person to list work experience and educational background. Most employers will require a completed job application a part of the hiring process.

Try It! As a group, discuss which form of workplace writing would be best for each of these purposes. Select the correct form for conveying your intended meaning to your audiences. Identify two or three types of information you would expect to include in a first draft.

- To inform the company that made your cell phone that it does not work properly
- To prepare information about your qualifications for a job search
- To create a plan for your group assignment in science class

Partner Talk

Share with a partner your experience with workplace and procedural writing. For example, have you ever written instructions, created a résumé, or completed a job application? What do you find are particular challenges with this type of writing?

Writing for Media

The world of communication has changed significantly in recent years. In addition to writing for print media such as magazines and books, writers also write for a variety of other **media,** in forms such as:

- Scripts for screenplays, video games, and documentaries
- Storyboards for graphic novels and advertisements
- Packaging for every kind of product
- Web sites and blogs

Scripts

Scripts are written for various media, such as documentaries, theater productions, speeches, and audio programs. Movies, television shows, and video games also have scripts.

- A good script focuses on a clearly expressed or implied **theme** and has a specific **purpose.**
- It also contains interesting details, which contribute to a definite **mood or tone.**
- A good script also includes a clear **setting, dialogue,** and well-developed **action.**

Blogs

Blogs address just about every purpose and interest. For example, there are blogs about local issues, pets, or food.

Advertisements

Advertisements are designed to persuade someone to buy a product or service. Advertisements use images, words, and music to support their message. Writers write the content of advertisements. In addition, they may help create music and design the sound and the images in the ad.

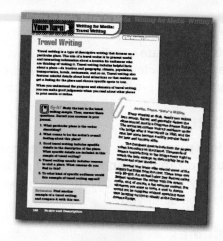

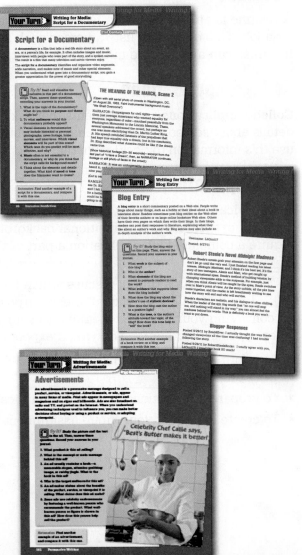

Creating Multimedia Projects

A **multimedia project** or presentation uses sound, video, and other media to convey a point or entertain an audience. No matter what type of project you choose as your own multimedia project, it is important to follow these steps:

- Decide on the project's **purpose** and your target **audience.**

- Choose **media** that will effectively convey your **message.**

- **Plan** your presentation. Will you work alone or with a partner or group? If you work with others, how will you assign the tasks?

- What **equipment** will you need? Will you produce artwork, record audio, and take photographs? Should you produce a storyboard to show the sequence of details in your presentation? Be sure to allow enough time to produce the text and all the other elements in your project.

- Keep the **writing process** in mind. There should be working and reworking along the way.

- **Assess** the progress of the project as you work. Ask questions, such as: Does my project incorporate appropriate writing genres? Will the presentation interest my audience? Have I kept my purpose in mind?

- **Rehearse!** Before presenting your project, be sure to do several "practice runs" to weed out and correct any errors.

- Keep an electronic record of your presentation for future reference.

- After your presentation, have others assess the project. Their critique will help you to do an even better job next time!

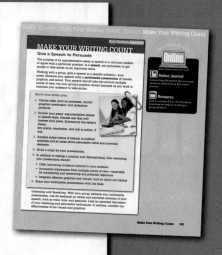

Partner Talk

Share with a partner your experience with writing for media or multimedia projects. Have you created a Web site or contributed to one? Have you had to complete multimedia projects for a class assignment or for a personal project on which you worked? Talk about how writing for media presents different challenges from more traditional writing and how you have dealt with those challenges.

Reflect on Your Writing

Learning more about the different types of writing can help you focus on the characteristics of each type so you can keep improving your own writing. Think about what you've learned in Chapter 2 as you answer these questions:

- What type of writing most interests you?
- What type of writing do you think is most useful? Why?

CHAPTER 3

THE WRITING PROCESS

Writing Traits

Good writing has specific qualities, or traits. In this chapter you will learn about these traits and how to use rubrics to evaluate your writing in terms of them. You will also learn how to address them during the writing process.

Ideas

The best writing is built from strong ideas. It shows original thinking and provides readers with interesting, significant information. It also sends a strong message or presents a clear "angle" or point of view on a subject. In good writing, ideas are well developed, or explained and supported with examples and other details.

Organization

A well-organized paper has an obvious plan. Ideas move from sentence to sentence and paragraph to paragraph in a logical way. For example, events in a story often appear in chronological order, the order in which they occurred. Some expository writing presents ideas in order of importance. Descriptive writing may use a spatial organization, describing something from top to bottom or left to right.

Voice

Voice is the combination of word choice and personal writing style that makes your writing unique. It shows your personality or "take" on a story. Voice connects a reader to the writer. While the content of your writing is critical, effective writing features a strong voice.

Word Choice

To best achieve your purpose in writing, choose words carefully. When you choose precise words, you choose words that express your exact meaning. When you choose vivid words, you choose words that create pictures for readers, words that describe how a subject looks, sounds, smells, and so on. You may also use figures of speech (direct or indirect comparisons of unlike things) to create memorable images of your subject.

Sentence Fluency

Sentence fluency refers to the rhythm and flow of writing. Keep the rhythm of your writing fresh by varying sentence patterns, and create flow by choosing sentence structures that match your meaning. For example, you might show the connection between two ideas by joining them in one longer sentence, or you might create emphasis by breaking off a series of long sentences with one short sentence.

Conventions

By following the rules of spelling, capitalization, punctuation, grammar, and usage, you help readers understand your ideas.

Overview of Writing Traits	
Ideas	• Significant ideas and informative details • Thorough development of ideas • Unique perspective or strong message
Organization	• Obvious plan • Clear sequence • Strong transitions
Voice	• Effective word choice expressing personality or perspective • Attention to style
Word Choice	• Precise, not vague, words • Vivid, not dull, words • Word choices suited to audience and purpose
Sentency Fluency	• Varied sentence beginnings, lengths, and structures • Smooth sentence rhythms used to support meaning
Conventions	• Proper spelling and capitalization • Correct punctuation, grammar, usage, and sentence structure

WRITING COACH

Online

www.phwritingcoach.com

 Online Journal

Try It! Record your answers and ideas in the online journal. You can also record and save your answers and ideas on pop-up sticky notes in the eText.

66 Writer to Writer 99

Good writing is a symphony of traits—all coming together to make the paper sing.

—Kelly Gallagher

Rubrics and How to Use Them

You can use rubrics to evaluate your writing. A rubric allows you to score your writing on a scale for each trait. You will use a six-point rubric like this to help evaluate your writing in chapters 5–12.

Writing Traits	Rating Scale
Ideas: How interesting, significant, or original are the ideas you present? How well do you develop, or explain, support, and extend, ideas?	Not very Very 1 2 3 4 5 6
Organization: How logically is your piece organized? How much sense do your transitions, or movements from idea to idea, make?	1 2 3 4 5 6
Voice: How authentic and original is your voice?	1 2 3 4 5 6
Word Choice: How precise and vivid are the words you use? How well does your word choice help achieve your purpose?	1 2 3 4 5 6
Sentence Fluency: How well do your sentences flow? How strong and varied is the rhythm they create?	1 2 3 4 5 6
Conventions: How correct is your punctuation? Your capitalization? Your spelling?	1 2 3 4 5 6

Each trait to be assessed appears in the first column. The rating scale appears in the second column. The higher your score for a trait, the better your writing exhibits that trait.

Using a Rubric on Your Own

A rubric can be a big help in assessing your writing while it is still in process. Imagine you are about to start writing a piece of narrative fiction. You consult a rubric, which reminds you that narrative fiction should have characters, a setting, and a conflict and resolution. As you write, you try to incorporate and develop each element. After drafting, you might check the rubric again to make sure you are on track. For example, after reviewing the rubric again, you might decide that you have not developed the conflict or its resolution well. You would then go back and revise to improve your writing and get a better score.

Narrative Fiction Elements	Rating Scale					
	Not very					Very
Interesting characters	1	2	3	4	5	6
Believable setting	1	2	3	4	5	6
Literary strategies	1	2	3	4	5	6
Well-developed conflict	1	2	3	4	5	6
Well-developed resolution	1	2	3	4	5	6

 Try It! If you checked your story against the rubric and rated yourself mostly 1s and 2s, what actions might you want to take?

Using a Rubric With a Partner

In some cases, building your own rubric can help you ensure that your writing will meet your expectations. For example, if your class has an assignment to write a poem, you and a partner might decide to construct a rubric to check one another's work. A rubric like the one shown here can help point out whether you should make any changes. Extra lines allow room for you to add other criteria.

Poetry Elements	Rating Scale					
	Not very					Very
Good sensory details	1	2	3	4	5	6
Colorful adjectives	1	2	3	4	5	6
	1	2	3	4	5	6
	1	2	3	4	5	6
	1	2	3	4	5	6

 Try It! What other elements might you add to the rubric?

Using a Rubric in a Group

It is also helpful to use a rubric in a group. That way you can get input on your writing from many people at the same time. If the group members' ratings of your piece are similar, you will probably have an easy time deciding whether to make changes. If the responses vary significantly, you might want to discuss the results with the group. Then, analyze what led to the differing opinions and make careful judgments about what changes you will make.

WRITING COACH

Online

www.phwritingcoach.com

Online Journal

Try It! Record your answers and ideas in the online journal. You can also record and save your answers and ideas on pop-up sticky notes in the eText.

What Is the Writing Process?

The five steps in the writing process are prewriting, drafting, revising, editing, and publishing. Writing is a process because your idea goes through a series of changes or stages before the product is finished.

Study the diagram to see how moving through the writing process can work. Remember, you can go back to a stage in the process. It does not always have to occur in order.

Prewriting

In prewriting, you will:
- Explore ideas
- Choose a purpose and an audience
- Gather details
- Sequence ideas

Drafting

In drafting, you will:
- Put ideas down
- Develop a thesis or controlling idea
- Structure ideas in a sustained way

In publishing, you will:
- Produce a final polished copy of your writing
- Share your writing

Publishing

In the editing phase, you will:
- Check the accuracy of facts
- Correct errors in spelling, grammar, usage, and mechanics

Revising

In revising, you will:
- Re-read draft to see what works and what does not
- Use a rubric to evaluate
- Analyze what you want to change or improve
- Make changes

Editing

Why Use the Writing Process?

Writing involves careful thinking, which means you will make changes as you write. Even professional writers don't just write their thoughts and call it a finished work of art. They use a process. For example, some writers keep going back to the revising stage many times, while others feel they can do the revision in just one step. It is up to each writer to develop the style that works best to produce the best results.

You might find that the writing process works best for you when you keep these tips in mind:

- Remember that the five steps in the writing process are equally important.
- Think about your audience as you plan your paper and develop your writing.
- Make sure you remember your topic and stick to your specific purpose as you write.
- Give your writing some time to "rest." Sometimes it can be good to work on a piece, walk away, and look at it later, with a fresh eye and mind.

The following pages will describe in more detail how to use each stage of the writing process to improve your writing.

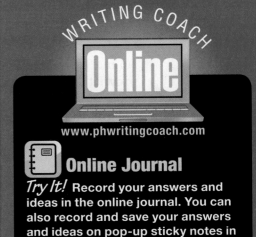

WRITING COACH

Online

www.phwritingcoach.com

Online Journal

Try It! Record your answers and ideas in the online journal. You can also record and save your answers and ideas on pop-up sticky notes in the eText.

66 Writer to Writer 99

Writing process gives us the freedom to write like mad, tinker like an engineer, evaluate like a judge—playing different roles at different stages. Most importantly it gives us the freedom to get our words out of our heads and into the world.

—Jeff Anderson

Prewriting

Prewriting

Drafting

Revising

Editing

Publishing

No matter what kind of writing you do, planning during the prewriting stage is crucial. During prewriting, you determine the topic of your writing, its purpose, and its specific audience. Then, you narrow the topic and gather details.

Determining the Purpose and Audience

What Is Your Purpose?

To be sure your writing communicates your ideas clearly, it is important to clarify why you are writing. Consider what you want your audience to take away from your writing. You may want to entertain them, or you may want to warn them about something. Even when you write an entry in a private journal, you're writing for an audience—you!

Who Is Your Audience?

Think about the people who will read your work and consider what they may already know about your topic. Being able to identify this group and their needs will let you be sure you are providing the right level of information.

Choosing a Topic

Here are just a few of the many techniques you can use to determine an appropriate topic.

- **Brainstorm**
  You can brainstorm by yourself, with a partner, or with a group. Just jot down ideas as they arise, and don't rule out anything. When brainstorming in a group, one person's idea often "piggy-backs" on another.

- **Make a Mind Map**
  A mind map is a quick drawing you sketch as ideas come to you. The mind map can take any form. The important thing is to write quick notes as they come to you and then to draw lines to connect relationships among the ideas.

- **Interview**

  A fun way to find a writing topic is to conduct an interview. You might start by writing interview questions for yourself or someone else. Questions that start with *what*, *when*, *why*, *how*, and *who* are most effective. For example, you might ask, "When was the last time you laughed really hard?" "What made you laugh?" Then, conduct the interview and discover the answers.

- **Review Resources and Discuss Ideas**

  You can review resources, such as books, magazines, newspapers, and digital articles, to get ideas. Discussing your initial ideas with a partner can spark even more ideas.

Narrowing Your Topic

Once you have settled on a topic idea you really like, it may seem too broad to tackle. How can you narrow your topic?

- **Use Graphic Organizers**

  A graphic organizer can help narrow a topic that's too broad. For example, you might choose "Animals" as a topic. You might make your topics smaller and smaller until you narrow the topic to "The Habitat of Emperor Penguins."

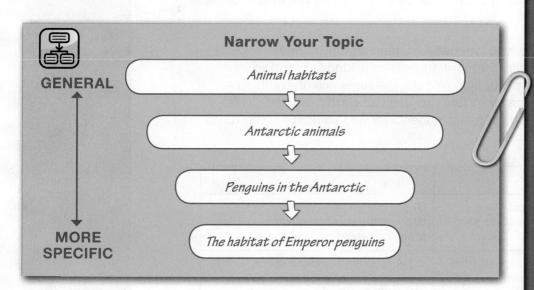

Narrow Your Topic

GENERAL

Animal habitats

Antarctic animals

Penguins in the Antarctic

MORE SPECIFIC

The habitat of Emperor penguins

WRITING COACH

Online

www.phwritingcoach.com

Online Journal

Try It! Record your answers and ideas in the online journal. You can also record and save your answers and ideas on pop-up sticky notes in the eText.

66 Writer to Writer 99

Put something down. Anything. Then, magic will happen.

—Jeff Anderson

Prewriting
Drafting
Revising
Editing
Publishing

Prewriting (continued)

- **Use Resource Materials**

  The resource materials you use to find information can also help you narrow a broad topic. Look up your subject online in an encyclopedia or newspaper archive. Scan the resources as you look for specific subtopics to pursue.

Gather Details

After you decide on a topic, you will want to explore and develop your ideas. You might start by looking through online resources again, talking with people who are knowledgeable about your topic, and writing everything you already know about the topic. It will be helpful to gather a variety of details. Look at these types:

- Facts
- Statistics
- Personal observations
- Expert opinions

- Examples
- Descriptions
- Quotations
- Opposing viewpoints

After you have narrowed your topic and gathered details, you will begin to plan your piece. During this part of prewriting, you will develop your essay's thesis or controlling idea—its main point or purpose. If you are writing a fiction or nonfiction story, you will outline the events of the story.

As you plan your piece, you can use a graphic organizer. Specific kinds of graphic organizers can help structure specific kinds of writing. For example, a plot map can help plot out the sequence of events in a mystery story. A pro-con chart like this one can clarify the reasons for and against an idea. It presents arguments for and against adding funds to a school music program.

Pro	Con
Adding funds to the school music budget would allow more students to learn to play instruments.	Giving more money to the music department would mean other programs would get less money.
Research shows that music helps the brain become more flexible.	Other programs, such as sports, are important in keeping students physically healthy.
Band members could stop selling gift-wrap materials at holiday time.	The school board has already approved the current budget allocations.

Drafting

In the drafting stage, you get your ideas down. You may consult an outline or your pre-writing notes as you build your first draft.

Prewriting

Drafting

Revising

Editing

Publishing

WRITING COACH

Online

www.phwritingcoach.com

Online Journal

Try It! **Record your answers and ideas in the online journal. You can also record and save your answers and ideas on pop-up sticky notes in the eText.**

The Introduction

Most genres should have a strong introduction that immediately grabs the reader's attention and includes the thesis. Even stories and poems need a "hook" to grab interest.

 *Try It!* Which of these first sentences are strong openers? Read these examples of first sentences. Decide which ones are most interesting to you. Explain why they grab your attention. Then, explain why the others are weak.

- Have you ever wondered what it would be like to wake up one morning to find you're someone else?
- There are many ways to paint a room.
- Yogi Berra, the famous baseball star, said, "You got to be careful if you don't know where you're going, because you might not get there."
- Autumn is a beautiful season.
- On Sunday, we went to the store.
- When I woke up that morning, I had no idea that it would be the best day of my life.

The Body

The body of a paper develops the main idea and details that elaborate on and support the thesis. As you tell your story or build an argument these details may include interesting facts, examples, statistics, anecdotes or stories, quotations, personal feelings, and sensory descriptions.

The Conclusion

The conclusion typically restates the thesis and summarizes the most important concepts of a paper.

Revising: Making It Better

Prewriting

Drafting

Revising

Editing

Publishing

No one gets every single thing right in a first draft. In fact, most people require more than two drafts to achieve their best writing and thinking. When you have finished your first draft, you're ready to revise.

Revising means "re-seeing." In revising, you look again to see if you can find ways to improve style, word choice, figurative language, sentence variety, and subtlety of meaning. As always, check how well you've addressed the issues of purpose, audience, and genre. Carefully analyze what you'd want to change and then go ahead and do it. Here are some helpful hints on starting the revision stage of the writing process.

Take a Break

Do not begin to revise immediately after you finish a draft. Take some time away from your paper. Get a glass of water, take a walk, or listen to some music. You may even want to wait a day to look at what you've written. When you come back, you will be better able to assess the strengths and weaknesses of your work.

Put Yourself in the Place of the Reader

Take off your writer's hat and put on your reader's hat. Do your best to pretend that you're reading someone else's work and see how it looks to that other person. Look for ideas that might be confusing and consider the questions that a reader might have. By reading the piece with an objective eye, you may find items you'd want to fix and improve.

Read Aloud to Yourself

It may feel strange to read aloud to yourself, but it can be an effective technique. It allows you to hear the flow of words, find errors, and hear where you might improve the work by smoothing out transitions between paragraphs or sections. Of course, if you're more comfortable reading your work aloud to someone else, that works, too.

Share Your Work to Get Feedback

Your friends or family members can help you by reading and reacting to your writing. Ask them whether you've clearly expressed your ideas. Encourage them to tell you which parts were most and least interesting and why. Try to find out if they have any questions about your topic that were not answered. Then, evaluate their input and decide what will make your writing better.

Use a Rubric

A rubric might be just what you need to pinpoint weaknesses in your work. You may want to think about the core parts of the work and rate them on a scale. If you come up short, you'll have a better idea about the kinds of things to improve. You might also use a rubric to invite peer review and input.

21st Century Learning

Collaborate and Discuss

When presenting and sharing drafts in the revision stage with a small group, it may be wise to set some ground rules. That way, the group is more likely to help each other analyze their work and make thoughtful changes that result in true improvements.

Here are some suggestions for reviewing drafts as a group:

- Cover the names on papers the group will review to keep the work anonymous.
- Print out copies for everyone in the group.
- Show respect for all group members and their writing.
- Be sure all critiques include positive comments.
- While it is fine to suggest ways to improve the work, present comments in a positive, helpful way. No insults are allowed!
- Plan for a second reading with additional input after the writer has followed selected suggestions.

WRITING COACH

Online

www.phwritingcoach.com

Online Journal

Try It! Record your answers and ideas in the online journal. You can also record and save your answers and ideas on pop-up sticky notes in the eText.

Partner Talk

After a group revision session, talk with a partner to analyze each other's feeling on how the session went. Discuss such issues as these: Did the group adhere to the ground rules? What suggestions could you and your partner make to improve the next session?

Revision RADaR

The Revision RADaR strategy, which you will use throughout this book, is an effective tool in helping you conduct a focused revision of your work.

You can use your Revision RADaR to revise your writing. The letters **R**, **A**, **D**, and **R** will help you remember to **r**eplace, **a**dd, **d**elete, and **r**eorder.

To understand more about the Revision RADaR strategy, study the following chart.

R Replace . . .	**A** Add . . .	**D** and Delete . . .	**R** Reorder . . .
• Words that are not specific • Words that are overused • Sentences that are unclear	• New information • Descriptive adjectives and adverbs • Rhetorical or literary devices	• Unrelated ideas • Sentences that sound good, but do not make sense • Repeated words or phrases • Unnecessary details	• So most important points are last • To make better sense or to flow better • So details support main ideas

 ## Replace

You can strengthen a text by replacing words that are not specific, words that are overused, and sentences that are unclear. Take a look at this before and after model.

BEFORE
As I ran to the finish line, my heart was beating.

AFTER
As I sprinted to the finish line, my heart was pounding in my chest.

Apply It! **How did the writer replace the overused verb *ran*? What other replacements do you see? How did they improve the text?**

A Add

You can add new information, descriptive adjectives and adverbs, and rhetorical or literary devices to make your piece more powerful. Study this before and after model.

BEFORE
Shadows made the night seem scary.
AFTER
Ominous shadows made the dark night seem even more sinister.

Apply It! **How did the second sentence make you feel, compared with the first? Explain.**

D Delete

Sometimes taking words out of a text can improve clarity. Analyze this before and after model.

BEFORE
The candidates talked about the issues, and many of the issues were issues that had been on voters' minds.
AFTER
The candidates talked about the issues, many of which had been on voters' minds.

Apply It! **Describe the revision you see. How did taking out unnecessary repetition of the word** *issues* **help the sentence flow more naturally?**

R Reorder

When you reorder, you can make sentences flow more logically. Look at this example.

BEFORE
Put the sunflower seeds over the strawberries, which are on top of the pineapple in a bowl. You'll have a delicious fruit salad!
AFTER
To make a delicious fruit salad, cut pineapple into a bowl. Add strawberries and then sprinkle a few sunflower seeds over the top.

Apply It! **Which of the models flows more logically? Why?**

" Writer to Writer "

Anyone can write a first draft, but revision is where the paper comes to life.

—Kelly Gallagher

USING TECHNOLOGY

Most word processing programs have a built-in thesaurus tool. You can use the thesaurus to find descriptive words that can often substitute for weaker, overused words.

Revision RADaR (continued)

Prewriting
Drafting
Revising
Editing
Publishing

Read the first draft of the Student Model—a review of the book *Technology Drives Me Wild!* Think about how you might use your Revision RADaR to improve the text in a second draft.

Kelly Gallagher, M. Ed.

KEEP REVISION ON YOUR RADaR

Technology Book Drives Reviewer Wild

As a technology fan, I always look for new books about the latest in technology, as soon as they come out. So, when I bought *Technology Drives Me Wild!* by James Frank, after reading other books by Mr. Frank, I had high hopes this would be another winner that would improve my life. Those high hopes were not met by reading this disappointing book.

This book, which dashed my high hopes of learning some new stuff, has many mistakes. One error is that computers were not invented in the early 1800s. Did Thomas Jefferson use a computer when he was president? I don't think so.

The one good thing about *Technology Drives Me Wild!* is the fact that it is a very short book. That way, you won't waste too much time, if you decide not to take my advice and read this boring book after all.

It would have helped to show more pictures when explaining how computer chips work. Besides that, the text is boring and there are no diagrams or photos to keep the text from being boring. In addition, the boring text is very wordy and many of the explanations are unclear and impossible to understand. Also, the photograph of Mr. Frank on the book jacket is out of focus.

Here's a summary of my recommendation about this book: don't read it! Use your time to find better information about technology in other sources.

> *Does my introduction grab reader interest?*

> *Are my word choices varied?*

After writing the first draft, the student used Revision RADaR and asked questions like these:

- What could I **replace**?
- What could I **add**?
- What words might I **delete**?
- Should I **reorder** anything?

The student writer created this second draft after using Revision RADaR.

Technology Book Drives Reviewer Wild

2ND DRAFT

There's no doubt about it. I find the expansion of technology fascinating. I'm always anxious to read the latest developments and to consider how they might enhance my own life. Having read James Frank's previous excellent books on technology, I rushed out to buy his latest—*Technology Drives Me Wild!* Unfortunately, this book turned out to be a grave disappointment.

> **R** *Replaced opening with more engaging sentences*

I'd hoped to glean new information and a fresh understanding of improvements in global positioning systems, netbooks, and cell phones from the book. What I discovered instead was a substandard account, fraught with errors. For example, I am quite certain that while some people may have dreamed of computers in the 1800s, I doubt any actually existed. Mr. Frank should have checked his facts.

> **D** *Deleted repetitive words*
> **A** *Added details about what would improve the text*

Perhaps additional diagrams, photographs, and other visuals would have helped clarify the weak explanations of how, for example, computer chips work. The addition of lively text would have also helped.

It's fortunate that *Technology Drives Me Wild!* is a short book. That way, even if you pick it up in error, you will not have wasted much of your valuable time.

Try It! What other words did the writer replace? Add? Delete? Reorder?

Partner Talk

Work with a partner to write as many substitutions for the verb *walk* as possible. Remember to consider the different ways people walk. For example, how does a young child walk? How does a successful team captain walk? How might a very elderly person walk? Discuss the value of using more specific words in your writing.

Editing: Making It Correct

Prewriting

Drafting

Revising

Editing

Publishing

Editing is the process of checking the accuracy of facts and correcting errors in spelling, grammar, usage, and mechanics. Using a checklist like the one shown here can help ensure you've done a thorough job of editing.

Editing Checklist	
Task	**Ask Yourself**
Check your facts and spelling	❑ Have I checked that my facts are correct? ❑ Have I used spell check or a dictionary to check any words I'm not sure are spelled correctly?
Check your grammar	❑ Have I written any run-on sentences? ❑ Have I used the correct verbs and verb tenses? ❑ Do my pronouns match their antecedents, or nouns they replace?
Check your usage	❑ Have I used the correct form of irregular verbs? ❑ Have I used object pronouns, such as *me*, *him*, *her*, *us*, and *them,* only after verbs or prepositions? ❑ Have I used subject pronouns, such as *I*, *he*, *she*, *we*, and *they,* correctly—usually as subjects?
Check for proper use of mechanics	❑ Have I used correct punctuation? ❑ Does each sentence have the correct end mark? ❑ Have I used apostrophes in nouns but not in pronouns to show possession? ❑ Have I used quotation marks around words from another source? ❑ Have I used correct capitalization? ❑ Does each sentence begin with a capital letter? ❑ Do the names of specific people and places begin with a capital letter?

Using Proofreading Marks

Professional editors use a set of proofreading marks to indicate changes in a text. Here is a chart of some of the more common proofreading marks.

Proofreader's Marks

(b.f.)	boldface
⌐	break text start new line
(caps)	capital letter
⊂	close up
℮	deletes
⌒/	insert ∧ word
⌐/	insert ∧ comma
=/	insert ∧ hyphen
+/	insert let∧er
⊙/	insert period∧
(ital)	italic type
(stet)	let stand as is
(l.f.)	lightface
(l.c.)	Lower case letter
⌐	move left
⌐	move right
¶	new paragraph
(rom)	roman type
	run text up
(sp)	spell out whole word
	transpoes

USING TECHNOLOGY

Many word processing programs have automatic spelling and grammar checks. While these tools can be helpful, be sure to pay attention to any suggestions they offer. That's because sometimes inappropriate substitutes are inserted automatically!

Editing: Making It Correct (continued)

WRITE GUY *Jeff Anderson, M. Ed.*

WHAT DO YOU NOTICE?

Using an editing checklist is a great way to check for correct grammar. However, using a checklist is not enough to make your writing grammatically correct. A checklist tells you what to look for, but not how to correct mistakes you find. To do that, you need to develop and apply your knowledge of grammar.

Looking closely at good writing is one way to expand your grammar know-how. The *What Do You Notice?* feature that appears throughout this book will help you zoom in on passages that use grammar correctly and effectively.

As you read this passage, from "One Dog's Feelings," zoom in on the sentences in the passage.

> *Bo clearly shows when he is angry. He gnashes his teeth, growls, and sometimes even spits! On the other hand, Bo, who can simultaneously chew on two pairs of shoes, is usually content. When he's happy, he simply smiles.*

Now, ask yourself: *What do you notice about the sentences in this passage?*

Maybe you noticed that the writer uses sentences of varying lengths and with different structures. Or perhaps you noticed that the writer varies the way sentences begin.

After asking a question that draws your attention to the grammar in the passage, the *What Do You Notice?* feature provides information on a particular grammar topic. For example, following the passage and question, you might read about simple and complex sentences, which are both used in the passage.

The *What Do You Notice?* feature will show you how grammar works in actual writing. It will help you learn how to make your writing correct.

Prewriting

Drafting

Revising

Editing

Publishing

One Dog's Feelings

Some people wonder if animals feel and show emotions. However, I am absolutely positive that dogs experience a full range of emotions. I owe this knowledge to my dog, Bo.

Bo clearly shows when he is angry. He gnashes his teeth, growls, and sometimes even spits! On the other hand, Bo, who can simultaneously chew on two pairs of shoes, is usually content. When he's happy, he simply smiles. The colors on his tan and white face seem to glow.

He and my cat often rest together on the mat near the door. When they are together, they both purr with happiness. Neither Bo nor the cat minds that cool air seeps under the door. They're just happy to be with one another.

If my brothers or I want to play fetch, Bo is always up for a game. We often throw a ball into the woods, where it sometimes gets buried under leaves and sticks. Bo always rushes for the ball. And running back to us with the stick in his mouth is obviously his great joy. As for the sticks, few are ever left unfound.

When I leave for school in the morning, Bo whimpers—an obvious sign of sadness. That makes me feel miserable. However, the big payoff comes when I return home. Then Bo jumps up on the door, his tail wagging enthusiastically with excitement. Everybody wants to be loved like that!

" Writer to Writer "

If I wonder how to write any kind of writing, I look at models— well-written examples of the kind of writing I want to do. Models are the greatest how-to lesson I have ever discovered.

—Jeff Anderson

Try It! Read "One Dog's Feelings." Then, zoom in on two more passages. Write a response to each question in your journal.

1 What do you notice about the pronouns (*he, they, one, another*) in the third paragraph?

2. How does the writer use transitions, such as the word *however*, to connect ideas in the last paragraph?

Publishing

Prewriting

Drafting

Revising

Editing

Publishing

When you publish, you produce a final copy of your work and present it to an audience. When publishing you'll need to decide which form will best reach your audience, exhibit your ideas, show your creativity, and accomplish your main purpose.

To start assessing the optimal way to publish your work, you might ask yourself these questions:

- What do I hope to accomplish by sharing my work with others?
- Should I publish in print form? Give an oral presentation? Publish in print form and give an oral presentation?
- Should I publish online, in traditional print, or both?
- What specific forms are available to choose from?

The answers to most of these questions will most likely link to your purpose for writing and your audience. Some choices seem obvious. For example, if you've written a piece to contribute to a blog, you'll definitely want to send it electronically.

Each publishing form will present different challenges and opportunities and each will demand different forms of preparation. For example, you may need to prepare presentation slides of your plan to give a speech, or you may want to select music and images if you will be posting a video podcast online.

Ways to Publish

There are many ways to publish your writing. This chart shows some of several opportunities you can pursue to publish your work.

Genre	Publishing Opportunities	
Narration: Nonfiction	• Blogs • Book manuscript • Audio recording	• Private diary or journal entries • Electronic slide show
Narration: Fiction	• Book manuscript • Film	• Audio recording • Oral reading to a group
Poetry and Description	• Bound collection • Visual display	• Audio recording • Oral reading to a group
Exposition and Persuasion	• Print or online article • Web site • Slide show • Visual display	• Film • Audio recording • Oral reading or speech
Response to Literature	• Print or online letters • Visual displays	• Blogs • Slide show
Research Writing	• Traditional paper • Print and online experiment journals	• Multimedia presentation

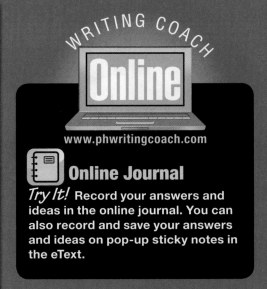

WRITING COACH

Online

www.phwritingcoach.com

Online Journal

Try It! Record your answers and ideas in the online journal. You can also record and save your answers and ideas on pop-up sticky notes in the eText.

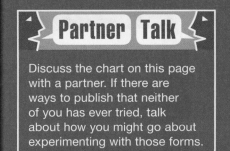

Partner Talk

Discuss the chart on this page with a partner. If there are ways to publish that neither of you has ever tried, talk about how you might go about experimenting with those forms.

Reflect on Your Writing

Think about what you learned in Chapter 3 as you answer these questions:

- What did you learn about the writing process?
- What steps in the writing process do you already use in your writing?
- Which stage do you think is the most fun? Which one may be most challenging for you? Explain.

SENTENCES, PARAGRAPHS, *and* COMPOSITIONS

Good writers know that strong sentences and paragraphs help to construct effective compositions. Chapter 4 will help you use these building blocks to structure and style excellent writing. It will also present ways to use rhetorical and literary devices and online tools to strengthen your writing.

The Building Blocks: Sentences and Paragraphs

A **sentence** is a group of words with two main parts: a subject and a predicate. Together, these parts express a complete thought.

A **paragraph** is built from a group of sentences that share a common idea and work together to express that idea clearly. The start of a new paragraph has visual clues—either an indent of several spaces in the first line or an extra line of space above it.

In a good piece of writing, each paragraph supports, develops, or explains the main idea of the whole work. Of course, the traits of effective writing—ideas, organization, voice, word choice, sentence fluency, and conventions—appear in each paragraph as well.

Writing Strong Sentences

To write strong paragraphs, you need strong sentences. While it may be your habit to write using a single style of sentences, adding variety will help make your writing more interesting. Combining sentences, using compound elements, forming compound sentences, and using subordination all may help you make your sentences stronger, clearer, or more varied.

Combine Sentences

Putting information from one sentence into another can make a more powerful sentence.

BEFORE
Video games can be effective educational tools. They can help teach many subjects.

AFTER
Video games, which can help teach many subjects, can be effective educational tools.

Use Compound Elements

You can form compound subjects, verbs, or objects to help the flow.

BEFORE
Students can play video games on their laptops. Students can also play video games on their cell phones.

AFTER
Students can play video games on their laptops and cell phones.

Form Compound Sentences

You can combine two sentences into a compound sentence.

BEFORE
Video games can motivate students to learn. They must have educational value.

AFTER
Video games can motivate students to learn, but they must have educational value.

Use Subordination

Combine two related sentences by rewriting the less important one as a subordinate clause.

BEFORE
Video games can take time away from exercise. That can be unhealthy.

AFTER
Video games can take time away from exercise, which can be unhealthy.

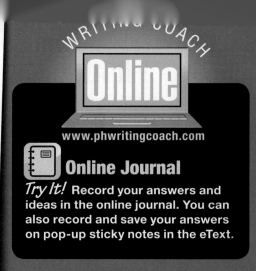

WRITING COACH

Online

www.phwritingcoach.com

Online Journal

Try It! Record your answers and ideas in the online journal. You can also record and save your answers on pop-up sticky notes in the eText.

LEARN MORE
- See Chapter 16, Effective Sentences, pages 410–411
- See Writing Coach Online

Writing Strong Paragraphs

If all the sentences in a paragraph reflect the main idea and work together to express that idea clearly, the result will be a strong paragraph.

Express Your Main Idea With a Clear Topic Sentence

A **topic sentence** summarizes the main idea of a paragraph. It may appear at the beginning, middle, or end of a paragraph. It may even be unstated. When the topic sentence comes at the beginning of a paragraph, it introduces the main idea and leads the reader naturally to the sentences that follow it. When it appears at the end of a paragraph, it can draw a conclusion or summarize what came before it. If the topic sentence is unstated, the rest of the paragraph must be very clearly developed, so the reader can understand the main idea from the other sentences.

Think about the topic sentence as you read this paragraph.

> Without a doubt, hiking must be the best sport in the world. Hiking is good exercise and makes me feel totally free. When I'm out on the trail, I can think more clearly than anywhere else. Even solving problems that seemed totally unsolvable at home becomes possible. I also use all of my senses when I hike. I hear birds singing, I notice strange plants, and I feel the soft underbrush beneath my boots. Sometimes I even think I can smell and taste the fresh air.

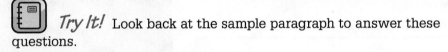 *Try It!* Look back at the sample paragraph to answer these questions.

1. What is the topic sentence?

2. Does the topic sentence introduce the main idea or draw a final conclusion? Explain.

3. What makes this topic sentence strong?

Write Effective Supporting Sentences

A clear topic sentence is a good start, but it needs to be accompanied by good details that support the paragraph's main idea. Your supporting sentences might tell interesting facts, describe events, or give examples. In addition, the supporting sentences should also provide a smooth transition, so that the paragraph reads clearly and logically.

Think about the topic sentences and supporting details as you read this paragraph.

What was life like before cell phones? It's barely imaginable! People were tied to land lines and could make and take calls only in homes, offices, or on pay phones. If there were an emergency, there could be unavoidable delays as people searched for an available phone. If they wanted to chat with friends, they usually had to wait until they got home. How did they ever live without being able to text? Some people send text messages to their friends about 50 times a day. What a different world it was way back then.

 Try It! Look at the paragraph and answer these questions.

1. What is the topic sentence of the paragraph?

2. Do you think it's an effective topic sentence? Why or why not?

3. What supporting details does the writer provide?

4. If you were the writer, what other supporting details might you add to strengthen the paragraph?

5. Which sentence in the paragraph breaks up the flow of ideas and does not provide a smooth transition to the next sentence?

WRITING COACH

Online

www.phwritingcoach.com

Online Journal

Try It! Record your answers and ideas in the online journal. You can also record and save your answers on pop-up sticky notes in the eText.

Include a Variety of Sentence Lengths, Structures, and Beginnings

To be interesting, a paragraph should include sentences of different lengths, types, and beginnings. Similarly, if every sentence has the same structure—for example, article, adjective, noun, verb—the paragraph may sound boring or dry.

21st Century Learning

Collaborate and Discuss

With a group, study this writing sample.

> The scene was tense as Carlos stepped to the plate. Looking confident, he took a few practice swings. Then he stopped and stared straight at the pitcher. The first pitch zoomed over home plate at about 90 miles an hour—right past Carlos. Strike one! The second pitch was high and outside. Ball one! Next Carlos took a deep breath; it was obvious he meant business now. He stared down the pitcher and raised his bat. Crack! Carlos hit that ball right over the fence behind second base and the game was over. It was a 4-2 victory for the home team, thanks to Carlos!

Discuss these questions about the paragraph.

1. What is the topic sentence? How does it draw in the reader?
2. What details support the topic sentence in each paragraph?
3. Point out some examples of varying sentence lengths and beginnings.
4. What examples can you find of sentences with a variety of sentence structures?
5. Which words help the transitions and flow of the paragraphs?

USING TECHNOLOGY

It's often better to use the tab key, rather than the space bar, to indent a paragraph. Using the tab key helps to ensure that the indents in all paragraphs will be uniform.

Composing Your Piece

You've learned that the building blocks of writing are strong sentences and paragraphs. Now it's time to use those building blocks to construct an effective composition. While the types of writing vary from short poems to long essays and research papers, most types have a definite structure with clearly defined parts.

The Parts of a Composition

Writers put together and arrange sentences and paragraphs to develop ideas in the clearest way possible in a composition. Some types of writing, such as poetry and advertisements, follow unique rules and may not have sentences and paragraphs that follow a standard structure. However, as you learned in Chapter 3, most compositions have three main sections: an introduction, a body, and a conclusion.

I. Introduction

The introduction of a composition introduces the focus of the composition, usually in a thesis statement. The introduction should engage the reader's interest, with such elements as a question, an unusual fact, or a surprising scene.

II. Body

Just as supporting statements develop the ideas of a topic sentence, the body of a composition develops the thesis statement and main idea. It provides details that help expand on the thesis statement. The paragraphs in the body are arranged in a logical order.

III. Conclusion

As the word implies, the conclusion of a composition concludes or ends a piece of writing. A good way to ensure the reader will remember your thesis statement is to restate it or summarize it in the conclusion. When restating the thesis, it's usually most effective to recast it in other words. Quotations and recommendations are other ways to conclude a composition with memorable impact. The conclusion should provide a parting insight or reinforce the importance of the main idea.

"Writer to Writer"

Strong, varied sentences and unified paragraphs are the building blocks of effective writing.

—Kelly Gallagher

Rhetorical and Literary Devices

Like any builders, good writers have a set of tools, or devices, at their fingertips to make their writing interesting, engaging, and effective. Writers can use the rhetorical devices of language and their effects to strengthen the power of their style. This section presents some tools you can store in your own writing toolbox to develop effective compositions.

Sound Devices

Sound devices, which create a musical or emotional effect, are most often used in poetry. The most common sound devices include these:

- **Alliteration** is the repetition of consonant sounds at the beginning of words that are close to one another.

  Example: Bees buzzed by both bouquets.

- **Assonance** is the repetition of vowel sounds in words that are close to one another.

  Example: My kite flew high into the sky.

- **Consonance** is the repetition of consonants within or at the end of words.

  Example: Each coach teaches touch football after lunch.

Structural Devices

Structural devices determine the way a piece of writing is organized. Rhyme and meter are most often used to structure poetry, as are stanzas and many other structural devices.

- **Rhyme** is the repetition of sounds at the ends of words. Certain poetry forms have specific rhyme schemes.
- **Meter** is the rhythmical pattern of a poem, determined by the stressed syllables in a line.
- **Visual elements**, such as stanzas, line breaks, line length, fonts, readability, and white space, help determine how a piece of writing is read and interpreted. These elements can also affect the emotional response to a piece.

Other Major Devices

You can use these devices in many forms of writing. They help writers express ideas clearly and engage their readers.

Device	Example
Figurative language is writing that means something beyond what the words actually say. Common forms of figurative language include these:	
• A **simile** compares two things using the words *like* or *as*.	*The fallen autumn leaves were like colorful jewels.*
• A **metaphor** compares two things by mentioning one thing as if it is something else. It does not use *like* or *as*.	*Her smile was a beacon of good cheer.*
• **Personification** gives human characteristics to a non-human object.	*Shadows crawled over the sand just before dusk.*
Hyperbole is exaggeration used for effect.	*The elephant was as big as a house.*
Irony is a contradiction between what happens and what is expected.	In a famous story, a wife cuts her hair to buy her husband a watch fob, and he sells his watch to buy her a brush.
Paradox is a statement that contains elements that seem contradictory but could be true.	George Orwell said, "Ignorance is strength."
An **oxymoron** is word or phrase that seems to contradict itself.	I had jumbo shrimp for dinner.
Symbolism is an object that stands for something else.	An owl is often used as a symbol for wisdom.
An **allegory** is a narrative that has a meaning other than what literally appears.	Some say that his sci-fi story is actually an allegory for the effects of war.
Repetition (or tautology) occurs when content is repeated, sometimes needlessly—for effect.	The forest was dense, dense and dark as coal.

WRITING COACH

Online

www.phwritingcoach.com

Online Journal

Try It! Record your answers and ideas in the online journal. You can also record and save your answers on pop-up sticky notes in the eText.

USING TECHNOLOGY

Most word processing programs have a built-in thesaurus tool. You can use the thesaurus to find descriptive words that can often substitute for weaker, overused words.

Partner Talk

There are many online tools that can help you strengthen your writing. For example, you can search for examples of figurative language and sound devices. Then you can model your own writing after the samples. Just be sure that you don't plagiarize or copy the written work of others.

Using Writing Traits to Develop an Effective Composition

You read about rubrics and traits in Chapter 3. Now it's time to look at how they function in good writing.

Ideas

In an excellent piece of writing, the information presented is significant, the message or perspective is strong, and the ideas are original. As you read the sample, think about the ideas it presents and how it develops them.

Leaves of Three

Leaves of three. Let them be! It's an old rhyme that warns against the dangers of poison ivy—a plant with three waxy-looking leaves. If you've ever had a poison ivy rash, you know that the itching and pain it can cause are nothing to sneeze at. You may not know that the rash is caused by a colorless oil called urushiol or that not all people are allergic to this substance. However, those who are allergic never forget its effects.

Contracting the rash is, unfortunately, all too easy. Perhaps you've been outside, pulling up weeds on a sunny weekend. Because of the way poison ivy leaves bend down, you might not have even noticed them. Then it might have taken 12 to 48 hours before you felt a sharp itch and saw the telltale red blisters caused by even a brief brush with the plant.

What can you do for the discomfort of poison ivy? Applying ice helps some people. Others need anti-itch medication, especially if the reaction is intense or covers a large area. However, the best idea is to keep that old rhyme in mind and to be careful not to let those leaves of three ever come close to thee!

 Try It! Think about ideas in the sample as you respond to these prompts.

1. List two details that help readers relate to the topic.

2. List two significant pieces of information the writer includes.

3. List two details that clearly convey the writer's perspective.

Organization

A well-organized composition flows easily from sentence to sentence and paragraph to paragraph. It smoothly progresses from one idea to the next, indicating the connections between ideas with transitions. The paper also avoids needless repetition.

Think about organization as you reread "Leaves of Three" on page 56.

 Try It! Answer the questions about the writing sample on page 56.

1. Identify the transition the writer uses to move from the ideas in the first paragraph to the ideas in the second.

2. List three details in the third paragraph. Explain how each detail supports the first sentence in the paragraph.

3. Identify the topic of each paragraph, and explain whether the topics are presented in logical order.

Voice

Voice is the individual "sound" of a writer's writing, reflecting the writer's personality and perspective. A well-written piece has a distinctive voice that expresses the writer's individuality.

Read the writing sample. Think about voice as you read.

> What is it like to know a person who looks exactly like you? As identical twins, my brother, Ben, and I can tell you that it's totally great. There are many reasons why.
>
> First, it's great to have a special non-verbal communication with another person. Sometimes it's even scary. Take this morning. Ben and I never dress alike, since we like to show that we're individuals. So, each of us got dressed in our own room and then skipped down the stairs for breakfast. You guessed it! We'd chosen exactly the same clothes—right down to our striped socks.
>
> Second, we can have fun fooling people by pretending to be each other. It's great fun to see Dad's expression when he finds he's treated the wrong twin to a reward.

 Try It! Consider the writer's voice as you answer these questions.

1. Describe the writer's tone—his attitude toward his subject.

2. Which words and phrases create a voice in this sample? Explain.

Partner Talk

Analyze the composition about poison ivy on page 56 with a partner. Discuss how well it might score for the traits of ideas and organization—from ineffective (1), to somewhat effective (2), to fairly effective (3), to effective (4), to highly effective in parts (5), to highly effective throughout (6).

Word Choice

By choosing words with precision, and by using vivid words to create images, good writers give their writing energy and help readers understand their exact meaning.

Think about the writer's word choice as you read these two drafts:

Sally and Alice ran until they reached a place to make a turn. They headed off to the left, where the flowers were pretty and smelled nice.  **1ST DRAFT**

Sally and Alice jogged at a steady pace on the dirt path along the lake until they reached a fork in the trail. Without breaking stride, the two turned in unison and headed left, bound by their silent understanding that left was best—left, where the cream-and-gold honeysuckle blossoms, drooping with fragrance, filled the air with a drowsy sweetness. **2ND DRAFT**

 Try It! Answer the question about the two drafts.

1. List two vague or imprecise words in the first draft.

2. Explain which words in the second draft replace the words you listed. What do the words in the second draft help you understand?

Sentence Fluency

When you read the best writing aloud, you will find that the sentences flow smoothly; they do not sound choppy or awkward. The meaning and the rhythm of the sentences work together. To create and control rhythm in writing, good writers use a variety of sentence structures and patterns. Think about the rhythm of the sentences as you read this draft:

Since I first joined the student council in the ninth grade, I have been a tireless advocate for many important student causes. My experience makes me a good candidate for president of the council; my advocacy makes me a great one. No one else matches my record.

 Try It! Answer the question about the sample.

Describe the rhythm created by the sentences. How does the writer emphasize the final sentence?

Conventions

If a piece of writing reflects a good command of spelling, capitalization, punctuation, grammar, usage, and sentence structure, it is much more likely to communicate clearly to readers.

Pay attention to spelling, capitalization, punctuation, grammar, usage, and sentence structure in the following first draft.

Super-Hero III Doesn't Fly

If you're among the thousands who have been waiting for the latest installment of the popular Super-Hero movie series, you're in for a big disappointment. This sequel misses the boat—literally.

Me and my companion couldn't believe it! At the very beginning of the movie, as usual, our "hero" runs for the ship on his quest to capture the evil warlord. However, this time he misreads, the schedule and it took off for asia without his assistant and he.

Now, read this section of the reviewer's second draft.

Super-Hero III Doesn't Fly

If you're among the thousands who have been waiting for the latest installment of the popular Super-Hero movie series, you're in for a big disappointment. This sequel misses the boat—literally.

My companion and I couldn't believe it! At the very beginning of the movie, as usual, our "hero" runs for the ship on his quest to capture the evil warlord. However, this time he misreads the schedule, and the ship takes off for Asia without his assistant and him.

 Try It! Answer these questions about both drafts.

1. What errors in convention did the writer correct in the second draft?

2. Why is the last sentence easier to read in the second draft?

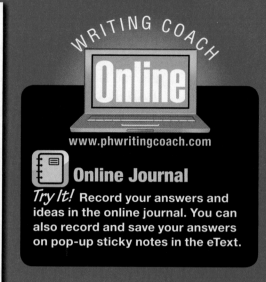

WRITING COACH

Online

www.phwritingcoach.com

Online Journal

Try It! Record your answers and ideas in the online journal. You can also record and save your answers on pop-up sticky notes in the eText.

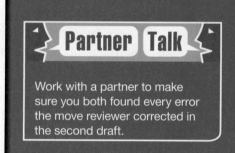

Partner Talk

Work with a partner to make sure you both found every error the move reviewer corrected in the second draft.

Using Interactive Writing Coach

As you learned in Chapter 3, you can use rubrics and your Revision RADaR to check how well your paragraphs and essays read. With Writing Coach, you also have another tool available to evaluate your work: the Interactive Writing Coach.

The Interactive Writing Coach is a program that you can use anywhere that you have Internet access. Interactive Writing Coach functions like your own personal writing tutor. It gives you personalized feedback on your work.

The Interactive Writing Coach has two parts: **Paragraph Feedback** and **Essay Scorer**.

- Paragraph Feedback gives you feedback on individual paragraphs as you write. It looks at the structure of sentences and paragraphs and gives you information about specific details, such as sentence variety and length.

- Essay Scorer looks at your whole essay and gives you a score and feedback on your entire piece of writing. It will tell you how well your essay reflects the traits of good writing.

This chart shows just a few questions that Paragraph Feedback and Essay Scorer will answer about your writing. The following pages explain Paragraph Feedback and Essay Scorer in more detail.

Sentences	• Are sentences varied in length? • Do sentences have varied beginnings? • Which sentences have too many ideas? • Are adjectives clear and precise? • Is the sentence grammatically correct? • Is all spelling correct in the sentence?
Paragraphs	• Does the paragraph support its topic? • Does the paragraph use transitions? • Does the paragraph contain the right amount of ideas and information?
Compositions	• Does the essay reflect characteristics of the genre? • Does it demonstrate the traits of good writing? • Is the main idea clear? • Is the main idea well supported? • Is the essay cohesive—does it hold together?

Interactive Writing Coach and the Writing Process

You can begin to use Essay Scorer during the drafting section of the writing process. It is best to complete a full draft of your essay before submitting to Essay Scorer. (While you are drafting individual paragraphs, you may want to use Paragraph Feedback.) Keep in mind, however, that your draft does not need to be perfect or polished before you submit to Essay Scorer. You will be able to use feedback from Essay Scorer to revise your draft many times. This chart shows how you might use the Interactive Writing Coach and incorporate Essay Scorer into your writing process.

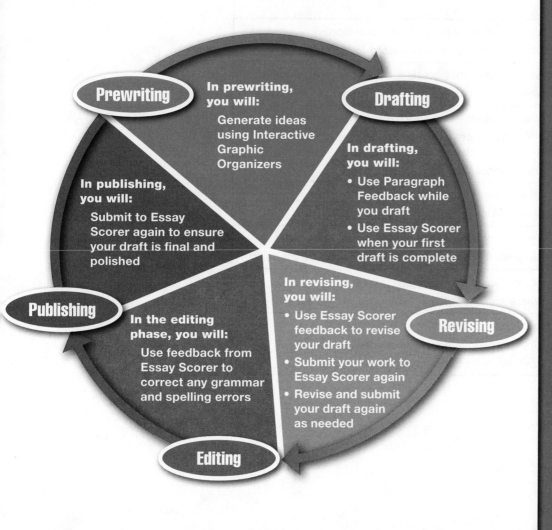

Prewriting

In prewriting, you will:

Generate ideas using Interactive Graphic Organizers

Drafting

In drafting, you will:

• Use Paragraph Feedback while you draft
• Use Essay Scorer when your first draft is complete

Revising

In revising, you will:

• Use Essay Scorer feedback to revise your draft
• Submit your work to Essay Scorer again
• Revise and submit your draft again as needed

Editing

In the editing phase, you will:

Use feedback from Essay Scorer to correct any grammar and spelling errors

Publishing

In publishing, you will:

Submit to Essay Scorer again to ensure your draft is final and polished

Paragraph Feedback With Interactive Writing Coach

The Paragraph Feedback assesses the ideas and topic support for each paragraph you write. You can enter your work into Paragraph Feedback one paragraph at a time. This makes it easy to work on individual paragraphs and get new feedback as you revise each one. Here are some things that Paragraph Feedback will be able to tell you.

Overall Paragraph Support	• Does the paragraph support the main idea? • Which sentences do not support the main idea?
Transitions	• Which sentences contain transition words? • Which words are transition words?
Ideas	• How well are ideas presented? • Which sentences have too many ideas?
Sentence Length and Variety	• Which sentences are short, medium, and long? • Which sentences could be longer or shorter for better sense or variety? • Are sentences varied?
Sentence Beginnings	• How do sentences begin? • Are sentence beginnings varied?
Sentence Structure	• Are sentence structures varied? • Are there too many sentences with similar structures?
Vague Adjectives	• Are any adjectives vague or unclear? • Where are adjectives in sentences and paragraphs?
Language Variety	• Are words repeated? • Where are repeated words located? • How can word choice be improved?

Essay Scoring With Interactive Writing Coach

Essay Scorer assesses your essay. It looks at the essay as a whole, and it also evaluates individual paragraphs, sentences, and words. Essay Scorer will help you evaluate the following traits.

Interactive Writing Coach™

Interactive Writing Coach provides support and guidance to help you improve your writing skills.

- Select a topic to write about from the Topic Bank.
- Use the interactive graphic organizers to narrow your topic.
- Go to Writing Coach Online and submit your work, paragraph by paragraph or as a complete draft.
- Receive immediate, personalized feedback as you write, revise, and edit your work.

Ideas	• Are the ideas original? Is a clear message or unique perspective presented? • Is the main idea clearly stated? • Is the main idea supported by informative details?
Organization	• Is the organization logical? • Is the introduction clear? Is the conclusion clear? • What transitions are used, and are they effective?
Voice	• Does the writer create a unique voice, expressing his or her personality or perspective? • Does the tone match the topic, audience, and purpose?
Word Choice	• Are precise words used? • Are vivid words used? • Do the word choices suit the purpose and audience?
Sentence Fluency	• Are sentence beginnings, lengths, and structures varied? • Do the sentences flow smoothly?
Conventions	• Is spelling correct? • Is capitalization used properly? • Is all punctuation (ending, internal, apostrophes) accurate? • Do subjects and verbs agree? • Are pronouns used correctly? • Are adjectives and adverbs used correctly? • Are plurals formed correctly? • Are commonly confused words used correctly?

Whenever you see the Interactive Writing Coach icon you can go to Writing Coach Online and submit your writing, either paragraph by paragraph or as a complete draft, for personalized feedback and scoring.

CHAPTER 5

NONFICTION NARRATION

What Do You Remember?

What interesting events have happened in your life? What makes these events special?

To tell a story about an event, you will need to remember details of the experience. Using vivid details to describe your memories will make them more interesting to others.

Try It! Think about an interesting event in your life. What story could you tell about it? Consider these questions as you participate in an extended discussion with a partner. Take turns expressing your ideas and feelings.

- What happened?
- Where were you and who was there?
- How did you feel during the experience?
- What did you see, smell, feel, taste, or hear?

Review the list you made, and then think about how you would include these details when telling someone about the interesting event in your life. Tell your story to a partner. As you listen to your partner's story, see if you can answer the questions listed above.

What's Ahead

In this chapter, you will review two strong examples of a narrative nonfiction text: a Mentor Text and a Student Model. Then, using the examples as guidance, you will write a narrative nonfiction text of your own.

WRITING COACH

Online

www.phwritingcoach.com

Online Journal
Try It! Record your answers and ideas in the online journal.

You can also record and save your answers and ideas on pop-up sticky notes in the eText.

THE BIG QUESTION

Connect to the Big Questions

Discuss these questions with your partner:

1 **What do you think?** What stories do sports tell best?

2 **Why write?** What should we put in and leave out to be accurate and honest?

NARRATIVE NONFICTION

Narrative nonfiction is writing that tells a true story. In this chapter, you will explore a special type of narrative nonfiction, the memoir. Like a fictional story, a memoir has a plot, or a series of events; characters; and a setting. A memoir has sensory details, or details that relate to the five senses of touch, taste, smell, sight, and sound, to help make the events seem real to readers. It may even include dialogue—characters' exact words. However, a memoir is a true story about someone's life.

You will develop your memoir by taking it through each of the steps of the writing process: prewriting, drafting, revising, editing, and publishing. You will also have an opportunity to create a script for a documentary about a musician, artist, or actor. To preview the criteria for how your memoir will be evaluated, see the rubric on page 83.

FEATURE ASSIGNMENT

Narrative Nonfiction: Memoir

An effective piece of narrative nonfiction has these characteristics:

- A true, **engaging story** that holds readers' attention

- A well-developed **conflict,** or problem to be solved

- A well-developed **resolution,** the outcome of the conflict, that shows how the problem was solved

- Complex and non-stereotypical **characters,** including yourself

- A specific **mood** or emotion that the narrative suggests

- A unique **tone** that communicates the writer's attitude toward the subject or events

- **Literary strategies** and **devices** to enhance the plot, such as dialogue and suspense, that make your narrative stand out

- **Sensory details**—details related to the five senses of sight, scent, sound, taste, and touch—that help build the story's mood and tone

- A clear **theme,** or larger meaning

- **Effective sentence structure** and correct spelling, grammar, and usage

A memoir also includes:

- Specific **details** about the writer's personal experiences

- Strong **characterization** of real people—your characters

Other Forms of Narrative Nonfiction

In addition to a memoir, there are other forms of narrative nonfiction, including these:

Autobiographical narratives are stories that share facts about your own life. Short autobiographical narratives might be published in magazines, while longer ones are published as books.

Biographical narratives are stories that share facts about someone else's life.

Blogs, or comments that writers share in online forums, may include autobiographical narratives (short or long), reflections, opinions, and other types of comments. Blogs often invite responses, and they usually are not considered a "permanent" form of writing.

Diary entries, which are highly personal, include experiences, thoughts, and feelings—but the audience is private, unless writers choose to share the entries.

Narrative essays use one or more biographical or autobiographical narratives to illustrate or prove a point (the main idea).

Reflective essays present personal experiences (either events that happened to the writers themselves or that they learned about from others), but they focus more on sharing the observations and insights that writers had while thinking about those experiences. Reflective essays often appear as features in magazines and newspapers.

Try It! For each audience and purpose described, choose a form, such as a biographical narrative, blog, or reflective essay, that is appropriate for conveying your intended meaning to the audience. Explain your choices.

- To let classmates know how your trip to the mountains changed your feelings about conservation
- To share with online friends a story about meeting a celebrity
- To record for your family your grandmother's childhood experiences

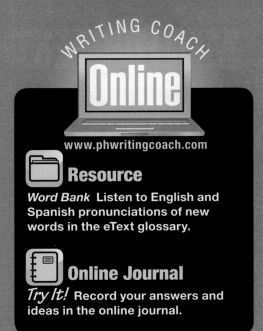
 **WORD BANK**

People often use these basic and content-based vocabulary words when they talk about narrative nonfiction writing. Work with a partner. Take turns saying each word aloud. Then write one sentence using each word. If you are unsure of the meaning of a word, use the Glossary or a dictionary to check the definition.

character	narrative
literary	sensory
mood	tone

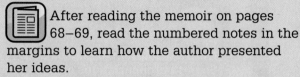

MENTOR TEXT   **Memoir**

Learn From Experience

 After reading the memoir on pages 68–69, read the numbered notes in the margins to learn how the author presented her ideas.

Answer the *Try It!* questions online or in your notebook.

---

1 The author uses **literary devices** in the introduction to her memoir. Her use of **figurative language** makes the description vivid and interesting.

Try It! To what does the author compare the Pacific Ocean? What point about the ocean does the comparison make?

2 A **conflict,** or problem, is introduced at this point: The author was mistakenly assigned to the fifth grade at age eight.

Try It! Why does the author introduce conflict early in the memoir? How does the content of the first paragraph prepare readers for the conflict that follows?

3 The author's misinterpretation of the Pledge of Allegiance helps set a certain **mood**. It also makes the author a more **interesting character** in her own story.

Try It! What mood, or feeling, does the misinterpretation convey?

Extension Find another example of a memoir, and compare it with this one.

Introduction

by Bette Bao Lord

1 My voyage to America began in the autumn of 1946. I was eight years old, sporting pigtails—an innocent, not even armed with a passing acquaintance of A, B, or C. To my chagrin, the ocean was not the vast jade lagoon that I had always envisioned
5 but about as pacific as a fierce dragon with chilies up its snout. And so I bravely cowered in my bunk battling to keep down what I assumed was an authentic American delicacy—spaghetti with meatballs.

Only yesterday, resting my chin on the rails of the S.S.
10 *Marylinx,* I peered into the mist for *Mei Guo,* beautiful country. It refused to appear. Then, within a blink, there was the golden gate, more like the portals to heaven than the arches of a manmade bridge.

2 I arrived in Brooklyn, New York, on a Sunday. On Monday
15 I was enrolled at P.S. 8. By putting up 10 fingers, I found myself sentenced to the fifth grade. It was a terrible mistake. By American reckoning, I had just turned eight. And so I was the shortest student by a head or two in class. In retrospect, I suppose that everyone just supposed that Chinese were supposed to be
20 small.

3 Only yesterday, holding my hand over my heart, I joined schoolmates to stare at the Stars and Stripes and say along: "I pledge a lesson to the frog of the United States of America. And to the wee puppet for witches' hands. One Asian, in the
25 vestibule, with little tea and just rice for all."

Only yesterday, rounding third base in galoshes, I swallowed a barrelful of tears wondering what wrong I had committed to anger my teammates so. Why were they all madly screaming at me to go home, go home?

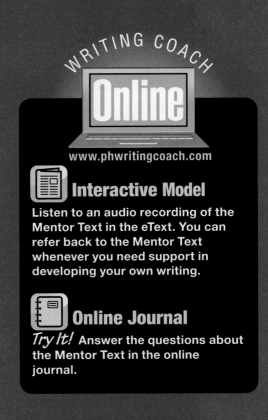

www.phwritingcoach.com

WRITING COACH

Online

Interactive Model
Listen to an audio recording of the Mentor Text in the eText. You can refer back to the Mentor Text whenever you need support in developing your own writing.

Online Journal
Try It! Answer the questions about the Mentor Text in the online journal.

30   ❹ Only yesterday, parroting the patter on our Philco radio, I mastered a few mouthfuls of syllables and immediately my teacher began eliciting my opinions. . . . I was amazed by the fact that an exalted teacher would solicit the opinion of a lowly student. Teachers in China never did that.

35   Eventually, I came to realize that the merits of one's opinions were not the determining goal of the exercise. The goal was to nurture a civil society where everyone is free to speak. Today, when political correctness threatens the rigor of our intellectual debates, how I value this aspect of my early education! To me, 40 the cacophony of puddingheads spewing their views is preferable to the clarion call of even the greatest emperor.

Only yesterday, standing still a head or two short at graduation, I felt as tall as the Statue of Liberty as I recited Walt Whitman: "I hear America singing, the varied carols I hear. . . . Each singing 45 what belongs to him or her and to none else."

❺ Thus I have never forgotten that one need not lose one's native culture in order to become an American. On the contrary, this individual feels doubly blessed. For to me, Americans— though as different as sisters and brothers are—belong to the 50 same family. For to me, America is a road cleared by the footfalls of millions of immigrants and paved with something far more precious than gold—grit and hope.

❹ The **resolution** to the conflict is simple. As the author learned English and American customs, she began to feel at home in the United States.

Try It! How does the author feel about America's tradition of free speech?

❺ In the **conclusion** to the memoir, the author shares insights that her experiences as an immigrant have given her.

Try It! What insights does the writer share? Why is this an effective way to conclude the memoir? What insights have you gained as a result of reading this memoir?

STUDENT MODEL Memoir

With a small group, take turns reading this Student Model aloud. As you read, practice newly acquired vocabulary by correctly producing the word's sound. Also notice how the writer uses dialogue and creates suspense.

Use a Reader's Eye

Now, reread the Student Model. On your copy of the Student Model, use the Reader's Response Symbols to react to what you read.

Reader's Response Symbols

+ **I like where this is going.**

– **This isn't clear to me.**

? **What will happen next?**

! **Wow! That is really cool/weird/ interesting!**

Discuss with a partner the author's use of dialogue, and express your opinion about how well the dialogue enhances the story. Note and discuss responses that were the same for both of you, as well as responses that were different.

A Misunderstanding

by Hector Gutierrez

One day last summer, my greatest fear came back to bite me. My cousin Brandon's neighbor, Mr. Goodman, offered the two of us work cleaning out an old basement. The only problem was that
5   I was terrified of spiders…and I was pretty sure there'd be a lot of them in a musty, old basement.

Mr. Goodman popped his head over the fence and offered us the job. Brandon laughed. I elbowed him, silently praying that he wouldn't tell my secret. "I'm your
10 man," he said, "but Hector here can't help you. He's afraid of spiders. I bet that old basement is full of them."

"Brandon's just messing with you," I said. "I'll help, too."

Mr. Goodman was glad to have the help and said he'd
15 see us on Monday morning.

"Thanks for being such a great friend," I said, but Brandon just shrugged.

"Hey, it's true," he said. "You won't last five minutes in that basement."

20 When I got home, my uncle Tito was in the kitchen making chili. I looked at his muscular arms and chiseled face. "I bet you've never been afraid of anything," I said.

"Everybody's afraid of something," Tito said. "Remember when I went to college? At first, I was so
25 scared I thought I would pass out. I thought everyone would see how stupid I was."

"You're not stupid!" I said.

"I know that now," Tito said. "That's what most fears are—just misunderstandings."

1

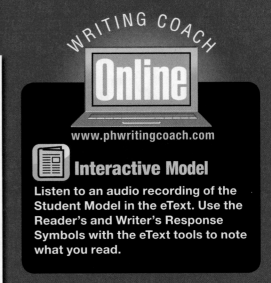

www.phwritingcoach.com

Interactive Model

Listen to an audio recording of the Student Model in the eText. Use the Reader's and Writer's Response Symbols with the eText tools to note what you read.

30   Uncle Tito had given me an idea. I went to the library and read about spiders. I found out most of them are harmless. I checked out a book and stared at photos of spiders until I fell asleep.

    On Monday, Brandon was surprised to see me at
35 Mr. Goodman's house. My knees felt wobbly, but I marched straight down to the basement. I turned on my flashlight and looked in all the corners for webs. Then I looked at the piles of junk on the floor and moved things around. I didn't see any sign of brown
40 recluse spiders, which are highly poisonous.

    Brandon and I covered our noses with bandannas and started hauling stuff outside. After a while, I heard Brandon yell. He was staring at a brown spider on his arm. I felt kind of queasy, but I acted
45 confident. "Don't worry," I told him. "It's just a wolf spider. It can't hurt you." When I brushed it off his arm, I knew spiders would never "bug" me again.

Use a Writer's Eye

Now, evaluate the piece as a writer. On your copy of the Student Model, use the Writer's Response Symbols to react to what you read. Identify places where the student writer uses characteristics of an effective memoir.

Writer's Response Symbols	
E.S.	Engaging story
C.R.	Clear, well-developed conflict and resolution
B.C.	Believable characters
S.D.	Specific and vivid details

2

Prewriting

Plan a first draft of your memoir **by determining an appropriate topic.**
You may select from the Topic Bank or come up with an idea of your own.

 Choose From the Topic Bank

TOPIC BANK

Milestone Milestones should be remembered because they are times
of great personal growth and achievement. Starting high school is a
significant milestone. In an essay, write about this experience and
explain how it has affected you.

Influential Person Think of a family member who has influenced your
life. Write a memoir in which you describe your relationship with this
person and explain the influence he or she has had in your life.

First Job Think of your first job. It might have been paid or volunteer
work. You might have worked after school, part time, or during the
summer. Write a memoir about how you got the job, what you did, and
what you learned from it.

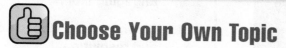 Choose Your Own Topic

Determine an appropriate topic on your own by using the following
range of strategies to generate ideas.

Interview and Reflect

- Interview close friends and family, asking them what events or
  experiences they think changed your life or attitudes.

- If you write in a journal or on an online blog, review your old entries.
  Ask yourself which of these posts records something significant about
  you and consider expanding that post into a memoir.

- Make a list of the things that make you who you are and write a
  memoir that explains why or how these things are important to you.

Review your responses and choose a topic.

Narrow Your Topic

Choosing a topic that is too broad will keep you from providing the sorts of specific details that make readers feel as though they were there when the story was taking place.

Apply It! Use a graphic organizer like the one shown to narrow your topic.

- Record your general topic—your broadest story idea—in the top box; then narrow your topic as you move down the chart.
- Your final box should hold your narrowest story idea, the new focus of your memoir.

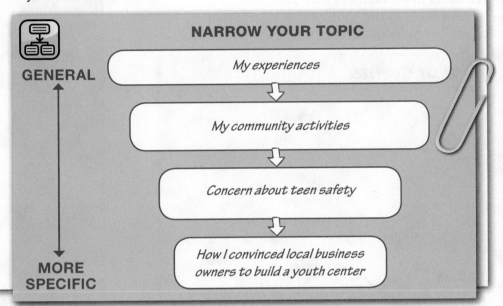

NARROW YOUR TOPIC

GENERAL

My experiences

My community activities

Concern about teen safety

How I convinced local business owners to build a youth center

MORE SPECIFIC

WRITING COACH

Online

www.phwritingcoach.com

 **Interactive Writing Coach™**

- Choosing from the Topic Bank gives you access to the Interactive Writing Coach™.
- Submit your writing and receive instant personalized feedback and guidance as you draft, revise, and edit your writing.

Interactive Graphic Organizers

Use the interactive graphic organizers to help you narrow your topic.

Online Journal

Try It! Record your answers and ideas in the online journal.

 # Consider Multiple Audiences and Purposes

Before writing, think about your audiences and purposes. Consider the views of others as you ask yourself these questions.

Questions for Audience	Questions for Purpose
• Who are the people in my audiences?	• What is my purpose? Do I want to be humorous, thought-provoking, or something else?
• Will the topic of my narrative engage each audience's interest?	
• What might each audience want to know about me—and why?	• As I develop my purpose, how much about myself do I want to share with each audience?
• What literary devices might help me hold each audience's attention?	

Record your answers in your writing journal.

Plan Your Piece

You will use a graphic organizer like the one shown to state your theme, organize your plot events, and define your story elements. When it is complete, you will be ready to write your first draft.

Develop Your Theme To develop a theme, or the controlling idea, for your topic, think about what you learned from the experience or what you want your audience to learn. In narrative nonfiction, your theme might be the lesson that came from experiencing an event.

Map Out Your Plot Use a graphic organizer like this one to help you develop a draft that **structures ideas** in a sustained way. Note the events that will lead to the highest point in the conflict and then reveal the resolution. You may make additional notes here, too.

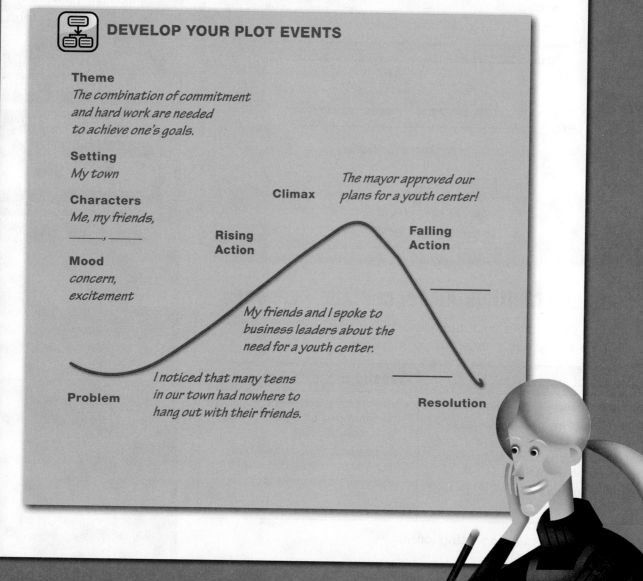

DEVELOP YOUR PLOT EVENTS

Theme
The combination of commitment and hard work are needed to achieve one's goals.

Setting
My town

Characters
Me, my friends,
_____, _____

Mood
concern,
excitement

Climax
The mayor approved our plans for a youth center!

Rising Action

Falling Action

My friends and I spoke to business leaders about the need for a youth center.

Problem

I noticed that many teens in our town had nowhere to hang out with their friends.

Resolution

Gather Details

Writers of memoirs usually build upon the story elements of character, setting, and plot by using a range of literary strategies. Look at these examples.

- **Dialogue** (character's speech): *"Why don't you speak to the business owners' club?" Dad asked. "Maybe they would be willing to fund a youth center."*

- **Mood** (emotion suggested): *The dingy street lit up as we began painting the old house bright blue and yellow. Mrs. Morales brought some flowers from her nursery, and we planted them in the yard. When we were done, the youth center was a warm, cheery place.*

- **Suspense** (uncertainty, tension, and excitement): *I stood up and walked to the podium, my heart pounding. I adjusted the microphone and looked up at a sea of serious adults. My mouth felt dry, and I didn't think I could make a sound. I closed my eyes and took a deep breath. "Thank you," I began, "for allowing me to speak to you this evening."*

Try It! Read the Student Model excerpt and identify what elements the author uses to engage the readers' interest and suggest a theme.

 **STUDENT MODEL** from **A Misunderstanding**
page 70; lines 1–6

> One day last summer, my greatest fear came back to bite me. My cousin Brandon's neighbor, Mr. Goodman, offered the two of us work cleaning out an old basement. The only problem was that I was terrified of spiders…and I was pretty sure there'd be a lot of them in a musty, old basement.

Apply It! As you review the elements on which a narrative writer often focuses, think about how your story details apply to these elements.

- Decide which **sensory details** are most likely to help you define the **mood** and **tone** and write an **engaging story** with well-developed characters, setting, and action.

- Add these details to your graphic organizer, matching each detail to the right part of the story so that you create a well-developed **conflict** and **resolution**.

Drafting

During the drafting stage, you will start to write your ideas for your memoir. You will follow an outline that will help you write a focused, organized, and coherent memoir in an open-ended or untimed situation.

The Organization of a Nonfiction Narrative

The chart shows an organizational strategy for a nonfiction narrative. Look back at how the Mentor Text follows this organizational strategy. Then, use this chart to help you outline your draft.

Outline for Success

I. Beginning

See Mentor Text, p. 68.

- Engaging opening
- Theme
- Introduction to the conflict

Grab Your Reader

- A rhetorical device, such as a rhetorical question, analogy, or a catchy phrase, will engage the readers' interest.
- A memoir may have a subtle point, but the beginning of a story offers at least a hint about the deeper meaning, or theme, of the story.

II. Middle

See Mentor Text, pp. 68–69.

- Well-developed conflict
- Complex characters
- Literary devices and strategies, such as suspense and dialogue
- Sensory details

Develop Your Plot

- Plot events are usually presented in chronological order, or the order in which they occurred, to build up the conflict.
- Dialogue helps to make characters true to life and helps readers to identify with them.
- Vivid details—about characters, setting, and action—make readers feel as if they're experiencing the story as it happens.

III. End

See Mentor Text, p. 69.

- Well-developed resolution
- Ending that reflects the theme and is memorable

Wrap It Up

- The resolution shows how the problem was solved or how events ended it.
- A good ending to a story ties back to the theme, and the writer reflects on how the events in the story affected him or her.

 **Start Your Draft**

To complete your draft, use the checklist. Use the graphic organizer that shows your plot events and the Outline for Success as guides.

While drafting, aim at writing your ideas, not on making your writing perfect. Remember, because you are developing your draft in an open-ended situation, you will have the chance to improve your draft when you revise and edit.

√ Start by drafting an attention-getting opening sentence. Use a **rhetorical device,** such as an analogy or a rhetorical question, to convey meaning and draw your readers into the story.

√ Continue your **beginning** by giving **details** that hint at the theme of your narrative. Make readers curious!.

√ Introduce your **conflict,** or problem, and your **characters.**

√ Develop the **middle** of your memoir. Present a series of plot events that create a well-developed **conflict,** using transitions to clarify the order of events.

√ Use **literary strategies and devices**, such as suspense and dialogue, to further enhance the plot.

√ Avoid creating dull characters. Be sure to describe the people in your story well, in order to build complex and non-stereotypical **characters.** Make your characters come alive to your readers!

√ Enhance the narrative by providing **sensory details** about the characters, setting, and events to establish a mood—the feeling created in the reader. At the same time, pay attention to tone—the writer's attitude toward the subject. Make sure each element of the story is described in a way that is specific and detailed to draw readers into the story.

√ At the **end** of your memoir, offer a well-developed **resolution**—how the conflict worked out.

√ Finish in a way that is satisfying and that recalls the beginning of your true story. Share an **insight** with your reader about how the events of your narrative affected you or your life.

WRITING COACH

Online

www.phwritingcoach.com

Interactive Model

Outline for Success View pop-ups of Mentor Text selections referenced in the Outline for Success.

Interactive Writing Coach™

Use the Interactive Writing Coach to receive the level of support you need:
- Write one paragraph at a time and submit each one for immediate, detailed feedback.
- Write your entire first draft and submit it for immediate, personalized feedback.

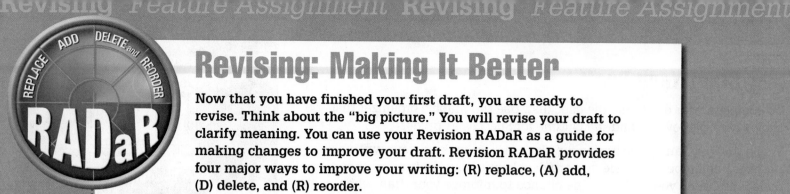

Revising: Making It Better

Now that you have finished your first draft, you are ready to revise. Think about the "big picture." You will revise your draft to clarify meaning. You can use your Revision RADaR as a guide for making changes to improve your draft. Revision RADaR provides four major ways to improve your writing: (R) replace, (A) add, (D) delete, and (R) reorder.

Kelly Gallagher, M. Ed.

KEEP REVISION ON YOUR RADAR

Read part of the first draft of the Student Model "A Misunderstanding." Then, look at the questions the writer asked himself as he thought about how well his draft was organized and how well his audience would understand it.

A Misunderstanding

 1ST DRAFT

"... would see how stupid I was."

I told my uncle he wasn't stupid. He said he knew that now, and that most fears are really just misunderstandings.

Uncle Tito had given me an idea. I went to the library and read about spiders. I found out most of them are harmless. I checked out a book and stared at photos of spiders until I fell asleep.

On Monday, Brandon was surprised to see me at Mr. Goodman's house. I marched straight down to the basement. I turned on my flashlight and looked in all the corners for webs. Then I looked at the piles of junk on the floor and moved things around. I didn't see any sign of brown recluses, highly poisonous spiders.

Brandon and I covered our noses with bandannas and started hauling stuff outside. After a while, I heard Brandon yell. I wondered what was wrong. He was staring at a brown spider on his arm. I felt kind of queasy, but I acted confident. "Don't worry," I told him. "It's just a wolf spider. It can't hurt you." Then I brushed it off his arm. I had learned a lesson.

Would this information be more interesting if I used dialogue?

Does this paragraph include sensory details that set the mood or tone and tell the reader how I felt?

Is my resolution of the conflict well-organized, and is my conclusion memorable?

Now look at how the writer applied Revision RADaR to write an improved second draft.

A Misunderstanding

"... would see how stupid I was."

"You're not stupid!" I said.

"I know that now," Tito said. "That's what most fears are—just misunderstandings."

Uncle Tito had given me an idea. I went to the library and read about spiders. I found out most of them are harmless. I checked out a book and stared at photos of spiders until I fell asleep.

On Monday, Brandon was surprised to see me at Mr. Goodman's house. My knees felt wobbly, but I marched straight down to the basement. I turned on my flashlight and looked in all the corners for webs. Then I looked at the piles of junk on the floor and moved things around. I didn't see any sign of brown recluses, highly poisonous spiders.

Brandon and I covered our noses with bandannas and started hauling stuff outside. After a while, I heard Brandon yell. He was staring at a brown spider on his arm. I felt kind of queasy, but I acted confident. "Don't worry," I told him. "It's just a wolf spider." When I brushed it off his arm, I knew spiders would never "bug" me again.

R *Replaced a general description with dialogue to make the information more interesting to my audience*

A *Added a sensory detail about my wobbling knees to show how frightened I was*

D *Deleted the unnecessary detail about the narrator wondering why Brandon was yelling*

R *Replaced a vague statement of resolution with a memorable, specific, and catchy phrase*

 Apply It! Now revise your draft to **clarify your meaning.**

- First, determine if you have included a well-developed conflict and resolution and sensory details that define the mood or tone of the story. Then make sure that your plot details are clear for your audience and that your organization of those details is logical.

- Then apply Revision RADaR to make needed changes. Remember— you can use the steps in the strategy in any order.

Look at the Big Picture

Use the chart to evaluate how well each section of your memoir achieves **logical organization**. When necessary, use the suggestions in the chart to revise your memoir.

Section	Evaluate	Revise
Beginning	• Decide whether your opening sentence is **engaging,** making your audience want to read on.	• Add a catchy phrase, an interesting quotation, or a personal observation to draw readers in.
	• Consider your **theme.** Readers should know why you're writing, even if your theme is subtle.	• Sum up the point of your narrative in one sentence; then, decide whether you want to include that sentence or hint at its idea.
Middle	• Review the plot of your narrative. Do you have a well-developed **conflict?** Do the events clearly present a problem that involves you?	• Add details and plot events to strengthen your conflict, or problem. Rearrange events to ensure chronological order. Add, change, or even delete details to keep readers in suspense about the conflict's resolution.
	• Underline details that show your characters in action in one or more settings. Do these descriptive details make the characters and settings interesting and believable? Do they help set the **mood** or **tone**?	• To define the mood or tone, add vivid sensory details about characters and settings. Make sure that your characters are complex and non-stereotypical.
	• Look at the middle as a whole and evaluate your use of a range of **literary strategies** and **devices** to enhance the plot and to hold readers' interest.	• Review the dialogue and the level of suspense you have built. To add more interest, experiment with figures of speech, such as irony. (See page 81.)
End	• Check for a well-developed **resolution**—one that clearly reveals the conflict's outcome.	• Add or revise details to show how the problem was solved or how events ended it.
	• Evaluate your **closing** to see if it reflects the beginning and brings the narrative full circle.	• Add a sentence or words that connect the theme with the outcome of the conflict.

Focus on Craft: Irony

Irony is a **trope,** or figure of speech, in which what is said is the opposite of what is meant. Because readers can tell that the opposite, or ironic, statement is ridiculous in the situation, they understand that the writer is emphasizing the real meaning. For instance, if a writer has a character that is freezing say, "I'm all toasty warm," the reader knows that the character is emphasizing how cold she is.

Think about irony as you read this sentence from the Student Model.

 **STUDENT MODEL** from **A Misunderstanding**
page 70; lines 16–17

> "Thanks for being such a great friend," I said, but Brandon just shrugged.

 Try It! Now, ask yourself these questions. Record your answers in your journal.

- Do you think this sentence would have been stronger or weaker if Hector had said, "That was unkind of you"? Explain.
- Does the dialogue sound like something a real person would say? Why or why not?

Fine-Tune Your Draft

 Apply It! Use the revision suggestions to prepare your final draft. Decide whether you have built a draft with a clear organization.

- **Employ Tropes** Add deliberate uses of language, such as irony or repetition, to express an emotional reaction and add interest to your narrative.
- **Use Transitions** Help readers understand how the events in your story are related by including transitions like *next, suddenly,* and *before I knew it,* to convey meaning and connect ideas.
- **Ensure Logical Organization** If necessary, rearrange words, sentences, and paragraphs to create logical organization and to clarify your meaning.

Peer Feedback Read your final draft to a group of peers. Ask the group to give you feedback on the problem and its resolution. Think about their responses and revise your final draft as needed.

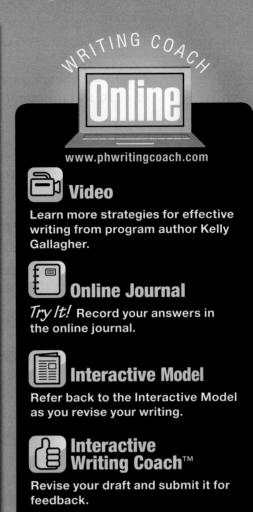

WRITING COACH

Online

www.phwritingcoach.com

Video

Learn more strategies for effective writing from program author Kelly Gallagher.

Online Journal

Try It! Record your answers in the online journal.

Interactive Model

Refer back to the Interactive Model as you revise your writing.

Interactive Writing Coach™

Revise your draft and submit it for feedback.

Editing: Making It Correct

To edit your work, read your draft carefully to correct errors in spelling and grammar. It can be helpful to read your draft aloud.

As you edit your final draft, think about how you can **use adverbial clauses** to make transitions. Keep in mind the rules for using commas to punctuate clauses. Then edit your draft by correcting any factual errors and errors in **grammar, mechanics, and spelling**.

WRITE GUY *Jeff Anderson, M. Ed.*

WHAT DO YOU NOTICE?

Zoom in on Conventions Focus on the use of adverbial clauses as you zoom in on this passage from the Student Model.

> 📰 **STUDENT MODEL** from **A Misunderstanding** page 70; lines 16–22
>
> "Thanks for being such a great friend," I said, but Brandon just shrugged.
>
> "Hey, it's true," he said. "You won't last five minutes in that basement."
>
> When I got home, my uncle Tito was in the kitchen making chili. I looked at his muscular arms and chiseled face. "I bet you've never been afraid of anything," I said.

> To learn more about adverbial clauses, see Chapter 15 of your Grammar Handbook.

Now, ask yourself: *How does the adverbial clause* When I got home *help you follow the sequence of events?*

Perhaps you said that the adverbial clause links the paragraphs.

When I got home is an **adverbial clause,** a subordinate clause that works like an adverb by modifying a verb, adjective, or verbal. It begins with a subordinating conjunction (e.g., *after, although, before, where*) and contains a subject and a verb.

Writers use adverbial clauses to make transitions between sentences or paragraphs. *When I got home* makes a transition between the end of the narrator's conversation with Brandon and the beginning of his conversation with Tito. It helps readers understand when and where the second conversation took place.

Partner Talk Discuss this question with a partner: *How can adverbial clauses help readers follow events in a text?*

Grammar Mini-Lesson: Commas With Clauses

To learn more, see Chapter 23.

Adverbial clauses used as transitions usually precede the main clause in a sentence. When an adverbial clause precedes the main clause, set it off with a **comma**. However, do not use a comma when the adverbial clause comes after the main clause. Study the following sentence from the Student Model. Notice how the author uses a comma to set off the adverbial clause.

STUDENT MODEL from **A Misunderstanding**
page 71; lines 46–47

> When I brushed it off his arm, I knew spiders would never "bug" me again.

 Try It! Place a comma if needed to **correctly punctuate** the adverbial clause in each sentence. Write the answers in your journal.

1. Before Jake came home he stopped off at the market.
2. We waited for Nicole until the bell rang.
3. While I went to answer the door the dog ate my sandwich.

 Apply It! Edit your draft for grammar, mechanics, and spelling. If necessary, revise some sentences to use adverbial clauses as transitions. Check to ensure that you have consistently punctuated adverbial clauses correctly.

 Use the rubric to evaluate your piece. If necessary, rethink, rewrite, or revise.

Rubric for Narrative Nonfiction: Memoir	Rating Scale
Ideas: How well do you narrate a single, important event?	Not very Very 1 2 3 4 5 6
Organization: How logically organized is your sequence of events?	1 2 3 4 5 6
Voice: How authentic and engaging is your voice?	1 2 3 4 5 6
Word Choice: How effectively do you use details to show characters and setting?	1 2 3 4 5 6
Sentence Fluency: How well have you used transitions when moving from idea to idea?	1 2 3 4 5 6
Conventions: How correct are your adverbial clauses?	1 2 3 4 5 6

WRITING COACH

Online

www.phwritingcoach.com

Video
Learn effective editing techniques from program author Jeff Anderson.

Online Journal
Try It! Record your answers in the online journal.

Interactive Model
Refer back to the Interactive Model as you edit your writing.

Interactive Writing Coach™
Edit your draft. Check it against the rubric and then submit it for feedback.

Publishing

Share your experience and what it means to you by publishing your memoir. First, prepare your narrative for presentation. Then, choose ways to **publish it for appropriate multiple audiences.**

Wrap Up Your Presentation

Is your narrative handwritten or written on a computer? If your narrative is handwritten, you may need to make a new, clean copy. If so, be sure to **write legibly.** Also be sure to add a title to your narrative that grabs the reader's attention and indicates your story's topic.

Publish Your Piece

Use the chart to identify ways to publish your memoir.

If your audience is...	...then publish it by...
Classmates and teachers at school	• Reading it aloud and creating an audio recording that can be checked out from the library as a CD or posted as a podcast • Posting it on your school's Web site
People (in your town or around the world) that you may never meet	• Submitting it to a print or online literary magazine • Posting it to a blog for people who share some of your experiences

Reflect on Your Writing

Now that you are done with your memoir, read it over and use your writing journal to answer the following questions.

- Does your memoir accurately capture the events and your emotions during and after the events? Explain.

- Are any parts of your story boring or slow-moving? If so, how can you change this in your next writing assignment?

- What do you like best about your memoir? How will you use this in the future?

 The Big Question: Why Write?
What did you decide to put in or leave out to be accurate and honest?

Manage Your Portfolio You may wish to include your published memoir in your writing portfolio.

MAKE YOUR WRITING COUNT

Make a Memoir Storyboard

Some of the most entertaining films for young people have been based on written memoirs. Prepare a memoir for the silver screen by creating a **storyboard**—a sequence of sketches representing the elements of each scene.

In an open-minded group discussion, review your memoirs and choose the one that might translate best to film. Present your storyboard as a **multimedia presentation** that blends media including sound, graphics, and images. You can also write out a brief script for a scene from the storyboard, or you can video-record a short film.

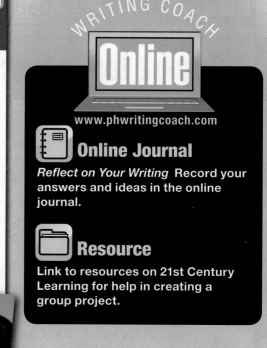

Here's your action plan.

1. Choose group roles and set objectives. You'll need to write the scenes, compose or select songs for the soundtrack, draft a storyboard, cast characters, and identify locations.

2. Create a storyboard. Try to **appeal to your audience** as you:

   - Sketch the basic visual set-up of the scene. Synthesize ideas from different team members' points of view.

   - Make notes about the script, location, and music beneath each sketch. Convey a clear and distinct perspective.

   - Note camera directions, such as "close-up" and "fade out."

   - Search online for additional tips on storyboarding.

3. Write the script, including all dialogue and narration. As you draft aim to produce a focused presentation based on solid reasoning.

4. As a group, review the script and the storyboard. Adjust each one as needed so that the two go hand in hand.

5. Present a video-recorded or live version of the memoir to the class.

Listening and Speaking Rehearse your script and stage each scene according to the directions in the storyboard, including music and sound effects. Try to synthesize, or blend, the multiple points of view expressed in your peers' feedback as you act out each scene live for the class or video-record the memoir.

WRITING COACH

Online

www.phwritingcoach.com

Online Journal

Reflect on Your Writing Record your answers and ideas in the online journal.

Resource

Link to resources on 21st Century Learning for help in creating a group project.

Your Turn

**Short Assignment:
Documentary Script**

21st Century Learning

Script for a Documentary

A **documentary** is a film that tells a story about real events or people. Documentary filmmakers may use filmed reenactments, video of scenes or places, interviews, still images, music or other sounds, and graphics. Most documentaries have a narrator—someone who tells the story from his or her own distinctive point of view.

A **script for a documentary** tells what viewers will see and hear and in what order. The power of a documentary's story depends on how effectively the filmmaker puts together the information.

 Try It! Read and visualize the narrative in this part of a documentary script. Then, answer these questions. Record your answers in your journal.

1. What is the topic of the documentary? What do you think its purpose and **theme** might be? Is the theme explicit (stated directly) or implicit (implied)?

2. To what **specific audiences** would this documentary probably appeal?

3. **Visual elements** in documentaries may include photographs, news footage, and interviews. Which visual elements are part of this scene?

4. What **literary techniques** does the filmmaker use in the script? How do they add value to the documentary?

Extension Find another example of a script, and compare it with this one.

BUILDING AN URBAN EDEN, Scene 1

(Open with a 1-minute time-lapse shot of plants sprouting, growing, and flowering in one of Kevin Chang's rooftop gardens. Instrumental background music: Vivaldi's "Spring.")

(Cut to the Chatham Street Food Pantry to show people moving from one table piled with fresh produce to another. Continue same background music.)

NARRATOR: This may look like a farmer's market. People stroll in with recyclable bags to pick out fresh, delicious fruits and vegetables and chat with the farmers. In fact, this is the Chatham Street Food Pantry, and everything here is free. The farmers are part of Master Gardener Kevin Chang's Eden Project, which has transformed downtown Hudson City.

(NARRATOR continues as he walks down the city street with Kevin Chang, passing beds and containers of vegetables and fruit in front of businesses, in window boxes, and in the small front yards of homes.)

NARRATOR: So how did this idea come to you, Kevin?

CHANG: When I was a child, I didn't understand the difference between ornamental and food plants. They looked equally beautiful to me! And you know, I never got the difference. Why plant something you can't eat, especially when people need the food?

(Chang stops and kneels at a planter full of red peppers in front of a fancy hotel.)

CHANG: You don't need a lot of space to grow vegetables. The doormen get to take these peppers home!

Create a Script for a Documentary

Follow these steps to create a 5-minute scene for your own documentary script. Keep in mind the theme of the documentary, as well as the mood or tone you hope to convey. To plan your script, review the graphic organizers on R24–R27 and choose one that suits your needs.

Prewriting

- Choose a topic for your documentary, such as a newsworthy event, an interesting local character, or a beautiful or intriguing place.
- Decide on your purpose for presenting this documentary. Think about your story and your **theme**. Will the theme be explicit and directly stated, or implicitly suggested?
- List the kinds of **literary techniques** that you might include—narration, dialogue, suspense, and so on—and note potential visual and sound elements, such as types of still or moving images, music, location, and camera angle direction.
- Research your topic, gathering information for the narration as well as for the visual elements, music, and so on. Document your sources.

Drafting

- Make an outline to organize the elements in a way that is varied but that still makes sense.
- Write a script that identifies the placement of each element and that uses narration to connect the elements.
- Keep your purpose, audience, theme, and mood or tone in mind.

Revising and Editing

- Review your draft to ensure that your documentary is accurate and appealing; add or remove details as needed. Make sure you have used a variety of **literary techniques** in your script.
- Check that spelling, grammar, and mechanics are correct, especially in the narrator's words. Also make sure that the narrator's words are specific and interesting.

Publishing

Publish your script by creating a video recording of it. Before recording, you might want to spend some time planning and talking with the subjects of your documentary. Afterward, present it to the class. Ask classmates to share their responses with you.

WRITING COACH Online
www.phwritingcoach.com

Online Journal
Try It! Record your answers in the online journal.

 ### Interactive Graphic Organizers

Choose from a variety of graphic organizers to plan and develop your project.

Partner Talk

Before you start drafting, explain your documentary to a partner. Use specific details to describe and explain your ideas. Increase the specificity of your details based on the type of information you are delivering. Ask for feedback. What ideas about the film's elements does your partner have?

Writing for Assessment

Many tests include a prompt that asks you to write an essay that relates to your personal experience. Use these prompts to practice. Respond using the characteristics of your memoir. (See page 66.)

 Try It! Read the **narrative nonfiction** prompt and the information on format and academic vocabulary. Then, use the ABCDs of On-Demand Writing to help you plan and write your essay.

Format

The prompt directs you to write a *narrative nonfiction essay.* Be sure to include a beginning that introduces your main idea and sets the scene for your narrative; a middle with a well-developed conflict; and an end that presents a well-developed resolution and reflects your main idea.

Narrative Nonfiction Prompt

What was the last contest you attended? Was it a sports event, a school debate, a dance contest, or something else? Write a narrative nonfiction essay about this event. Tell a narrative about the conflict between contestants. Include an explanation of the resolution.

Academic Vocabulary

Remember that a *conflict* is a struggle between people or forces, and a *resolution* is the struggle's outcome. Narrative nonfiction should always include a well-developed conflict and resolution.

The ABCDs of On-Demand Writing

Use the following ABCDs to help you respond to the prompt.

Before you write your draft:

A ttack the prompt [1 MINUTE]

- Circle or highlight important verbs in the prompt. Draw a line from the verb to what it refers to.
- Rewrite the prompt in your own words.

B rainstorm possible answers [4 MINUTES]

- Create a graphic organizer to generate ideas.
- Use one for each part of the prompt if necessary.

C hoose the order of your response [1 MINUTE]

- Think about the best way to organize your ideas.
- Number your ideas in the order you will write about them. Cross out ideas you will not be using.

After you write your draft:

D etect errors before turning in the draft [1 MINUTE]

- Carefully reread your writing.
- Make sure that your response makes sense and is complete.
- Look for spelling, punctuation, and grammar errors.

👍 More Prompts for Practice

Apply It! Respond to Prompts 1 and 2 in timed or open-ended situations by writing **narrative nonfiction** essays that present an **engaging story** in support of a main idea. As you write, be sure to:

- Fully develop complex and non-stereotypical characters
- Give your narrative a well-developed **conflict** and **resolution**
- Include a range of **literary strategies and devices,** such as suspense and dialogue to enhance the **plot** of the narrative
- Use **transitions** and appropriate **rhetorical devices,** such as rhetorical questions and analogies to convey meaning
- Include **sensory details** that define the mood or tone of the story and help your readers feel as if they were there as the events took place

> **Prompt 1** Think of something you loved to do as a child. Why did you love it? What made it exciting for you? Write a narrative nonfiction essay that tells a story and sums up your feelings about that activity.

> **Prompt 2** We all have a person or people in our lives who have affected us in powerful ways. Write a narrative nonfiction essay that tells a story about you and an important person in your life.

More Strategies for Writing for Assessment

- Consider several possible topics and quickly list details that you might use in your response. Then, choose the topic for which you have the strongest ideas.
- If you do not understand any words in the prompt, use context clues to determine the meaning of any unfamiliar words.
- Be sure to follow the ABCDs of writing to a prompt. Planning is an important part of writing.
- Make sure to reread your piece after you have completed it. This will give you a chance to find and correct errors. If you are in a timed situation be sure to leave enough time for this step.

WRITING COACH
Online
www.phwritingcoach.com

👍 Interactive Writing Coach™

Plan your response to the prompt. If you are using the prompt for practice, write one paragraph at a time or your entire draft and then submit it for feedback. If you are using the prompt as a timed test, write your entire draft and then submit it for feedback.

Remember ABCD

Attack the prompt

Brainstorm possible answers

Choose the order of your response

Detect errors before turning in the draft

CHAPTER 6

FICTION NARRATION

What's the Story?

What is happening in the photo? What do you think will happen next? What story can you tell about it?

Many stories have realistic settings. Believable details about setting, such as a description of a rickety bridge, help get the reader interested and add to the story. Conflict is also important. Conflict is a challenge or problem the main character faces.

Try It! Think about the events of these people's day. What events led up to this moment?

Consider these questions as you participate in an extended discussion with a partner. Take turns expressing your ideas and feelings.

- What is the setting of this story?
- How do you think these people feel?
- Do you think these people are crossing the bridge for fun or out of necessity?
- What other activities might they have done on this day?

Review your notes. Use your notes to tell a story about the people. Be sure to use many details to make your story believable.

What's Ahead

In this chapter, you will review two strong examples of a short story: a Mentor Text and a Student Model. Then, using the examples as guidance, you will write a fiction story of your own.

WRITING COACH

Online

www.phwritingcoach.com

 Online Journal

Try It! Record your answers and ideas in the online journal.

You can also record and save your answers and ideas on pop-up sticky notes in the eText.

 Connect to the Big Questions

Discuss these questions with your partner:

1 **What do you think?** Do we adapt our environment or adapt to it?

2 **Why write?** What can fiction do better than nonfiction?

SHORT STORY

A short story is a brief work of fiction that develops and resolves a single conflict or problem. In this chapter, you will explore a special type of short story called historical fiction. Historical fiction is set during a real historical time period and may include characters or events of historical importance. Like any short story, historical fiction explores a central conflict or problem faced by the main character. The plot develops to a climax, or turning point, and is resolved at the end of the story.

You will develop your work of historical fiction by taking it through each of the steps of the writing process: prewriting, drafting, revising, editing, and publishing. You will also have an opportunity to create a pitch for a historical fiction screenplay. To preview the criteria for how your historical fiction will be evaluated, see the rubric on page 111.

FEATURE ASSIGNMENT

Short Story: Historical Fiction

An effective and imaginative short story has these characteristics:

- An **engaging story**

- A **well-developed conflict** and **resolution**

- Complex and non-stereotypical **characters**

- A range of **literary strategies and devices,** such as dialogue and suspense, to enhance the **plot** and help develop characters' personalities

- **Sensory details** that define the **mood** or **tone**

- A clearly described **setting** that correctly establishes the time and place

- **Effective pacing,** or the rhythm and speed at which the plot unfolds

- Effective **sentence structure** and correct spelling, grammar, and usage

An effective work of historical fiction also includes:

- **Imaginary characters** who live in real places and times in history

- **Descriptive details** that help readers identify the historical time and place

- Characters who may interact with famous people in history and participate in **important historical events**

Other Forms of Short Stories

In addition to historical fiction, there are other forms of short stories, including:

Fantasy stories stretch the imagination and take readers to unreal worlds. Animals may talk, people may fly, or characters may have superhuman powers.

Mysteries focus on unexplained or strange events that one of the characters tries to solve. These stories are often full of suspense and surprises.

Myths and legends are traditional stories that different cultures have told to explain natural events, human nature, or the origins of things. They often include gods and goddesses from ancient times and heroes who do superhuman things.

Realistic fiction portrays invented characters and events in everyday life that most readers would find familiar.

Science fiction stories focus on real or imagined developments in science and technology and their effects on the way people think and live. Space travel, robots, and life in the future are popular topics for science fiction.

Tall tales tell about larger-than-life characters in realistic settings. The characters perform amazing acts of strength, bravery, or even silliness. Often tall tales explain how the main character solves a problem or reaches a goal by doing something wild and fantastic that normal people could never do.

Try It! For each audience and purpose described, choose a story form, such as a tall tale, science fiction, or myth, that is appropriate for conveying your intended meaning to the audience. Explain your choices.

- To explain in a story why rain falls from clouds
- To show readers what it might be like to live on a distant planet
- To amuse your friends by exaggerating an event that happened in school or your neighborhood

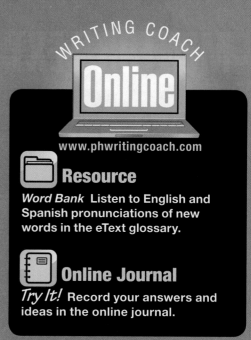

WORD BANK

People often use these vocabulary words when they talk about short story writing. Work with a partner. Take turns saying each word aloud. Then write one sentence using each word. If you are unsure of the meaning of a word, use the Glossary or a dictionary to check the definition.

characterization	mood
climax	resolution
conflict	tone

MENTOR TEXT

Historical Fiction

Learn From Experience

 Read the historical fiction on pages 94–97. As you read, take notes to develop your understanding of basic sight and English vocabulary. Then, read the numbered notes in the margins to learn about how the author presented her ideas.

Answer the *Try It!* questions online or in your notebook.

1 Like all historical fiction, this story takes place during a real historical time period—the Civil War. This paragraph gives an overview of the **setting**.

Try It! Who are the Rebs? Who are the Yankees? Is the narrator a Reb or a Yankee?

2 In these passages, the author mentions Major General Buell, General Braxton Bragg, and Major General Rosencrans. These characters were **real people of historical importance**, and the battles that are described actually took place.

Try It! Why might a writer of historical fiction include real people or events in her story? Can a modern author accurately portray historical events? Why or why not?

3 The author uses **sensory details** to describe the scene and define the **mood**.

Try It! What details appeal to the reader's sense of hearing? Touch? Sight?

Extension Find another example of a short story, and compare it with this one.

The Song of Stones River

by Jennifer Armstrong

1 By July of 1862 the War Between the States had already torn fifteen months off the calendar. Our boys had fought bloodily in the battlefields of Virginia and on the other side of the Appalachians, too, in Tennessee, Kentucky, and Missouri. With all the cards against them—fewer men, fewer guns, fewer supplies of all kinds—the rebel army of the Confederacy had won battle after battle. Our powerful army of the United States was getting kicked all over the map. The Rebs were beating us Yankees.

2 Over in Murfreesboro, Tennessee, Federal troops under Major General Buell were looking to hold control of the railroad lines so the supply trains could come through from Kentucky with food for men, horses, and mules. Like a summer storm, Confederate cavalry crashed down upon them, overwhelmed the garrison, and forced a surrender. The way was now clear for the Rebels to invade northward.

And northward they ran, into Kentucky, hastening upward toward Ohio like a burning fuse, even as the sun beat down from a cloudless sky and squeezed every particle of moisture from the landscape. **2** My brother was in a Union regiment at Green River Bridge in September when the advancing Confederate Army under General Braxton Bragg broke upon them and forced another surrender. The rebel cavalry watered their dry horses at the river's edge while the defeated boys of the Union garrison were made prisoners of war, my brother among them.

Now more divisions of the Union army under Major General Rosencrans, and me and my drum with them, had to trudge south along the rail lines to beat back the Confederate invasion of Kentucky. By early October, the drought had burned the ground coal-hard, and we were worn to a thread before we'd even met the Rebels. **3** Me beating cadence on my drum was the only beating going on at that warm time. From north and from south, footsore soldiers marched under a blistering sun, and we shook the last drops of water from our canteens; the bugler was too dry to blow his horn. We came upon a creek in Perryville, with a unit

(Line numbers in margin: 5, 10, 15, 20, 25, 30)

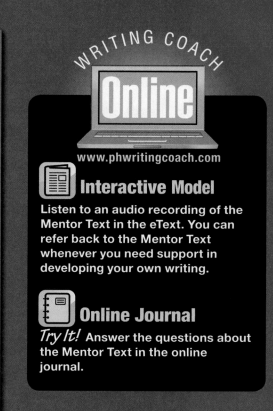

WRITING COACH

Online

www.phwritingcoach.com

Interactive Model

Listen to an audio recording of the Mentor Text in the eText. You can refer back to the Mentor Text whenever you need support in developing your own writing.

Online Journal

Try It! Answer the questions about the Mentor Text in the online journal.

35 of Arkansas soldiers refreshing themselves in the shade, and this lit off a huge battle that ended with victory for us at last. By nightfall the scorched Confederates were beating a retreat back toward the Cumberland Gap, back into Tennessee. The summer campaign had beaten us all as dry and thin as leather straps, and
40 them weary Confederate troops were looking forward to settling in for their winter camp and singing restful songs.

   ❹ But we was on our way to the Cumberland Gap, too. Throughout the fall, I drummed us after the retreating rebels, southward across the mountains into east Tennessee, and
45 then dogged them west on the road to Nashville. Our pickets skirmished with theirs, kicking up the dust in the dry lanes as the leaves began to fall. Autumn's crops lay forgotten in the fields—pumpkins and apples abuzz with yellow jackets while the people in the countryside tried to keep out of the way of us
50 bluecoats. Woodpeckers drummed their warning through deep thickets, and mourning doves sang their melancholy laments as we passed by. When late December's darkness closed in around us, we and the Confederates both camped outside Murfreesboro, Tennessee, in the rocky cedar glades along the banks of the
55 narrow Stones River.

❹ The author's **pacing** is unhurried in this passage and throughout most of the story.

Try It! Why is the pacing effective in this story? What contributes to the slow pacing?

5 The author uses descriptive details to create the **mood** in this passage.

Try It! How would you describe the mood? What details help create the mood?

6 The author develops the narrator's **character** in this passage and reveals his inner **conflict**.

Try It! What brought the narrator to the war, and what is he questioning now? How does the language that he uses help characterize him? Would he use different words if he were a character in a modern book you know? Explain.

7 The author uses the literary device of **foreshadowing** in this sentence.

Try It! How do you think music might affect the soldiers and their actions?

8 This passage is important to the **plot**. The author creates **conflict** between the groups of soldiers.

Try It! What effect does the "song fight" have on the soldiers?

Discuss the story with a partner. Consider that it was written many years after the Civil War. What modern ideas does the author seem to emphasize in the story? What do you think the literature suggests about the historical period and cultural contexts in which it was *written*?

There would be another battle. Not a man among us doubted it, though we in the ranks was too far below the officers to be informed to the level of certainty. Even though the summer and fall had been one long weary march broken up with bitter fighting, 60 there would be no rest for us. Even though it was Christmas, there would be no rest for us. In our camp, men wrote letters to their wives and mothers as they crouched near the cookfires. **5** And I had no misgivings but that General Bragg's boys were doing the same over where they lay, in their bivouacs on the 65 cold limestone. In the rope corrals, the bony mules who pulled our baggage wagons brayed their complaints into the darkness, and it seemed to me that I could let out just as desolate a cry without much effort. In the fields beyond the woods, a cold wind blew through the last ragged tatters of cotton stuck on the dry 70 and trembling stems. Christmas came, and with it came the heartache and lonesomeness. The chill breeze brought tears to my eyes. **6** Or maybe it was thoughts of home—my ma, my little sisters. I'd been so proud to show off my drum and rattle the sticks for them. I did not know music could lead me to such 75 a place. Why am I here? I wondered as I thought of my home, my dog, my companions in tag and school sums. What is this war for? From each encampment, the spark and flash would be artillery blasts and musket fire, and winter sunlight would glitter on the bayonets. From each encampment, the low murmur of 80 voices mingled with the mutter of water over stones; tomorrow the stones would resound with the din and discord of shots and screams, and I would play the cadence that drove men forward into death.

7 To raise our spirits, the regimental band began to play. Our 85 fellows let loose with "Yankee Doodle," and it rang like metal in the frosty air. I blew on my fingers to warm them before I could get a proper grasp on the drumsticks.

Then we heard a band on the rebel side strike up "Dixie," vying to drown us out.

90 Our boys hollered to our band to play "The Star-Spangled Banner," and in between the bars our ears caught the strains of "Bonnie Blue Flag."

8 Back and forth we fought with songs, fighting ourselves into the kind of hot excitement a man needs to carry him into 95 deadly battle. The fellows grabbed their muskets by the hand, as if they was sweethearts at a square dance, and breathed hard and

WRITING COACH

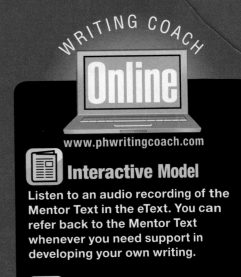

www.phwritingcoach.com

Interactive Model

Listen to an audio recording of the Mentor Text in the eText. You can refer back to the Mentor Text whenever you need support in developing your own writing.

Online Journal

Try It! Answer the questions about the Mentor Text in the online journal.

9 In the **resolution**, the narrator reflects on what has happened.

Try It! What message does the narrator take from the soldiers' singing "There's No Place Like Home"? What is the theme of the story?

remembered the fights they'd already seen and the lead they'd already let fly.

100 But then, in a lull, one of the bands—and I can't say which side it come from—began a quieter tune, and all around me the fellows felt their hearts catch in their throats. I lowered my drum. The words of the familiar song came to our lips, where moments before we had been thirsty for battle cries.

"'Mid pleasures and palaces though I may roam,

105 Be it ever so humble, there's no place like home!"

The tender words rose into the air with the sparks of the campfires on both sides, and our hearts were soothed and gentled. "Home!" we sang, all of us, Yankee and Rebel alike. "Home! Sweet, sweet home! There's no place like home!" If

110 there is a sweeter tune, it has not been sung for living ears.

9 When the sun arose, the dread war would start anew, but for the moment in Tennessee we were all just Americans, singing in harmony, and our country was whole again.

STUDENT MODEL

Historical Fiction

With a small group, take turns reading this Student Model aloud. As you read draw conclusions about the story's structure and the elements of fiction the author uses. Take note of how the author creates imagery and mood.

Use a Reader's Eye

Now, reread the Student Model. On your copy of the Student Model, use the Reader's Response Symbols to react to what you read.

Reader's Response Symbols

+ This is a good description.

— This isn't clear to me.

! This is really cool/weird/interesting!

? What will happen next?

Partner Talk

Participate in an extended discussion with a partner. Express your opinions and share your responses to the Student Model. Focus especially on how the author's use of language and sensory details creates imagery, or word pictures.

Out of This World

by Lily Thompson

"Wake up, Arnetta. It's time to go." My mother gently shook my shoulder.

My eyes popped open, and I leapt out of bed. "I'm up. Let's go, let's go!" I shouted with excitement.

5   I dashed down the hall to wake my little brother Jeffrey. He's only six—ten years younger than me—and we don't have much in common. My parents say that he's my responsibility, but I don't like having him hanging around me all the time.

10 Especially today! Today is simply too important. Today is the launch of *Apollo 11*. It's my dream to someday be the first female astronaut in space. I've watched every single rocket launch that has taken place at the Kennedy Space Center, near my home in Florida. And today, July

15 16, 1969, is the most important launch of all because today *Apollo 11* will carry three astronauts to the moon.

Later, when we at last made it to the viewing area, the voices of thousands of people buzzed in the air. They were all waiting for the big event. We spread our blanket in

20 a good location and settled in to watch.

An hour later, Jeffrey was fidgety and whimpering. "I'm *bored*," he said. "I want to go *home*." My mother suggested I take him for a walk, so I grabbed his hand and dragged him around. When we'd walked for a while, I dropped his

25 hand and gazed at the *Apollo*, dreaming about my thrilling future.

When I turned around, Jeffrey was gone. While I'd been distracted, my brother had simply disappeared. Blood rushed in my ears, and fear gnawed at my stomach. There

30 were thousands of faces in that crowd, but none was my brother's. I heard the countdown begin, but I couldn't watch. I frantically looked for Jeffrey. Then I heard an awestruck gasp and saw the rocket firing out of the corner of my eye while I ran to a policeman. Together, we searched

1

35   the area and finally found Jeffrey crying under a tree.

"I'm sorry, Arnetta," Jeffrey sobbed. "I thought I saw Mom, but it wasn't her. And then I couldn't find you again. And now we missed the launch, and I ruined everything!" I gave him a huge hug and explained that
40   he was more important to me than even the *Apollo*.

Days later, Jeffrey and I sat on our couch, watching in amazement as Neil Armstrong walked on the moon.

"Do you think you'll ever make it into space?" he asked.

"Definitely," I replied. "But do you know what's really
45   out of this world? You!"

2

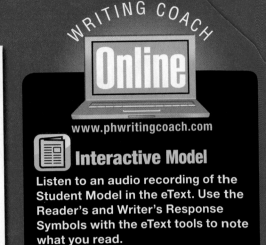

WRITING COACH

Online

www.phwritingcoach.com

 Interactive Model

Listen to an audio recording of the Student Model in the eText. Use the Reader's and Writer's Response Symbols with the eText tools to note what you read.

Use a Writer's Eye

Now, evaluate the piece as a writer. On your copy of the Student Model, use the Writer's Response Symbols to react to what you read. Identify places where the student writer uses characteristics of an effective work of historical fiction.

Writer's Response Symbols	
H.S.	**Details that reveal historical setting**
R.D.	**Realistic and believable dialogue**
S.D.	**Vivid sensory details**
W.C.	**Well-developed, interesting characters**

Prewriting

Plan a first draft of your historical fiction story **by determining an appropriate topic.** You can select from the Topic Bank or come up with an idea of your own, as long as it shows people or events from history.

Choose From the Topic Bank

TOPIC BANK

Unique Challenge Think about a challenge people faced in the past. For example, what obstacles did pioneer families encounter as they traveled west? Write a story that shows how characters conquered a unique challenge in the past.

Unusual Setting Write a historical fiction story that places your main character in an unusual setting from the past. You might even have your character jump into a work of art, literature, or a famous sporting event.

Famous Person Who inspires or intrigues you? Choose a famous person who lived long ago, such as Amelia Earhart, as the main character or as a person with whom your main character interacts in a historical fiction story.

Choose Your Own Topic

Determine an appropriate topic on your own by using the following **range of strategies** to generate ideas.

Skim and Research

- Skim your history book for topics or time periods that interest you. Think about books and movies that are set in the past.

- Then make a list of events, people, or places that spark ideas. Circle your favorite.

- Search your library's database and the Internet for information about your top choice. Can you find enough information to create a background for your story? If not, move on to another topic.

Review your responses and choose a topic.

Narrow Your Topic

Choosing a topic that is too broad will make your story lack focus and intensity.

Apply It! Use a graphic organizer like the one shown to narrow your topic.

- Write your general topic in the top box. This phrase might describe a time period or event from the past.
- Write a more specific, related idea in the next box, and keep narrowing your topic as you move down the chart.
- Your last box should hold your narrowest or "smallest" topic, the focus of your historical fiction short story.

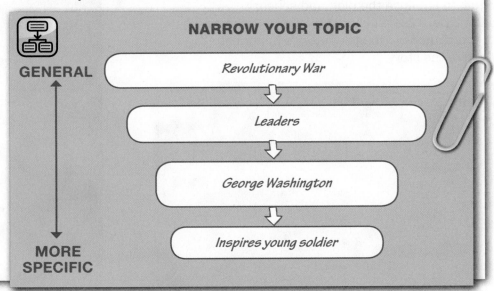

NARROW YOUR TOPIC

GENERAL

Revolutionary War

Leaders

George Washington

Inspires young soldier

MORE SPECIFIC

Consider Multiple Audiences and Purposes

Before writing, think about your audiences and purposes. Consider the views of others as you ask yourself these questions.

Questions for Audience	Questions for Purpose
• Who might my various audiences be? • What impressions of my topic do my audiences already have? • What kind of historical background information will my audiences need to understand my story?	• How will I use historical details to tell a compelling story? • How will I make my story engaging for my audiences? • What story elements, approaches, and techniques will I include to create a well-developed conflict and resolution?

Record your answers in your writing journal.

WRITING COACH

Online

www.phwritingcoach.com

Interactive Graphic Organizers

Use the interactive graphic organizers to help you narrow your topic.

Online Journal

Try It! Record your answers and ideas in the online journal.

Plan Your Piece

You will use a graphic organizer like the one shown to state your theme, organize your plot events, and define your story elements. When it is complete, you will be ready to write your first draft.

Develop the Plot Use a graphic organizer like the one shown to develop a basic outline of the plot. Ask yourself, "How should the story begin? What will happen next? What will be the climax? How should the conflict be resolved?" Make sure you create a well-developed conflict and resolution. Avoid including bland or predictable people and events. Instead, plan to build complex, non-stereotypical characters who take part in the action.

Identify Literary Elements Identify **literary strategies and devices,** such as suspense and dialogue, to enhance the plot, and **sensory details** that define the mood or tone. Take a moment to choose a theme, or message for the story. As you plan, describe your story's historical setting, and describe the mood of the story.

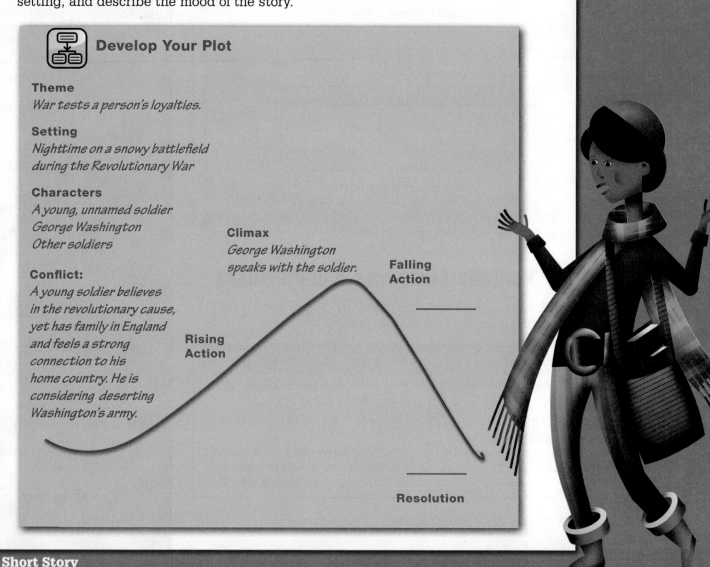

Develop Your Plot

Theme
War tests a person's loyalties.

Setting
Nighttime on a snowy battlefield during the Revolutionary War

Characters
A young, unnamed soldier
George Washington
Other soldiers

Conflict:
A young soldier believes in the revolutionary cause, yet has family in England and feels a strong connection to his home country. He is considering deserting Washington's army.

Rising Action

Climax
George Washington speaks with the soldier.

Falling Action
_____

Resolution
_____

Gather Details

Writers of historical fiction use certain elements to create an engaging story. Look at these examples:

- **Central Conflict:** *The soldier supports the revolution in theory but has a hard time fighting against his home country.*
- **Complex Characters:** *"What shall I do?" the soldier thought. "I can't let the cause down, but how can I fight against my home country?"*
- **Historical Setting:** *Jon watched the soldiers settle into their bedrolls. Across the ridge he could see the fires from the Redcoats' camp.*
- **Effective Literary Strategies and Devices** (such as dialogue, suspense, imagery): *"We're fighting for freedom, young man. Surely you're on the side of freedom!"*
- **Defined Mood:** *The soldier paced the ridge with quick, short steps. His head ached as the words "Shall I?" repeated in his mind.*
- **Analogy:** *The soldiers stood in straight, tight rows like piano keys.*
- **Rhetorical Question:** *Would the army turn him away?*

Try It! Read this excerpt from the Student Model and identify details of setting that describe the historical time and place.

 **STUDENT MODEL** from **Out of This World**
page 98; lines 10–16

Especially today! Today is simply too important. Today is the launch of *Apollo 11.* It's my dream to someday be the first female astronaut in space. I've watched every single rocket launch that has taken place at the Kennedy Space Center, near my home in Florida. And today, July 16, 1969, is the most important launch of all because today *Apollo 11* will carry three astronauts to the moon.

 Apply It! Review the literary devices and elements that good writers use as they generate ideas and create historical fiction.

- Identify **sensory details** you can use in your story to establish the historical setting and create the mood. Remember that sensory details are words and phrases that appeal to the reader's senses of sight, smell, taste, touch, and sound.
- Add these details to your graphic organizer.

WRITING COACH

Online

www.phwritingcoach.com

 **Interactive Graphic Organizers**

Use the interactive graphic organizers to help you create a plan for your writing.

 Interactive Model

Refer back to the Interactive Model in the eText as you plan your writing.

Drafting

During the drafting stage, you will start to write your ideas for your historical fiction story. You will follow an outline that provides an organizational strategy that will help you **structure your ideas in a sustained way** to write a focused, organized, and coherent work of historical fiction.

The Organization of a Historical Fiction Story

This chart shows how most works of historical fiction are organized. Look back at how the Mentor Text follows this organizational strategy. Then, use this chart to help you outline your draft.

Outline for Success

Beginning
See Mentor Text, p. 94.

- Introduction of setting and characters
- Introduction of conflict
- Sensory details to build description

Middle
See Mentor Text, pp. 95–96.

- Development of conflict
- Climax
- Literary strategies and devices, including rhetorical devices

End
See Mentor Text, p. 97.

- Falling action
- Resolution

Start Out Strong

- A strong beginning will hook the reader's attention with a description of the historical setting and characters.
- Sensory details—details related to touch, taste, sight, sound, and smell—create a story's mood or tone.
- The conflict, or central problem, of the story is introduced in the beginning.

Build to a Climax

- Literary devices and strategies, such as dialogue and suspense, help to develop the conflict and the plot.
- Rhetorical devices, such as point of view, analogies, and metaphors comparing two usually unrelated things, help to make writing interesting.
- The development of characters and the conflict in a story continues until the climax, or high point of the story.

Come to a Satisfying Resolution

- The final paragraphs show what happens after the climax and how the conflict is resolved.
- Loose ends of the story are tied up at the end, and writers often work to create a memorable and interesting conclusion.

Start Your Draft

Use the checklist to help complete your draft. Use the graphic organizer that shows the elements of your story, and the Outline for Success as guides.

While drafting, aim at getting your ideas down, not on making your writing perfect. Remember, because you are writing in an open-ended situation, you will have the chance to improve your draft when you revise and edit.

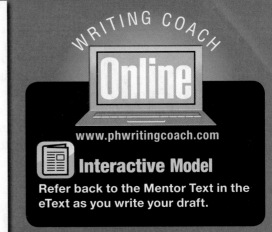

WRITING COACH

Online
www.phwritingcoach.com

Interactive Model
Refer back to the Mentor Text in the eText as you write your draft.

√ In the **beginning** of your story, introduce readers to the historical setting and the main characters. Be sure to present **complex, non-stereotypical characters** who grow over the course of the story.

√ Use **sensory details** to establish your story's mood or tone.

√ Begin to develop the **conflict.** Remember, conflict can be between your character and another person or outside force, or within him- or herself.

√ In the **middle,** build your story to create **a well-developed conflict.** Use literary strategies, and devices such as dialogue and suspense, to build the conflict and enhance the plot.

√ Keep building tension at a good pace until you reach the story's **climax.** The reader should care about how things will turn out.

√ Include **rhetorical devices,** such as rhetorical questions and analogies, in your story. They will help you to convey meaning to your readers and will keep your writing engaging, lively, and interesting.

√ At the **end,** offer **a well-developed resolution.** Show how the conflict is resolved and work out any final details.

Revising: Making It Better

Now that you have finished your first draft, you are ready to revise. Think about the "big picture." You will clarify the meaning of your writing by adding transitional words and phrases. You can use your Revision RADaR as a guide for making changes to improve your draft. Revision RADaR provides four major ways to improve your writing: (R) replace, (A) add, (D) delete, and (R) reorder.

Kelly Gallagher, M. Ed.

KEEP REVISION ON YOUR RADAR

Read part of the first draft of the Student Model "Out of This World." Then, look at the questions the writer asked herself as she thought about how well her draft addressed issues of audience, purpose, and genre.

Out of This World

Today is simply too important. I want to be an astronaut one day. Space is a fascinating place. I love watching rocket launches at the Kennedy Space Center. And today is a very important launch, because the shuttle will carry three astronauts to the moon.

Have I created complex characters, and have I made my historical setting clear?

Later, when we at last made it to the viewing area, there were a lot of people there, waiting for the big event. We spread our blanket in a good location and settled in to watch.

Have I used sensory details to help define the mood of the story?

Jeffrey was fidgety and whimpering. "I'm *bored*," he said. "I want to go *home*." My mother suggested I take him for a walk, so I grabbed his hand and dragged him around. When we'd walked for a while, I dropped his hand and gazed at the *Apollo*, dreaming about my thrilling future.

Is my story well organized? Have I included transitions to tie ideas together and to show that time has gone by?

When I turned around, Jeffrey was gone. While I'd been distracted, my baby brother had simply disappeared. I was nervous and started to look for him.

Have I established a well-developed conflict?

Out of This World

2ND DRAFT

Today is simply too important. It's my dream to someday be the first female astronaut in space. I've watched every single rocket launch that has taken place at the Kennedy Space Center, near my home in Florida. And today, July 16, 1969, is the most important launch of all because today *Apollo 11* will carry three astronauts to the moon.

Later, when we at last made it to the viewing area, the voices of thousands of people buzzed in the air. They were all waiting for the big event. We spread our blanket in a good location and settled in to watch.

An hour later, Jeffrey was fidgety and whimpering. "I'm *bored*," he said. "I want to go *home*." My mother suggested I take him for a walk, so I grabbed his hand and dragged him around. When we'd walked for a while, I dropped his hand and gazed at the *Apollo*, dreaming about my thrilling future.

When I turned around, Jeffrey was gone. While I'd been distracted, my baby brother had simply disappeared. Blood rushed in my ears, and fear gnawed at my stomach. There were thousands of faces in that crowd, but none were my brother's. I heard the countdown begin, but I couldn't watch. I frantically looked for Jeffrey.

D *Deleted unnecessary information about space that doesn't enhance the plot*
A *Added specific details to create a well-developed character and to clearly establish the historical setting*

A *Added sensory detail about the sound to help establish the mood of excitement at the event*

A *Added the transition* <u>an hour later</u> *to show that time has gone by*

R *Replaced general language with sensory details and clearer description to increase the effect of the rising action and establish a mood of fear and panic*

Apply It! Now revise your draft to **clarify** your story's **meaning**.

- First, determine if your story has **a well-developed conflict and resolution** and **complex and non-stereotypical characters**.
- Then apply your Revision RADaR to make needed changes. Look for places where you can add or revise words and sentences to clarify your meaning. Remember—you can use the revision steps in any order.

Look at the Big Picture

Use the chart and your analytical skills to evaluate how well each section of your historical fiction story addresses purpose, audience, and genre. When necessary, use the suggestions in the chart to revise your piece.

Section	Evaluate	Revise
Beginning	• Make sure the **historical setting** is established.	• Add specific details of time and place.
	• Underline details or dialogue that reveals the personality of the **main character.**	• Replace generic or vague terms with descriptive words for the character's appearance, thoughts, and behavior to create more complex, non-stereotypical characters.
	• Check that you have introduced the character's main problem, or **conflict.**	• What issue is the character facing? Clearly show his or her problem.
Middle	• Circle words used to establish the **mood or tone.**	• Add sensory details to define the story's mood or tone to make it more vivid.
	• Check whether the story is **well organized** and that the climax is the high point of the story.	• Reorder events if they don't appear to be in time order. Rework early passages to build suspense and tension and to create a well-developed conflict.
	• Make sure **literary strategies and devices** enhance the plot.	• Add foreshadowing, or hints about what will happen next, to build suspense. Rework dialogue to move the plot forward.
	• Make sure the **pacing** is appropriate.	• If your story is adventurous, make it fast-paced, with events moving quickly from one to the next. If it is quiet, include more description and build slowly. Delete information that does not support the action.
End	• Check that the **resolution** is well developed and clearly shows the solution to the problem.	• Tie up any loose ends and add details to provide a satisfying ending.

Focus on Craft: Repetition

A **scheme** is a writing style feature that is a deliberate change in standard word order for effect. Using **repetition**, one type of scheme, in a short story will help you to clarify meaning and emphasize a character's feelings or important events in the story. Repeating a word, phrase, or sentence helps to enhance essential ideas or character traits. For example, a character might say: "I'm sorry. I am so, so sorry!" The repetition of the words *sorry* and *so* emphasize the character's distress and regret. Look at this example.

 **STUDENT MODEL** from **Out of This World**
page 98; lines 3–4

> My eyes popped open, and I leapt out of bed. "I'm up. Let's go, let's go!" I shouted with excitement.

 Try It! Now, ask yourself these questions:

- Which word or phrase is repeated in the passage?
- What does the repetition suggest about the narrator's emotions?

Fine-Tune Your Draft

Apply It! Use the revision suggestions to prepare your final draft after rethinking how well questions of purpose, audience, and genre have been addressed.

- **Employ Schemes** Use schemes, such as repetition, to emphasize certain parts of your story and to help readers see key ideas.
- **Clarify Meaning** Make sure your readers understand your story's message. Clearly explain all of your story elements, being specific and detailed. Rearrange words, sentences, and paragraphs if necessary to make your meaning clear.
- **Use Clear Transitions** Add transitional words and phrases such as *first, next, above, mainly, likewise, yet,* and *because* to show connections between details and ideas.

Peer Feedback Ask a partner to read your story. Have him or her summarize its sequence of events, central conflict, and theme and share any concerns about the character development. Then **revise your final draft in response to his or her feedback.**

WRITING COACH

Online

www.phwritingcoach.com

Online Journal
Try It! Record your answers in the online journal.

Interactive Model
Refer back to the Interactive Model as you revise your writing.

Editing: Making It Correct

Editing means polishing your work and correcting errors. When editing, you may want to read through your work several times.

During the editing process, think about whether your **verb tenses** are consistent and whether you have used **a variety of sentence structures, including compound, complex, and compound-complex.** Then edit your final draft for any errors in **grammar, mechanics, and spelling.**

WRITE GUY *Jeff Anderson, M. Ed.*

WHAT DO YOU NOTICE?

Zoom in on Conventions Focus on verb tenses as you zoom in on these lines from the Student Model.

> **STUDENT MODEL** | from **Out of This World** page 98; lines 27–28
>
> When I turned around, Jeffrey was gone. While I'd been distracted, my baby brother had simply disappeared.

Now, ask yourself: *How are the verbs in each sentence alike?*

Perhaps you said that the author uses a consistent tense within each sentence. The first sentence is written in the **past tense,** and the second sentence uses the **past perfect tense.**

Past tense verbs show actions that began at a point in the past. **Present tense verbs** show present or continuing actions. Verbs in the **future tense** express actions that have not yet occurred.

A perfect tense is created by adding a form of the word *have* before the past participle of the main verb. The **present perfect tense** shows a completed action or action continuing to the present. A **past perfect tense** shows an action that happened before another in the past. A verb in **future perfect tense** shows an action that will happen before another future action.

> To learn more about verb tenses, see Chapter 17 of your Grammar Handbook.

Verb tenses help establish consistency in a narrative by advancing the plot and letting readers know the sequence of events. Verb tenses may not always be consistent between sentences, but they should usually be consistent within sentences.

Partner Talk Discuss this question with a partner: *Why might it be confusing if a story writer uses the wrong tenses?*

Grammar Mini-Lesson: Consistent Tenses

Writers use a **variety of sentence structures—compound, complex, and compound-complex—**and must at times vary the verb tense to express sequence. However, writers usually avoid switching tenses within a sentence. Notice how the Mentor Text author uses the past tense consistently to express a sequence of events.

 **MENTOR TEXT** from **The Song of Stones River**
page 94; lines 12–14

> Like a summer storm, Confederate cavalry crashed down upon them, overwhelmed the garrison, and forced a surrender.

 Try It! Choose the correct verb tenses in the following compound, complex, and compound-complex sentences. Write the answers in your journal.

1. Lucinda (wanted, wants) to be a chef, and she (was, will be) one someday. (compound)

2. Manuel (was, had been) upset when his team lost the game, but then he (had thought, thought) about how to improve his performance for next time. (compound-complex)

Apply It! Edit your draft for **grammar, mechanics, and spelling.** If necessary, rewrite to ensure that you use a **variety of sentences** with consistent and correct verb tenses.

Use the rubric to evaluate your piece. If necessary, rethink, rewrite, or revise.

Rubric for Short Story: Historical Fiction	Rating Scale					
Ideas: How well do you narrate a story with a clear characters and plot?	Not very					Very
	1	2	3	4	5	6
Organization: How clearly organized is the sequence of events?	1	2	3	4	5	6
Voice: How authentic and engaging is your voice?	1	2	3	4	5	6
Word Choice: How effective is your word choice in creating tone and style?	1	2	3	4	5	6
Sentence Fluency: How well have you used transitions to show connections among ideas?	1	2	3	4	5	6
Conventions: How consistent and correct are your verb tenses in a variety of sentence structures?	1	2	3	4	5	6

To learn more, see Chapter 17.

WRITING COACH

 **Online**

www.phwritingcoach.com

 Video

Learn effective editing techniques from program author Jeff Anderson.

Online Journal

Try It! Record your answers in the online journal.

Interactive Model

Refer back to the Interactive Model as you edit your writing.

Publishing

Now it's time to let others enjoy your story. First, get it ready for publication. Then, choose a way to **publish your written work for appropriate audiences.**

Wrap Up Your Presentation

Once your final draft is complete, put the finishing touches on your story. Choose a readable font—a font without any fancy, potentially confusing elements. Also be sure to add a title to your story that grabs the reader's attention and indicates the story's topic.

Publish Your Piece

Use the chart to find ways to publish your story for multiple audiences.

If your audience is...	...then publish it by...
Students and teachers at school	• Submitting it to your school's literary journal • Using a desktop publishing program to create a book and submitting it to your class
Family, friends, and others who enjoy historical fiction	• Posting it to your own Web site or blog • Submitting it to an online literary magazine

 ## Reflect on Your Writing

Now that you are done with your historical fiction story, read it over and use your writing journal to answer these questions. Use specific details to describe and explain your ideas. Increase the specificity of your details based on the type of information you are recording.

- Do your characters "come alive" in your story? Does your completed story live up to your expectations?
- What are you most proud of in your story? How will you apply what you have done in this story to other stories?
- How has writing a story set in the past changed your perspective about the time period? What did you learn about the time period? Where could you learn more?

Manage Your Portfolio You may wish to include your published historical fiction story in your writing portfolio.

 The Big Question: Why Write?
What can fiction do better than non-fiction?

21st Century Learning

MAKE YOUR WRITING COUNT

Convey Historical Themes in a Script

Good historical fiction evokes a specific time and place, making history come to life in the reader's imagination. Bring a historical era to life by preparing a **script** based on your own historical fiction.

As a group, analyze the historical fiction you wrote and adapt it as a television script. Your script should include dialogue, narration, stage directions, and sound effects that reflect the era's themes. Present your script live or as a video.

Here's your action plan.

1. As a group, review your peers' historical fiction and choose one to adapt as a script. Choose roles, such as script writer, director, stage/costume designer, and sound-effects manager.

2. Look online for examples of scripts. Pay attention to their formatting.

3. Adapt your chosen story as a script by:

   - Choosing dialogue to keep and deciding where to add dialogue
   - Identifying important historical details that can be expressed through dialogue, narration, or stage directions
   - Suggesting explicitly and directly or implicitly through suggestions a theme about the era
   - Using literary techniques and sound effects to convey the era's atmosphere

4. As a group, read the draft. Revise until the script evokes the era.

Listening and Speaking With your group, rehearse the script. Listen carefully and give one another constructive feedback on pacing, intonation, and expression. Before your performance, practice gestures and staging, and prepare costumes and sets. During the performance, work as a team to convey the themes of another historical era. Record your performance with an audio- or video-recording device.

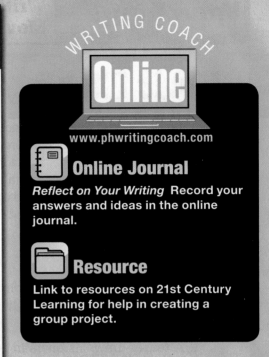

WRITING COACH

Online

www.phwritingcoach.com

Online Journal

Reflect on Your Writing Record your answers and ideas in the online journal.

Resource

Link to resources on 21st Century Learning for help in creating a group project.

21st Century Learning

Movie Pitch

You might have seen many historical fiction movies at the theater—including movies set in ancient Greece, the Old West, or World War II. How did each of these stories get turned into movies? They each began with a pitch. A **movie pitch** is a short oral presentation that a screenwriter makes to convince a producer to turn his or her screenplay into a movie. A pitch summarizes the script and focuses on the main characters and conflict.

Try It! Study the pitch shown here. Then answer the questions. Record your answers in your journal.

1. A **teaser** draws listeners in by describing the story. The last sentence leaves the listener wanting to know more about the script. Does it achieve its purpose? Explain.

2. The **character summary** introduces the film's main characters. How does this character summary show how Henson's role changes during the movie?

3. The **conflict summary** explains the main characters' central problem. Does the conflict described here translate well into the movie format?

4. The **resolution** shares the movie's ending, including any surprise endings or plot twists. What is surprising about this movie's ending?

5. The **target audience** describes the people who may see the film. Why might boys ages 11–17 enjoy this movie?

Extension Find another example of a movie pitch, and compare it with this one. Alternatively, look for a movie advertisement and contrast the two different forms.

Proposed Film Title: The Wasteland

Teaser: In 1908, in the frozen wasteland of the Arctic, Robert Peary, Matthew Henson, and their team set out to be the first to reach the as-yet unexplored North Pole. The team's chances of success are slim. Will they reach their destination, and more importantly, will they live to tell the tale?

Characters: Matthew Henson is the African American assistant to Robert Peary, a Navy officer and explorer who is driven to reach the North Pole. Henson emerges as a savior figure throughout the story—his skills make it clear that the party would never have made it to the Pole without his help. Other characters include Inuit and other team members.

Conflict: Henson and Peary must race against time and face terrifying dangers to reach the North Pole. The high-drama dangers they will face include: sub-freezing temperatures, sudden storms, dwindling supplies, and dangerous cracks in the ice.

Resolution: Henson is the first person to ever reach the North Pole, and Peary is furious that he wasn't the first. The two reach an uneasy truce because they know they'll need each other to survive the trek home. The movie closes with Henson on board the USS Roosevelt, staring out at the frozen wasteland. Famous lines from Henson's autobiography are heard in the background: "The lure of the Arctic is tugging at my heart. To me the trail is calling. The old trail. The trail that is always new."

Target audience: Boys, ages 11–17; women ages 30–55; men ages 30–55

Create a Pitch for a Historical Fiction Screenplay

Follow these steps to create your own pitch. To plan your pitch, review the graphic organizers on R24–R27 and choose one that suits your needs.

Prewriting

- Research the film market by viewing trailers of historical fiction films currently playing in theaters. Also research the top-grossing historical films of all time. Think about what they had in common.
- To help you brainstorm for ideas, think about these questions: What era or event in history is the most interesting to you? What elements of this era or event would be best for creating an engaging story? Do you want to create fictional characters to place in that time period, or do you want to create a story based on a real historical figure?
- Choose the best ideas and plan an outline for creating a well-developed conflict and resolution and interesting characters.

Drafting

- Get your basic ideas on paper, following the sample pitch's format.
- Focus on the teaser. This brief passage must capture a producer's interest. It has to sound intriguing!
- Write 1–3 sentences for your teaser and no more than a paragraph for each of the remaining sections. Make sure to use sensory details in some of your descriptions to grab the audience's attention.

Revising and Editing

- Review the teaser. Does it describe the characters, conflict, and genre? Polish the final sentence to leave the audience wanting more. Rhetorical questions like the one in the sample are often useful in creating suspense.
- Add details to your character summary to flesh out personalities.
- Take out information that is not crucial to each summary.
- Re-evaluate your target audience information and consider whether you've left anyone out of your list.
- Check that your spelling, grammar, and mechanics are correct.

Publishing

Create a video recording of yourself presenting your pitch. Include graphics, images, and sounds. Then present the video to your class.

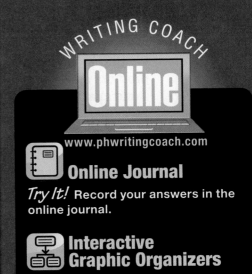

WRITING COACH

Online

www.phwritingcoach.com

Online Journal

Try It! Record your answers in the online journal.

Interactive Graphic Organizers

Choose from a variety of graphic organizers to plan and develop your project.

Partner Talk

Before you begin drafting, ask a partner's opinion about your movie idea. Get your partner's feedback about the characters, conflict, and resolution. Monitor your partner's spoken language by asking follow-up questions to confirm your understanding.

Writing for Assessment

Writing a good short story takes a lot of practice. You can use the prompts on these pages to practice. Your responses should include the same characteristics as your historical fiction story. (See page 92.)

Try It! To begin, read the prompt and the information on format and academic vocabulary. Then, use the ABCDs of On-Demand Writing to help you plan and write your **story**.

Format

The prompt directs you to write a *short story*. Be sure to introduce your characters, historical setting, and conflict in the beginning, describe the mood and the climax in the middle, and provide a satisfying resolution at the end.

Short Story Prompt

Life during the Civil War period was difficult as families split apart and the war intruded on everyday life. Write a short story about a family during the Civil War. Be sure to include a well-developed conflict and resolution, and literary devices such as dialogue to keep your story interesting.

Academic Vocabulary

Remember that the *conflict* is the story's central problem. The *resolution* is when the conflict is resolved and loose ends are tied up. *Dialogue* is written conversation between characters.

The ABCDs of On-Demand Writing

Use the following ABCDs to help you respond to the prompt.

Before you write your draft:

Attack the prompt [1 MINUTE]

- Circle or highlight important verbs in the prompt. Draw a line from the verb to what it refers to.
- Rewrite the prompt in your own words.

Brainstorm possible answers [4 MINUTES]

- Create a graphic organizer to generate ideas.
- Use one for each part of the prompt if necessary.

Choose the order of your response [1 MINUTE]

- Think about the best way to organize your ideas.
- Number your ideas in the order you will write about them. Cross out ideas you will not be using.

After you write your draft:

Detect errors before turning in the draft [1 MINUTE]

- Carefully reread your writing.
- Look for spelling, punctuation, and grammar errors.
- Make sure that your response makes sense and is complete.

More Prompts for Practice

Apply It! Respond to Prompts 1 and 2 by writing **engaging** stories. As you write, be sure to:

- Include **complex and non-stereotypical characters** who grow over the course of the story
- Create **a well-developed conflict** over the course of the story and provide a satisfying **well-developed resolution** at the end
- Provide interesting **details** to establish the historical time period
- Use a range of **literary strategies and devices,** such as dialogue and suspense, **to enhance the plot**
- Include **sensory details** to define the mood or tone of your story

> **Prompt 1** Write a short story about a character who is a passenger on the *Titanic*. Remember that the passengers on the doomed ship were varied—poor and rich, young and old. Consider the mood of the story, its central conflict, and how it will be resolved.

> **Prompt 2** Write a short story about a young man who sets out to make his fortune during the California Gold Rush. Provide details about the main character, his central conflict, and its resolution.

Spiral Review: Narrative Respond to Prompt 3 by writing an **autobiographical narrative.** Make sure your narrative is an **engaging story** that reflects all the characteristics described on page 66, including:

- A well-developed **conflict and resolution**
- Complex and interesting **characters**
- A range of **literary strategies and devices** to enhance the plot
- **Sensory details** that define the mood or tone

> **Prompt 3** Write an autobiographical narrative about a time you did something courageous or a time when you saw someone doing something courageous. In your narrative, explain how this moment affected you.

WRITING COACH

www.phwritingcoach.com

👍 Interactive Writing Coach™

Plan your response to the prompt. If you are using the prompt for practice, write one paragraph at a time or your entire draft and then submit it for feedback. If you are using the prompt as a timed test, write your entire draft and then submit it for feedback.

Remember **ABCD**

Attack the prompt

Brainstorm possible answers

Choose the order of your response

Detect errors before turning in the draft

CHAPTER 7

POETRY and DESCRIPTION

What Do You See?

People see different things when they look at something. Some people may look at this photograph and see a conductor. Others might see excitement or freedom.

People use different words to describe what they see. Words can be a powerful way to capture experiences or feelings.

Try It! Take a few minutes to list what you see in the photograph. Remember, you might describe the actual image or you might describe how it makes you feel.

Consider these questions as you participate in an extended discussion with a partner. Take turns expressing your ideas and feelings.

- What do you actually see?
- What emotions does this photograph make you feel?
- What would you feel if you were conducting an orchestra?

Review the list you made. Use your list to describe to a partner what you see in this photograph. Think about how you would use these words to make a poem.

What's Ahead

In this chapter, you will review some strong examples of poems: Mentor Texts and Student Models. Then, using the examples as guidance, you will write a poem of your own.

Connect to the Big Questions

Discuss these questions with your partner:

1 **What do you think?** What do music, art, and poetry best communicate?

2 **Why write?** How do we best convey feelings through words on a page?

POETRY AND DESCRIPTION

In this chapter, you will focus on writing a poem. Poetry is a form of writing that uses special language to communicate ideas and feelings. To make every word count, a poet carefully chooses language that is vivid, precise, and often musical, or pleasing to hear. An especially important part of poetry—and most other kinds of writing—is description. Descriptive details create imagery that helps readers picture what something looks like or imagine its smell, sound, texture, or taste.

You will develop a poem by taking it through each of the steps of the writing process: prewriting, drafting, revising, editing, and publishing. You will also have an opportunity to use what you have learned about descriptive writing to write a definition essay. To preview the criteria for how your poem will be evaluated, see the rubric on page 137.

FEATURE ASSIGNMENT

Poem

An effective poem has these characteristics:

- A clear **topic, theme,** or **controlling idea**
- A clear **point of view**
- **Poetic conventions,** or special poetic techniques, such as sound devices, sensory details, and figurative language (See page 129.)
- **Structural elements,** such as rhyme and meter (See page 129.)
- Specific **forms** based on **poetic traditions,** such as ballads, lyric, or free verse poems, that follow strict organizational patterns and rules

A ballad also has these characteristics (See page 130):

- A simple **rhyme pattern** and regular **rhythm**
- A narrative that tells **a story,** often an adventure or romance
- A song-like **structure,** often with a refrain, or a regularly repeated line or group of lines

A free verse poem also has these characteristics (See page 130):

- Text written to imitate the rhythms of **everyday speech**
- No specific rhyme pattern
- No specific meter
- No specific length

Other Forms of Poetry and Description

There are many forms of poetry and description, including these forms:

Ballads are poems that tell a story and are usually meant to be sung. Ballads often contain repetition and have a simple, regular rhyme pattern and meter, or "beat."

Descriptive essays use imagery and vivid details to help readers imagine a person, place, thing, or event. Like all essays, they are made up of an introduction, body, and conclusion.

Free verse is poetry that imitates the rhythms of everyday speech. Freed of set rhythm and rhyme patterns, free verse uses figurative language and sound devices to convey ideas and feelings.

Haiku are three-line poems that originated in Japan. In a haiku, the first and last lines consist of five syllables, and the middle line consists of seven syllables. Classic haiku are usually about nature.

Lyric poems are poems that express a speaker's feelings about a particular person, place, thing, or event. Unlike ballads, lyric poems usually do not tell a story. Sonnets and free verse poems are types of lyric poems.

Prose poems look like prose, or regular text you might find in a story or essay, but use poetic conventions to create a memorable description of a person, place, thing, or event.

Sonnets are 14-line poems written in a regular meter and pattern of rhyme. One kind of sonnet—the English sonnet—consists of three four-line stanzas and a final couplet, or two rhyming lines. In each stanza, alternating lines rhyme.

 *Try It!* For each audience and purpose described, choose a form, such as a haiku or lyric poem, that is appropriate for conveying your intended meaning to the audience. Explain your choices.

- To describe the beauty of a flower to readers of a magazine
- To tell the story of an amazing adventure to entertain children
- To express feelings about your childhood home on a blog

📁 **WORD BANK**

People often use these basic and content-based vocabulary words when they talk about poetry. Work with a partner. Take turns saying each word aloud. Then, write one sentence using each word. If you are unsure of the meaning of a word, use the Glossary or a dictionary to check the definition.

couplet	metaphor
figurative	refrain
imagery	sensory

MENTOR TEXT

Ballad and Free Verse Poem

Learn From Experience

 After reading the ballad and free verse poem on pages 122–123, read the numbered notes in the margins to learn how the poets presented their ideas.

Answer the *Try It!* questions online or in your notebook.

① Like most **ballads,** this one tells a story. Here, the story's **conflict** is introduced.

Try It! What is the conflict? What does conflict add to the story?

② Here, the setting for this scene is introduced, and **sensory imagery** makes the scene more vivid.

Try It! What are the sensory images in this stanza? To which of the five senses do they appeal?

③ Rhyming words create a musical effect. So does the regular **rhythm,** or "beat."

Try It! Read aloud the fifth and sixth stanzas. Do the same lines rhyme in the fifth stanza as in the sixth stanza? Is this rhyme scheme, or pattern, used throughout the ballad? Explain.

Extension Find another example of a poem, and compare it with these. Look at a range of poems from American, European, and world literatures.

The Bailiff's Daughter of Islington

A Traditional Ballad

① There lived a youth, and a well-beloved youth,
    And he was the squire's son;
And he loved the bailiff's daughter dear,
    Who lived in Islington.

5 But she was coy and never would
    On him her love bestow,
Till he was sent to London town
    Because he loved her so.

When seven long years had passed away,
10   She put on ragged attire,
And forth she went to Islington,
    Her true love to inquire.

② And as she went along the high road,
    The weather being hot and dry,
15 She sat her down upon a green bank,
    And her true love came riding by.

She started up, and with a color so red,
    And caught hold of his bridle rein,
"One penny, one penny, kind sir," she said,
20   "Will ease me of much pain."

③ "Before I give you a penny, sweetheart,
    Pray tell me where you were born."
"At Islington, kind sir," she said,
    "Where I have dwelt with many a scorn."

25 "I prithee, sweetheart, oh tell to me,
    Oh tell me if you know,
The bailiff's daughter of Islington?"
    "She's dead, sir, long ago."

"If she be dead, then take my horse,
30   My saddle and bridle also,
For I will into some far country go,
    Where no man shall me know."

"Oh stay, oh stay, thou goodly youth,
    She standeth by thy side.
35 She is not dead; she is here alive
    And ready to be thy bride."

Olivia

by Kathleen Thompson

4 When they brought Olivia home,
Mother holding her as though she were
made all of soft light feathers,
40 I thought she was mine, like my bear,
like my slippers that looked like baby penguins.
It turns out she belongs to herself,
although, in a way, to me, too.

Now I see her running with her friends,
45 twirling and turning and falling, breathless.
5 Grass as soft as innocence
cushions their elbows and knees, and they laugh.
Our love cushions them, too, protecting them
from the hard ground of life. Soon enough,
50 their joys will be different, strong and deep.
Their sorrows will make them who they need to be.

But now she is noise and laughter,
first joys and new discoveries,
and I wish it could last forever.

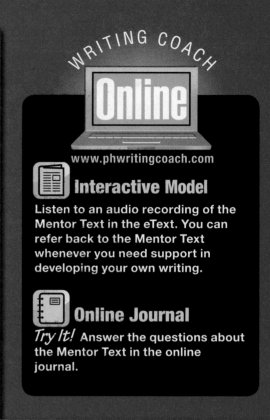

4 Throughout the poem, the poet maintains a very **clear, consistent point of view.**

Try It! Who might the speaker be in this poem? What do you think the speaker's relationship is to Olivia?

5 The poet uses **figurative language** that contributes to the mood of the poem.

Try It! What type of figurative language is used in the highlighted lines? What emotion does this figure of speech convey?

STUDENT MODEL
Ballad and Free Verse Poems

With a small group, take turns reading the Student Models aloud. As you read, practice newly acquired vocabulary by correctly producing the word's sound. Also note structures and elements of poetry. You may want to take a look at the Poet's Toolbox on page 129. Ask yourself how the poetic language informs and shapes your understanding of the poem.

Use a Reader's Eye

Now, reread the Student Models. On your copies of the Student Models, use the Reader's Response Symbols to react to what you read.

Reader's Response Symbols

+   **I can picture this.**

−   **This image could be stronger.**

?   **I wonder what this means.**

!   **This is cool!**

Express your ideas and feelings about the Student Models with a partner. Note and discuss responses that were the same for both of you, as well as responses that were different.

My Friend Sam
A Ballad by Joe Morris

My friend Sam could swing a bat
and throw a ball, could he.
We played ball on summer nights,
just stars and him and me.

5   But then one day we had a fight,
over whose turn it was to bat,
And Sam turned 'round
spat on the ground
threw down his favorite hat.
10   "The game is over!" he declared,
along with a dirty look.
Storming off without looking back,
I shouted, "You're a crook!"

My friend Sam could swing a bat
15   and throw a ball, could he.
We played ball on summer nights,
just stars and him and me.

I've never known a friend like Sam,
who could swing a bat and throw.
20   A cooler guy and nicer friend,
you could never know.
I wish I'd handed him the bat
and let the whole thing go.
Oh, I wish I'd handed him the bat
and let the whole thing go.

1

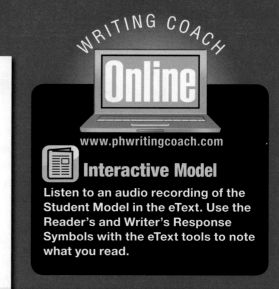

Online

www.phwritingcoach.com

Interactive Model

Listen to an audio recording of the Student Model in the eText. Use the Reader's and Writer's Response Symbols with the eText tools to note what you read.

Friends

A Free Verse Poem by Andrea Harrison

Friends can be as frail as birds.

Birds,
with their one bite beaks
and wings of silk thin feathers
5   and feet not heavy enough even to leave prints.

Birds,
with their deadened or bright colors—
depending on the season, the region
depending on the size of their hearts.

10 Birds,
if they'd allow you the blessing of holding them,
could fit in the palms of your hands
among the creases and lines, among
the fingers and knuckles.

15 Birds feast on a single worm,
a few crumbs of bread or the
round corners of pretzels,
or nothing at all
if nature hasn't been kind.

20 Most everything they do,
eat, touch,
or sing
is fragile.

Friends are similar.

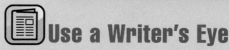

2

Use a Writer's Eye

Now, evaluate the poems as a writer. On your copies of the Student Models, use the Writer's Response Symbols to react to what you read. Identify places where the student writers use characteristics of an effective ballad and free verse poem.

Response Key Head

R.R.   **Rhythm or rhyme fits the poem's form**

S.D.   **Effective use of sound devices**

F.L.   **Figurative language conveys a mood**

I.D.   **Images and details appeal to the senses**

**Feature Assignment:
Ballad or Free Verse Poem**

Prewriting

Plan a first draft of your poem by deciding which form of poem—
ballad, free verse, or other form—you want to write and then
determining an appropriate topic. Select a topic from the Topic
Bank or come up with an idea of your own.

Choose From the Topic Bank

TOPIC BANK

The Table of Contents for Your Life Write a poem to describe the most
important events in or parts of your life. Each stanza of your poem could
focus on an important part of your life.

High Adventure Write a poem about an adventure you have had.
Describe the adventure using the conventions of poetry, such as
figurative language, sensory details, and rhyme or rhythm.

A Seasonal Moment Describe a favorite season or memorable moment
during a specific season, such as the first snowfall, a spring evening,
or sunrise at the beach. Use the conventions of poetry to describe the
seasonal moment.

Choose Your Own Topic

Determine an appropriate topic of your own by using the following
range of strategies to generate ideas.

Read and Discuss

- Read several free verse poems written by a poet you like. Note the
  important ideas and how they are expressed in each. Jot down the
  ideas that these poems inspire in you.

- Think about people, places, and things that are important in your life.
  Consider whether any of them would make a good topic for a poem.

- Discuss local current events with your friends or family members.
  Write down topics that interest you.

Review your responses and choose a topic.

Narrow Your Topic

A narrow topic will help you create a focused, interesting poem.

Apply It! Use a graphic organizer like the one shown to narrow your topic.

- Begin by writing your general topic in the top box and then sharpen your topic by making it more and more specific as you move down the chart.
- The last box shows the most precise topic, the focus of your poem.

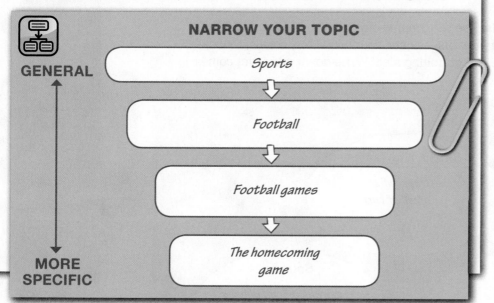

NARROW YOUR TOPIC

GENERAL

Sports

Football

Football games

The homecoming game

MORE SPECIFIC

Consider Multiple Audiences and Purposes

Before writing think about your audiences and purposes. Consider how the form you selected conveys the intended meaning to multiple audiences. Consider the views of others as you ask yourself these questions. Record your answers in your writing journal.

Questions for Audience	Questions for Purpose
• Who might read my poem? • What will they need to know to understand and appreciate my poem? • What ideas, impressions, or feelings might they have while reading my poem? • What form of poem would best convey my meaning to them?	• What idea or emotion would I like to convey? • How would I like readers to react to this idea or emotion? • How will I express the main idea or emotion?

WRITING COACH

Online

www.phwritingcoach.com

Interactive Graphic Organizers

Use the interactive graphic organizers to help you narrow your topic.

Online Journal

Try It! Record your answers and ideas in the online journal.

Plan Your Piece

You will use a graphic organizer like the one shown to develop your topic and organize your details. When it is complete, you will be ready to write your first draft.

Develop a Topic, Theme, or Controlling Idea To focus your poem, review your notes and write a clear statement of your topic, theme, or controlling idea. Name the most important idea or feeling you want to communicate. Add your statement to the center of a graphic organizer like the one shown.

Develop Ideas and Details Use the graphic organizer to identify ideas, feelings, events, and sensory details—sights, sounds, tastes, smells, touch—related to your topic, theme, or controlling idea. Write down whatever comes to you.

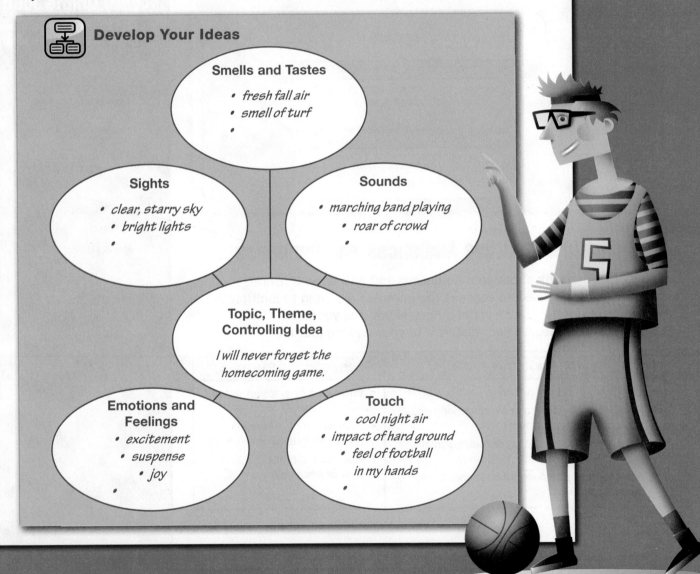

Develop Your Ideas

Smells and Tastes
- *fresh fall air*
- *smell of turf*
-

Sights
- *clear, starry sky*
- *bright lights*
-

Sounds
- *marching band playing*
- *roar of crowd*
-

Topic, Theme, Controlling Idea
I will never forget the homecoming game.

Emotions and Feelings
- *excitement*
- *suspense*
- *joy*
-

Touch
- *cool night air*
- *impact of hard ground*
- *feel of football in my hands*
-

Poet's Toolbox

Poets use a variety of techniques to make their ideas vivid and clear. Techniques vary according to the **conventions and traditions** of particular forms of poetry. For instance, a narrative poem like a ballad uses some of the techniques of fiction. Here are some techniques you might use in your poem.

Figurative Language is writing that means something beyond what the words actually say.	
Simile: comparison using *like* or *as*	*The defensive line came at us like a freight train.*
Metaphor: comparison made by saying that one thing is something else	*The roar of the crowd was a huge wave of sound.*
Personification: human characteristics applied to non-human objects	*The night came alive.*
Symbols add depth and insight to poetry.	
An object that stands for something else	The team's victory could symbolize strength.
Sound Devices create a musical or emotional effect.	
Alliteration: repetition of consonant sounds at the beginning of nearby words	***T**en **t**ons of **T**iger defense hit me.*
Assonance: repetition of vowel sounds in nearby words	*I was like **i**ce as all **eye**s turned to me.*
Consonance: repetition of consonants in the middle or at the end of words	*The bra**sh** lineba**ck**er ru**sh**ed the da**sh**ing quarterba**ck**.*
Structural Elements help build the framework for poetic language.	
Rhyme: repetition of sounds at the ends of lines of poetry	*I caught the football, small and **brown,** Then ran and ran—touch**down!***
Meter: rhythmical pattern of a poem. It is determined by stressed syllables in a line. Some forms of poetry have specific patterns of stressed syllables.	*ˇ **Í** ˇ ˇ **Í** ˇ **Í** ˇ ˇ **Í*** *I **caught** the **foot**ball, **small** and **brown*** (Stressed syllables in poetry are marked with a ´, while unstressed syllables are marked with a ˇ.)
Graphic Elements position the words on a page.	
Arrangement of words on a page	Capital letters, line spacing, and line breaks

 Apply It! Review the ideas, feelings, and sensory details in the graphic organizer you created.

- Decide what techniques from the Poet's Toolbox you would like to use in your poem.

- Keep in mind that some poetic techniques are traditionally used in specific forms. For example, ballads often include rhyme, while free verse does not.

- As you draft your poem, you will study the conventions of your form and finalize the techniques you will use.

WRITING COACH

Online

www.phwritingcoach.com

 Interactive Graphic Organizers

Use the interactive graphic organizers to help you create a plan for your writing.

 Interactive Model

Refer back to the Interactive Model in the eText as you plan your writing.

Drafting

During the drafting stage, you will start to write your ideas for a ballad, free verse poem, or other form of poetry. You will use the ideas you developed in prewriting and structure them in a sustained way according to the traditions required for the particular poetic form you chose.

Drafting a Free Verse Poem or Ballad

Each poetic form has specific characteristics, or **traditions**. You will write your poem using these traditions, the **conventions** from the Poet's Toolbox, and the ideas, feelings, and sensory details you developed in your graphic organizer.

These charts show the characteristics of each form. Review the characteristics. Then answer the questions in the right column as you draft your poem.

Free Verse Characteristics	Questions to Answer While Drafting
• Varied number of lines • Varied number of stanzas • No meter used; follows natural patterns of speech • Rhyme not often used • Poetic conventions, such as figurative language, used • Feelings or emotions conveyed • Vivid descriptions and sensory details	• How long do I want my poem to be? **Tip**: You don't have to decide the exact number of stanzas and lines. • What sound devices will I use? • What poetic conventions will I use? • What feelings or emotions will I express? • How will I make my descriptions vivid?

Ballad Characteristics	Questions to Answer While Drafting
• Varied length, but usually four stanzas or more • Plot, or story line • Rhyme often used • Regular rhythm • Refrain often repeated • Poetic and narrative conventions such as plot used • Feelings or emotions conveyed • Vivid descriptions	• What story will I tell? • What do I want to describe or express in each stanza? • What words will I rhyme in each stanza? **Tip:** Consult a rhyming dictionary and thesaurus. • Do my lines follow a regular rhythm? **Tip:** Read aloud as you write. • What poetic and narrative conventions will I use? • What feelings or emotions will I express? • How will I make my descriptions vivid?

Start Your Draft

To complete your draft, follow each of these steps. Use the graphic organizer that shows your topic, ideas, and sensory details and the Poet's Toolbox as guides.

While developing your poem, aim at writing your ideas, not on making your writing perfect. Remember, because you are writing in an open-ended situation, you will have the chance to improve your poem when you revise and edit.

WRITING COACH

Online

www.phwritingcoach.com

Interactive Model
Refer back to the Mentor Text in the eText as you write your draft.

Before You Write

√ Choose the **poetic form** you want to use—free verse, a sonnet, or another poetic form.

√ Review the **poetic traditions** of your poetic form that are listed in Drafting a Free Verse Poem or Sonnet. Make sure you use these characteristics when you write your draft.

√ Think of a striking image, figurative language, or other **poetic convention** to start your poem that will attract readers' attention.

While You Write

√ State or imply the **topic** or controlling idea. It does not have to be mentioned in each line, but should be sustained through the poem as a whole.

√ Include your **ideas** from prewriting. If a particular feeling, emotion, sensory detail, or other idea does not seem to work, try a different approach.

√ Review the **poetic conventions** in the Poet's Toolbox. Use some of these conventions to express your ideas. If you experiment with a convention and it does not seem to work, try another.

√ Include **rhetorical devices,** such as similes, metaphors, and personification, to convey meaning to your audience and to keep your writing interesting.

√ Make sure that you make careful word choices in your poem, including words that offer **sensory details** to ensure that your audience can fully experience the emotion in your poem.

√ Read your poem aloud to listen to the **sound devices** and evaluate their effects.

Revising: Making It Better

Now that you have finished your first draft, you are ready to revise. Think about the "big picture" of how well your audience will understand and connect to your poem. You can use your Revision RADaR as a guide for making changes to improve your draft. Revision RADaR provides four major ways to improve your writing: (R) replace, (A) add, (D) delete, and (R) reorder.

Kelly Gallagher, M. Ed.

KEEP REVISION ON YOUR RADaR

Read part of the first draft of the Student Model "Friends." Then look at questions the writer asked herself as she thought about how her draft will affect her audience.

Friends

1ST DRAFT

Birds and friends are the same—they are frail.

Birds,
with their tiny beaks
and wings of thin feathers
and tiny feet.

Birds,
with their deadened or bright colors—
depending on the season, the region
depending on the size of their hearts.

Birds,
If they'd let you, they,
could fit in the palms of your hands
among the creases and lines, among the
fingers and knuckles.

> Have I captured my reader's attention in my *opening*?

> Have I included *sensory details*?

> Do these words add to my *controlling idea*?

Now, look at how the writer applied her Revision RADaR to write an improved second draft.

Friends

2ND DRAFT

Friends can be as frail as birds.

Birds,
with their one bite beaks
and wings of silk thin feathers
and feet not heavy enough even to leave prints.

Birds,
with their deadened or bright colors—
depending on the season, the region
depending on the size of their hearts.

Birds,
if they'd allow you the blessing of holding them,
could fit in the palms of your hands among the
creases and lines, among the fingers and knuckles.

R *Reordered the words in the first line to add a simile to capture the reader's attention*

R *Replaced bland adjectives with vivid, sensory details*

D *Deleted confusing words*
A *Added a clear description, so my audience will better understand the theme*

WRITING COACH

Online

www.phwritingcoach.com

Video

Learn more strategies for effective writing from program author Kelly Gallagher.

Apply It! Use your Revision RADaR to revise your draft.

- First, determine whether you have addressed the needs of your audiences and purpose, and included the **poetic traditions,** or characteristics, of a ballad, a free verse poem or the form you have chosen.

- Then, make sure you have included a variety of **poetic conventions** to make your writing interesting.

- Finally, apply your Revision RADaR to make needed changes. Focus especially on revising figurative language, such as similes, metaphors, and personification, to improve your poem's **style**—your unique way of expressing ideas through writing. And remember—you can use the Revision RADaR steps in any order.

Look at the Big Picture

Use the chart and your analytical skills to evaluate how well each section of your poem is organized and meets the needs of your audience. When necessary, use the suggestions in the chart to revise your poem.

	Evaluate	Revise
Topic and Sensory Details	• Make sure your controlling idea or **theme** is clear in the poem. • Check that the **sensory details** you have chosen support the controlling idea or theme.	• Think about the most important idea or feeling you want to convey. If needed, add a statement or a suggestion of theme. • Replace sensory details that do not support the controlling idea. Add new details that help paint a clearer picture.
Structural Elements	• Ensure the **poetic traditions** of your chosen form have been included in your poem. • If you are writing a free verse poem, check to see if the **language** reflects normal speech. • If you are writing a ballad: • Check the rhythm and **rhyme**. • Consider whether to include a **refrain**. • Decide whether you have used enough **transitions** to convey meaning and connect events.	• Review the poetic traditions for your chosen poetic form in Drafting a Free Verse Poem or Ballad. Revise your poem to include any missing characteristics. • Replace any words that you wouldn't normally use in speaking aloud. • If you are writing a ballad: • Add or delete lines and replace and reorder words to improve the rhyme and rhythm. • Add a refrain, if appropriate. • Add words and phrases such as *then, next,* and *at last* to connect ideas in your poem.
Poetic Conventions	• Make sure **poetic conventions,** such as figurative language, help convey your meaning and purpose to your audience. • Read aloud to check that your **sound devices** are effective.	• Replace boring or vague words with figurative language, vivid words, and sensory details. • Use a dictionary or thesaurus to find words that create a more musical quality.

Focus on Craft: Simile

A **trope** is a deliberate use of language for effect. For example, figurative language, such as a simile, is writing that means something beyond what the words actually say. A **simile** is a kind of trope that uses a connecting word, such as *like* or *as,* to compare two usually unrelated things. For instance, the statement *life is like a winding road* is a simile because it uses the word *like* to compare life to a road. Including similes in poems is an effective way to help readers see things in new ways.

Think about how similes affect how a reader might experience a poem as you read this excerpt from the Student Model.

 **STUDENT MODEL** | from **Friends**
page 124; line 1

Friends can be as frail as birds.

 Try It! Now, ask yourself these questions. Record your answers in your journal.

- What two things are being compared in this line?
- What makes these things very different? What might they have in common? How does the comparison help you to see friends in a new way? Explain.

Fine-Tune Your Draft

Apply It! Use the revision suggestions to prepare your final draft after rethinking how well questions of audience and purpose have been addressed.

- **Employ Tropes** Use figurative language, such as similes, to help readers pull meaning from your poem. If necessary, rearrange words as you work to employ these tropes.
- **Include Transitions** Use transitions, if necessary, to clarify your meaning. For instance, in a ballad you might use a transition such as *finally* to show the sequence of events.

Teacher or Peer Feedback Explain to your teacher or a group of your peers the theme or controlling idea that you are trying to express in your poem. Then, read your poem aloud. Ask if the meaning you hoped to express in your poem is clear. Think about the feedback you receive and revise your final draft as needed.

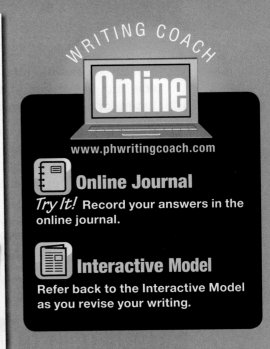

WRITING COACH

Online

www.phwritingcoach.com

Online Journal

Try It! Record your answers in the online journal.

Interactive Model

Refer back to the Interactive Model as you revise your writing.

Editing: Making It Correct

To edit your work, read your draft carefully to correct errors in spelling and grammar. It can be helpful to read your draft aloud to listen for where the writing needs correction.

As you edit your draft, consider using **different kinds of phrases,** such as **adjectival, adverbial, verbal, and infinitive phrases.** A phrase is a group of words that act as a single part of speech. Then edit your final draft for errors in **grammar, mechanics, and spelling.**

WRITE GUY *Jeff Anderson, M. Ed.*

WHAT DO YOU NOTICE?

Zoom in on Conventions Focus on phrases as you zoom in on lines from the Student Model.

> To learn more about phrases, see Chapter 15 of your Grammar Handbook.

STUDENT MODEL from **Friends** page 125; lines 10–12

Birds,

if they'd allow you the blessing of holding them,

could fit in the palms of your hands

Now, ask yourself: *As what part of speech does each highlighted phrase serve?*

Perhaps you said the first and last phrases serve as adjectives and the second phrase as an adverb. **Adjectival phrases** are prepositional phrases that modify nouns or pronouns. The adjectival phrase *of holding them* modifies *blessing,* and *of your hands* modifies *palms.* **Adverbial phrases** are prepositional phrases that modify adjectives, adverbs, and verbs. The adverbial phrase *in the palms* modifies the verb *fit.*

Verbal phrases function as adjectives, adverbs, and nouns. Participial phrases are made up of the past or present participle and its modifiers. They function as adjectives, as in: The door, *opened by the wind,* should be closed. Gerund phrases are made up of the *-ing* verb form and its modifiers. They function as nouns, as in: *Playing on the football team* is his favorite activity.

Infinitive phrases are a kind of verbal phrase consisting of *to,* the base form of a verb, and related modifiers. They function as nouns, adjectives, and adverbs. In this example, the infinitive phrase acts as a noun: It was her hope *to play flawlessly.*

Partner Talk Discuss this question with a partner: *How do phrases help make the poem more vivid?*

Grammar Mini-Lesson: Commas With Phrases

Phrases are sometimes set off with a comma, especially introductory phrases. Place a comma after a participial or infinitive phrase that introduces a sentence. Place a comma after most introductory adjectival and adverbial phrases, too. However, you may choose not to place a comma after very short adjectival or adverbial phrases such as *on the way* or *in 2002*. Notice how the author of the Mentor Text uses a comma to set off an introductory participial phrase.

 **STUDENT MODEL** from **My Friend Sam**
page 124; lines 12-13

Storming off without looking back, I shouted, "You're a crook!"

Try It! Tell where commas might be added to these sentences. Write the answers in your journal.

1. To be helpful Alana quizzed me on the driving test exam questions.
2. Swinging the bat the batter loosened up before stepping up to the plate.

Apply It! Edit your draft for **grammar, mechanics, and spelling.** Check that you have used different types of phrases and consistently **punctuated** them correctly.

To learn more, see Chapter 23.

WRITING COACH

Online

www.phwritingcoach.com

Video
Learn effective editing techniques from program author Jeff Anderson.

 Online Journal
Try It! Record your answers in the online journal.

 Interactive Model
Refer back to the Interactive Model as you edit your writing.

Use the rubric to evaluate your piece. If necessary, rethink, rewrite, or revise.

Rubric for Poetry: Ballad or Free Verse Poem	Rating Scale
Ideas: How well is the poem's subject or controlling idea defined and developed?	Not very Very 1 2 3 4 5 6
Organization: How organized are your ideas?	1 2 3 4 5 6
Voice: How effectively do you use figurative language and poetic techniques to create a unique voice?	1 2 3 4 5 6
Word Choice: How well do the specific words you have chosen convey your meaning?	1 2 3 4 5 6
Sentence Fluency: How naturally does your writing flow in the form you've chosen?	1 2 3 4 5 6
Conventions: How correct is your use of phrases?	1 2 3 4 5 6

Publishing

Give your poem a chance to inspire someone—publish it! First, get your poem ready for presentation. Then, choose a way to publish it for the appropriate audience.

Wrap Up Your Presentation

Is your poem handwritten or written on a computer? If your poem is handwritten, you may need to make a new, clean copy. If so, be sure to write legibly. Add a title to your poem that grabs the reader's attention.

Publish Your Piece

Use the chart to identify a way to publish your poem.

If your audience is...	...then, publish it by...
Teens around the world	• Researching literary journals that publish young writers and submitting your poem for publication • Posting your poem online and inviting responses
The community	• Submitting your poem to local magazines that publish creative writing • Posting your poem on community billboards

 ## Reflect on Your Writing

Now that you are done with your poem, read it over and use your writing journal to answer these questions.

- Which parts of the poem do you feel are the strongest? Which are the weakest? How can you improve your writing in your next assignment?
- How does writing a poem help you to appreciate the work of other poets?
- Compare your poem to another piece of writing that expresses a similar theme. As you evaluate what these works have in common, consider what you might learn from both pieces.

Manage Your Portfolio You may wish to include your poem in your writing portfolio. If so, consider what this poem reveals about your growth as a writer.

The Big Question: Why Write?
How do we best convey feeling through words on a page?

21st Century Learning

MAKE YOUR WRITING COUNT

Engage Viewers' Senses With a Poetry Collage

A poem is a collage of sensory effects. Poetic language creates vivid images and sounds that appeal to our eyes and ears as well as our other senses. Help a specific audience—your classmates—experience poetry in a new way by creating a multimedia **collage.**

In groups, produce a **multimedia presentation** incorporating still images, sound, and graphics. You can center your presentation on a traditional paper collage, adding sound in a live presentation. Alternatively, you can use Web authoring tools to more easily blend your media elements. The collage should include the full text of each poem in your group.

Here's your action plan.

1. As a group, identify common themes, images, or tone among your poems, so that your collage reflects a unified point of view.

2. Choose group roles. Put one person in charge of each of the following tasks:

   - Finding original graphics that reflect the poems' common themes, images, or tone

   - Finding magazine, newspaper, or Web images that reflect the poems' common ideas

   - Choosing typefaces appropriate to the poems

   - Selecting appropriate sounds, such as music. For online collages, record your peers' readings of their own poems.

3. Meet to approve or reject each of the collected graphics, images, typefaces, or sounds.

4. Assemble the collage, including the full text of each poem. If you are posting your presentation online, record your final product.

5. Present your collage to the class, either live or by projecting your Web site on a large screen.

Listening and Speaking During your multimedia presentations, each group member should read his or her own poem expressively. After each presentation, participate in a class discussion to evaluate how well the graphics, images, typeface, and layout of the collage and the sounds fit the common themes, images, or tone of the poems.

WRITING COACH

Online

www.phwritingcoach.com

Online Journal

Reflect on Your Writing Record your answers and ideas in the online journal.

Resource

Link to resources on 21st Century Learning for help in creating a group project.

Your Turn ▶ **Writing for Media: Definition Essay**

21st Century Learning

Definition Essay

A **definition essay** is an analytical essay that defines a word or concept. In a definition essay, the writer provides personal context and opinions to extend the literal, or dictionary, definition of a term. Most definition essays focus on abstract terms, such as democracy, prejudice, or love. These essays follow the standard format of introduction, body, and conclusion. Definition essays are often found in literary and news magazines, as well as on the Internet.

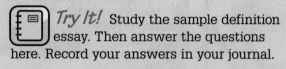

Try It! Study the sample definition essay. Then answer the questions here. Record your answers in your journal.

1. What does the essay define?

2. Does the essay include both a **literal definition** and **figurative definition**, that is, one that goes beyond the literal meaning?

3. What is the **thesis**, or main idea, of the definition essay?

4. Good essays include **specific details** to support their main idea. What specific details are included in this essay?

5. If you were to define the subject of this essay in a **poem**, how would you do it? How would your poem differ from the essay?

Extension Find another example of a definition essay, and compare it with this one.

Home

I recently saw a sign that said, "Home for Sale," and my first thought was: That's impossible! You can't sell a home! But of course you can sell a home. There are "For Sale" signs in front of homes all over this country—or are they just houses? To me the word *home* refers to much more than the literal structure in which a person lives—the four walls and a roof. Home, to use a cliché, is where the heart is.

When I think of home, I don't usually think of the actual house I live in, a modest single-story house on a quiet street. I think instead of the people and animals who live inside that house—my family and my pets. The ones I love. I think of the feeling I get returning from a busy day at school to a place that provides not only shelter but comfort, relaxation, and acceptance. My dog doesn't care what kind of shoes I'm wearing or how well I did on my test.

My mom loves me whether I look my best or not. This is what home means to me. It's not just the place I live, but also the place I belong. And you can't buy that!

Create a Definition Essay

Follow these steps to create a definition essay. To plan your definition essay, review the graphic organizers on R24–R27 and choose one that suits your needs.

Prewriting

- Identify a word that you would like to define. It should be a word that has meaning beyond just its literal definition.
- Identify the literal definition of the word and then consider any figurative definitions.
- Review your notes and create a thesis or main idea that states why your word or concept has meaning beyond its literal meaning. List examples and details that you can use to support your main idea.

Drafting

- Create an outline with an introduction, body, and conclusion to guide you as you write your essay. You can use comparison and contrast, cause and effect, or order of importance to organize your ideas.
- Consider your purpose—to define—and your audience. As you draft, include examples and details that help you achieve your purpose and that will appeal to your audience.

Revising and Editing

- Review your draft to ensure that your word is fully defined, that the definition is logically organized, and that details and examples support your thesis.
- Make sure that you have included both the literal and figurative meanings of your word and have explained them in detail.
- Check that spelling, grammar, and mechanics are correct.

Publishing

- Compile a class "dictionary" that includes everyone's definition essays.
- Create a multimedia presentation with graphics, images, and sound.
- Enhance your presentation by drawing ideas from several different areas. To do this, clearly show the literal definition of your concept and then explain how different people feel about the concept. In the body of your presentation, stress your ideas and perspective.

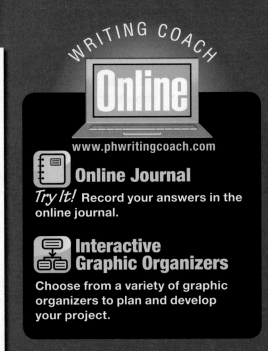

WRITING COACH

Online

www.phwritingcoach.com

Online Journal

Try It! Record your answers in the online journal.

Interactive Graphic Organizers

Choose from a variety of graphic organizers to plan and develop your project.

Partner Talk

Before you start drafting, explain the literal and figurative meanings of the word in your definition essay to a partner. Use specific details to describe and explain your ideas. Increase the specificity of your details based on the type of information you are delivering. Ask for feedback about your explanation. For example, does it make sense?

Writing for Assessment

Writing a good poem can take a lot of practice. You can use these prompts to do just that—practice writing poems. Your responses should include the same characteristics as your free verse poem or ballad. Look back at page 120 to review these characteristics.

 Try It! Begin by reading the **poetry** prompt and the information on format and academic vocabulary. Then, use the ABCDs of On-Demand Writing to help you plan and write your poem.

Format

The prompt directs you to write a *poem*. Develop your topic, theme, or controlling idea by deciding on ideas and sensory details you would like to use in your poem.

Poetry Prompt

Some of our happiest times live in our hearts and minds as memories. Think of a time when you were happy. Write a poem describing the time and explaining why you felt so good. Be sure to construct a poem that has a clear theme or controlling idea and uses the traditions of the poetic form you chose.

Academic Vocabulary

When you use a specific poetic form, such as the sonnet, lyric poem, ballad, or free verse, you need to follow the *traditions* of that form. For instance, a sonnet has fourteen lines, while a ballad, as you learned in this chapter, usually has a refrain.

The ABCDs of On-Demand Writing

Use the following ABCDs to help you respond to the prompt.

Before you write your draft:

A ttack the prompt [1 MINUTE]

- Circle or highlight important verbs in the prompt. Draw a line from the verb to what it refers to.
- Rewrite the prompt in your own words.

B rainstorm possible answers [4 MINUTES]

- Create a graphic organizer to generate ideas.
- Use one for each part of the prompt if necessary.

C hoose the order of your response [1 MINUTE]

- Think about the best way to organize your ideas.
- Number your ideas in the order you will write about them. Cross out ideas you will not be using.

After you write your draft:

D etect errors before turning in the draft [1 MINUTE]

- Carefully reread your writing.
- Make sure that your response makes sense and is complete.
- Look for spelling, punctuation, and grammar errors.

More Prompts for Practice

Apply It! Respond to Prompts 1 and 2 by writing **poems** that reflect an awareness of poetic conventions and poetic traditions within different forms. As you write, be sure to:

- Identify your audience
- Choose a poetic form and use the **traditions, or characteristics,** of that form
- Include a variety of **poetic conventions,** such as figurative language and sound devices, to make your meaning clear to your audience
- Establish a clear **topic, theme,** or **controlling idea**

> **Prompt 1** There are many forms of dance, such as hip hop, jazz, and ballet. Each form expresses movement differently and affects its audience in some way. Write a poem about a particular form of dance. Be sure to construct a poem that uses poetic conventions.

> **Prompt 2** Often, people use hobbies to relieve stress or just to enjoy themselves. Write a poem about a hobby or something you like to do. Be sure to construct a poem that uses poetic conventions.

Spiral Review: Narrative Respond to Prompt 3 by writing an **autobiographical narrative** that meets these criteria:

- Develop an engaging **story,** including a well-developed **conflict** that is resolved
- Present interesting and believable **characters**
- Use a range of **literary strategies** and **devices** to enhance the plot
- Include **sensory details** that define the **mood** and **tone**

> **Prompt 3** We face challenges in different ways. Write an autobiographical narrative about a problem you overcame. Develop the conflict in your narrative, explaining what steps you used to solve it. Be sure to include dialogue and other literary devices to tell the story.

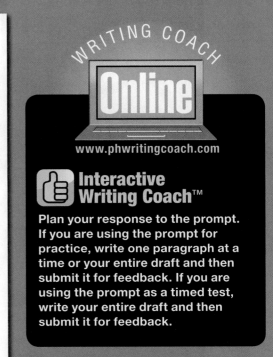

WRITING COACH

Online

www.phwritingcoach.com

Interactive Writing Coach™

Plan your response to the prompt. If you are using the prompt for practice, write one paragraph at a time or your entire draft and then submit it for feedback. If you are using the prompt as a timed test, write your entire draft and then submit it for feedback.

Remember **ABCD**

Attack the prompt

Brainstorm possible answers

Choose the order of your response

Detect errors before turning in the draft

CHAPTER 8

EXPOSITION

How Can You Explain This?

What do you know about snowboarding? What information and ideas about snowboarding could you share with others?

Information can be presented many ways. For example, you can compare two things, you can discuss the positives and negatives of an idea, or you can present a problem and a solution.

Try It! Imagine that you wanted to explain your ideas about snowboarding. How would you describe your opinion about this sport?

Consider these questions as you participate in an extended discussion with a partner. Take turns expressing your ideas and feelings.

- Consider the benefits: What makes snowboarding exciting or worthwhile?
- Think about the drawbacks: What makes snowboarding risky or dangerous?
- Are there any other factors to consider?
- Do any of your ideas outweigh the others?

Review the ideas you wrote. Tell your partner your ideas about snowboarding.

What's Ahead

In this chapter, you will review two strong examples of an analytical essay: a Mentor Text and a Student Model. Then, using the examples as guides, you will write an analytical essay in the pro-con form.

WRITING COACH

Online

www.phwritingcoach.com

 Online Journal
Try It! Record your answers and ideas in the online journal.

You can also record and save your answers and ideas on pop-up sticky notes in the eText.

 **Connect to the Big Questions**

Discuss these questions with your partner:

1 **What do you think?** What is the best way to learn?

2 **Why write?** What should we tell and what should we describe to make information clear?

ANALYTICAL ESSAY

An analytical essay is a type of expository essay that explores a topic to inform the reader about the topic. In this chapter, you will learn to write a type of analytical essay known as a pro-con essay. A pro-con essay explores the advantages and disadvantages of a topic. It may address personal choices; business or consumer decisions; or local, national, or global issues. Pro-con essays often include opinions, like persuasive essays, but their purpose is to give balanced and fair information in order to aid the reader in making his or her own informed decision.

You will develop your pro-con essay by taking it through each of the steps of the writing process: prewriting, drafting, revising, editing, and publishing. You will also have an opportunity to write a summary of a feature article. To preview the criteria for how your pro-con essay will be evaluated, see the rubric on page 163.

FEATURE ASSIGNMENT

Analytical Essay: Pro-Con Essay

An effective analytical essay has these characteristics:

- **Effective introductory** and **concluding paragraphs**

- A **clear thesis statement** or **controlling idea**

- A **clear organizing structure for conveying ideas**

- **Relevant and substantial evidence,** or proof, **and well-chosen details** that support the thesis

- A **variety of sentence structures,** and **rhetorical devices,** such as analogies and rhetorical questions, that express ideas clearly and effectively

- Smooth **transitions** between paragraphs

- **Effective sentence structure** and correct spelling, grammar, and usage

A pro-con essay also includes:

- **Information on multiple relevant perspectives**

- A clear **analysis** of benefits and drawbacks

- **Valid and reliable sources,** such as experts in the field or research studies

- **Sources that are relevant,** or timely and closely related to the topic and point of view

Other Forms of Analytical Essays

In addition to pro-con essays, there are other forms of analytical essays, including:

Cause-and-effect essays trace the results of an event or the reasons an event happened.

Classification essays organize subjects into categories or classes and investigate the similarities that comprise these classes.

Compare-and-contrast essays explore similarities and differences between two or more topics.

Newspaper and magazine articles are printed or published on the Internet and supply relevant information about a particular topic by analyzing the topic's elements. They may also reflect genres other than analytical essays, such as persuasive or narrative nonfiction writing.

Problem-solution essays identify problems and propose one or more solutions.

Try It! For each audience and purpose described, choose a form, such as a compare-and-contrast, cause-and-effect, or problem-solution essay, that is appropriate for conveying your intended meaning to multiple audiences. Explain your choices.

- To explain how to resolve a problem with litter in your neighborhood
- To describe to your history class three main events that led to U.S. involvement in World War II
- To explore in your English class the similarities and differences between two works by the same author

WORD BANK

People often use these vocabulary words when they talk about expository writing. Work with a partner. Take turns using each word in a sentence. If you are unsure of the meaning of a word, use the Glossary or a dictionary to check the definition.

advantage	relevant
convey	substantial
perspective	suitable

MENTOR TEXT

Learn From Experience

 After reading the analytical essay on pages 148–149, read the numbered notes in the margins to learn how the author presented her ideas. Later you will read a Student Model, which shares these characteristics and also has the characteristics of a pro-con essay.

Answer the *Try It!* questions online or in your notebook.

---

1 The **introduction** introduces the topic by describing a situation to which its audience can relate.

Try It! What is the topic of the essay? Who is the audience for the essay?

2 The **thesis,** or controlling idea, narrows the general topic to a few specifics about the topic.

Try It! What is the thesis, or controlling idea, of the essay? From the thesis, what aspects of the topic will the author analyze in the rest of the essay? What will be the purpose of the essay?

3 The **organizational structure** of this passage is cause and effect. The analysis of the cause and effect provides **relevant evidence** to support the thesis.

Try It! What other organizational structures have you seen in essays? How are those structures different from this cause-and-effect structure?

Extension Find another example of an analytical essay, and compare it with this one.

From Sleep Is One Thing Missing in Busy Teenage Lives

by Denise Grady

1 At 6:30 in the morning, a strapping teenager on the cusp of manhood can look an awful lot like a newborn puppy, with eyes that won't open and a powerful instinct to curl up under something warm. Is this the same person who swore he wasn't
5 tired at 10:30 the night before while he traded instant messages with six different friends at once, and who will probably do it again tonight?

Parents know the adolescent drill all too well: stay up past 11 or 12 on school nights, stagger out of bed at 6 or 7, shower
10 interminably, eat a token breakfast and bolt. Yawn through school, perk up for sports or clubs, fight sleep while doing homework. Come to life at 9 p.m., deny fatigue and stay up well after parents have collapsed into bed. Holidays and weekends, stay up half the night and then "binge sleep" until noon or
15 beyond. Sunday night, restart the cycle of late to bed and early to rise.

2 Americans are said to be a sleep-deprived people, and teenagers are the worst of the lot. Most are lucky to get 6, 7 or 8 hours of sleep a night, even though studies have shown
20 repeatedly that people in their teens and possibly even early 20's need 9 to 10 hours. Many live in a state of chronic sleep deficit that can affect mood, behavior, schoolwork and reaction time.

Dr. Mary Carskadon, a sleep researcher at Brown University, describes sleep-deprived teenagers as existing in a "kind of gray
25 cloud."

"We just ignore these bad feelings from not enough sleep and get used to it," she said. "We forget what it's like to feel good, and how much more efficiently you can do things." Physical, emotional and social factors seem to conspire against letting
30 adolescents get enough sleep.

3 When teenagers insist that they are not tired at 9 or 10 p.m., they are very likely telling the truth. For reasons that are

35 not fully understood, Dr. Carskadon said, their body clocks shift, so that their natural tendency is to stay up later at night and wake up later in the morning than when they were younger. But that inner clock often clashes with the outer world: early starting times in high school and demanding schedules of sports, clubs, music lessons, homework and part-time jobs.

40 There are consequences. For one thing, lack of sleep can interfere with learning: tired students have a hard time paying attention, and even if they do somehow manage to focus, they may forget what they were taught because memory formation takes place partly during sleep.

45 In *Adolescent Sleep Patterns*, a book published in August and edited by Dr. Carskadon, she wrote, "The students may be in school, but their brains are at home on their pillows."

④ Tired teenagers can be as cranky as tired 2-year-olds, and even less fun to deal with. More seriously, sleep deprivation can bring on feelings of stress, anger, and sadness.

50 Dr. Carskadon said studies had repeatedly linked sleep deprivation to depressed mood—a temporary case of the blues, not the same as clinical depression.

"In every study where we've looked at it, it's crystal clear that kids who sleep less report more depressed mood," she said.

55 ⑤ In one experiment, Dr. Carskadon said, teenagers were shown various photographs, and a researcher gauged their emotional reactions.

"Kids not getting enough sleep are less likely to respond in a positive way to positive things in the environment, and more

60 likely to respond in a negative way to negative things," she said.

---

④ A **variety of sentence structures** and **rhetorical devices** help make this passage interesting and easy to read.

Try It! Which sentence structures are used in the passage? Simple? Compound? Complex? Compound-complex? Give examples of the structures you find. What figurative language does the author use?

⑤ In the **conclusion,** the author quotes Dr. Carskadon.

Try It! How does the quotation support the thesis of the essay?

STUDENT MODEL

Pro-Con Essay

With a small group, take turns reading the Student Model aloud. Ask yourself if the topic is clearly stated and the pros and cons are thoroughly covered.

Use a Reader's Eye

Now, reread the Student Model. On your copy of the Student Model, use the Reader's Response Symbols to react to what you read.

> **Reader's Response Symbols**
>
> **+** **Aha! That makes sense to me.**
>
> **−** **This isn't clear to me.**
>
> **?** **I have a question about this.**
>
> **!** **Wow! That is cool/weird/ interesting.**

Participate in an extended discussion with a partner. Express your opinions and share your responses to the Student Model. Discuss the main ideas and the author's purpose with a partner.

Studying Abroad: TO GO OR NOT TO GO?

by Marcus Thompson

Leaving home for a summer, semester, or year to study abroad is a major decision—one that only you and your family can make. When students have to make these decisions, it's important to be well
5 informed. Information about study abroad programs is available from many sources—guidance counselors, libraries, the Internet, exchange program brochures, and others who have studied abroad. An important step in the decision-making process is considering
10 the pros and cons of studying abroad to determine whether it is the right choice for you and your family.

One thing to consider when deciding whether or not to study abroad is the educational experience you'll have in that country. Studying in another country will allow you
15 to gain fluency in a foreign language. Although learning a new language is challenging, most students find the experience rewarding in the end. In addition to learning a new language, students will be attending regular classes, such as science and history. Because this can be a very
20 challenging way to learn, it is important to think carefully about how well you would learn in this environment. "If you aren't prepared for hard work, study abroad is not for you," warns guidance counselor Phil Sergeant.

Living abroad also gives you access to a new
25 culture. Exchange student Amanda Purcell explains, "I learned so much about Spain from my host family. They introduced me to Spanish customs and showed me places I would never have found on my own." Many students find the experience of learning about a new

1

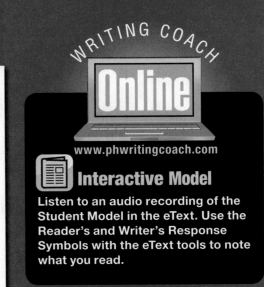

WRITING COACH

Online

www.phwritingcoach.com

Interactive Model

Listen to an audio recording of the Student Model in the eText. Use the Reader's and Writer's Response Symbols with the eText tools to note what you read.

30 culture and exploring museums and historical landmarks fascinating. Conversely, others find that these cultural differences are overwhelming. They often become homesick, missing their friends and family and normal routine. Ultimately, you have to decide whether leaving
35 friends and family behind is worth the experience.

In addition to the emotional factors, you and your family must consider the cost of the program. Exchange programs can be expensive, and they often do not include the price of meals, entertainment, and travel.
40 Additional expenses add up. At first, the fee may seem too costly. However, partial and full scholarships are often available. With careful research and planning, a student who wants to study abroad can get financial assistance.

There are many benefits and drawbacks of studying
45 abroad. Embarking on such an adventure can be quite exciting because it gives you the opportunity to learn a new language, experience a new culture, and make new friends. However, with those pros come the cons of a difficult learning environment,
50 spending months away from your family and friends, and a high price tag. There is no "right" or "wrong" decision about studying abroad: the challenge is to decide whether such an experience is right for you.

Use a Writer's Eye

Now evaluate the piece as a writer. On your copy of the Student Model, use the Writer's Response Symbols to react to what you read. Identify places where the student writer uses characteristics of an effective pro-con essay.

Writer's Response Symbols

C.T. Clear thesis

I.C. Effective introduction and conclusion

R.D. Good use of rhetorical devices

S.E. Effective supporting evidence

2

**Feature Assignment:
Pro-Con Essay**

Prewriting

Plan a first draft of your pro-con essay by **determining an appropriate topic**. Choose from the Topic Bank or come up with a topic of your own.

 Choose From the Topic Bank

TOPIC BANK

Effects of the Internet The Age of the Internet has been the cause of many changes in people's lives. Its effects are not limited to adults; children are affected, too. Consider both the positive and negative effects the use of the Internet has on children and write a pro-con essay that discusses these effects.

Study Techniques Different study techniques work for different people. Choose a particular study technique, such as flashcards or study groups. Write a pro-con essay in which you discuss the advantages and disadvantages of the study technique you've chosen.

School Days Traditionally students go to school from fall through spring with a long break in the summer. Some school districts are rethinking this plan and have students going to school all year with short breaks in between sessions. Write a pro-con essay on which of these plans you think is best.

 Choose Your Own Topic

Determine an appropriate topic on your own by using the following **range of strategies** to generate ideas.

Read and Discuss

- Visit the library or search the Internet for issues that interest you and that have both pros and cons. Spend time reading about the different perspectives presented about these issues.

- Discuss topics with friends or family members who might have information about a topic that interests you.

Review your responses and choose a topic.

Narrow Your Topic

If your topic is too broad in a pro-con essay, you cannot adequately cover all the benefits and drawbacks of the topic. By narrowing your topic, you can focus on presenting two or three important pros and cons.

Apply It! Use a graphic organizer like the one shown to narrow your topic.

- Write your general topic in the top box and then record specific aspects of your topic in the next row of boxes.
- Choose the specific aspect, or controlling idea, that most interests you and narrow it further, recording the focus of your pro-con essay in the last box.

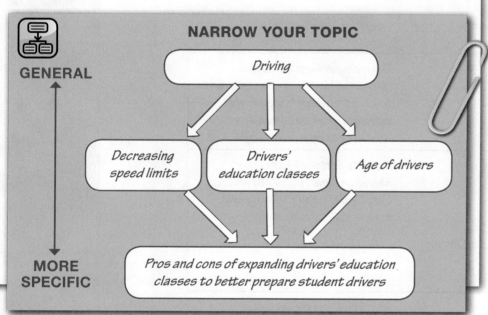

NARROW YOUR TOPIC

GENERAL

Driving

Decreasing speed limits

Drivers' education classes

Age of drivers

MORE SPECIFIC

Pros and cons of expanding drivers' education classes to better prepare student drivers

Consider Multiple Audiences and Purposes

Before writing, think about your audiences and purposes. Consider the views of others as you ask yourself these questions.

Questions for Audience	Questions for Purpose
• Who are my various audiences? • How familiar are these audiences with the topic? • What might my various audiences need to know to come to an informed opinion?	• How can I make the information clear to my audiences? • How will I organize and balance my information about multiple perspectives?

Record your answers in your writing journal.

www.phwritingcoach.com

👍 Interactive Writing Coach™

- **Choosing from the Topic Bank gives you access to the Interactive Writing Coach™.**
- **Submit your writing and receive instant personalized feedback and guidance as you draft, revise, and edit your writing.**

 Interactive Graphic Organizers

Use the interactive graphic organizers to help you narrow your topic.

📓 Online Journal

Try It! Record your answers and ideas in the online journal.

Plan Your Piece

You will use the graphic organizer to state your thesis, organize the pros and cons, and identify supporting details. When it is complete, you will be ready to write your first draft.

Develop a Clear Thesis Evaluate your preliminary ideas and information to develop a thesis that concisely identifies the topic and explains why it is under consideration. List it on a graphic organizer like this one to help you develop an effective essay and introduction.

Organize Your Ideas Use a graphic organizer to develop a clear scheme, or plan, for your essay. Decide whether presenting pros and cons point-by-point or discussing pros and then cons will best convey your ideas.

Develop Your Pro-Con Essay

Clear Thesis	*Expanding drivers' education classes will better prepare students to take the wheel; however, this extra preparation comes at a cost of both money and time.*
Pro and/or Con	*Pro: Students will have more hands-on time behind the wheel. Con: Parents and students will have to adjust schedules.*
Supporting Evidence/Details	
Pro and/or Con	*Pro: Students will be better prepared to drive alone. Con: The expense for drivers' education will increase.*
Supporting Evidence/Details	
Conclusion	*The benefits of expanding drivers' education are clear, but whether they are necessary or worth the cost in time and money is still undecided.*

Gather Details

To provide strong evidence to support your thesis, writers use many kinds of details. Look at these examples.

- **Facts:** *According to national insurance company reports, teenage drivers are among the most likely to have multiple accidents.*

- **Personal Observations:** *"A few more sessions with my instructor would have made me more comfortable, but I think I was sufficiently ready to drive on my own," says one teenager.*

- **Expert Opinions:** *Drivers' Education teacher Mrs. Frankel claims that even three additional sessions would bring about marked improvement in teenagers' driving habits.*

As you conduct research on your topic, consult different resources:

- **Primary Sources** *like reports of research results, newspaper articles, interviews, and photographs can provide first-hand accounts of events.*

- **Secondary Sources** *like textbooks and commentaries provide analysis and perspective on events the author did not personally witness.*

Try It! Read the Student Model excerpt and identify the kinds of details the author used to support his ideas.

 STUDENT MODEL from **Studying Abroad: To Go or Not To Go?** page 150; lines 15–23

> Although learning a new language is challenging, most students find the experience rewarding in the end. … "If you aren't prepared for hard work, study abroad is not for you," warns guidance counselor Phil Sergeant.

Apply It! Review the kinds of support an analytical essay can use. Think about examples of each kind that you might include to develop ideas in the draft of your pro-con essay.

- Review the advantages and disadvantages of your topic, taking notes on the most important information. Then, list **relevant and substantial evidence,** or the most important, related, and timely ideas that are based on facts, first-hand knowledge, or expert opinions, and well-chosen details to support your thesis or controlling idea.

- Be sure to include information on multiple **relevant perspectives.** Include enough detail to address both the benefits and drawbacks.

- Consider the validity, reliability, and relevance of your **primary and secondary sources** and the details you obtain from them. Only use trustworthy sources.

WRITING COACH

Online

www.phwritingcoach.com

Interactive Graphic Organizers

Use the interactive graphic organizers to help you create a plan for your writing.

Interactive Model

Refer back to the Interactive Model in the eText as you plan your writing.

Drafting

During the drafting stage, you will start to write your ideas for your pro-con essay. You will follow an outline that provides an **organizational strategy** that will help you **convey and structure ideas in a sustained way** to write a focused, organized, and coherent pro-con essay.

The Organization of an Analytical Essay

This chart provides an organizing structure for an analytical essay. As you adapt it for your particular pro-con essay, be sure to keep in mind your audience and purpose.

Outline for Success

I. Introduction

See Student Model, p. 150.

- Clear thesis statement
- An explanation of the topic

II. Body

See Student Model, pp. 150–151.

- Balanced analysis of pros and cons
- Logically organized evidence and details
- A variety of sentence structures and rhetorical devices

III. Conclusion

See Student Model, p. 151.

- A restatement of the thesis
- A recap of the major pros and cons

Establish Your Analysis

A strong, clear thesis statement states the general pros and cons that will be considered.

Develop Your Ideas

- An unbiased, or fair, essay includes the same number of pros and cons and considers multiple perspectives.

- Transitions, such as *however* and *on the other hand,* help link ideas, evidence, details, and paragraphs.

- A well-organized essay discusses the pros and cons of one idea or aspect per paragraph, or it discusses all the pros and then all the cons.

- Using sentences with clauses and phrases makes writing more memorable and detailed and keeps the reader interested.

- Using rhetorical devices, such as analogies, helps the reader understand your meaning.

End Effectively

A memorable conclusion restates the thesis and reminds the reader of the major pros and cons of the topic or issue.

Start Your Draft

Use the checklist to help you complete your draft. Use the graphic organizer that shows your thesis, pros and cons, and supporting details, and the Outline for Success as guides.

While drafting, aim at writing your ideas, not on making your writing perfect. Remember, because you are drafting in an open-ended situation, you will have the chance to improve your draft when you revise and edit.

√ Start by identifying the **issue** and its importance.

√ Continue building an **effective introduction** by establishing the structure and the general premise of your analysis. Include a clear thesis statement.

√ Develop the **body** of your pro-con essay by describing the **advantages** and **disadvantages** associated with your topic.

√ Be sure to use a variety of **sentence structures** to keep your writing clear, interesting, and lively.

√ Use a clear **organizational structure** for conveying your ideas— either point-by-point or block organization. In point-by-point, each paragraph includes both the pros and cons of one idea or point. In block organization, all the pros are discussed and then all the cons.

√ Support your ideas with substantial and relevant evidence. Include sufficient evidence to make certain your reader clearly understands each point. Use carefully chosen details to explain your main points and be sure that everything you include is timely and is clearly related to the topic. Also be sure to include information on multiple **relevant perspectives** so that your essay is well supported and balanced.

√ Be sure to use **rhetorical devices,** such as analogies, to make your argument more effective and to convey meaning.

√ Carefully check that your primary and secondary **sources** are valid, reliable, and relevant before using any details from them.

√ End with an **effective conclusion** that restates your explanation and summarizes your main ideas.

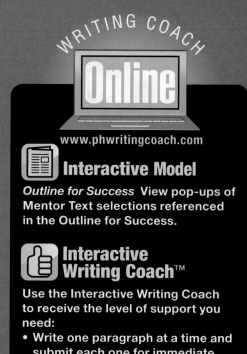

WRITING COACH

Online

www.phwritingcoach.com

Interactive Model

Outline for Success View pop-ups of Mentor Text selections referenced in the Outline for Success.

Interactive Writing Coach™

Use the Interactive Writing Coach to receive the level of support you need:
- Write one paragraph at a time and submit each one for immediate, detailed feedback.
- Write your entire first draft and submit it for immediate, personalized feedback.

Revising: Making It Better

Now that you have finished your first draft, you are ready to revise. Think about the "big picture." You will consider the logical organization and clarity of meaning in your writing. You can use the Revision RADaR strategy as a guide for making changes to improve your draft. Revision RADaR provides four major ways to improve your writing: (R) replace, (A) add, (D) delete, and (R) reorder.

Kelly Gallagher, M. Ed.

KEEP REVISION ON YOUR RADaR

Read part of the first draft of the Student Model "Studying Abroad: To Go or Not To Go?" Then look at questions the writer asked himself as he thought about how well his draft addressed issues of audience, purpose, genre, logical organization, and clarity of meaning.

Studying Abroad: To Go or Not To Go?

Many students think about whether or not to study abroad. You can find information about studying abroad from many sources—guidance counselors, libraries, the Internet, exchange program brochures, and others who have studied abroad. You should consider the pros and cons of studying abroad.

Studying in another country will allow you to gain fluency in a foreign language. Although learning a new language is challenging, most students find the experience rewarding in the end. Students will be attending regular classes, such as science and history. Because this can be a very challenging way to learn, it is important to think carefully about how well you would learn in this environment. So one thing to consider when deciding whether or not to study abroad is the educational experience you'll have in that country.

*Do I effectively explain why the **topic** is under consideration?*

*Have I developed a **thesis** that clearly states the issue and why it is important?*

*Is my **organization** logical and fluid? Do I provide relevant and clear **details**?*

Now look at how the writer applied Revision RADaR to write an improved second draft.

Studying Abroad:
TO GO OR NOT TO GO?

2ND DRAFT

Leaving home for a summer, semester, or year to study abroad is a major decision—one that only you and your family can make. When students have to make these decisions, it's important to be well informed. We can find information about studying abroad from many sources—guidance counselors, libraries, the Internet, exchange program brochures, and others who have studied abroad. An important step in the decision-making process is considering the pros and cons of studying abroad to determine whether it is the right choice for you and your family.

One thing to consider when deciding whether or not to study abroad is the educational experience you'll have in that country. Studying in another country will allow you to gain fluency in a foreign language. In addition to learning a new language, students will be attending regular classes, such as science and history. Because this can be a very challenging way to learn, it is important to think carefully about how well you would learn in this environment. "If you aren't prepared for hard work, study abroad is not for you," warns guidance counselor Phil Sergeant.

A *Added an explanation of why the topic should be examined*

R *Replaced a weak thesis with a clear one to describe what should be considered and why*

R *Reordered text to put the topic sentence at the beginning of the paragraph*

A *Added transitions to link ideas and added an expert opinion to strengthen support and clarify meaning*

WRITING COACH

Online

www.phwritingcoach.com

Interactive Writing Coach™

Use the Revision RADaR strategy in your own writing. Then submit your paragraph or draft for feedback.

 Apply It! Use your Revision RADaR to revise your draft.

- First, determine if your draft is logically organized, if your meaning is clearly expressed, and if you have included all the elements of a pro-con essay.

- Then apply the Revision RADaR strategy to make needed changes. Remember—you can use the steps in the strategy in any order. Be sure to focus on important elements, such as an effective introduction and a clear thesis, and use a variety of sentence structures, rhetorical devices, and transitions between ideas.

Look at the Big Picture

Use the chart and your analytical skills to evaluate whether your pro-con essay is **logically organized** and your **meaning** is clearly **conveyed**. When necessary, use the suggestions in the chart to revise your piece.

Section	Evaluate	Revise
Introduction	• Make sure your **thesis** clearly identifies the issue and explains why it should be considered.	• In one sentence, answer the questions "What specific issue am I examining? Why should a person consider the issue?" This will help you build an effective introduction.
Body	• Check the number of **pros** and **cons** you have included to be sure they are balanced.	• Highlight pros in one color and cons in another. Add one or the other to achieve balance in representing multiple perspectives.
	• Check that your **information** is valid, reliable, and relevant by finding the same information in multiple sources.	• Carefully choose your details from primary and secondary sources while keeping their origin in mind.
	• Check that your essay is well-supported and that your **evidence** and details are well-chosen.	• Add substantial evidence to reflect multiple perspectives. Delete any details that aren't relevant.
	• Make sure that you have used **rhetorical devices** to strengthen your writing.	• Add analogies, or comparisons, to convey ideas in a different way.
	• Check that your **organizational schema**, or plan, is clear and logically conveys ideas.	• Consider whether point-by-point or block organization best suits your purpose. Reorder details accordingly.
	• Evaluate the variety of your **sentence structures** and make sure transitions between paragraphs are included.	• Combine or divide sentences and add transition words and phrases to clearly connect ideas.
Conclusion	• Check that you have restated the issue and summed up your major pros and cons to build an effective **concluding paragraph**.	• Compare your introductory paragraph and topic sentences in body paragraphs to the information in your summary. Delete repetitive phrases and replace with different wording. Add ideas as needed.

Focus on Craft: Transitional Words and Phrases

Transitional words and phrases convey the connections between ideas and events. *First, after,* and *yesterday* express time-order relationships. *Because, therefore,* and *as a result* express cause-and-effect relationships. *Similarly, on the other hand,* and *in contrast* establish similarities and differences. As you construct an essay, use transitions to establish connections between paragraphs.

Look for a transitional word or phrase as you read these sentences from the Student Model.

 **STUDENT MODEL** from **Studying Abroad: To Go or Not To Go?** pages 150–151; lines 28–32

> Many students find the experience of learning about a new culture and exploring museums and historical landmarks fascinating. Conversely, others find that these cultural differences are overwhelming.

 Try It! Now, ask yourself these questions. Record your answers in your journal.

- What relationship does the transitional word *conversely* express?
- What other transitional words or phrases would work in this sentence?

 Fine-Tune Your Draft

Apply It! Use these revision suggestions to prepare your final draft.

- **Add Transitional Words and Phrases** Make sure you use transitions to clarify connections and convey meaning.
- **Improve Logical Organization** Make sure your paragraphs and ideas flow in a way that makes sense. Reorder words, sentences, and paragraphs to improve the logical flow of ideas. Consider ordering ideas chronologically or by strength of purpose.
- **Evaluate Consistency of Tone** Check your tone, or the attitude you take toward your subject or audience, to make sure it remains consistent throughout your essay. For example, you could use a formal tone throughout, or a friendly, casual one, but avoid moving back and forth between the two.

Teacher Feedback Ask your teacher if you have an effective introduction and conclusion. Consider the response and revise your final draft.

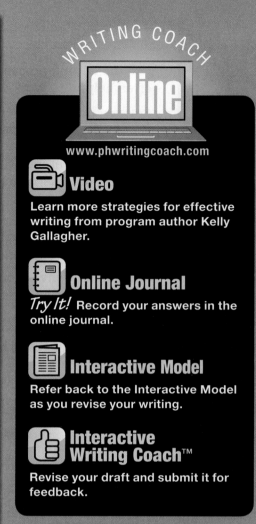

WRITING COACH

Online

www.phwritingcoach.com

Video
Learn more strategies for effective writing from program author Kelly Gallagher.

Online Journal
Try It! Record your answers in the online journal.

Interactive Model
Refer back to the Interactive Model as you revise your writing.

Interactive Writing Coach™
Revise your draft and submit it for feedback.

Editing: Making It Correct

Use the editing process to polish your work and correct errors. It is often helpful to work with a partner when editing your drafts.

Before editing, consider using **a variety of correctly structured sentences**—including **simple compound, complex,** and **compound-complex sentences**—to add interest to your writing and express connections between ideas clearly. Then, edit your final draft for any errors in **grammar, mechanics, and spelling.**

WRITE GUY *Jeff Anderson, M. Ed.*

WHAT DO YOU NOTICE?

Zoom in on Conventions Focus on sentence structures as you zoom in on these lines from the Mentor Text.

 **MENTOR TEXT** from **Sleep Is One Thing Missing in Busy Teenage Lives** pages 148–149; lines 17–18, 31–31, 39

> Americans are said to be a sleep-deprived people, and teenagers are the worst of the lot. . . . When teenagers insist that they are not tired at 9 or 10 p.m., they are very likely telling the truth. . . . There are consequences.

Now, ask yourself: *How does the structure of each sentence differ?*

Perhaps you said that each structure contains different kinds of clauses. Sentences consist of independent and subordinate clauses. An independent clause can stand on its own, whereas a subordinate clause cannot.

A **simple sentence** has one independent clause and no subordinate clauses. Simple sentences allow a writer to express ideas succinctly.

A **compound sentence** has two or more independent clauses joined by commas and conjunctions (e.g., *and, but, or*) or by a semicolon. A compound sentence has no subordinate clauses. Compound sentences join ideas of equal weight.

A **complex sentence** has one independent clause and at least one subordinate clause. Complex sentences allow a writer to include information about a subject or express relationships between ideas.

A **compound-complex sentence** has at least two independent clauses and at least one subordinate clause. By using compound-complex sentences, writers can closely connect ideas and achieve a variety of sentence lengths.

Partner Talk Discuss this question with a partner: *What is the effect of having sentence variety in writing?*

To learn more about sentence structure, see Chapter 15 of your Grammar Handbook.

Grammar Mini-Lesson:
Commas in Sentence Structures

To learn more, see Chapter 23.

Compound, complex, and compound-complex sentences use **commas** to combine clauses. Use a comma before a coordinating conjunction (e.g., *and, but, or*) that connects the independent clauses in a compound or compound-complex sentence. In complex and compound-complex sentences, use commas to set off nonessential subordinate clauses and after an introductory adverbial clause. Notice how the author uses commas in the Mentor Text.

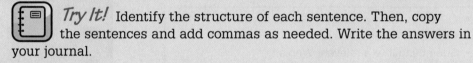 **MENTOR TEXT** from **Sleep Is One Thing Missing In Busy Teenage Lives** page 148; lines 18–21

> Most are lucky to get 6, 7, or 8 hours of sleep a night, even though studies have shown repeatedly that people in their teens and possibly even early 20's need 9 to 10 hours.

 Try It! Identify the structure of each sentence. Then, copy the sentences and add commas as needed. Write the answers in your journal.

1. Some students decide to study abroad but others remain at home.
2. Though it takes a long time to organize study abroad the benefits are worth it.

 Apply It! **Edit your draft for grammar, mechanics, and spelling**. Ensure that you have used **a variety of correctly structured sentences** with **correct punctuation**.

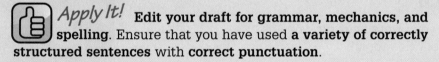 Use the rubric to evaluate your piece. If necessary, rethink, rewrite, or revise.

Rubric for Analytical Essay: Pro-Con Essay	Rating Scale
Ideas: How clearly are the pros and cons of your topic developed?	Not very Very 1 2 3 4 5 6
Organization: How well are your ideas organized?	1 2 3 4 5 6
Voice: How well have you engaged your reader?	1 2 3 4 5 6
Word Choice: How effective is your word choice in conveying a consistent tone?	1 2 3 4 5 6
Sentence Fluency: How well do you use transitions to create sentence fluency?	1 2 3 4 5 6
Conventions: How correct is the structure and punctuation of your sentences?	1 2 3 4 5 6

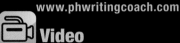

WRITING COACH

www.phwritingcoach.com

 Video
Learn effective editing techniques from program author Jeff Anderson.

 Online Journal
Try It! Record your answers in the online journal.

 Interactive Model
Refer back to the Interactive Model as you edit your writing.

Interactive Writing Coach™
Edit your draft. Check it against the rubric and then submit it for feedback.

Publishing

Prepare your pro-con essay for presentation so you can share your ideas with others. Choose a way to **publish** it **for appropriate audiences**.

Wrap Up Your Presentation

Before you can publish your essay, you may need to make a new, clean copy. Be sure to add images that grab your reader's attention and an interesting title that indicates the topic of your essay.

Publish Your Piece

Use the chart to identify a way to publish your essay.

If your audience is...	...then publish it by...
Your teachers or classmates	• Submitting it in the assigned format • Giving a multimedia class presentation • Sharing it at an assembly or student meeting
An online community	• Creating a blog or posting your essay on an established blog • Submitting it to a relevant Web site • Making a podcast available for download

 Extend Your Research

Think more about the topic on which you wrote your pro-con essay. What else would you like to know about this topic?

- Use specific details to describe and explain your ideas. Increase the specificity of your details based on the type of information you are recording. Brainstorm for several questions you would like to research and then consult, or discuss, with others.

- Formulate, or develop, a plan about how you will answer these questions. Decide where you will find more information— on the Internet, at the library, or through other sources.

- Finally, learn more about your topic by following through with your research plan.

 The Big Question: Why Write?
What should we tell and what should we describe to make information clear?

MAKE YOUR WRITING COUNT

Produce a Pro-Con Analysis Television Report

Pro-con essays analyze the benefits and drawbacks of decisions, actions, or events. For a **television report,** help classmates interpret and draw conclusions about a decision or event at your school.

With a group, write a **script** for a **multimedia presentation** for a specific audience—peers. The presentation should include graphics, images, and sound and synthesize information from multiple points of view—pro and con. Your script should draw on information covered in one of your pro-con essays. Present your script to a live audience or make a video.

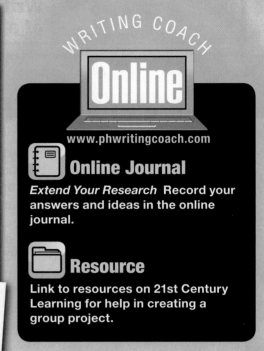

WRITING COACH

Online

www.phwritingcoach.com

Online Journal

Extend Your Research Record your answers and ideas in the online journal.

Resource

Link to resources on 21st Century Learning for help in creating a group project.

Here's your action plan.

1. Choose group roles and set objectives. You will need a reporter, a director, and a video producer.

2. First, review your peers' pro-con essays. Choose one whose topic affects your school.

3. View news shows for ideas on presenting a pro-con analysis in visual formats.

4. Write a script based on the essay. The script should:

   - Introduce the topic
   - State a clear thesis telling viewers why the issue is important
   - Use a variety of literary techniques, such as analogies, and state a theme either explicitly and directly or suggested implicitly
   - Make reference to or quote analysis from the original essay
   - Include notes for incorporating graphic and sound elements

5. Rehearse the presentation of your script. Practice your pacing, matching words to visuals and sounds.

6. Present your pro-con analysis, recording it on video if possible.

Listening and Speaking In groups, rehearse your script. First, discuss how and why scripted news sounds different from conversation or from a class lecture. Take turns reading scripts aloud, practicing to develop the speaking style of a professional newsreader. Incorporate feedback from your rehearsal into your final multimedia presentation.

21st Century Learning

Summary of a Feature Article

A feature article is a nonfiction article that is meant to inform, entertain, or persuade readers of a publication, such as a newspaper or magazine. In contrast to news articles, feature articles often analyze current events and focus on human interest. Some feature articles discuss the benefits and drawbacks of recent events, community actions, or political decisions. A **summary of a feature article** is a relatively brief restatement of the main ideas of a feature article. When you summarize a feature article, you should include the name of the article and the author, the publication it appeared in, and the publication date and focus on only the main ideas and the most important supporting details. Learning to summarize will help you better understand and remember what you read.

 Try It! Read the sample summary of a feature article. Then, answer the questions about it. Record your answers.

1. What **feature article** does this summarize? Who is the author of the feature article? Where was it published?

2. What is the topic of the article? What is the **topic sentence** of the summary?

3. What three main supporting ideas about the topic of the article are explained in the summary? What **details** are included to support these points?

4. What **transitional words and phrases** are used to identify the main ideas and connect ideas?

5. What memorable **concluding point** does the summary include?

Extension Find another example of a summary of a feature article, and compare it with this one.

A Summary of "Escape from AlCATraz"

The feature article "Escape from AlCATraz" appeared in the November 10 edition of the *Local Gazette*. In the article, writer Tina Li examines the rising adoption rate of cats and kittens from local shelters. Li investigates several reasons for the rising number of feline adoptions.

To begin, she cites advertisements that promote the importance of adopting homeless animals instead of ads endorsing specific shelters. Li also notes the rise in popularity of owning cats because of their ease of care—cats need just a litter box, food and water, and plenty of love. Finally, Li studies the population data of the area, noting the rising number of elementary children. She connects kitten and cat adoptions to homes with children who are getting their first pet.

In the conclusion, Li admits that many other factors contribute to cats finding new homes. However, she emphasizes that the causes are not as important as the effect—loving homes for homeless pets.

Create a Summary of a Feature Article

Follow these steps to create your own summary of a feature article. To plan your summary, review the graphic organizers on pages R24–R27 and choose one that suits your needs.

Prewriting

- Choose a feature article to summarize. Look in your favorite magazine, local newspapers, or national newspapers for articles that interest you.
- Record the name of the author and publication, the date, and the edition.
- Read through the article once. Then reread the article, highlighting or underlining the description of the topic or argument and the main ideas that support that argument.
- Take notes on the article, restating the sentences you underlined in your own words.

Drafting

- Begin your draft by identifying the publication, the date, the edition, and the author.
- Summarize the article's main ideas, presenting your restatement of the topic first. Mimic the article's organization of main ideas in your summary.
- Include transitional words and phrases to show how the ideas are connected within the article.

Revising and Editing

- Reread the article and then your summary. Make sure you have used your own words to summarize the main points.
- Make sure you have included the main points in your summary. Take out unimportant details and add details that are missing.
- Check that your organization reflects that of the feature article. Reorder ideas if needed.
- Check that spelling, grammar, and mechanics are correct.

Publishing

Type or write legibly to make a clean copy of your summary. Present it to the class or post it on the school Web site.

WRITING COACH

Online

www.phwritingcoach.com

Online Journal

Try It! **Record your answers in the online journal.**

 **Interactive Graphic Organizers**

Choose from a variety of graphic organizers to plan and develop your project.

Partner Talk

Discuss your choice of a feature article with a partner. Share the ideas you highlighted and ask whether your partner thinks that you have identified the main ideas. Monitor your partner's spoken language by asking follow-up questions to confirm your understanding.

Writing for Assessment

Many standardized tests include a prompt that asks you to write an analytical essay. Use these prompts to practice. Your responses should include most of the same characteristics as your pro-con essay. (See page 146.)

 Try It! To begin, read the **analytical essay** prompt and the information on format and academic vocabulary. Then write an essay by following instructions shown in the ABCDs of On-Demand Writing.

Format

The prompt directs you to write an *analytical essay* that explains *pros* and *cons*. Be sure to include a thesis, supporting evidence, and an effective conclusion.

Analytical Essay Prompt

Some people today keep wild animals as household pets. Write an analytical essay that explains the pros and cons of having these wild animals as pets. Be sure to use transitions to show the relationship between ideas.

Academic Vocabulary

Remember that *pros* are arguments supporting an idea, and *cons* are arguments against an idea. *Transitions* express the connections between ideas.

The ABCDs of On-Demand Writing

Use the following ABCDs to help you respond to the prompt.

Before you write your draft:

A ttack the prompt [1 MINUTE]

- Circle or highlight important verbs in the prompt. Draw a line from the verb to what it refers to.
- Rewrite the prompt in your own words.

B rainstorm possible answers [4 MINUTES]

- Create a graphic organizer to generate ideas.
- Use one for each part of the prompt if necessary.

C hoose the order of your response [1 MINUTE]

- Think about the best way to organize your ideas.
- Number your ideas in the order you will write about them. Cross out ideas you will not be using.

After you write your draft:

D etect errors before turning in the draft [1 MINUTE]

- Carefully reread your writing.
- Make sure that your response makes sense and is complete.
- Look for spelling, punctuation, and grammar errors.

 More Prompts for Practice

Apply It! Respond to Prompts 1 and 2 in timed or open-ended situations by writing **analytical essays** that have sufficient length to address the topics. As you write, be sure to:

- Construct an **effective introduction and conclusion**
- Establish a **clear thesis** or controlling idea
- Include **rhetorical devices,** such as parallel structure or analogies, and **transitions** between paragraphs
- Use a variety of **sentence structures**
- Include information on **multiple views** related to both sides of your topic
- Support ideas with relevant, substantial, and carefully chosen **evidence and details**
- Choose a logical **organizational structure**
- If appropriate, check that **primary and secondary sources** are valid, reliable, and relevant

www.phwritingcoach.com

Interactive Writing Coach™

Plan your response to the prompt. If you are using the prompt for practice, write one paragraph at a time or your entire draft and then submit it for feedback. If you are using the prompt as a timed test, write your entire draft and then submit it for feedback.

Prompt 1 Some people today question the safety of teenage drivers and are considering raising the age at which people can get driver's licenses. Write an analytical essay that explains the pros and cons of teenagers being able to get their licenses while in high school.

Prompt 2 Most high schools today evaluate students based on their grade-point averages. Write an analytical essay about the advantages and disadvantages of being evaluated in this way. Include substantial evidence and well-chosen details to support your thesis.

Spiral Review: Poetry Respond to Prompt 3 by writing a **poem** that includes all the characteristics listed on page 120, including an awareness of **poetic conventions** and **traditions** within different poetic **forms**.

Prompt 3 Imagine that you are at the beach to observe the ocean. Write a poem about the ocean. Be sure to include sensory details about the sights, smells, and sounds.

CHAPTER 9

PERSUASION

What Do You Think?

Sports are a topic about which most people have an opinion. Some people think sports help young adults mature. Others think schools should require students to spend more time engaged in schoolwork.

You probably have an opinion on this topic. You may want to convince someone to share your opinion. In order to persuade someone to share your opinion, you must use facts and details to support your point of view.

Try It! List reasons why teens should participate in sports or reasons why schools should put less emphasis on sports.

Consider these questions as you participate in an extended discussion with a partner. Take turns expressing your ideas and feelings.

- What are the benefits of sports for teenagers?
- What are the negative results of teenagers' participating in sports?
- Why should schools continue to invest money in sports?
- Why should schools cut back on the money they spend on sports?

Review the list you made. Choose a position on the issue by deciding which side to take. Write a sentence that states which position, or side, you will take. Then take turns talking about your ideas and positions with a partner.

What's Ahead

In this chapter, you will review two strong examples of an argumentative essay: a Mentor Text and a Student Model. Then, using the examples as guidance, you will write an argumentative essay of your own.

WRITING COACH

Online

www.phwritingcoach.com

Online Journal

Try It! Record your answers and ideas in the online journal.

You can also record and save your answers and ideas on pop-up sticky notes in the eText.

 Connect to the Big Questions

Discuss these questions with your partner:

1 What do you think? In team sports, how important is the individual?

2 Why write? What is your point of view?
How will you know if you have convinced others?

ARGUMENTATIVE ESSAY

An argumentative essay argues a position or viewpoint and attempts to persuade others to agree. In this chapter, you will explore a special type of argumentative essay, the speech. In a speech, the speaker presents a position on an issue and backs up that position with facts, examples, and other evidence. He or she delivers the speech orally, or speaks it aloud, to the audience. By doing this, the speaker tries to get the audience to agree with the position or to take action in some way.

You will develop the speech by taking it through each of the steps of the writing process: prewriting, drafting, revising, editing, and publishing. You will also have an opportunity to create a persuasive proposal. To preview the criteria for how your speech will be evaluated, see the rubric on page 189.

FEATURE ASSIGNMENT

Argumentative Essay: Speech

An effective argumentative essay has these characteristics:

- A clear **thesis statement** that defines the position, based on logical reasons

- **Precise and relevant evidence** that supports the position, such as facts, expert opinions, quotations, and commonly accepted beliefs—ideas that most people accept as true

- An **accurate and honest representation** of different views

- Information on the **complete range of relevant perspectives**— including the many ways of looking at the issue

- A **consideration of all sources**, making sure information included is correct and applies to the topic

- **Persuasive language** that is crafted to move an audience that may not care or agree. The text might include rhetorical devices (such as rhetorical questions and analogies) to back up the assertions and ideas it presents.

- An **organizing structure** appropriate to the persuasive purpose, audience, and context

- **Effective sentence structure** and correct spelling, grammar, and usage

A speech also includes:

- A use of specific and **precise words** that the audience will understand

- **Anecdotes** that help the audience personalize the information presented

- An **oral** (or spoken aloud) presentation

Other Forms of Argumentative Writing

In addition to speeches, there are other forms of argumentative writing, including:

Advertisements are paid announcements that try to convince people to do or buy something.

Editorials state the opinion of the editors and publishers of news organizations. Editorials are usually about current issues and appear in newspapers, magazines, or on television, radio, or the Internet.

Letters to the editor are written by readers who express an opinion in response to an article that has been published in a newspaper or magazine.

Persuasive essays use logic and reasoning to persuade readers to adopt a certain action or point of view.

Propaganda uses emotional appeals and often biased, false, or misleading information to persuade people to think or act in a certain way. Propaganda is often about political issues.

Reviews evaluate items and activities such as books and movies. A review often states an opinion on whether people should spend time and money on the item or activity.

Try It! For each audience and purpose described, select the correct form, such as a letter, review, or advertisement, that is appropriate for conveying your intended meaning to the audience. Discuss your ideas with a partner and explain your choices.

- To encourage classmates to attend a movie at a local theater
- To promote membership in an academic club
- To disagree with an article in the school newspaper

MENTOR TEXT

Speech

Learn From Experience

 Read the speech on pages 174–175. As you read, take notes to develop your understanding of basic sight and English vocabulary. Then, read the numbered notes in the margins to learn about how the author presented her ideas.

Answer the *Try It!* questions online or in your notebook.

---

1 In her introduction, Susan B. Anthony explains her situation and presents a **clear thesis statement.** The thesis gives her **position** about whether she committed a crime.

Try It! Does Anthony believe she is guilty of a crime? Consider the historical and cultural context. What does her situation suggest about women's rights in nineteenth-century American society?

2 Anthony supports her position with **logical reasons.**

Try It! On what right does Anthony say the U.S. government is based? What do people who form a government pledge to do?

3 Anthony supports her position with **relevant evidence,** including a **quotation** from the Declaration of Independence.

Try It! Do you think the quotation strengthens her argument or weakens it? Why?

Extension Find another example of a persuasive speech, and compare it with this one.

From Woman's Right to Suffrage

by Susan B. Anthony

1 Friends and fellow citizens: I stand before you tonight under indictment for the alleged crime of having voted at the last presidential election, without having a lawful right to vote. It shall be my work this evening to prove to you that in thus doing,
5 I not only committed no crime, but, instead, simply exercised my citizen's rights, guaranteed to me and all United States citizens by the National Constitution, beyond the power of any State to deny.

2 Our democratic-republican government is based on the
10 idea of the natural right of every individual member thereof to a voice and a vote in making and executing the laws. We assert the province of government to be to secure the people in the enjoyment of their inalienable right. We throw to the winds the old dogma that government can give rights.
15 No one denies that before governments were organized each individual possessed the right to protect his own life, liberty, and property. **2** When 100 to 1,000,000 people enter into a free government, they do not barter away their natural rights; they simply pledge themselves to protect each other in the enjoyment
20 of them through prescribed judicial and legislative tribunals. They agree to abandon the methods of brute force in the adjustment of their differences and adopt those of civilization.

3 "All men are created equal, and endowed by their Creator with certain inalienable rights. Among these are life, liberty,
25 and the pursuit of happiness. To secure these, governments are instituted among men, deriving their just powers from the consent of the governed."

Here is no shadow of government authority over rights, or exclusion of any class from their full and equal enjoyment.
30 Here is pronounced the right of all men, and "consequently," as the Quaker preacher said, "of all women," to a voice in the government. And here, in this first paragraph of the Declaration, is the assertion of the natural right of all to the ballot; for how can "the consent of the governed" be given, if the right to vote
35 be denied?

* * *

The preamble of the Federal Constitution says: "We, the people of the United States, in order to form a more perfect union, establish justice, insure domestic tranquility, provide for the common defense, promote the general welfare, and secure
40   the blessings of liberty to ourselves and our posterity, do ordain and establish this Constitution for the United States of America."
4 It was we, the people; not we, the white male citizens; nor we, the male citizens; but we, the whole people, who formed the Union. And we formed it, not to give the blessings of liberty, but
45   to secure them; not to the half of ourselves and the half of our posterity, but to the whole people—women as well as men. And it is a downright mockery to talk to women of their enjoyment of the blessings of liberty while they are denied the use of the only means of securing them provided by this democratic-republican
50   government—the ballot.

* * *

For any State to make sex a qualification, which must ever result in the disfranchisement of one entire half of the people, is to pass a bill of attainder, an ex post facto law, and is therefore a violation of the supreme law of the land. **5** By it the blessings
55   of liberty are forever withheld from women and their female posterity. For them, this government has no just powers derived from the consent of the governed. For them this government is not a democracy; it is not a republic. It is the most odious aristocracy ever established on the face of the globe.

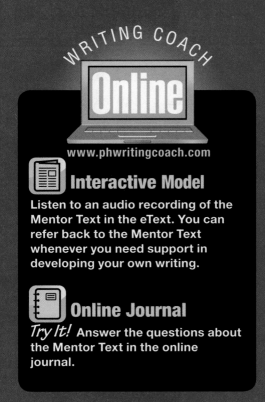

WRITING COACH
Online
www.phwritingcoach.com

Interactive Model
Listen to an audio recording of the Mentor Text in the eText. You can refer back to the Mentor Text whenever you need support in developing your own writing.

Online Journal
Try It! Answer the questions about the Mentor Text in the online journal.

4 Anthony uses effective **persuasive language** and **rhetorical devices**.

Try It! What examples can you find of parallel structure in the highlighted passage? What does this rhetorical device add to Anthony's argument?

5 In making her argument, Anthony appeals to her **audience's emotions**.

Try It! How might the word *blessing* stir the audience's emotions? Which words in the last sentence are likely to spark strong emotional reactions? Why?

STUDENT MODEL | Speech

With a small group, take turns reading this Student Model aloud. As you read, practice newly acquired vocabulary by correctly producing the word's sound. Also ask yourself if you find the writer's arguments convincing. Consider which evidence from the text helps you decide.

Use a Reader's Eye

Now, reread the Student Model. On your copy of the Student Model, use the Reader's Response Symbols to react to what you read.

Reader's Response Symbols

+   **I strongly agree with this.**

−   **I strongly disagree with this.**

?   **I have a question about this.**

!   **Wow! This is cool/weird/interesting.**

With a partner, discuss how the writer presents information. Consider the quality of the evidence and the logic.

The Virtual Classroom Is Online, Anytime!

by Amy Callahan

Many schools now offer students the opportunity to complete their classes online. I'm convinced that online learning offers students great advantages, and when you hear about these advantages, I'm sure
5   you'll be convinced, too.

One of the biggest advantages of online learning is that students can learn anytime, anywhere. Do you know a teenager who is a "morning person"? I don't. With online learning, there's no need to be up at the
10   crack of dawn for classes! The classes fit to each student's schedule. In addition, each student sets his or her own learning pace. Students can spend extra time on the parts of a lesson they don't understand.

This kind of student-focused learning has other
15   advantages. Students learn in many different ways. Some students learn best by reading. Others learn best by hearing instruction. In online lessons, the teacher can address the different learning styles of each student.

Another advantage to online learning is that more
20   information can be taught. A variety of subjects can be included in one online lesson. In addition, using technology in this way teaches students the skills we need to succeed in the 21st Century. That's an advantage a single-subject textbook just can't match.

25   Now, some might say that online learning can never replace the classroom and face-to-face communication. However, according to researchers from Cornell University, "the Internet provides significant new functionality in transmitting information to the student
30   and providing forums for exchange." In other words, students can connect and work with teachers and with other students in chat rooms. Having a chance to

1

communicate like this is an advantage for students who might be shy about raising their hand in the classroom.

35   There are others who say that online learning is not practical because not everyone has access to a personal computer or the Internet. This is true. At this point, online learning is still new and is commonly considered a way of learning that should be used along
40 with traditional learning in a classroom. But the growth of online education can mean fewer natural resources used for paper and for transportation of books.

    Maybe you've already taken a class online. Perhaps you've worked online for a class or a project. If so, you
45 already know about some of these advantages. If not, I urge you to consider giving online learning a try!

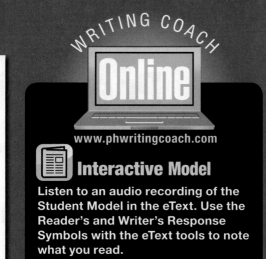

WRITING COACH
Online
www.phwritingcoach.com

 **Interactive Model**

Listen to an audio recording of the Student Model in the eText. Use the Reader's and Writer's Response Symbols with the eText tools to note what you read.

Use a Writer's Eye

Now, evaluate the speech as a writer. Analyze the strength of the evidence used by the author, judge the logic of the presentation, and consider the credibility of the argument. On your copy of the Student Model, use the Writer's Response Symbols to react to what you read. Identify places where the student writer uses characteristics of an effective speech.

Writer's Response Symbols	
C.T.	**Clearly stated thesis**
P.A.	**Good persuasive arguments**
S.E.	**Effective supporting evidence**
C.A.	**Good responses to readers' counter-arguments**

2

Your Turn ▶ **Feature Assignment: Speech**

Prewriting

Plan a first draft of your speech by **determining an appropriate topic.** You can select from the Topic Bank or come up with an idea of your own.

 ## Choose From the Topic Bank

TOPIC BANK

Dress Codes High schools, restaurants, work places, and the military all use dress codes. Think about the reasons for instituting dress codes and why they might be enforced in each case. Then, select one example of the use of dress codes. Write a speech or essay in which you argue the benefits or drawbacks of a dress code in that situation.

Dollars and Sense Your family's tax dollars are used for many things in your community. They support your local library and public schools. They help with the upkeep of roads and encourage new business development. Think about how you'd like your family's tax dollars to be spent. Write a speech in which you explain how you think taxes should be used in your community.

Work Force Many teenagers who are still in school have already entered the job market. Think about the advantages or disadvantages of having a part-time job. Write a speech that argues for or against teens having jobs while they are still in school.

 ## Choose Your Own Topic

Determine an appropriate topic on your own by using the following **range of strategies** to generate ideas.

Interview and Research

- Interview family members on issues that concern or worry them. Take detailed notes and during your interview ask your family members to explain their reasoning.
- Read through your notes and circle key words and phrases that describe the issues that interest you. Research these issues in a library.

Review your responses and choose a topic.

Narrow Your Topic

Choosing a topic that is too broad results in writing that is general and could be boring. Remember that in a persuasive speech, you are trying to get an audience to agree with your idea.

Apply It! Use a graphic organizer like the one shown to narrow your topic.

- Write your general topic in the top box, and keep narrowing your topic as you move down the chart.
- Your last box should hold your narrowest or "smallest" topic, the new focus of your speech.

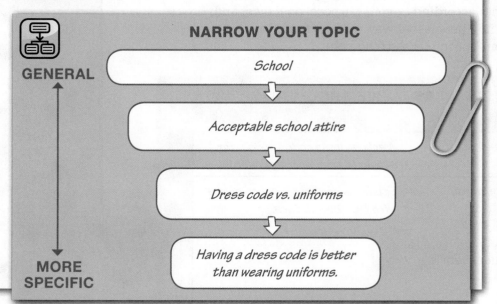

NARROW YOUR TOPIC

GENERAL

School

Acceptable school attire

Dress code vs. uniforms

Having a dress code is better than wearing uniforms.

MORE SPECIFIC

 ## Consider Multiple Audiences and Purposes

Before writing your speech, think about your specific audiences and purposes. Consider **the complete range of perspectives** related to your topic as you ask these questions. To avoid bias give an **accurate and honest representation of divergent, or differing, views.**

Questions for Audience	Questions for Purpose
• Who is my audience?	• How can I identify my topic and viewpoint?
• What might my audience need to know to understand the topic fully?	• What attitudes do I want to influence?
• What views might my audience have about the topic?	• What actions do I want to influence the audience to take?

Record your answers in your writing journal.

WRITING COACH

Online

www.phwritingcoach.com

 Interactive Writing Coach™

- Choosing from the Topic Bank gives you access to the Interactive Writing Coach™.
- Submit your writing and receive instant personalized feedback and guidance as you draft, revise, and edit your writing.

Interactive Graphic Organizers

Use the interactive graphic organizers to help you narrow your topic.

Online Journal

Try It! Record your answers and ideas in the online journal.

Plan Your Piece

You will use a graphic organizer, like this one, to state your thesis, organize your arguments, and identify details. When it is complete, you will be ready to write your first draft.

Develop a Clear Thesis To present your position to your audience, review your notes and develop **a clear thesis**—one sentence that states your position or sums up your argument. Add your thesis statement to a graphic organizer like the one shown. All the points and evidence in your speech should contribute to this controlling idea.

Logically Organize Your Arguments Fill in the graphic organizer to structure your arguments according to your purpose, audience, and context. Order your ideas in a persuasive way, such as from least to most important, to end your speech on a strong point.

DEVELOP YOUR PERSUASIVE ARGUMENTS

Clear Thesis	*A school dress code is better for students than wearing uniforms.*
First Persuasive Argument	*Students can express themselves with their own clothes.*
Supporting Evidence/Details	
Second Persuasive Argument	*Teachers don't have a uniform, and they can wear their own clothes.*
Supporting Evidence/Details	
Opposing Viewpoint	*Students who wear uniforms focus more on learning and less on their appearance.*
Response to Opposing Viewpoint	

Gather Details

To provide supporting evidence for their arguments, writers use a variety of types of details. Look at these examples:

- **Logical Reasoning, Including Facts:** *It is important for students to express their individual personality. Students should be able to express that personality through their clothing.*

- **Expert Opinions:** *According to a researcher at Forestville High School in Virginia, students "rebelled because they were afraid wearing uniforms was going to take away their individuality."*

- **Personal Observations and Commonly Accepted Beliefs:** *Among my friends, many girls think that wearing dresses should be an option.*

- **Rhetorical Devices:** *School is a place where students have to do what the teachers tell them to do. Why are they taking away our only creative outlet?* (Rhetorical Question)

You may need to do research as you gather details. Good writers don't accept everything they read—they **consider the validity and reliability** of any outside sources they use. They also keep careful records of each.

- **Research reports** are useful for facts, statistics, and expert opinions.

- **Magazines** are a good source for information on your topic.

Try It! Read the Student Model excerpt and identify which details the author used to support the argument.

 STUDENT MODEL from **The Virtual Classroom Is Online, Anytime!** page 176; lines 21–24

In addition, using technology in this way teaches students the skills we need to succeed in the 21st Century. That's an advantage a single-subject textbook just can't match.

 Apply It! Review the types of support a persuasive writer can use. Then, identify at least one detail for each of your arguments.

- Use details such as facts, expert opinions, quotations, and expressions of commonly held beliefs to provide **precise and relevant supporting evidence of your thesis.**

- Identify and consider the **validity and reliability** of all your primary— firsthand—and secondary—secondhand—sources.

- Then, add your details to your graphic organizer.

WRITING COACH

Online

www.phwritingcoach.com

Interactive Graphic Organizers

Use the interactive graphic organizers to help you create a plan for your writing.

Interactive Model

Refer back to the Interactive Model in the eText as you plan your writing.

Drafting

During the drafting stage, you will start to write your ideas for your persuasive speech. You will follow an outline that provides a **persuasive organizational strategy** that will help you write a focused, organized, and coherent persuasive speech.

The Organization of an Argumentative Essay

The chart shows an organizational strategy for an argumentative essay. Look back at how the Mentor Text follows this organizational strategy. Ask your teacher whether you will write the draft in a timed situation or in an open-ended situation with unlimited time constraints. Then, use this chart to help you outline your draft.

Outline for Success

I. Introduction

See Mentor Text, p. 174.

- Interesting opening
- Clear thesis or position

Grab Your Reader

- An interesting opening might include a question, an anecdote, or a vivid detail.
- A clear statement of your thesis or position on the issue shows your audience what you are supporting.

II. Body

See Mentor Text, pp. 174–175.

- Persuasive arguments
- Logically organized supporting evidence
- Responses to different views and information

Build Your Case

- Each argument and its supporting evidence are presented in one paragraph.
- Different views and perspectives show that you considered many positions but still can make a case that your position is strongest.
- Paragraphs are ordered from least to most important idea so the best case is last.

III. Conclusion

See Mentor Text, p. 175.

- Restatement of position
- Memorable ending, including a call to action

Wrap It Up

- The restatement of a position helps a writer solidify an argument. Echoing the language of the thesis statement helps cement it in readers' minds.
- A call to action uses specific language to request the audience to act in a certain manner.

Start Your Draft

To complete your draft, follow each step in the process. Use the graphic organizer that shows your thesis, persuasive arguments, and supporting evidence, and the Outline for Success as guides.

While drafting, aim at writing your ideas, not on making your writing perfect. Remember, you will have the chance to improve your draft when you revise and edit.

√ Start by drafting an engaging **opening.** Use the opener to immediately grab your audience's attention and introduce your viewpoint.

√ Continue to build your **introduction** by telling readers what to expect in the rest of your speech. Include a **clear thesis statement**.

√ Shape the **body** of your speech by using an **organizing structure** appropriate to your audience, purpose, and context.

√ Develop a focused paragraph for each logically reasoned argument. Support your arguments with **precise and relevant evidence,** including facts, expert opinions, quotations, and/or expressions of commonly accepted beliefs.

√ Include information on the **complete range of perspectives.** Avoid bias by providing an accurate and honest representation of divergent views.

√ Be sure to check the **validity and reliability of all primary and secondary sources** in which you find your evidence.

√ Remember to use persuasive language, including **rhetorical strategies** such as repetition, to reach audience members who may be uninterested and not care about the issue or even opposed to your views and disagree.

√ End with a strong **conclusion** that restates your position and finishes on a memorable note.

√ To be sure you can **influence your audience's attitudes**, call them to action. Make a concrete suggestion by naming people, places, events, and activities.

WRITING COACH

Online

www.phwritingcoach.com

Interactive Model

Outline for Success View pop-ups of Mentor Text selections referenced in the Outline for Success.

Interactive Writing Coach™

Use the Interactive Writing Coach to receive the level of support you need:

- **Write one paragraph at a time and submit each one for immediate, detailed feedback.**
- **Write your entire first draft and submit it for immediate, personalized feedback.**

Revising: Making It Better

Now that you have finished your draft, you are ready to revise. Think about the "big picture." You will consider the logical organization and clarity of meaning in your writing. You can use your Revision RADaR as a guide for making changes to improve your draft. Revision RADaR provides four major ways to improve your writing: (R) replace, (A) add, (D) delete, and (R) reorder.

Kelly Gallagher, M. Ed.

KEEP REVISION ON YOUR RADaR

Read part of the first draft of the Student Model "The Virtual Classroom Is Online, Anytime!" Then look at questions the writer asked herself as she thought about how well her draft addressed issues of audience, purpose, and genre, as well as logical organization and clarity of meaning.

The Virtual Classroom Is Online, Anytime!

There are many advantages to online learning. There are also disadvantages. In this speech, I will tell you about the advantages and why it would be a good idea to try a class online.

One of the biggest advantages to online learning is that students can learn anytime anywhere. Do you know a student who is a "morning person"? I don't. Most teenagers do not like to get up and be on a set schedule. Online learning has more flexibility for scheduling and pace of learning. This kind of student-focused learning has other advantages. Students learn in many different ways. Online learning offers different kinds of teaching methods. Another advantage to online learning is that more subjects can be taught. A variety of subjects can be included in one online lesson.

Does the introduction grab my audience?

Have I used persuasive language to sway my audience?

Have I provided enough evidence to support my arguments?

Now look at how the writer applied Revision RADaR to write an improved second draft.

The Virtual Classroom Is Online, Anytime!

Many schools now offer students the opportunity to complete their classes online. I'm convinced that online learning offers students great advantages, and when you hear about these advantages, I'm sure you'll be convinced, too.

R *Replaced dull wording with language that is more personal and will relate better to students*

One of the biggest advantages of online learning is that students can learn anytime, anywhere. Do you know a teenager who is a "morning person"? I don't. With online learning, there's no need to be up at the crack of dawn for classes! The classes fit to each student's schedule. In addition, each student sets his or her own learning pace. Students can spend extra time on the parts of a lesson they don't understand.

A *Added persuasive language to convince the audience of the position*

This kind of student-focused learning has other advantages. Students learn in many different ways. Some students learn best by reading. Others learn best by hearing instruction. In online lessons, the teacher can address the different learning styles of each student.

A *Added additional evidence to expand upon and support my arguments*

Another advantage to online learning is that more subjects can be taught. A variety of subjects can be included in one online lesson....

R *Reordered one body paragraph into three arguments with evidence*

 Apply It! Use your Revision RADaR to revise your draft.

- First, check to see that your paragraphs are logically organized and that your meaning is clear. To **clarify meaning,** try rearranging words, sentences, and paragraphs to have a logical flow of ideas.
- Then, apply your Revision RADaR to make any other needed changes. Remember—you can use the steps in Revision RADaR in any order.

Look at the Big Picture

Use the chart and your analytical skills to evaluate how well each section of your speech demonstrates **logical organization and clarity of meaning.** When necessary, use the suggestions in the chart to revise your piece.

Section	Evaluate	Revise
Introduction	• Check your **opening**. Will it grab listeners' attention and make them want to hear more?	• Add a question, anecdote, quotation, or strong detail to make your lead more interesting.
	• Make sure the **thesis** clearly identifies your position on the issue and is based on logical reasons.	• Turn the thesis statement into a question and answer it by stating your opinion. If your opinion does not match the question, revise your thesis statement as needed.
Body	• Check that you have **organized** your persuasive arguments in a logical way that will be clear for your audience, purpose, and context.	• Rearrange your arguments so that the strongest argument is last.
	• Underline details that offer supporting evidence. Make sure your evidence is **precise and relevant** and includes at least one of the following: facts, examples, statistics, expert opinions, or quotations.	• Rearrange any details that do not appear in the same paragraph as the argument they support. When necessary, add or take out details.
	• Make sure that your primary and secondary sources for your evidence are **valid and reliable.**	• Delete any facts or information that may be wrong or that came from an untrustworthy or biased source.
	• Check that you have included any **alternative viewpoints** and that you have addressed them accurately and honestly.	• Add information to include a complete range of perspectives. Delete or add information to address any bias.
	• Make sure you have used language, including **rhetorical devices,** that will sway your audience, particularly those who are uninterested or opposed.	• Add rhetorical questions, analogies, or repetition to enhance the style and presentation of your argument.
Conclusion	• Check the **restatement** of your thesis.	• If necessary, clarify your position.
	• Check that your conclusion ends with a **call to action.**	• Include direct language to tell readers how they can help.

Focus on Craft: Rhetorical Questions

A rhetorical question is a question that is posed without an expectation of an answer. This device is often used to persuade a reader or audience. For example, the question *Does it get any better than that?* intends to persuade an audience that what they are experiencing is the best. In an argumentative essay, using **tropes** (or rhetorical devices), such as rhetorical questions, can help you make your point.

Think about rhetorical questions as you read the following sentences from the Student Model.

 **STUDENT MODEL** from **The Virtual Classroom Is Online, Anytime!** page 176; lines 6–10

> One of the biggest advantages of online learning is that students can learn anytime, anywhere. Do you know a teenager who is a "morning person"? I don't. With online learning, there's no need to be up at the crack of dawn for classes!

 Try It! Now, ask yourself these questions. Record your answers in your journal.

- When does the speaker use a rhetorical question?
- How does the use of the rhetorical question enhance the speaker's point? How does it impact the author's tone, or attitude, in the passage?

 Fine-Tune Your Draft

Apply It! Use the revision suggestions to prepare your final draft.

- **Add Rhetorical Questions** Use rhetorical questions and employ other tropes to enhance your argument by making your audience think. This will help you meet your specific rhetorical purpose—to persuade.
- **Ensure Consistency of Tone** Choose words that convey a consistent tone, which is your attitude toward your audience and toward the subject of your speech. If your speech has a formal tone, make sure that the rhetorical question you pose is consistent with that tone.

Peer Feedback Read your final draft to a group of peers. Ask if you have organized your ideas logically and made the meaning of your position clear. Think about their responses and revise your final draft as needed.

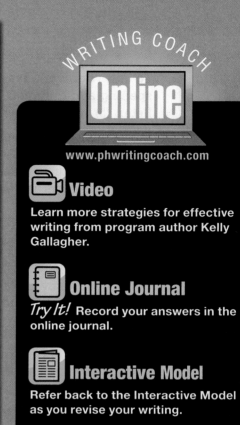

WRITING COACH

Online

www.phwritingcoach.com

Video
Learn more strategies for effective writing from program author Kelly Gallagher.

Online Journal
Try It! Record your answers in the online journal.

Interactive Model
Refer back to the Interactive Model as you revise your writing.

Interactive Writing Coach™
Revise your draft and submit it for feedback.

Editing: Making It Correct

To edit your work, read your draft carefully to correct errors in spelling and grammar. It can be helpful to read your draft aloud to listen for where the writing needs correction.

Before editing your final draft, think about using **different types of clauses**, including adjectival, adverbial, and noun clauses. Also think about using **parallel structures** within sentences. Then edit your draft by correcting any factual errors and errors in **grammar, mechanics, and spelling**.

WRITE GUY *Jeff Anderson, M. Ed.*

WHAT DO YOU NOTICE?

Zoom in on Conventions Focus on clauses as you zoom in on this sentence from the Student Model.

> **STUDENT MODEL** from **The Virtual Classroom Is Online, Anytime!** page 176; lines 7–8
>
> Do you know a teenager who is a "morning person"?

> To learn more about clauses, see Chapter 15 of your Grammar Handbook.

Now, ask yourself: *Who or what does the highlighted clause describe?*

Perhaps you said the clause describes *teenager*. Because *teenager* is used as a noun, the words describing him or her are an adjectival clause. An **adjectival clause** is a set of words that stand in for an adjective and modify a noun. Adjectival clauses usually begin with relative pronouns: *who, whom, whose, which,* or *that*.

An **adverbial clause** is a set of words that stand in for an adverb. Adverbial clauses modify verbs, adjectives, or other adverbs. Adverbial clauses begin with a subordinating conjunction, such as *after, although, because, if, unless,* or *while*. For example, in the sentence *After she hit the alarm clock, she went back to sleep*, the underlined adverbial clause tells when the rest of the action of the sentence took place.

A **noun clause** is a set of words that name a person, place, or thing. Noun clauses may function as the subject or object of a sentence. They often begin with a relative pronoun or words such as *how, what, where, when, whether, who, whoever,* and *why*. For example, in the sentence *We didn't know when she would wake up*, the underlined noun clause acts as the object of the verb *know*.

Partner Talk Discuss this question with a partner: *Why might a writer use clauses in place of nouns, adjectives, and adverbs?*

Grammar Mini-Lesson: Parallel Structures

Using **parallel structures** in a sentence means that equal ideas are expressed in words, phrases, clauses, or sentences of similar types. Parallel structure can add to the persuasive force of writing. Notice how the author used parallel structure in sentences of similar types.

 **STUDENT MODEL** from **The Virtual Classroom Is Online, Anytime!** page 177; lines 43–44

> <u>Maybe you've</u> already taken a class online. <u>Perhaps you've</u> worked online for a class or a project.

Try It! Tell whether these sentences include adjectival, adverbial, or noun clauses. Then identify the items that have parallel structure. Write the answers in your journal.

1. When school is over, we're going to the movies, and when the movie ends, we'll have to go home.

2. The dog, whose brown eyes begged for a treat, sat obediently and waited patiently.

3. I don't know what time it is. I don't know what day it is!

Apply It! **Edit your draft for grammar, mechanics, and spelling.** If necessary, rewrite some sentences to ensure that your sentences use **different types of clauses** and parallel structures.

 Use the rubric to evaluate your piece. If necessary, rethink, rewrite, or revise.

Rubric for Argumentative Essay: Speech	Rating Scale					
Ideas: How clearly are the issue and your position stated?	Not very 1	2	3	4	5	Very 6
Organization: How organized are your arguments and supporting evidence?	1	2	3	4	5	6
Voice: How authoritative and persuasive is your voice?	1	2	3	4	5	6
Word Choice: How persuasive is the language you have used?	1	2	3	4	5	6
Sentence Fluency: How well have you used transitions to convey meaning?	1	2	3	4	5	6
Conventions: How effective is your use of parallel structures?	1	2	3	4	5	6

To learn more, see Chapter 16.

WRITING COACH

 **Online**

www.phwritingcoach.com

Video
Learn effective editing techniques from program author Jeff Anderson.

 Online Journal
Try It! Record your answers in the online journal.

 Interactive Model
Refer back to the Interactive Model as you edit your writing.

 Interactive Writing Coach™
Edit your draft. Check it against the rubric and then submit it for feedback.

Publishing

Give your speech a chance to change someone's mind—publish it! First, get your speech ready for presentation. Then, choose a way to **publish or present it to the appropriate audience.**

Wrap Up Your Presentation

Is your speech handwritten or written on a computer? If your speech is handwritten, you may need to make a new, clean copy. If so, be sure to **write legibly**.

Publish Your Piece

Use the chart to identify a way to publish or present your speech.

If your audience is...	...then publish it by...
Students or adults at school	• Delivering a speech to your classmates • Producing a multimedia presentation with graphics, images, and sound
People in your neighborhood or city	• Posting your speech on a community blog • Presenting your speech to residents at a senior center

 Extend Your Research

Think more about the topic on which you wrote your speech. What else would you like to know about this topic?

- Brainstorm for several questions you would like to research and then consult, or discuss, with others. Then decide which question is your major research question.

- Formulate, or develop, a plan about how you will answer these questions. Decide where you will find more information—on the Internet, at the library, or through other sources.

- Finally, learn more about your topic by following through with your research plan.

 The Big Question: Why Write?
What is your point of view? How do you know if you have convinced others?

MAKE YOUR WRITING COUNT

Give a Speech to Persuade

The purpose of an argumentative essay or speech is to convince readers to agree with a particular position. In a **speech,** use persuasion to get people to take action on an important issue.

Working with a group, give a speech to a specific audience—your peers. Enhance your speech with a **multimedia presentation** of visuals, graphics, and sound. Your speech should take into account multiple points of view, but your group's position should dominate as you work to convince your audience to take action.

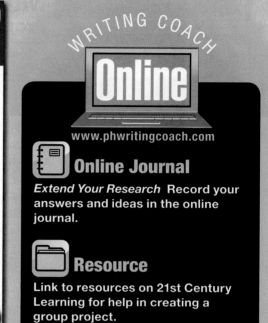

www.phwritingcoach.com

Online Journal

Extend Your Research Record your answers and ideas in the online journal.

Resource

Link to resources on 21st Century Learning for help in creating a group project.

Here's your action plan.

1. Choose roles, such as presenter, charts/graphics coordinator, and slideshow producer.

2. Review your peers' argumentative essays or speech texts. Choose one that will interest your peers. Summarize the essay's thesis, key points, conclusion, and call to action, if any.

3. Analyze online videos of historic or political speeches and jot notes about persuasive verbal and nonverbal elements.

4. Write a script for your presentation.

5. In addition to stating a position and demonstrating clear reasoning, your presentation should:

   - Offer convincing evidence tailored to your audience
   - Synthesize information from multiple points of view—especially by anticipating and answering any potential objections
   - Integrate effective graphics and visuals, such as charts and photos

6. Share your multimedia presentation with the class.

Listening and Speaking With your group, rehearse your multimedia presentation. Ask for feedback on verbal and nonverbal elements of your speech, such as voice, tone, and gestures. Lead an extended discussion of your reasoning and persuasive techniques. In addition, consider the effectiveness of the visuals and graphics.

**Writing for Media:
Proposal**

Proposal

A **proposal** is a formal persuasive message designed to recommend a specific action or set of actions. Proposals frequently make a recommendation to address an oversight or to solve a problem. Business and community groups often use proposals to help individuals present ideas and plans to larger groups. When you understand how proposals are used, you can write one yourself to improve a situation or recommend a solution to a problem.

Try It! Study the sample proposal on this page. Then, answer these questions. Record your answers in your journal.

1. What **action** does the writer propose?

2. What is the **problem** the writer aims to solve?

3. What **evidence** does the writer present to convince the reader that the recommended action is necessary?

4. What is the **call to action** in the last paragraph? What does the writer want the principal to do after reading the proposal?

Extension Find another example of a proposal, and compare it with this one.

To: Principal Elaine Fischer

From: Luis Marquez, Student Government President

In reference to: Student Government Fundraising Through a Talent Show

This year's student government car wash fundraiser did not meet expectations. To raise more funds for our school library, it's time to change the type of event we host. I propose that we consider hosting a talent show. This event could be more successful for several reasons.

- A talent show is likely to bring in more people. If we open admission to all students and their families, we are guaranteed to have a better turnout than we did at the car wash.

- A talent show is an event that people will enjoy attending, whereas a car wash does not generate the same amount of excitement.

- Finally, in our role as student government members, we would meet our goal of boosting school spirit by hosting a talent show.

The time to change is now! Please consider this proposal as we vote on events for next year's student government.

Luis Marquez

Create a Proposal

Follow these steps to create your own proposal. To plan your proposal, review the graphic organizers on R24–R27 and choose one that suits your needs.

Prewriting

- Identify a specific action you think a group or individual needs to take. Your proposal should address an oversight, solve a problem, or present an action to improve an existing situation.
- Identify your target audience.
- List the evidence you will include in your proposal to convince the audience to take action.

Drafting

- Begin your proposal in a way that will grab your audience's attention.
- As you develop your draft, structure your ideas in a persuasive way. Keep a clear focus.
- Include evidence in well-organized paragraphs to convince your audience that the idea you propose is necessary.
- Conclude your proposal with a call to action, telling your audience what they should do next.
- Sign your proposal to show that you are responsible for the contents of the proposal.

Revising and Editing

- Review your draft to ensure that your ideas are organized logically.
- Make sure the action you propose is clearly presented.
- Take out material that distracts from your message.
- Check that spelling, grammar, and mechanics are correct.

Publishing

- Type up your proposal and share it with friends, classmates, or committee members.
- Consider posting your proposal on a blog or Web site. As an alternative, read your proposal to others who might join your cause.

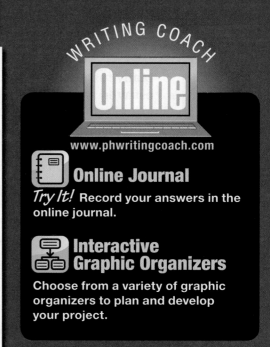

WRITING COACH

Online

www.phwritingcoach.com

Online Journal

Try It! Record your answers in the online journal.

Interactive Graphic Organizers

Choose from a variety of graphic organizers to plan and develop your project.

Partner Talk

Before you start drafting, describe your proposal to a partner. Use specific details to describe and explain your ideas. Increase the specificity of your details based on the type of information you are delivering. Ask for feedback about your plan. For example, is your recommended action clear?

Writing for Assessment

SAT/PSAT PREP ACT

Many tests include a prompt that asks you to write a persuasive essay in a timed situation. You can use the prompts on these pages to practice. Your responses should include the same characteristics as your speech. (See page 172.)

 Try It! To begin, read the **persuasive** prompt and the information on format and academic vocabulary. Use the ABCDs of On-Demand Writing to help you plan and write your essay.

Format

The prompt directs you to write a *persuasive essay*. Include a clear thesis, body paragraphs with supporting evidence, and a conclusion.

Persuasive Prompt

Think about a book that you would recommend to others. Write a **persuasive essay** to convince someone to read that book. Include **evidence** to support your **opinion**.

Academic Vocabulary

An *opinion* is a personal belief or judgment about something. An opinion should be supported by *evidence*—facts, details, and examples..

The ABCDs of On-Demand Writing

Use the following ABCDs to help you respond to the prompt.

Before you write your draft:

A ttack the prompt [1 MINUTE]

- Circle or highlight important verbs in the prompt. Draw a line from the verb to what it refers to.
- Rewrite the prompt in your own words.

B rainstorm possible answers [4 MINUTES]

- Create a graphic organizer to generate ideas.
- Use one for each part of the prompt if necessary.

C hoose the order of your response [1 MINUTE]

- Think about the best way to organize your ideas.
- Number your ideas in the order you will write about them. Cross out ideas you will not be using.

After you write your draft:

D etect errors before turning in the draft [1 MINUTE]

- Carefully reread your writing.
- Make sure that your response makes sense and is complete.
- Look for spelling, punctuation, and grammar errors.

More Prompts for Practice

Apply It! Respond to Prompt 1 in a timed or open-ended situation by writing a **persuasive essay** meant to influence the attitudes or actions of a specific audience on a specific issue. As you write, be sure to:

- Establish a clear and logically reasoned **thesis** or position
- Include information on a range of **relevant perspectives**
- Avoid bias by **accurately and honestly** representing others' views, even when they are divergent from your own
- Gather **precise and relevant evidence** to support your position, including facts, expert opinions, and commonly held beliefs
- **Logically organize** your arguments and evidence so that they support your viewpoint as well as your purpose, audience, and context
- Consider the **validity and reliability** of all primary and secondary sources
- Craft language using **rhetorical devices** to back up your assertions and to move an audience that may be uninterested or opposed

> **Prompt 1** What's your position on space exploration? Is it still necessary or simply costly? Write an essay arguing your position on the issue.

Spiral Review: Analytical Respond to Prompt 2 by writing an **analytical essay.** Make sure your essay reflects all the characteristics listed on page 146, including:

- Effective **introductions and conclusions** and a variety of **sentence structures**
- **Rhetorical devices and transitions** between paragraphs
- A clear **thesis statement** or controlling idea and an essay of sufficient length to support your ideas
- A clear **organizational schema** for conveying ideas
- **Relevant, substantial evidence** and well-chosen details
- Information on multiple **relevant perspectives**
- A consideration of the validity, reliability, and relevance of **primary and secondary sources**

> **Prompt 2** Write an essay about the problem of bullying and possible solutions. Provide ample evidence to support your viewpoint.

WRITING COACH

Online

www.phwritingcoach.com

Interactive Writing Coach™

Plan your response to the prompt. If you are using the prompt for practice, write one paragraph at a time or your entire draft and then submit it for feedback. If you are using the prompt as a timed test, write your entire draft and then submit it for feedback.

Remember **ABCD**

A ttack the prompt

B rainstorm possible answers

C hoose the order of your response

D etect errors before turning in the draft

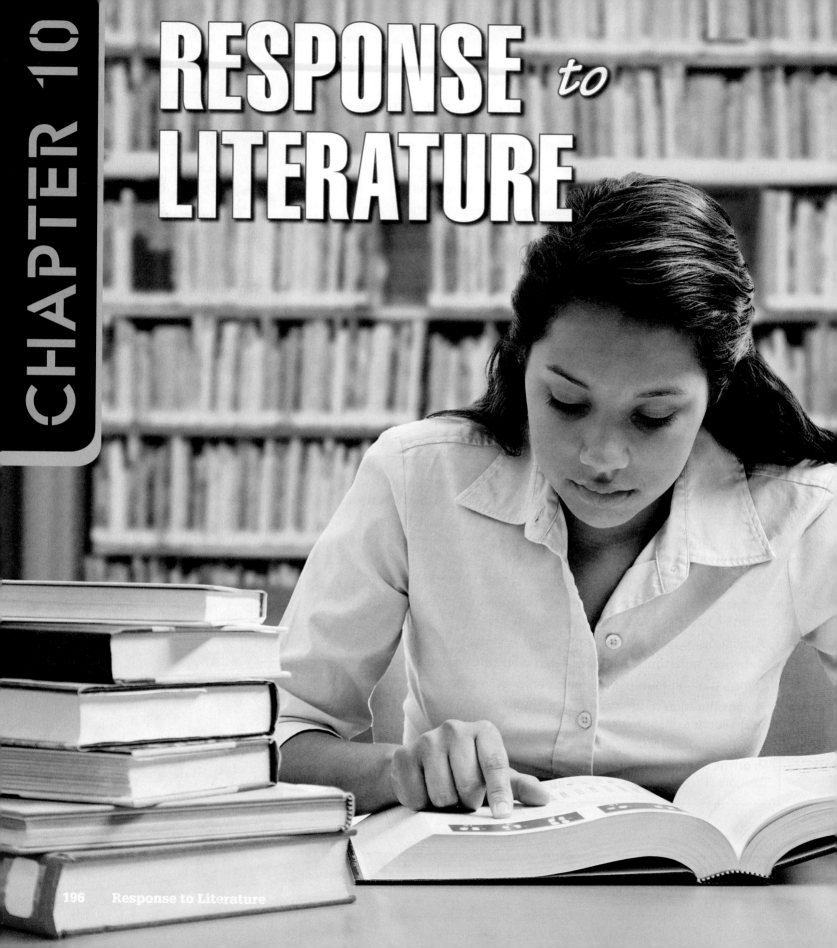

CHAPTER 10

RESPONSE *to* LITERATURE

What Do You Think?

Authors have purposes for writing. Some authors write to inform. Some write to entertain. Others write to persuade.

Part of being an active reader is analyzing the author's purpose. You think about the author's purpose and use details to show how the author achieves that purpose.

Try It! Think about your favorite book. What do you think the author was trying to communicate by writing this book? Consider these questions as you reflect on the book.

- How did you feel when reading this book?
- How did the author achieve his or her purpose?
- Do you think the author did a good job achieving his or her purpose? Why or why not?
- What details support your answer?

Review your answers to the questions. Then participate in an extended discussion with a partner. Take turns expressing your ideas and feelings.

What's Ahead

In this chapter, you will review two strong examples of an interpretative response essay: a Mentor Text and a Student Model. Then, using the examples as guides, you will write an interpretative response essay of your own.

 Connect to the Big Questions

Discuss these questions with your partner:

1 What do you think? How much does literature change people's lives?

2 Why write? What should you write about to make others interested in a text?

INTERPRETATIVE RESPONSE

An interpretative response analyzes an author's work. In this chapter, you will explore a special type of interpretative response, the response to literature essay. When you write a response to literature, you analyze the author's use of story elements, as well as stylistic and rhetorical devices and how these devices contribute to the work. A response to literature also explains your reactions to and feelings about the work.

You will develop the response to literature essay by taking it through each of the steps of the writing process: prewriting, drafting, revising, editing, and publishing. You will also have an opportunity to write a movie scene script about a short story you have read. To preview the criteria for how your response to literature essay will be evaluated, see the rubric on page 215.

FEATURE ASSIGNMENT

Interpretative Response: Response to Literature Essay

An effective interpretative response has these characteristics:

- A clear **thesis statement**

- Writing that addresses the writing skills for an **analytical essay,** including references to and commentary on **quotations from the text** and the use of **rhetorical devices**

- **Analysis of the aesthetic,** or beautiful or artistic, **effects of an author's use of stylistic or rhetorical devices,** such as symbolism and analogies

- **Analysis of the ambiguities, nuances, complexities** in the text—those parts of the writing that make it confusing, difficult, or complicated

- **Anticipation of and response to readers' questions or contradictory information,** or information that doesn't agree

- **Effective sentence structure** and correct spelling, grammar, and usage

A response to literature essay can address expository or literary texts and may also include:

- Analysis of **story elements,** such as character, plot, setting, and theme

- Writing that extends **beyond a summary and literal analysis** to examine how the elements of a written work blend to communicate information to the reader

Other Forms of Interpretative Response

In addition to a response to literature essay, there are other forms of interpretative responses, including:

Blog comments on an author's Web site share readers' ideas about an author's work. Readers express their opinions and give their interpretations of what an author's work means.

Comparison essays compare and contrast two or more literary works. A comparison essay might compare two novels with the same theme, or it might compare several thematically related short stories to a movie. The basis for the comparison is often related to the author's use of stylistic or rhetorical devices.

Critical reviews evaluate books, plays, poetry, and other literary works. They appear in newspapers and magazines, on television and radio, and on the Internet. These kinds of interpretative works present the writer's opinions and support them with specific examples.

Letters to an author address a writer directly. They offer the reader's thoughts and feelings about the work and discuss what the work communicated to the reader. They also examine how the author's writing style added to the work. A letter includes a greeting and a closing and may ask the author questions or make requests of the author.

Try It! For each audience and purpose described, choose a form, such as a comparison essay or critical review, that is appropriate for conveying your intended meaning to the audience. Explain your choices.

- To compare an author's use of symbolism in two separate works
- To inform an author that you didn't like his latest book
- To review a book you liked and want to recommend to others

WRITING COACH

Online

www.phwritingcoach.com

Resource

Word Bank Listen to English and Spanish pronunciations of new words in the eText glossary.

Online Journal

Try It! Record your answers and ideas in the online journal.

WORD BANK

People often use these vocabulary words when they talk about interpretative response writing. Work with a partner. Take turns using each word in a sentence. If you are unsure of the meaning of a word, use the Glossary or a dictionary to check the definition.

analysis	evaluate
commentary	point of view
determine	summary

A root word is the most basic part of a word. An affix is a word part that is added to the beginning of a word, as a prefix, or at the end of a word, as a suffix. Prefixes and suffixes change the meaning of the root word in some way.

Think about how the words below are related to the words above.

analyze	evaluation
comment	summarize

MENTOR TEXT

Response to Literature Essay

Learn From Experience

 Read the response to literature essay on pages 200–201. As you read, take notes to develop your understanding of basic sight and English vocabulary. Then, read the numbered notes in the margins to learn about how the author presented her ideas.

 Answer the *Try It!* questions online or in your notebook.

---

❶ The **introduction** ends with a **thesis statement** that tells the controlling idea of the essay.

Try It! What is the thesis statement? What three points will the essay explain?

❷ The author analyzes the **aesthetic,** or pleasing, **effects** of Whitman's writing style, in this case, Whitman's word choice and his ability to structure his ideas in interesting ways.

Try It! How does the author feel about Whitman's writing style? What examples from the text does she use to support her feelings?

❸ The author **goes beyond a summary and literal analysis** to analyze a concept in Whitman's poem.

Try It! How does the analysis help you to understand the author's point?

Extension Find another example of a response to literature essay, and compare it with this one.

A Response to Walt Whitman's "Song of Myself"

by Andria Cole

In his poem "Song of Myself," when Walt Whitman writes, "Hoping to cease not till death," he means that he wishes to truly *live* until he dies. This passion for life, this determination to experience all that life has to offer, is found in every crease of the poem. Whitman expresses it clearly in the "I celebrate myself, and sing myself" lines, as well as more indirectly, in the poem's overall tone of optimism. "Song of Myself" is a collection of stanzas that honor every aspect of existence—the beautiful, the painful, and the silent. The poem explains over and over—through metaphors, imagery, and descriptions of experience—that all living things are connected. Human beings are both distinct elements of the Earth and absolutely indistinguishable from it. **❶** Whitman constructs the poem with a similar sense of dualism—focusing on both the concrete and the abstract—and his poem achieves greatness through its presentation of celebration and humility.

Dualism is a significant characteristic of "Song of Myself." Most poems are constructed with duality, with a top or literal layer that is enhanced by a deeper, more abstract layer. **❷** With "Song of Myself," it's not the characteristic of dualism itself that makes the poem so grand and original, rather it is Whitman's great skill with words that creates such an exquisite work. He balances literal descriptions such as, "The dried grass of the harvest time loads the slow-drawn wagon," with abstract lines such as, "I am integral with you, I too am of one phase and all phases." **❸** These examples represent "literal" and "abstract," but there are plenty of lines that bear both labels: "If you want me again look for me under your boot soles." The reader is urged to consider the very physical idea of Whitman's bodily remains being in the dirt beneath him or her. But he or she must also contemplate what the concept means on a deeper level—that our cyclical connectedness with the Universe reveals both our nothingness and our supremeness.

These concepts of duality and the interconnectedness of the Universe are presented throughout the poem as a celebration of life. To begin, the reader is given the impression that life is a most fantastical blessing. Whitman accomplishes this impression by peppering the poem with energy. Section 6 of the poem goes so far as to say, "there is really no death." Whitman allows the "smallest sprout" to demonstrate this. When a sprout reaches its end and

is returned to the soil, another will rise in its place, or perhaps it
40 will be eaten and then used to sustain life within another creature
that will pass the energy on again. "All goes onward and outward,
nothing collapses," says Whitman.

The poem's celebration of life is matched by its humility.
❹ When a child asks, "What is the grass?" the poet admits, "How
45 could I answer the child? I do not know what it is any more than
he." The poet humbly admits that he doesn't have all the answers.
Still, even in humility, there is dualism. Humility has another side;
it can also present a clear sense of worth. Whitman knows he is
not fit to define grass, but he also knows he is *of* the grass and
50 at least qualified to attempt an explanation for it: "I guess it must
be the flag of my disposition, out of hopeful green stuff woven."
Later, in section 14, he sees himself in the sharp-hoof'd moose,
the chickadee, and the grunting sow. Here, the sense of humility
is highlighted again. He calls himself the "commonest, cheapest,
55 nearest, easiest," and then reminds the reader that not one of
man's thoughts is original. Even the lines, "I am large, I contain
multitudes" and "I too am not a bit tamed, I too am untranslatable"
affirm humility as they reflect the poet's understanding of his value
and relationship to what surrounds and is within him. According
60 to Whitman, he is both nothing and everything and is thrilled about
the complexity of it all.

❺ With this concept of complexity, Whitman effortlessly
juggles celebration, humility, and dualism in "Song of Myself." He
urges the reader to see both duality and the interconnectedness of
65 the Universe. But, perhaps most importantly, he urges the reader
to celebrate life: "Do you see O my brothers and sisters? / It is not
chaos or death—it is form, union, plan—it is eternal life—it is
HAPPINESS."

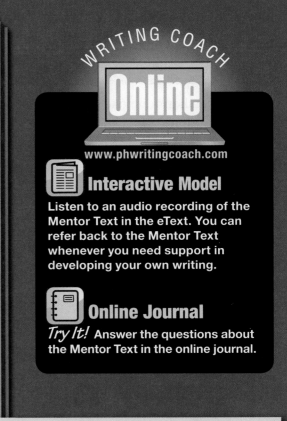

www.phwritingcoach.com

Interactive Model
Listen to an audio recording of the Mentor Text in the eText. You can refer back to the Mentor Text whenever you need support in developing your own writing.

Online Journal
Try It! Answer the questions about the Mentor Text in the online journal.

❹ Here and elsewhere, the author uses **embedded quotations** to support her thesis.

Try It! Why are quotations from literature strong evidence in a response to literature essay?

❺ The **conclusion** makes its point by quoting lines from Whitman's poem.

Try It! Why does the last line make an especially appropriate and effective ending?

STUDENT MODEL — Response to Literature Essay

Use a Reader's Eye

Now, reread the Student Model. On your copy of the Student Model, use the Reader's Response Symbols to react to what you read.

Reader's Response Symbols

+ **I agree with this point.**

− **This isn't clear to me.**

? **I have a question about this.**

! **Well said!**

Participate in an extended discussion with a partner. Express your opinions and share your responses to the Student Model. Work to find all the quotations used as evidence. Discuss how the quotations work to support the writer's ideas.

Point of View in "An Occurrence at Owl Creek Bridge"

by Briana Collins

I just finished reading "An Occurrence at Owl Creek Bridge." Just when I thought I had the whole story figured out, the surprise ending showed me I was wrong. After rereading the story to see how
5 I got tricked, I realized that Ambrose Bierce, the author, told the story using different points of view. The switch from one point of view to another set me up to expect one thing, then gave me another.

The first part of the story is told from an objective
10 point of view. The narrator is almost like a TV reporter on the scene, describing what he sees without telling any of the characters' thoughts. From the narrator's description, we learn that Union soldiers are about to hang a man, but we don't know why. The narrator
15 says, "The man who was engaged in being hanged was apparently about thirty-five years of age. He was a civilian, if one might judge from his habit, which was that of a planter." This objective viewpoint gives facts but not reasons for them. That builds interest and suspense.

20 In the second part of the story, an omniscient narrator fills in background information. We find out that the man is from the South and that his name is Peyton Farquhar. Before he was captured, he had plotted with a Confederate soldier to burn Owl
25 Creek Bridge. What Farquhar didn't know, though, was that the "grey-clad soldier" he had plotted with was actually a Federal scout in disguise.

In the third part of the story, the omniscient narrator reveals more personal details by telling what Farquhar
30 thinks and feels at the hanging. For several paragraphs, the narrator describes Farquhar's daring escape:

1

"Farquhar dived—dived as deeply as he could. The water roared in his ears like the voice of Niagara." Because the narrator told me how Farquhar felt, I could sympathize with him, and I was rooting for him to get away. Then, the last line of the story crashed any hopes back to reality: "Peyton Farquhar was dead; his body, with a broken neck, swung gently from side to side beneath the timbers of Owl Creek Bridge."

Peyton Farquhar hadn't escaped at all! His escape was just a fantasy, all in his mind, in the seconds before he died. Though this ending surprised me, it also made the story more interesting to me. The different points of view make "An Occurrence at Owl Creek Bridge" more than just another Civil War story.

2

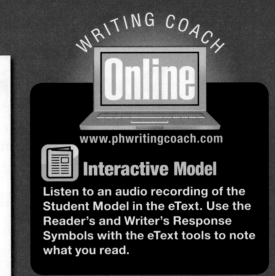

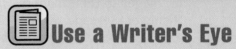
www.phwritingcoach.com

Interactive Model

Listen to an audio recording of the Student Model in the eText. Use the Reader's and Writer's Response Symbols with the eText tools to note what you read.

Use a Writer's Eye

Now, evaluate the piece as a writer. On your copy of the Student Model, use the Writer's Response Symbols to react to what you read. Identify places where the student writer uses characteristics of an effective response to literature essay.

Writer's Response Symbols	
C.T.	Clearly stated thesis
I.A.	In-depth analysis
S.E.	Effective supporting evidence
E.Q.	Effective quotations

Prewriting

Begin to plan a first draft of your response to literature essay by choosing a topic from the Topic Bank or coming up with a topic of your own.

 ## Choose From the Topic Bank

TOPIC BANK

Theme Authors use theme to communicate universal ideas and messages to their readers. Choose a piece of writing that has a strong theme or message. Write a response to literature essay in which you explore how effectively the author develops that theme.

Response to a Mentor Text Read "The Song of Stones River" by Jennifer Armstrong on pages 94–97. Write a response to literature essay that explores the author's style and analyzes its effectiveness.

Rhetoric Rhetoric refers to elements such as figures of speech, idioms, analogies, rhetorical questions, and so on. Choose a piece of writing you found particularly interesting or persuasive. Write a response to literature essay in which you analyze the effectiveness of the author's rhetorical style.

 ## Choose Your Own Topic

Use the following **range of strategies** to generate your own topic ideas.

Brainstorm and Discuss

- List books you found interesting, compelling, confusing, or just amazing. Generate a list of possible topics based on works of literature you have read, taking notes on anything that comes to mind.

- Then, discuss with a partner which topic would create the most effective essay.

Review your responses and choose a topic.

Narrow Your Topic

If your topic is too broad, you will find it difficult to develop a clear thesis statement or controlling idea.

Apply It! Use a graphic organizer like the one shown to narrow your topic.

- Write your general topic in the top box, and keep narrowing your topic as you move down in the chart.
- Your last box should hold your narrowest or "smallest" topic for your response to literature essay.

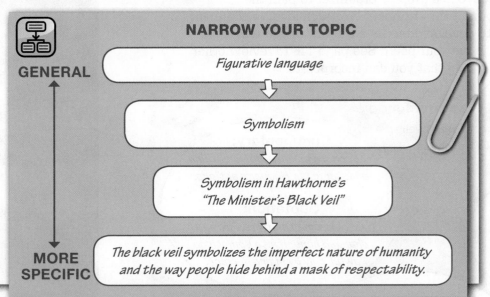

NARROW YOUR TOPIC

GENERAL

Figurative language

↓

Symbolism

↓

Symbolism in Hawthorne's "The Minister's Black Veil"

↓

MORE SPECIFIC

The black veil symbolizes the imperfect nature of humanity and the way people hide behind a mask of respectability.

 ## Consider Multiple Audiences and Purposes

Before writing, think about your audiences and purposes. Consider how your writing will convey the intended meaning to multiple audiences—friends, classmates, teachers, or others. Consider their views as you ask yourself these questions.

Questions for Audience	Questions for Purpose
• Who are my audiences? • Can I assume that my audiences have read the literary work about which I am writing? • What questions or contradictory information might my audiences have about my topic? How will I respond to those ideas?	• What reaction do I want from my audiences? • What approaches, forms, and rhetorical techniques do I want to use to demonstrate my purpose?

Record your answers in your writing journal.

Plan Your Piece

You will use the graphic organizer to state your thesis and organize your supporting evidence. When it is complete, you will be ready to write your first draft.

Develop a Clear Thesis As part of an open-ended writing situation, develop a clear **thesis statement** or controlling idea that sums up your response to the literature. Add your thesis statement to a graphic organizer like the one shown.

Gather Relevant Evidence Use a graphic organizer to plan the evidence you will use to build your argument. For each idea, or comment on the text that you plan to develop, identify a **quotation** you will reference from the text to prove your point. See page 146 to review other skills of analytical essay writing that you can incorporate.

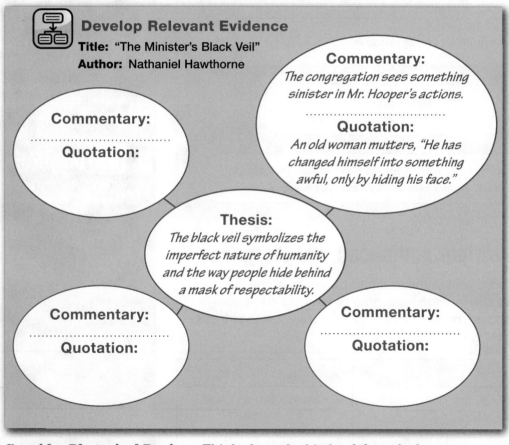

Develop Relevant Evidence
Title: "The Minister's Black Veil"
Author: Nathaniel Hawthorne

Commentary:
The congregation sees something sinister in Mr. Hooper's actions.

Quotation:
An old woman mutters, "He has changed himself into something awful, only by hiding his face."

Commentary:
Quotation:

Thesis:
The black veil symbolizes the imperfect nature of humanity and the way people hide behind a mask of respectability.

Commentary:
Quotation:

Commentary:
Quotation:

Consider Rhetorical Devices Think about the kinds of **rhetorical devices** you will use in your essay **to convey meaning.** Rhetorical devices, such as analogies, rhetorical questions, figurative language, point of view, metaphors, and similes, make writing interesting and lively.

Gather Details

To provide evidence from the text to support their ideas, writers use many kinds of details. Look at these examples:

- **Commentary:** *The black veil literally cast a shadow over everything the minister saw, but it also cast a symbolic shadow that changed his opinion of the world.*

- **Quotations From the Text:** *"[The black veil] probably did not intercept his sight, farther than to give a darkened aspect to all living and inanimate things."*

- **Personal Observations:** *A friend once lied about a mistake she had made. By "hiding behind her black veil," she made the situation much worse.*

- **Rhetorical Devices:** "Why would a minister dress in a way that frightened his flock?"(Rhetorical Question)

Try It! Read the Student Model excerpt and identify which details the author used to support her thesis.

 **STUDENT MODEL** from **Point of View in "An Occurrence at Owl Creek Bridge"** page 202; lines 14–19

> The narrator says, "The man who was engaged in being hanged was apparently about thirty-five years of age. He was a civilian, if one might judge from his habit, which was that of a planter." This objective viewpoint gives facts but not reasons for them. That builds interest and suspense.

 Apply It! Review the types of details a writer can use as relevant evidence.

- Look for points of difficulty in the text. Specifically find the **ambiguities, nuances, and complexities** that make the work interesting, or those points that cause debate or discussion among you and your classmates. These points are worth your analysis and commentary. Take notes as you find likely quotations.

- Look not only at what the selection says, but also how the author writes it. Prepare to discuss and analyze the **aesthetic effects** of any **stylistic** or **rhetorical devices,** such as word choice, rhetorical questions, analogies, and so on.

- Add these details to your graphic organizer. Use specific language in your supporting details to best describe and explain your ideas.

WRITING COACH

Online

www.phwritingcoach.com

Interactive Graphic Organizers

Use the interactive graphic organizers to help you create a plan for your writing.

Interactive Model

Refer back to the Interactive Model in the eText as you plan your writing.

Drafting

During the drafting stage, you will start to write your ideas for your response to literature essay. You will follow an outline that provides an organizational strategy that will help you write a focused, organized, and coherent response to literature essay.

The Organization of an Interpretative Response

The chart shows an organizational strategy for an interpretative response. Look back at how the Mentor Text follows this organizational strategy. Then use this chart to help you outline your draft.

Outline for Success

I. Introduction

See Mentor Text, p. 200.

- Opening statement
- Clear thesis statement
- Identification of the literary work and its author

II. Body

See Mentor Text, pp. 200–201.

- Quotations from text that offer relevant support
- Logically organized details and analysis of the text
- Rhetorical devices

III. Conclusion

See Mentor Text, p. 201.

- Restatement of thesis
- Memorable or powerful ending

Grab Your Reader

- A strong opening statement captures the reader's attention.
- A clear thesis statement defines the purpose for writing.
- An introduction for a response to literature essay always includes the title of the work being discussed and its author.

Develop Relevant Evidence

- One organizational strategy is to include one paragraph for each point that supports the thesis statement, using quotations, your thoughts, and careful analysis of the text.
- Another way to organize the body paragraphs is to put them in chronological, or time, order based on the plot, following the same order as the literature.
- Rhetorical devices, such as analogies, rhetorical questions, figurative language, and metaphors and similes, make writing lively and interesting.

Wrap It Up

- A restatement of the ideas presented in the thesis one last time concludes your essay.
- A rhetorical question to make readers think further about the text, or an analogy that puts the information into perspective for them, will create a memorable ending.

Start Your Draft

Use the checklist to help you complete your draft. Use the graphic organizer that shows your thesis and your commentary and quotations from the text, and the Outline for Success as guides.

While drafting, focus on writing your ideas, not on making your writing perfect. Remember, you will have the chance to improve your draft when you revise and edit.

√ Start by drafting an **opening statement** to catch your reader's attention.

√ Continue to develop an *introduction* that identifies the work of the literature and its author and lets your reader know what to expect in the rest of your essay. Include your **thesis statement.**

√ Develop the *body* of your essay by writing a **focused paragraph** for each point that supports your thesis statement.

√ Be sure to address the writing skills for an **analytical essay** (see page 146), including references to and commentary on quotations from the text.

√ Your writing should identify and analyze the ambiguities, nuances, and **complexities** of the text.

√ Your body should also include an analysis of the **aesthetic effects** of the author's use of stylistic or rhetorical devices, such as analogies, rhetorical questions, figurative language, point of view, metaphors, and similes.

√ Your analysis should anticipate and respond to readers' questions or **contradictory information**. Think carefully about how the audience might respond to your analysis, as well as how you will respond to their questions and comments.

√ Also be sure to use your own **rhetorical devices** in your writing to convey meaning and keep your writing interesting.

√ End with a strong *conclusion* that restates your **thesis.**

√ Leave readers with a memorable **insight** to encourage them to remember or think further about what you wrote.

WRITING COACH

Online

www.phwritingcoach.com

Interactive Model

Outline for Success View pop-ups of Mentor Text selections referenced in the Outline for Success.

Interactive Writing Coach™

Use the Interactive Writing Coach to receive the level of support you need:
- Write one paragraph at a time and submit each one for immediate, detailed feedback.
- Write your entire first draft and submit it for immediate, personalized feedback.

Revising: Making It Better

Now that you have finished your first draft, you are ready to revise. Think about the "big picture" of the logical organization of your writing. You can use your Revision RADaR as a guide for making changes to improve your draft. Revision RADaR provides four major ways to improve your writing: (R) replace, (A) add, (D) delete, and (R) reorder.

Kelly Gallagher, M. Ed.

KEEP REVISION ON YOUR RADaR

Read these two separate paragraphs, which are part of the first draft of the Student Model "Point of View in 'An Occurrence at Owl Creek Bridge.'" Then, look at questions the writer asked herself as she thought about how well her draft addressed issues of logical organization and clarity of meaning.

Point of View in "An Occurrence at Owl Creek Bridge"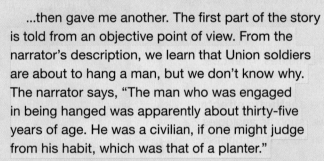

...then gave me another. The first part of the story is told from an objective point of view. From the narrator's description, we learn that Union soldiers are about to hang a man, but we don't know why. The narrator says, "The man who was engaged in being hanged was apparently about thirty-five years of age. He was a civilian, if one might judge from his habit, which was that of a planter."

For several paragraphs, the narrator describes Farquhar's daring escape: "Farquhar dived—dived as deeply as he could. The water roared in his ears like the voice of Niagara." That's where the omniscient narrator gets personal by telling what Farquhar thinks and feels at the hanging. Because the narrator told me how Farquhar felt, I could sympathize with him, and I was rooting for him to get away. Then the last line of the story crashed any hopes back to reality. I found out that Farquhar was actually dead; he didn't escape.

*Have I provided enough **relevant information** for my audience to understand my points?*

*Have I fully analyzed the **author's style** and have I included commentary on **quotations** from the text?*

*Are my thoughts logically **organized?***

Have I included enough examples from the text to back up my interpretation?

Now look at how the writer applied her Revision RADaR to write an improved second draft.

Point of View in "An Occurrence at Owl Creek Bridge"

...then gave me another. The first part of the story is told from an objective point of view. The narrator is almost like a TV reporter on the scene, describing what he sees without telling any of the characters' thoughts. From the narrator's description, we learn that Union soldiers are about to hang a man, but we don't know why. The narrator says, "The man who was engaged in being hanged was apparently about thirty-five years of age. He was a civilian, if one might judge from his habit, which was that of a planter." This objective viewpoint gives facts but not reasons for them. That builds interest and suspense.

In the third part of the story, the omniscient narrator reveals more personal details by telling what Farquhar thinks and feels at the hanging. For several paragraphs, the narrator describes Farquhar's daring escape: "Farquhar dived—dived as deeply as he could. The water roared in his ears like the voice of Niagara." Because the narrator told me how Farquhar felt, I could sympathize with him, and I was rooting for him to get away. Then the last line of the story crashed my hopes back to reality: "Peyton Farquhar was dead; his body, with a broken neck, swung gently from side to side beneath the timbers of Owl Creek Bridge."

A — *Added an analogy to better explain my point and help the audience make a connection to my point*

A — *Added commentary to provide a full analysis of the author's use of a rhetorical device: point of view*

R — *Reordered sentences to make sure my topic sentence appeared first in the paragraph. This sets up a logical flow of ideas*

D — *Deleted vague description*
R — *Replaced it with a quotation from the text for more emphasis and support*

WRITING COACH

Online

www.phwritingcoach.com

Interactive Writing Coach™

Use the Revision RADaR strategy in your own writing. Then submit your paragraph or draft for feedback.

 Apply It! Use your Revision RADaR to revise your draft.

- First, determine if you have written a **clear thesis statement** and have included **quotations** from the text and **commentary** on these lines.
- Then, apply your Revision RADaR to make needed changes. Focus especially on reordering or rearranging words, sentences, and paragraphs to achieve **logical organization**.

REPLACE ADD DELETE and REORDER

RADaR

Look at the Big Picture

Use the chart and your analytical skills to evaluate how well each section of your response to literature essay addresses and logically organizes your ideas. When necessary, use the suggestions in the chart to revise your piece.

Section	Evaluate	Revise
Introduction	• Look at your **opening statement.** Will it capture the attention of your audience?	• You can make your opening statement more interesting by adding a strong detail or fact.
	• Make sure you have written a clear **thesis statement** that communicates your controlling idea. Try reading your thesis statement aloud to a peer to see if someone else can identify your controlling idea.	• Revise your thesis statement so that someone else can identify your controlling idea. Sometimes you can make your thesis clearer by using simpler language.
Body	• Check to see if you have ordered your ideas logically and included **transitions**.	• Add transitions if they are missing. Transitions tie together concepts within and between paragraphs.
	• Make sure that each quotation you use as evidence includes your **commentary** to ensure that you have fully explained your evidence. See page 146 for other analytical essay writing skills.	• Do not assume your readers will know why you have included each reference. Tell them why. Add commentary that identifies and analyzes the ambiguities, nuances, and complexities within the text.
	• Check that you have studied the **aesthetic effects** of the author's use of stylistic or rhetorical devices.	• Add quotations and/or commentary on important text elements you may have missed.
	• Reread your quotations and commentary to make sure that they anticipate or respond to readers' questions or **contradictory information**.	• Substitute quotations that will allow you to address readers' concerns, and add additional commentary to address readers' possible questions.
Conclusion	• Check that your body paragraphs prove the ideas you have presented in your thesis. Then, be sure you have clearly restated your **thesis**.	• If necessary, revisit the wording of your thesis to ensure readers will understand your controlling idea.
	• Make sure that your **conclusion** is memorable.	• Add something that gives your reader something to think about, such as an analogy or a rhetorical question.

Focus on Craft: Analogies

An **analogy** is a **trope,** or a deliberate use of language that makes a comparison to help readers understand an idea.

Using analogies in your writing is an effective way to help your reader understand a difficult concept. When you use an analogy, you make a comparison to show how two things are alike. For example, you might compare learning how to write with learning how to ride a bicycle.

Think about analogies as you read the following sentences from the Student Model.

 STUDENT MODEL from **Point of View in "An Occurrence at Owl Creek Bridge"** page 202; lines 10–14

> The narrator is almost like a TV reporter on the scene, describing what he sees without telling any of the characters' thoughts. From the narrator's description, we learn that Union soldiers are about to hang a man, but we don't know why.

 Try It! Now, ask yourself these questions:

- What two things is the author comparing? Does the comparison help you understand what the author is trying to say?
- Would the statement be more or less effective without the analogy? Why?

 Fine-Tune Your Draft

Apply It! Use the revision suggestions to prepare your final draft.

- **Employ Tropes** Use analogies or other kinds of figurative language to make comparisons that will help your readers better understand your controlling idea. This will help you to achieve your specific rhetorical purpose—to communicate your response to a piece of literature.

- **Use Effective Transitions** If necessary, add transition words and phrases such as *therefore*, *however*, and *although* to show your readers how sentences and paragraphs are connected.

Teacher Feedback Share your final draft with your teacher. Ask if your teacher found anything hard to follow, and whether your examples, quotations, and commentary helped establish your main ideas. Listen carefully to and think about your teacher's response and revise your final draft as needed.

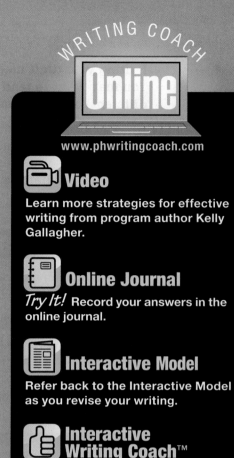

WRITING COACH

Online

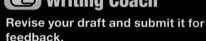

www.phwritingcoach.com

Video

Learn more strategies for effective writing from program author Kelly Gallagher.

Online Journal

Try It! Record your answers in the online journal.

Interactive Model

Refer back to the Interactive Model as you revise your writing.

Interactive Writing Coach™

Revise your draft and submit it for feedback.

Editing: Making It Correct

Editing your draft means polishing your work and correcting errors. You may want to read through your work several times, looking for different errors and issues each time.

As you edit your work, pay special attention to the **punctuation and capitalization** of quotations in your essay. You should also make sure that the quotations you used are smoothly integrated into your writing. Then, edit your final draft for any errors in **grammar, mechanics, and spelling.**

WRITE GUY *Jeff Anderson, M. Ed.*

WHAT DO YOU NOTICE?

Zoom in on Conventions Focus on the punctuation of quotations as you zoom in on these lines from the Mentor Text.

 **MENTOR TEXT** | from **A Response to Walt Whitman's "Song of Myself"** page 201; lines 17–20

> But, perhaps most importantly, he urges the reader to celebrate life: "Do you see O my brothers and sisters? / It is not chaos or death—it is form, union, plan—it is eternal life—it is HAPPINESS."

Now, ask yourself: *What part of the sentence is quoted?*

The part of the sentence beginning, "Do you suppose…" is a **quotation**. The quoted material is enclosed in quotation marks. This quotation is preceded by an **introductory tagline**. Introductory taglines are punctuated with a comma or a colon just before the quoted material.

You can also identify quotations with a **concluding tagline**. If the quotation ends with a period, replace the period with a comma (the comma goes inside the quotation mark), and then add the concluding tagline. However, if the quotation ends with an exclamation point or question mark, do not change the end punctuation. For example: "Can you stay for dinner?" my mother asked.

You can also use a **medial tagline,** which falls in the middle of the quoted material. Choose a natural pause in the quotation to insert the tagline. End the first part of the quotation with a comma inside the quotation marks, and place a comma after the tagline.

Partner Talk Discuss this question with a partner: *Why is it important to properly punctuate quotations?*

> To learn more about punctuation and capitalization, see Chapters 22 and 23 of your Grammar Handbook.

Grammar Mini-Lesson: Quotation Capitalization

To learn more, see Chapter 22.

In a quotation, keep the same **capitalization** that was in the original text. If the quotation could stand alone as a sentence, the beginning of the quote should be capitalized, even though the quotation comes in the middle of your sentence. If you quote a fragment that does not include the sentence's first word, do not capitalize the first word of the quotation. Notice how the author of the Mentor Text does not capitalize the first word of the quoted sentence fragment.

 MENTOR TEXT | from **A Response to Walt Whitman's "Song of Myself"** page 201; lines 1–3

> He calls himself the "commonest, cheapest, nearest, easiest," and then reminds the reader that not one of man's thoughts is original.

Try It! Revise each sentence using the correct capitalization and punctuation. Write the answers in your journal.

1. Rose was creative states the narrator. "all the students envied her."

2. "she was a blue sky on a summer's day" says the narrator.

 Apply It! Edit your draft for **grammar, mechanics, and spelling.** Check for effective taglines for quotations as well as consistently appropriate **punctuation and capitalization**. If necessary, revise some sentences to improve the way quoted material is integrated.

Use the rubric to evaluate your piece. If necessary, rethink, rewrite, or revise.

Rubric for Interpretive Response: Response to Literature Essay	Rating Scale
Ideas: How well does your response present a focused statement and analysis of the work?	Not very Very 1 2 3 4 5 6
Organization: How clearly organized is your analysis?	1 2 3 4 5 6
Voice: How well have you engaged the reader and sustained his or her interest?	1 2 3 4 5 6
Word Choice: How precisely do your word choices accurately reflect your purpose?	1 2 3 4 5 6
Sentence Fluency: How well have you varied sentence structure and length?	1 2 3 4 5 6
Conventions: How correct is your use of punctuation, quotation marks, and capitalization?	1 2 3 4 5 6

WRITING COACH

Online

www.phwritingcoach.com

 Video

Learn effective editing techniques from program author Jeff Anderson.

 Online Journal

Try It! Record your answers in the online journal.

 Interactive Model

Refer back to the Interactive Model as you edit your writing.

 Interactive Writing Coach™

Edit your draft. Check it against the rubric and then submit it for feedback.

Publishing

Share your response to literature essay—publish it! First, get your essay ready for publication. Then, choose a way to **publish it for appropriate audiences**.

Wrap Up Your Presentation

Now that you have finished your draft, add the final details. Include page numbers on each page of your draft. This will help readers as they read through your work. Also be sure to add a title that grabs the reader's attention and indicates the topic of your essay.

Publish Your Piece

Use the chart to identify a way to publish your essay.

If your audience is...	...then publish it by...
Students or adults in your school	• Compiling your essay and other interpretative responses into a booklet • Posting your essay online and inviting readers to respond to it
People in your community	• Submitting it to a local literary magazine • Reading it to a group of people at your local library

 Extend Your Research

Think more about the topic on which you wrote your essay. What else would you like to know about this topic? Use specific details to describe and explain your ideas. Increase the specificity of your details based on the type of information you are recording.

- Brainstorm for several questions you would like to research and then consult, or discuss, with others. Then, decide which question is your major research question.

- Formulate, or develop, a plan about how you will answer these questions. Decide where you will find more information—on the Internet, at the library, or through other sources.

- Finally, learn more about your topic by following through with your research plan.

 The Big Question: Why Write?
What should you write about to make others interested in a text?

MAKE YOUR WRITING COUNT

Produce a Movie Trailer Ad for a Favorite Story

Response to literature essays offer interpretations on pieces of literature based on details in the work. Encourage classmates to read a literary work you have interpreted by showing them a **trailer.**

A traditional trailer is a film advertisement, shown in a movie theater. Instead of promoting a film, your trailer will promote a literary work. However, you will use the trailer director's tools to create a **multimedia presentation** that includes text, graphics, images, and sound that convey a distinctive point of view. The trailer, which you can present live or video-record, should be designed to "sell" your story to a specific audience—your peers.

Here's your action plan.

1. Choose roles, such as director, scriptwriter, storyboard writer and illustrator, and actors. If you are filming, you will need a camera operator.

2. Review your peers' response to literature essays. Choose a piece of literature to advertise.

3. View movie trailers online for inspiration.

4. Create a storyboard, a series of sketches representing each scene in the trailer, with notes about voiceover and other dialogue, camera angles, graphics, and sound. In your 3-minute storyboard, include:

   - An attention-grabbing "first act" that establishes the situation and characters
   - A suspenseful second act that hints at the climax
   - An emotional third act that doesn't "give away" the ending but creates drama using swelling music

5. Using the storyboard, develop the trailer with actors, a narrator, sound, and graphics to communicate your point of view.

6. Present or record your trailer.

Listening and Speaking As a group, practice presenting your trailer. Act out each scene, tying in music, other sound, and graphics wherever appropriate. Listeners should provide feedback and constructive criticism, and actors should adjust their presentation accordingly.

WRITING COACH

Online

www.phwritingcoach.com

Online Journal

Extend Your Research Record your answers and ideas in the online journal.

Resource

Link to resources on 21st Century Learning for help in creating a group project.

Your Turn

Writing for Media:
Script Adaptation

Script Adaptation

A **script** is the written version of words spoken in a play, a movie, a television show, or a commercial. A script can be written to entertain, inform, or persuade, and it uses a variety of literary techniques, such as dialogue and symbolism, to convey meaning. As in other written works, the theme of a script can be either explicitly and directly included, or just implicitly suggested, leaving audiences to work the theme out for themselves. Because scripts are delivered orally, they are usually written in dialogue format. Sometimes scripts include special directions called *stage directions* that give the speakers extra information about how, when, or where to move.

Try It! Study the sample script, which was based on the short story "The Minister's Black Veil" by Nathaniel Hawthorne. Then, answer these questions. Record your answers in your journal.

- What is the **theme** of this movie script?

- Identify two examples of **stage directions** to the actors in the movie. What kind of print indicates that the words are directions rather than dialogue?

- Compare the script to the first several pages of the short story. How does this **adaptation** condense the information from the short story in this script?

- Which information is an example of a direction that instructs the speaker about the type of **emotion** he or she should show when speaking the line?

- The author did not pick up the **dialogue** from the story word for word. Why do you think the author changed some of the dialogue?

Extension Find another example of a script adaptation, and compare it with this one.

The Minister's Black Veil

(The sexton stands on the porch of the meetinghouse, pulling the bell. People from the village arrive dressed in their Sunday best. The Reverend Mr. Hooper arrives wearing a black veil covering his face.)

THE SEXTON: But what does good Parson Hooper have on his face? *(spoken in an astonished voice)*

GOODMAN GRAY: Are you sure it is our parson?

THE SEXTON: Of course I'm sure, but it is hard to believe that good Mr. Hooper's face is behind that veil.

OLD WOMAN: I don't like it. He has changed himself into something awful by hiding his face.

GOODMAN GRAY: Our parson has gone insane!

(They all follow Mr. Hooper into the meetinghouse.)

(Later, the congregation exits the meetinghouse. They are all discussing the black veil worn by Mr. Hooper.)

A LADY: How strange that a veil should become such a terrible thing on Mr. Hooper's face! I felt like he was looking right at all of my secrets when he started talking about secret sins that we hide.

HER HUSBAND: Yes. Did you see that several ladies needed to leave before the service ended? The strangest part is the effect of the veil. Even a quiet man like myself would feel the influence. It makes him ghostlike from head to foot. Did you feel it?

Create a Script Adaptation

Follow these steps to create your own script adaptation based on a work of literature. To plan your script, review the graphic organizers on R24–R27 and choose one that suits your needs.

Prewriting

- Choose a short story that you enjoyed reading. A short story with a lot of dialogue will work best. Determine the explicit or implicit theme your script will project, based on the theme of the short story.
- Identify your target audience.
- Decide which details you will use from the story, and how you will present those details. Will it be as stage direction or dialogue?
- As you plan your adaptation, identify dialogue that can be used in your script. Then, identify descriptive writing that can be converted into dialogue.

Drafting

- First, write stage directions that create a sense of setting. Put the directions in parentheses and italic font at the start of your script.
- Add usable dialogue from the short story to your script. You may need to make some adjustments to be sure the dialogue will be understood by your audience. Next, turn some descriptive writing into dialogue.
- Include stage directions to give the speakers extra information about movement and emotion in the scene.

Revising and Editing

- Review your draft to ensure that the events are ordered logically and that the dialogue of your script communicates the story. Be sure that your adaptation includes all key events from the original.
- Read the dialogue aloud to make sure it will sound natural when spoken. Revise the dialogue as necessary and remove any dialogue that does not advance the plot.
- Check spelling, grammar, and mechanics.

Publishing

With your classmates, act out the movie script. If technology allows, make a video of the performance.

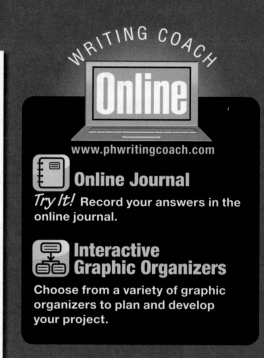

WRITING COACH

Online

www.phwritingcoach.com

Online Journal

Try It! **Record your answers in the online journal.**

Interactive Graphic Organizers

Choose from a variety of graphic organizers to plan and develop your project.

Partner Talk

Read your script aloud with a partner. Ask your partner to interpret the message and identify the position of one or more of the speakers. Monitor your partner's spoken language by asking follow-up questions to confirm your understanding.

Writing for Assessment

You may be asked to write a response to a prompt that asks you to respond to literature. Use these prompts to practice. Your responses should include the same characteristics as your response to literature essay. (See page 198.)

 Try It! First read the interpretative response prompt and the information on format and academic vocabulary. Then, use the ABCDs of On-Demand Writing to help you plan and write your essay.

Format

The prompt directs you to write an interpretative response in the form of a *critical review*. Create an introduction with a clear thesis, a body that includes an analysis of the work, and a conclusion that is memorable.

Critical Review Prompt

Choose a book, short story, or poem that you felt was especially well written. Write an interpretative response that is a critical review of that work of literature. In your essay, focus on a rhetorical device used by the author to convey meaning.

Academic Vocabulary

Remember that a *rhetorical device* is a way of using language to achieve some sort of effect. Rhetorical devices include elements such as symbolism, point of view, rhetorical questions, and analogies.

The ABCDs of On-Demand Writing

Use the following ABCDs to help you respond to the prompt.

Before you write your draft:

Attack the prompt [1 MINUTE]

- Circle or highlight important verbs in the prompt. Draw a line from the verb to what it refers to.
- Rewrite the prompt in your own words.

Brainstorm possible answers [4 MINUTES]

- Create a graphic organizer to generate ideas.
- Use one for each part of the prompt if necessary.

Choose the order of your response [1 MINUTE]

- Think about the best way to organize your ideas.
- Number your ideas in the order you will write about them. Cross out ideas you will not be using.

After you write your draft:

Detect errors before turning in the draft [1 MINUTE]

- Carefully reread your writing.
- Look for spelling, punctuation, and grammar errors.
- Make sure that your response makes sense and is complete.

More Prompts for Practice

Apply It! Respond to Prompt 1 in timed or open-ended situations by writing an interpretative response essay about an expository or literary work. As you write, be sure to:

- Establish a clear **thesis statement**
- Address the writing skills for an **analytical essay** (see page 146), including references to and commentary on **quotations** from the text
- Analyze the **aesthetic effects** of the author's use of **stylistic** or **rhetorical devices**
- Include **transitions** and **rhetorical devices** to convey meaning
- Identify and analyze the **ambiguities, nuances,** and **complexities** within the text
- Anticipate and respond to **readers' questions** or **contradictory information**

> **Prompt 1** Write an interpretative response essay that analyzes a theme in a short story, book, expository text, or poem. Be sure to include examples from the text to back up your analysis.

Spiral Review: Persuasive Respond to Prompt 2 by writing an **argumentative essay.** Make sure your essay reflects all the characteristics described on page 172, including:

- A clear **thesis** or position based on logical reasons that is supported by precise and relevant **evidence**
- Accurate and honest representation of **divergent views**
- An **organizing structure** appropriate to the purpose, audience, and context
- Information on the complete range of relevant **perspectives**
- Consideration of the validity and reliability of all **primary and secondary sources**
- **Persuasive language** to move disinterested or opposed audiences

> **Prompt 2** Managing money is a lifelong skill. Write an essay to convince others of the benefits of budgeting and saving money.

WRITING COACH

Online

www.phwritingcoach.com

Interactive Writing Coach™

Plan your response to the prompt. If you are using the prompt for practice, write one paragraph at a time or your entire draft and then submit it for feedback. If you are using the prompt as a timed test, write your entire draft and then submit it for feedback.

Remember **ABCD**

Attack the prompt

Brainstorm possible answers

Choose the order of your response

Detect errors before turning in the draft

CHAPTER 11

RESEARCH WRITING

What Do You Want To Know?

How do people find out more information about interesting topics? They do research to gather, organize, and present information.

One of the first steps of research writing is to identify a topic that interests you and then formulate open-ended research questions. Open-ended research questions ask what you want to find out about the topic. For example, if you want to find out more about space travel, you would first decide what you want to know about it.

Try It! Take a few minutes to list some things you want to know about the astronaut. Consider these questions as you participate in an extended discussion with a partner. Take turns expressing your ideas and feelings.

- What do you want to know about the astronaut?
- What research do you think the astronaut is conducting?
- How does the information the astronaut gathers help us?

Review your list of questions with a partner. Compare lists to determine which ideas overlap or how you might build off each other's ideas. Then, discuss where you would go to research answers to your questions.

What's Ahead

In this chapter, you will review a strong example of an informational research report. Then, using the examples as guidance, you will develop your own research plan and write your own informational research report.

Connect to the Big Questions

Discuss these questions with your partner:

1 What do you think? How important is it to explore the unknown?

2 Why write? Do you understand a subject well enough to write about it? How will you find out what the facts are?

RESEARCH WRITING

Research writing is a way to gather information from various sources, and evaluate, organize, and synthesize that information into a report for others to read. In this chapter, you will write an informational research report that conveys what you have learned about a topic that interests you. Before you write, you will search for information about your topic in different kinds of sources. You will evaluate the information you find, choose the best facts and details for your report, and organize your ideas so that you can clearly communicate them to your audience.

You will develop your informational research report by taking it through each of the steps of the writing process: prewriting, drafting, revising, editing, and publishing. You will also have an opportunity to use your informational research report in an oral or multimedia presentation that uses graphics, images, and sound to share what you have learned. To preview the criteria for how your research report will be evaluated, see the rubric on page 247.

FEATURE ASSIGNMENT

Research Writing: Informational Research Report

An effective informational research report has these characteristics:

- A clear **thesis statement** supported by **evidence,** such as facts synthesized from a variety of sources

- An **analysis** that supports and develops personal opinions and goes beyond restatement of information while maintaining a clearly stated **point of view**

- **A progression of ideas** developed logically within the organization structure of **introduction, body,** and **conclusion**

- **Rhetorical strategies** that help develop the argument

- Anticipation of audience questions and refutation of **counter-arguments**

- **Sufficient length** to address the complexity of the topic

- Proper documentation and **citation of sources** to show where the author found the information

- Correct **formatting,** or presentation, of written materials according to a style guide

- Effective **sentence structure** and correct **spelling, grammar, and usage**

Other Forms of Research Writing

In addition to an informational research report, there are other forms of research writing, including:

Annotated bibliographies list sources of information about a topic and provide a summary or evaluation of the main ideas of each source. Full publication information is given, including the title, author, date, and publisher of each source.

Biographical profiles give specific details about the life and work of a real person. The person may be living or dead, someone famous, or someone familiar to the writer.

Documentaries are filmed reports that focus on a specific topic or issue. These multimedia presentations use spoken and written text as well as photographs, videos, music, and sound effects.

Health reports present the latest information, data, and research about a specific disease or issue in human health.

Historical reports give in-depth information about a past event or situation. These kinds of reports focus on a narrow topic and may discuss causes and effects.

Scientific reports analyze information and data concerning a current, past, or future scientific issue or theory. A **lab report** describes a scientific experiment, including observations and conclusions.

Try It! For each research report described, brainstorm for possible topics with others. Then, consult with others to decide on and write a major research question for each topic. As you write, keep your audience and purpose in mind.

- A historical report about the effects of the Civil War
- A health report about new findings concerning the long-term effects of exercise
- A biographical profile of a U.S. president

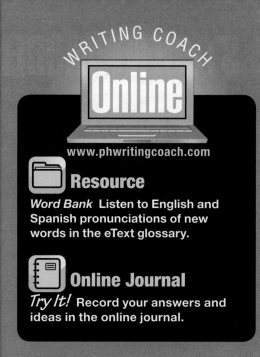

WRITING COACH

Online

www.phwritingcoach.com

📁 **Resource**

Word Bank Listen to English and Spanish pronunciations of new words in the eText glossary.

📓 **Online Journal**

Try It! Record your answers and ideas in the online journal.

📁 **WORD BANK**

People use these basic and content-based words when they talk about writing that reports information. Work with a partner. Take turns saying and writing each word in a sentence. If you are unsure of the meaning of a word, use the Glossary or a dictionary to check the definition.

citation	relevant
primary	secondary
quote	valid

STUDENT MODEL — Informational Research Report

Use a Reader's Eye

Read the Student Model. On your copy of the Student Model, use the Reader's Response Symbols to react to what you read.

Reader's Response Symbols

√ **OK. I understand this. It's very clearly explained.**

? **I don't follow what the writer is saying here.**

+ **I think the writer needs more details here.**

− **This information doesn't seem relevant.**

! **Wow! That is cool/weird/interesting.**

Learn From Experience

Read the numbered notes in the margins as you reread the Student Model to learn about how the writer presented her ideas.

Answer the *Try It!* questions online or in your notebook.

❶ This report follows correct formatting styles. **Page numbers** and author's name appear at the top right of every page. The **author masthead,** with the author's name, teacher's name, class, and date, appears on the left of only the first page.

❷ The **thesis statement** gives the controlling, or main, idea of the report and how it will be supported with evidence.

Try It! What main ideas will the report cover? Summarize them. What do you think are the purpose and audience for the report?

❶ Camilla Juarez
Ms. Kingsley
Science
14 February 2010

The Space Race: A Voyage From Competition to Comfort

On October 4, 1957, the U.S.S.R. launched into space *Sputnik I,* the first Earth orbiting satellite, which looked like a big, shiny basketball with four antennae (see figure 1). Just a little over a decade after World War II, the Soviet Union, with this
5 launch, catapulted itself into the lead of the space race and the Cold War. As a result, the United States reacted quickly and comprehensively. Millions of dollars and hundreds of people were used to put the U.S. back in the running. Within four months, *Explorer I* (see figure 2) was successfully launched from Cape
10 Canaveral. A new age of space exploration and technological advancement began. ❷ Though partially motivated by public fear and a desire to defeat the Soviet Union, the United States' dedication to winning the space race resulted in technological advancements that make our lives on Earth more comfortable
15 and safer today.

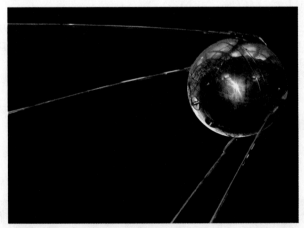

Figure 1. *Sputnik I,* from NASA. JPG file.

Juarez 2

WRITING COACH

Online

www.phwritingcoach.com

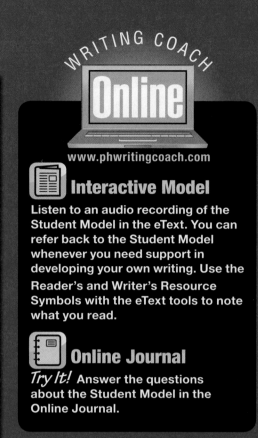

③ Figure 2. *Explorer I,* from NASA. JPG file.

Interactive Model

Listen to an audio recording of the Student Model in the eText. You can refer back to the Student Model whenever you need support in developing your own writing. Use the Reader's and Writer's Resource Symbols with the eText tools to note what you read.

Online Journal

Try It! Answer the questions about the Student Model in the Online Journal.

Perhaps Joan Johnson-Freese, chair of the National Security Decision Making Department, explains the impact of the space race best: "The technological advancements made during that time transformed civil society . . . in ways still evolving" (David).

20 According to Neal, Smith, and McCormick, the passage of the Space Act of 1958, which created the National Aeronautics and Space Administration (NASA), was a direct result of the Sputnik launch (3). Results of the research and development carried out by NASA affect not only the space program but people's lives

25 every day. From smoke alarms to laser surgery to skin care products, NASA has provided the basic science and technology that play a large role in daily living. *NASA Solutions*, an online publication of Marshall Space Flight Center in Alabama, classifies the effects of NASA research based on the area of life

30 it affects: *home, hospital, firehouse, airport,* and more. ④ Life is safer today as a direct result of NASA's work: We have clean drinking water at home, better diagnostic tools at the hospital, improved breathing apparatus for firefighters, and planes that are less likely to collide.

③ Photographs and captions provide visual support and may include additional information.

Try It! How do the photographs and captions support the written information? What additional information do they provide? Explain.

④ Specific **evidence,** such as examples of the technological advancements, support the thesis statement.

Try It! How does this evidence work to support the thesis? Explain.

Juarez 3

5 The author provides an **analysis** of the impact of the space race, discussing not only the decisions that were made but the effects that they have on our lives today.

Try It! How does this analysis support the thesis? Explain.

6 **Proper documentation** shows where the student writer found information. The name in the introductory sentence and the page number in parentheses refer to a source in the Works Cited list. Notice the writer has used proper formatting and set off a quote of more than four lines.

Try It! Turn to the Works Cited list on page 229. To which source does the parenthetical citation refer?

7 Here and elsewhere, the report is written with a clear **point of view.**

Try It! What conclusions can you draw about the writer's point of view concerning the overall impact of the space race?

8 The **conclusion** sums up the **logical progression** of ideas in the report.

Try It! What main ideas does the writer summarize in the conclusion?

9 The Works Cited list provides proper **documentation** by listing publication information for each source used to write the report. The formatting of the list follows the MLA style manual.

Extension Locate one of the sources from the Works Cited page, and write a brief synopsis of it in your own words.

35 **5** Although these inventions and discoveries play a very important role in everyday life, the most influential effect of the space race may be "the way [it] changed the educational system" ("Living in an Atomic Age"). Politicians and citizens alike understood that the only way to maintain a presence in the space

40 race was to prepare the nation's children to lead the way: "[T]he public began calling for a greater emphasis on math and science in the nation's schools" ("Living in an Atomic Age"). In other words, the country needed more scientists, mathematicians, and engineers to join the ranks of the men and women dedicated to

45 winning the space race. In the end, the nation's children benefited and still benefit from the decisions inspired by *Sputnik I.*

As with any undertaking of this magnitude, the decisions made to fund space exploration eventually came under public scrutiny. At first, the news of the Soviet victory in space

50 motivated Americans to support any and all means to reach orbit. **6** Paul Dickson reports on public reaction to the events:

> Polls taken within days of the launch showed that Americans were concerned—so concerned that almost every person surveyed was willing to see the national debt
> 55 limit raised and forgo a proposed tax cut in order to get the United States moving in space. . . . J. Allen Hynek . . . had the impression that Americans . . . felt they had "lost the ball on [their] own 40-yard line but would still win the game" (23).

60 In 1959, Congress responded to public sentiment by "increas[ing] funding for the National Science Foundation (NSF) to $134 million, from a figure of just $34 million the year before" (Neal, Smith, and McCormick 3). However, while the investment in science and technology spiked, public sentiment changed as

65 time progressed and the heated politics of the Cold War waned. Critics argued that the benefits and advances made during space exploration did not warrant the cost. Others argued that our tax dollars would be better spent on anything from exploration of our own planet to welfare programs. As Steven J. Dick, chief historian

70 of NASA, explains, many people believed the money spent on

Juarez 4

space flight was "a diversion of resources better used on earthly problems" (Wilford). **7** These critics, however, do not realize just how many "earthly problems" are addressed as a result of the research and work for the space program.

75 **8** Certainly the Cold War, with the seemingly imminent threat of atomic warfare, had a negative impact on a global scale. But out of the ashes of this war without weapons came the race for space that bred scientific and technological advancement beyond our nation's wildest dreams. From a global competition

80 fed by fear came the conveniences, comforts, and necessities for personal safety that feed our delight. As a result of the space race and the research that followed, our knowledge and understanding of space and Earth increase daily. As time goes on, NASA continues to work toward further space exploration,

85 as well as to improve life here on Earth.

---

9 Works Cited

David, Leonard. "Sputnik 1: The Satellite That Started It All." *Space.com*. Imaginova, 4 Oct. 2002. Web. 4 Feb. 2010.

Dickson, Paul. *Sputnik: The Shock of the Century*. New York: Walker, 2001. Print.

"Explorer I: America's First Spacecraft." *NASA.gov*. NASA, 30 Jan. 2008. Web. 7 Feb. 2010.

"Living in an Atomic Age: The Space Race." *Nebraskastudies. org*. n.p., n.d. Web. 6 Jan. 2010.

NASA. "Benefits of the Space Program" *NASA Solutions*. NASA, n.d. Web. 6 Jan. 2010.

Neal, Homer A., Tobin Smith, and Jennifer McCormick. *Beyond Sputnik: U.S. Science Policy in the 21st Century*. Ann Arbor: U of Michigan, 2008. Print.

Wilford, John Noble. "Remembering When U.S. Finally (and Really) Joined the Space Race." *New York Times*. 29 Jan. 2008. New York Times, 2008. Web. 15 Jan. 2010.

WRITING COACH

Online

www.phwritingcoach.com

Interactive Model

Listen to an audio recording of the Student Model in the eText. You can refer to the Mentor Text whenever you need support in developing your own writing. Use the Reader's and Writer's Response Symbols with the eText tools to note what you read.

Use a Writer's Eye

Now go back to the beginning of the Student Model and evaluate the piece as a writer. On your copy of the Student Model, use the Writer's Response Symbols to react to what you read. Identify places where the student writer uses characteristics of an effective informational research report.

Writer's Response Symbols

T.S.   Clear thesis statement

S.E.   Supporting evidence

R.G.   Relevant graphic

D.S.   Proper documentation of sources

Your Turn ▷ Feature Assignment:
Informational Research Report

Prewriting

Begin to plan a first draft by determining an appropriate topic. You
can select from the Topic Bank or come up with an idea of your own.

 Choose From the Topic Bank

TOPIC BANK

Movies, Music, and the Law Has technology changed the government's
involvement in and laws related to entertainment and media industries for
the better or worse? Choose an aspect of media regulation to research and
present your position on the effects of the changes over the last decade.

A Positive Impact Research a conservation project that you believe affects
the environment in a positive way, such as stocking trout streams, preserving
land, or rebuilding wetlands. Does the research support your opinion?

Increasing Populations More and more people live on Earth each year.
How is this impacting the planet? Research the effects that population
increases are having on one of Earth's subsystems, such as water, air, or
land. What are we doing to control the problem? Is the problem worse in
more populated areas?

 Choose Your Own Topic

Determine a topic of your own using the following range of **strategies**
to generate ideas.

Brainstorm and Browse

- **Brainstorm for** possible topics using strategies such as listing,
  freewriting, or webbing. **Consult with others** to narrow your list of
  possibilities and ultimately decide upon **a topic.**

- **Formulate** several **open-ended research questions** about the topic.
  Circle key words in your questions. Use your key words and phrases
  to browse the library. Note what sparks your curiosity and may make
  a good research topic.

- Search the Internet, using the same key words and phrases. Work with a
  partner to decide which questions provide results that interest you most.

- Review your work and choose a topic.

Formulate Your Research Question

A broad, general topic is almost impossible to research well and cover thoroughly. Plan to do some preliminary research in order to narrow your topic and formulate your research question.

Apply It! Use a printed or online graphic organizer like the one shown to narrow your topic.

- Write your general topic in the top box, and keep narrowing your topic with research questions as you move down the chart.
- Your last box should hold your narrowest or "smallest" research questions. They will be the focus of your informational research report.

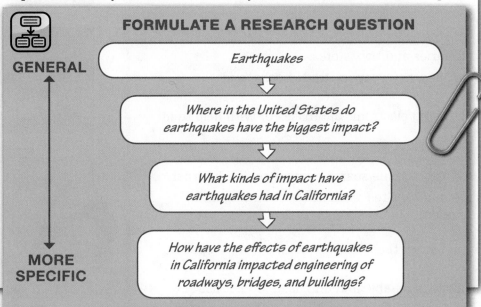

FORMULATE A RESEARCH QUESTION

GENERAL

Earthquakes

Where in the United States do earthquakes have the biggest impact?

What kinds of impact have earthquakes had in California?

MORE SPECIFIC

How have the effects of earthquakes in California impacted engineering of roadways, bridges, and buildings?

Consider Multiple Audiences and Purposes

Before conducting research, think about your audiences and purposes. Then, think about the kinds of information you'll look for in order to meet your audiences' needs and your purposes.

Questions About Audiences	Questions About Purposes
• Who are my audiences? • What background information will they need to understand my report? • What jargon or technical language will I need to explain or define?	• What information do I want to share and interpret? • What attitude toward my subject do I want to present? • How can I use word choice to achieve my purpose?

Record your answers in your writing journal.

WRITING COACH

Online

Interactive Writing Coach™

- **Choosing from the Topic Bank gives you access to the Interactive Writing Coach™.**
- **Submit your writing paragraph by paragraph and receive detailed feedback and guidance as you draft, revise, and edit your writing.**

Interactive Graphic Organizers

Use the interactive graphic organizers to help you narrow your topic.

Online Journal

Record your answers and ideas in the online journal.

Make a Research Plan

Once you formulate your major research question, you are ready to make a research plan. As part of your plan, you will create a timeline for finishing your report.

Find Authoritative, Objective Sources For your report, you will need to **gather evidence from experts on the topic**. Consider the range of relevant resources and choose **texts written for informed audiences.** Make sure the sources you plan to use are **authoritative**—written or put together by experts on your topic. All your resources should be **reliable**—trustworthy and valid. Consider a variety of sources, using these tips:

Print Resources

- Find print resources in libraries and bookstores.
- Use encyclopedias, magazines, newspapers, trade books, and textbooks.
- Search for print resources using electronic databases or with help from the reference librarian.

Electronic Resources

- Find electronic resources using online search engines on the Internet.
- Choose only authoritative reliable sites, such as those ending in:
    .edu (educational institution)
    .gov (government agency)
    .org (not-for-profit organization; these may be biased toward specific purposes)
- If you are not sure that a site is reliable and unbiased, do not use it.

Interviews With Experts

- Ask questions of an expert on your topic.
- Set up a short in-person, e-mail, or telephone interview.
- Record the interview and take good notes.

Multimedia Resources

- Watch movies about your topic.
- Listen to podcasts or seminars related to the topic.
- Search for relevant photos, diagrams, charts, and graphs.

Evaluate Your Sources Do not assume that all sources of information on your topic are useful, good, or trustworthy. Use the checklist on page 233 to evaluate sources of information you find. The more questions that you can answer with a yes, the more likely you should use the source.

Checklist for Evaluating Sources

Does the source of information:

❑ Provide **relevant** and **accurate** information written or compiled by experts on the topic?

❑ Address an **audience** that is **informed** in the field?

❑ Support **theories** with **strong evidence?**

❑ Tell all sides of a story, including opposing viewpoints?

❑ **Create a cogent—or persuasive—argument** from the theories and the supporting evidence?

❑ Have a recent **publication date,** indicating that it is up-to-date?

WRITING COACH

Online

www.phwritingcoach.com

Online Journal

Record your answers and ideas in the online journal.

Distinguish Between Types of Sources As you research, you will discover two kinds of sources: primary sources and secondary sources. Your teacher may require that you use both kinds of sources.

- A **primary source** is an original document presented without interpretation by another person. For example, a letter or a journal written by a historical figure, such as Christopher Columbus, is a primary source, as is an official record.

- A **secondary source** provides an interpretation or analysis of a primary source. For example, a book about Christopher Columbus or about his journals is a secondary source. Be aware that secondary sources present one author's interpretation of a primary source.

Apply It! Create a **research plan** and timeline for finishing your informational report. Avoid over-reliance on one source by listing at least four sources of information, including evidence from experts and texts written for audiences informed on the topic.

- Work with your teacher to determine deadlines for completing your research, thesis statement, draft, and final report.

- Confirm that your topic is complex and multi-faceted.

- For each source you plan to use, give full publication information.

- Evaluate the **authority** of each source by answering the Checklist for Evaluating Sources questions.

Modify Your Plan As you engage in in-depth research, you may find it necessary to **modify your major research question** and **refocus** the emphasis of **your research plan**. For example, you may not find the resources you need for the topic you've selected. **Critique the research process** at each step to **implement changes** as the need occurs and is identified.

Collect and Organize Data

For your informational research report, you will need to use **multiple sources** of information originating from experts on the topic and written for informed audiences in the field. As you investigate, you will need to **systematically organize** relevant and accurate information. You will also need to prepare to **cite** all researched information.

Keep Track of Multiple Sources As you gather information from **multiple sources,** you will need to keep track of the sources. One way to make sure you accurately cite all researched information is to use source cards. Number each source card and include the publication information according to a standard format. The example shown is from the Student Model. It matches MLA style used in the Works Cited on page 229.

Take Notes As you take notes, follow these guidelines:

- Organize the notes using headings that sum up the main ideas of each group of notes
- **Summarize** and **paraphrase** information, being careful to restate ideas in your own words
- Separate facts from opinions and inferences
- Evaluate information, determining how the evidence will help you create a cogent argument
- Copy direct **quotations** exactly as they appear, place them within quotation marks, and record the exact location of the quotation within your source

Apply It! Use the bulleted list on note-taking to record notes on information that is accurate and relevant to your research report.

- Categorize the information to support your report's **central ideas, concepts, and themes.** You may also want to create **timelines or conceptual maps,** such as a web, to help you organize your ideas.
- Be sure to **paraphrase and summarize,** using your own words.
- As you gather information, include **direct quotations** within quotation marks and **accurately cite** the publication information.

Source 1

"Explorer I: America's First Spacecraft." <u>*Nasa.gov.*</u> *NASA, 30 Jan. 2008. Web. 7 Feb. 2010*

Notes From Source 1

<u>*Explorer I*</u>

- *launched Jan. 31, 1958*
- *first U.S. satellite*
- *dimensions: 80 inches long; 6.25 inches in diameter*
- *Include photograph of <u>Explorer I</u>*

Avoid Plagiarism

Plagiarism refers to claiming someone else's work as your own. Often plagiarism is unintentional, but its consequences are severe. Plagiarism can occur in many ways. For example, presenting someone else's ideas as your own or copying sentence structures and only changing a few words are forms of plagiarism.

Careful Note-taking Matters To avoid plagiarism, take good notes. Make sure you put direct quotations in quotation marks and clearly identify the sources of ideas that are not your own. Use good paraphrasing skills and accurate citations. The student who wrote this note card made two mistakes. She followed the original source too closely, and she did not include correct publication information.

> *Explorer 1* was the first satellite launched by the United States when it was sent into space on January 31, 1958. Following the launch of the Soviet Union's *Sputnik 1* on October 4, 1957, the U.S. Army Ballistic Missile Agency was directed to launch a satellite. . . .

Original Source

> ### Notes From Source 1
>
> *Explorer I was the first satellite sent into space by the U.S. It was launched on January 31, 1958. It followed Russia's Sputnik I, which was launched on October 4, 1957.*
>
> *from "Explorer: America"*

Plagiarized Notes

Partner Talk

Review taking notes with a partner. Explain why each of these is essential:

- A source card for each source
- A source card number on each note card
- Your own words to summarize ideas
- Large quotation marks for direct quotations

Use these strategies to avoid plagiarism.

- **Paraphrase** Use your own words to restate information from a text. Read the text, look away as you think about what the author means, and then write the ideas in your own words. Be sure to revisit the original text to make sure you have not copied the sentence structure too closely.

- **Summarize** A summary should include only the main ideas of a passage. As you read, identify the main ideas and then state them briefly in your own words.

- **Quote** When you use a **direct quotation,** be sure to enclose the words in quotation marks, identify the speaker or writer, and **accurately cite** the publication information.

Try It! Look at the Notes From Source 1 in the example. Highlight the parts that plagiarize the original. Now, write a new note based on the original source. Be sure to avoid plagiarizing the content.

Document Your Sources

When you write a research report, you have to tell your readers where you found information. You need to accurately cite all researched information that is not common knowledge and cite it according to a standard format.

Works Cited Your research report should end with a Works Cited page that lists all the sources you used. Do not include sources you investigated but did not use. Your teacher will identify the standard format for citation, such as that of the Modern Language Association (MLA) or American Psychological Association (APA).

Look at the example citations shown. Use these and MLA Style for Listing Sources on page R16 as a guide for writing your citations. Pay attention to formatting including italics, abbreviations, and punctuation.

Book With One Author

Author's last name, author's first name followed by the author's middle name or initial (if given). *Full title of book.* City where book was published: Name of publisher, date of publication. Medium of publication.

Dickson, Paul. *Sputnik: The Shock of the Century.* New York: Walker, 2001. Print.

Book With More Than One Author

First listed author's last name, first listed author's first name followed by the author's middle name or initial (if given), second author's first and last names, and third author's first and last names. *Full title of book.* City where book was published: Name of publisher, date of publication. Medium of publication.

Neal, Homer A., Tobin Smith, and Jennifer McCormick. *Beyond* Sputnik: *U.S. Science Policy in the 21st Century.* Ann Arbor: U of Michigan, 2008. Print.

Web Page

Author's last name, author's first name followed by author's middle name or initial (if given) OR name of editor or compiler (if given). "Name of page." *Name of the site.* Publisher or N.p. if none given, date page was published or n.d. if none given. Medium of publication. Date on which you accessed the page.

"Benefits of the Space Program." *NASA Solutions.* NASA, n.d. Web. 18 Dec. 2009.

Parenthetical Citations A parenthetical citation is a quick reference to a source on the Works Cited page. These citations give the author's last name or title and the page number on which the information is located. Here is an example of a parenthetical citation from the Student Model.

 **STUDENT MODEL** | from **"The Space Race: A Voyage From Competition to Comfort"**
page 228; lines 60–63

In 1959, Congress responded to public sentiment by "increas[ing] funding for the National Science Foundation (NSF) to $134 million, from a figure of just $34 million the year before" (Neal, Smith, and McCormick 3).

If the author is mentioned in the sentence, only the page number is given in parentheses.

According to Neal, Smith, and McCormick the passage of the Space Act of 1958, which created the National Aeronautics and Space Administration (NASA), was a direct result of the Sputnik launch (3).

When the author's name is not given, use a title or a word from the title.

Although these inventions and discoveries play a very important role in everyday life, the most influential effect of the space race may be "the way [it] changed the educational system" ("Living in an Atomic Age").

 Try It! Use MLA style to create a short Works Cited page based on the sources described.

- A Web article titled "First Contact: Sputnik" located on NASA's Web site. The article was published on October 2, 2007. The researcher accessed the article on December 29, 2009.

- A book published by Harper Collins in New York in 2006 titled *Space Race: The Epic Battle Between America and the Soviet Union for Dominion of Space.* It is written by Deborah Cadbury.

Critique Your Research Process

At every step in the research process, be prepared to modify or change your research plan. If you can't find enough information to write your thesis statement, try rewording your research question. Don't get bogged down in the research step. Stick to your timeline. You're ready to wrap up prewriting and start drafting your paper.

Apply It! Review your sources to ensure that you have included both **primary** and **secondary sources.** Make adjustments to your research if needed. Then, write an entry for the Works Cited page for every source you have consulted for your informational research report. To format your sources correctly, use MLA style or the style your teacher has directed you to use. Confirm that you have done enough research to begin your draft.

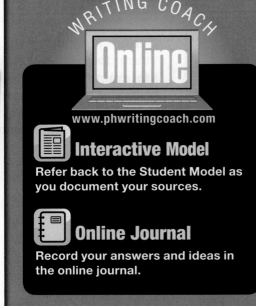

WRITING COACH

Online

www.phwritingcoach.com

Interactive Model
Refer back to the Student Model as you document your sources.

Online Journal
Record your answers and ideas in the online journal.

 **Partner Talk**

Participate in an extended discussion with a partner to discuss research sources and express your ideas and opinions.

- Where have you looked for information on your topic?
- What sources have been most useful?
- Which sources haven't been reliable?
- How have you been keeping track of them?

Drafting: Organize and Write

During the drafting stage, you will start to write your ideas for your **informational research report.** You will write a **clear thesis statement.** You will follow an outline that provides an **organizational strategy** to help you write a focused, organized, and coherent research report. As you write your draft or prepare your notes for an oral presentation, remember to keep your **audience** in mind.

The Organization of an Informational Research Report

The chart shows an organizational strategy for a research report. Look back at how the Student Model follows this same strategy. Then, create a detailed outline for your informational research report. Use the outline template shown on page R26 to develop your outline. Also, refer to the Outline for Success as you work.

Outline for *Success*

I. Introduction
See Student Model, p. 226.

- Attention-grabbing introduction
- Clear thesis statement

II. Body
See Student Model, pp. 227–229.

- Synthesis of information from multiple sources
- Logical progression of ideas
- A variety of formats and rhetorical strategies to argue for the thesis
- An argument that incorporates the complexities of information from multiple sources and perspectives
- Graphics or illustrations to explain concepts
- Anticipation and refutation of counter-arguments

III. Conclusion
See Student Model, p. 229.

- A summation of the argument and its main points
- A memorable ending that inspires further thought

Introduce Your Thesis Statement
- A quotation or interesting fact related to the thesis will grab the reader's attention.
- A clear thesis statement is often the last sentence in the introduction and answers the research question.

Support Your Thesis Statement
- The entire body of a research report supports the opinion presented in the thesis statement.
- Each paragraph expresses a major point in the argument and supports that argument with a variety of rhetorical strategies.
- Paragraphs build on preceding paragraphs to logically develop the argument. As the paper progresses, different perspectives present and support the argument.

Add a Final Thought
- The conclusion includes a restatement of the thesis and a review of the major points of the argument.
- A memorable conclusion ends with a final thought that makes readers ponder the topic or ask further questions.

👍 Start Your Draft

Use the checklist below to help complete your draft. Use your specific thesis statement; your detailed outline listing your supporting evidence, logical progression of ideas, graphics, and illustrations; and the Outline for Success as guides.

While drafting, aim at writing your ideas, not on making your writing perfect. Remember, you will have the chance to improve your draft when you revise and edit.

√ Start your **introduction** with background information on your topic.

√ End this part of your draft with a clear **thesis statement** that is based on your research question. Your thesis should be the road map for your report.

√ Develop the **body** one paragraph at a time. Organize and present your ideas to suit the purpose of your research and the needs of your specific audience. Begin with a topic sentence that states the main idea.

√ Each paragraph should analyze evidence to **support and develop your opinions,** rather than just restating existing information.

√ Use formats such as graphics to enhance your writing and support the thesis.

√ Develop your arguments to discuss the **complexities and discrepancies** or inconsistencies in information you've gathered. Your report should analyze and present multiple sources and perspectives.

√ Anticipate and refute counter-arguments.

√ Work on your use of language. Use **rhetorical strategies,** such as repetition, to reinforce your thesis and engage the audience.

√ Draft a **conclusion** that sums up, restates, and adds a final thought.

WRITING COACH

Online

www.phwritingcoach.com

Interactive Model

Outline for Success View pop-ups of Student Model selections referenced in the Outline for Success.

👍 **Interactive Writing Coach™**

Submit your draft one paragraph at a time and receive immediate, detailed feedback.

Provide and Document Evidence

As you draft, you will present an analysis that supports and develops your thesis. You will provide evidence to support your claims, or personal opinions and ideas. As you draft, avoid simply restating existing information. Instead, develop an argument that incorporates the complexities of and discrepancies in information you found in multiple sources. Be sure to differentiate between your opinions and ideas and those of others. Document the words and ideas of other people as you provide evidence.

Give Facts and Statistics To present convincing opinions and ideas, support them with facts and statistics. Facts are convincing because they can be proven. Make sure statistics, or facts stated in numbers, come from authoritative sources. Document facts and statistics that are not common knowledge.

Give Examples You can make abstract or complicated ideas easy to understand by providing concrete examples. Document examples from particular sources as shown in the Student Model.

STUDENT MODEL from **"The Space Race: A Voyage From Competition to Comfort"** page 228; lines 35–38

> Although these inventions and discoveries play a very important role in everyday life, the most influential effect of the space race may be "the way [it] changed the educational system" ("Living in an Atomic Age").

Quote Authorities The exact words of experts on your topic also provide convincing support. Whenever you use a quotation, make sure it fits smoothly into a sentence and be sure to use your own words to identify the expert. Follow these guidelines:

- Only quote if you must use an expert's exact words.
- Do not quote if paraphrasing is just as clear.
- Separate and inset quotes of four lines or more.
- Always indicate who said or wrote the quote and why that person is an expert.
- Be sure to punctuate quotes correctly. (See page 247.)
- Follow quotes with a proper parenthetical citation.

Try It! Review Notes From Source 3. Write a paragraph using the quotation from Joan Johnson-Freese, incorporating it into a sentence instead of setting it apart with a colon. You do not have to use the entire quotation, but do include the parenthetical citation and use proper punctuation.

Notes From Source 3

Perhaps Joan Johnson-Freese, chair of the National Security Decision-Making Department, explains the impact of the space race best: "The technological advancements made during that time transformed civil society . . . in ways still evolving" (David).

Use Graphics and Illustrations

Visual elements not only add interest to your writing but can also provide important information that would be difficult to express in words. As you draft, consider how you can create visual elements, such as graphs, charts, photographs, or diagrams, to convey ideas and information. Link the figure to your text by referring to it in the body of your report. Then, label your visuals with a figure or table number, caption, and source citations for the data. Use caution when copying an existing graphic because you will need permission from the copyright holder if you publish your work for use outside school.

- **Photographs** Include photographs to help your audience visualize your topic. Be sure to label the photograph with a figure number, include a caption, and provide source information.

- **Maps** To clarify ideas about locations or routes traveled, include a map. Remember to include a legend and a compass with your map in addition to the figure number, caption, and source information.

- **Charts, Tables, and Graphs** Create a chart, table, or graph to provide information in a more visual or organized way. Give each a title that tells what it shows. If you include more than one, number them in chronological order. Include a complete citation for the source of information you used to create the chart, table, or graph. Put it below after the word *Source* and a colon.

Table 1. Early Events in the Space Race (based on data from NASA)

Date	Mission Name	Country	Achievement
October 4, 1957	*Sputnik I*	U.S.S.R.	First artificial satellite
November 3, 1957	*Sputnik II*	U.S.S.R.	Carried Laika, first animal in space
December 6, 1957	*Vanguard TV-3*	U.S.A.	Explodes on launch pad
January 31, 1958	*Explorer 1*	U.S.A.	First successful American satellite launched into orbit
February 3, 1958	*Sputnik III*	U.S.S.R	Failed to launch
March 17, 1958	*Vanguard I*	U.S.A	First solar powered satellite

Source: National Aeronautics and Space Administration, "Chronology of Sputnik/Vanguard/Explorer Events," NASA, 1957–58. Web. 10 Nov. 2011.

 Apply It! Identify two visual elements to include in your research report.

- Think about which kind of graphic or visual would be most helpful in conveying information about your topic concisely.

- Find or create the two graphics and add them to your report.

- Reference them within the text and label them with figure numbers, captions, and sources.

- Use a style manual to correctly format and document your graphics.

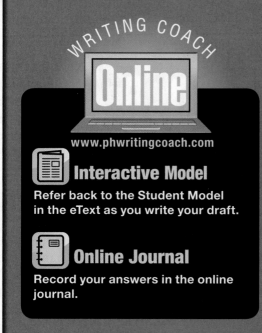

WRITING COACH

Online

www.phwritingcoach.com

Interactive Model

Refer back to the Student Model in the eText as you write your draft.

Online Journal

Record your answers in the online journal.

 **Partner Talk**

Before you create or find graphics, talk over your ideas with a partner. Explain how each graphic will enhance your report. Consider feedback from your partner as you move forward to find or create graphics.

Revising: Making It Better

Now that you have finished your draft, you are ready to revise. Think about the "big picture" of **audience, pupose,** and **genre.** You can use the Revision RADaR strategy as a guide for making changes to improve your draft. Revision RADaR provides four major ways to **improve your writing:** (R) replace, (A) add, (D) delete, and (R) reorder.

Kelly Gallagher, M. Ed.

KEEP REVISION ON YOUR RADaR

Read part of the first draft of the Student Model "The Space Race: A Voyage From Competition to Comfort." Then, look at questions the writer asked herself as she thought about how well her draft addressed issues of logical organization and clarity of meaning.

The Space Race: A Voyage From Competition to Comfort

Just a little over a decade after World War II, the Soviet Union, with its launch of *Sputnik I,* catapulted itself into the lead of the space race and the Cold War. On October 4, 1957, the U.S.S.R. launched into space *Sputnik I*, which looked like a big, shiny basketball with four antennae (see figure 1). The United States reacted quickly and comprehensively. Millions of dollars and hundreds of people were used to put the U.S. back in the running. Within four months, *Explorer I* (see figure 2) was successfully launched from Cape Canaveral. A new age of space exploration and technological advancement began. The United States was dedicated to winning the space race. This resulted in technological advancements that make our lives on Earth more comfortable and safer today.

Have I provided enough background information? Do I need to clarify terms or explain concepts?

Is my information logically organized? Do I arrange ideas and use transitions to develop an argument?

Does my thesis statement clearly express my personal ideas and opinion, or does it simply restate existing information?

Now look at how the writer applied Revision RADaR to write an improved second draft.

The Space Race: A Voyage from Competition to Comfort **2ND DRAFT**

On October 4, 1957, the U.S.S.R. launched into space *Sputnik I*, the first Earth orbiting satellite, which looked like a big, shiny basketball with four antennae (see figure 1). Just a little over a decade after World War II, the Soviet Union, with this launch, catapulted itself into the lead of the space race and the Cold War. As a result, the United States reacted quickly and comprehensively. Millions of dollars and hundreds of people were used to put the U.S. back in the running. Within four months, *Explorer I* (see figure 2) was successfully launched from Cape Canaveral. A new age of space exploration and technological advancement began. Though partially motivated by public fear and a desire to defeat the Soviet Union, the United States' dedication to winning the space race resulted in technological advancements that make our lives on Earth more comfortable and safer today.

R *Reordered sentences to make ideas flow logically*
A *Added the first Earth orbiting satellite to clarify meaning*

A *Added the transition as a result to connect ideas and develop the argument*

D *Deleted two sentences that simply stated facts*
R *Replaced them with one sentence that clearly expressed a personal opinion*

 Apply It! Use your Revision RADaR to revise your draft.

- First, determine whether your meaning is clear and your ideas are arranged logically. Confirm that your writing meets the needs of your audience and purpose.
- Then, apply Revision RADaR to make needed changes. Remember—you can use the steps in the strategy in any order.

Look at the Big Picture

Use the chart and your analytical skills to evaluate how well each section of your informational research report addresses **logical organization** and **clarity of meaning.** When necessary, use the suggestions in the chart to revise your piece.

Section	Evaluate	Revise
Introduction	• Have you included enough **background information** and presented it in logical order?	• Add information necessary for understanding and reorder information as needed.
	• Check that your **thesis statement** clearly expresses your opinion.	• Ask yourself, "What am I arguing?" If your thesis doesn't answer this question, revise it.
Body	• Does each **paragraph** provide an analysis that supports and develops the **thesis**?	• Delete unnecessary repetition of others' ideas. Add your own ideas and delete evidence that does not directly support your ideas or the thesis. Add graphics as needed.
	• Does your writing include **rhetorical strategies** to argue the thesis?	• Make effective use of language. Add similes or metaphors to help readers see your ideas in a new way. Add repetition or other rhetorical strategies to strengthen your writing style. (See page 245.)
	• Do you explore the **complexities and discrepancies** in information gathered from multiple sources? Do you anticipate and address counter-arguments?	• Share what you have learned. • Add new sources and perspectives to represent multiple views. Add details to refute counter-arguments.
	• Do you cite and **document** your **sources** accurately? Check that your report is correctly formatted according to a **style manual.**	• Add parenthetical citations as needed. Use a style manual to check your documentation and format.
Conclusion	• Does your conclusion restate and review the **major points** of your argument?	• Review your thesis statement and topic sentences. Confirm that your thesis traces logically through your report, with all paragraphs supporting your main idea.
	• Does your research report end with a new **insight** or leave the reader with a final thought?	• Add a statement or question that makes readers contemplate your ideas further.
Works Cited/ Bibliography	• Have you formatted your **Works Cited** entries according to a standard format?	• Be sure that you have included all your sources and checked your Works Cited entries against a style guide.

Focus on Craft: Schemes: Antithesis

Antithesis is a scheme, or rhetorical strategy that presents opposing ideas in a parallel grammatical pattern. A familiar example is Charles Dickens's introduction to *A Tale of Two Cities*: "It was the best of times, it was the worst of times." The first clause presents the "thesis," and the second, by changing the word *best* to *worst,* is the antithesis. As you revise, consider adding the rhetorical scheme of antithesis to your writing in order to create a bigger impact with your ideas. Think about antithesis as you read this excerpt from the Student Model.

 **STUDENT MODEL** from **"The Space Race: A Voyage From Competition to Comfort"** page 229; lines 79–81

> From a global competition fed by fear came the conveniences, comforts, and necessities for personal safety that feed our delight.

 Try It! Now, ask yourself these questions. Record your answers in your journal.

- How does the writer describe the "thesis" or cause in this sentence?
- Which words create the parallelism and introduce the antithesis?

Fine-Tune Your Draft

Apply It! Use the revision suggestions to prepare your final draft. Make sure you consider clarity of meaning as you introduce rhetorical strategies into your writing.

- **Employ Schemes** Consider using schemes, such as antithesis, to create a big impact on your audience and to help you achieve your rhetorical purpose of informing your audience about your topic.

- **Use a Consistent Tone** Your tone, or attitude toward your subject, should remain the same throughout your report. Most often, a research report should use a formal or serious tone. Review your writing to ensure consistency.

- **Add Transitions** Organize and present your ideas and information to suit your audience and purpose. To help your audience follow the path of your analysis, add transitions—as words, phrases, or even sentences or paragraphs.

Teacher and Family Feedback Share your draft with your teacher or a family member. Ask for feedback on your report's length and complexity. Are they sufficient to address the topic completely? Review the comments, and revise your final draft as needed.

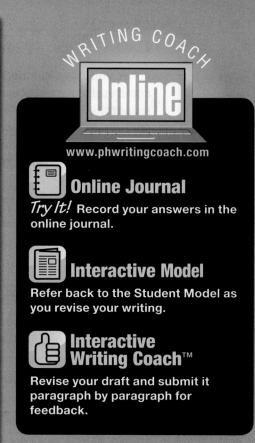

WRITING COACH

Online

www.phwritingcoach.com

Online Journal

Try It! Record your answers in the online journal.

Interactive Model

Refer back to the Student Model as you revise your writing.

Interactive Writing Coach™

Revise your draft and submit it paragraph by paragraph for feedback.

Editing: Making It Correct

After you have revised your report, check to see that you have accurately **paraphrased, summarized, quoted,** and **cited** all researched information. Then, edit your draft using a **style manual,** such as *MLA Handbook for Writers of Research Papers,* to document sources and format the materials, including quotations. Finally, edit your final draft for **errors in grammar, mechanics, and spelling.**

WRITE GUY *Jeff Anderson, M. Ed.*

WHAT DO YOU NOTICE?

Zoom in on Conventions Focus on quotations as you zoom in on these lines from the Student Model.

 **STUDENT TEXT** | from **"The Space Race: A Voyage From Competition to Comfort"** page 228; lines 35–38

> Although these inventions and discoveries play a very important role in everyday life, the most influential effect of the space race may be "the way [it] changed the educational system" ("Living in an Atomic Age").

Now, ask yourself this question: *What techniques has the writer used to integrate the quotation?*

- The introductory phrase provides transition from previous ideas to the quotation.
- The writer prepares the reader for the information in the quote.
- The writer has properly cited the source, using correct format and punctuation.

Partner Talk Discuss this question with a partner: *How does the writer ensure that the quotation flows smoothly with the sentences that surround it?* Monitor your partner's spoken language by asking follow-up questions to confirm your understanding.

> To learn more about integrating quotations, see Grammar Game Plan Error 18, page 290.

Grammar Mini-Lesson: Punctuation

Punctuating Quotations With Citations Quotations follow specific rules for punctuation. Study these sentences from the Student Model. Notice how the writer punctuated the quotation with a citation.

To learn more, see Grammar Game Plan, Error 3, p. 275.

  **STUDENT MODEL**

from **"The Space Race: A Voyage From Competition to Comfort"**
pages 228–229; lines 69–72

As Steven J. Dick, chief historian of NASA, explains, many people believed the money spent on space flight was "a diversion of resources better used on earthly problems" (Wilford).

Try It! Correct the punctuation and citation format in the quotations below. Write the answers in your journal.

1. Paul Dickson reports that "polls taken within days of the launch showed that Americans were concerned." (Dickson 23)

2. According to Dickson, "J. Allen Hynek . . . had the impression that Americans . . . felt they had 'lost the ball on [their] own 40-yard line but would still win the game.'" (23)

Apply It! Edit your draft for grammar, mechanics, and spelling. If necessary, rewrite sentences with quotations to ensure you've integrated them properly, and punctuated and cited them according to a standard format. Use a style manual to check your formatting and documentation of sources.

 Use the rubric to evaluate your piece. If necessary, rethink, rewrite, or revise.

Rubric for Informational Research Report	Rating Scale					
Ideas: How clearly have you expressed and developed your thesis statement?	Not very					Very
	1	2	3	4	5	6
Organization: How logical is the progression of your ideas?	1	2	3	4	5	6
Voice: How clearly have you expressed your point of view?	1	2	3	4	5	6
Word Choice: How well have you used precise language to develop your supporting evidence?	1	2	3	4	5	6
Sentence Fluency: How well have you used sentence variety in your report?	1	2	3	4	5	6
Conventions: How correct is the formatting of sources that you used?	1	2	3	4	5	6

WRITING COACH

 Online

www.phwritingcoach.com

 Video
Learn effective editing techniques from program author Jeff Anderson.

 Interactive Model
Refer back to the Student Model as you edit your writing.

 Online Journal
Try It! Record your answers in the online journal.

Interactive Writing Coach™
Edit your draft and check it against the rubric. Submit it paragraph by paragraph for feedback.

Publishing

Now that you have researched, compiled, and refined your report, you can share your information. When you've finished your final draft, **publish it for multiple audiences.**

Wrap Up Your Presentation

Your teacher may require a word-processed final report. Follow the guidelines provided. Create a cover sheet, table of contents, and a Works Cited list.

Publish Your Piece

You may be publishing a written report or presenting your report as an oral or multimedia presentation.

If your audience is...	...then publish it by...
Your teacher or classmates	• Submitting a written report • Posting your writing on a classroom blog or Web site
A school club or special interest group	• Giving an oral presentation of your information • Presenting a multimedia presentation

 ## Reflect on Your Writing

Now that you are done with your informational research report, read it over and use your writing journal to answer these questions.

- Which parts of your research report are the strongest or most insightful? Which parts could you improve?
- What will you do differently the next time you are assigned a research report?
- What are the most important things you learned about the research process?

 The Big Question: Why Write? Do you understand a subject well enough to write about it? How did you find out what the facts were?

Manage Your Portfolio You may wish to include your published informational research report in your writing portfolio. If so, consider what this piece reveals about your writing and your growth as a writer.

21st Century Learning

MAKE YOUR WRITING COUNT

Write a Script Based on a Research Report

Research reports answer complex questions about the world by providing evidence from a variety of credible sources. Help your schoolmates learn about a topic from one of your research reports by scripting a documentary or docudrama narrated by an important person related to the topic.

Documentaries are films that use text, images, and interviews to share information about specific topics. A docudrama is a television movie based on real events. With your group, craft a **script** for a documentary or docudrama. Then, present the script as a **multimedia presentation.** Read aloud your script or record and present it as a podcast.

Here's your action plan.

1. Choose roles, such as writer, editor, narrator, and, if recording, sound engineer.

2. Review your research reports. Choose one that cites an expert or important person close to the topic who can narrate your script. The topic should also appeal to a specific audience.

3. View online scripts to see how to format yours. Locate appropriate images, graphics, and sounds.

4. Work together to write a script that:

   - Synthesizes information from multiple points of view to convey a single, distinctive point of view
   - Presents information logically and appeals to a specific audience
   - Identifies text to be read by the narrator
   - Shows notes about visuals and sound effects

5. Rehearse your presentation. Practice matching words to visuals.

6. Record your script if you intend to share it as a podcast.

Listening and Speaking Meet with your group to discuss how to present your script or podcast to the class. Then, practice presenting your script. Include music, other sound, and graphics wherever appropriate. Listeners should provide feedback. Presenters should adjust their delivery accordingly. During the presentation, work as a team to engage and inform your audience.

WRITING COACH

Online

www.phwritingcoach.com

Online Journal

Reflect on your writing. Record your answers and ideas in the online journal.

Resource

Link to resources on 21st Century Learning for help in creating a group project.

Your Turn

Writing For Media:
Television Interview Script

Television Interview Script

Every day new things are discovered and research results are published on topics ranging from fuel-efficient vehicles to new species of life. Often these discoveries are discussed on television news programs in an interview format. In this assignment, you will create your own **television interview script** about a recent discovery or newly published research results. You will formulate a research question and follow a research plan to systematically organize relevant and accurate information for your script. You will put your information together to inform your audience about your chosen discovery or research results.

Try It! Study the excerpt from the television interview script shown on this page. Then, answer these questions. Record your answers in your journal.

1. Who is **interviewed** in this script? What are his **credentials?**

2. What is the **purpose,** or goal, of the script? Who is the intended **audience?**

3. A **television interview script** provides information about a specific topic. What topic is discussed here? What new information is given?

4. What **format** does the script follow? What kinds of questions does the interviewer ask?

5. What **improvements** to the questions might you suggest?

Interview with Dr. Jeff Wood
from the Royal Botanic Gardens

HOST: Forests are in danger as a result of logging and irresponsible farming across the world. Borneo's forests are no exception. However, help is on the way in the form of a beautiful flower. That's right—a flower. Today we have with us an expert on orchids, Dr. Jeff Wood from the Royal Botanic Gardens, located in the United Kingdom. Good afternoon, Dr. Wood.

DR. WOOD: Good afternoon, Jack. It's a pleasure to be here.

HOST: Where have you been conducting your research this year?

DR. WOOD: This past year was spent on Mount Kinabalu in Borneo. I have been working there for over ten years now.

HOST: That is a long time to linger in one place. It must be vast. Has this been a productive year for you and your colleague Dr. Phil Cribb?

DR. WOOD: Kinabalu is unbelievably rich. In an area of just 1,200 square kilometers, 866 different orchids grow, including 13 new species described this year alone ("Orchid Doctor").

HOST: Your work has not gone unnoticed, Dr. Wood. As a result of your discoveries, progress is being made in keeping the mountains of Borneo safe from destruction (*Borneo Today*).

Create a Television Interview Script

Follow these steps to create your own **television interview script**. To plan your television interview script, review the graphic organizers on pages R24–R27 and choose one that suits your needs.

Prewriting

- **Brainstorm for** a list of topics and consult with classmates. Then, choose a topic and formulate a major **open-ended research question**.

- Before you begin to research, formulate a **research plan,** including the investigation you need to do and the timetable in which you must complete your work.

- Gather information from experts on the topic and from texts written for audiences who are **informed in the field** of research. Use multiple sources to avoid over-reliance on one source and any resulting bias or inaccuracy.

- Evaluate each source, determining whether a source is **reliable** and whether the evidence is strong. Differentiate between a source's major theories and the supporting evidence. Then, determine how and if the evidence creates a cogent, or persuasive, argument.

- Use an outline, **conceptual map,** or other graphic organizer to **systematically organize accurate and** relevant information. Use headings to categorize your notes to ensure they support your **central ideas, concepts, and themes.**

- As you take notes, **separate facts from inferences** and opinions. **Paraphrase** ideas, restating them in your own words. **Summarize** articles, recording only main ideas. **Quote** experts and authoritative texts. Be sure to cite all researched information according to a **standard format**.

- Look for **graphics and sound** to enhance your television interview script. Be sure to record source information.

Extension Find another example of an interview script and compare it with the one shown as a model.

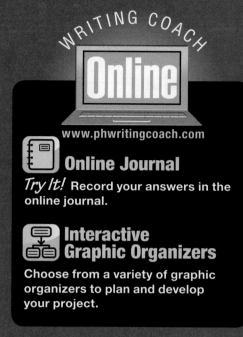

WRITING COACH

Online
www.phwritingcoach.com

Online Journal
Try It! Record your answers in the online journal.

 **Interactive Graphic Organizers**

Choose from a variety of graphic organizers to plan and develop your project.

Partner Talk

Ask a partner to critique your research plan. Does your partner have questions you hadn't thought about asking? Modify your research questions to refocus your research plan and implement changes as needed.

Writing for Media: Television Interview Script (*continued*)

Drafting

- Identify who the speakers will be in your script. You will need a host, or interviewer. Take the role of the person being interviewed, who is considered an expert on the topic.

- Begin by setting up the topic and answering your research question. Since the format is an interview, you will have to set up your argument as answers to the host's leading questions.

- Do not **plagiarize.** Be sure to express ideas in your own words or add a reference to the original speaker or writer in your dialogue.

- Develop your argument logically, using information from **multiple sources** and examining **multiple perspectives**. Use the host to present counter-arguments for you to address and refute. Use the **complexities and discrepancies** and any other inconsistencies like repetition, figurative language, and parallelism from the information you have gathered to convincingly create counter-arguments.

- Responses should provide **analyses that develop and support personal opinions,** rather than just restating existing information.

- Use **rhetorical strategies** to argue for your thesis and engage your audience.

- Use a **variety of formats,** such as graphics, images, and sounds, in your script to develop and support your thesis and add interest.

Revising

Use Revision RADaR techniques as you review your draft carefully.

- **Replace** general terms with vivid details and unclear explanations with precise ideas.

- **Add** specific details or missing information to support your argument.

- **Delete** information that does not support your thesis or develop your argument.

- **Reorder** sentences and paragraphs to present ideas clearly and logically.

- Use a **style manual** to check that you have correctly documented sources and formatted your work.

- Review your script to check that its **length and complexity are sufficient** to fully address your research topic.

Editing

Before you publish your television interview script, check it for errors in grammar, usage, and mechanics. Read through your script several times, focusing on a particular kind of error each time. Look for these common errors:

- Errors in subject-verb agreement
- Errors in pronoun usage
- Run-on sentences and sentence fragments
- Spelling and capitalization mistakes
- Omitted punctuation marks
- Improper script format
- Missing citations of sources

If you are unsure about how to correct errors, consult traditional and electronic references, such as grammar handbooks or dictionaries.

Publishing

- Prepare a final copy of your television script. With another student, act out the script for your class or school. If possible, display graphics and images to enhance the interview.

- Work with a small group of students to create the television program based on your script. Assign responsibilities to group members, identifying who will video-record your interview and who will speak.

- Submit your script or video-recorded program to a public access television station or post it online.

- Print copies of your script for friends and relatives.

Partner Talk

Exchange drafts with a partner, and give each other some feedback. Is your television interview script logically organized and clearly written? Does it give enough specific information? Consider your partner's suggestions as you revise your draft.

Writing for Assessment

Many standardized tests include a prompt that asks you to write or critique a research plan. Use these prompts to practice. Respond using the characteristics of your informational research report. (See page 224.)

 Try It! Read the prompt carefully, and create a detailed **research plan**. List all of the actions you will take to research this topic. Tell where you will look for sources, and how you will evaluate them. Be as specific as you can.

Format

Write your *research plan* in parts. Organize the plan based on the writing process. You might divide it into sections, such as topic, research, and drafting.

Research Plan Prompt

Choose a person or event related to the Abolitionist Movement and formulate **a major research question.** Write a research plan about your chosen topic. Your plan should include: a research topic and question, a list of possible sources, the audience, and the steps you'll take following a timeline. [30 minutes]

Academic Vocabulary

To begin any research plan, you must *formulate*, or devise, a question to research. As you investigate, you try to find the answer to your question in different sources, or publications of information. Remember to list possible primary and secondary sources as you develop your plan.

The ABCDs of On-Demand Writing

Use the following ABCDs to help you respond to the prompt.

Before you write your draft:

A ttack the prompt [1 MINUTE]

- Circle or highlight important verbs in the prompt. Draw a line from the verb to what it refers to.
- Rewrite the prompt in your own words.

B rainstorm possible answers [4 MINUTES]

- Create a graphic organizer to generate ideas.
- Use one for each part of the prompt if necessary.

C hoose the order of your response [1 MINUTE]

- Think about the best way to organize your ideas.
- Number your ideas in the order you will write about them. Cross out ideas you will not be using.

After you write your draft:

D etect errors before turning in the draft [1 MINUTE]

- Carefully reread your writing.
- Make sure that your response makes sense and is complete.
- Look for spelling, punctuation, and grammar errors.

 **More Prompts for Practice**

Apply It! Work with a partner to **critique the research plans** in Prompt 1. In a written response, make specific suggestions to improve each research plan.

- Has the **research plan** covered all of the prewriting steps?
- Is there a limited **topic?** Is it appropriate for the audience and purpose?
- Is the writer planning to find enough **sources?** Are the sources varied?
- Does the research plan say anything about **evaluating** sources?

Prompt 1 Ellen wrote the following research plan. Explain what she did well and what needs improvement.

My Topic: I will research to learn about the space station and then, formulate a question based on my findings.

My Research: Search for current information on the NASA Web site and other reputable sources. Search the library for historical information on the space station.

My Writing: After a week of research, I will use my notes to write a draft. Then, I'll show my teacher before revising it.

My Draft: Organize the information I find in an outline.

Spiral Review: Narrative If you choose to write a **personal narrative** in response to Prompt 2, make sure your story reflects the characteristics described on page 66.

Prompt 2 Write about a time you learned a new and unfamiliar skill. Include details about how you felt and what happened. Were there surprises? Disappointments? How can you use these newfound skills? Do you now have the ability to teach the skill to someone else?

Spiral Review: Response to Literature If you choose to write a response to Prompt 3, make sure your **interpretative response** reflects all of the characteristics described on page 198, including **extending beyond a summary** and literal analysis; addressing the writing skills for an **analytical essay** (see page 146); providing evidence from the text using **embedded quotations;** and analyzing the **aesthetic effects** of the author's use of stylistic or rhetorical devices.

Prompt 3 Choose an expository or literary text that you feel strongly about. Write an interpretative response about how the writer has created an emotional narrative. Include information about word choice, vivid imagery, and sensory details, as well as an analysis of why the plot is important to the story.

WRITING COACH

Online

www.phwritingcoach.com

Interactive Writing Coach™

Plan your response to the prompt. If you are using the prompt for practice, write one paragraph at a time or your entire draft and then submit it for feedback. If you are using the prompt as a timed test, write your entire draft and then submit it for feedback.

Remember **ABCD**

Attack the prompt

Brainstorm possible answers

Choose the order of your response

Detect errors before turning in the draft

CHAPTER 12

WORKPLACE WRITING

What's Ahead

In this chapter, you will learn to write several practical documents, including work-related documents, and procedural documents, which explain how to do something. You will also learn about responses to prompts like those found on employment applications or college application essays. All of these documents should contain accurately written information presented in a reader-friendly format. The language used in these documents should be clear, formal, and polite.

Characteristics of Writing

Effective workplace writing has these characteristics:

- **Well-organized, accurate** information
- **Reader-friendly formatting techniques** such as clearly defined sections
- Detailed and clear language that is **formal and polite**
- Correct **grammar, punctuation, and spelling** appropriate to the form of writing

Forms of Writing

Forms of workplace writing that you will learn are:

College application essays are written in response to a prompt. They should thoroughly address each part of the prompt and demonstrate both critical thinking and good writing skills.

Cover letters and business letters are written to explain the purpose of other materials in a mailing, such as a college application or a résumé.

Letters of request are formal correspondence written to a business or outside organization. They are written to ask for information or action for the recipient, such as to write a letter of recommendation.

Proposals are used in business to obtain work. They are broken into formal sections that address phases of the project and project budget.

Other forms of workplace writing include:

Business e-mails are an electronic form of correspondence used for informal business communication.

User's manuals are procedural texts that tell customers how to use and maintain a product. Manufacturers provide user's manuals for the products they create.

 Try It! For each audience and purpose described, select the form, such as a user's manual, a memo, or letter—that would best convey your intended meaning. Explain your choices.

- To tell your parents how to access your grades online
- To recommend a friend for a job in your grandfather's company

STUDENT MODEL

College Application Essay

Learn From Experience

Many colleges require applicants to write an essay as part of the admissions process. This essay prompt said: Write a 300- to 350-word essay that describes a specific incident in your life and explain how it prepared you to thrive in a university environment.

 After reading the college application essay on this page, read the numbered notes in the margin to learn about how the writer presented his ideas. As you read, take notes to develop your understanding of basic sight and English vocabulary.

Try It! Record your answers and ideas in the online journal.

---

❶ Introduction: The first paragraph **clearly states the purpose** of the essay and **addresses the prompt.** Notice that the writer repeats key words from the prompt.

❷ Body: The writer asks a **question to engage readers.** The question shows that he has **anticipated his readers' need** to know what he learned from his experience. The writer shows his ability to analyze an experience, and his writing suggests that he can write well enough to succeed in college.

❸ Conclusion: The writer uses an **appropriate organizational structure** for his essay. The last paragraph ties the details in paragraphs 2 and 3 to the purpose of the essay.

Try It! Relate the model application essay to the prompt.

- Does the writer stay within the 350-word limit?
- Does he adequately explain how an incident in his life has prepared him to live in an international community? Explain.

Essay prompt: Write a 300- to 350-word essay that describes a specific incident in your life and explain how it prepared you to thrive in a university environment.

Finding My Place

by Kevin Smythe

❶ Who would have guessed that a month with a hammer would prepare me for the rest of my life? The university environment is the perfect place for someone with my experience and interests to thrive and contribute in significant ways. In return, I know that South Central Business College will give me the academic and business tools I need to succeed in the future.

One experience stands out as great preparation for my fitting in at SCBC—and in the world. Two years ago, my father and I spent a month as volunteers, helping to build houses in rural Mexico. We worked alongside people from countries all over the world, such as Chile, South Africa, Belgium, and Japan. Every evening, the group met for dinner, and we discussed our lives back home. We all shared stories about educational experiences, community celebrations, and important friendships. ❷ What did I learn from those talks? I learned that people around the world have a lot in common. We all want what is best for our families, our towns, our countries, and the world.

After my trip to Mexico, I knew that I wanted to work and live in a diverse community. I believe that when people from different backgrounds come together in peace and productivity, the world, bit-by-bit, becomes a better place. This conviction has inspired me to work toward a profession as an organizer in an international nonprofit group. Already, I have a history of making important organizational contributions to several extracurricular clubs.

❸ My experience in Mexico and my passion to participate in a united world community will allow me to make real and important contributions at SCBS. I am especially interested in joining SCBS's United Nations Club, as well as pursuing the International Business Degree program. This will dovetail nicely with my new part-time job working in the offices of the Habitat for Humanity nonprofit group. Ultimately, I plan to transform my SCBS degree into a tool that allows me to help people who need it most—the poor and homeless around the world.

Your Turn ▷ **Feature Assignment: College Application Essay**

Prewriting

- Plan a first draft of your **college application essay**. You can select from the Topic Bank or come up with an idea of your own.

TOPIC BANK

Impact of a Personal Experience Relate a significant experience, achievement, risk you have taken, or ethical dilemma you have faced, and evaluate its impact on you.

Person of Influence Describe a person who has had a significant influence on you, and analyze that influence.

- Identify the words in the prompt that tell you where your focus should be. For example, the sample prompt asked you to *describe* and *explain* an incident that prepared the applicants to thrive at the school.
- Write a sentence that clearly states the **purpose** of your essay. In this sentence, include key words from the prompt.

Drafting

- In the body of your essay give **facts** and details to build a well-supported **viewpoint.**
- Take this opportunity to show your analytical skills—instead of simply describing an experience or event, be sure to share the insight you gained. Remember, reviewers are trying to learn about you and your strengths as a student. Consider and answer relevant and engaging **questions** that meet your audience's needs.
- Use **appropriate formatting** and **organizational structures.** Each paragraph should have a clear topic sentence that states the purpose.

Revising and Editing

Review your draft to ensure you meet the requirements of the prompt. Think about your reader's **viewpoint.** If you provide **technical information,** use **accessible language** to do so. Proofread your work carefully to correct any errors in grammar or spelling.

Publishing

- If you plan to mail the application, print it on suitable paper.
- If you plan to submit it electronically either using e-mail or posting it online, create a PDF of the essay before submitting it.

WRITING COACH

Online

www.phwritingcoach.com

 Interactive Model
Listen to an audio recording of the Student Model.

 Online Journal
Try It! Record your answers and ideas in the online journal.

 Interactive Writing Coach
Submit your writing and receive personalized feedback and support as you draft, revise, and edit.

 Video
Learn strategies for effective revising and editing from program authors Jeff Anderson and Kelly Gallagher.

 **Partner Talk**

Read your final draft to a partner. Ask if your essay responds to the prompt effectively. What might you need to change to make sure every part of the prompt is addressed?

STUDENT MODEL   Cover Letter

Learn From Experience

After reading the cover letter on this page, read the numbered notes in the margin to learn about how the writer presented his ideas.

Try It! Record your answers and ideas in the online journal.

---

1 The **return address** lists the name of the writer, the writer's address, and the date on which the letter was written.

2 The **inside address** lists the name of the recipient and his business address.

3 The **purpose** of the cover letter is clearly stated in the first paragraph.

4 The writer helps fulfill the letter's purpose by providing **supporting facts and details.**

5 The writer explains when and how he will contact the potential employer and emphasizes **how he can contribute to the organization.**

Try It! Do you think the cover letter is persuasive? Explain why or why not.

Extension Inferring from the letter's tone, consider the way a recipient might respond. Use the letter's tone to help you distinguish fact from opinion. First, identify the facts the author presents. Next, look for any opinions he provides. Then, write a response from the recipient that summarizes the issue and responds to the original writer's request.

---

1 Terrence Jefferson
224 E. First Street
El Paso, TX 79901
April 7, 2010

2 Matthew Van Riper
Skate-Town USA
892 N. Washington Ave.
El Paso, TX 79901

Dear Mr. Van Riper:

I was very happy to see your advertisement in Sunday's newspaper seeking a part-time disc jockey. **3** As the attached résumé shows, my skills and experience have prepared me well for a disc jockey position at Skate-Town USA skating rink.

4 I have two years of experience spinning music at weddings and private parties. I am familiar with many types of music, and I know how to set different moods or change the mood at a party. I am also an excellent skater. Last but not least, I am trained to administer first aid and CPR. Although these are skills I hope I never need, they are skills that could be an asset to Skate-Town.

5 I look forward to learning more about your business. I will call the morning of Monday, April 11, to discuss how I might contribute to the success of Skate-Town USA. You can also reach me at 915-555-7184 at your convenience to schedule a time when we can talk.

Sincerely,

Terrence Jefferson

Terrence Jefferson

 **Feature Assignment:
Cover Letter**

Prewriting

- Plan a first draft of your **cover letter**. You can select from the Topic Bank or come up with an idea of your own.

TOPIC BANK

College Preparation Program Imagine that you are applying to a summer program that helps prepare students for college or the workplace. Write a cover letter that describes your experience and highlights the qualities that make you an excellent candidate for the program.

Résumé Cover Letter Write a cover letter to accompany a résumé for the job of your choice. Use a business letter format, and be sure to tell why you are a good candidate for the position.

- Brainstorm for **facts and details,** such as a list of experiences and qualities, that make you qualified for the job or program.
- Be sure to locate and use accurate contact information.

 **Drafting**

- Write a first paragraph that includes a clearly stated **purpose.** In your second paragraph, ask and answer **relevant questions** your **audience** may have or will find engaging. End with a paragraph suggesting a course of action.
- A cover letter is a work-related document. It should be formal and concise. Use the **organizational structures** of business letters.
- If you provide **technical information,** use accessible language to address the needs of the reader.

 Revising and **Editing**

Check that you have supported your point of view. Have you addressed questions your recipient is likely to ask? Have you followed standard business letter **format?**

Publishing

- If you plan to mail the letter, print the letter on paper that is suitable for business correspondence.
- Attach your résumé and any other relevant documents.
- If you plan to e-mail the letter, confirm the correct e-mail address and attach your letter to a message as a PDF.

 WRITING COACH

Online

www.phwritingcoach.com

 Interactive Model

Listen to an audio recording of the Student Model.

 Online Journal

Try It! Record your answers and ideas in the online journal.

 Interactive Writing Coach

Submit your writing and receive personalized feedback and support as you draft, revise, and edit.

Video

Learn strategies for effective revising and editing from program authors Jeff Anderson and Kelly Gallagher.

 **Partner Talk**

Work with a partner to edit your cover letter. Ask if you appear to be a good candidate.

STUDENT MODEL Proposal

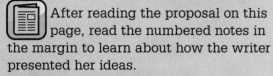

Learn From Experience

 After reading the proposal on this page, read the numbered notes in the margin to learn about how the writer presented her ideas.

Try It! Record your answers and ideas in the online journal.

---

❶ This **subhead** and the others are **appropriate formatting** techniques.

- They make it easy to understand the **organizational structure** of the proposal.
- The **purpose** of the proposal is clearly stated in the opening background section.

❷ The plan helps **support the writer's viewpoint** that she should study abroad. **Numbered steps** are another **appropriate formatting** technique.

❸ The **facts** in the resource section **support the purpose** of the proposal.

❹ The summary briefly restates the main ideas of the proposal.

Try It!

- What is the audience and purpose?
- How does the organization of the proposal meet readers' needs?
- What impression do you think the writer makes in her proposal? Why do you say so?
- Does the writer get her message across in this persuasive text?

Proposal: *Study Abroad*

Janelle Samuels—January 24, 2010

❶ Background

I have the opportunity to spend a month this summer in Spain, learning Spanish from native speakers. I would live with a host family approved by my school. To study abroad, I need $3,000 and the approval of the community grant office. **❶** This proposal explains why I am a strong candidate for this award.

❷ Project Plan

1. I will work hard to raise money (see Resources).
2. I will continue to be a good student, employee, and member of the Student Government Association.
3. I will stay safe during travel and in Spain by carrying a cell phone, practicing the buddy system, and staying with an approved family.
4. I will become fluent in Spanish, which will help me in college and the world of work.
5. When I return from my trip, I will become a mentor for others who wish to have a similar experience.

❸ Resources

I will contribute half the money—$1500—by saving $250 a month from the salary I make at my part-time job. The other $1,500 would be matching funds from the community grant office. My family is prepared to help with any emergency expenses.

❹ Summary

I will earn the right to study abroad by working to help pay for the trip and earning good grades. I believe that this opportunity will provide me with great experiences. I can share what I have learned with others in the town, and I know the trip will help me be a success in the future.

Your Turn > Feature Assignment: Proposal

Prewriting

- Plan a first draft of your **proposal**. You can select from the Topic Bank or come up with an idea of your own for this work-related text.

TOPIC BANK

Classroom Funding Use One of your teachers has been awarded $200 for use in the classroom. Write a proposal about how you think it should be spent.

Gardening Job Your neighbors are building a garden in the backyard. They are taking proposals from contractors who want to build it. Write a proposal about why you should be allowed to do the work.

- Brainstorm for a list of things your audience will need to know about your proposal. List the steps necessary to accomplish your plan.
- Gather **accurate facts and details** for the resources section. Back up your budget with research on what things cost.

Drafting

- As you plan and write your draft, ask and answer **relevant questions** that engage readers and consider their needs.
- Use appropriate **organizational and formatting structures,** including the section heads for proposals shown in the Student Model.
- Organize the information so that your first and last sections include a clearly stated **purpose** and a well-supported **point of view.**
- Provide **technical information** in accessible language. Consider the needs of your audience.

 **Revising** and **Editing**

Consider how well you have addressed your purpose and audience. Is your purpose clear? Will your audience understand technical information? Is your proposal structured correctly? Then, revise your draft as needed. Correct any errors in spelling or grammar.

Publishing

- Print the proposal on paper that is suitable for business correspondence.
- Deliver the proposal to the appropriate audience.

WRITING COACH

Online

www.phwritingcoach.com

 Interactive Model

Listen to an audio recording of the Student Model.

 Online Journal

Try It! Record your answers and ideas in the online journal.

 Interactive Writing Coach

Submit your writing and receive personalized feedback and support as you draft, revise, and edit.

 Video

Learn strategies for effective revising and editing from program authors Jeff Anderson and Kelly Gallagher.

Partner Talk

Work with a partner to edit your proposal. Ask if your project plan and resources support your proposal.

MAKE YOUR WRITING COUNT

Present a Research Report for College Day

Proposals, college application essays, and cover letters help people communicate important information. These documents may involve the seeds that will help classmates learn more. Make a **research report** and presentation to share with your classmates.

With a group, **brainstorm** for several topics drawn from your work in this chapter that you can explore further. Have a discussion with others to **decide upon a topic** that will be helpful to someone thinking about future college options. Work together to formulate **an open-ended research question** that will help you produce a research report about the topic. Consider topics like campus location and activities, academic requirements, or the application process and documents.

As you develop your report, you may need to **modify research questions** and **evaluate collected information** as necessary. Group members should **consult** one another to **critique the process** as you work. Be prepared to implement changes as needed. Focus on researching information related to choosing a college that is a good fit. Remember that a research report should:

- State a clear thesis
- Consider audience and purpose
- Express a clear point of view
- Provide supporting evidence
- Present ideas in a logical way
- Document sources properly

Organize a College Day to present your research to students in your school. Share the information you have gathered in a **multimedia presentation** that uses graphics, images, and sound.

Here's your action plan.

1. Research takes time. In a group, make a plan for several group meetings. Set objectives and choose roles for each member.

2. Work together to develop a **research plan** involving:

   - Gathering evidence from **experts on the topic** and from **texts written for informed audiences**
   - Choosing reliable sources and strong evidence over unreliable sources and weak evidence
   - Using a variety of sources to avoid error due to over-reliance on one source
   - Separating inferences and theories from supporting evidence and factual data in your sources
   - Understanding how your sources use supporting evidence to develop a cogent—persuasive—argument

3. Discuss your findings. Use a system such as headings or sub-topics to organize the **relevant and accurate information** you have gathered to support your central ideas, concepts, and themes. Use **conceptual maps** and **timelines** to organize complex ideas. Differentiate between primary and secondary sources. Next, work together to create a clear thesis statement.

4. Outline the content of the report. Assign sections of the outline to each group member. You may need to research further before you write a draft. Be sure to **paraphrase, summarize, quote,** and **accurately cite sources** according to a standard format, such as MLA style.

5. Work together to compile data and write a rough draft. Develop an argument based on **complex information** gathered from multiple sources and perspectives. Use this data and any **discrepancies**—inconsistencies—to anticipate and refute counter-arguments.

6. As a group, revise the draft's language and style. Check that your **analysis** is original and that it supports and develops **personal opinions,** instead of simply restating existing information. Use a style manual for **documenting sources** and **formatting materials.**

7. Revise and edit to ensure that the thesis is supported by evidence presented through a variety of **formats** and **rhetorical strategies.** Check that the report **length and complexity** are sufficient to address the topic.

8. Finally, add audio-visual support, such as music and video clips.

9. Present your report to interested students, counselors, and teachers.

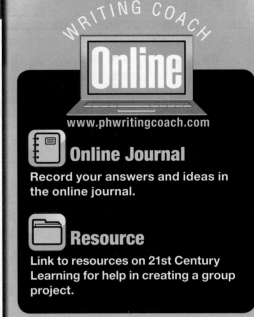

WRITING COACH

Online

www.phwritingcoach.com

Online Journal

Record your answers and ideas in the online journal.

Resource

Link to resources on 21st Century Learning for help in creating a group project.

Listening and Speaking Practice the presentation in front of another group or each other. Listen to feedback and make improvements. On College Day, speak clearly and confidently to your audience.

Your Turn

Writing for Media: Request for a Letter of Recommendation

Request for a Letter of Recommendation

21st Century Learning

When applying for college or for certain jobs, you may need to **request letters of recommendation** from people outside your school. If you need to make a general request to anyone in a group you have worked with, a blog may provide a convenient forum. A **blog** is a periodically updated Web site, often linking members of a group with a common interest. It provides information using text and graphics, and may include audio and video.

In this message, the student who wrote the college application essay on page 258 is requesting a letter of recommendation for his application to South Central Business College. The writer posts his request on his own blog called MiCasa for a group of volunteers he worked with in Mexico.

Try It! Study the request for a letter of recommendation on this page. Then, answer these questions. Record your answers in your journal.

1. How does the writer state the **purpose** of the posting? Is the purpose clear? Explain.

2. What **formatting and organizational structures** does the writer use that are appropriate for a blog?

3. How does the **photograph** support the writer's purpose? How does it appeal to the writer's audience?

4. What additional information does the writer include to answer **relevant questions** the audience may have?

Extension Find another example of a letter of request and compare it with this one.

New Post—9/30/10

Dear MiCasa subscribers:

Once again I want to tell you all just how much I enjoyed volunteering with you in Mexico. I have posted a photo of us building a home together. The experience was very good for my character and my understanding of the world.

Now it is my hope that this experience will also contribute to my efforts to get into the college of my choice: South Central Business College. I'm hoping some of you will consider writing a letter of recommendation to the college on my behalf. It would help me greatly if you could address how well I am prepared for the international community at the college. I've also included an audio link to my college application essay for your reference.

Please use the college's standard form. If you fill out the form, please note in the comments section of this blog that you have done so. I truly appreciate your help with this!

Sincerely,

Kevin

Listen to My Application Essay

Create a Request for a Letter of Recommendation

Follow these steps to create your work-related document—a **letter of request** on a blog post. To plan your blog post, review the graphic organizers on pages R24–R27 to select one best suited to your needs.

Prewriting

- Identify a group you have worked with. If that group subscribes to a blog, use that as a starting point. If no blog exists for the group, consider starting one, or assume a fictitious one.

- Consider the needs of your specific audience. Ask and answer **relevant questions** that engage readers and consider their needs. What does your audience already know about you and the college you are applying to? What **facts and details** does the audience need to know?

- Think about images, sound files, or other documents you can include with your post to help your audience write a recommendation.

Drafting

- Use **appropriate formatting and organizational structures.** In correspondence requesting a letter of recommendation, this often includes your address and the address of the recipient. Since this request will be posted on a blog, begin with an appropriate salutation.

- Write paragraphs that include a **clearly stated purpose** along with a **well-supported viewpoint.**

Revising and Editing

- As you revise your blog, include the contact information that your readers will need in their letters of recommendation.

- If you must convey **technical information,** such as how to navigate the blog, use accessible language that readers will understand.

- Finally, identify and fix any spelling or grammar errors.

Publishing

- Post the letter online where your recipients will read it. Make sure to include a call to action, along with contact information. Attach any other relevant documents.

- Present your blog to classmates. Speak clearly and allow time for your audience to ask questions.

WRITING COACH

Online

www.phwritingcoach.com

Online Journal

Try It! Record your answers and ideas in the online journal.

Interactive Graphic Organizers

Use the graphic organizers to plan your multimedia presentation.

> **Partner Talk**

Before publishing, review your request with a partner. Ask for feedback about the effectiveness of your blog and whatever graphics and sound files you have included. Monitor your partner's spoken language by asking follow-up questions to confirm your understanding.

Writing for Assessment

Many standardized tests include a prompt that asks you to write a procedural text. Use these prompts to practice. Respond using the characteristics of your proposal covered on pages 262–263.

 Try It! Read the procedural text prompt and the information on the format and academic vocabulary. Use the ABCDs of On-Demand Writing to help you plan and write your procedural text.

Format

The prompt directs you to write a *procedural text*. Describe the purpose of the text in the first section. Be sure to include steps that organize information using reader-friendly formatting techniques such as a numbered list or materials lists. Anticipate reader questions and answer them in the text.

Procedural Text Prompt

Your friend wants to write an essay for application to a college. He needs to have written instructions about how to do so. Write a procedural text that anticipates and answers reader questions.

Academic Vocabulary

A procedural text is a kind of text that tells somebody how to perform a task. *Anticipate* means to foresee something and deal with it in advance.

The ABCDs of On-Demand Writing

Use the following ABCDs to help you respond to the prompt.

Before you write your draft:

A ttack the critical review prompt [1 MINUTE]

- Circle or highlight important verbs in the prompt. Draw a line from the verb to what it refers to.
- Rewrite the prompt in your own words.

B rainstorm possible answers [4 MINUTES]

- Create a graphic organizer to generate ideas.
- Use one for each part of the prompt if necessary.

C hoose the order of your response [1 MINUTE]

- Think about the best way to organize your ideas.
- Number your ideas in the order you will write about them. Cross out ideas you will not be using.

After you write your draft:

D etect errors before turning in the draft [1 MINUTE]

- Carefully reread your writing.
- Look for spelling, punctuation, and grammar errors.
- Make sure that your response makes sense and is complete.

More Prompts for Practice

Apply It! Respond to Prompt 1 by writing a **procedural text** in a timed or open-ended situation. As you write, be sure to take these steps.

- Clearly state the **purpose** of the text you are writing and provide a well-supported **point of view**
- Consider and answer questions about what your **audience** knows and needs to know about the procedure as well as what it will find engaging
- Use appropriate **formatting and organizational structures** to develop information in accurate and clearly explained steps or paragraphs supported by **facts and details**
- Develop a draft with **transitions,** such as *first, next,* and *finally,* that clearly **convey meaning**
- Define any **technical terms** accurately, in language your audience will understand

> **Prompt 1** Your aunt wants to have a party in a local restaurant, but she is not familiar with online research. Write a procedural text that includes stepped-out instructions for finding information about locations, menus, and prices online along with directions for finding customer reviews.

Spiral Review: Research Respond to Prompt 2 by writing a **critique of the research process** it describes. Your critique should determine if the research plan:

- Addresses a major topic and **research question**
- Sets up to do research on a **complex, multifaceted topic**
- Contains plans for compiling data from **reliable sources**
- Mentions organizing information using **graphics and forms**
- References using a **standard format** from an appropriate style manual

> **Prompt 2** Li wrote the following research plan. Critique the plan, explaining what he did well and what needs improvement.
> *My Topic:* Zora Neale Hurston.
> *My Research:* I read *Their Eyes Were Watching God,* which involved a flood. I want to find out if the flood really occurred and what other historical events informed her writing. The librarian can find sources for me.
> *My Writing:* In my draft, I will include a timeline.

WRITING COACH

Online

www.phwritingcoach.com

Interactive Writing Coach™

Plan your response to the prompt. If you are writing the prompt for practice, write one paragraph at a time or your entire draft and submit it for feedback. If you are using the prompt for a timed test, write your entire draft and submit it for feedback.

Remember **ABCD**

Attack the prompt

Brainstorm possible answers

Choose the order of your response

Detect errors before turning in the draft

nd Predicates **PHRASES AND CLAUSES** *Phrases* **EFFECTIVE SENTENCES**

GREEMENT *Subject-Verb Agreement* **THE PARTS OF SPEECH** *Nouns and*

Phrases **EFFECTIVE SENTENCES** *The Four Functions of a Sentence* **VERB**

t **THE PARTS OF SPEECH** *Nouns and Pronouns* **BASIC SENTENCE PARTS**

e Fou ctions of a Sentence **VERB USAGE** *Verb Tenses* **PRONOUN USA**

onou **ES AND**

B US E Ve **ect-Verb**

S Su **CTIVE S**

SAG a AGREEMEN ed *Ve* **RTS OF SPEECH**

Grammar

Find It FIX IT

Grammar Game Plan

This handy guide will help you find and fix errors in your writing!

20 Major Grammatical Errors and How to Fix Them

GAME PLAN Use the right words to add clarity and authority to your writing. Make sure your words say exactly what you mean them to say.

CLARIFY MEANING Do not confuse the meanings of words with similar spellings. Also, words with similar definitions can have important shades of meaning. Check that words you found in a thesaurus are used correctly.

I always pay attention to the ~~advise~~ advice my mother gives me.

No one ~~beside~~ besides me packed a tent for the camping trip.

SPELL-CHECK ERRORS Computer spell-checkers often correct a misspelling with a different, similarly spelled word. Be sure to proofread your work carefully to catch these errors. In each of the following examples, the word with a strikethrough represents an inappropriate spell-checker correction.

She told me ~~where~~ there was a tornado watch for the county.

The cause-and-~~affect~~ effect chart we made for class was due yesterday.

Tech Tip

Be your own "spell-checker"! Proofread! Your computer's spell-checker will not identify every misspelling or incorrectly used word.

LEARN MORE

• See Chapter 21, Miscellaneous Problems in Usage, pages 524–540
• See Writing Coach Online

✓ Check It

Use a current or completed draft of your work to practice using words correctly.

✓ **READ carefully.** Take the time to read your draft closely. For a double-check, have someone else read your work.

✓ **IDENTIFY possible mistakes.** Mark any difficult or commonly misused words in your draft.

✓ **USE a dictionary.** If you are not sure of a word's meaning, consult a dictionary.

2

Missing Comma After Introductory Element

LEARN MORE
- See Chapter 23, Punctuation, pages 574–577
- See Writing Coach Online

GAME PLAN Place a comma after the following introductory elements in your work.

WORDS Place a comma after introductory words of direct address, words of permission, and interjections.

> Mom, will you drive me to the library?
>
> Yes, we will leave soon.
>
> Oh, please bring my coat.

PHRASES Place a comma after introductory prepositional, participial, and infinitive phrases.

> Before the storm, we boarded our windows.
>
> Speaking quickly, I rushed through my speech.
>
> To write a book, he will need to devote a lot of time.

CLAUSES Introductory adverbial clauses should be followed by a comma.

> After we drive to the store, we will buy our groceries.

✓ Check It

Use a current or completed draft of your work to practice placing commas after introductory elements.

✔ **SCAN your draft.** Look for introductory words, phrases, and clauses.

✔ **IDENTIFY missing commas.** Mark sentence starters that might need a comma.

✔ **USE your textbook.** Consult the grammar section of your textbook if you are not sure whether or not to use a comma.

GAME PLAN Provide complete citations for borrowed words and ideas. Use the citation style (such as MLA) that your teacher recommends.

MISSING CITATIONS Cite sources of direct quotes and statistics. Remember—when in doubt, cite the source.

The mayor said, "We will build a better tomorrow"ᴧ(Alex 53).

Thomas concluded the work force has been cut back by 15 percentᴧ(Thomas 86).

INCOMPLETE CITATIONS Make sure your citations include complete source information. This information will vary depending on the source and the citation style, but it may include the author's name, the source's title, and the page number or other location information.

The author called the review "completely inaccurate" (Donaldᴧ14). (incomplete citation)

Most of its readers claimed to have skimmed the book (Albertᴧ18).

Tech Tip

Be sure to include the citations attached to sentences when you cut and paste text.

LEARN MORE

* See Chapter 11, Research Writing, pages 234–237
* See Writing Coach Online

✓ *Check It*

Use a current or completed draft of your work to practice documenting your sources.

✔ **REVIEW your draft.** Look for places where you are referencing someone else's ideas.

✔ **USE a style guide.** Check the appropriate format and contents for your citations in the style guide your teacher recommends.

4

Vague Pronoun Reference

LEARN MORE

• See Chapter 19, Agreement, pages 500–504
• See Writing Coach Online

GAME PLAN Create clear pronoun-antecedent relationships to make your writing more accurate and powerful.

VAGUE IDEA Pronouns such as *which, this, that,* and *these* should refer to a specific idea. Sometimes, changing a pronoun to an adjective that modifies a specific noun can avoid a vague reference.

The presidential candidate visited his hometown to discuss his goals for office. These ∧goals will either get him elected or be the cause of his defeat.

UNCLEAR USE OF *IT, THEY,* AND *YOU* Be sure that the pronouns *it, they,* and *you* have a clearly stated antecedent. Replacing the personal pronoun with a specific noun can make a sentence clearer.

The candidate is traveling the country as part of his campaign. I̶t̶ ∧The campaign will be his most effective yet.

When the staff members met with voters, t̶h̶e̶y̶ ∧the voters asked many questions.

To run for president, y̶o̶u̶ ∧a candidate must be willing to devote several months, even years, to campaigning.

✔ **Check It**

Use a current or completed draft of your work to practice identifying vague pronoun references.

✔ **READ** carefully. Read your draft slowly to locate pronouns.

✔ **IDENTIFY** possible errors. Mark any vague pronoun references.

✔ **REVISE** your draft. Rewrite sentences with vague pronoun-antecedent relationships.

GAME PLAN Spelling errors can change the meaning of a sentence. Proofread your work after spell-checking to be sure you have used the correct words.

SPELL-CHECK ERRORS Computer spell-checkers often replace misspelled words with others close in spelling but different in meaning. Proofread your work carefully to correct these errors.

When my twin sister gets embarrassed, her ~~checks~~ ₌cheeks turn bright pink!

After the award recipient received a standing ovation, she said ~~think~~ ₌thank you many times.

HOMOPHONES Words that are pronounced the same but have different spellings and meanings are called homophones. Check that you have used the correct homophones to convey your intended meaning.

My dad's car was ~~toad~~ ₌towed when it got a flat tire and he didn't have a spare.

My aunt says she always sees ~~dear~~ ₌deer in her backyard at dusk.

Tech Tip

Proper nouns are not checked by a computer spell-checker. Proofread to make sure that you have spelled people's names correctly.

LEARN MORE

• See Chapter 21, Miscellaneous Problems in Usage, pages 524–540
• See Writing Coach Online

✔ Check It

Use a current or completed draft of your work to practice spelling words correctly.

✔ **READ** carefully. Read your draft word by word looking for spelling errors.

✔ **IDENTIFY** possible mistakes. Mark any incorrect words or words that are misspelled.

✔ **USE** a dictionary. If you are not certain how to spell a word or think a homophone has been used incorrectly, consult a dictionary.

6

Punctuation Error With a Quotation

Tech Tip

If you cut and paste quotations, remember to copy the taglines to make sure you have included all of the correct punctuation marks that accompany direct quotations.

LEARN MORE

- See Chapter 23, Punctuation, pages 593–599
- See Writing Coach Online

GAME PLAN Quotation marks are used to identify direct quotations. Proper punctuation helps to identify quotations and relate them to your work.

DIRECT AND INDIRECT QUOTATIONS A direct quotation is enclosed in quotation marks. Indirect quotations do not need quotation marks.

Maria said, "I like to volunteer at soup kitchens."

Maria said she likes to volunteer at soup kitchens.

QUOTATION MARKS WITH OTHER PUNCTUATION When commas or periods end a quotation, the punctuation goes inside the quotation marks. Question marks and exclamation marks go either inside or outside the quotation marks, depending on the sentence structure. Colons and semicolons used after quoted material should be placed outside the quotation marks.

"Students who want to volunteer this weekend must sign up today," the volunteer coordinator said.

Sami said, "You have to sign up right now if you want to go on this trip!"

Did she say, "Only ten students can volunteer"?

Mr. Jacobson said, "Volunteering is a great way to help your community"; we all agree!

✔ Check It

Use a current or completed draft of your work to practice punctuating quotations correctly.

✔ **READ** carefully. If you used indirect quotations, make sure that they are not set in quotation marks.

✔ **IDENTIFY** direct quotations. Mark each direct quotation in your work. Is each quotation punctuated correctly?

✔ **REVISE** your sentences. Correct all punctuation errors in your quotations.

7

Unnecessary Comma

GAME PLAN Before you insert a comma, think about how your ideas relate to one another. Make sure the comma is necessary.

ESSENTIAL ELEMENTS Appositives, participial phrases, and adjectival clauses that are essential to the meaning of a sentence are not set off by commas.

My friend, Latoya, is rehearsing her part in the upcoming school musical.

The student, singing the solo, is a junior in high school.

The musical, that many students are participating in, takes place in Paris.

COMPOUND PREDICATE Commas should not break apart a compound predicate.

He traveled to Thailand, but lived in Japan.

The author visited many schools, and signed many copies of his book.

 **Check It**

Use a current or completed draft of your work to practice correctly punctuating essential elements.

✔ **SCAN** Mentor Texts. Notice how professional writers use commas.

✔ **IDENTIFY** essential elements. Did you use commas to indicate these elements?

✔ **REVISE** your sentences. Delete any commas that set off essential elements.

Tech Tip

As you restructure sentences by cutting and pasting from different parts of a sentence or paragraph, remember to add or delete commas.

LEARN MORE
- See Chapter 23, Punctuation, pages 576–577, 583–584
- See Writing Coach Online

8

Unnecessary or Missing Capitalization

LEARN MORE
- See Chapter 22, Capitalization, pages 543–562
- See Writing Coach Online

GAME PLAN Follow the rules of capitalization, such as capitalizing proper nouns, the first word of a sentence, and titles of works of art.

PROPER NOUNS Names, geographical locations, and organizations are examples of nouns that should be capitalized.

Neil Armstrong was a NASA astronaut who landed on the moon.

I saw a space shuttle take off when I was in Florida.

TITLES OF WORKS OF ART The first word and all other key words in the titles of books, poems, stories, plays, paintings, and other works of art are capitalized.

We were assigned to read *The Grapes of Wrath* by Steinbeck.

Have you ever seen the painting *The Starry Night* by Vincent van Gogh?

✔ Check It

Use a current or completed draft of your work to practice correctly capitalizing words.

✔ **SCAN** your draft. Look for words that are capitalized.

✔ **IDENTIFY** incorrect capitalization. Mark words that might be capitalized incorrectly.

✔ **USE** your textbook. Consult the grammar section of your textbook if you are not sure if a word should be capitalized.

9

Missing Word

GAME PLAN Make sure there are no missing words in a text. This will allow ideas to flow smoothly and will help readers understand the text.

ARTICLES In order to make sure that ideas follow smoothly and sentences are coherent, you must proofread your work. A missing word, even a missing article (*a, an, the*), is enough to confuse a reader.

 The heavy snowfall caused the airport to cancel the flight I was scheduled to take home.

KEY IDEAS When copying and pasting text, you might miss moving a word in a sentence. If that word is central to the main idea of the sentence, the intended meaning could be lost.

 The police force was outfitted with new uniforms this past week.

Some of the officers preferred the style of the old uniforms, but they welcomed the change.

✔ *Check It*

Use a current or completed draft of your work to practice proofreading.

✔ **READ** carefully. Read your draft word by word to make sure that you did not omit a word.

✔ **IDENTIFY** unclear sentences. Mark any sentences you find that do not make sense. Are they unclear because of a missing word?

✔ **REVISE** your sentences. Add words to your sentences to make the meaning clear.

Tech Tip

When cutting and pasting sentences, you may accidentally insert the same word twice, one right after the other. While spell checkers generally highlight duplicate words, proofread to be sure the sentence reads as you intended.

LEARN MORE
- See Editing sections in the writing chapters
- See Writing Coach Online

10

Faulty Sentence Structure

LEARN MORE
• See Chapter 16, Effective Sentences, pages 415–420
• See Writing Coach Online

GAME PLAN Sentences should express complex ideas using similar structures and appropriate tenses.

FAULTY PARALLELISM When you express complex ideas, it is important that you use parallel grammatical structures to express ideas in phrases, clauses, or sentences of similar types.

> On her vacation, Jennifer plans to sightsee, to swim, and ‸to hike ~~hiking~~.
>
> Allie thought that she could go shopping, that the sale was still on, and ‸that she could afford the coat.

FAULTY COORDINATION Ideas that are not of equal importance should not be connected with *and.* Instead, use multiple sentences or turn one idea into a subordinate clause.

> Before we went to bed, we played a board game. ~~and~~ ‸When my dad won, ~~and~~ my brother thought it was surprising because my dad had never played the game before.
>
> Mr. Hart took his daughter to see the ballet ~~and~~ ‸because she was enrolled in dance classes.

✓ Check It

Use a current or corrected draft of your work to practice correctly structuring sentences.

✔ **SCAN** Mentor Texts. Notice how professional writers present complex ideas.

✔ **IDENTIFY** possible mistakes. Mark any sentences that have faulty parallelism or faulty coordination.

✔ **REVISE** your sentences. Rewrite any sentences that do not have correct sentence structure.

GAME PLAN Use commas to set off nonessential elements of sentences.

APPOSITIVE If an appositive is not essential to the meaning of a sentence, it should be set off by commas.

 Thomas Jefferson, <u>a United States president</u>, built a home in Virginia.

PARTICIPIAL PHRASE A participial phrase not essential to the meaning of a sentence is set off by commas.

 The Louisiana Purchase,∧completed in 1803,∧was a memorable event in Jefferson's presidency.

ADJECTIVAL CLAUSE Use commas to set off an adjectival clause if it is not essential to the meaning of a sentence.

 Jefferson, <u>who signed the Declaration of Independence</u>, was the third U.S. president.

✔ *Check It*

Use a current or completed draft of your work to practice using commas correctly with nonessential elements.

✔ **SCAN** Mentor Texts. Notice how professional writers use commas to set off nonessential elements.

✔ **IDENTIFY** nonessential elements. Did you use commas to indicate these words, phrases, or clauses?

✔ **REVISE** your sentences. Use commas to set off nonessential elements.

Tech Tip

When you cut part of a sentence and paste it to another, be sure to include the correct punctuation. Proofread these sentences carefully.

LEARN MORE
- See Chapter 23, Punctuation, pages 576–577
- See Writing Coach Online

12

Unnecessary Shift in Verb Tense

Tech Tip

When you cut text from one section to paste to another, the new sentence may have verbs that are not consistent in tense. Proofread revised sentences to make sure they use consistent tenses.

LEARN MORE
- See Chapter 17, Verb Usage, pages 444–450
- See Writing Coach Online

GAME PLAN Use consistent verb tenses in your work. Shift tenses only to show that one event comes before or after another.

SEQUENCE OF EVENTS Do not shift tenses unnecessarily when showing a sequence of events.

We will buy a house, and then we will move to Colorado.

She watered the plants in the front of the house for 15 minutes and ~~waters~~ watered the plants in the back of the house for 30 minutes.

SUBORDINATE CLAUSE The verb in the subordinate clause should follow logically from the tense of the main verb. The verbs require a shift in tense if one event happens before or after another.

She thinks that she ~~dances~~ danced better as a young girl in Lisbon.

Abby knows that we will go to the theater without her this weekend.

✓ Check It

Use a current or completed draft of your work to practice using consistent tenses.

✓ **SCAN** mentor text. Notice how professional writers use consistent tenses within a sentence.

✓ **IDENTIFY** possible mistakes. Mark any shift in verb tense within a sentence.

✓ **USE** your textbook. Consult the grammar section of your textbook if you are not sure that you have used consistent tenses.

GAME PLAN Use a comma before a coordinating conjunction to separate two or more main clauses in a compound sentence.

MAIN CLAUSES Place a comma before a coordinating conjunction (e.g. *and, but, or, nor, yet, so, for*) in a compound sentence.

Ms. Jennings is running for mayor,ₐand she has a lot of support from the city.

BRIEF CLAUSES The main clauses in some compound sentences are brief and do not need a comma if the meaning is clear.

He parked the car and she got out.

COMPOUND SUBJECTS AND VERBS Commas should *not* be used to separate compound subjects and compound verbs in a sentence.

The men, and women were all dressed for the occasion.

He walked to his new neighbor's house, and knocked on the front door.

✓ *Check It*

Use a current or completed draft of your work to practice using commas in compound sentences.

✔ **SCAN** your draft. Look for compound sentences.

✔ **IDENTIFY** missing commas. Mark any compound sentences that should be punctuated with a comma.

✔ **REVISE** your sentences. Add commas before coordinating conjunctions to separate main clauses.

14

Unnecessary or Missing Apostrophe

Tech Tip

Proofread your draft carefully. Not all computer grammar checkers will point out incorrect uses of apostrophes.

LEARN MORE
- **See Chapter 18, Pronoun Usage, pages 467–468**
- **See Chapter 23, Punctuation, pages 612–617**
- **See Writing Coach Online**

GAME PLAN Use apostrophes correctly to show possession.

SINGULAR NOUNS To show the possessive case of most singular nouns, add an apostrophe and -s.

 The university's team colors were not his favorite to wear.

PLURAL NOUNS Add an apostrophe to show the possessive case for most plural nouns ending in -s or -es. For plural nouns that do not end in -s or -es, add an apostrophe and -s.

 All of the phones' batteries need recharging.

The women's locker room was noisy and crowded.

POSSESSIVE PRONOUNS Possessive pronouns (e.g. *his, hers, its, our, their*) show possession without the use of an apostrophe. Remember that the word *it's* means "it is" while *its* shows possession.

 The restaurant is our favorite because of its view.

✓ Check It

Use a current or completed draft of your work to practice showing possession.

✓ **SCAN** Mentor Texts. Notice when professional writers use apostrophes to indicate possession.

✓ **IDENTIFY** possible mistakes. Mark each apostrophe in your draft. Did you use them correctly to show possession?

✓ **REVISE** your sentences. Make sure to delete any apostrophes you used with possessive pronouns.

GAME PLAN Use correct punctuation to avoid run-on sentences, which are two or more sentences punctuated as if they were a single sentence.

FUSED SENTENCE A fused sentence contains two or more sentences joined with no punctuation. To correct a fused sentence, place a period (and capitalize the following word) or a semicolon between the main clauses.

The figure skater will not be able to compete in tomorrow's competition she ∧. She sprained her ankle during practice.

The fans were on the edge of their seats; ∧ the game was going into overtime.

RUN-ON SENTENCE Make sure you place a comma before coordinating conjunctions that join main clauses to avoid run-on sentences.

My library books are overdue, ∧ and I seem to have misplaced one.

✔ Check It

Use a current or completed draft of your work to practice correcting run-on sentences.

✔ **SCAN** your draft. Look for run-on sentences.

✔ **IDENTIFY** missing punctuation. Mark sentences that might need a period or a semicolon to separate main clauses.

✔ **REVISE** your sentences. When correcting fused sentences, vary your sentence structure.

Tech Tip

Remember to proofread your work. Not all grammar checkers identify run-on sentences.

LEARN MORE

- See Chapter 16, Effective Sentences, pages 410–411
- See Writing Coach Online

Find It / FIX IT

16

Comma Splice

GAME PLAN Use correct punctuation to avoid comma splices. A comma splice happens when two or more complete sentences are joined only with a comma.

PERIOD Replace the comma with a period (and capitalize the following word) to separate two complete thoughts.

My mom's favorite season is winter, she. She likes to ski more than she likes to swim.

SEMICOLON Replace the comma with a semicolon if the ideas are similar.

He was the best tennis player on our team, he practiced for three hours every day.

COORDINATING CONJUNCTION A comma splice can be corrected by placing a coordinating conjunction (e.g. *and, or, but, yet, nor*) after the comma.

The wind blew my map away, but I think I remember how to get to her house.

Check It

Use a current or completed draft of your work to practice correcting comma splices.

✔ **READ** carefully. Take time to read your draft carefully. Have someone else read your work for a double-check.

✔ **IDENTIFY** possible mistakes. Mark any comma splices you find.

✔ **REVISE** your sentences. Fix comma splices in different ways to vary your sentence structure.

Tech Tip

Some grammar checkers will not catch comma splices. Proofread your work carefully to avoid comma splices.

LEARN MORE

- See Chapter 16, Effective Sentences, pages 410–411
- See Chapter 23, Punctuation, page 570
- See Writing Coach Online

17

Lack of Pronoun-Antecedent Agreement

GAME PLAN Check that pronouns agree with their antecedents in number, person, and gender. When the gender is not specified, the pronoun must still agree in number.

GENDER NEUTRAL ANTECEDENTS When gender is not specific, use *his or her* to refer to the singular antecedent.

> Each <u>driver</u> must pass a written and practical exam before ~~their~~ his or her driver's license is issued.

OR, NOR, AND When two or more singular antecedents are joined by *or* or *nor*, use a singular personal pronoun. Use a plural personal pronoun when two or more antecedents are joined by *and*.

> Either Mary <u>or</u> Susie will sign up for ~~their~~ her violin lessons.
>
> Dave <u>and</u> Charlie wish that ~~he~~ they could play the saxophone as well as Carlos.

INDEFINITE PRONOUNS When a plural indefinite pronoun is an antecedent, use a plural personal pronoun to agree with it. When a singular indefinite pronoun is the antecedent, use a singular personal pronoun to agree with it.

> <u>All</u> of the girls left ~~her~~ their sheet music at home.
>
> <u>One</u> of the female musicians had ~~their~~ her clarinet tuned before the concert.

✔ Check It

Use a current or completed draft of your work to practice pronoun-antecedent agreement.

✔ **READ** carefully. Take time to read your draft carefully. For a double-check, have someone else read your work.

✔ **IDENTIFY** possible mistakes. Mark any pronouns that do not agree with their antecedents in a sentence.

✔ **USE** your textbook. Consult the grammar section of your textbook if you are not sure whether your pronouns and antecedents agree.

Tech Tip

When you cut and paste text from one sentence to another, check that the pronouns agree with the antecedent in the new sentence you create.

LEARN MORE

- See Chapter 19, Agreement, pages 491–504
- See Writing Coach Online

GAME PLAN Quotations should flow smoothly into the sentences that surround them. Add explanatory information to link quotes to the rest of your work.

QUOTE IN A SENTENCE Prepare the reader for the information contained in the quote by introducing the quote's idea.

In her book review, the critic ∧spoke about the conclusion: "The ending was abrupt and did not provide closure for each of the character's lives" (24).

Victoria ∧says that highly motivated students should be recognized: **"We need to take time to notice the students who do their best in the classroom."**

QUOTE AS A SENTENCE Place an introductory phrase before or after a quotation that stands alone. In most cases, this phrase should identify the quote's author or speaker.

∧According to Mr. Thompson, "The cost of attending a private school is steadily increasing" (Thompson 12).

Tech Tip

When you cut a quote from one sentence and paste it in another, remember to revise the surrounding sentence to integrate the quote into the text.

LEARN MORE
- See Chapter 23, Punctuation, pages 593–599
- See Writing Coach Online

✔ Check It

Use a current or completed draft of your work to practice integrating quotations.

✔ **SCAN Mentor Texts.** Notice how professional writers integrate quotations into their work.

✔ **IDENTIFY quotes.** Mark each quote in your work. Does each quote flow smoothly with the surrounding sentence?

✔ **REVISE your sentences.** Add explanatory information and introductions as needed.

GAME PLAN Use hyphens correctly in your writing, including with compound words and compound adjectives.

COMPOUND WORDS Hyphens can connect two or more words that are used as one compound word. Some compound words do not require a hyphen. Check a current dictionary if you are unsure about hyphenating a word.

That ~~highrise~~ˌhigh-rise building is the newest ~~sky-scraper~~ˌskyscraper in the city.

My ~~step-mother~~ˌstepmother went to the ~~parentteacher~~ˌparent-teacher conference.

COMPOUND ADJECTIVES A compound adjective that appears before a noun should be hyphenated. Remember not to hyphenate a compound proper noun acting as an adjective.

The blueˌeyed dog was the prettiest I have ever seen.

The World War II attack on Pearl Harbor occurred in 1941.

Tech Tip

The automatic hyphenation setting in word processors causes words that break at the end of a line of text to hyphenate automatically. Be sure to turn off this setting when you are writing a standard essay.

LEARN MORE
• See Chapter 23, Punctuation, pages 605–611
• See Writing Coach Online

✔ *Check It*

Use a current or completed draft of your work to practice hyphenating words.

✔ **IDENTIFY** possible errors. Mark any compound adjectives before a noun that are not hyphenated.

✔ **REVISE** your sentences. Add a hyphen to words that should be hyphenated.

✔ **USE** a dictionary. Consult a dictionary if you are not sure if a word should be hyphenated.

20

Sentence Fragment

LEARN MORE

- See Chapter 14, Basic Sentence Parts, pages 339–342
- See Chapter 16, Effective Sentences, pages 407–411
- See Writing Coach Online

GAME PLAN Use complete sentences when writing. Make sure you have a subject and a complete verb in each and that each sentence expresses a complete thought.

LACKING A SUBJECT OR VERB A complete sentence must have a subject and a verb.

The doctor was known as the best pediatrician in town. ~~And~~ She always had a long list of patients to prove it!

The flamingo in the pond had been standing on one leg.

SUBORDINATE CLAUSE A subordinate clause cannot stand on its own as a complete sentence because it does not express a complete thought.

Ariel was chosen to be the team captain. ~~Because~~ because she was the most responsible person on the team.

Jordan decided to run for class treasurer. ~~Although~~ although he originally wanted to run for vice president.

✔ Check It

Use a current or completed draft of your work to practice writing complete sentences.

✔ **SCAN** your draft. Look for incomplete sentences.

✔ **IDENTIFY** missing words. Mark sentences that have missing subjects or verbs.

✔ **REVISE** your sentences. Rewrite any sentences that are missing subjects or verbs or that are subordinate clauses standing on their own.

CHAPTER 13

THE PARTS of SPEECH

Use each part of speech to help you build sentences that are meaningful and interesting.

WRITE GUY *Jeff Anderson, M.Ed.*

WHAT DO YOU NOTICE?

Uncover the parts of speech as you zoom in on these sentences from the myth "The Earth on Turtle's Back" retold by Michael Caduto and Joseph Bruchac.

MENTOR TEXT

> She was not as strong or as swift as the others, but she was determined. She went so deep that it was all dark, and still she swam deeper.

Now, ask yourself the following questions:

- How do the two coordinating conjunctions in the first sentence link parts of the sentence?
- What is the purpose of the coordinating conjunction *and* in the second sentence?

In the first sentence, the word *or* connects the phrases *as strong* and *as swift*. The word *but* connects the main clauses *she was not as strong or as swift as the others* and *she was determined*. In the second sentence, the word *and* connects the clauses *she went so deep that it was all dark* with another clause, *still she swam deeper*.

Grammar for Writers Pay attention to how each part of speech can help you craft memorable sentences. Less noticeable words like conjunctions and prepositions play just as important a role as prominent words like adjectives and adverbs.

I'm going to watch a movie or go to a friend's house.

Why not use and so that you can do both?

13.1 Nouns and Pronouns

Nouns and pronouns make it possible for people to label everything around them.

WRITING COACH

Online

www.phwritingcoach.com

Grammar Tutorials
Brush up on your Grammar skills with these animated videos.

Grammar Practice
Practice your grammar skills with Writing Coach Online.

Grammar Games
Test your knowledge of grammar in this fast-paced interactive video game.

Nouns

The word *noun* comes from the Latin word *nomen*, which means "name."

RULE 13.1.1 ➤ A **noun** is the part of speech that names a person, place, thing, or idea.

Nouns that name a *person* or *place* are easy to identify.

PERSON	Uncle Mike, neighbor, girls, Bob, swimmer, Ms. Yang, Captain Smith
PLACE	library, Dallas, garden, city, kitchen, James River, canyon, Oklahoma

The category *thing* includes visible things, ideas, actions, conditions, and qualities.

VISIBLE THINGS	chair, pencil, school, duck, daffodil, fort
IDEAS	independence, democracy, militarism, capitalism, recession, freedom
ACTIONS	work, research, exploration, competition, exercise, labor
CONDITIONS	sadness, illness, excitement, joy, health, happiness
QUALITIES	kindness, patience, ability, compassion, intelligence, drive

Concrete and Abstract Nouns

Nouns can also be grouped as *concrete* or *abstract*. A **concrete noun** names something you can see, touch, taste, hear, or smell. An **abstract noun** names something you cannot perceive through any of your five senses.

CONCRETE NOUNS	person, cannon, road, city, music
ABSTRACT NOUNS	hope, improvement, independence, desperation, cooperation

See Practice 13.1A

Collective Nouns

A **collective noun** names a *group* of people or things. A collective noun looks singular, but its meaning may be singular or plural, depending on how it is used in a sentence.

COLLECTIVE NOUNS			
army	choir	troop	faculty
cast	class	crew	legislature

Do not confuse collective nouns—nouns that name a collection of people or things acting as a unit—with plural nouns.

Compound Nouns

A **compound noun** is a noun made up of two or more words acting as a single unit. Compound nouns may be written as separate words, hyphenated words, or combined words.

COMPOUND NOUNS	
Separate	life preserver coffee table bird dog
Hyphenated	sergeant-at-arms self-rule daughter-in-law
Combined	battlefield dreamland porthole

Check a dictionary if you are not sure how to write a compound noun.

Common and Proper Nouns

Any noun may be categorized as either *common* or *proper*.
A **common noun** names any one of a class of people, places, or things. A **proper noun** names a specific person, place, or thing. Proper nouns are capitalized, but common nouns are not.
(See Chapter 22 for rules of capitalization.)

COMMON NOUNS	building, writer, nation, month, leader, place, book, war
PROPER NOUNS	Jones, Virginia, *Leaves of Grass,* Revolutionary War, White House, Mark Twain, France, June

A noun of direct address—the name of a person to whom you are directly speaking—is always a proper noun, as is a family title before a name. In the examples below, common nouns are highlighted in yellow, and proper nouns are highlighted in orange.

COMMON NOUNS	My **mom** is a **doctor** .
	Our **teacher** is always early.
	My favorite **person** is my **grandma** .
DIRECT ADDRESS	Please, **Dad** , tell us a story before bed.
	Dad , can you take me there?
	Eva , please bring your vegetable dip when you come to the party.
FAMILY TITLE	**Aunt Deb** works in Washington, D.C.
	Grandpa bakes great fruit tarts, and his apple tart is my favorite.
	My favorite person is **Grandma Jones** .

See Practice 13.1B

PRACTICE 13.1A Identifying and Labeling Nouns as Concrete or Abstract

Read each item. Then, label each item *concrete noun* or *abstract noun*, and write another similar concrete or abstract noun.

EXAMPLE   frustration

ANSWER   *abstract noun,* **exasperation**

1. coin
2. dreams
3. tennis racket
4. liberty
5. thought
6. information
7. beach
8. misery
9. toy
10. thrill

PRACTICE 13.1B Recognizing Kinds of Nouns (Collective, Compound, Proper)

Read each sentence. Then, write whether the underlined nouns are *collective*, *compound*, or *proper*. Answer in the order the words appear.

EXAMPLE   <u>Sam</u> is one of four kids in his <u>family</u>.

ANSWER   *proper, collective*

11. Kristen's <u>brother-in-law</u> was raised in <u>Kentucky</u>.
12. The <u>station wagon</u> is so large, the entire <u>squad</u> could almost fit in it.
13. <u>Burt</u> hiked all the way to the top of the inactive volcano.
14. In <u>Montreal</u>, it seems that you are in the <u>minority</u> if you don't like hockey.
15. The field looked far away to some of the <u>crowd</u>.
16. I had to take my <u>great-grandfather</u> to see a doctor.
17. There was a <u>swarm</u> of bees behind our house.
18. The restaurant was named *<u>Timmy's</u>* after the owner.
19. <u>Tony</u> reads the <u>newspaper</u> as soon as he gets home.
20. The <u>audience</u> cheered loudly for the singer.

SPEAKING APPLICATION

Take turns with a partner. Name an object in the room, and say abstract nouns that could be connected with it. Move on to another object and do the same.

WRITING APPLICATION

Using one common, one collective, one compound, and one proper noun from Practice 13.1B, write an original paragraph on any subject.

Pronouns

Pronouns help writers and speakers avoid awkward repetition of nouns.

RULE 13.1.2

> **Pronouns** are words that stand for nouns or for words that take the place of nouns.

Antecedents of Pronouns Pronouns get their meaning from the words they stand for. These words are called **antecedents.**

RULE 13.1.3

> **Antecedents** are nouns or words that take the place of nouns to which pronouns refer.

The arrows point from pronouns to their antecedents.

EXAMPLES   **Kristy** said **she** lost **her** list after the meeting.

When the **Woods** moved, **they** gave **their** furniture to me.

Attending the town concert was tiring, but **it** was fun!

Antecedents do not always appear before their pronouns, however. Sometimes an antecedent follows its pronoun.

EXAMPLE   Because of **its** history, **Jerusalem** , Israel, is my favorite city.

There are several kinds of pronouns. Most of them have specific antecedents, but a few do not.

See Practice 13.1C

Personal Pronouns The most common pronouns are the
personal pronouns.

> **Personal pronouns** refer to the person speaking
> (first person), the person spoken to (second person), or the
> person, place, or thing spoken about (third person).

RULE 13.1.4

PERSONAL PRONOUNS		
	SINGULAR	**PLURAL**
First Person	I, me my, mine	we, us our, ours
Second Person	you your, yours	you your, yours
Third Person	he, him, his she, her, hers it, its	they, them their, theirs

In the first example below, the antecedent of the personal
pronoun is the person speaking. In the second, the antecedent of
the personal pronoun is the person being spoken to. In the last
example, the antecedent of the personal pronoun is the thing
spoken about.

**FIRST
PERSON**   **My** name is not Greg.

**SECOND
PERSON**   When **you** left, **you** forgot **your** wallet.

**THIRD
PERSON**   The car is new, but **its** windows are dirty.

Reflexive and Intensive Pronouns These two types of pronouns
look the same, but they function differently in sentences.

> A **reflexive pronoun** ends in *-self* or *-selves* and indicates that
> someone or something in the sentence acts for or on itself.
> A reflexive pronoun is essential to the meaning of a sentence.
> An **intensive pronoun** ends in *-self* or *-selves* and simply adds
> emphasis to a noun or pronoun in the sentence.

RULE 13.1.5

REFLEXIVE AND INTENSIVE PRONOUNS		
	SINGULAR	PLURAL
First Person	myself	ourselves
Second Person	yourself	yourselves
Third Person	himself, herself, itself	themselves

REFLEXIVE   The children prepared **themselves** for the upcoming presentation.

INTENSIVE   Ricky Stanley **himself** wrote an account of the transformation.

See Practice 13.1D

Reciprocal Pronouns **Reciprocal pronouns** show a mutual action or relationship.

> The **reciprocal pronouns** *each other* and *one another* refer to a plural antecedent. They express a mutual action or relationship.

EXAMPLES   The two students quizzed **each other**.
The class shared their answers with **one another**.

See Practice 13.1E

Demonstrative Pronouns **Demonstrative pronouns** are used to point out one or more nouns.

> A **demonstrative pronoun** directs attention to a specific person, place, or thing.

There are four demonstrative pronouns.

DEMONSTRATIVE PRONOUNS	
SINGULAR	PLURAL
this, that	these, those

Demonstrative pronouns may come before or after their antecedents.

BEFORE **That** is the **country** I would like to visit.

AFTER I hope to visit **Texas** and **New Mexico** . **Those** are my first choices.

One of the demonstrative pronouns, *that*, can also be used as a relative pronoun.

Relative Pronouns

Relative pronouns are used to relate one idea in a sentence to another. There are five main relative pronouns.

> A **relative pronoun** introduces an adjective clause and connects it to the word that the clause modifies.

RULE 13.1.8

RELATIVE PRONOUNS				
that	which	who	whom	whose

EXAMPLES She watched a **movie that** portrayed a character's childhood memories.

The **writer who** had lived it explained her childhood.

The **vacation** , **which** they knew would be exciting, was quickly approaching.

See Practice 13.1F

Read each sentence. Then, write the antecedent of each underlined pronoun.

EXAMPLE   My mother told me to give my sister <u>her</u> books.

ANSWER   *sister*

1. As the boy made his way up the hill, <u>he</u> whistled.

2. Tony must get <u>himself</u> ready soon if <u>he</u> wants to make it to the game.

3. Martin <u>himself</u> admitted to hiding the ball.

4. The three sisters packed <u>themselves</u> plenty of supplies for <u>their</u> weekend at camp.

5. <u>Those</u> are the dishes Mom likes, but <u>she</u> isn't sure the colors are right.

6. We rode in a cab <u>whose</u> driver told us about the city.

7. Conor told <u>himself</u> that there was nothing <u>he</u> could do about the bad weather.

8. I saw the outraged bull tossing <u>its</u> head and kicking wildly.

9. Terik and Colleen, allow <u>yourselves</u> one hour to get there.

10. <u>These</u> are the watches Miguel likes best.

Read each sentence. Then, write each pronoun, and label it *personal, reflexive,* or *intensive.*

EXAMPLE   Lucas spoke to the professor and persuaded him to delay the quiz.

ANSWER   *him — personal*

11. Jim was surprised when he learned the truth.

12. Just imagine yourself in a foreign land.

13. She didn't know the coat was mine.

14. With their love for rolling around in mud, pigs themselves aren't very clean.

15. You owe yourself a night out on the town.

16. Scientists are surprised themselves when they discover new species.

17. Robin made his decision.

18. The children themselves were responsible for making breakfast.

19. Everyone has different talents, and running track is one of hers.

20. The vast majority of worker bees sacrifice themselves for their queen.

SPEAKING APPLICATION

Take turns with a partner. Tell about someone you would like to meet and why. Use three or more pronouns that refer to that person. Your partner should identify the pronouns and their antecedents.

WRITING APPLICATION

Write a paragraph about a trip you have taken, using personal, reflexive, and intensive pronouns in your paragraph.

PRACTICE 13.1E ▷ **Identifying Reciprocal Pronouns**

Read each sentence. Then, write the reciprocal pronoun in each sentence.

EXAMPLE   Linda and Fabio are going to help each other study for the midterms.

ANSWER   *each other*

1. The couple laughed at each other as they finished their meal.

2. My brothers and sisters are very fond of one another.

3. Talia and I have known each other for years.

4. Robert and Eileen wrote to each other for a long time.

5. I think we have learned a lot about one another this year.

6. Brian and Vallon supported each other through tough times.

7. They have each other, don't they?

8. We gave presents to one another.

9. Celia and Jennifer always say goodbye to each other.

10. They write to each other once a month.

PRACTICE 13.1F ▷ **Recognizing Demonstrative and Relative Pronouns**

Read each sentence. Then, write each underlined pronoun and label it *demonstrative* or *relative*.

EXAMPLE   <u>These</u> are my two favorite records.

ANSWER   *These* — demonstrative

11. The quarterback <u>who</u> played last night was a close friend.

12. Jackson's father gave him an old watch <u>that</u> he had worn.

13. Marla, <u>whose</u> car was in the shop, rode with us to the dance.

14. The play <u>that</u> the cast performed was written by Alexis.

15. <u>This</u> belongs to my best friend.

16. <u>That</u> is the upper section of the stadium.

17. <u>Those</u> are the new shoes I want to buy.

18. The community meeting, <u>which</u> started at 7:00, ended hours later.

19. <u>These</u> are the library books I still have to return.

20. Sandy, <u>whom</u> I met this summer, is joining me for dinner.

SPEAKING APPLICATION

Take turns with a partner. Describe the relationship between two friends in a book that you have read. Show that you understand reciprocal pronouns by using some in your description. Your partner should listen for and identify the reciprocal pronouns that you use.

WRITING APPLICATION

Write a paragraph describing an upcoming school event, using at least two demonstrative and two relative pronouns.

Interrogative Pronouns

Interrogative pronouns are used to ask questions.

RULE 13.1.9

> **An interrogative pronoun is used to begin a question.**

The five interrogative pronouns are *what*, *which*, *who*, *whom*, and *whose*. Sometimes the antecedent of an interrogative pronoun is not known.

EXAMPLE   **Who** picked up the cups for the party?

See Practice 13.1G

Indefinite Pronouns

Indefinite pronouns sometimes lack specific antecedents.

RULE 13.1.10

> **An indefinite pronoun refers to a person, place, or thing that may or may not be specifically named.**

INDEFINITE PRONOUNS				
SINGULAR			PLURAL	BOTH
another	everyone	nothing	both	all
anybody	everything	one	few	any
anyone	little	other	many	more
anything	much	somebody	others	most
each	neither	someone	several	none
either	nobody	something		some
everybody	no one			

Indefinite pronouns sometimes have specific antecedents.

NO SPECIFIC ANTECEDENT   **Each** brought one friend.

SPECIFIC ANTECEDENTS   **One** of the **students** didn't pass.

Some indefinite pronouns can also function as adjectives.

ADJECTIVE   **Few** authors are as famous as this one.

See Practice 13.1H

PRACTICE 13.1G > Recognizing Interrogative Pronouns

Read each sentence. Then, write the interrogative pronoun needed to complete the sentence.

EXAMPLE _____ needs a pen?

ANSWER *Who*

1. _____ of the Nelson boys plays soccer?

2. _____ led the symphony during the performance?

3. _____ led Tiffany to miss her brother's recital?

4. _____ was the total cost of your vacation?

5. _____ of the students came in late?

6. _____ 's going on?

7. _____ can we ask about adopting the kitten?

8. To _____ are you speaking?

9. _____ are those stickers?

10. _____ of the performances was canceled?

PRACTICE 13.1H > Identifying Indefinite Pronouns

Read each sentence. Then, write the indefinite pronoun(s) used in each sentence.

EXAMPLE All of the teachers met in the faculty staff room.

ANSWER *All*

11. Everyone had some of the fruit salad.

12. After the meeting, few of the attendees stayed to interview the speaker.

13. Most of the travelers were weary at the end of the day.

14. No one failed to make a contribution.

15. I believe that much could be accomplished at this point.

16. Does either of your backup plans sound reasonable?

17. Neither of the disks we had was formatted.

18. Everyone worked so hard during the campaign that no one left early.

19. Both of us agreed it should end in a tie.

20. There isn't much to do since everybody has finished.

SPEAKING APPLICATION

With a partner, take turns trying to find out what the other did over the weekend. Use interrogative pronouns in your questions.

WRITING APPLICATION

Rewrite sentences 11, 18, and 19, replacing the indefinite pronouns with different indefinite pronouns. Make sure that the new sentences still make sense.

13.2 Verbs

Every complete sentence must have at least one **verb**, which may consist of as many as four words.

RULE 13.2.1

A **verb** is a word or group of words that expresses time while showing an action, a condition, or the fact that something exists.

Action Verbs and Linking Verbs

Action verbs express action. They are used to tell what someone or something does, did, or will do. **Linking verbs** express a condition or show that something exists.

RULE 13.2.2

An **action verb** tells what action someone or something is performing.

ACTION VERBS

Deanna **read** about European cities.

The stereo **blared** the lyrics of the new CD.

We **chose** to visit Austin and Houston.

They **remember** the book about Israel.

The action expressed by a verb does not have to be visible. Words expressing mental activities—such as *learn, think,* or *decide*—are also considered action verbs.

The person or thing that performs the action is called the *subject* of the verb. In the examples above, *Deanna, stereo, we,* and *they* are the subjects of *read, blared, chose,* and *remember.*

A **linking verb** is a verb that connects its subject with a noun, pronoun, or adjective that identifies or describes the subject.

LINKING VERBS

The woman **is** a famous singer.

The chair **seems** to be clean.

The verb *be* is the most common linking verb.

THE FORMS OF *BE*			
am	am being	can be	have been
are	are being	could be	has been
is	is being	may be	had been
was	was being	might be	could have been
were	were being	must be	may have been
		shall be	might have been
		should be	shall have been
		will be	should have been
		would be	will have been
			would have been

Most often, the forms of *be* that function as linking verbs express the condition of the subject. Occasionally, however, they may merely express existence, usually by showing, with other words, where the subject is located.

EXAMPLE Dinner **is** on the table.

Other Linking Verbs A few other verbs can also serve as linking verbs.

OTHER LINKING VERBS		
appear	look	sound
become	remain	stay
feel	seem	taste
grow	smell	turn

EXAMPLES   The car **stayed** clean and unscratched.

The food **smelled** irresistible.

The dress **appeared** appropriate.

The situation on the field **remained** tense.

The teachers **grew** apprehensive.

Some of these verbs may also act as action—not linking—verbs. To determine whether the word is functioning as an action verb or as a linking verb, insert *am*, *are*, or *is* in place of the verb. If the substitute makes sense while connecting two words, then the original verb is a linking verb.

LINKING VERB   The air **felt** humid. (The air **is** humid.)

ACTION VERB   The gardener **felt** a moist raindrop.

LINKING VERB   The lemons **taste** sour. (The lemons **are** sour.)

ACTION VERB   I **taste** the oranges.

See Practice 13.2A
See Practice 13.2B

PRACTICE 13.2A > Identifying Action and Linking Verbs

Read each sentence. Write the action verb in each sentence.

EXAMPLE   The telephone rings in both offices.

ANSWER   *rings*

1. Mary grew cucumbers during the summer.
2. The injured man stumbled into the hospital.
3. Brian memorized the opening line of his speech.
4. The kitten raced around the living room.
5. I pushed open the squeaky, old door.

Read each sentence. Write the linking verb in each sentence.

EXAMPLE   Milk spoils quickly unless it is refrigerated.

ANSWER   *is*

6. The express bus may be late this evening.
7. Our dinner tasted delicious.
8. The accident victim remained alert.
9. Your behavior should have been less rude.
10. The huge dog was ferocious.

PRACTICE 13.2B > Distinguishing Between Action and Linking Verbs

Read each sentence. Write *action* or *linking* for each underlined verb.

EXAMPLE   He submitted his latest poems for the contest.

ANSWER   *action*

11. The flowers smelled delightful.
12. Federick leaned back in his chair.
13. Camilla repeatedly waved at Aaron.
14. The room seemed dark and oppressive.
15. The famished swimmers smelled the bacon and eggs.
16. Jose will buy lunch for the four of us.
17. The cat is the neighborhood stray.
18. You should be thinking about college.
19. Arabella seemed to be a talkative person.
20. Jake suffered through the grueling match.

SPEAKING APPLICATION

Take turns with a partner. Tell about a television show you saw recently. Your partner should listen for and name three action verbs that you use.

WRITING APPLICATION

Write four sentences, two sentences with action verbs and two sentences with linking verbs. Then, exchange papers with a partner and underline the verbs in your partner's sentences. Label each verb *action* or *linking*.

Transitive and Intransitive Verbs

All verbs are either **transitive** or **intransitive,** depending on whether or not they transfer action to another word in a sentence.

RULE 13.2.4

> A **transitive verb** directs action toward someone or something named in the same sentence. An **intransitive verb** does not direct action toward anyone or anything named in the same sentence.

The word toward which a transitive verb directs its action is called the *object* of the verb. Intransitive verbs never have objects. You can determine whether a verb has an object by asking *whom* or *what* after the verb.

TRANSITIVE   Felix **hit** the ball.
                  (Hit what? ball)

                  We **ate** the hummus.
                  (Ate what? hummus)

INTRANSITIVE   The cast **practiced** on the stage.
                  (Practiced what? [no answer])

                  The mother **shouted** quickly.
                  (Shouted what? [no answer])

RULE 13.2.5

> Because linking verbs do not express action, they are always intransitive. Most action verbs can be either transitive or intransitive, depending on the sentence. However, some action verbs can only be transitive, and others can only be intransitive.

TRANSITIVE   I **wrote** a postcard from Florida.

INTRANSITIVE   The editor **wrote** quickly.

| ALWAYS TRANSITIVE | European oranges **rival** those of America. |

See Practice 13.2C

| ALWAYS INTRANSITIVE | They **winced** at the sound of the thunder. |

Verb Phrases

A verb that has more than one word is a **verb phrase.**

> **A verb phrase consists of a main verb and one or more helping verbs.**

RULE 13.2.6

Helping verbs are often called auxiliary verbs. One or more helping verbs may precede the main verb in a verb phrase.

| VERB PHRASES | I **will be taking** an extended vacation in Italy.

I **should have been watching** when I ran down the stairs. |

All the forms of *be* listed in this chapter can be used as helping verbs. The following verbs can also be helping verbs.

OTHER HELPING VERBS			
do	have	shall	can
does	has	should	could
did	had	will	may
		would	might
			must

A verb phrase is often interrupted by other words in an sentence.

| INTERRUPTED VERB PHRASES | I **will** definitely **be taking** an extended vacation in Italy.

Should I **take** an extended vacation in Italy? |

See Practice 13.2D

PRACTICE 13.2C > Distinguishing Between Transitive and Intransitive Verbs

Read each sentence. Then, write *transitive* or *intransitive* for each underlined verb.

EXAMPLE	Keith placed the heavy metal box on his desk.
ANSWER	*transitive*

1. Clouds swirled near the top of the volcano.
2. After much delay, the judge rendered an unpopular decision.
3. For a good analysis, read *Understanding Fiction*.
4. Dimitri rehearsed his speech many times.
5. The runaway skateboard careened into a stone wall.
6. The orchestra began with a loud overture.
7. The townspeople took a siesta each afternoon.
8. The mother smiled at the infant in her arms.
9. The eel slid along the floor of the fishing boat.
10. The crew ate lunch under an old oak tree.

PRACTICE 13.2D > Recognizing Verb Phrases

Read each sentence. Then, write the verb phrase in each sentence.

EXAMPLE	By now, we should have been in Houston.
ANSWER	*should have been*

11. The police department has already been notified.
12. We can expect a letter from them in a month.
13. The flood has not blocked the main highway.
14. Their roles have not been clearly defined.
15. Will you remind them of our change in plans?
16. The hunting dogs were howling with excitement.
17. The horses could not jump the high hedges.
18. She might have won with a better partner.
19. The ship will be sailing soon.
20. Ying should have known better than that.

SPEAKING APPLICATION

Take turns with a partner. Say two sentences with a transitive verb and two sentences with an intransitive verb. Your partner should identify each type of verb.

WRITING APPLICATION

Rewrite sentences 12 and 13, keeping the subject but changing the verb phrases. Make sure the sentences still make sense.

13.3 Adjectives and Adverbs

Adjectives and **adverbs** are the two parts of speech known as *modifiers*—that is, they slightly change the meaning of other words by adding description or making them more precise.

Adjectives

An **adjective** clarifies the meaning of a noun or pronoun by providing information about its appearance, location, and so on.

> **An adjective is a word used to describe a noun or pronoun or to give it a more specific meaning.**

An adjective answers one of four questions about a noun or pronoun: *What kind? Which one? How many? How much?*

EXAMPLES **high-heeled** shoes (What kind of shoes?)

that car (Which car?)

five shirts (How many shirts?)

four inches of rain (How many inches?)

When an adjective modifies a noun, it usually precedes the noun. Occasionally, the adjective may follow the noun.

EXAMPLES The professor was **impressed** with my prior knowledge.

I considered the professor **impressed**.

An adjective that modifies a pronoun usually follows it. Sometimes, however, the adjective precedes the pronoun as it does in the example on the next page.

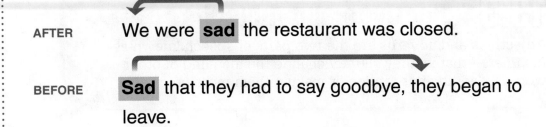

AFTER   We were **sad** the restaurant was closed.

BEFORE   **Sad** that they had to say goodbye, they began to leave.

More than one adjective may modify a single noun or pronoun.

EXAMPLE   We hired an **efficient, knowledgeable** manager.

Articles Three common adjectives—*a, an,* and *the*—are known as **articles.** *A* and *an* are called **indefinite articles** because they refer to any one of a class of nouns. *The* refers to a specific noun and, therefore, is called the **definite article.**

INDEFINITE EXAMPLES	DEFINITE EXAMPLES
a daisy	**the** stem
an orchid	**the** mask

Remember that *an* is used before a vowel sound; *a* is used before a consonant sound.

EXAMPLES   **a** one-stoplight town (*w* sound)

a universal feeling (*y* sound)

an honest pastor (no *h* sound)

See Practice 13.3A

Nouns Used as Adjectives Words that are usually nouns sometimes act as adjectives. In this case, the noun answers the questions *What kind?* or *Which one?* about another noun.

NOUNS USED AS ADJECTIVES	
flower	**flower** garden
lawn	**lawn** mower

See Practice 13.3B

Proper Adjectives Adjectives can also be proper. **Proper adjectives** are proper nouns used as adjectives or adjectives formed from proper nouns. They usually begin with capital letters.

PROPER NOUNS	PROPER ADJECTIVES
Monday	Monday morning
San Francisco	San Francisco streets
Europe	European roses
Rome	Roman hyacinth

Compound Adjectives Adjectives can be compound. Most are hyphenated; others are combined or are separate words.

HYPHENATED	**rain-forest** plants
	water-soluble pigments
COMBINED	**airborne** pollen
	evergreen shrubs
SEPARATE	**North American** rhododendrons

See Practice 13.3C

Pronouns Used as Adjectives Certain pronouns can also function as adjectives. The seven personal pronouns known as either **possessive adjectives** or **possessive pronouns** do double duty in a sentence. They act as pronouns because they have antecedents. They also act as adjectives because they modify nouns by answering *Which one?* The other pronouns become adjectives instead of pronouns when they stand before nouns and answer the question *Which one?*

> **A pronoun is used as an adjective if it modifies a noun.**

RULE
13.3.2

Possessive pronouns, demonstrative pronouns, interrogative pronouns, and indefinite pronouns can all function as adjectives when they modify nouns.

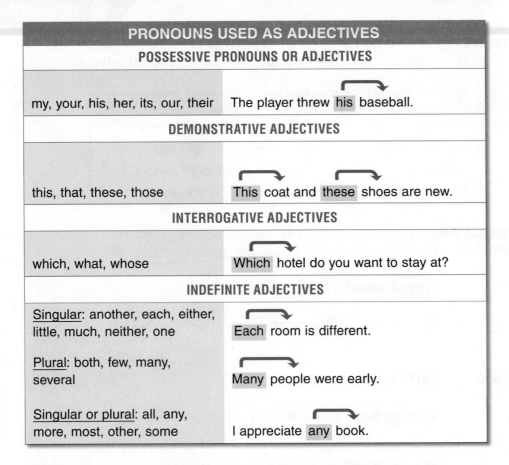

PRONOUNS USED AS ADJECTIVES

POSSESSIVE PRONOUNS OR ADJECTIVES	
my, your, his, her, its, our, their	The player threw his baseball.

DEMONSTRATIVE ADJECTIVES	
this, that, these, those	This coat and these shoes are new.

INTERROGATIVE ADJECTIVES	
which, what, whose	Which hotel do you want to stay at?

INDEFINITE ADJECTIVES	
Singular: another, each, either, little, much, neither, one	Each room is different.
Plural: both, few, many, several	Many people were early.
Singular or plural: all, any, more, most, other, some	I appreciate any book.

Verb Forms Used as Adjectives Verb forms used as adjectives usually end in *-ing* or *-ed* and are called **participles.**

EXAMPLE   I petted the **barking** puppy.

Nouns, pronouns, and verb forms function as adjectives only when they modify other nouns or pronouns. The following examples show how their function in a sentence can change.

	REGULAR FUNCTION	AS AN ADJECTIVE
Noun	The new floor was wet.	I sat on the floor mat.
Pronoun	This was a peaceful house.	This house was peaceful.
Verb	The rain melted the ice	The melted ice flooded the gutter.

See Practice 13.3D

> **PRACTICE 13.3A** **Recognizing Adjectives and Articles**

Read each sentence. Then, write the adjective(s) and the article(s) in each sentence.

EXAMPLE   I remember the man with the raspy voice.

ANSWER   *raspy; the, the*

1. The box with the yellow bow is a present.
2. An oral report is due next week.
3. A lizard has weak jaws.
4. The woman in the blue sneakers ran the fastest.
5. An error of judgment can result in bad consequences.
6. An author can also be a great illustrator.
7. A well-known theory is the theory of relativity.
8. The colorful sign above the desk inspires me.
9. The small children ran down a field in the rain.
10. The nurse spoke in a soft voice.

> **PRACTICE 13.3B** **Identifying Nouns Used as Adjectives**

Read each sentence. Then, write each noun that is used as an adjective and the noun that it modifies.

EXAMPLE   The school bus arrived.

ANSWER   *school, bus*

11. Next Monday is a vacation day.
12. The weather report called for snow today.
13. He received a laptop computer for his birthday.
14. This juice comes from Florida oranges.
15. My mother uses lots of household products.
16. My little sister enjoys story hour at the town library.
17. Dad picked up a magazine at the newspaper stand.
18. Magda put a spider crab in her metal bucket.
19. Our summer vacation is here at last.
20. Karell's new car has leather seats.

SPEAKING APPLICATION

Take turns with a partner. Tell about your favorite character from a book. Use different kinds of adjectives. Your partner should listen for and name the adjectives that you use.

WRITING APPLICATION

Write three sentences that have the following nouns: *weather*, *newspaper*, and *summer*. Then, write three additional sentences, using each noun as an adjective.

PRACTICE 13.3C ▸ Recognizing Proper and Compound Adjectives

Read each sentence. Then, identify each underlined adjective as *proper* or *compound*.

EXAMPLE   The <u>Navajo</u> weaver made a blanket.

ANSWER   *proper*

1. The quartet sang several <u>Irish</u> songs.
2. France is a part of the <u>European</u> continent.
3. We need to develop a <u>fund-raising</u> activity.
4. The class watched a <u>Victorian</u> drama today.
5. The vanilla yogurt had a <u>long-lasting</u> flavor.
6. You must reference an <u>up-to-date</u> encyclopedia.
7. My family visited a <u>Hawaiian</u> island last summer.
8. Woven <u>Peruvian</u> blankets are warm.
9. My mother enjoys reading <u>self-help</u> books.
10. We bought <u>Indian</u> rugs at the import store.

PRACTICE 13.3D ▸ Recognizing Pronouns and Verbs Used as Adjectives

Read each sentence. Then, write each pronoun or verb used as an adjective and the noun that it modifies.

EXAMPLE   The carpenter fixed the dilapidated roof.

ANSWER   *dilapidated, roof*

11. The wailing baby could be heard by all of the shoppers.
12. Some potters use a shaping tool.
13. The remaining contestants were nervous.
14. The smiling bridesmaid happily displayed her fragrant bouquet.
15. The tugboat saved the sinking ship.
16. This computer is very fast.
17. The attending physician examined twenty patients last night.
18. The race cars waited at the starting line.
19. These ingredients are for the birthday cake.
20. Several plants bloomed after the rain.

SPEAKING APPLICATION

Take turns with a partner. Say sentences using the following words as adjectives: *French*, *American*, *self-starting*, and *ever-lasting*. Your partner should identify the nouns as proper or compound.

WRITING APPLICATION

Write four sentences, include pronouns used as adjectives and verbs used as adjectives.

Adverbs

Adverbs, like adjectives, describe other words or make other words more specific.

> **An adverb** is a word that modifies a verb, an adjective, or another adverb.

RULE 13.3.3

When an adverb modifies a verb, it will answer any of the following questions: *Where? When? In what way? To what extent?*

An adverb answers only one question when modifying an adjective or another adverb: *To what extent?* Because it specifies the degree or intensity of the modified adjective or adverb, such an adverb is often called an **intensifier.**

The position of an adverb in relation to the word it modifies can vary in a sentence. If the adverb modifies a verb, it may precede or follow it or even interrupt a verb phrase. Normally, adverbs modifying adjectives and adverbs will immediately precede the words they modify.

ADVERBS MODIFYING VERBS	
Where? The puppy played outside. The puppy played there. The cat ran everywhere.	**When?** Sophie never ate her treats. Later, we toured the farm. The puppy chews the bone daily.
In what way? She quickly sold the puppy. She graciously let us hold her. Joe left quietly after the show.	**To what extent?** The landscapers still worked after dark. She always read with expression. Be sure you wash completely after playing.

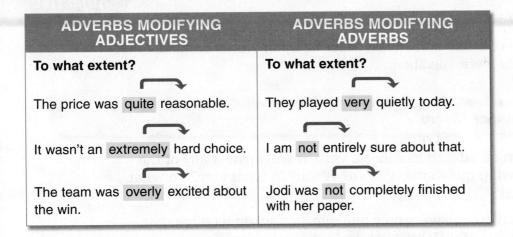

ADVERBS MODIFYING ADJECTIVES	ADVERBS MODIFYING ADVERBS
To what extent?	**To what extent?**
The price was quite reasonable.	They played very quietly today.
It wasn't an extremely hard choice.	I am not entirely sure about that.
The team was overly excited about the win.	Jodi was not completely finished with her paper.

Adverbs as Parts of Verbs Some verbs require an adverb to complete their meaning. Adverbs used this way are considered part of the verb. An adverb functioning as part of a verb does not answer the usual questions for adverbs.

EXAMPLES   The child **backed up** because she was scared.

Be sure to **point out** which painting is yours.

Jonathan had to **run out** to get some different color paints.

See Practice 13.3E

Nouns Functioning as Adverbs
Several nouns can function as adverbs that answer the questions *Where?* or *When?* Some of these words are *home, yesterday, today, tomorrow, mornings, afternoons, evenings, nights, week, month,* and *year.*

NOUNS USED AS ADVERBS	
NOUNS	**AS ADVERBS**
Afternoons are always slower.	I nap afternoons.
My week off was relaxing.	Let's go shopping this week.
Tomorrow will be a busy day.	I will see them tomorrow at the show.

Adverb or Adjective?

Adverbs usually have different forms from adjectives and thus are easily identified. Many adverbs are formed by the addition of *-ly* to an adjective.

ADJECTIVES   The father looked **happy**.

The dog ran through the **open** door.

ADVERBS   The father looked at his daughters **happily**.

Paul and I discussed our concerns **openly**.

Some adjectives, however, also end in *-ly*. Therefore, you cannot assume that every word ending in *-ly* is an adverb.

ADJECTIVES   an **elderly** person

a **lively** debate

a **leisurely** stroll

oily fish

Some adjectives and adverbs share the same form. You can determine the part of speech of such words by checking their function in the sentence. An adverb will modify a verb, adjective, or adverb; an adjective will modify a noun or pronoun.

ADVERB   The ceremony ran **late**.

ADJECTIVE   We enjoyed the **late** breakfast.

ADVERB   The bears walked **straight** through the camp.

See Practice 13.3F   ADJECTIVE   The line of students was **straight**.

PRACTICE 13.3E > Recognizing Adverbs

Read each sentence. Then, write the adverb in each sentence, and tell whether it modifies a *verb, adjective, or adverb.*

EXAMPLE   The man spoke sharply.

ANSWER   *sharply — verb*

1. The play was extremely funny.
2. Rafe was really trying to win.
3. We decided that we will go tomorrow.
4. That pitcher throws really hard.
5. James will probably call us.
6. Shawn runs quickly.
7. My grandparents are exceedingly generous.
8. I could hardly believe how the book ended.
9. The dog is unusually alert this evening.
10. News of the wedding traveled rapidly.

PRACTICE 13.3F > Identifying Adverbs and the Words They Modify

Read each sentence. Then, write the adverb in each sentence and the word it modifies.

EXAMPLE   Sammy's bike is very fast.

ANSWER   *very, fast*

11. She was nearly starving after the camping trip.
12. Mom is an extremely early riser.
13. I predict that our team will be hugely victorious.
14. My new computer arrived yesterday from the seller.
15. The dog ferociously ate his meal.
16. She laughed loudly.
17. We couldn't help arriving late.
18. Tatum seldom chats over the Internet.
19. I can barely see without my contact lenses.
20. The ecology club toiled hard to make Earth Day a success.

SPEAKING APPLICATION

Take turns with a partner. Tell about something that you enjoy doing. Your partner should name adverbs that you use.

WRITING APPLICATION

Use sentence 15 as a model to write three sentences of your own. Replace the adverb in sentence 15 with other adverbs.

13.4 Prepositions, Conjunctions, and Interjections

Prepositions and conjunctions function in sentences as connectors. **Prepositions** express relationships between words or ideas, whereas **conjunctions** join words, groups of words, or even entire sentences. **Interjections** function by themselves and are independent of other words in a sentence.

WRITING COACH

Online

www.phwritingcoach.com

Grammar Tutorials
Brush up on your Grammar skills with these animated videos.

Grammar Practice
Practice your grammar skills with Writing Coach Online.

Grammar Games
Test your knowledge of grammar in this fast-paced interactive video game.

Prepositions and Prepositional Phrases

Prepositions make it possible to show relationships between words. The relationships may involve, for example, location, direction, time, cause, or possession. A preposition may consist of one word or multiple words. (See the chart on the next page.)

> **A preposition** relates the noun or pronoun that appears with it to another word in the sentence.

RULE 13.4.1

Notice how the prepositions below, highlighted in pink, relate to the words highlighted in yellow.

LOCATION   Paintings **are displayed** **around** the **house**.

TIME   Some artists aren't **famous** **during** their **lifetimes**.

CAUSE   Karen is **late** **because of** the long **test**.

> **A prepositional phrase** is a group of words that includes a preposition and a noun or pronoun.

RULE 13.4.2

The noun or pronoun with a preposition is called the **object of the preposition.** Objects may have one or more modifiers. A prepositional phrase may also have more than one object. In the example below, the objects of the prepositions are highlighted in blue, and the prepositions are in pink.

EXAMPLE   Michael and Heather applied **for** a marriage **certificate** **on** **Monday**.

PREPOSITIONS			
aboard	before	in front of	over
about	behind	in place of	owing to
above	below	in regard to	past
according to	beneath	inside	prior to
across	beside	in spite of	regarding
across from	besides	instead of	round
after	between	into	since
against	beyond	in view of	through
ahead of	but	like	throughout
along	by	near	till
alongside	by means of	nearby	to
along with	concerning	next to	together with
amid	considering	of	toward
among	despite	off	under
apart from	down	on	underneath
around	during	on account of	until
aside from	except	onto	unto
as of	for	on top of	up
as	from	opposite	upon
atop	in	out	with
barring	in addition to	out of	within
because of	in back of	outside	without

See Practice 13.4A

Preposition or Adverb?
Many words may be used either as prepositions or adverbs.
Words that can function in either role include *around*, *before*,
behind, *down*, *in*, *off*, *on*, *out*, *over*, and *up*. If an object
accompanies the word, the word is used as a preposition.

PREPOSITION   My friends gathered **around** the dog.

ADVERB   The dog ran **around** and **around** .

See Practice 13.4B

PRACTICE 13.4A > Identifying Prepositions and Prepositional Phrases

Read each sentence. Then, write each prepositional phrase, and underline each preposition.

EXAMPLE   I saw a rabbit in the thicket.

ANSWER   *in the thicket*

1. In the evening, my friends and I finished unpacking.
2. Tina arrived early for the concert.
3. The trunk beside the bed is full of old treasures.
4. Long ago, my grandfather fished in this lake.
5. The reference books are on the first floor of the library.
6. With a beep of the car's horn, Mom got my attention.
7. You're the one with the incredible golf swing!
8. We were all tired after the long trip.
9. The students waited patiently at the door.
10. The ball rolled toward the fence.

PRACTICE 13.4B > Distinguishing Between Prepositions and Adverbs

Read each sentence. Then, label the underlined word in each sentence as *preposition* or *adverb*.

EXAMPLE   I showed the new student <u>around</u>.

ANSWER   *adverb*

11. She asked me to wait <u>outside</u>.
12. Cars lined up <u>outside</u> the train station.
13. We got confused and drove <u>past</u> the entrance.
14. As we waited at the red light, we were shocked to see an elephant run <u>past</u>!
15. Subway trains roared beneath our feet, and skyscrapers towered <u>above</u>.
16. We could hear the geese honking <u>above</u> the clouds.
17. We put our rain gear <u>on</u> quickly.
18. Ducks paddled peacefully <u>on</u> the pond.
19. The doghouse is <u>behind</u> the garden.
20. When you went home, you left your homework <u>behind</u>.

SPEAKING APPLICATION

With a partner, take turns describing the locations of objects in the room. Your partner should listen for and identify the prepositional phrases that you use and the preposition in each phrase.

WRITING APPLICATION

Write a sentence using the word *inside* as a preposition. Then, write another sentence using *inside* as an adverb.

Conjunctions

There are three main kinds of conjunctions: **coordinating, correlative,** and **subordinating.** Sometimes a type of adverb, the **conjunctive adverb,** is also considered a conjunction.

> A **conjunction** is a word used to connect other words or groups of words.

Coordinating Conjunctions The seven coordinating conjunctions are used to connect similar parts of speech or groups of words of equal grammatical weight.

COORDINATING CONJUNCTIONS						
and	but	for	nor	or	so	yet

EXAMPLES My sister **and** mother ran the shop.

Bonnie left late, **so** I waited for her.

Correlative Conjunctions The five paired correlative conjunctions join elements of equal grammatical weight.

CORRELATIVE CONJUNCTIONS		
both . . . and	either . . . or	neither . . . nor
not only . . . but also	whether . . . or	

EXAMPLES She was buying **both** a Yorkie **and** a poodle.

Neither Marco **nor** Liz came to the party.

I don't know **whether** to meet them for lunch **or** for dinner.

Subordinating Conjunctions Subordinating conjunctions join two complete ideas by making one of the ideas subordinate to, or dependent upon, the other.

SUBORDINATING CONJUNCTIONS

after	because	lest	till
although	before	now that	unless
as	even if	provided	until
as if	even though	since	when
as long as	how	so that	whenever
as much as	if	than	where
as soon as	inasmuch as	that	wherever
as though	in order that	though	while

The subordinate idea in a sentence always begins with a subordinating conjunction and makes up what is known as a subordinate clause. A subordinate clause may either follow or precede the main idea in a sentence.

EXAMPLES   We will be waiting for you at the airport **whenever** your plane arrives.

As soon as the speaker arrived, we started the lecture.

Conjunctive Adverbs Conjunctive adverbs act as transitions between complete ideas by indicating comparisons, contrasts, results, and other relationships. The chart below lists the most common conjunctive adverbs.

CONJUNCTIVE ADVERBS

accordingly	finally	nevertheless
again	furthermore	otherwise
also	however	then
besides	indeed	therefore
consequently	moreover	thus

Punctuation With Conjunctive Adverbs Punctuation is usually required both before and after conjunctive adverbs.

EXAMPLES   The exam was unusually hard. **Furthermore**, there were topics that we didn't cover in class.

Bonnie was an excellent sculptor; **however**, painting was her favorite medium.

I left early; **nevertheless**, I still got there late.

See Practice 13.4C
See Practice 13.4D
See Practice 13.4E

Interjections

Interjections express emotion. Unlike most words, they have no grammatical connection to other words in a sentence.

RULE
13.4.4

> An **interjection** is a word that expresses feeling or emotion and functions independently of a sentence.

Interjections can express a variety of sentiments, such as happiness, fear, anger, pain, surprise, sorrow, exhaustion, or hesitation.

SOME COMMON INTERJECTIONS				
ah	dear	hey	ouch	well
aha	goodness	hurray	psst	whew
alas	gracious	oh	tsk	wow

EXAMPLES   **Ouch**! Those peppers burned my mouth.

Wow! That was close!

Oh! I didn't see it.

Whew! What a relief to finish the long race.

See Practice 13.4F

Read each sentence. Then, write the conjunction in each sentence, and label it *coordinating*, *correlative*, *subordinating*, or *conjunctive*.

EXAMPLE   As soon as the rain stopped, we went out.

ANSWER   *As soon as* — subordinating

1. I wanted to go to the concert, but I could not.
2. Both my brother and my sister play soccer.
3. My cousin has been traveling since he graduated.
4. It began to snow; therefore, the game was canceled.
5. When the winner was announced, Gaby cheered.
6. My dog Comet follows me wherever I go.
7. He had to leave; otherwise, he'd miss his train.
8. Julio swam well; indeed, he won every race.
9. Either you tell me, or I'll find out from someone else.
10. I like living here because the ocean is nearby.

Write new sentences using the conjunctions and conjunctive adverbs provided.

EXAMPLE   not only . . . but also

ANSWER   *Not only the faculty but also the entire junior class saw Josh catch the football.*

11. yet
12. or
13. as if
14. neither . . . nor
15. furthermore
16. for
17. unless
18. however
19. whether . . . or
20. whenever

SPEAKING APPLICATION

Take turns with a partner. Tell about something that you did with a friend. Your partner should name conjunctions that you use and tell what kind of conjunction each one is.

WRITING APPLICATION

Write a paragraph comparing the features of two or more versions of a product you'd like to buy (for example, a cell phone). Use all four types of conjunctions in your analysis.

PRACTICE 13.4E > Using Different Conjunctions

Read each sentence. Write a conjunction that makes sense to fill in each blank. Then, identify the conjunction as *coordinating, subordinating, correlative,* or *conjunctive.*

EXAMPLE   I like pizza, _____ I really could not eat another bite.

ANSWER   *but — coordinating*

1. I will call Pat back _____ I eat dinner.

2. _____ you wear a life preserver, _____ you stay on shore.

3. _____ Jeff says he studied, his grade suggests otherwise.

4. Winnie walked the dog, _____ then she went to a movie.

5. Fred likes to stay up all night; _____, he became an astronomer.

6. _____ we can swim, _____ we can hike—the choice is yours.

7. _____ Kyle loves cauliflower, he planted a vegetable garden.

8. The food was _____ bad _____ expensive.

9. I waited days for good weather; _____, the sun came out.

10. Raul was determined to train daily, _____ he ran six miles in a downpour.

PRACTICE 13.4F > Supplying Interjections

Read each sentence. Then, write an interjection that shows the feeling expressed in the sentence.

EXAMPLE   _____, the cat got out!

ANSWER   *Oh, no*

11. _____, where did I leave my keys?

12. _____, is that someone famous?

13. _____! We won again!

14. _____, that salesperson is calling again!

15. _____, the queen has produced an heir!

16. _____! I don't approve of that behavior.

17. _____! I thought we'd never get out of there.

18. _____! I tripped and sprained my ankle.

19. _____, come in out of the rain.

20. _____, wait for me!

SPEAKING APPLICATION

Work with a partner. Take turns reading the sentences you completed in Practice 13.4E. Discuss how different conjunctions can change the meaning of a sentence.

WRITING APPLICATION

Write three sentences using interjections.

Test Warm-Up

DIRECTIONS
Read the introduction and the passage that follows. Then, answer the questions to show that you understand the function of conjunctions and interjections in reading and writing.

Ali wrote this paragraph about an ancient Roman city. Read the paragraph and think about conjunctions and interjections. When you finish reading, answer the questions that follow.

Pompeii

(1) In Italy, the town of Pompeii lay buried in the earth for centuries. (2) Pompeii was an ancient Roman city located near Mount Vesuvius, and it erupted in 79 A.D., covering the town in thick layers of ash. (3) Before the eruption, Pompeii was a prosperous trading town because it was situated on the Bay of Naples. (4) When the volcano began to erupt, most of the residents began to flee. (5) The town's inhabitants not only tried to escape by land but also tried to escape by sea. (6) Alas, with the overwhelming heat and amount of ash from the volcano, few people survived. (7) When archaeologists rediscovered the town in 1748, they found it well preserved, and it has since provided valuable insights into ancient Roman city life.

1 The word *and* in sentence 2 is a(n) —

   A coordinating conjunction

   B subordinating conjunction

   C correlative conjunction

   D interjection

2 The word *because* in sentence 3 is a —

   F coordinating conjunction

   G subordinating conjunction

   H correlative conjunction

   J conjunctive adverb

3 The phrase *not only . . . but also* in sentence 5 is a —

   A coordinating conjunction

   B subordinating conjunction

   C correlative conjunction

   D conjunctive adverb

4 The word *alas* in sentence 6 is a(n) —

   F coordinating conjunction

   G subordinating conjunction

   H conjunctive adverb

   J interjection

13.5 Words as Different Parts of Speech

Words are flexible, often serving as one part of speech in one sentence and as another part of speech in another.

Identifying Parts of Speech

To *function* means "to serve in a particular capacity." The function of a word may change from one sentence to another.

RULE 13.5.1

> **The way a word is used in a sentence determines its part of speech.**

The word *well* has different meanings in the following sentences.

As a Noun	The well was overflowing.
As a Verb	After winning the tournament, tears welled in Meena's eyes.
As an Adjective	Tia didn't feel well yesterday.

Nouns, Pronouns, and Verbs A **noun** names a person, place, or thing. A **pronoun** stands for a noun. A **verb** shows action, condition, or existence.

The chart below reviews the definition of each part of speech.

PARTS OF SPEECH	QUESTIONS TO ASK YOURSELF	EXAMPLES
Noun	Does the word name a person, place, or thing?	Their trip to Yellowstone Park delighted Tina.
Pronoun	Does the word stand for a noun?	They lent the car to him.

PARTS OF SPEECH	QUESTIONS TO ASK YOURSELF	EXAMPLES
Verb	Does the word tell what someone or something did? Does the word link one word with another word that identifies or describes it? Does the word show that something exists?	We played tennis. That game was fun. Our host appeared relaxed. Our guest is here.

See Practice 13.5A

The Other Parts of Speech An **adjective** modifies a noun or pronoun. An **adverb** modifies a verb, an adjective, or another adverb. A **preposition** relates a noun or pronoun that appears with it to another word. A **conjunction** connects words or groups of words. An **interjection** expresses emotion.

PARTS OF SPEECH	QUESTIONS TO ASK YOURSELF	EXAMPLES
Adjective	Does the word tell *what kind, which one, how many,* or *how much*?	Those two fruit bars have an unusual taste.
Adverb	Does the word tell *where, when, in what way,* or *to what extent*?	Go home. Apply now. Walk very slowly. I am extremely excited.
Preposition	Is the word part of a phrase that includes a noun or pronoun?	Behind the fence, the children were on the swings.
Conjunction	Does the word connect other words in the sentence or connect clauses?	Both Sara and I will cook because they need food; besides, it will be fun!
Interjection	Does the word express feeling or emotion and function independently of the sentence?	Hey, where's that from? Wow! That was a bargain!

See Practice 13.5B

PRACTICE 13.5A ▷ Identifying Nouns, Pronouns, and Verbs

Read each sentence. Then, label the underlined word *noun*, *pronoun*, or *verb*.

EXAMPLE   Ted lives in the biggest house in <u>our</u> neighborhood.

ANSWER   *pronoun*

1. The senior musical was a big <u>hit</u> with the community.

2. The pitcher threw the ball, and Eduardo <u>hit</u> it out of the park.

3. Bart said <u>he</u> doesn't like jazz music.

4. <u>We</u> have a question for the teacher.

5. I hope no one <u>spots</u> me here when I should be sleeping.

6. Mom says a leopard never changes its <u>spots</u>.

7. I am so glad <u>our</u> project is finished.

8. Stephen offered to take his little cousin to the <u>park</u>.

9. I'll wait here while you <u>park</u> the car.

10. Ask your friends if <u>they</u> want to come in.

PRACTICE 13.5B ▷ Recognizing All the Parts of Speech

Read each sentence. Then, write which part of speech the underlined words are in each sentence.

EXAMPLE   Rosa didn't win the award, but an article was written <u>about</u> her in the <u>newspaper</u>.

ANSWER   *preposition, noun*

11. Mom is home, <u>but</u> Dad is not.

12. Let's stop and <u>visit</u> our friends <u>while</u> we're here.

13. <u>Hey</u>, where were <u>you</u> earlier?

14. She got <u>home</u> at three, and she's been studying ever <u>since</u>.

15. We stayed up to watch the <u>late</u> movie.

16. I was on time, but you arrived <u>late</u>.

17. <u>After</u> the storm, the air was <u>very</u> still.

18. Dad will talk to <u>him</u> <u>after</u> we get home.

19. Ted had an <u>early</u> breakfast and headed to school.

20. Have you <u>finished</u> your assignments <u>yet</u>?

SPEAKING APPLICATION

Take turns with a partner. Tell about something that you did earlier today. Your partner should identify the nouns, pronouns, and verbs that you use.

WRITING APPLICATION

Write the part of speech of each word in sentence 18.

Pair strong subjects and verbs to form creative sentences, and use descriptive complements to add interest.

WRITE GUY *Jeff Anderson, M.Ed.*

WHAT DO YOU NOTICE?

Focus on sentence parts as you zoom in on these lines from Act 4 of the play *The Crucible* by Arthur Miller.

MENTOR TEXT

> **Danforth,** *suspiciously:* What is he about here?
> **Herrick:** He goes among them that will hang, sir. And he prays with them. He sits with Goody Nurse now. And Mr. Parris with him.

Now, ask yourself the following questions:

- What is the sentence fragment in these lines, and what is missing that makes it a fragment?
- What reason do you think the playwright had for using a sentence fragment here?

The sentence fragment in these lines is *And Mr. Parris with him.* Although the line has a subject, *Mr. Parris*, it lacks a verb to make it a complete sentence. Miller probably decided to use a sentence fragment here because he wanted the dialogue to sound natural. People often use sentence fragments in conversation.

Grammar for Writers When you are writing formally, it is best to use complete sentences. However, if you are writing dialogue, it is acceptable to use an occasional sentence fragment to echo real speech.

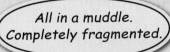

All in a muddle. Completely fragmented.

Know what you mean. Me too.

14.1 Subjects and Predicates

A **sentence** is a group of words that expresses a complete unit of thought. *The cereal in the bowl* is not a complete unit of thought because you probably wonder what the writer wanted to say about the cereal. *The cereal in the bowl is soggy*, however, does express a complete unit of thought.

RULE
14.1.1

> A **sentence** is a group of words that has two main parts: a complete subject and a complete predicate. Together, these parts express a complete thought or paint a complete picture.

The **complete subject** contains a noun, pronoun, or group of words acting as a noun, plus its modifiers. These words tell *who* or *what* the sentence is about. The **complete predicate** consists of the verb or verb phrase, plus its modifiers and complements. These words tell what the complete subject is or does.

COMPLETE SUBJECTS	COMPLETE PREDICATES
Snakes	slither.
A bell-clanging streetcar	moved through the turn.
Wood or cellulose	makes a delicious meal for a termite.
The candidate's approach to fiscal problems	impressed the voters attending the rally.

Sometimes, part of the predicate precedes the complete subject.

EXAMPLES   **At midnight , the cluster of stars**
                complete   complete subject

was visible .
predicate

Tonight my book club
complete   complete subject

visited a coffee shop .
predicate

See Practice 14.1A

WRITING COACH

Online
www.phwritingcoach.com

Grammar Tutorials
Brush up on your Grammar skills with these animated videos.

Grammar Practice
Practice your grammar skills with Writing Coach Online.

Grammar Games
Test your knowledge of grammar in this fast-paced interactive video game.

Simple Subjects and Predicates

The most essential parts of a sentence are the **simple subject** and the **simple predicate.** These words tell you the basics of what you need to know about the topic of the sentence. All of the other words in the sentence give you information about the simple subject and simple predicate.

> The **simple subject** is the essential noun, pronoun, or group of words that acts as a noun in a complete subject. The **simple predicate** is the essential verb or verb phrase in a complete predicate.

RULE 14.1.2

Note: When sentences are discussed in this chapter, the term *subject* will refer to a simple subject, and the term *verb* will refer to a simple predicate.

SUBJECTS	VERBS
Small shoes	fit nicely into the closets.
Many Broadway shows	have used colored lights to show effect.
Jars of honey	were hanging from the tree branch.
A colorful sign	covered the door.
The author's editor	published all of her books.
Studies of other cultures	have certainly revealed much about their lifestyles.

In the last example, the simple subject is *studies,* not *cultures; cultures* is the object of the preposition *of.* Objects of prepositions never function as simple subjects. In this same example, the simple predicate is a verb phrase. In addition, the word *certainly* is not part of the simple predicate because it does not provide essential information.

See Practice 14.1B

PRACTICE 14.1A ▷ Recognizing Complete Subjects and Predicates

Read each sentence. Then, rewrite the sentence, and draw a vertical line between the complete subject and the complete predicate.

EXAMPLE The player with the ball tagged the runner.

ANSWER *The player with the ball | tagged the runner.*

1. My friends are starting a business.

2. We will need a tent and some sleeping bags.

3. Arriving at the mall, we saw a crowd near the main entrance.

4. Everyone has an opportunity to get involved.

5. The beginning of the book was not very interesting.

6. The path across the desert was hot and dusty.

7. The pilot flew the hot-air balloon above the hilltops.

8. They learned to water ski on the lake this summer.

9. An old dog slept on the front porch.

10. My father has written many stories of his childhood.

PRACTICE 14.1B ▷ Identifying Simple Subjects and Predicates

Read each sentence. The complete subject is underlined. The rest of the sentence is the complete predicate. Write the simple subject and simple predicate.

EXAMPLE That girl on the diving board is in my Spanish class.

ANSWER *girl, is*

11. Three of us from the hiking club traveled across the country.

12. Mrs. Irwin finished painting her house today.

13. The price of that car is more than I can pay.

14. The tiny bird was rescued by one of our neighbors.

15. The temperature rarely falls below freezing in southern Florida.

16. Three homes on our block were recently sold.

17. Tanya wanted to e-mail her parents.

18. A child holding a paper bag stared up at me.

19. Too many errors have been left in this report.

20. A terrible blizzard took people by surprise that winter.

SPEAKING APPLICATION

Take turns with a partner. Tell about something interesting that happened to you. Your partner should tell the complete subject and complete predicate in each of your sentences.

WRITING APPLICATION

Write a paragraph about your favorite place to visit. In each sentence, underline the simple subject, and double underline the simple predicate.

Fragments

A **fragment** is a group of words that does not contain either a complete subject or a complete predicate, or both. Fragments are usually not used in formal writing. You can correct a fragment by adding the parts needed to complete the thought.

> A **fragment** is a group of words that lacks a subject or a predicate, or both. It does not express a complete unit of thought.

14.1.3 RULE

FRAGMENTS	COMPLETE SENTENCES
bowl of cherries (complete predicate missing)	The bowl of cherries was eaten quickly . (complete predicate added)
splash in water (complete subject missing)	Children splash in water. (complete subject added)
from the playground (complete subject and predicate missing)	Kids from the playground swarmed into the house . (subject and complete predicate added)

In conversations, fragments usually do not present a problem because tone of voice, gestures, and facial expressions can add the missing information. A reader, however, cannot ask a writer for clarification.

Fragments are sometimes acceptable in writing that represents speech, such as the dialogue in a play or short story. Fragments are also sometimes acceptable in elliptical sentences.

> An **elliptical sentence** is one in which the missing word or words can be easily understood.

14.1.4 RULE

EXAMPLES   Until June.

Why such an anxious face?

Locating Subjects and Verbs

To avoid writing a fragment, look for the subject and verb in a sentence. To find the subject, ask, "Which word tells *what* or *who* this sentence is about?" Once you have the answer (the subject), then ask, "What does the subject do?" or "What is being done to the subject?" This will help you locate the verb.

In some sentences, it's easier to find the verb first. In this case, ask, "Which word states the action or condition in this sentence?" This question should help you locate the verb. Then ask, "*Who* or *what* is involved in the action of the verb?" The resulting word or words will be the subject.

EXAMPLE   Dogs often eat dry and wet food.

To find the subject first, ask, "Which word or words tell what or whom this sentence is about?"

ANSWER   Dogs (*Dogs* is the subject.)

Then ask, "What do dogs do?"

ANSWER   eat (*Eat* is the verb.)

To find the verb first, ask, "Which word or words state the action or condition in the sentence?"

ANSWER   eat (*Eat* states the action, so it is the verb.)

Then ask, "Who or what eats?"

ANSWER   Dogs (*Dogs* is the subject.)

To easily locate the subject and verb, mentally cross out any adjectives, adverbs, and prepositional phrases you see. These words add information, but they are usually less important than the simple subject and verb.

EXAMPLE   ~~Our~~ **flowers** **should grow** ~~rapidly~~
           simple subject   verb phrase
           ~~in the next ten weeks.~~

Sentences With More Than One Subject or Verb

Some sentences contain a **compound subject** or a
compound verb, or a subject or verb with more than one part.

> **A compound subject** consists of two or more subjects. These
> subjects may be joined by a conjunction such as *and* or *or*.

14.1.5 RULE

EXAMPLES

The **campers** and **hikers** carried water bottles.

Cars, motorcycles , and **trucks** are all employing
new fuel technology.

Neither the **teacher** nor the **student**
looked happy.

> **A compound verb** consists of two or more verbs. These verbs
> may be joined by a conjunction such as *and, but, or,* or *nor*.

14.1.6 RULE

EXAMPLES

I neither **wrote** them nor **called** them.

Kelly **left** work and **ran** to dance class.

The baby **screamed** and **cried** through the
entire play.

Some sentences contain both a compound subject and a
compound verb.

EXAMPLES

Jill and **Peter** **planned** the party but
disagreed on what food to serve.

The **chef** and his **student** **eyed** their staff,
turned warily, and **walked** into the kitchen.

See Practice 14.1C
See Practice 14.1D

PRACTICE 14.1C > **Locating Subjects and Verbs**

Read each sentence. Then, write subjects(s) and verb(s) in each sentence. Underline the subject.

EXAMPLE   All of my relatives live and work in the Southwest.

ANSWER   *All; live, work*

1. Either Max or Ellen will get the best grade.
2. In this theater, the best seats are on the right.
3. The salad and drinks are in the refrigerator.
4. Pete mixed water into the paint and spread it on the canvas.
5. The thunder and lightning signaled a violent storm.
6. Haley gave it her best and won the contest.
7. Plumbers and electricians can make a very good living.
8. We left early and sped home.
9. They held a meeting on the first night of camp.
10. Bud made corn bread and took it to the party.

PRACTICE 14.1D > **Fixing Sentence Errors**

Read each fragment. Then, use each fragment in a sentence.

EXAMPLE   in the morning

ANSWER   *I eat breakfast in the morning.*

11. sang a song
12. the statue in front of the school
13. at lunch
14. another clean shirt
15. with my help
16. wrote a poem
17. at the beach
18. the truck
19. swam in the lake
20. our second try

SPEAKING APPLICATION

Take turns with a partner. Tell about your favorite possessions. Your partner should name the subject and the verb in each of your sentences.

WRITING APPLICATION

Write a fragment of your own. Use the fragment in three different sentences.

14.2 Hard-to-Find Subjects

While most sentences have subjects that are easy to find, some present a challenge.

Subjects in Declarative Sentences Beginning With *Here* or *There*

When the word *here* or *there* begins a declarative sentence, it is often mistaken for the subject.

> ***Here*** **and** ***there*** **are never the subject of a sentence.**

RULE 14.2.1

Here and *there* are usually adverbs that modify the verb by pointing out *where* something is located. However, *there* may occasionally begin a sentence simply as an introductory word.

In some sentences beginning with *here* or *there*, the subject appears before the verb. However, many sentences beginning with *here* or *there* are **inverted.** In an inverted sentence, the subject follows the verb. If you rearrange such a sentence in subject–verb order, you can identify the subject more easily.

INVERTED   There **are** the **groceries** . (verb–subject order)

REARRANGED   The **groceries** **are** there. (subject–verb order)

SENTENCES BEGINNING WITH *HERE* OR *THERE*	SENTENCES REARRANGED IN SUBJECT–VERB ORDER
There are the new condo buildings .	The new condo buildings are there.
Here is the ticket for the show.	The ticket for the show is here.
There is money in the jar.	Money is in the jar there.

> **In some declarative sentences, the subject is placed after the verb in order to give the subject greater emphasis.**

RULE 14.2.2

Because most sentences are written in subject–verb order, changing that order makes readers stop and think. Inverted sentences often begin with prepositional phrases.

SENTENCES INVERTED FOR EMPHASIS	SENTENCES REARRANGED IN SUBJECT–VERB ORDER
Toward the open doors rushed the hungry crowd.	The hungry crowd rushed toward the open doors.
Around the corner careened the racing bicyclist.	The racing bicyclist careened around the corner.

Subjects in Interrogative Sentences

Some interrogative sentences use subject–verb order. Often, however, the word order of an interrogative sentence is verb–subject.

EXAMPLES   Which **television gets** the best picture?
(subject–verb order)

When **are we** going there?
(verb–subject order)

In interrogative sentences, the subject often follows the verb.

An inverted interrogative sentence can begin with a verb, a helping verb, or one of the following words: *how, what, when, where, which, who, whom, whose,* or *why.* Some interrogative sentences divide the helping verb from the main verb. To help locate the subject, mentally rearrange the sentence into subject–verb order.

INTERROGATIVE SENTENCES	REARRANGED IN SUBJECT–VERB ORDER
Is the Museum of Art open this afternoon?	The Museum of Art is open this afternoon.
Do they own that boat?	They do own that boat.
Where will the party be held?	The party will be held where?

Subjects in Imperative Sentences

The subject of an imperative sentence is usually implied rather than specifically stated.

> In imperative sentences, the subject is understood to be *you*.

RULE 14.2.4

IMPERATIVE SENTENCES	SENTENCES WITH *YOU* ADDED
First, tour the movie studios.	First, [you] tour the movie studios.
After the tour, come back for the rides.	After the tour, [you] come back for the rides.
Peri, show me the park map.	Peri, [you] show me the park map.

In the last example, the name of the person being addressed, *Peri,* is not the subject of the imperative sentence. Instead, the subject is still understood to be *you*.

Subjects in Exclamatory Sentences

In some **exclamatory sentences,** the subject appears before the verb. In others, the verb appears first. To find the subject, rearrange the sentence in subject–verb order.

> In exclamatory sentences, the subject often appears after the verb, or it may be understood.

RULE 14.2.5

EXAMPLES   What **do they know**!
(**They do know** what.)

Come now!
(Subject understood: [**You**] come now!)

In other exclamatory sentences, both the subject and verb may be unstated.

EXAMPLES   Lightning! ([**You watch** out for the] lightning!)

See Practice 14.2A
See Practice 14.2B

Bear! ([**I see**] a bear!)

PRACTICE 14.2A >	Identifying Hard-to-Find Subjects

Read each sentence. Then, write the subject of each sentence.

EXAMPLE   Here is your new car!

ANSWER   *car*

1. There is a strange odor in here.
2. Has the last bus left yet?
3. Near the center of town is the old courthouse.
4. Where can my umbrella be?
5. Here is the tool you were looking for.
6. In the forest sleep wild animals.
7. There are no bananas in the kitchen.
8. Will someone be available to answer questions?
9. Beyond the house is a small pond.
10. There goes the last of the geese.

PRACTICE 14.2B >	Locating Hard-to-Find Verbs

Read each sentence. Then, write the verb in each sentence.

EXAMPLE   Look for Gary's house.

ANSWER   *Look*

11. Can you verify the facts from the case?
12. Why would anyone tell such bad jokes?
13. In the morning, wake up happy.
14. Before the game, show me your special pitch.
15. With great stealth, the animal stalked its prey.
16. During a hurricane, can lightning strike?
17. Hey, take the bread out of the oven!
18. Where are your parents?
19. Against the wall stood the tall ladder.
20. At dusk, turn on the lights.

SPEAKING APPLICATION

Take turns with a partner. Say sentences that describe someone doing something. Your partner should name the subject in each of your sentences.

WRITING APPLICATION

Write three imperative sentences. Underline the subject and double underline the verb in each sentence.

14.3 Complements

Some sentences are complete with just a subject and a verb or with a subject, verb, and modifiers: *The crowd cheered.* Other sentences need more information to be complete.

WRITING COACH

Online

www.phwritingcoach.com

Grammar Practice

Practice your grammar skills with Writing Coach Online.

Grammar Games

Test your knowledge of grammar in this fast-paced interactive video game.

The meaning of many sentences, however, depends on additional words that add information to the subject and verb. For example, although *The satellite continually sends* has a subject and verb, it is an incomplete sentence. To complete the meaning of the predicate—in this case, to tell *what* a satellite sends—a writer must add a **complement.**

> A **complement** is a word or group of words that completes the meaning of the predicate of a sentence.

RULE 14.3.1

There are five kinds of complements in English: **direct objects, indirect objects, object complements, predicate nominatives,** and **predicate adjectives.** The first three occur in sentences that have transitive verbs. The last two are often called **subject complements.** Subject complements are found only with linking verbs. (See Chapter 13 for more information about action and linking verbs.)

Direct Objects

Direct objects are the most common of the five types of complements. They complete the meaning of action verbs by telling *who* or *what* receives the action.

> A **direct object** is a noun, pronoun, or group of words acting as a noun that receives the action of a transitive verb.

RULE 14.3.2

EXAMPLES   I **visited** the **Kennedy Space Center**.

                        direct object

         Ice and **hail broke** the **gutters** this winter.

                                 direct object

Direct Objects and Action Verbs The direct object answers the question *Whom?* or *What?* about the action verb. If you cannot answer the question *Whom?* or *What?* the verb may be intransitive, and there is no direct object in the sentence.

EXAMPLES

The sprinters **can run** around the track.
(Ask, "Sprinters can run *what*?" No answer; the verb is intransitive.)

The top **spun** around the table.
(Ask, "The top spun *what*?" No answer; the verb is intransitive.)

RULE 14.3.3

In some inverted questions, the direct object may appear before the verb. To find the direct object easily, rearrange inverted questions in subject–verb order.

INVERTED QUESTION

Which **shows** **did** **they** **see**?
direct object

REARRANGED IN SUBJECT–VERB ORDER

They **did see** which **shows**?
direct object

Some sentences have more than one direct object, known as a **compound direct object.** If a sentence contains a compound direct object, asking *Whom?* or *What?* after the action verb will yield two or more answers.

EXAMPLES

The climbers **wore** **helmets** and
direct object
gloves.
direct object

The theater company **has performed** **plays**
direct object
and **musicals** around the country.
direct object

In the last example, *country* is the object of the preposition *around.* The object of a preposition is never a direct object.

348   **Basic Sentence Parts**

Indirect Objects

Indirect objects appear only in sentences that contain transitive verbs and direct objects. Indirect objects are common with such verbs as *ask, bring, buy, give, lend, make, show, teach, tell,* and *write.* Some sentences may contain a compound indirect object.

> An **indirect object** is a noun or pronoun that appears with a direct object. It often names the person or thing that something is given to or done for.

14.3.4 RULE

EXAMPLES   The **professor** **gave** the **student** the corrected
                                      indirect object
paper.
direct object

I **showed** my **cousin** and **friend** the new
                        compound indirect object
DVD.
direct object

To locate an indirect object, make sure the sentence contains a direct object. Then, ask one of these questions after the verb and direct object: *To* or *for whom?* or *To* or *for what?*

EXAMPLES   The **instructor** **taught** our **class** **yoga**.
(The instructor taught yoga *to whom*? ANSWER: our class)

We **bought** our **puppy** a **bed**.
(Bought a bed *for what*? ANSWER: our puppy)

An indirect object almost always appears between the verb and the direct object. In a sentence with subject–verb order, the indirect object never follows the direct object, nor will it ever be the object of the preposition *to* or *for.*

EXAMPLES   **Erin** **sent** the **book** to **me**.
                                direct object   object of preposition

Theo **sent** **me** the **DVD**.
              indirect object   direct object

Theo **gave** **Dan** a **review** of the song.
              indirect object   direct object

See Practice 14.3A
See Practice 14.3B

Object Complements

While an indirect object almost always comes *before* a direct object, an **object complement** almost always *follows* a direct object. The object complement completes the meaning of the direct object.

RULE 14.3.5

> An **object complement** is an adjective or noun that appears with a direct object and describes or renames it.

A sentence that contains an object complement may seem to have two direct objects. However, object complements occur only with such verbs as *appoint, call, consider, declare, elect, judge, label, make, name, select,* and *think.* The words *to be* are often understood before an object complement.

EXAMPLES   The **organizers** of the conference **declared** **it**
direct object

successful in the end.
object complement

The **coach** **appointed** **him** **captain**
          direct object   object
                          complement
of the team.

I **consider** **Bonnie** a loyal **friend** and
            direct object   object
                                  complement
sensitive **mother**.
object complement

Subject Complements

Linking verbs require **subject complements** to complete their meaning.

RULE 14.3.6

> A **subject complement** is a noun, pronoun, or adjective that appears with a linking verb and gives more information about the subject.

There are two kinds of subject complements: **predicate nominatives** and **predicate adjectives**.

Predicate Nominatives

The **predicate nominative** refers to the same person, place, or thing as the subject of the sentence.

> A **predicate nominative** is a noun or pronoun that appears with a linking verb and renames, identifies, or explains the subject. Some sentences may contain a compound predicate nominative.

14.3.7 RULE

EXAMPLES   **Tara Penn** **is** a **doctor** at the hospital.
predicate nominative

The **winner** of the show **will be** the **poodle** .
predicate nominative

Michael Stoll **was** a **coach** and
former **hockey player** .
compound predicate nominative

Predicate Adjectives

A **predicate adjective** is an adjective that appears with a linking verb. It describes the subject in much the same way that an adjective modifies a noun or pronoun. Some sentences may contain a compound predicate adjective.

> A **predicate adjective** is an adjective that appears with a linking verb and describes the subject of the sentence.

14.3.8 RULE

EXAMPLES   Your **reasoning** **seems** **fair** .
predicate adjective

The **soccer player** **was** **fast** .
predicate adjective

The **ocean** **sounded** **loud** and **fierce** .
compound predicate adjective

See Practice 14.3C
See Practice 14.3D

The navy **uniforms** **are** **blue** and **white** .
compound predicate adjective

Read each sentence. Then, write and label each direct object and indirect object.

EXAMPLE   The students brought posters.

ANSWER   *posters* — *direct object*

1. I promised James and Lara a trip to the park.

2. Tell the doctor your symptoms.

3. The teacher asked me a question.

4. Sasha bought a sweater and a pair of shoes.

5. Why did you tell him the secret?

6. Which program are you watching?

7. My family runs an Italian restaurant in the city.

8. Teach the children the poem.

9. What destination do you recommend?

10. After class, the teacher gave us the news.

Read each sentence. Then, write each indirect object. If a sentence does not have an indirect object, write *none*.

EXAMPLE   You should give Sue a call before noon.

ANSWER   *Sue*

11. Venetra handed Jerry a pencil in class.

12. Are you giving Marta a gift for her birthday?

13. Gonzalez threw a fastball to the new catcher.

14. Send me a text message when you arrive.

15. Justin handed his key to his sister.

16. Did Juanito lend you his MP3 player?

17. I put together a special playlist for him.

18. Heather borrowed Anita's suitcase for her trip.

19. You should sing us a song.

20. When Anna won the award, friends sent her flowers.

SPEAKING APPLICATION

Take turns with a partner. Tell about a family event. Your partner should name the direct object and indirect object, if any, in each of your sentences.

WRITING APPLICATION

Use sentence 19 in Practice 14.3B as a model to write a conversation between two people. Underline and label each direct and indirect object in your sentences.

PRACTICE 14.3C ► Locating Object and Subject Complements

Read each sentence. Then, write the complement, and label it *object complement* or *subject complement*.

EXAMPLE   The coach named Albert team leader.

ANSWER   *leader* — object complement

1. Mr. Johnson labeled the mail "First Class."

2. Suddenly, the old man seemed friendlier.

3. Sean became our neighbor last year.

4. Of all countries, India is the most beautiful.

5. Shelly painted her room blue.

6. Was the house unusual?

7. She remained my friend for many years.

8. He is extremely sensitive to heat.

9. The principal appointed Ravi spokesperson.

10. Our teacher often calls us brilliant.

PRACTICE 14.3D ► Identifying Complements

Read each sentence. Identify each direct object, indirect object, object complement, predicate nominative, and predicate adjective that you find.

EXAMPLE   Some people consider themselves leaders.

ANSWER   *themselves* — direct object; *leaders* — predicate nominative

11. My cat is crazy.

12. The club elected me president.

13. Crocheting became my favorite pastime.

14. Li sent Brenda a message.

15. The weather seemed chilly to me.

16. The judges named Rover the best of his breed.

17. The class awarded Ricardo a prize for best artist.

18. He is both a painter and a sculptor.

19. Bob told Joseph the secret.

20. Hugo grew bored with the TV show.

SPEAKING APPLICATION

Take turns with a partner. Describe something you did this week using direct objects, indirect objects, object complements (noun or adjective), predicate nominatives, and predicate adjectives. Your partner should identify the objects and predicates that you use.

WRITING APPLICATION

Use sentences 11 and 12 in Practice 14.3D as models to write similar sentences. Underline and label the complement in each of your sentences.

Test Warm-Up

DIRECTIONS

Read the introduction and the passage that follows. Then, answer the questions to show that you can use and understand the function of complements in reading and writing.

Adam wrote this paragraph about a basketball game in which he recently played. Read the paragraph and think about complements. When you finish reading, answer the questions that follow.

A Tense Moment

(1) We were trailing the Tornados by two points when Guillermo passed me the ball. (2) I was feeling tense right about then. (3) I was not the best shooter on the team and had, in fact, missed my last two shots. (4) With only seconds left in the game, I charged down the court. (5) Then I saw a clear shot, and I took it. (6) The ball made a beautiful arc into the basket—nothing but net! (7) Even though I am not an outside shooter, I had sunk a three-pointer. (8) People called me a hero for helping to win the game.

1 Which is the indirect object in the second clause of sentence 1?

  A Tornados

  B Guillermo

  C me

  D ball

2 In sentence 2, the word **tense** is a(n) —

  F predicate adjective

  G predicate nominative

  H direct object

  J object complement

3 In sentence 3, the word **shooter** is a(n) —

  A predicate adjective

  B predicate nominative

  C direct object

  D object complement

4 In sentence 8, the word **hero** is a(n) —

  F direct object

  G indirect object

  H object complement

  J predicate nominative

CHAPTER 15

PHRASES *and* CLAUSES

Combine related clauses into sentences to add variety to your writing, and include phrases that add vivid description.

WRITE GUY *Jeff Anderson, M.Ed.*

WHAT DO YOU NOTICE?

Hunt for phrases as you zoom in on this sentence from the book *Moby-Dick* by Herman Melville.

MENTOR TEXT

Silently obeying the order, the three harpooners now stood with the detached iron part of their harpoons, some three feet long, held, barbs up, before him.

Now, ask yourself the following questions:

- What participle modifies the noun *part* in the sentence?
- Which noun does the participial phrase *silently obeying the order* modify?

A participle is a form of a verb that can act as an adjective. In this sentence, *detached* is a participle that acts as an adjective modifying the noun *part*. The participial phrase *silently obeying the order* contains the present participle *obeying*; the entire phrase modifies the noun *harpooners*.

Grammar for Writers Writers can add or take away phrases and clauses to adjust their sentence lengths and to add information. Think of phrases and clauses as movable parts that help you form your sentences.

This adjective isn't enough on its own.

Well then, make it part of a phrase!

15.1 Phrases

When one adjective or adverb cannot convey enough information, a phrase can contribute more detail to a sentence. A **phrase** is a group of words that does not include a subject and verb and cannot stand alone as a sentence.

There are several kinds of phrases, including **prepositional phrases, appositive phrases, participial phrases, gerund phrases,** and **infinitive phrases.**

Prepositional Phrases

A **prepositional phrase** consists of a preposition and a noun or pronoun, called the object of the preposition. *Over their heads, until dark,* and *after the baseball game* are all prepositional phrases. Prepositional phrases often modify other words by functioning as adjectives or adverbs.

Sometimes, a single prepositional phrase may include two or more objects joined by a conjunction.

EXAMPLES between the **shower** and the **sink**
preposition   object   object

with the **sand** and the **ocean**
preposition object   object

beside the **grass** and **trees**
preposition   object   object

See Practice 15.1A

Adjectival Phrases
A prepositional phrase that acts as an adjective is called an **adjectival phrase.**

RULE 15.1.1

> An **adjectival phrase** is a prepositional phrase that modifies a noun or pronoun by telling *what kind* or *which one.*

ADJECTIVES	ADJECTIVAL PHRASES
An important book was displayed in the library.	A book of great importance was displayed in the library. *(What kind of book?)*
Mike had a chicken taco.	Mike had a taco with chicken. *(What kind of sandwich?)*

Like one-word adjectives, adjectival phrases can modify subjects, direct objects, indirect objects, or predicate nominatives.

**MODIFYING
A SUBJECT**

The house **across the road** is for sale.

**MODIFYING
A DIRECT OBJECT**

Let's take a picture **of the Empire State Building**.

**MODIFYING AN
INDIRECT OBJECT**

I gave the people **on the trolley** a tour.

**MODIFYING
A PREDICATE
NOMINATIVE**

Italy is a country **with many traditions**.

A sentence may contain two or more **adjectival phrases.** In some cases, one phrase may modify the object of the preceding phrase. In others, two phrases may modify the same word.

EXAMPLES

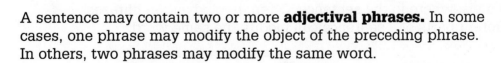

We bought tickets **for the rides** **in the park**.

The photograph **of the tree** **in the library** was beautiful.

Adverbial Phrases

A prepositional phrase that acts as an adverb is called an **adverbial phrase.**

RULE 15.1.2

> An **adverbial phrase** is a prepositional phrase that modifies a verb, an adjective, or an adverb by pointing out *where, why, when, in what way,* or *to what extent.*

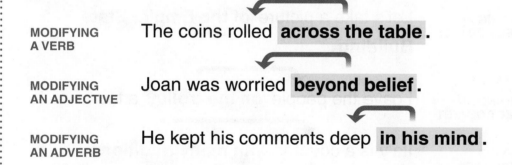

ADVERBS	ADVERBIAL PHRASES
She drove swiftly. (Drove *in what way?*)	She drove with speed.
I was scared then. (Scared *why?*)	I was scared by the loud noise.
The hawk flew overhead. (Flew *where?*)	The hawk flew over our house.

Adverbial phrases can modify verbs, adjectives, or adverbs.

MODIFYING
A VERB
The coins rolled **across the table**.

MODIFYING
AN ADJECTIVE
Joan was worried **beyond belief**.

MODIFYING
AN ADVERB
He kept his comments deep **in his mind**.

An adverbial phrase may either follow the word it modifies or be located elsewhere in the sentence. Often, two adverbial phrases in different parts of a sentence can modify the same word.

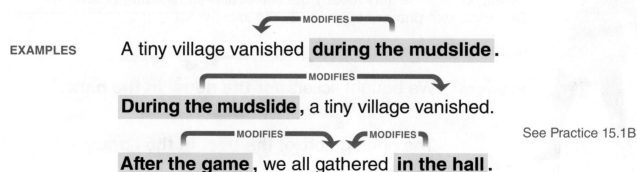

EXAMPLES

A tiny village vanished **during the mudslide**.

During the mudslide, a tiny village vanished.

After the game, we all gathered **in the hall**.

See Practice 15.1B

PRACTICE 15.1A ▷ **Identifying Prepositional Phrases**

Read each sentence. Write the prepositional phrase in each sentence and underline the preposition. Then, use the phrase in a sentence of your own.

EXAMPLE   The book cover on that novel is interesting.

ANSWER   *on that novel; I left the key on that novel.*

1. She wore a jacket of soft cashmere.
2. In the car, she began to sing softly.
3. I moved the trash cans across the driveway.
4. My parents arrived late for the gathering.
5. She worked on Tuesday.
6. The room in the attic is empty.
7. I remember the man with the big smile.
8. The children were hungry after the play date.
9. The jacket with the silver buttons is hers.
10. The hotels in Las Vegas are very large and ornate.

PRACTICE 15.1B ▷ **Identifying Adjectival and Adverbial Phrases**

Read each sentence. Write the adjectival or adverbial phrase. Then, label the phrase *adjectival* or *adverbial*. Finally, use the phrase in a sentence of your own.

EXAMPLE   You can make time for the things you want.

ANSWER   *for the things you want — adjectival; Sometimes you must wait for the things you want.*

11. A glass of water will satisfy your thirst.
12. Even ten years later, the memory still remains in my mind.
13. Gillian sat by the pool and read her magazine.
14. Conduct rules for all employees must be followed.
15. Vanessa will take the test on Monday.
16. The man in the black shorts ran the fastest.
17. The study of dinosaurs is fascinating.
18. Ryan left for Mexico.
19. Bruno was very excited about the good news.
20. The team with the red caps is ours.

SPEAKING APPLICATION

With a partner, take turns describing the location of the furniture in the classroom. Your partner should listen for the prepositional phrases that you use and indicate the function of each phrase (adjectival or adverbial) by telling the words that they modify.

WRITING APPLICATION

Show that you understand the function of adjectival and adverbial phrases. Write four sentences using adjectival and adverbial phrases. Explain the function of each phrase by identifying the word it modifies. Read your sentences to a partner, who should identify the phrases as you speak.

Practice   359

Appositives and Appositive Phrases

The term *appositive* comes from a Latin verb that means "to put near or next to."

Appositives Using **appositives** in your writing is an easy way to give additional meaning to a noun or pronoun.

RULE 15.1.3 ▷

> An **appositive** is a group of words that identifies, renames, or explains a noun or pronoun.

As the examples below show, appositives usually follow immediately after the words they explain.

EXAMPLES Some members, **the old-timers**, don't like change.

The home team, **the Panthers**, won the tournament title.

Notice that commas are used in the examples above because these appositives are **nonessential.** In other words, the appositives could be omitted from the sentences without altering the basic meaning of the sentences.

Some appositives, however, are not set off by any punctuation because they are **essential** to the meaning of the sentence.

EXAMPLES The poet **Lord Byron** was a British citizen.
(The appositive is essential because it identifies which specific poet.)

My neighbor **Beth** is a talented painter.
(The appositive is essential because you might have several neighbors.)

Note About Terms: Sometimes, the terms *nonrestrictive* and *restrictive* are used in place of *nonessential* and *essential.*

Appositive Phrases When an appositive is accompanied by its own modifiers, it is called an **appositive phrase.**

> An **appositive phrase** is a noun or pronoun with modifiers that adds information by identifying, renaming, or explaining a noun or pronoun.

15.1.4 RULE

Appositives and appositive phrases may follow nouns or pronouns used in almost any role within a sentence. The modifiers within an appositive phrase can be adjectives, adjective phrases, or other groups of words functioning as adjectives.

EXAMPLES   Mrs. Vanas, **my guidance counselor** , picked three colleges for me to visit.

Tara explained genetics, **the study of heredity and genes** .

ROLES OF APPOSITIVE PHRASES IN SENTENCES	
Identifying a Subject	Leonardo da Vinci, a famous artist, painted many murals.
Identifying a Direct Object	The chef prepared snails, a French delicacy.
Identifying an Indirect Object	I brought my cousin Isabella, a girl of seven, a DVD.
Identifying an Object Complement	I chose the color neon blue, an unusual color for a car.
Identifying a Predicate Nominative	My favorite snack is an orange, a citrus fruit.
Identifying the Object of a Preposition	Store the books in the basement, a cool, dry place.

Compound Appositives Appositives and appositive phrases can also be compound.

EXAMPLES   The entire team—**writers**, **editors**, and **designers**—worked on the book.

All books, **fiction** and **non-fiction**, are on sale at the store.

Casey visited her favorite cities, **London** and **Oslo**, on her summer vacation.

See Practice 15.1C

Grammar and Style Tip When **appositives** or **appositive phrases** are used to combine sentences, they help to eliminate unnecessary words. One way to streamline your writing is to combine sentences by using an appositive phrase.

TWO SENTENCES	COMBINED SENTENCE
New Jersey is located in North America. The state is an exporter of cranberries.	New Jersey, an exporter of cranberries, is located in North America.
The ballet was a sixteenth-century masterpiece. It was first seen in the French king's courts.	The ballet, a sixteenth-century masterpiece, was first seen in the French king's courts.
New York City is one of the busiest cities in the United States. It is located on the East Coast.	New York City, one of our busiest cities, is on the East Coast of the United States.

Read aloud the pairs of sentences in the chart. Notice how the combined sentences, which began as two choppy sentences, include the same information. However, they flow much more smoothly once the information in both sentences is clearly linked.

See Practice 15.1D

PRACTICE 15.1C Identifying Appositives and Appositive Phrases

Read each sentence. Then, write the appositive or appositive phrase in each sentence. Finally, identify the function of the phrase—explain which word it tells more about.

EXAMPLE Jackie's favorite team, the Bulldogs, won the championship game.

ANSWER *the Bulldogs; Jackie's favorite team*

1. Miss Smith, a music teacher, decided to play on Broadway.

2. My favorite cousin, a circus performer, lives far away.

3. I sold my old car, the Road Warrior.

4. My sister Tonya just graduated from college.

5. I stared at her face, a study of pride.

6. Her plants, all roses, are exquisite.

7. Gazpacho, a spicy soup, is my favorite.

8. Her favorite meal, roast chicken, will be served today.

9. Most people will never play polo, a challenging game.

10. My friends Tiffany and Jing are going with me.

PRACTICE 15.1D Using Appositives and Appositive Phrases

Read each pair of sentences. Then, combine the sentences using an appositive or an appositive phrase.

EXAMPLE Austin is a rapidly changing city. It is the capital of Texas.

ANSWER *Austin, a rapidly changing city, is the capital of Texas.*

11. Dr. Kim is retiring. She is our family doctor.

12. A box was in the basement. It was small but large enough for the gift.

13. The birds sat within a foot of the window. They were cardinals.

14. She suffers from claustrophobia. Claustrophobia is a fear of enclosed spaces.

15. We finally reached the campsite. It was a meadow surrounded by trees.

16. Her hobby is gardening. It keeps her busy.

17. Ecuador is a country in South America. It straddles the equator.

18. The prize was a plastic magnet. It disappointed me.

19. The dress is on the bed. It is my favorite.

20. My brothers are Dean and Michael. They are very different people.

SPEAKING APPLICATION

Take turns with a partner. Read aloud an article from a newspaper. Your partner should tell the function of the appositives and appositive phrases by indicating which words they tell more about.

WRITING APPLICATION

Write two sentences about the same subject. Then, combine the sentences with an appositive or an appositive phrase.

Verbal Phrases

When a verb is used as a noun, an adjective, or an adverb, it is called a **verbal.** Although a verbal does not function as a verb, it retains two characteristics of verbs: It can be modified in different ways, and it can have one or more complements. A verbal with modifiers or complements is called a **verbal phrase.**

Participles

Many of the adjectives you use are actually verbals known as **participles.**

> A **participle** is a form of a verb that can act as an adjective.

The most common kinds of participles are **present participles** and **past participles.** These two participles can be distinguished from one another by their endings. Present participles usually end in -ing *(frightening, entertaining).* Past participles usually end in -ed *(frightened, entertained),* but many have irregular endings, such as -t or -en *(burnt, written).*

PRESENT PARTICIPLES	PAST PARTICIPLES
The swaying boxer held his aching head.	Confused, Mary returned to her interrupted conference call.

Like other adjectives, participles answer the question *What kind?* or *Which one?* about the nouns or pronouns they modify.

EXAMPLES   Maggie's **tearing** eyes betrayed her happiness.
(*What kind* of eyes? Answer: *tearing* eyes)

The **broken** door needs to be replaced.
(*Which* door? Answer: *broken* door)

Participles may also have a **present perfect** form.

EXAMPLES   **Having decided**, Christina packed her bags.

Having greeted the press, the star walked into the awards show.

Verb or Participle? Because **verbs** often have endings such as -*ing* and -*ed,* you may confuse them with **participles.** If a word ending in -*ed* or -*ing* expresses the action of the sentence, it is a verb or part of a verb phrase. If it describes a noun or pronoun, it is a participle.

> A **verb** shows an action, a condition, or the fact that something exists. A **participle** acting as an adjective modifies a noun or a pronoun.

15.1.6 RULE

ACTING AS VERBS	ACTING AS ADJECTIVES
The cat is crying at the door. (What is the cat doing?)	The crying cat clawed at the door. (Which cat?)
The people were delighted with the new laws. (What delighted the people?)	Delighted, the people approved of the new laws. (What kind of people?)

Participial Phrases

A participle can be expanded by adding modifiers and complements to form a **participial phrase.**

> A **participial phrase** is a participle modified by an adverb or adverbial phrase or accompanied by a complement. The entire participial phrase acts as an adjective.

15.1.7 RULE

The following examples show different ways that participles may be expanded into phrases.

WITH AN ADVERB
Working quickly, we built the house in three weeks.

WITH AN ADVERB PHRASE
Working at a fast pace, we built the house in three weeks.

WITH A COMPLEMENT
Avoiding stops, we built the house in three weeks.

A participial phrase that is nonessential to the basic meaning of a sentence is set off by commas or other forms of punctuation. A participial phrase that is essential is not set off by punctuation.

NONESSENTIAL PHRASES	ESSENTIAL PHRASES
Here is Tina, waiting at the counter .	The girl waiting at the counter is Tina.
Built in 1800 , the bridge was the first in town.	The bridge built in 1800 is the one that needs the most repair.

In the first sentence on the left side of the chart above, *waiting at the counter* merely adds information about Tina, so it is nonessential. In the sentence on the right, however, the same phrase is essential because many different girls might be in view.

In the second sentence on the left, *Built in 1800* is an additional description of *bridge,* so it is nonessential. In the sentence on the right, however, the phrase is essential because it identifies the specific bridge that is being discussed.

RULE

15.1.8

Participial phrases can often be used to combine information from two sentences into one.

TWO SENTENCES
We were exhausted from the ride to California.
We rested by the side of the road.

COMBINED
Exhausted by the ride to California ,
we rested by the side of the road.

TWO SENTENCES
We ate dinner. We shared stories about our day.

COMBINED
Eating dinner , we shared stories about our day.

See Practice 15.1E
See Practice 15.1F

Notice how part of the verb in one sentence is changed into a participle in the combined sentence.

PRACTICE 15.1E ▷ Identifying Verbal Phrases

Read each sentence. Then, write the verbal phrase and the word it modifies.

EXAMPLE   Walking quickly, we soon reached our car.

ANSWER   *Walking quickly, we*

1. Searching in the dark, Ann finally found the light switch.
2. The manager, arriving at ten, will unlock the door.
3. The well-known performer, contacted at home, answered all the questions.
4. This tale, first told to me by my mother, has always been my favorite.
5. A dog named Norbert walked across the state to find his family.
6. The highest peak in North America is Mount McKinley, located in Alaska.
7. Exhausted by the rehearsal, the actor took a long nap.
8. Hitting the shelf, I almost knocked over the glass.
9. The contest, lasting all day and night, finally came to an end.
10. Carla, having auditioned yesterday, waited eagerly for the results.

PRACTICE 15.1F ▷ Recognizing Participial Phrases

Read each sentence. Write the participial phrase in each sentence. Then, write *E* for *essential* or *N* for *nonessential*. Finally, use the phrase in a new sentence of your own.

EXAMPLE   Chosen by her peers, Natalie was the recipient of the award.

ANSWER   *Chosen by her peers — N;*
Chosen by her peers, Tasha became class president.

11. Painting quickly, he completed the mural.
12. Shivering with fright, the puppy was lost.
13. The first important invention made by Einstein advanced telegraphy.
14. Having won by a landslide, the team cheered.
15. The key witness, protected by guards, entered the room.
16. The White House, built on swampland, has sunk one-quarter inch in thirty years.
17. Weighing over one hundred pounds, the pumpkin was sold at auction.
18. The chef, having added olive oil, put the vegetables in the oven.
19. Impeached by the panel, the disgraced politician headed home.
20. Expecting good news, I answered the phone.

SPEAKING APPLICATION

With a partner, take turns telling about your favorite after-school activities. Your partner should identify the verbal phrases that you use and indicate the function of each by telling the words that they modify.

WRITING APPLICATION

Write three sentences with nonessential phrases and three sentences with essential phrases. Then, rewrite the sentences so that the nonessential phrases become essential phrases and the essential phrases become nonessential phrases.

Gerunds

Many nouns that end in -ing are actually **verbals** known as **gerunds.** Gerunds are not difficult to recognize: They always end in -ing, and they always function as **nouns.**

RULE 15.1.9

> A **gerund** is a form of a verb that ends in **-ing** and acts as a **noun.**

FUNCTIONS OF GERUNDS	
Subject	Reading is my favorite pastime.
Direct Object	I enjoy reading.
Indirect Object	The coach gave running a new meaning.
Predicate Nominative	My sister's favorite activity is running.
Object of a Preposition	Their well-behaved horses showed signs of training.
Appositive	Dan's profession, acting, is very competitive.

Verb, Participle, or Gerund? Words ending in -ing may be parts of verb phrases, participles acting as adjectives, or gerunds.

RULE 15.1.10

> Words ending in **-ing** that act as **nouns** are called **gerunds.** Unlike verbs ending in **-ing**, gerunds do not have helping verbs. Unlike participles ending in **-ing,** they do not act as adjectives.

VERB	Gabby is **singing** in her seat.
PARTICIPLE	The **singing** girl is very joyful.
GERUND	**Singing** is very soothing.
VERB	My brother was **yelling**, and that upset me.
PARTICIPLE	**Yelling**, my brother upset me.
GERUND	My brother's **yelling** upset me.

Gerund Phrases Like participles, gerunds may be joined by other words to make **gerund phrases.**

> A **gerund phrase** consists of a gerund and one or more modifiers or a complement. These phrases act together as a noun.

15.1.11 RULE

GERUND PHRASES	
With Adjectives	His constant, angry ranting made the commander difficult to tolerate.
With an Adverb	Speaking loudly is not always a good idea.
With a Prepositional Phrase	Walking on the grass is prohibited here.
With a Direct Object	Blane was incapable of remembering the speech .
With an Indirect and a Direct Object	The literature professor tried giving her students praise .

Note About Gerunds and Possessive Pronouns: Always use the possessive form of a personal pronoun in front of a gerund.

See Practice 15.1G

INCORRECT	We never listen to **him** shouting.
CORRECT	We never listen to **his** shouting.
INCORRECT	**Them** refusing to wear knee pads is dangerous.
CORRECT	**Their** refusing to wear knee pads is dangerous.

Infinitives

The third kind of verbal is the **infinitive.** Infinitives have many different uses. They can act as nouns, adjectives, or adverbs.

> An **infinitive** is a form of a verb that generally appears with the word *to* in front of it and acts as a noun, an adjective, or an adverb.

15.1.12 RULE

The librarian asked the people **whisper**.

INFINITIVES USED AS NOUNS	
Subject	To teach requires practice and patience.
Direct Object	The prisoners decided to rebel.
Predicate Nominative	The girl's only option was to drive home.
Object of a Preposition	I have no goal in life except to sing.
Appositive	You have only one option, to wait.

Unlike gerunds, infinitives can also act as adjectives and adverbs.

INFINITIVES USED AS MODIFIERS	
Adjective	The team showed a willingness to cooperate.
Adverb	Some people were unable to sing.

Prepositional Phrase or Infinitive? Although both **prepositional phrases** and **infinitives** often begin with *to*, you can tell the difference between them by analyzing the words that follow *to*.

RULE 15.1.13

A **prepositional phrase** always ends with a noun or pronoun that acts as the object of the preposition. An **infinitive** always ends with a verb.

PREPOSITIONAL PHRASE	INFINITIVE
The students listened to the instructions.	The purpose of the headmaster is to instruct.
We went to the back of the store.	Make sure to back up your inventory list.

Note About Infinitives Without *to*: Sometimes infinitives do not include the word *to*. When an infinitive follows one of the eight verbs listed below, the *to* is generally omitted. However, it may be understood.

VERBS THAT PRECEDE INFINITIVES WITHOUT *TO*			
dare	help	make	see
hear	let	please	watch

EXAMPLES   He won't dare **[to] go** without a flight plan.

Please help me **[to] reach** the top shelf.

Bob helped Mike **[to] see** the game.

Infinitive Phrases Infinitives also can be joined with other words to form phrases.

> An **infinitive phrase** consists of an infinitive and its modifiers, complements, or subject, all acting together as a single part of speech.

15.1.14   RULE

INFINITIVE PHRASES	
With an Adverb	Tim's family likes to read quietly.
With an Adverb Phrase	To run on the sand is sometimes difficult.
With a Direct Object	Annie hated to leave San Francisco.
With an Indirect and a Direct Object	She promised to show us the video indirect direct object from her soccer game. object
With a Subject and a Complement	I want him to decide his own future. subject complement

See Practice 15.1H

PRACTICE 15.1G ▶ **Identifying and Using Gerunds and Gerund Phrases**

Read each sentence. Then, write the gerund or gerund phrase in each sentence. Tell how it functions in the sentence—as the *subject*, *direct object*, *subject complement*, and so on. Finally, use the gerund or gerund phrase in a sentence of your own.

EXAMPLE   Cooking together is a family tradition.

ANSWER   *Cooking together* — subject *is what my father and grandmother do best.*

1. Sailing has always been Nina's favorite activity.

2. He often talks about growing older.

3. Todd enjoys dancing to fast music.

4. Developing a new system is Pablo's dream.

5. I avoid eating too much sugar.

6. I was tired of waiting all day.

7. Working harder is usually the answer.

8. I just finished writing my short story.

9. The performer's best trick was juggling.

10. Ashley spent the afternoon babysitting her nephew.

PRACTICE 15.1H ▶ **Identifying and Using Infinitives and Infinitive Phrases**

Read each sentence. Then, write the infinitive phrase in each sentence. Tell how it functions in the sentence—as the *subject*, *direct object*, *subject complement*, and so on. Finally, use the phrase in a sentence of your own.

EXAMPLE   To win at chess requires skill.

ANSWER   *To win at chess* — subject *I have always wanted to win at chess.*

11. The magician's best trick was to saw a woman in half.

12. Would you like to see the new calves?

13. Nate was practicing daily to improve his typing.

14. Jane had hoped to win the contest.

15. To plan an exciting party is no easy task.

16. We would like to see the opera tomorrow.

17. Here are the directions to get to the park.

18. Elaine left to catch her flight to Oregon.

19. His daily goal, to run five miles, is not always possible.

20. I bought a new dress to wear to dinner.

SPEAKING APPLICATION

Take turns with a partner. Say sentences with gerund phrases. Your partner should identify each gerund phrase.

WRITING APPLICATION

Write three sentences with infinitive phrases about what you would like to do when you graduate.

15.2 Clauses

Every **clause** contains a subject and a verb. However, not every clause can stand by itself as a complete thought.

> **A clause** is a group of words that contains a subject and a verb.

RULE **15.2.1**

Independent and Subordinate Clauses

The two basic kinds of clauses are **independent** or **main clauses** and **subordinate clauses.**

> An **independent** or **main clause** can stand by itself as a complete sentence.

RULE **15.2.2**

Every sentence must contain an independent clause. The independent clause can either stand by itself or be connected to other independent or subordinate clauses.

STANDING ALONE

Mrs. Vera teaches grammar .
$\qquad$ independent clause

WITH ANOTHER INDEPENDENT CLAUSE

Mrs. Vera teaches grammar , and
$\qquad$ independent clause

her friend teaches writing .
$\qquad$ independent clause

WITH A SUBORDINATE CLAUSE

Mrs. Vera teaches grammar , while her friend
$\qquad$ independent clause $\qquad$ subordinate clause

teaches writing .

When you subordinate something, you give it less importance.

> A **subordinate clause,** although it has a subject and verb, cannot stand by itself as a complete sentence.

RULE **15.2.3**

Subordinate clauses can appear before or after an independent clause in a sentence or can even split an independent clause.

LOCATIONS OF SUBORDINATE CLAUSES	
In the Middle of an Independent Clause	The woman to whom I introduced you teaches English.
Preceding an Independent Clause	Unless the flood stops soon , the town will be underwater.
Following an Independent Clause	They asked that they be excused .

See Practice 15.2A

Like phrases, subordinate clauses can function as adjectives, adverbs, or nouns in sentences.

Adjectival Clauses

One way to add description and detail to a sentence is by adding an **adjectival clause.**

> **RULE**
> **15.2.4**
>
> An **adjectival clause** is a subordinate clause that modifies a noun or pronoun in another clause by telling *what kind* or *which one.*

An adjectival clause usually begins with one of the relative pronouns: *that, which, who, whom,* or *whose.* Sometimes, it begins with a relative adverb, such as *before, since, when, where,* or *why.* Each of these words connects the clause to the word it modifies.

> **RULE**
> **15.2.5**
>
> An **adjectival clause** often begins with a **relative pronoun** or a **relative adverb** that links the clause to a noun or pronoun in another clause.

The adjectival clauses in the examples on the next page answer the questions *What kind?* and *Which one?* Each modifies the noun in the independent clause that comes right before the adjectival clause. Notice also that the first two clauses begin with relative pronouns and the last one begins with a relative adverb.

EXAMPLES   I read the magazine **that you gave me**.

We gave skiing, **which we found challenging**, another try.

In England, we visited the town **where my mother grew up**.

Adjectival clauses can often be used to combine information from two sentences into one. By using adjectival clauses, you can indicate the relationship between ideas as well as add detail.

TWO SENTENCES	COMBINED SENTENCES
The artist set up her easel. The artist is ready to paint.	The artist, who is ready to paint, set up her easel.
My brother won the wrestling match in less than three minutes. He is on the varsity team.	My brother, who is on the varsity team, won the wrestling match in less than three minutes.

Essential and Nonessential Adjectival Clauses Adjectival clauses are set off by punctuation only when they are not essential to the meaning of a sentence. Commas are used to indicate information that is not essential. When information in an adjectival clause is essential to the sentence, no commas are used.

NONESSENTIAL CLAUSES	ESSENTIAL CLAUSES
One of Dickens's best characters is Pip, who is a main character in *Great Expectations*.	The project that everyone must complete by Wednesday promises to be challenging.
Jenna Vance, who studied every night for a week, passed the test.	A teacher who prepares faithfully usually finds teaching easy.

See Practice 15.2B

PRACTICE 15.2A > Identifying Independent and Subordinate Clauses

Read each sentence. Identify the underlined clause as *independent* or *subordinate*. Explain the function of each clause by telling whether it states a main idea all by itself or whether it adds more information to a main idea.

EXAMPLE   All the roads will be flooded <u>unless the storm stops soon</u>.

ANSWER   *subordinate—adds more information to a main idea*

1. <u>My older sister drives</u>, but my younger one does not.

2. My class has too many students now, but <u>that will change next week</u>.

3. <u>Since I left</u>, the town has changed a lot.

4. <u>As I walked up the stairs</u>, I felt optimistic.

5. <u>Lindsay loved the flowers</u> because they made the room smell sweet.

6. That book was not very good, but <u>I did enjoy the characters</u>.

7. Take the book to the publisher <u>who gives the best compensation</u>.

8. When the holiday season begins, <u>the stores are overflowing with buyers</u>.

9. Anyone <u>who wants a ride</u> needs to tell me now.

10. The roast <u>we are having for dinner</u> smells wonderful.

PRACTICE 15.2B > Identifying Adjectival Clauses

Read each sentence. Then, write the adjectival clause in each sentence. Explain the function of each clause by telling which word it modifies.

EXAMPLE   The book that you mentioned is sold out.

ANSWER   *that you mentioned; book*

11. The building, which we visited, is very old.

12. This is the architectural style that I prefer.

13. I bought the painting, which was on sale.

14. The man whom you described is my neighbor.

15. Sophie, who is in my science class, used to live in Singapore.

16. This is the table that I want.

17. The speaker who visited our school was very interesting.

18. I prefer a radio station that plays all types of music.

19. I used the printer that had plenty of ink.

20. The people who live on that street are kind.

SPEAKING APPLICATION

Take turns with a partner. Say three sentences from Practice 15.2A, changing the underlined clauses from subordinate clauses to independent clauses or from independent clauses to subordinate clauses.

WRITING APPLICATION

Write two sentences that could be combined with an adjectival clause. Exchange papers with a partner. Combine your partner's sentences with an adjectival clause.

Relative Pronouns **Relative pronouns** help link a subordinate clause to another part of a sentence. They also have a function in the subordinate clause.

> **Relative pronouns** connect adjectival clauses to the words they modify and act as subjects, direct objects, objects of prepositions, or adjectives in the subordinate clauses.

15.2.6 RULE

To tell how a relative pronoun is used within a clause, separate the clause from the rest of the sentence, and find the subject and verb in the clause.

FUNCTIONS OF RELATIVE PRONOUNS IN CLAUSES	
As a Subject	A bridge that is built on a strong foundation is built subject to last.
As a Direct Object	Kevin, whom my brother met in the military, is direct object an officer. (Reworded clause: my brother met *whom* in the military)
As an Object of a Preposition	This is the play about which I heard excellent reviews. object of a preposition (Reworded clause: I heard excellent reviews about *which*)
As an Adjective	The student whose behavior was in question spoke to adjective the principal.

Sometimes in writing and in speech, a relative pronoun is left out of an adjectival clause. However, the missing word, though simply understood, still functions in the sentence.

EXAMPLES   The generals [**whom**] we studied were great leaders.

See Practice 15.2C

The changes [**that**] they made were successful.

Relative Adverbs Like relative pronouns, **relative adverbs** help link the subordinate clause to another part of a sentence. However, they have only one use within a subordinate clause.

Relative adverbs connect adjectival clauses to the words they modify and act as adverbs in the clauses.

15.2.7

EXAMPLE The passenger yearned for the minute **when** she'd be off the ship.

In the example, the adjectival clause is *when she'd be off the ship.* Reword the clause this way to see that *when* functions as an adverb: *she'd be off the ship when.*

Adverbial Clauses

Subordinate clauses may also serve as adverbs in sentences. They are introduced by subordinating conjunctions. Like adverbs, **adverbial clauses** modify verbs, adjectives, or other adverbs.

Subordinate **adverbial clauses** modify verbs, adjectives, adverbs, or verbals by telling *where, when, in what way, to what extent, under what condition,* or *why.*

An adverbial clause begins with a subordinating conjunction and contains a subject and a verb, although they are not the main subject and verb in the sentence. In the chart that follows, the adverbial clauses are highlighted in orange. Arrows point to the words they modify.

ADVERBIAL CLAUSES	
Modifying a Verb	After you visit Houston, you should begin your report. (Begin *when?*)
Modifying an Adjective	Max seemed peaceful wherever he was. (Peaceful *where?*)
Modifying a Gerund	Driving a car if you have a license is legal. (Driving *under what condition?*)

> **Adverbial clauses** begin with **subordinating conjunctions** and contain subjects and verbs.

EXAMPLE   **Whenever** it snows, my dog loves to go outdoors.
            subordinating
            conjunction

Recognizing the subordinating conjunctions will help you identify adverbial clauses. The following chart shows some of the most common subordinating conjunctions.

SUBORDINATING CONJUNCTIONS			
after	because	so that	when
although	before	than	whenever
as	even though	though	where
as if	if	unless	wherever
as long as	since	until	while

Where an adverbial clause appears in a sentence can affect meaning.

EXAMPLES   **Before spring,** Tim made plans to visit Spain.

             Tim made plans to visit **before spring** .

Like adjectival clauses, adverbial clauses can be used to combine the information from two sentences into one. The combined sentence shows a close relationship between the ideas.

See Practice 15.2D
See Practice 15.2E
See Practice 15.2F
See Practice 15.2G
See Practice 15.2H

TWO   **It was stormy** . They did not go swimming.
SENTENCES

COMBINED   **Because** it was stormy, they did not go swimming.
             subordinating
             conjunction

PRACTICE 15.2C › Identifying Relative Pronouns and Adjectival Clauses

Read each sentence. Then, write the adjectival clause in each sentence, and underline the relative pronoun that introduces the clause. Finally, explain the function of each clause by telling which word it modifies.

EXAMPLE   The contest, which includes a free prize, is open to everyone.

ANSWER   *which includes a free prize — contest*

1. The badge that I earned last summer is in my closet.

2. My sister, whom you met last week, went back to college.

3. The theater, which is twenty miles away, is easily reached by train.

4. The manager who hosted the open house was happy with the large turnout.

5. The recipe that you asked for is in my cookbook.

6. The man who created this game is Irish.

7. The chicken that I roasted was delicious.

8. She is the person who works at the park.

9. The shirt, which costs only a few dollars, is pink.

10. The cup that holds pencils tipped over.

PRACTICE 15.2D › Recognizing Adverbial Clauses

Read each sentence. Then, write the adverbial clause in each sentence. Finally, explain the function of each clause by telling which word it modifies.

EXAMPLE   The principal will make his announcement when classes are over.

ANSWER   *when classes are over — make*

11. Everyone stopped talking when she walked into the room.

12. I will reply as soon as I get a chance.

13. We will take them swimming so that they can cool off.

14. She is upset when she misses her daily workout.

15. To be able to travel whenever you like is a luxury.

16. She is happy when she hears from you.

17. Because many people were confused, the president explained why we needed to pass the new law.

18. When everyone arrived, we began the show.

19. The front of the stage creaks when you step on it.

20. While riding the tram, he took lots of photographs of the scenery.

SPEAKING APPLICATION

Take turns with a partner. Tell about a book you have read recently. Use at least two adjectival clauses beginning with relative pronouns. Your partner should listen for and identify the relative pronouns that you use that answer *which*, *who*, and *whose*.

WRITING APPLICATION

For each of the relative adverbs *when*, *where*, and *why*, write a sentence using the relative adverb in an adverbial clause.

PRACTICE 15.2E **Identifying and Using Adjectival Clauses**

Read each sentence. Identify its adjectival clause and tell which word it modifies. Then, construct a clause of your own that starts with the same relative pronoun or relative adverb. Write a sentence using your new clause.

EXAMPLE   The pitcher, who was exhausted, threw a wild pitch.

ANSWER   *who was exhausted* — modifies <u>pitcher</u>
My brother, who is five years old, goes to kindergarten.

1. That's the spot where I last saw him.

2. The tree that I planted is now 20 feet tall.

3. My keys, which I had a minute ago, are missing.

4. Have you seen the new video game that gives players a workout?

5. Terri, whose bad temper is legendary, was surprisingly calm.

6. Mark, whom Serena usually beats at tennis, won the last match.

7. It was Ron who invented our new game.

8. Fish, which is one of my favorite foods, is nutritious.

9. The movie that we watched last night was boring.

10. Ms. Ramirez, whom I had called earlier, texted me.

PRACTICE 15.2F **Using Adjectival Clauses to Combine Sentences**

Read each pair of sentences. Write a new sentence that combines each pair by turning one sentence into an adjectival clause. Start the clause with the relative pronoun or adverb given. Tell which word the new clause modifies.

EXAMPLE   The chef specializes in Asian cooking. She just opened her own restaurant. (who)

ANSWER   *The chef, who specializes in Asian cooking, just opened her own restaurant.* (modifies <u>chef</u>)

11. This is the corner. We are to meet at 8. (where)

12. The paper is due today. It is on the desk. (that)

13. I upgraded my computer. It was working very slowly. (which)

14. You have met Julio. He is coming with us. (who)

15. You should e-mail the company. It sold you the bicycle. (that)

16. The man lives upstairs. He is loud. (who)

17. The play will be staged in April. It has roles for six actors. (which)

18. The vehicle hit the tree. The vehicle was a silver SUV. (that)

19. Omar is applying for a scholarship. Omar's grades are good. (whose)

20. The tree towered above the house. Its leaves had turned red. (whose)

SPEAKING APPLICATION

Describe a person using at least three adjectival clauses. Have a partner identify the adjectival clauses that you use.

WRITING APPLICATION

Write a paragraph about someone whom you admire. Use at least three adjectival clauses.

PRACTICE 15.2G Identifying and Using Adverbial Clauses

Read each sentence. Identify its adverbial clause and tell which word it modifies. Then, construct a clause of your own that starts with the same subordinating conjunction. Write a sentence using your new clause.

EXAMPLE   Before George ran, he drank water.

ANSWER   *Before George ran* — modifies <u>drank</u>
Before I got my driver's license, I walked everywhere.

1. John smiled when he saw Bernadette.

2. Because Raul forgot his wallet, he borrowed money from me.

3. Eric's shirt faded even though it was new.

4. Madison tripped while she ran for the bus.

5. Ty enjoys himself when he rides his horse.

6. I ask questions in class if I do not understand an assignment.

7. Children attend preschool until they are five years old.

8. Before we go to school, we eat breakfast.

9. Lin tapped her foot as she listened to music.

10. He has phoned once since he left.

PRACTICE 15.2H Using Adverbial Clauses to Combine Sentences

Read each pair of sentences. Write a new sentence that combines each pair by turning one sentence into an adverbial clause. Start the clause with the subordinating conjunction given. Then, tell which word the new clause modifies.

EXAMPLE   Emma left. It was getting late. (because)

ANSWER   *Emma left because it was getting late.* (modifies <u>left</u>)

11. Wash the dishes. You eat dinner. (after)

12. Call your mother. You arrive home. (when)

13. George stayed home. He hates crowds. (because)

14. The cat purred. Federico brushed it. (while)

15. Claire runs every day. She dislikes exercise. (even though)

16. She has a good idea. She writes it in her journal. (whenever)

17. Mandy practices the piano. She has time. (if)

18. Neil played music. His workout went faster. (so that)

19. Work on the test. Your teacher tells you to stop. (until)

20. She danced. He sang. (as)

SPEAKING APPLICATION

Take turns with a partner. Describe a concert or game using at least three adverbial clauses. Your partner should identify the adverbial clauses that you use and explain their function.

WRITING APPLICATION

Write a how-to paragraph. Do not use any adverbial clauses. Then, add at least three adverbial clauses to show connections between ideas. Compare your two drafts and comment on the differences between them.

Elliptical Adverbial Clauses Sometimes, words are omitted in adverbial clauses, especially in those clauses that begin with *as* or *than* and are used to express comparisons. Such clauses are said to be *elliptical*.

> An **elliptical clause** is a clause in which the verb or the subject and verb are understood but not actually stated.

15.2.10 RULE

Even though the subject or the verb (or both) may not appear in an elliptical clause, they make the clause express a complete thought.

In the following examples, the understood words appear in brackets. The sentences are alike, except for the words *she* and *her*. In the first sentence, *she* is a subject of the adverbial clause. In the second sentence, *her* functions as a direct object of the adverbial clause.

VERB UNDERSTOOD Her brother resembles their father more **than she [does]**.

See Practice 15.2I

SUBJECT AND VERB UNDERSTOOD Her brother resembles their father more **than [he resembles] her**.

When you read or write elliptical clauses, mentally include the omitted words to clarify the intended meaning.

Noun Clauses

Subordinate clauses can also act as nouns in sentences.

> A **noun clause** is a subordinate clause that acts as a noun.

15.2.11 RULE

A noun clause acts in almost the same way a one-word noun does in a sentence: It tells what or whom the sentence is about.

RULE 15.2.12

In a sentence, a noun clause may act as a subject, direct object, indirect object, predicate nominative, object of a preposition, or appositive.

EXAMPLES **Whatever you lost** can be found in the closet.

subject

My friends remembered **what I wanted to do on my birthday** .

direct object

The chart on the next page contains more examples of the functions of noun clauses.

Introductory Words

Noun clauses frequently begin with the words *that, which, who, whom,* or *whose*—the same words that are used to begin adjective clauses. *Whichever, whoever,* or *whomever* may also be used as introductory words in noun clauses. Other noun clauses begin with the words *how, if, what, whatever, where, when, whether,* or *why.*

RULE 15.2.13

Introductory words may act as subjects, direct objects, objects of prepositions, adjectives, or adverbs in noun clauses, or they may simply introduce the clauses.

SOME USES OF INTRODUCTORY WORDS IN NOUN CLAUSES	
FUNCTIONS IN CLAUSES	EXAMPLES
Adjective	She couldn't decide which dress was her favorite .
Adverb	We want to know how the game is played .
Subject	I want the pattern from whoever knitted that sweater .
Direct Object	Whatever my manager suggested , I did.
No Function	The doctor determined that she had passed .

Note that in the following chart the introductory word *that* in the last example has no function except to introduce the clause.

FUNCTIONS OF NOUN CLAUSES IN SENTENCES	
Acting as a Subject	Whoever is last must turn the lights out.
Acting as a Direct Object	Please tell whomever you want about the good news!
Acting as an Indirect Object	Her joyful personality made whoever met her smile.
Acting as a Predicate Nominative	The question is whether he will win or lose.
Acting as an Object of a Preposition	Use the DVD for whatever movie you would like.
Acting as an Appositive	The counsel rejected the plea that more money be given away to charity.

Some words that introduce noun clauses also introduce adjectival and adverbial clauses. It is necessary to check the function of the clause in the sentence to determine its type. To check the function, try substituting the words *it, you, fact,* or *thing* for the clause. If the sentence retains its smoothness, you probably replaced a noun clause.

NOUN CLAUSE	I said **that it was at 6 P.M**.
SUBSTITUTION	I said it.

In the following examples, all three subordinating clauses begin with *where,* but only the first is a noun clause because it functions in the sentence as a direct object.

NOUN CLAUSE	Mr. James told the players **where they would gather for the game**. (Told the players *what?*)
ADJECTIVAL CLAUSE	They took the player to the medical bench, **where a doctor examined his injury**. (*Which* bench?)
ADVERBIAL CLAUSE	She lives **where the weather is cloudy most days**. (Lives *where?*)

Note About Introductory Words: The introductory word *that* is often omitted from a noun clause. In the following examples, the understood word *that* is in brackets.

EXAMPLES	The teacher suggested **[that] I write my name in large print**.
	After her professor chose her for the debate team, Tia knew **[that] she would have a very busy year**.
	She remembered **[that] you wanted to run in the morning**.

See Practice 15.2J

PRACTICE 15.2I ▷ Identifying Elliptical Adverbial Clauses

Read each sentence. Then, write the adverbial clause in each sentence. For the adverbial clauses that are elliptical, add the understood words in parentheses. Finally, explain the function of each adverbial clause by telling which word it modifies.

EXAMPLE   My handwriting is neater than Julia's handwriting.

ANSWER   *than Julia's handwriting (is); neater*

1. The length of Mark's arms is shorter than the length of David's arms.

2. My braces will come off sooner than Juanita's braces.

3. Graham's sister is younger than Peter's sister.

4. Don's son is as tall as Don.

5. The cat ran faster than my dog.

6. The sidewalk is hotter than a frying pan.

7. That juice is as sour as a lemon.

8. That color is brighter than neon pink.

9. Nathalia's hair is as smooth as silk.

10. Alexa plays the piano as well as Drew.

PRACTICE 15.2J ▷ Recognizing Noun Clauses

Read each sentence. Then, write the noun clause and label it with its function—*subject, direct object, indirect object, object of a preposition, predicate nominative,* or *appositive.*

EXAMPLE   I wonder how he expects to leave.

ANSWER   *how he expects to leave* — direct object

11. This announcement is exactly what we anticipated.

12. My plan, that the team will practice every night, was rejected.

13. How the animals hunt every night is completely unknown.

14. Do you agree with what they recommend?

15. The repairman will show up on whatever day you indicate.

16. I agree with her idea, that we start another project.

17. Whatever time they set is probably too early.

18. A strict exercise routine is what Timothy needs.

19. Brenda gave whoever showed up all the prizes.

20. I think about how I can make them laugh.

SPEAKING APPLICATION

Take turns with a partner. Say sentences that include adverbial clauses. Your partner should listen for and identify each clause.

WRITING APPLICATION

Show that you understand the function of noun clauses. Write four sentences with noun clauses. Then, trade sentences with a partner. Identify the noun clauses in each other's sentences, and explain the part of speech it functions as.

15.3 The Four Structures of Sentences

Independent and subordinate clauses are the building blocks of sentences. These clauses can be combined in an endless number of ways to form the four basic sentence structures: **simple, compound, complex,** and **compound-complex.**

WRITING COACH

Online

www.phwritingcoach.com

Grammar Practice

Practice your grammar skills with Writing Coach Online.

Grammar Games

Test your knowledge of grammar in this fast-paced interactive video game.

RULE 15.3.1

> A **simple sentence** contains a single independent or main clause.

Although a simple sentence contains only one main or independent clause, its subject, verb, or both may be compound. A simple sentence may also have modifying phrases and complements. However, it cannot have a subordinate clause.

In the following simple sentences, the subjects are highlighted in yellow, and the verbs are highlighted in orange.

ONE SUBJECT AND VERB
The **athlete** **ran**.

COMPOUND SUBJECT
George and **Tom** **administered** the test.

COMPOUND VERB
The **car** **sputtered** and **stalled**.

COMPOUND SUBJECT AND VERB
Neither the **instructor** nor the **class** **felt** or **heard** the earthquake.

RULE 15.3.2

> A **compound sentence** contains two or more main clauses.

The main clauses in a compound sentence can be joined by a comma and a coordinating conjunction (*and, but, for, nor, or, so, yet*) or by a semicolon (;). Like a simple sentence, a compound sentence contains no subordinate clauses.

EXAMPLE
The **puppy** **carried** his bone into the yard, and **he** **dug** a hole to hide it.

See Practice 15.3A

RULE
15.3.3

A **complex sentence** consists of one independent or main clause and one or more subordinate clauses.

The independent clause in a complex sentence is often called the main clause to distinguish it from the subordinate clause or clauses. The subject and verb in the independent clause are called the subject of the sentence and the main verb. The second example shows that a subordinate clause may fall between the parts of a main clause. In the examples below, the main clauses are highlighted in blue, and the subordinate clauses are highlighted in pink.

EXAMPLES   No one answered the intercom when it buzzed .

The vase of flowers that the girl placed on the counter doesn't have any tulips .

Note on Complex Sentences With Noun Clauses: The subject of the main clause may sometimes be the subordinate clause itself.

EXAMPLE   That I wanted to leave bothered them .

RULE
15.3.4

A **compound-complex sentence** consists of two or more independent clauses and one or more subordinate clauses.

In the example below, the independent clauses are highlighted in blue, and the subordinate clause is highlighted in pink.

See Practice 15.3B
See Practice 15.3C
See Practice 15.3D

EXAMPLE   The dog barked when he saw a rabbit ,

and he ran through the trees after it .

PRACTICE 15.3A Distinguishing Between Simple and Compound Sentences

Read each sentence. Then, label each sentence *simple* or *compound*.

EXAMPLE   She will show up, or Don will call her parents.

ANSWER   *compound*

1. My younger brother plays on the tennis team, but my older one is in the band.

2. I am partial to foreign films; my best friend likes horror movies.

3. Have you finished your report on hurricanes?

4. Did Lacy order the shipment today, or will she do it tomorrow?

5. At the end of the cul-de-sac near the mail drop is an abandoned building.

6. In my town, most refuse is buried in a landfill, but the landfill is now in danger of overflowing.

7. The owl serves as a sign of the goddess Athena and wisdom.

8. Stacy and Art shoot hoops in the gym.

9. I earned every merit badge, so I received an award.

10. You could go to the grocery store, or you could pick up the dry cleaning.

PRACTICE 15.3B Identifying the Four Structures of Sentences

Read each sentence. Then, label each sentence *simple, compound, complex,* or *compound-complex*.

EXAMPLE   Layla ran into her bedroom.

ANSWER   *simple*

11. All the highways will be covered unless the snow stops soon.

12. I need to go to the library, but I'm feeling too tired to drive.

13. I looked for Dennis and Kenyon at the train station.

14. The audience in the courtroom is large now, but it will get smaller once the case ends.

15. I hope to start my own company, and I want to offer insurance to my employees.

16. Since I started, the processes have changed very little.

17. I enjoy a cup of tea in the morning.

18. You could act like a child, or you could clean up your mess.

19. This is the album that I have been hoping to find.

20. When I start my new job, I will sell my old car, and I will buy another one that is better on gas mileage.

SPEAKING APPLICATION

Take turns with a partner. Tell about your dream jobs. Use both simple and compound sentences. Your partner should listen for and identify each sentence as simple or compound.

WRITING APPLICATION

Write a paragraph about what you think you will be doing ten years from now. Your paragraph should include a variety of correctly structured sentences: simple, compound, complex, and compound-complex.

PRACTICE 15.3C Creating Simple and Compound Sentences

Read each sentence. Identify it as *simple* or *compound*. Then, change each simple sentence into a compound one by adding a new independent clause. Change each compound sentence into two simple ones by dividing clauses.

EXAMPLE   Joe went to the concert.

ANSWER   *simple Joe went to the concert, and he had a good time.*

1. The Yankees won the game, but they did not win the series.

2. We cooked hamburgers on Monday.

3. Ed, Geraldo, and I attended the meeting.

4. I want to major in business or accounting in college.

5. I lost my cell phone, so I have to buy a new one.

6. We played baseball and soccer last weekend.

7. I will call him, or you can send him a text message.

8. We went to Chicago and St. Louis last year.

9. I love Austin; the city has a great music scene.

10. Neither Michael nor Max was at the party.

PRACTICE 15.3D Creating Complex and Compound-Complex Sentences

Read each sentence. Identify it as *simple* or *compound*. Then, change each simple sentence to complex and each compound sentence to compound-complex by adding a subordinate clause.

EXAMPLE   Ed practiced all week, but he lost the game.

ANSWER   *compound Ed practiced all week, but he lost the game because his shoulder hurt.*

11. Our collie is very playful.

12. Fran went to a poetry reading, and she had fun.

13. I have not seen Will or any of the other students.

14. It rained hard in the morning, but then the weather cleared up.

15. You might enjoy the stories of Sandra Cisneros.

16. My brother was tired, so I put him to bed.

17. Mom painted our living room purple.

18. I did not feel energetic, and I did not have much of an appetite.

19. Eve greeted her with a big smile and a hug.

20. I love mariachi music; I grew up listening to it.

SPEAKING APPLICATION

Take turns with a partner. Discuss a favorite song and reasons that you like it. Use a variety of sentence structures. Your partner should listen for and identify the structure of each sentence.

WRITING APPLICATION

Using only simple and compound sentences, write a paragraph about a trip you want to take. Then, rewrite the paragraph using a variety of sentence structures. Compare the two drafts and comment on the differences.

Test Warm-Up

DIRECTIONS

Read the introduction and the passage that follows. Then, answer the questions to show that you can identify and use a variety of correctly structured sentences (e.g., compound, complex, and compound-complex).

Anna wrote this paragraph about the work she did over summer vacation. Read the paragraph and think about the kinds of sentences that are in it as well as changes you would suggest as a peer editor. When you finish reading, answer the questions that follow.

Summer Work

(1) Last summer, I worked at a day camp for children ages six to eight. (2) Although I worked long hours, I enjoyed myself. (3) I want to be a teacher someday, and I think that my experience working with the children will help me succeed. (4) I plan to work at the camp again next summer for I would like to get even more experience.

1 What kind of sentence is sentence 1?

  A simple

  B compound

  C complex

  D compound-complex

2 What kind of sentence is sentence 2?

  F simple

  G compound

  H complex

  J compound-complex

3 What kind of sentence is sentence 3?

  A simple

  B compound

  C complex

  D compound-complex

4 What change, if any, should be made to sentence 4?

  F Omit the conjunction *for*

  G Insert a comma before the conjunction *for*

  H Insert a period after *summer* and capitalize the conjunction *for*

  J Make no change

PRACTICE 1 > Identifying Nouns

Read the sentences. Then, label each underlined noun either *concrete* or *abstract*. If the noun is concrete, label it *collective*, *compound*, or *proper*.

1. The <u>firefighters</u> quickly climbed the <u>fire escape</u>.

2. Sal's greatest <u>wish</u> is to live in <u>Paris</u>.

3. An <u>army</u> would often dig <u>foxholes</u> in which to sleep during World War II.

4. Many <u>onlookers</u> stared in awe at the <u>superstructure</u> before them.

5. The <u>bylaw</u> is up for vote in the <u>legislature</u> this week.

PRACTICE 2 > Identifying Pronouns

Read the sentences. Then, label each underlined pronoun *reciprocal*, *demonstrative*, *relative*, *interrogative*, or *indefinite*.

1. What on Earth is <u>that</u> over there?

2. The coach is looking for a student <u>who</u> likes to pitch.

3. <u>Whom</u> should I call?

4. <u>Someone</u> has to know what's going on.

5. Fred and Hal have never met <u>each other</u>.

PRACTICE 3 > Classifying Verbs and Verb Phrases

Read the sentences. Then, write the verb or verb phrase in each sentence. Label each either *action verb* or *linking verb*. If the verb is an action verb, label it *transitive* or *intransitive*.

1. The train stopped mere inches from the station.

2. *Dubliners* became my favorite book when I read it last year.

3. The sink appears broken; we need a plumber.

4. My dog Rex can smell anything.

5. Shelly rarely drives after dark.

PRACTICE 4 > Identifying Adjectives and Adverbs

Read the sentences. Then, identify the underlined word as an *adjective* or *adverb*. Write the word that is modified.

1. Malcolm plays the banjo quite <u>well</u>.

2. I never shy away from a <u>friendly</u> face.

3. She was <u>disturbed</u> when she heard the news.

4. I <u>never</u> eat before I work out.

5. Manny is looking forward to <u>successfully</u> completing college next year.

PRACTICE 5 > Using Conjunctions and Interjections

Read the sentences. Then, write the conjunction or interjection. If there is a conjunction in the sentence, label it *coordinating*, *correlative*, or *subordinating*.

1. Finally! I can go home.

2. Clarice had to take the subway because her car broke down.

3. The restaurant serves not only Italian food but also Mexican food.

4. Brian doesn't like hot dogs, nor does he like sausages.

5. After Fey left the meeting, she went to get a cup of coffee.

PRACTICE 6 > Recognizing Direct and Indirect Objects and Object of a Preposition

Read the sentences. Then, identify the underlined items as *direct object*, *indirect object*, or *object of a preposition*.

1. Delia mailed her <u>mother</u> a <u>card</u> for Mother's Day.

Continued on next page ▶

2. Luke left his <u>jacket</u> in the <u>house</u>.

3. Helen told <u>Julio</u> and <u>me</u> about the new movie.

4. Jennifer bought <u>Chris</u> a sweater for their <u>anniversary</u>.

5. Each of <u>us</u> will take a <u>number</u> from the hat.

6. Don't give <u>me</u> the <u>news</u> until I'm ready.

7. Ned cleaned and polished the <u>table</u> and the <u>chairs</u>.

8. During the <u>night</u>, our dog Sammy hides under the <u>couch</u>.

9. Bonny will eat her <u>lunch</u> before the one o'clock <u>meeting</u>.

10. Jeremiah showed <u>Alicia</u> and <u>me</u> the rough draft of his short story.

PRACTICE 7 Identifying Phrases

Write the phrases contained in the following sentences. Identify each phrase as a *prepositional phrase, appositive phrase, participial phrase, gerund phrase,* or *infinitive phrase.*

1. The car quickly disappeared around the corner.

2. Sprinting to the finish line, Terrance felt elated.

3. To ride a bike without a helmet is not safe.

4. The Enlightenment, a fascinating period, influenced many policies of the U.S. Constitution.

5. The bus stopped to let the children cross the street.

6. Darryl, a man of thirty-two, volunteers at the fire department down the street.

7. Swimming laps in a pool is great exercise.

8. When the nurse takes your blood pressure, he slips a cuff around your arm.

9. Amazed by the light show, Joan asked a technician how it was done.

10. Taking a chance, Keith applied for the job after the deadline.

PRACTICE 8 Recognizing Clauses

Label the underlined clauses in the following sentences *independent* or *subordinate.* Identify any subordinate clause as *adjectival, adverbial,* or *noun clause.* Then, label any adjectival clauses as *essential* or *nonessential.*

1. The dog <u>that has a black collar</u> is very well behaved.

2. <u>Sam's baseball crashed through the window</u> to everyone's annoyance.

3. <u>That the road is covered with potholes</u> has been the talk of town hall for months.

4. <u>While the concert was going on</u>, Larry left to answer his cellphone.

5. Mildred likes spiders <u>because they keep pests out of her garden</u>.

6. <u>Oscar, our pet parrot, flew away last week</u> because someone left his cage open.

7. The auto show, <u>which was never well attended</u>, was canceled this year.

8. <u>Even if the stadium were freezing</u>, James would still go to the hockey game.

9. The most fascinating thing about Benjamin Franklin is <u>how he became such a great politician and scientist</u>.

10. The CN Tower, <u>which is in Toronto, Canada</u>, is the tallest tower in North America.

CHAPTER 16

EFFECTIVE SENTENCES

Use sentences of varying lengths and complexities to add dimension to your writing.

WRITE GUY *Jeff Anderson, M.Ed.*

WHAT DO YOU NOTICE?

Observe how the author crafted his sentences as you zoom in on this passage from *Life on the Mississippi* by Mark Twain.

MENTOR TEXT

> Before these events, the day was glorious with expectancy; after them, the day was a dead and empty thing. Not only the boys, but the whole village, felt this.

Now, ask yourself the following questions:

- How does the first sentence reflect the author's use of parallelism?
- What purpose does parallelism serve in this passage?

The prepositional phrases at the beginning of each clause of the first sentence and the parallel clauses *the day was glorious with expectancy* and *the day was a dead and empty thing* are both parallel structures. The author uses parallelism to compare people's feelings before and after certain events, thus showing how important these events are to his characters.

Grammar for Writers Writers use different sentence structures to engage and guide their readers. Start your sentences in different ways to add variety to your writing, and use parallelism to help your readers connect ideas.

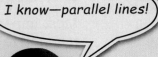

What do math and grammar have in common?

I know—parallel lines!

16.1 The Four Functions of a Sentence

Sentences can be classified according to what they do—that is, whether they state ideas, ask questions, give orders, or express strong emotions.

WRITING COACH

Online

www.phwritingcoach.com

Grammar Practice
Practice your grammar skills with Writing Coach Online.

Grammar Games
Test your knowledge of grammar in this fast-paced interactive video game.

Declarative sentences are used to declare, or state, ideas.

RULE 16.1.1
> **A declarative sentence** states an idea and ends with a period.

DECLARATIVE   Jerusalem is a city in Israel.

To *interrogate* means "to ask." An **interrogative sentence** is a question.

RULE 16.1.2
> **An interrogative sentence** asks a question and ends with a question mark.

INTERROGATIVE   On which continent do elephants live?

Imperative sentences give commands or directions.

RULE 16.1.3
> **An imperative sentence** gives an order or a direction and ends with either a period or an exclamation mark.

Most imperative sentences start with a verb. In this type of imperative sentence, the subject is understood to be *you*.

IMPERATIVE   Stack the dinner china carefully.

Exclamatory sentences are used to express emotions.

RULE 16.1.4
> **An exclamatory sentence** conveys strong emotion and ends with an exclamation mark.

EXCLAMATORY   That is wonderful!

See Practice 16.1A
See Practice 16.1B

PRACTICE 16.1A > **Identifying the Four Types of Sentences**

Read each sentence. Then, label each sentence *declarative, interrogative, imperative,* or *exclamatory.*

EXAMPLE　　When was your house built?

ANSWER　　*interrogative*

1. That was amazing!

2. The upper level is still under construction.

3. How much did you pay for that shirt?

4. Listen closely to me.

5. What is your favorite color?

6. The candidate is someone I trust completely.

7. What a menacing sight!

8. Put on your warmest pair of socks.

9. Who wrote this poem?

10. This was one of the hardest marathons that I've ever run.

PRACTICE 16.1B > **Punctuating the Four Types of Sentences**

Read each sentence. Then, label each sentence *declarative, interrogative, imperative,* or *exclamatory,* and, in parentheses, write the correct end mark.

EXAMPLE　　What a great time we had

ANSWER　　*exclamatory (!)*

11. This part of the city gets poor cellphone reception

12. Do you want to arrive Tuesday or Wednesday morning

13. This is baffling

14. My professor does not appreciate tardiness

15. When will my car be ready

16. Turn off the air conditioner when you leave the house

17. I have always wondered what college he attended

18. Ask Ronaldo to hand in his paper

19. Wow, that was exciting

20. Would you hand me the broom, please

SPEAKING APPLICATION

Take turns with a partner. Describe an exciting event that you have experienced. Make sure to use all four sentence types in your description. Your partner should identify each type of sentence in your description.

WRITING APPLICATION

Write a paragraph about your first day of high school. Use at least one declarative, one interrogative, and one imperative sentence in your paragraph.

Practice　　**397**

16.2 Sentence Combining

Too many short sentences can make your writing choppy and disconnected.

WRITING COACH

Online

www.phwritingcoach.com

Grammar Practice
Practice your grammar skills with Writing Coach Online.

Grammar Games
Test your knowledge of grammar in this fast-paced interactive video game.

One way to avoid the excessive use of short sentences and to achieve variety is to combine sentences.

RULE 16.2.1

> Sentences can be combined by using a **compound subject,** a **compound verb,** or a **compound object.**

TWO SENTENCES	Kevin enjoyed the concert tonight. Andrew enjoyed the concert tonight.
COMPOUND SUBJECT	Kevin and Andrew enjoyed the concert tonight.
TWO SENTENCES	Jen practiced hard. Jen won the game.
COMPOUND VERB	Jen practiced hard and won the game.
TWO SENTENCES	Joshua saw the plane. Joshua saw the fighter jet.
COMPOUND OBJECT	Joshua saw the plane and the fighter jet.

See Practice 16.2A

RULE 16.2.2

> Sentences can be combined by joining two **main** or **independent clauses** to create a **compound sentence.**

Use a compound sentence when combining ideas that are related but independent. To join main clauses, use a comma and a coordinating conjunction (*for, and, but, or, nor, yet,* or *so*) or a semicolon.

EXAMPLE	The child was looking for her shoes. She did not notice them outside.
COMPOUND SENTENCE	The child was looking for her shoes, yet she did not notice them outside.

Sentences can be combined by changing one into a subordinate clause to create a complex sentence.

To show the relationship between ideas in which one depends on the other, use a **complex sentence.** The subordinating conjunction will help readers understand the relationship. Some common subordinating conjunctions are *after, although, because, if, since, when,* and *while.*

EXAMPLE	We were tired. We couldn't sleep on the bumpy flight.
COMBINED WITH A SUBORDINATE CLAUSE	We were tired **because we couldn't sleep on the bumpy flight**.

Sentences can be combined by changing one of them into a phrase.

EXAMPLE	My sister will present her paper today. The paper is on insects.
COMBINED WITH PREPOSITIONAL PHRASE	My sister will present her paper **on insects** today.
EXAMPLE	My sister will present her paper on insects today. It is the final paper of the year.
COMBINED WITH APPOSITIVE PHRASE	Today, my sister will present her paper, **the final one of the year**, on insects.

See Practice 16.2B
See Practice 16.2C

Read each set of sentences. Then, combine each set of sentences, using one sentence that contains a compound subject, verb, or object.

EXAMPLE   The team lost the game.
            They finished in last place.

ANSWER   *The team lost the game and finished in last place.*

1. Carrie could not sleep last night. She was late for her doctor's appointment.

2. Mars is known as the red planet. Mars is named after the Roman god of war.

3. Aneeta earns impressive grades. She is also a natural leader.

4. Vernon likes to read science fiction novels. Theresa likes to read science fiction novels.

5. Tyler ate breakfast at home. He had lunch at home. He ate dinner at home.

Read each set of sentences. Combine each set by turning one sentence into a phrase—prepositional, participial, or appositive—that adds detail to the other.

EXAMPLE   The witness spoke to an officer.
            He identified the suspect.

ANSWER   *The witness who spoke to an officer identified the suspect.*

6. Percy waited underneath the tree. A friend was with him.

7. Our team captain arrived early. He did warm-up exercises to pass the time.

8. All drivers must navigate the course. The course was designed by professional racers.

9. Stewart Manning is our student body representative. He will speak at tomorrow's pep rally.

10. Many books have been written about time travel. This is a very interesting topic.

SPEAKING APPLICATION

Take turns with a partner. Say two related sentences. Your partner should combine these two sentences into one logical sentence.

WRITING APPLICATION

Write two sentences that relate to each other. Then, combine these two sentences into one. Repeat with two other related sentences.

PRACTICE 16.2C > **Combining Sentences by Forming Compound or Complex Sentences**

Read each set of sentences. Then, combine the sentences, using a coordinating or subordinating conjunction. Underline the conjunction that you use and label it *coordinating* or *subordinating*.

EXAMPLE   I wanted to sit in the front row. I ordered my tickets early.

ANSWER   *I wanted to sit in the front row, so I ordered my tickets early.* — *coordinating*

1. Julio enjoys reading mystery novels. He has a love for suspense.

2. My brother loves to eat apples. He eats one almost every day.

3. You might not make it to the show on time. The train station is only one block away.

4. Rory and Hanne left early. I did not see them when I arrived at the party.

5. Wendy traveled to Mexico last summer. She did not visit the Pyramid of the Moon.

6. Geoff was able to get on an earlier flight. Geoff's conference ended early.

7. Yusef really enjoys listening to jazz music. His girlfriend prefers classical music.

8. Bears hibernate during winter. Butterflies migrate south.

9. I waited in line to buy the album. I read the last chapter of my book.

10. Scientists have learned much about the universe. Scientists still send craft into outer space to gather more information.

SPEAKING APPLICATION

Take turns with a partner. Describe a memorable event. Be sure to include at least four complex or compound sentences that contain coordinating or subordinating conjunctions.

WRITING APPLICATION

Write a paragraph about a favorite relative. Use compound and complex sentences with coordinating and subordinating conjunctions in your paragraph.

PRACTICE 16.2D ▷ **Combining Sentences in Two Different Ways**

Read each sentence. Combine each pair of sentences to create two *different*, correctly structured compound or complex sentences. Explain how they differ in meaning.

EXAMPLE   Bob wanted to win this time. Chris always wins.

ANSWER   Complex: *Bob wanted to win this time because Chris always wins.*

Compound: *Bob wanted to win this time, but Chris always wins.*

The first sentence suggests Bob has a chance to win, but the second makes that seem unlikely.

1. Sue texted Greg at 3 A.M. He was annoyed.

2. Most people think robins fly north in spring. Many robins stay year-round.

3. Sandy decided to be a veterinarian. She works hard in her biology class.

4. I will bring paper. Ellie will bring pens.

5. Do the geometry problems. You will be able to understand the formulas.

6. Bill is working today. Ask him to help you.

7. Javier is a good baseball player. He has difficulty playing basketball.

8. You need help studying. You should call me.

PRACTICE 16.2E ▷ **Combining Sentences by Forming Complex or Compound-Complex Sentences**

Read each sentence. Combine each group of sentences to create a correctly structured complex or compound-complex sentence.

EXAMPLE   Pavel stood in the doorway. He watched the rain. It soaked into the earth.

ANSWER   *Pavel stood in the doorway, and he watched the rain as it soaked into the earth.*

9. I like that book. I think you will too. It is funny.

10. I found a cat in a Catalpa tree. I adopted him. I named him after the tree.

11. Val plays in a band. It is called Teen Turmoil. It plays this Friday.

12. Deb's car is old. It is rusty. It still runs well.

13. It became cold last night. The roses froze. The roses are in our garden.

14. Vacation starts tomorrow. I can hardly wait. We are going to Hawaii!

15. My computer crashed. My paper was due. I printed it at a friend's.

16. We have a team. It won first place last year. I think it will win this year also.

SPEAKING APPLICATION

Take turns with a partner. Tell a brief story on a topic of your choice. Combine sentences as your partner suggests. Discuss how the two versions differ in meaning.

WRITING APPLICATION

Write a paragraph about a hobby or sport. Revise your draft by combining two or more sentences into a compound or complex sentence. Write a few sentences analyzing the differences between versions.

Test Warm-Up

DIRECTIONS
Read the introduction and the passage that follows. Then, answer the questions to show that you can combine sentences in writing.

Ron wrote this paragraph about a thoughtful teen. Read the paragraph and think about the changes you would suggest as a peer editor. When you finish reading, answer the questions that follow.

Oops!

(1) Jasmine blushed. (2) She had dropped her cafeteria tray. (3) Now all her friends were laughing. (4) She looked at Chris. (5) He saw the embarrassment in her eyes. (6) He acted quickly. (7) He pretended to slip. (8) He slid across the floor. (9) Then, he jumped to his feet. (10) Now everyone was laughing at *him*. (11) The students had already forgotten Jasmine's mishap. (12) When Chris bowed, they applauded. (13) Jasmine smiled at him. (14) She breathed a sigh of relief.

---

1 What is the most effective way to combine sentences 2 and 3?

 A She had dropped her cafeteria tray, and now all her friends were laughing.

 B Since she had dropped her cafeteria tray; and now all her friends were laughing.

 C Although she had dropped her cafeteria tray, now all her friends were laughing.

 D She had dropped her cafeteria tray, for now all her friends were laughing.

2 What is the most effective way to combine sentences 4 and 5?

 F She looked at Chris, yet he saw the embarrassment in her eyes.

 G She looked at Chris seeing the embarrassment in her eyes.

 H She looked at Chris because he saw the embarrassment in her eyes.

 J She looked at Chris, who saw the embarrassment in her eyes.

3 What is the most effective way to combine sentences 6 and 7?

 A He acted quickly, but he pretended to slip.

 B Slipping, he quickly pretended to act.

 C Acting quickly, he pretended to slip.

 D Quickly acting and pretending to slip, he.

4 What is the most effective way to combine sentences 13 and 14?

 F Breathing a sigh of relief and smiling at him was Jasmine.

 G Smiling at him, Jasmine breathed a sigh of relief.

 H At him, Jasmine smiled and breathing a sigh of relief.

 J Jasmine smiling at him and breathing a sigh of relief.

16.3 Varying Sentences

Vary your sentences to develop a rhythm, to achieve an effect, or to emphasize the connections between ideas. There are several ways you can vary your sentences.

WRITING COACH
Online
www.phwritingcoach.com

Grammar Tutorials
Brush up on your Grammar skills with these animated videos.

Grammar Practice
Practice your grammar skills with Writing Coach Online.

Grammar Games
Test your knowledge of grammar in this fast-paced interactive video game.

Varying Sentence Length

To emphasize a point or surprise a reader, include a short, direct sentence to interrupt the flow of long sentences. Notice the effect of the last sentence in the following paragraph.

EXAMPLE The Jacobites derived their name from *Jacobus,* the Latin name for King James II of England, who was dethroned in 1688 by William of Orange during the Glorious Revolution. Unpopular because of his Catholicism and autocratic ruling style, James fled to France to seek the aid of King Louis XIV. In 1690, James, along with a small body of French troops, landed in Ireland in an attempt to regain his throne. His hopes ended at the Battle of the Boyne.

Some sentences contain only one idea and can't be broken. It may be possible, however, to state the idea in a shorter sentence. Other sentences contain two or more ideas and might be shortened by breaking up the ideas.

LONGER SENTENCE Many of James II's predecessors were able to avoid major economic problems, but James had serious economic problems.

MORE DIRECT Unlike many of his predecessors, James II was unable to avoid major economic problems.

LONGER SENTENCE James tried to work with Parliament to develop a plan of taxation that would be fair and reasonable, but members of Parliament rejected his efforts, and James dissolved the Parliament.

SHORTER SENTENCES James tried to work with Parliament to develop a fair and reasonable taxation plan. However, because members of Parliament rejected his efforts, James dissolved the Parliament.

Varying Sentence Beginnings

Another way to create sentence variety is to start sentences with different parts of speech.

WAYS TO VARY SENTENCE BEGINNINGS	
Start With a Noun	Houses are difficult to build.
Start With an Adverb	Naturally, houses are difficult to build.
Start With an Adverbial Phrase	Because of their complexity, houses are difficult to build.
Start With a Participial Phrase	Having tried to build several houses, I know how hard it is.
Start With a Prepositional Phrase	For the average person, houses are very difficult to build.
Start With an Infinitive Phrase	To build a safe and durable house was my goal.

See Practice 16.3A

Using Inverted Word Order

You can also vary sentence beginnings by reversing the traditional subject–verb order to create verb–subject order. You can reverse order by starting the sentence with a **participial phrase** or a **prepositional phrase.** You can also move a verb or a complement to the beginning of the sentence.

SUBJECT–VERB ORDER

The command to leave was posted on the wall.

The soldier drove into the hot, barren desert.

If I were to tell you, you would not believe me.

The sounds were terrible.

VERB–SUBJECT ORDER

Posted on the wall was the command to leave.
participial phrase

Into the hot, barren desert drove the soldier.
prepositional phrase

Were I to tell you, you would not believe me.
verb

Terrible were the sounds.
complement

See Practice 16.3B

PRACTICE 16.3A > **Revising to Vary Sentence Beginnings**

Read each sentence. Rewrite each sentence to begin with the part of speech or phrase indicated in parentheses. You may need to add a word or phrase.

EXAMPLE Certain types of diseases have recurred throughout history. (prepositional phrase)

ANSWER *Throughout history, certain types of diseases have recurred.*

1. Lidia accepted the invitation. (adverb)

2. Search the Internet. (infinitive phrase)

3. Some cities are using street-cars to reduce pollution. (infinitive phrase)

4. Cheering fans threw confetti onto the field. (prepositional phrase)

5. The president did many great things. (prepositional phrase)

6. We finally reached camp. (participial phrase)

7. The wind blew violently through the trees. (adverb)

8. Lots of acorns tumbled out of the trees. (adverb)

9. Many sets of twins were born on that day. (prepositional phrase)

10. Michael stood at the foot of the stairs. (prepositional phrase)

PRACTICE 16.3B > **Inverting Sentences to Vary Subject–Verb Order**

Read each sentence. Rewrite each sentence by inverting subject-verb order to verb-subject order. Use the word in parentheses to start the new sentence.

EXAMPLE The baby slept in a crib. (In)

ANSWER *In a crib slept the baby.*

11. A great, dark bird flew over my head. (Over)

12. Celebrities are rarely willing to talk. (Rarely)

13. Bertha's brother announced, "I will pay the airfare for the trip." (I)

14. The heroes of the Battle of San Jacinto are listed here. (Listed)

15. My lost catcher's mitt was there in the closet. (There)

16. A loud roar came from deep inside the cave. (From)

17. I have felt so comfortable with no one but you. (With)

18. Players were never so determined to win. (Never)

19. The great emperor Julius Caesar was born on July 12, 100 BC. (On)

20. The word "beware" was carved into the stone. (Carved)

SPEAKING APPLICATION

Take turns with a partner. Read three sentences from Practice 16.3A, but change the directive in parentheses. Your partner should follow the directive to revise how the sentence begins.

WRITING APPLICATION

Write three sentences about your morning routine. Then, exchange papers with a partner. Your partner should invert the order of your sentences from subject–verb order to verb–subject order to vary the beginnings.

16.4 Avoid Fragments and Run-ons

Hasty writers sometimes omit crucial words, punctuate awkwardly, or leave their thoughts unfinished, causing two common sentence errors: **fragments** and **run-ons**.

Find It/ FIX IT

20

Grammar
Game Plan

www.phwritingcoach.com

Grammar Tutorials
Brush up on your
Grammar skills with
these animated
videos.

Grammar Practice
Practice your
grammar skills with
Writing Coach Online.

Grammar Games
Test your knowledge
of grammar in this
fast-paced interactive
video game.

Recognizing Fragments

Although some writers use them for stylistic effect, **fragments** are generally considered errors in standard English.

> **Do not capitalize and punctuate phrases, subordinate clauses, or words in a series as if they were complete sentences.**

 16.4.1 RULE

Reading your work aloud to listen for natural pauses and stops should help you avoid fragments. Sometimes, you can repair a fragment by connecting it to words that come before or after it.

> **One way to correct a fragment is to connect it to the words in a nearby sentence.**

 16.4.2 RULE

PARTICIPIAL FRAGMENT	inspired by the talent of the singer
ADDED TO A NEARBY SENTENCE	**Inspired by the talent of the singer** , Deb went to the concert twice.
PREPOSITIONAL FRAGMENT	before their band
ADDED TO A NEARBY SENTENCE	The trio of singers came on stage **before their band** .
PRONOUN AND PARTICIPIAL FRAGMENT	the one on the bed
ADDED TO NEARBY SENTENCE	The warm woolen blanket I want is **the one on the bed** .

Another way to correct a fragment is to add any sentence part that is needed to make the fragment a complete sentence.

Remember that every complete sentence must have both a subject and a verb and express a complete thought. Check to see that each of your sentences contains all of the parts necessary to be complete.

NOUN
FRAGMENT
the team of young soccer players

COMPLETED
SENTENCES
The team of young soccer players
subject

ran **across the field.**
verb

We **excitedly** **watched**
subject   verb

the team of young soccer players .
direct object

Notice what missing sentence parts must be added to the following types of phrase fragments to make them complete.

	FRAGMENTS	COMPLETED SENTENCES
Noun Fragment With Participial Phrase	the fruit eaten by us	The fruit was eaten by us.
Verb Fragment	will be at the conference tomorrow	I will be at the conference tomorrow.
Prepositional Fragment	in the bathroom closet	I put the towels in the bathroom closet.
Participial Fragment	found under the table	The magazines found under the table are mine.
Gerund Fragment	teaching children to swim	Teaching children to swim is exciting.
Infinitive Fragment	to meet the new instructor	I expect to meet the new instructor.

You may need to attach a **subordinate clause** to a main clause to correct a fragment.

A **subordinate clause** contains a subject and a verb but does not express a complete thought and cannot stand alone as a sentence. Link it to a main clause to make the sentence complete.

ADJECTIVAL CLAUSE FRAGMENT	which was being read inside the store
COMPLETED SENTENCE	I planned on hearing the author's excerpt, **which was being read inside the store**.
ADVERBIAL CLAUSE FRAGMENT	after she read the first book
COMPLETED SENTENCE	**After she read the first book**, she was ready for the sequel.
NOUN CLAUSE FRAGMENT	whatever movie we see in this theater
COMPLETED SENTENCE	We always enjoy **whatever movie we see in this theater**.

Series Fragments A fragment is not always short. A long series of words still needs to have a subject and a verb and express a complete thought. It may be a long fragment masquerading as a sentence.

SERIES FRAGMENT	COMPLETE SENTENCE
after reading Shakespeare's play, with its probing look at love and family, in the style so typical of this well-known playwright	After reading Shakespeare's play, with its probing look at love and family, in the style so typical of this well-known playwright, I was able to form an interesting character assessment.

See Practice 16.4A

Avoiding Run-on Sentences

A **run-on** sentence is two or more sentences capitalized and punctuated as if they were a single sentence.

> **Use punctuation and conjunctions to correctly join or separate parts of a run-on sentence.**

There are two kinds of **run-ons: fused sentences,** which are two or more sentences joined with no punctuation, and **comma splices,** which have two or more sentences separated only by commas rather than by commas and conjunctions.

FUSED
SENTENCE
The student studied every day she was the valedictorian of the class.

COMMA SPLICE
Only one check arrived in the mail, the other checks never came.

As with fragments, proofreading or reading your work aloud will help you find run-ons. Once found, they can be corrected by adding punctuation and conjunctions or by rewording the sentences.

FOUR WAYS TO CORRECT RUN-ONS		
	RUN-ON	**CORRECTION**
With End Marks and Capitals	The storm hit with full force in the basement the family was huddled together.	The storm hit with full force. In the basement, the family was huddled together.
With Commas and Conjunctions	The food needed to be cooked we could not locate the pans.	The food needed to be cooked, but we could not locate the pans.
With Semicolons	We have many colleges around the country, for example, Pennsylvania is sometimes called the college state.	We have many colleges around the country; for example, Pennsylvania is sometimes called the college state.
By Rewriting	The movie began late, the projector wasn't working.	The movie began late because the projector wasn't working.

See Practice 16.4B

PRACTICE 16.4A Identifying and Correcting Fragments

Read each sentence. If an item contains a fragment, rewrite it to make a complete sentence. If an item contains a complete sentence, write *correct*.

EXAMPLE   Reluctantly chose to lead the team.

ANSWER   *Reluctantly, he chose to lead the team.*

1. A strong wind blowing from the south.

2. An invasion from Mars was the movie's theme.

3. Coming around the next bend.

4. Raised her hand eagerly.

5. Listen to me, please.

6. Sitting quietly, reading a book.

7. Safe drivers always.

8. Acted without a thought for his own safety.

9. We went down the hill.

10. Unless it is refrigerated.

PRACTICE 16.4B Revising to Eliminate Run-on Sentences

Read each sentence. Correct each run-on by correctly joining or separating the sentence parts.

EXAMPLE   Mrs. Ladner spoke softly I listened carefully.

ANSWER   *Mrs. Ladner spoke softly, so I listened carefully.*

11. We opened the box it contained dishes.

12. This is my answer I won't change my mind.

13. The trains are quicker the buses are cheaper.

14. The electricity went out I looked for the flashlight.

15. What time is the play, will you come and get me?

16. I ran after him however he had already driven away.

17. I lost the first wrestling match I won the second.

18. Is this your paper it's really well-written.

19. My cousin collects baseball cards I collect seashells.

20. I waved, Raisa waved back.

SPEAKING APPLICATION

Take turns with a partner. Use different words to make the fragments in Practice 16.4A into complete sentences.

WRITING APPLICATION

Write four run-on sentences. Then, exchange papers with a partner, and correct your partner's run-on sentences.

PRACTICE 16.5A **Identifying and Correcting Misplaced Modifiers**

Read each sentence. Then, rewrite each sentence, putting the misplaced modifier closer to the words it should modify. If a sentence is correct, write *correct*.

EXAMPLE   The conductor gave instructions with his baton in hand.

ANSWER   *The conductor, with his baton in hand, gave instructions.*

1. The store is on the corner that just opened.

2. The book won an award with many colorful illustrations.

3. The treasure chest was buried filled with jewels.

4. The shirt that you want will cost thirty dollars.

5. The team won from our school.

6. The man asked for help standing by the highway.

7. The room with a fireplace has been rented.

8. Vanessa reminded me to bring my notebook twice.

9. The pianist played a new composition sitting on the piano bench.

10. Please give the ice cream to my sister with hot fudge sauce.

PRACTICE 16.5B **Identifying and Correcting Dangling Modifiers**

Read each sentence. Then, rewrite the sentences, correcting any dangling modifiers by supplying missing words or ideas.

EXAMPLE   Walking to school, her notebook was lost.

ANSWER   *Walking to school, she lost her notebook.*

11. To enter the race, a form must be completed.

12. To knit a hat, all the yarn must be bought at once.

13. Having solved the problem, liftoff could take place.

14. To get the job, references must be verified.

15. While taking inventory, the store was closed.

16. Cutting out all the wordiness, the essay was improved.

17. When not talking, the room was filled with silence.

18. After examining the evidence, the accused was released.

19. Wrapped in my blanket, the cold was no problem.

20. After washing the clothes, the clothes needed to be folded.

SPEAKING APPLICATION

Take turns with a partner. Tell about an exciting experience that you have had. Use modifiers in your sentences. Your partner should listen for and identify the modifiers and tell whether they are correctly placed.

WRITING APPLICATION

Use sentences 18, 19, and 20 as models to write similar sentences with dangling modifiers. Then, rewrite each sentence to correct the dangling modifiers.

16.6 Faulty Parallelism

Good writers try to present a series of ideas in similar grammatical structures so the ideas will read smoothly. If one element in a series is not parallel with the others, the result may be jarring or confusing.

Find It / FIX IT

10

Grammar Game Plan

Recognizing the Correct Use of Parallelism

To present a series of ideas of equal importance, you should use parallel grammatical structures.

Parallelism involves presenting equal ideas in words, phrases, clauses, or sentences of similar types.

RULE 16.6.1

PARALLEL WORDS	The dancer looked **graceful** , **fit** , and **agile** .
PARALLEL PHRASES	The greatest feeling I know is **to dance on the stage flawlessly** and **to have the audience and all my friends applaud graciously** .
PARALLEL CLAUSES	The ballet slippers **that you recommended** and **that my daughter wants** are on sale.
PARALLEL SENTENCES	**It couldn't be** , of course. **It could never, never be** . –Dorothy Parker

Correcting Faulty Parallelism

Faulty parallelism occurs when a writer uses unequal grammatical structures to express related ideas.

Correct a sentence containing faulty parallelism by rewriting it so that each parallel idea is expressed in the same grammatical structure.

RULE 16.6.2

Faulty parallelism can involve words, phrases, and clauses in a series or in comparisons.

Nonparallel Words, Phrases, and Clauses in a Series

Always check for parallelism when your writing contains items in a series.

Correcting Faulty Parallelism in a Series

NONPARALLEL STRUCTURES

Planning, **filming**, and **edit** are all steps in
gerund · · · · · · · · · gerund · · · · · · · · · noun
the movie process.

CORRECTION

Planning, **filming**, and **editing** are all steps
gerund · · · · · · · · · gerund · · · · · · · · · gerund
in the movie process.

NONPARALLEL STRUCTURES

I could not wait **to see the new show**,
infinitive phrase
to get dressed up, and **visiting the theater**.
infinitive phrase · · · · · · · · · · · · · · · participial phrase

CORRECTION

I could not wait **to see the new show**, **to get
infinitive phrase
dressed up**, and **to visit the theater**.
infinitive phrase · · · · · · · · · · · · · infinitive phrase

NONPARALLEL STRUCTURE

Some experts feel **that cheering is not a**
noun clause
contact sport, but **it requires caution and**
independent clause
athleticism.

CORRECTION

Some experts feel **that cheering is not a**
noun clause
contact sport but **that it requires caution**
noun clause
and athleticism.

Another potential problem involves correlative conjunctions, such as *both ... and* or *not only ... but also*. Though these conjunctions connect two related items, writers sometimes misplace or split the first part of the conjunction. The result is faulty parallelism.

NONPARALLEL	Anne **not only** won the gymnastics championship **but also** the national title.
PARALLEL	Anne won **not only** the gymnastics championship **but also** the national title.

Nonparallel Words, Phrases, and Clauses in Comparisons
As the saying goes, you cannot compare apples with oranges. In writing comparisons, you generally should compare a phrase with the same type of phrase and a clause with the same type of clause.

Correcting Faulty Parallelism in Comparisons

NONPARALLEL
STRUCTURES

Many people prefer potatoes to eating
            noun   gerund phrase
broccoli .

CORRECTION

Many people prefer potatoes to broccoli .
        noun   noun

NONPARALLEL
STRUCTURES

I left my office at 9:00 P.M. rather than
        prepositional phrase
stopping work at 4:30 P.M.
      gerund phrase

CORRECTION

I left my office at 9:00 P.M. rather than
        prepositional phrase
at the usual 4:30 P.M.
      prepositional phrase

NONPARALLEL
STRUCTURES

Jenny delights in snowy days as much as
subject   prepositional phrase
sunny days delight other people .
subject   direct object

CORRECTION

Jenny delights in snowy days as much as
subject   prepositional phrase
other people delight in sunny days .
subject   prepositional phrase

See Practice 16.6A

16.7 Faulty Coordination

When two or more independent clauses of unequal importance are joined by *and*, the result can be faulty **coordination**.

WRITING COACH

Online

www.phwritingcoach.com

Grammar Practice

Practice your grammar skills with Writing Coach Online.

Grammar Games

Test your knowledge of grammar in this fast-paced interactive video game.

Recognizing Faulty Coordination

To *coordinate* means to "place side by side in equal rank." Two independent clauses that are joined by the coordinating conjunction *and*, therefore, should have equal rank.

RULE

16.7.1

> **Use *and* or other coordinating conjunctions only to connect ideas of equal importance.**

CORRECT COORDINATION   Tim designed a ship, **and** Jake built it.

Sometimes, however, writers carelessly use *and* to join main clauses that either should not be joined or should be joined in another way so that the real relationship between the clauses is clear. Faulty coordination puts all the ideas on the same level of importance, even though logically they should not be.

FAULTY COORDINATION   Demand for computers accelerated in the twenty-first century, **and** the computer became an important factor in offices.

I didn't do well, **and** the run was easy.

Mark Twain was one of our greatest authors **and** he was born in Missouri.

Occasionally, writers will also string together so many ideas with *and*'s that the reader is left breathless.

STRINGY SENTENCE   The helicopter that flew over the city did a few dips and turns, **and** the people on the ground craned their necks to watch, **and** everyone laughed and cheered.

Correcting Faulty Coordination

Faulty coordination can be corrected in several ways.

> **One way to correct faulty coordination is to put unrelated ideas into separate sentences.**

When faulty coordination occurs in a sentence in which the main clauses are not closely related, separate the clauses and omit the coordinating conjunction.

FAULTY COORDINATION	Demand for computers accelerated in the twenty-first century, **and** the computer became an important factor in offices.
CORRECTION	Demand for computers accelerated in the twenty-first century. The computer became an important factor in offices.

> **You can correct faulty coordination by putting less important ideas into subordinate clauses or phrases.**

If one main clause is less important than, or subordinate to, the other, turn it into a subordinate clause. You can also reduce a less important idea to a phrase.

FAULTY COORDINATION	I didn't do well, **and** the run was easy.
CORRECTION	I didn't do well, **even though** the run was easy.
FAULTY COORDINATION	The road was bumpy, **and** it made me feel sick.
CORRECTION	I was feeling sick, because the road was bumpy.

Stringy sentences should be broken up and revised using any of the three methods just described. Following is one way that the stringy sentence on the previous page can be revised.

REVISION OF A STRINGY SENTENCE	The helicopter that flew over the city did a few dips and turns. Craning their necks to watch, the people on the ground laughed and cheered.

See Practice 16.6B

PRACTICE 16.6A Revising to Eliminate Faulty Parallelism

Read each sentence. Then, rewrite each sentence to correct any nonparallel structures.

EXAMPLE   I left work tired, cold, and wanting a meal.

ANSWER   *I left work tired, cold, and hungry.*

1. Today, I have classes to attend, a meeting to lead, and cleaning my room.

2. I like my little sister because she is smart, funny, and I like to play cards with her.

3. Theresa will stay overnight and cooking breakfast in the morning.

4. Kent did a poor job washing the car more because he was rushed than that he did not know how to do it.

5. I prefer Greek mythology to reading nonfiction.

6. I will not go to the play because I would have to buy a ticket, and you have to dress up.

7. The story that Dad told about me was funny, interesting, and I was entertained.

8. I have a dog, Ning has a cat, but a goldfish is Roger's only pet.

9. The ice skater landed her jumps but makes other mistakes.

10. I both cleaned my room and the garage.

PRACTICE 16.6B Revising to Eliminate Faulty Coordination

Read each sentence. Then, rewrite each sentence to correct the faulty coordination.

EXAMPLE   The waiter brought the main course, and it is lasagna.

ANSWER   *The waiter brought the main course, lasagna.*

11. The Carlsbad Caverns are in New Mexico, and we visited them last year.

12. I'm nervous and the audition is today.

13. Misty is a talented singer, and people like to hear her perform.

14. Bijou found a kitten, and it is white.

15. Amy is afraid of honeybees, and they are necessary for cross-pollination.

16. Albert Einstein was a brilliant scientist, and he left Germany before World War II.

17. I jogged in the park, and crowds filled the paths there.

18. Our bags were packed, and we left for home.

19. Jim was searching for a job, and he had graduated from college last week.

20. The alarm clock woke me this morning, and it was still dark.

SPEAKING APPLICATION

Take turns with a partner. Tell about something you plan to do with your family or friends. Try to include two or three activities in each sentence. Your partner should listen for and correct any faulty parallelism.

WRITING APPLICATION

Use sentences 18, 19, and 20 as models to write three similar sentences that contain faulty coordination. Exchange papers with a partner, and correct each other's work.

CHAPTER 17

VERB USAGE

Use verbs strategically to shape how you present the events in your writing.

WRITE GUY *Jeff Anderson, M.Ed.*

WHAT DO YOU NOTICE?

Size up the verbs as you zoom in on these sentences from the inaugural address of President John F. Kennedy.

MENTOR TEXT

> In your hands, my fellow citizens, more than in mine, will rest the final success or failure of our course. Since this country was founded, each generation of Americans has been summoned to give testimony to its national loyalty.

Now, ask yourself the following questions:

- Is the first sentence written in the active voice or passive voice?
- In the second sentence, which voice is used in each of the two clauses, and what might be the reason for using this voice?

The first sentence is written in the active voice, or tense, because the subject *success or failure* performs the action of the verb *will rest*. The second sentence is written in the passive voice, or tense, because the subject of each clause does not perform the action of the verb. The passive verbs are *was founded* and *has been summoned*. The passive voice is used here because the speaker is focused on the future, not on who founded the country or who summoned the people.

Grammar for Writers When you have a choice between active and passive voice, you should usually choose the active voice. Because it is more direct, the active voice makes your writing more vibrant and powerful.

The song was sung by the singer, and she was accompanied by the band.

Hmm . . . and the concert was enjoyed by all?

17.1 Verb Tenses

Besides expressing actions or conditions, verbs have different **tenses** to indicate when the action or condition occurred.

RULE 17.1.1

A **tense** is the form of a verb that shows the time of an action or a condition.

The Six Verb Tenses

There are six tenses that indicate when an action or a condition of a verb is, was, or will be in effect. Each of these six tenses has at least two forms.

RULE 17.1.2

Each tense has a **basic** and a **progressive** form.

The chart that follows shows examples of the six tenses.

THE BASIC FORMS OF THE SIX TENSES	
Present	Bill writes for magazines.
Past	He wrote about the economy for news magazines.
Future	He will write about new economic trends.
Present Perfect	He has written for many newspapers, too.
Past Perfect	He had written for his school newspaper when he was in college.
Future Perfect	He will have written about many subjects during his writing career.
Present	Marie runs track.
Past	She ran track last year.
Future	She will run in this week's meet.
Present Perfect	She has run in every meet this year.
Past Perfect	She had run relay races, too.
Future Perfect	She will have run throughout high school.

See Practice 17.1A

Basic Verb Forms or Tenses

Verb tenses are identified simply by their tense names.
The **progressive tenses,** however, are identified by their tense names plus the word *progressive*. Progressive tenses show that an action is or was happening for a period of time.

The chart below shows examples of the six tenses in their progressive form or tense. Note that all of these progressive tenses end in *-ing*. (See the section on verb conjugation later in this chapter for more about the progressive tense.)

THE PROGRESSIVE TENSES	
Present Progressive	Mark is writing about history.
Past Progressive	He was writing in the library.
Future Progressive	He will be writing at home tonight.
Present Perfect Progressive	He has been writing since he was in elementary school.
Past Perfect Progressive	He had been writing about sports before he began writing about history.
Future Perfect Progressive	Next year, he will have been writing for magazines for a decade.

The Emphatic Form

There is also a third form or tense, the **emphatic,** which exists only for the present and past tenses. The **present emphatic** is formed with the helping verb *do* or *does,* depending on the subject. The **past emphatic** is formed with *did.* The purpose of the emphatic tense is to put more emphasis on, or to stress, the action of the verb.

THE EMPHATIC TENSES OF THE PRESENT AND THE PAST	
Present Emphatic	Our team does play better defense than Central's team. Most of my family does like to go to the shore during the summer.
Past Emphatic	I did exercise last night to work on my endurance. Mona did wonder what had happened to her backpack.

See Practice 17.1B

PRACTICE 17.1A > **Identifying Verb Tenses**

Read each sentence. Then, write the tense of the underlined verb in each sentence.

EXAMPLE   Liz <u>has balanced</u> perfectly on the beam many times.

ANSWER   *present perfect*

1. We did not know the team <u>practiced</u> yesterday afternoon.

2. We hope the honeybees <u>will make</u> more honey by next spring.

3. Ben <u>takes</u> algebra this year.

4. Blanca <u>had left</u> for the day.

5. Sam <u>will learn</u> to play the piano.

6. Dan <u>takes</u> swimming lessons at the town pool.

7. Mary <u>will have sung</u> in the shower this morning.

8. I <u>will join</u> the choir next semester.

9. My father <u>has worked</u> very hard at his job.

10. I <u>will have gone</u> to college.

PRACTICE 17.1B > **Recognizing Tenses or Forms of Verbs**

Read each sentence. Then, write the verb and the tense of the verb.

EXAMPLE   I was mowing the lawn all day yesterday.

ANSWER   *was mowing* — *past progressive*

11. Sasha will have been watching television in the evening.

12. Matthew will be playing for a different team next spring.

13. The teacher did return our tests before the bell rang.

14. It had been snowing since 1:00 P.M.

15. I did tell my sister the truth.

16. Latoya and her friends will have been studying.

17. The play will have been over by 8:00 P.M.

18. The blue paint does look better than the green.

19. I will be ordering lunch for you.

20. Miguel is taking karate classes after school.

SPEAKING APPLICATION

Take turns with a partner. Tell what you did yesterday and what you plan to do today. Use past, present, and future forms of verb tenses. Your partner should listen for and identify each verb tense that you use.

WRITING APPLICATION

Write your own sentences, using different verb tenses. Then, underline the verb or verb phrase in each sentence, and write the tense of each verb.

The Four Principal Parts of Verbs

Every verb in the English language has four **principal parts** from which all of the tenses are formed.

> **A verb has four principal parts: the present, the present participle, the past, and the past participle.**

17.1.3 RULE

The chart below shows the principal parts of the verbs *wait*, *laugh*, and *run*.

THE FOUR PRINCIPAL PARTS			
PRESENT	PRESENT PARTICIPLE	PAST	PAST PARTICIPLE
wait	waiting	waited	(have) waited
laugh	laughing	laughed	(have) laughed
run	running	ran	(have) run

The first principal part, the present, is used for the basic forms of the present and future tenses, as well as for the emphatic forms or tenses. The present tense is formed by adding an -*s* or -*es* when the subject is *he, she, it,* or a singular noun. The future tense is formed with the helping verb *will. (I will wait. Mary will laugh. Carl will run.)* The present emphatic is formed with the helping verb *do* or *does. (I do wait. Mary does laugh. Carl does run.)* The past emphatic is formed with the helping verb *did. (I did wait. Mary did laugh. Carl did run.)*

The second principal part, the present participle, is used with helping verbs for all of the progressive forms. *(I am waiting. Mary is laughing. Carl is running.)*

The third principal part, the past, is used to form the past tense. *(I waited. Mary laughed. Carl ran.)* As in the example *ran,* the past tense of a verb can change its spelling. (See the next section for more information.)

See Practice 17.1C
See Practice 17.1D

The fourth principal part, the past participle, is used with helping verbs to create the perfect tenses. *(I have waited. Mary had laughed. Carl had run.)*

PRACTICE 17.1C > **Recognizing the Four Principal Parts of Verbs**

Read each sentence. Then, write the principal part and label as *present, present participle, past,* or *past participle.*

EXAMPLE   We were just walking past the school.

ANSWER   *walking* — *present participle*

1. Sue and Eric wash the dishes after dinner.
2. Liam is reading in bed for a while.
3. The team practiced soccer for several hours.
4. I had quoted that profound speech.
5. It is raining lightly.
6. Jing and Grace reached the end of the trail.
7. The storm had flooded the streets.
8. Jen had better grades than Seth.
9. I drove you home after practice.
10. Taylor is taking world history this semester.

PRACTICE 17.1D > **Identifying the Four Principal Parts of Verbs**

Read each sentence. Then, identify the principal part used to form each verb.

EXAMPLE   They are playing chess.

ANSWER   *present participle*

11. I fell on the slippery path.
12. They have read a play by William Shakespeare.
13. The glass vase shattered.
14. I believe in miracles.
15. She is smiling happily.
16. He is running to the library.
17. I promised earnestly.
18. She is forgetting about the dinner party.
19. They arrived on time.
20. You are leading the procession.

SPEAKING APPLICATION

Take turns with a partner. Tell about a place that you have visited. Your partner should listen for and identify the principal parts that you use.

WRITING APPLICATION

Write four sentences that use each of the four principal parts. Then, circle the principal part in each sentence, and write the name of that principal part.

Regular and Irregular Verbs

The way the past and past participle forms of a verb are formed determines whether the verb is **regular** or **irregular.**

Regular Verbs The majority of verbs are regular. Regular verbs form their past and past participles according to a predictable pattern.

> **A regular verb** is one for which the past and past participle are formed by adding *-ed* or *-d* to the present form.

RULE 17.1.4

In the chart below, notice that a final consonant is sometimes doubled to form the present participle, the past, and the past participle. A final *e* may also be dropped to form the participle.

See Practice 17.1E

See Practice 17.1F

PRINCIPAL PARTS OF REGULAR VERBS			
PRESENT	PRESENT PARTICIPLE	PAST	PAST PARTICIPLE
manage	managing	managed	(have) managed
describe	describing	described	(have) described
slip	slipping	slipped	(have) slipped

Irregular Verbs Although most verbs are regular, many of the most common verbs are irregular. Irregular verbs do not use a predictable pattern to form their past and past participles.

> **An irregular verb** is one whose past and past participle are *not* formed by adding *-ed* or *-d* to the present form.

RULE 17.1.5

Usage Problems Remembering the principal parts of irregular verbs can help you avoid usage problems. One common usage problem is using a principal part that is not standard.

INCORRECT Kim **sleeped** late this morning.

CORRECT Kim **slept** late this morning.

A second usage problem is confusing the past and past participle when they have different forms.

INCORRECT Tamara **done** her research in the library.

CORRECT Tamara **did** her research in the library.

Some common irregular verbs are shown in the charts that follow. Use a dictionary if you are not sure how to form the principal parts of an irregular verb.

IRREGULAR VERBS WITH THE SAME PRESENT, PAST, AND PAST PARTICIPLE			
PRESENT	PRESENT PARTICIPLE	PAST	PAST PARTICIPLE
burst	bursting	burst	(have) burst
cost	costing	cost	(have) cost
cut	cutting	cut	(have) cut
hit	hitting	hit	(have) hit
hurt	hurting	hurt	(have) hurt
let	letting	let	(have) let
put	putting	put	(have) put
set	setting	set	(have) set
shut	shutting	shut	(have) shut
split	splitting	split	(have) split
spread	spreading	spread	(have) spread

Note About *Be: Be* is one of the most irregular of all of the verbs. The present participle of *be* is *being*. The past participle is *been*. The present and the past vary depending on the subject.

CONJUGATION OF *BE*		
	SINGULAR	PLURAL
Present	I am . You are . He, she, or it is .	We are . You are . They are .
Past	I was . You were . He, she, or it was .	We were . You were . They were .
Future	I will be . You will be . He, she, or it will be .	We will be . You will be . They will be .

IRREGULAR VERBS WITH THE SAME PAST AND PAST PARTICIPLE			
PRESENT	PRESENT PARTICIPLE	PAST	PAST PARTICIPLE
bring	bringing	brought	(have) brought
build	building	built	(have) built
buy	buying	bought	(have) bought
catch	catching	caught	(have) caught
fight	fighting	fought	(have) fought
find	finding	found	(have) found
get	getting	got	(have) got or (have) gotten
hold	holding	held	(have) held
keep	keeping	kept	(have) kept
lay	laying	laid	(have) laid
lead	leading	led	(have) led
leave	leaving	left	(have) left
lose	losing	lost	(have) lost
pay	paying	paid	(have) paid
say	saying	said	(have) said
sell	selling	sold	(have) sold
send	sending	sent	(have) sent
shine	shining	shone or shined	(have) shone or (have) shined
sit	sitting	sat	(have) sat
sleep	sleeping	slept	(have) slept
spend	spending	spent	(have) spent
stand	standing	stood	(have) stood
stick	sticking	stuck	(have) stuck
sting	stinging	stung	(have) stung
strike	striking	struck	(have) struck
swing	swinging	swung	(have) swung
teach	teaching	taught	(have) taught
win	winning	won	(have) won
wind	winding	wound	(have) wound

Verb Tenses **429**

IRREGULAR VERBS THAT CHANGE IN OTHER WAYS			
PRESENT	PRESENT PARTICIPLE	PAST	PAST PARTICIPLE
arise	arising	arose	(have) arisen
become	becoming	became	(have) become
begin	beginning	began	(have) begun
bite	biting	bit	(have) bitten
break	breaking	broke	(have) broken
choose	choosing	chose	(have) chosen
come	coming	came	(have) come
do	doing	did	(have) done
draw	drawing	drew	(have) drawn
drink	drinking	drank	(have) drunk
drive	driving	drove	(have) driven
eat	eating	ate	(have) eaten
fall	falling	fell	(have) fallen
fly	flying	flew	(have) flown
give	giving	gave	(have) given
go	going	went	(have) gone
grow	growing	grew	(have) grown
know	knowing	knew	(have) known
lie	lying	lay	(have) lain
ride	riding	rode	(have) ridden
ring	ringing	rang	(have) rung
rise	rising	rose	(have) risen
run	running	ran	(have) run
see	seeing	saw	(have) seen
sing	singing	sang	(have) sung
sink	sinking	sank	(have) sunk
speak	speaking	spoke	(have) spoken
swim	swimming	swam	(have) swum
take	taking	took	(have) taken
tear	tearing	tore	(have) torn
throw	throwing	threw	(have) thrown
wear	wearing	wore	(have) worn
write	writing	wrote	(have) written

See Practice 17.1G
See Practice 17.1H

PRACTICE 17.1E > Recognizing Principal Parts of Regular Verbs

Read each regular verb. Then, add the missing principal parts. The order of the parts should be present, present participle, past, and past participle.

EXAMPLE ____ ____ cluttered ____

ANSWER *clutter*
cluttering
cluttered
(have) cluttered

1. ____ applauding ____ ____
2. measure ____ ____ ____
3. produce ____ ____ ____
4. ____ ____ replaced ____
5. ____ smelling ____ ____
6. ____ ____ ____ (have) cheated
7. ____ embarrassing ____ ____
8. improve ____ ____ ____
9. ____ ____ ____ (have) squeezed
10. ____ ____ noticed ____

PRACTICE 17.1F > Using the Correct Form of Regular Verbs

Read each sentence. Then, fill in each blank by choosing the correct verb form from those given in parentheses.

EXAMPLE I ____ you were not in attendance at the meeting. (realizing, realized)

ANSWER *realized*

11. Vic ____ for a salad. (opt, opted)
12. Yesterday, I ____ Ling that she could come over after school today. (promise, promised)
13. The cheerleaders ____ chants during the football games. (shouting, shout)
14. I ____ that we should be allowed to leave books in our lockers. (agreeing, agree)
15. The ball ____ high. (bounced, bouncing)
16. The hurricane ____ an evacuation of the city. (has forced, forcing)
17. Please ____ me for dinner. (join, joined)
18. Mr. Turner is ____ the food and clothing drive. (managing, managed)
19. Mia ____ the award more times than any other student. (earning, has earned)
20. I ____ the furniture. (dusting, dusted)

SPEAKING APPLICATION

Take turns with a partner. Tell about something you did last summer. Use a different principal part in each of your sentences. Your partner should listen for and identify the principal parts in your sentences.

WRITING APPLICATION

Use your completion of sentence 20 as a model to write three sentences of your own. Replace the verb in sentence 20 with other participle forms of regular verbs.

PRACTICE 17.1G > **Recognizing Principal Parts of Irregular Verbs**

Read each word. Then, write the present participle, the past, and the past participle of each verb.

EXAMPLE   awake

ANSWER   *awaking, awoke, (have) awoken*

1. bring _____

2. fly _____

3. put _____

4. make _____

5. draw _____

6. hear _____

7. sing _____

8. break _____

9. tear _____

10. sit _____

PRACTICE 17.1H > **Supplying the Correct Form of Irregular Verbs**

Read each sentence. Then, write the appropriate form of each irregular verb indicated in parentheses.

EXAMPLE   NASA _____ the risks involved with a mission to the moon. (understand)

ANSWER   *understood*

11. The first steps on the moon were _____ by Neil Armstrong on July 20, 1969. (take)

12. He _____ the first man to walk on the surface of the moon. (become)

13. Armstrong _____ his way out of the *Eagle* and onto the moon. (make)

14. He later said that the ground _____ like powdered charcoal. (feel)

15. Armstrong _____ his first few minutes on the moon taking photographs. (spend)

16. He then _____ an American flag into the moon's surface. (stick)

17. Millions of Americans _____ the landing on their television screens. (see)

18. They _____ Armstrong speak from the moon. (hear)

19. Armstrong _____, "That's one small step for man, one giant leap for mankind." (say)

20. The United States had _____ the space race against the Soviet Union. (win)

SPEAKING APPLICATION

Take turns with a partner. Say the present form of five irregular verbs. Your partner should tell the present participle, past, and past participle of each verb.

WRITING APPLICATION

Write three sentences about what you think of the first moon landing. Include the correct form of at least three irregular verbs in your writing.

Verb Conjugation

The **conjugation** of a verb displays all of its different forms.

17.1.6 RULE

> A **conjugation** is a complete list of the singular and plural forms of a verb in a particular tense.

The singular forms of a verb are used with singular subjects (*I, you, he, she, it,* and singular nouns), and the plural forms are used with plural subjects (*we, you, they,* and plural nouns).

To conjugate a verb, you need the four principal parts: the present (*pay*), the present participle (*paying*), the past (*paid*), and the past participle (*paid*). You also need various helping verbs, such as *has, have,* or *will.*

Notice that only three principal parts—the present, the past, and the past participle—are used to conjugate all six of the basic forms.

CONJUGATION OF THE BASIC FORMS OF *PAY*		SINGULAR	PLURAL
Present	First Person Second Person Third Person	I pay. You pay. He, she, or it pays.	We pay. You pay. They pay.
Past	First Person Second Person Third Person	I paid. You paid. He, she, or it paid.	We paid. You paid. They paid.
Future	First Person Second Person Third Person	I will pay. You will pay. He, she, or it will pay.	We will pay. You will pay. They will pay.
Present Perfect	First Person Second Person Third Person	I have paid. You have paid. He, she, or it has paid.	We have paid. You have paid. They have paid.
Past Perfect	First Person Second Person Third Person	I had paid. You had paid. He, she, or it had paid.	We had paid. You had paid. They had paid.
Future Perfect	First Person Second Person Third Person	I will have paid. You will have paid. He, she, or it will have paid.	We will have paid. You will have paid. They will have paid.

See Practice 17.1I

Conjugating the Progressive Tense With *Be*

As you learned earlier, the **progressive tense** shows an ongoing action or condition. To form the progressive tense, use the present participle form of the verb (the *-ing* form) with a form of the verb *be*.

CONJUGATION OF THE PROGRESSIVE FORMS OF *PAY*		SINGULAR	PLURAL
Present Progressive	First Person Second Person Third Person	I am paying. You are paying. He, she, or it is paying.	We are paying. You are paying. They are paying.
Past Progressive	First Person Second Person Third Person	I was paying. You were paying. He, she, or it was paying.	We were paying. You were paying. They were paying.
Future Progressive	First Person Second Person Third Person	I will be paying. You will be paying. He, she, or it will be paying.	We will be paying. You will be paying. They will be paying.
Present Perfect Progressive	First Person Second Person Third Person	I have been paying. You have been paying. He, she, or it has been paying.	We have been paying. You have been paying. They have been paying.
Past Perfect Progressive	First Person Second Person Third Person	I had been paying. You had been paying. He, she, or it had been paying.	We had been paying. You had been paying. They had been paying.
Future Perfect Progressive	First Person Second Person Third Person	I will have been paying. You will have been paying. He, she, or it will have been paying.	We will have been paying. You will have been paying. They will have been paying.

See Practice 17.1J

PRACTICE 17.1I ▶ **Conjugating the Basic Forms of Verbs**

Read each verb. Then, complete the conjugations for all six basic forms of the verb, using the subject indicated in parentheses.

EXAMPLE   run (I)

ANSWER   *I run, I ran, I will run, I have run, I had run, I will have run*

1. sing (I) _____

2. jump (you) _____

3. see (she) _____

4. prepare (we) _____

5. think (they) _____

6. believe (he) _____

7. control (I) _____

8. fight (we) _____

9. laugh (she) _____

10. inspire (you) _____

PRACTICE 17.1J ▶ **Conjugating the Progressive Forms of Verbs**

Read each verb. Then, complete the conjugations for all six progressive forms of the verb, using the subject indicated in parentheses.

EXAMPLE   run (I)

ANSWER   *I am running, I was running, I will be running, I have been running, I had been running, I will have been running*

11. watch (they) _____

12. join (we) _____

13. kick (you) _____

14. collect (she) _____

15. wish (I) _____

16. choose (they) _____

17. learn (he) _____

18. cheer (we) _____

19. smile (you) _____

20. blush (she) _____

SPEAKING APPLICATION

Choose six verbs not used in Practice 17.1I. With a partner, take turns conjugating each verb for all six basic forms.

WRITING APPLICATION

Choose three verbs not used in Practice 17.1J. Conjugate each verb for all six progressive forms.

17.2 The Correct Use of Tenses

The basic, progressive, and emphatic forms of the six tenses show time within one of three general categories: **present**, **past**, and **future**. This section will explain how each verb form has a specific use that distinguishes it from the other forms.

WRITING COACH

Online

www.phwritingcoach.com

Grammar Tutorials
Brush up on your Grammar skills with these animated videos.

Grammar Practice
Practice your grammar skills with Writing Coach Online.

Grammar Games
Test your knowledge of grammar in this fast-paced interactive video game.

Present, Past, and Future Tense

Good usage depends on an understanding of how each form works within its general category of time to express meaning.

Uses of Tense in Present Time
Three different forms can be used to express present time.

RULE 17.2.1

The three forms of the **present tense** show present actions or conditions as well as various continuing actions or conditions.

EXPRESSING PRESENT TENSE	
Present	I study .
Present Progressive	I am studying .
Present Emphatic	I do study .

The main uses of the basic form of the present tense are shown in the chart below.

EXPRESSING PRESENT TENSE	
Present Action	Emma is swimming in a meet.
Present Condition	She wants to win.
Regularly Occurring Action	She practices every afternoon.
Regularly Occurring Condition	She is a strong swimmer.
Constant Action	People swim in pools all year.
Constant Condition	Some pools are open to the public.

See Practice 17.2A

Historical Present The present tense may also be used to express historical events. This use of the present, called the **historical present tense,** is occasionally used in narration to make past actions or conditions sound more lively.

THE HISTORICAL PRESENT TENSE	
Past Actions Expressed in Historical Present Tense	The Union soldier crawls up the hill and looks for enemy soldiers.
Past Condition Expressed in Historical Present Tense	The armies of the North and the South are at war with one another during the Civil War.

The **critical present tense** is most often used to discuss deceased authors and their literary achievements.

THE CRITICAL PRESENT TENSE	
Action Expressed in Critical Present	Walt Whitman writes about exploring the natural world.
Condition Expressed in Critical Present	In addition, Whitman is the author of several volumes of poetry.

The **present progressive tense** is used to show a continuing action or condition of a long or short duration.

USES OF THE PRESENT PROGRESSIVE TENSE	
Long Continuing Action	Keisha is working at the store.
Short Continuing Action	She is learning how to work the cash register.
Continuing Condition	She is hoping to become a manager.

The **present emphatic tense** has several specific uses.

USES OF THE PRESENT EMPHATIC TENSE	
Emphasizing a Statement	Peter does like to cook meals.
Denying a Contrary Assertion	No, he does not like to clean up after cooking.
Asking a Question	Does he know your recipe for spaghetti?
Stating a Negative	He does not have a sauce recipe he likes.

See Practice 17.2B

PRACTICE 17.2A > **Identifying the Tense in Present Time**

Read each sentence. Then, label the form of the underlined verb *present, present progressive,* or *present emphatic.*

EXAMPLE   My mother is making dinner in the kitchen.

ANSWER   *present progressive*

1. That flight <u>leaves</u> daily from Gate B at 3:00 P.M.

2. Many businesses <u>are offering</u> deals to fight the competition.

3. The shuttle bus <u>waits</u> to transport passengers.

4. The doctor's office <u>is</u> always busy.

5. A letter of congratulations <u>does seem</u> appropriate.

6. Dan <u>anticipates</u> a lengthy involvement.

7. I <u>notice</u> a new ship in the harbor.

8. John Williams <u>composes</u> with an attention to detail.

9. My brothers <u>are playing</u> video games in the den.

10. Professors <u>are</u> usually experts on their subjects.

PRACTICE 17.2B > **Supplying Verbs in Present Tense**

Read each sentence. Then, complete each sentence with an appropriate verb in the present tense.

EXAMPLE   First thing in the morning, Pete usually _____ his teeth.

ANSWER   *brushes*

11. Every afternoon after school, Jaya _____ her homework at the kitchen table.

12. The president of the United States _____ in the White House.

13. Connor _____ his teacher he will succeed in science class.

14. Stella, Jen, and Maria _____ to remain best friends forever.

15. Doug _____ his grandfather to the supermarket every Saturday morning.

16. Marcus _____ to his favorite radio station while eating breakfast every morning.

17. Jamie _____ his lunch to school instead of buying it in the cafeteria.

18. Jose and his brother _____ groceries after school.

19. Cara _____ to the National Honor Society at her high school.

20. Raj _____ the winning serve for the volleyball team.

SPEAKING APPLICATION

Take turns with a partner. Tell about things that happen in your school community. Your partner should listen for and name the use of present-tense verbs in your sentences.

WRITING APPLICATION

Write five sentences that use verbs in the present tense. Underline the verbs in your sentences.

Uses of Tense in Past Time
There are seven verb forms that express past actions or conditions.

> The seven forms that express **past tense** show actions and conditions that began at some time in the past.

FORMS EXPRESSING PAST TENSE	
Past	I drew.
Present Perfect	I have drawn.
Past Perfect	I had drawn.
Past Progressive	I was drawing.
Present Perfect Progressive	I have been drawing.
Past Perfect Progressive	I had been drawing.
Past Emphatic	I did draw.

The uses of the most common form, the past, are shown below.

USES OF THE PAST TENSE	
Completed Action	Kate edited Bob's paper.
Completed Condition	She was careful to catch Bob's errors.

Notice in the chart above that the time of the action or the condition could be changed from indefinite to definite if such words as *last week* or *yesterday* were added to the sentences.

See Practice 17.2C

Present Perfect The **present perfect tense** always expresses indefinite time. Use it to show actions or conditions continuing from the past to the present.

USES OF THE PRESENT PERFECT TENSE	
Completed Action (Indefinite Time)	They have rehearsed their parts.
Completed Condition (Indefinite Time)	They have been in this theater.
Action Continuing to Present	The tickets have been selling well.
Condition Continuing to Present	I have been hoping people would enjoy the play.

Past Perfect The **past perfect tense** expresses an action that took place before another action.

USES OF THE PAST PERFECT TENSE	
Action Completed Before Another Action	My teacher had created the final exam before she gave us study guidelines.
Condition Completed Before Another Condition	The student had been until she began to have doubts.

These charts show the **past progressive** and **emphatic tenses.**

USES OF THE PROGRESSIVE TENSE TO EXPRESS PAST TIME	
Past Progressive	LONG CONTINUING ACTION We were planing a seaside vacation. SHORT CONTINUING ACTION We were trying to surf. CONTINUOUS CONDITION I was being brave, even if a bit scared.
Present Perfect Progressive	CONTINUING ACTION We have been swimming all winter to increase our endurance.
Past Perfect Progressive	CONTINUING ACTION INTERRUPTED We had been dreaming of big waves, but then we decided that small ones would be fine.

USES OF THE PAST EMPHATIC TENSE	
Emphasizing a Statement	My guitar playing did improve after I tried your technique.
Denying a Contrary Assertion	Yes, I did practice the chords!
Asking a Question	Where did you learn how to play so well?
Making a Sentence Negative	I did not appreciate how hard it was to play the guitar.

See Practice 17.2D

PRACTICE 17.2C Identifying Tense in Past Time

Read each sentence. Then, write the verb in each sentence that shows past time and identify the tense form.

EXAMPLE   The police officer rerouted all traffic.

ANSWER   *rerouted— past*

1. The visitor had left after knocking on the door for several minutes.
2. We played Central High's basketball team twice this season.
3. We did follow all of the rules of the game.
4. I have been in a great mood all week.
5. The first settlers lived a much simpler life.
6. After a few days, we had adjusted to the new schedule.
7. A small crowd was gathering in the courtyard.
8. My first class started at 8:00 A.M.
9. We had finished reviewing our notes just before the fire drill.
10. The class officers have been meeting about the theme for the spring dance.

PRACTICE 17.2D Supplying Verbs in Past Time

Read each sentence. Then, write the form of each verb indicated in parentheses.

EXAMPLE   We _____ the Vatican during our trip to Rome. (visit; past progressive)

ANSWER   *were visiting*

11. I _____ the test long before the time was up. (complete; past perfect)
12. The baby _____ through the night. (sleep; past perfect progressive)
13. I was happy to see that it _____ during the night. (snow; past perfect progressive)
14. We _____ years for the eclipse to reoccur. (wait; past perfect progressive)
15. It _____ unusually cold out when I left my house this morning. (be; past perfect)
16. The new movie theater in town _____. (open; past perfect)
17. The game _____ when we got to the arena. (start; past progressive)
18. I _____ at the student council assembly yesterday. (speak; past emphatic)
19. Frank worried that he _____ to a hasty conclusion. (jump; past perfect)
20. We _____ in the library for hours. (study; past emphatic)

SPEAKING APPLICATION

Take turns with a partner. Identify the use of the past-tense verbs in the sentences in Practice 17.2C.

WRITING APPLICATION

Use your correction of sentence 17 as a model to write three sentences of your own. Replace the verb in your corrected sentence with other past progressive forms of verbs.

Uses of Tense in Future Time

The **future tense** shows actions or conditions that will happen at a later date.

RULE
17.2.3

> The future tense expresses actions or conditions that have not yet occurred.

FORMS EXPRESSING FUTURE TENSE	
Future	I will drive .
Future Perfect	I will have driven .
Future Progressive	I will be driving .
Future Perfect Progressive	I will have been driving .

USES OF THE FUTURE AND THE FUTURE PERFECT TENSE	
Future	I will jog every afternoon. I will take different routes.
Future Perfect	I will have jogged ten miles every day this week. At the end of this month, I will have jogged for four years.

Notice in the next chart that the **future progressive** and the **future perfect progressive tenses** express only future actions.

USES OF THE PROGRESSIVE TENSE TO EXPRESS FUTURE TIME	
Future Progressive	Janice will be playing tennis today.
Future Perfect Progressive	When she graduates, she will have been playing for four years on the high school team.

The basic forms of the present and the present progressive tense are often used with other words to express future time.

EXAMPLES   The movie **opens** downtown next week.

My friends **are waiting** to see it.

See Practice 17.2E
See Practice 17.2F

PRACTICE 17.2E > **Identifying Future Tense**

Read each sentence. Then, write the future-tense verbs in each sentence and identify the form of the tense.

EXAMPLE   The train will be arriving shortly.

ANSWER   *will be arriving — future progressive*

1. The convention will have continued for another five days.
2. The play will be running for ten years.
3. They will have played the other team by then.
4. We will be traveling over Pike's Peak.
5. This will have been my first airplane ride.
6. Tomorrow night we will adjust our clocks.
7. We will be at the beach soon.
8. He will have been working at the ranch.
9. The guests will have arrived at the party by noon.
10. Susan will compete in the swim meet on Saturday.

PRACTICE 17.2F > **Supplying Verbs in Future Tense**

Read each sentence. Then, rewrite each sentence, filling in the blank with the future tense of the verb indicated in parentheses.

EXAMPLE   The children _____ outside tonight. (sleep, future)

ANSWER   *The children will sleep outside tonight.*

11. The paint _____ by tomorrow. (dry, future progressive)
12. She _____ to Europe. (travel, future perfect)
13. The doctor said that she _____ before next week. (heal, future perfect)
14. The school day _____ at 3:00. (end, future)
15. Caitlyn _____ home by 5:00 P.M. (walk, future perfect)
16. Tonight, I _____ the entire house. (clean, future progressive)
17. The cast _____ all day today. (practice, future)
18. By the end of the year, I _____ at the same job for four years. (work, future perfect progressive)
19. He _____ his paper after school. (write, future progressive)
20. The clowns _____ at the rodeo by this weekend. (perform, future perfect progressive)

SPEAKING APPLICATION

Take turns with a partner. Tell about your career plans or what you hope to be doing in ten years. Use future-tense verbs in your sentences. Your partner should listen for and name the future-tense verbs that you use.

WRITING APPLICATION

Rewrite your corrections for sentences 11, 12, and 13, changing the verbs to include other future-tense verbs. Make sure your sentences still make sense.

Sequence of Tenses

A sentence with more than one verb must be consistent in its
time sequence.

> When showing a sequence of events, do not shift tenses
> unnecessarily.

EXAMPLES   Jim **will wait** for me, then we **will walk** home.

My dog **has brought** me her ball and **has gotten**
her leash.

I **swam** all afternoon and **slept** all night.

Sometimes, however, it is necessary to shift tenses, especially
when a sentence is complex or compound-complex. The tense
of the main verb often determines the tense of the verb in the
subordinate clause.

Verbs in Subordinate Clauses It is frequently necessary to look
at the tense of the main verb in a sentence before choosing the
tense of the verb in the subordinate clause.

> The tense of a verb in a subordinate clause should follow
> logically from the tense of the main verb.

INCORRECT   I **thought** that Marta **will go** downtown.

CORRECT   I **thought** that Marta **went** downtown.

As you study the combinations of tenses in the charts on the next
pages, notice that the choice of tenses affects the logical relationship
between the events being expressed. Some combinations indicate
that the events are **simultaneous**—meaning that they occur at
the same time. Other combinations indicate that the events are
sequential—meaning that one event occurs before or after the other.

SEQUENCE OF EVENTS		
MAIN VERB	**SUBORDINATE VERB**	**MEANING**
MAIN VERB IN PRESENT TENSE		
I understand...	**PRESENT** that she cooks delicious meals. **PRESENT PROGRESSIVE** that she is cooking delicious meals. **PRESENT EMPHATIC** that she does cook delicious meals.	Simultaneous events: All events occur in present time.
I understand...	**PAST** that she cooked delicious meals. **PRESENT PERFECT** that she has cooked delicious meals. **PAST PERFECT** that she had cooked delicious meals. **PAST PROGRESSIVE** that she was cooking delicious meals. **PRESENT PERFECT PROGRESSIVE** that she has been cooking delicious meals. **PAST PERFECT PROGRESSIVE** that she had been cooking delicious meals. **PAST EMPHATIC** that she did cook delicious meals.	Sequential events: The cooking comes before the understanding.
I understand...	**FUTURE** that she will cook delicious meals. **FUTURE PERFECT** that she will have cooked delicious meals. **FUTURE PROGRESSIVE** that she will be cooking delicious meals. **FUTURE PERFECT PROGRESSIVE** that she will have been cooking delicious meals.	Sequential events: The understanding comes before the cooking.

SEQUENCE OF EVENTS

MAIN VERB	SUBORDINATE VERB	MEANING
MAIN VERB IN PAST TENSE		
I understood…	**PAST** that she cooked delicious meals. **PAST PROGRESSIVE** that she was cooking delicious meals. **PAST EMPHATIC** that she did cook delicious meals.	Simultaneous events: All events take place in the past.
I understood…	**PAST PERFECT** that she had cooked delicious meals. **PAST PERFECT PROGRESSIVE** that she had been cooking delicious meals.	Sequential events: The cooking came before the understanding.
MAIN VERB IN FUTURE TENSE		
I will understand…	**PRESENT** if she cooks delicious meals. **PRESENT PROGRESSIVE** if she is cooking delicious meals. **PRESENT EMPHATIC** if she does cook delicious meals.	Simultaneous events: All events take place in future time.
I will understand…	**PAST** if she cooked delicious meals. **PRESENT PERFECT** if she has cooked delicious meals. **PRESENT PERFECT PROGRESSIVE** if she has been cooking delicious meals. **PAST EMPHATIC** if she did cook delicious meals.	Sequential events: The cooking comes before the understanding.

Time Sequence With Participles and Infinitives Frequently, the form of a participle or infinitive determines whether the events are simultaneous or sequential. Participles can be present (*watching*), past (*watched*), or perfect (*having watched*). Infinitives can be present (*to watch*) or perfect (*to have watched*).

> **The form of a participle or an infinitive should logically relate to the verb in the same clause or sentence.**

17.2.6 RULE

To show simultaneous events, you will generally need to use the present participle or the present infinitive, whether the main verb is present, past, or future.

Simultaneous Events

| IN PRESENT TIME | **Watching** the movie, she **cries**. |
| | present · · · present |

| IN PAST TIME | **Watching** the movie, she **cried**. |
| | present · · · past |

| IN FUTURE TIME | **Watching** the movie, she **will cry**. |
| | present · · · future |

To show sequential events, use the perfect form of the participle and infinitive, regardless of the tense of the main verb.

Sequential Events

IN PRESENT TIME	**Having watched** the movie, she **is crying**.
	perfect · · · present progressive
	(She watched *before* she cried.)

IN PAST TIME	**Having watched** the movie, she **cried**.
	perfect · · · past
	(She watched *before* she cried.)

See Practice 17.2G
See Practice 17.2H
See Practice 17.2I
See Practice 17.2J

SPANNING PAST AND FUTURE TIME	**Having watched** the movie, she **will cry**.
	perfect · · · future
	(She will cry *after* watching.)

PRACTICE 17.2G > Identifying the Time Sequence in Sentences With More Than One Verb

Read each sentence. Then, write the verb of the event that happens second in each sentence.

EXAMPLE   Even though the alarm clock rings, I roll over in my bed.

ANSWER   *roll*

1. She had been working on the project for two years before she made her first discovery.

2. In the past, most people wanted big cars, but now many drive small ones.

3. I wanted a big minivan, but I will be getting a small sedan instead.

4. Most children learn to talk after they have learned to walk.

5. Greg likes to reminisce about the fish that he caught last summer.

6. Astronomers predict that the sun will stop giving off energy in about ten billion years.

7. When the crew saw land, they cheered.

8. People will buy homes when interest rates are lowered.

9. Students will get their prizes after we verify their scores.

10. I start my summer job as soon as I finish orientation.

PRACTICE 17.2H > Recognizing and Correcting Errors in Tense Sequence

Read each sentence. Then, if a sentence has an error in tense sequence, rewrite it to correct the error. If a sentence is correct, write *correct*.

EXAMPLE   The river flows down the valley and emptied into the lake.

ANSWER   *The river flows down the valley and empties into the lake.*

11. The wind changed directions and became stronger.

12. The volcano erupted and destroys the tiny island.

13. A robin catches worms and fed her young.

14. The nurses checked on their patients and give them their medicine.

15. All of the students studied hard and learn the material.

16. The puppets sang and dance to the music.

17. One of the horses kicked down the fence and ran toward the woods.

18. The skier turns and came to a stop on the slope.

19. The kitten hides under the bed and slept.

20. The rider got off her horse and removes the saddle.

SPEAKING APPLICATION

Take turns with a partner. Tell about something fun you like to do. Use two verbs in each of your sentences. Your partner should listen for and identify the sequence of events in all of your sentences.

WRITING APPLICATION

Use sentences 11, 13, and 15 as models to write your own sentences with incorrect tense sequence. Then, exchange papers with a partner. Your partner should rewrite your sentences, using the correct sequence in tense.

PRACTICE 17.2I ▷ Sequencing Tenses in Subordinate Clauses

Read each sentence. Then, for each subordinate clause, fill in the blank with the correct tense of the verb specified in parentheses.

EXAMPLE   Ana remembers the trail she _____ last winter. (ski; past)

ANSWER   *skied*

1. Frank already knows where he _____ college. (attend; future)

2. After Julio _____ the sauce, he put the meat in the oven. (make; past)

3. I realize that I _____ this before. (do; present perfect)

4. Renee went to New York, where she _____ before. (go; present perfect)

5. I wonder why Trent _____ so quickly. (run; past progressive)

6. Charles never wins a game, although he _____. (try; present)

7. If Tom _____ all day, why doesn't he sound better? (practice; present perfect progressive)

8. I expect that Jess _____ tomorrow. (arrive; future progressive)

9. When April _____, she forgets all her troubles. (dance; present progressive)

10. Though next week Dee _____ for six months, she still has much to learn. (work; future perfect progressive)

PRACTICE 17.2J ▷ Sequencing Tenses in Main Clauses

Read each sentence. Then, add a verb to finish the main clause attached to each phrase. Show whether events are simultaneous or sequential by putting the verb in the tense indicated in parentheses.

EXAMPLE   Having stayed up all night, Joe _____. (present progressive)

ANSWER   *Having stayed up all night, Joe is dozing off now.*

11. Listening to music, Rena _____. (present)

12. Having studied for the test, Tim _____. (future)

13. Reading a funny book, Steve _____. (past)

14. Having locked the door, Tina _____. (past)

15. Following his coach's advice, Les _____. (future)

16. Having finished his homework, Carlos _____. (present progressive)

17. Running as fast as he can, Roger _____. (present)

18. Having received an A on her paper, Maddy _____. (past)

19. Stalking her prey, the lion _____. (past)

20. Having heard about a summer job, Jenna _____. (future)

SPEAKING APPLICATION

Take turns with a partner. Say each sentence in Practice 17.2I. Have your partner identify the tense of the verb in each main clause.

WRITING APPLICATION

Review your sentences for Practice 17.2J. Rewrite them, providing a new phrase to start each sentence. Change the tense of the main clause as needed.

Test Warm-Up

DIRECTIONS
Read the introduction and the passage that follows. Then, answer the
questions to show that you can use and understand the correct sequence
of tenses in reading and writing.

*Charmain wrote this paragraph about a Nobel Peace Prize winner. Read
the paragraph and think about the changes you would suggest as a peer
editor. When you finish reading, answer the questions that follow.*

Planting Trees for Peace

(1) Parts of Africa are becoming deserts because forests were cleared.
(2) As trees will be cut down, women had to walk miles to gather
firewood. (3) In 1977, a Kenyan biologist named Wangari Maathai
addressed the problem and starts the Green Belt Movement. (4) Local
women began planting trees. (5) In less than 30 years, they have planted
30 million trees, which provide fuel, food, shelter, and income. (6) Maathai
was recognized for her work; in 2004, she wins the Nobel Peace Prize.

---

1 What is the most effective way to revise
sentence 2?

  A As trees will be cut down, women had to
walk miles to be gathering firewood.

  B As trees will be cut down, women will
have to walk miles to gather firewood.

  C As trees were cut down, women had to
walk miles to gather firewood.

  D Make no change

2 What change should be made in sentence 3?

  F Change *starts* to **started**

  G Change *addressed* to **addresses**

  H Change *addressed* to **addressing** and
starts to **starting**

  J Change *addressed* to **address** and
starts to **start**

3 What is the most effective way to revise
sentence 5?

  A In less than 30 years, they had planted
30 million trees, which had provided fuel,
food, shelter, and income.

  B In less than 30 years, they will be
planting 30 million trees, which provide
fuel, food, shelter, and income.

  C In less than 30 years, they will plant 30
million trees, which provide fuel, food,
shelter, and income.

  D Make no change

4 What change, if any, should be made in
sentence 6?

  F Change *was* to **will be**

  G Change *wins* to **won**

  H Change *was* to **is**

  J Make no change

Modifiers That Help Clarify Tense

The time expressed by a verb can often be clarified by adverbs such as *often*, *sometimes*, *always*, or *frequently* and phrases such as *once in a while*, *within a week*, *last week*, or *now and then*.

> **Use modifiers when they can help clarify tense.**

17.2.7 RULE

In the examples below, the modifiers that help clarify the tense of the verb are highlighted in orange. Think about how the sentences would read without the modifiers. Modifiers help to make your writing more precise and interesting.

EXAMPLES

Dogs **like** to run **every day**.

My dog **goes** to the park **once a day**.

My dog **goes** to the park **now and then**.
(These two sentences have very different meanings.)

Occasionally, I **walk** my dog all the way to the dog run.

She **always loves** to play with other dogs.

By tomorrow, we **will have gone** to the dog run three times this week.

My dog also **likes** to walk **twice a day**.

Playing catch **is now** one of her favorite sports.

Sometimes, she **attempts** to catch the ball before I throw it.

She **always pants** hard after she plays catch.

See Practice 17.2K
See Practice 17.2L

> **Identifying Modifiers That Help Clarify Tense**

Read each sentence. Then, write the modifier in each sentence that helps clarify the verb tense.

EXAMPLE   This morning, they cooked breakfast for the whole family.

ANSWER   *This morning*

1. Chad always has trouble getting up early.

2. Every morning, Shoshana makes her bed.

3. I never want to see another tragic drama again.

4. We finally finished our project at midnight.

5. He occasionally helps his mother in her garden.

6. I practice my karate movements every day.

7. My mother always includes a note in my lunch box.

8. It is just now time for dinner.

9. Suddenly, the door burst open.

10. My sister vacuums the house every week.

> **Supplying Modifiers to Clarify Meaning**

Read each sentence. Then, fill in the blank with a modifier that will clarify the meaning of each sentence.

EXAMPLE   _____, the bus departs at 9:15 A.M.

ANSWER   *Daily*

11. I _____ see a plane in the sky.

12. _____, the phone began to ring.

13. The little ducks jumped into the pond _____.

14. Keshaun _____ decided to return my phone call.

15. My father _____ wants to eat liver and onions.

16. _____, we watch movies and eat out on Friday nights.

17. Skyler goes to swim practice _____.

18. It is _____ time to put the turkey in the oven.

19. We _____ prepare a healthy meal for one another.

20. _____, my mother lets me stay up late.

SPEAKING APPLICATION

Take turns with a partner. Tell about trips that you have taken. Use modifiers that help clarify tense in your sentences. Your partner should listen for and identify the modifiers in your sentences.

WRITING APPLICATION

Use your corrections for sentences 11, 13, and 19 as models to write your own sentences. Rewrite the sentences to include different modifiers that clarify meaning.

17.3 The Subjunctive Mood

There are three **moods,** or ways in which a verb can express an action or condition: **indicative, imperative,** and **subjunctive.** The **indicative** mood, which is the most common, is used to make statements (*Karl is helpful.*) and to ask questions (*Is Karl helpful?*). The **imperative** mood is used to give orders or directions (*Be helpful.*).

Using the Subjunctive Mood

There are two important differences between verbs in the **subjunctive** mood and those in the indicative mood. First, in the present tense, third-person singular verbs in the subjunctive mood do not have the usual *-s* or *-es* ending. Second, the subjunctive mood of *be* in the present tense is *be;* in the past tense, it is *were,* regardless of the subject.

INDICATIVE MOOD	SUBJUNCTIVE MOOD
He practices his music.	I suggest that he practice every day.
We are here to perform.	We insist that everyone be ready to perform.
We are prepared.	If we were not prepared, we would not perform well.

Use the subjunctive mood (1) in clauses beginning with *if* or *that* to express an idea that is contrary to fact or (2) in clauses beginning with *that* to express a request, a demand, or a proposal.

17.3.1 RULE

Expressing Ideas Contrary to Fact Ideas that are contrary to fact are commonly expressed as wishes or conditions. Using the subjunctive mood in these situations shows that the idea expressed is not true now and may never be true.

EXAMPLES   Emma wishes that the sun **were** shining.

She wished that she **were** able to go to the beach.

She could have had more fun if the weather **were** clear.

Some *if* clauses do not take a subjunctive verb. If the idea expressed may be true, an indicative form is used.

EXAMPLES   I told my little brother that **if** the sun **was** shining, we'd go to the park.

If he **was** ready, we could leave.

Expressing Requests, Demands, and Proposals Verbs that request, demand, or propose are often followed by a *that* clause containing a verb in the subjunctive mood.

REQUEST   The instructor requests that the student **drive** carefully.

DEMAND   It is required that the student **drive** carefully.

PROPOSAL   He proposed that the student **drive** carefully.   See Practice 17.3A

Auxiliary Verbs That Express the Subjunctive Mood

Because certain helping verbs suggest conditions contrary to fact, they can often be used in place of the subjunctive mood.

Could, would, or *should* can be used with a verb to express the subjunctive mood.

The sentences on the left in the chart below have the usual subjunctive form of the verb *be: were.* The sentences on the right have been reworded with *could, would,* and *should.*

THE SUBJUNCTIVE MOOD WITH AUXILIARY VERBS	
WITH FORMS OF *BE*	**WITH *COULD, WOULD,* OR *SHOULD***
If the sky **were** to clear, we'd go out.	If the sky **should** be clear, we'd go out.
If she **were** to win the scholarship, she'd be happy.	If she **could** win the scholarship, she'd be happy.
If I **were** to write to you, would you answer me?	If I **should** write to you, would you answer me?

See Practice 17.3B

PRACTICE 17.3A Identifying Mood (Indicative, Imperative, Subjunctive)

Read each sentence. Then, identify whether each sentence expresses the *indicative, imperative*, or *subjunctive* mood.

EXAMPLE   If I were you, I would buy some land.

ANSWER   *subjunctive*

1. Sheila may demand a refund for the damaged goods.

2. Gary will bring flashlights on the company trip.

3. If I were tired, I would take a nap.

4. Julio was there at the park.

5. Do you recommend reading *The Grapes of Wrath?*

6. It is best that John and Jagger work together.

7. I need to leave soon.

8. Give me a hand with this leaking faucet.

9. It is necessary to keep an emergency kit in your car.

10. Be home by 9:00.

PRACTICE 17.3B Supplying Auxiliary Verbs to Express the Subjunctive Mood

Read each sentence. Then, rewrite each sentence, completing it by supplying an auxiliary verb to express the subjunctive mood.

EXAMPLE   If there were a concert tonight, we _____ go.

ANSWER   *If there were a concert tonight, we would go.*

11. John _____ prefer that his son go hiking.

12. If you checked with your mother first, I _____ be surprised.

13. If it were possible to help him, I _____ do it.

14. If he had come home early, we _____ have been supportive.

15. I _____ go to the game if the weather were better.

16. If you had studied, you _____ answer those questions.

17. If I were you, I _____ keep doing that.

18. If my earrings were gold, they _____ be worth a lot of money.

19. If this were Friday, we _____ be finished with our tests.

20. If your brother were a year or two older, he _____ join our team.

SPEAKING APPLICATION

With a partner, take turns saying sentences that express the indicative, imperative, and subjunctive moods. Your partner should listen for and identify which mood each sentence expresses.

WRITING APPLICATION

Use the auxiliary verbs that you used to rewrite sentences 12, 16, and 17 to write your own sentences. Make sure that your sentences express the subjunctive mood.

17.4 Voice

This section discusses a characteristic of verbs called **voice**.

RULE 17.4.1

Voice or tense is the form of a verb that shows whether the subject is performing the action or is being acted upon.

In English, there are two voices: **active** and **passive.** Only action verbs can indicate voice; linking verbs cannot.

Active and Passive Voice or Tense

If the subject of a verb performs the action, the verb is active; if the subject receives the action, the verb is passive.

Active Voice Any action verb can be used in the active voice. The action verb may be transitive (that is, it may have a direct object) or intransitive (without a direct object).

RULE 17.4.2

A verb is active if its subject performs the action.

In the examples below, the subject performs the action. In the first example, the verb *telephoned* is transitive; *team* is the direct object, which receives the action. In the second example, the verb *developed* is transitive; *pictures* is the direct object. In the third example, the verb *gathered* is intransitive; it has no direct object. In the last example, the verb *worked* is intransitive and has no direct object.

ACTIVE VOICE

The captain **telephoned** the **team**.
　　　　　　　transitive verb　　　direct object

Bill **developed** twenty-five **pictures** of the ocean.
　　　transitive verb　　　　　　direct object

Telephone messages **gathered** on the desk while
　　　　　　　　　　　intransitive verb
she was away.

Bill **worked** quickly.
　　intransitive verb

See Practice 17.4A
See Practice 17.4B

Passive Voice Most action verbs can also be used in the passive voice.

> **A verb is passive if its action is performed upon the subject.**

17.4.3 RULE

In the following examples, the subjects are the receivers of the action. The first example names the performer, the captain, as the object of the preposition *by* instead of the subject. In the second example, no performer of the action is mentioned.

PASSIVE VOICE

The **team** **was telephoned** by the captain.
receiver of action — verb

The **messages** **were gathered** into neat piles.
receiver of action — verb

> **A passive verb is always a verb phrase made from a form of *be* plus the past participle of a verb. The tense of the helping verb *be* determines the tense of the passive verb.**

17.4.4 RULE

The chart below provides a conjugation in the passive voice of the verb *choose* in the three moods. Notice that there are only two progressive forms and no emphatic form.

THE VERB *CHOOSE* IN THE PASSIVE VOICE	
Present Indicative	He is chosen.
Past Indicative	He was chosen.
Future Indicative	He will be chosen.
Present Perfect Indicative	He has been chosen.
Past Perfect Indicative	He had been chosen.
Future Perfect Indicative	He will have been chosen.
Present Progressive Indicative	He is being chosen.
Past Progressive Indicative	He was being chosen.
Present Imperative	(You) be chosen.
Present Subjunctive	(if) he be chosen
Past Subjunctive	(if) he were chosen

See Practice 17.2C

Using Active and Passive Voice

Writing that uses the active voice tends to be much more lively than writing that uses the passive voice. The active voice is usually more direct and economical. That is because active voice shows someone doing something.

RULE 17.4.5

Use the active voice whenever possible.

ACTIVE VOICE   Anthony **won** the trophy.

PASSIVE VOICE   The trophy **was won** by Anthony.

The passive voice has two uses in English.

RULE 17.4.6

Use the passive voice when you want to emphasize the receiver of an action rather than the performer of an action.

EXAMPLE   The boat **was rocked** by the ocean, and it felt like the boat might capsize.

RULE 17.4.7

Use the passive voice to point out the receiver of an action whenever the performer is not important or not easily identified.

EXAMPLE   Joe **was selected** to represent our school.

The active voice lends more excitement to writing, making it more interesting to readers. In the example below, notice how the sentence you just read has been revised to show someone doing something, rather than something just happening.

EXAMPLE   The ocean **rocked** the boat, and it felt like the boat might capsize.

(*What* rocked the boat and made it feel like it might capsize?)   See Practice 17.4D

PRACTICE 17.4A > **Recognizing Active Voice (Active Tense)**

Read each sentence. Then, write the active verb(s) in each sentence.

EXAMPLE   The storm battered and damaged the oak tree.

ANSWER   *battered, damaged*

1. My mother painted that picture and framed it herself.

2. The delivery person left a package on the front porch.

3. The detective examined and documented the evidence.

4. The airliner landed safely.

5. My aunt taught me the game of tennis.

6. The sanctuary houses and protects wild animals.

7. The two astronauts floated in space.

8. The man slowly opened the front door and then let the dog out.

9. A famous architect designed that building.

10. I planned and prepared tonight's meal with care.

PRACTICE 17.4B > **Using Active Verbs**

Read each item. Then, write different sentences, using each item as an active verb or verbs.

EXAMPLE   informed

ANSWER   *Cherie informed me about the quiz.*

11. cancels

12. journeyed

13. swarmed

14. smelled, ate

15. climbed, saw

16. sings, watches

17. returned

18. fishing, caught

19. paid, walked

20. spotted

SPEAKING APPLICATION

Take turns with a partner. Say sentences in the active voice. Your partner should listen for and identify the active verbs in each of your sentences.

WRITING APPLICATION

Write two sentences in the active voice, using more than one active verb in each sentence.

PRACTICE 17.4C > Forming the Tenses of Passive Verbs

Read each verb. Then, using the subject indicated in parentheses, conjugate each verb in the passive voice for the present indicative, past indicative, future indicative, present perfect indicative, and future perfect indicative.

EXAMPLE   bite (it)

ANSWER   *it is bitten, it was bitten, it will be bitten, it has been bitten, it had been bitten, it will have been bitten*

1. interrupt (he)

2. open (it)

3. select (she)

4. use (it)

5. alarm (we)

6. choose (he)

7. stop (she)

8. win (it)

9. sell (it)

10. convince (you)

PRACTICE 17.4D > Supplying Verbs in the Active Voice (Active Tense)

Read each sentence. Then, complete each sentence by supplying a verb in the active voice.

EXAMPLE   The San Antonio Spurs _____ the championship.

ANSWER   *won*

11. Georgia _____ the paper.

12. The students _____ the reports.

13. The quarterback _____ the football for more than forty yards.

14. Thousands of fans _____ the concert.

15. The people in the restaurant _____ the chef's special.

16. Vincent van Gogh _____ the picture.

17. The children's librarian _____ the story with great expression.

18. Jorge and I _____ the gifts.

19. The hungry children _____ the meal.

20. A famous author _____ the book.

SPEAKING APPLICATION

Take turns with a partner. Say active verbs. Your partner should say the basic forms of each verb in the passive voice.

WRITING APPLICATION

Choose five of the verbs that you supplied for Practice 17.4D. Write a new sentence for each verb. Be sure to use the active voice in your sentences.

CHAPTER 18

PRONOUN USAGE

Use pronouns correctly to craft sentences that readers can follow with ease.

WRITE GUY *Jeff Anderson, M.Ed.*

WHAT DO YOU NOTICE?

Track down the pronouns as you zoom in on these lines from the poem "The Negro Speaks of Rivers" by Langston Hughes.

MENTOR TEXT

> I heard the singing of the Mississippi when Abe Lincoln
>   went down to New Orleans, and I've seen its muddy
>   bosom turn all golden in the sunset.

Now, ask yourself the following questions:

- Why is the pronoun *I* used in the two places in which it appears?
- To which word does the pronoun *its* refer?

I is used because it is the subject performing the action of both the verb *heard* and the verb *seen*. The pronoun *I* also shows that the speaker is telling about his or her own experiences. The pronoun *its* refers to the Mississippi and shows ownership of the noun *bosom*.

Grammar for Writers Writers who understand important pronoun usage rules avoid common mistakes. For example, confusing *its* and *it's* is avoidable if you know that *its* is a possessive pronoun, whereas *it's* is a contraction that stands for the words *it is* or *it has*.

Is this book yours?

Yes, it's mine. And its sequel also belongs to me.

18.1 Case

Nouns and pronouns are the only parts of speech that have **case.**

RULE 18.1.1

Case is the form of a noun or a pronoun that shows how it is used in a sentence.

The Three Cases

Nouns and pronouns have three cases, each of which has its own distinctive uses.

RULE 18.1.2

The three cases of nouns and pronouns are the **nominative,** the **objective,** and the **possessive.**

CASE	USE IN SENTENCE
Nominative	As the Subject of a Verb, Predicate Nominative, or Nominative Absolute
Objective	As the Direct Object, Indirect Object, Object of a Preposition, Object of a Verbal, or Subject of an Infinitive
Possessive	To Show Ownership

Case in Nouns
The case, or form, of a noun changes only to show possession.

NOMINATIVE   The **box** had been hidden for months.

(*Box* is the subject of the verb *had been hidden*.)

OBJECTIVE   We tried to find the **box** .

(*Box* is the object of the infinitive *to find*.)

POSSESSIVE   The **box's** location could not be determined.

(The form changes when *'s* is added to show possession.)

Case in Pronouns

Personal pronouns often have different forms for all three cases. The pronoun that you use depends on its function in a sentence.

NOMINATIVE	OBJECTIVE	POSSESSIVE
I	*me*	*my, mine*
you	*you*	*your, yours*
he, she, it	*him, her, it*	*his, her, hers, its*
we, they	*us, them*	*our, ours*
		their, theirs

EXAMPLES   **I** watched the documentary about planes.

Ben sent the camera to **me**.

See Practice 18.1A   The documentary about planes is **mine**.

The Nominative Case in Pronouns

The **nominative case** is used when a personal pronoun acts in one of three ways.

> Use the **nominative case** when a pronoun is the subject of a verb, a predicate nominative, or part of a nominative absolute.

RULE 18.1.3

A **nominative absolute** consists of a noun or nominative pronoun followed by a participial phrase. It functions independently from the rest of the sentence.

EXAMPLE   **We having entered the kitchen,** the chef began to

cook according to the recipe.

NOMINATIVE PRONOUNS	
As the Subject of a Verb	I will consult the directions while she asks for help.
As a Predicate Nominative	The winners were he and she.
In a Nominative Absolute	We having landed on time, the flight attendant opened the cabin door.

Nominative Pronouns in Compounds

When you use a pronoun in a compound subject or predicate nominative, check the case either by mentally crossing out the other part of the compound or by inverting the sentence.

COMPOUND SUBJECT	The lawyer and **I** inspected the contracts. (**I** inspected the contracts.) **She** and her mother went shopping. (**She** went shopping.)
COMPOUND PREDICATE NOMINATIVE	The best cooks were Emily and **she**. (Emily and **she** were the best cooks.) The instructors were Bon and **I**. (Bon and **I** were the instructors.)

Nominative Pronouns With Appositives

When an appositive follows a pronoun that is being used as a subject or predicate nominative, the pronoun should stay in the nominative case. To check that you have used the correct case, either mentally cross out the appositive or isolate the subject and verb.

SUBJECT	**We** scientists use microscopes. (**We** use microscopes.)
PREDICATE NOMINATIVE	The champions were **we** Tigers. (**We** were the champions.)
APPOSITIVE AFTER NOUN	The hikers, **he** and **I**, climbed the mountain. (**He** and **I** climbed the mountain.)

See Practice 18.1B

PRACTICE 18.1A ▷ Identifying Case

Read each sentence. Then, label the underlined pronoun in each sentence *nominative*, *objective*, or *possessive*.

EXAMPLE   Are these blueberries <u>yours</u>?

ANSWER   *possessive*

1. Our teacher explained the problem to <u>me</u>. *Obj*
2. That jacket with the silk lining is <u>mine</u>. *poss*
3. <u>She</u> should have followed his advice. *Nom*
4. Please tell <u>me</u> the truth. *Obj*
5. We bought <u>him</u> some flowers. *obj*
6. Why are <u>they</u> always in a hurry? *nom*
7. This is <u>your</u> seat for the show. *poss*
8. You can buy strawberries or pick <u>them</u>. *obj*
9. By law, the land should be <u>hers</u>. *poss*
10. The man in that picture is <u>he</u>. *nom*

PRACTICE 18.1B ▷ Supplying Pronouns in the Nominative Case

Read each sentence. Then, write the correct pronoun from the choices in parentheses to complete each sentence.

EXAMPLE   When Jenny left the store, (she, her) forgot her keys.

ANSWER   *she*

11. (He, him) told the class about his cruise.
12. When (her, she) woke up, Heather's papers were scattered around the room.
13. I can't believe Shaun and (he, him) traveled all the way from another country.
14. (Them, They) are searching for information about their ancestors.
15. The first girl chosen was (she, her).
16. The treasure hunters, (he and her, he and she), were interviewed by reporters.
17. When the storm reached Texas, (it, its) intensified.
18. (Us, We) finished plowing our part of the field first.
19. While Tricia was there, (her, she) took advantage of the sunny weather.
20. Mike and (she, her) are leaving tomorrow.

SPEAKING APPLICATION

Take turns with a partner. Describe a fun time that you have had with friends or family members. Use sentences that contain one or more pronouns. Your partner should identify the case of each pronoun that you use.

WRITING APPLICATION

Write five sentences. Each sentence should contain a nominative pronoun in a compound subject.

The Objective Case

Objective pronouns are used for any kind of object in a sentence as well as for the subject of an infinitive.

> Use the **objective case** for the object of any verb, preposition, or verbal or for the subject of an infinitive.

OBJECTIVE PRONOUNS	
Direct Object	The tennis ball hit her on the foot.
Indirect Object	My grandmother sent me a bracelet from Nepal.
Object of Preposition	The conductor stood in front of us on the stage in the Opera House.
Object of Participle	Calling him from the garage, Kim tried to get Ben's attention.
Object of Gerund	Seeing them after all this time will be a relief.
Object of Infinitive	I promised to help him study this weekend.
Subject of Infinitive	The police chief wanted him to work tonight.

Objective Pronouns in Compounds

As with the nominative case, errors with objective pronouns most often occur in compounds. To find the correct case, mentally cross out the other part of the compound.

EXAMPLES

The threatening floods alarmed Ray and **her**.
(Threatening floods alarmed **her**.)

Bob wrote Jim and **me** instructions for the game.
(Bob wrote **me** instructions.)

Note About *Between*: Be sure to use the objective case after the preposition *between*.

INCORRECT   This conversation is between you and **I**.

CORRECT   This conversation is between you and **me**.

Objective Pronouns With Appositives

Use the objective case when a pronoun that is used as an object or as the subject of an infinitive is followed by an appositive.

we students were intimidated by the test

EXAMPLES	The biology test intimidated **us** students.
	My aunt brought **us** nephews baseball tickets.
	Our mother asked **us** children to be quiet.

See Practice 18.1C

The Possessive Case

One use for the **possessive case** is before gerunds. A **gerund** is a verbal form ending in *-ing* that is used as a noun.

> Use the **possessive case** before gerunds.

18.1.5 RULE

EXAMPLES	**Your** cooking was the best I've ever had.
	We disagreed with **his** assuming that we were late.
	Jon supports **our** deciding to leave.

Common Errors in the Possessive Case

Be sure not to use an apostrophe with a possessive pronoun because possessives already show ownership. Spellings such as *her's, our's, their's,* and *your's* are incorrect.

In addition, be sure not to confuse possessive pronouns and contractions that sound alike. *It's* (with an apostrophe) is the contraction for *it is* or *it has. Its* (without the apostrophe) is a possessive pronoun that means "belonging to it." *You're* is a contraction of *you are;* the possessive form of *you* is *your.*

POSSESSIVE PRONOUNS	The plan had served **its** purpose.
	Don't forget **your** banner.
CONTRACTIONS	**It's** possible we will go out tonight.
	You're the one who wouldn't stop and ask for directions.

See Practice 18.1D
See Practice 18.1E
See Practice 18.1F

Find It/ FIX IT
14
Grammar Game Plan

PRACTICE 18.1C > **Supplying Pronouns in the Objective Case**

Read each sentence. Then, write an objective pronoun to complete each sentence.

EXAMPLE   We all want _____ to win the prize.

ANSWER   *her*

1. We would like to talk to ~~you~~. *her* *him*
2. Paula gave *her* that recipe. *him*
3. Will you send *her* that article today? *him*
4. The heavy rain has Omar and *I* worried about flooding. *she* *her*
5. We got *her* a gift certificate. *him*
6. I had trouble choosing among _____.
7. Julio asked *me* to fix dinner. *us*
8. Mrs. Hernandez asked Tanya and *I* to *she* *he* distribute the books. *me*
9. Thank you for helping *me* with the task.
10. The conversation was between you and *I*. *her* *me* *him*

PRACTICE 18.1D > **Recognizing Pronouns in the Possessive Case**

Read each sentence. Then, write the correct pronoun from the choices in parentheses to complete each sentence.

EXAMPLE   I am happy with (my, mine) decision.

ANSWER   *my*

11. (Her, She) singing made everyone happy.
12. The boy could not prove that the mitt was (his, him).
13. (They, Their) umbrellas were blown by the wind.
14. The dog licked (its, it) paws.
15. Rai thought (she, her) painting was the best.
16. I don't know if it's (her, she) book that I found on the chair.
17. (Us, Our) volunteering resulted in getting a commendation from the mayor.
18. The plate with the rose decoration is (my, mine).
19. The town council is unlikely to approve (they, their) request.
20. That jacket could only be (her, hers).

SPEAKING APPLICATION

Take turns with a partner. Read each sentence in Practice 18.1C, omitting the objective pronoun. Your partner should complete each sentence, using a correct objective pronoun.

WRITING APPLICATION

Write a paragraph about something you own. Underline all the possessive pronouns in your paragraph.

PRACTICE 18.1E Supplying Pronouns in the Correct Case

Read each sentence. Then, write a pronoun in the correct case to complete each sentence.
More than one pronoun may be correct.

EXAMPLE   Dave and _____ looked for the map.

ANSWER   *I*

1. Mario says that backpack is _his_.
2. Could you pass this pencil to _her_? *him*
3. I think it is _her_ turn. *his*
4. _She_ has always been nice to me. *he*
5. The supervisor gave Herve and _I_ a call. *she / he*
6. Did you see that chipmunk attack _it_?
7. Between you and _I_, this is the easiest job I have ever had.
8. Bob told _her_ that the dog needs a bath. *him*
9. Katie acts as if nothing interests _her_, but I do not believe it.
10. We left _our_ phone numbers with the receptionist.

PRACTICE 18.1F Selecting the Correct Pronoun

Read each sentence. Then, choose the correct pronoun to complete each sentence.

EXAMPLE   The guitarist gave tickets to Graham and (I, me).

ANSWER   *me*

11. Lebron and (he, him) have been inseparable since third grade.
12. I plan to send (she, her) a message.
13. (We, Us) athletes burn many calories.
14. The strongest swimmers were Michael and (he, him).
15. Watching (they, them), he realized how talented they were.
16. Mom asked (she, her) to drive today.
17. I look forward to (us, our) planning a party.
18. They fed (he, him) grapes and peaches.
19. The choice was between Maureen and (she, her).
20. Tony, Andy, and (I, me) are going to the lake this weekend.

SPEAKING APPLICATION

Take turns with a partner. Tell about an activity you did with friends. Use at least one pronoun in each sentence. Your partner should identify the case of each pronoun.

WRITING APPLICATION

Use sentences 13, 15, and 16 in Practice 18.1F as models to write your own sentences with incorrect pronoun cases. Then, exchange papers with a partner. Your partner should rewrite your sentences using the correct cases.

Test Warm-Up

DIRECTIONS
Read the introduction and the passage that follows. Then, answer the questions to show that you can use and understand correct pronoun cases in reading and writing.

Ursula wrote this paragraph as the beginning of a science fiction story. Read the paragraph and think about the changes you would suggest as a peer editor. When you finish reading, answer the questions that follow.

Reaching the Red Planet

(1) I was fulfilling my greatest dream. (2) After a three-year journey, our ship was landing on Mars. (3) Our crew consisted of Jack Brown, Megan McDay, Casey Denton, and I. (4) Casey and Megan were piloting the ship. (5) He and she held their breath as the ship hovered over the landing site, it's engine whining. (6) Jack and me looked at each other, our eyes wide; if we crashed, there was no one to rescue us. (7) We landed with only a bump. (8) "We're heroes!" Jack shouted. (9) We then talked about our families. (10) We "heroes" agreed that it was them who were the real heroes, for patiently waiting for their loved ones to return.

---

1 What change, if any, should be made in sentence 3?

A Change *Our* to **We**

B Add **they** after *crew*

C Change *I* to **me**

D Make no change

2 How should sentence 5 be revised?

F He and she held their breath as the ship hovered over the landing site, its engine whining.

G Him and her held their breath as the ship hovered over the landing site, it's engine whining.

H He and her held their breath as the ship hovered over the landing site, it's engine whining.

J He and she held her breath as the ship hovered over the landing site, it's engine whining.

3 What change, if any, should be made in sentence 6?

A Change *me* to **I**

B Change *there* to **their**

C Change *us* to **we**

D Make no change

4 What change, if any, should be made in sentence 10?

F Change *We* to **Us**

G Change *them* to **they**

H Change *their* to **they're**

J Make no change

18.2 Special Problems With Pronouns

Choosing the correct case is not always a matter of choosing the form that "sounds correct," because writing is usually more formal than speech. For example, it would be incorrect to say, "John is smarter than *me*." because the verb is understood in the sentence: "John is smarter than *I [am]*."

Using *Who* and *Whom* Correctly

In order to decide when to use *who* or *whom* and the related forms *whoever* and *whomever*, you need to know how the pronoun is used in a sentence and what case is appropriate.

> ***Who*** is used for the nominative case. ***Whom*** is used for the objective case.

RULE 18.2.1

CASE	PRONOUNS	USE IN SENTENCES
Nominative	*who* *whoever*	As the Subject of a Verb or Predicate Nominative
Objective	*whom* *whomever*	As the Direct Object, Object of a Verbal, Object of a Preposition, or Subject of an Infinitive
Possessive	*whose* *whosever*	To Show Ownership

EXAMPLES   I know **who** has a new house.

Jon brought **whoever** was home Chinese food for dinner.

Anne did not know **whom** the director chose.

Whose shoes are sitting in the hallway?

The nominative and objective cases are the source of certain problems. Pronoun problems can appear in two kinds of sentences: direct questions and complex sentences.

In Direct Questions

Who is the correct form when the pronoun is the subject of a simple question. *Whom* is the correct form when the pronoun is the direct object, object of a verbal, or object of a preposition.

Questions in subject–verb word order always begin with *who*. However, questions in inverted order never correctly begin with *who*. To see if you should use *who* or *whom*, reword the question as a statement in subject–verb word order.

EXAMPLES	**Who** wants to have lunch at the deli?
	Whom did you ask to the party?
	(You did ask **whom** to the party.)

In Complex Sentences

Follow these steps to see if the case of a pronoun in a subordinate clause is correct. First, find the subordinate clause. If the complex sentence is a question, rearrange it in subject–verb order. Second, if the subordinate clause is inverted, rearrange the words in subject–verb word order. Finally, determine how the pronoun is used in the subordinate clause.

EXAMPLE	**Who**, may I ask, has seen the documentary?
REARRANGED	I may ask **who** has seen the documentary.
USE OF PRONOUN	(subject of the verb *has seen*)

EXAMPLE	The captain is the one **whom** they chose.
REARRANGED	They chose **whom**.
USE OF PRONOUN	(object of the verb *chose*)

Note About *Whose*: The word *whose* is a possessive pronoun; the contraction *who's* means "who is" or "who has."

POSSESSIVE PRONOUN	**Whose** DVD is this?
CONTRACTION	**Who's** [who has] taken my DVD?

See Practice 18.2A

Pronouns in Elliptical Clauses

An **elliptical clause** is one in which some words are omitted but still understood. Errors in pronoun usage can easily be made when an elliptical clause that begins with *than* or *as* is used to make a comparison.

RULE 18.2.2

> In **elliptical clauses** beginning with *than* or *as*, use the form of the pronoun that you would use if the clause were fully stated.

The case of the pronoun is determined by whether the omitted words fall before or after the pronoun. The omitted words in the examples below are shown in brackets.

WORDS OMITTED BEFORE PRONOUN	You bought Ben more than **me**. (You bought Ben more than [you bought] **me**.)
WORDS OMITTED AFTER PRONOUN	Anna is as hardworking as **she**. (Anna is as hardworking as **she** [is].)

Mentally add the missing words. If they come *before* the pronoun, choose the objective case. If they come *after* the pronoun, choose the nominative case.

CHOOSING A PRONOUN IN ELLIPTICAL CLAUSES
1. Consider the choices of pronouns: nominative or objective.
2. Mentally complete the elliptical clause.
3. Base your choice on what you find.

The case of the pronoun can sometimes change the entire meaning of the sentence.

NOMINATIVE PRONOUN	He liked dogs more than **I**. He liked dogs more than **I** [did].
OBJECTIVE PRONOUN	He liked dogs more than **me**. He liked dogs more than [he liked] **me**.

See Practice 18.2B

PRACTICE 18.2A > Choosing *Who* or *Whom* Correctly

Read each sentence. Then, write *who* or *whom* to complete each sentence.

EXAMPLE _____ is the president of your class?

ANSWER *Who*

1. There are several drummers *whom* the conductor has not heard.
2. Anyone *who* saw the play agrees it was great.
3. The quarterback *whom* we supported won the game.
4. Carl is a boy *who* knows how to sing.
5. Are you aware of *whom* the teacher selected?
6. *Who*, in your opinion, is the best qualified?
7. The jury has acquitted the man *who* was accused of stealing.
8. To *whom* did you report the robbery?
9. *Who* was there with you?
10. With *whom* did you have dinner last night?

PRACTICE 18.2B > Identifying the Correct Pronoun in Elliptical Clauses

Read each sentence. Then, complete each elliptical clause by choosing the correct pronoun in parentheses and adding the missing words in brackets.

EXAMPLE Tammi is a better skier than (I, me).

ANSWER *Tammi is a better skier than I [am].*

11. He was as surprised as (I, me). *[was]*
12. That waiter gave Damian more change than (I, me).
13. This painter has better style than (she, her). *has*
14. You are a better player than (he, him).
15. She was as close to the stage as (I, me). *was*
16. Jordan spoke to Emmanuel longer than to (him, he). *[spoke to him]*
17. We are farther along than (they, them). *are*
18. My sister has fewer pets than (she, her). *has*
19. You are less experienced than (she, her). *is*
20. Because Uncle Roy travels for work, he has visited many more cities than (I, me). *have visited*

SPEAKING APPLICATION

Take turns with a partner. Ask questions that use the word *who* or *whom*. Your partner should respond by also using *who* and *whom* correctly in his or her response.

WRITING APPLICATION

Write five sentences that contain elliptical clauses. Then, underline the pronoun in each elliptical clause and add the missing words in brackets.

CHAPTER 19

AGREEMENT

Knowing how to relate subjects and verbs and nouns and pronouns will help you to write expert sentences.

WRITE GUY *Jeff Anderson, M.Ed.*

WHAT DO YOU NOTICE?

Focus on agreement as you zoom in on this sentence from the story "Winter Dreams" by F. Scott Fitzgerald.

MENTOR TEXT

> He was a favorite caddy, and the thirty dollars a month he earned through the summer were not to be made elsewhere around the lake.

Now, ask yourself the following questions:

- To which noun does the second pronoun *he* refer?
- What is the subject and verb of the clause that comes after the comma and conjunction *and*? How do they agree?

The second pronoun *he* is the same favorite caddy to which the first pronoun *he* refers. In the second main, or independent, clause, the subject is the plural noun *dollars,* which agrees in number with the plural verb *were.* The intervening clause *he earned through the summer* does not affect the agreement of the subject and verb.

Grammar for Writers Writers use a variety of sentences to make their writing more interesting. When crafting complex sentences, writers should check that their verbs agree with their subjects and that their pronouns have clear antecedents.

Do you always make your subject agree with your verb?

Of course! They know who's boss.

19.1 Subject–Verb Agreement

For a subject and a verb to agree, both must be singular, or both must be plural. In this section, you will learn how to make sure singular and plural subjects and verbs agree.

Number in Nouns, Pronouns, and Verbs

In grammar, **number** indicates whether a word is singular or plural. Only three parts of speech have different forms that indicate number: nouns, pronouns, and verbs.

RULE 19.1.1

> **Number** shows whether a noun, pronoun, or verb is singular or plural.

Recognizing the number of most nouns is seldom a problem because most form their plurals by adding -s or -es. Some, such as *mouse* or *ox*, form their plurals irregularly: *mice, oxen*.

Pronouns, however, have different forms to indicate their number. The chart below shows the different forms of personal pronouns in the nominative case, the case that is used for subjects.

PERSONAL PRONOUNS		
SINGULAR	PLURAL	SINGULAR OR PLURAL
I	*we*	*you*
he, she, it	*they*	

The grammatical number of verbs is sometimes difficult to determine. That is because the form of many verbs can be either singular or plural, and they may form plurals in different ways.

SINGULAR   She **thinks** .

She **has thought** .

PLURAL   We **think** .

We **have thought** .

Some verb forms can be only singular. The personal pronouns *he*, *she*, and *it* and all singular nouns call for singular verbs in the present and the present perfect tense.

ALWAYS
SINGULAR

She **paints**.

She **has painted**.

Kate **paints**.

Kris **has painted**.

She **walks**.

She **has walked**.

The verb *be* in the present tense has special forms to agree with singular subjects. The pronoun *I* has its own singular form of *be*; so do *he*, *she*, *it*, and singular nouns.

ALWAYS
SINGULAR

I **am** working out.

He **is** fun.

Bette **is** early.

He **is** coming.

All singular subjects except *you* share the same past tense verb form of *be*.

ALWAYS
SINGULAR

I **was** going shopping.

She **was** editor in chief.

Christina **was** early to dinner.

See Practice 19.1A

He **was** boarding the airplane.

A verb form will always be singular if it has had an *-s* or *-es* added to it or if it includes the words *has*, *am*, *is*, or *was*. The number of any other verb depends on its subject.

The chart on the next page shows verb forms that are always singular and those that can be singular or plural.

VERBS THAT ARE ALWAYS SINGULAR	VERBS THAT CAN BE SINGULAR OR PLURAL
(he, she, Jane) sees	(I, you, we, they) see
(he, she, Jane) has seen	(I, you, we, they) have seen
(I) am	(you, we, they) are
(he, she, Jane) is	(you, we, they) were
(I, he, she, Jane) was	

Singular and Plural Subjects

When making a verb agree with its subject, be sure to identify the subject and determine its number.

RULE
19.1.2

A singular subject must have a singular verb. A plural subject must have a plural verb.

SINGULAR SUBJECT AND VERB	PLURAL SUBJECT AND VERB
The English teacher works in China.	These English teachers work in China.
He was being mysterious about their anniversary dinner.	They were being mysterious about their anniversary dinner.
Daphne looks through an encyclopedia for term-paper topics.	Daphne and Dan look through an encyclopedia for term-paper topics.
Israel is a small country in the Middle East.	Israel and Jordan are small countries in the Middle East.
Halley takes American literature.	Halley and Rachael take American literature.
Michael is planning a vacation to the Grand Canyon.	Michael and Alan are planning a vacation to the Grand Canyon.
Jennifer plays trumpet in the school band.	Jennifer and Jess play in the school band.
He looks through the magazines.	They look through the magazines.
Amanda has been studying how to garden successfully.	They have been studying how to garden successfully.

See Practice 19.1B

PRACTICE 19.1A Identifying Number in Nouns, Pronouns, and Verbs

Read each word or group of words. Write whether the word or words are *singular*, *plural*, or *both*.

EXAMPLE   lunch

ANSWER   *singular*

1. they
2. learns
3. have seen
4. you understand
5. fish
6. computers
7. rummages
8. we
9. man
10. he

PRACTICE 19.1B Identifying Singular and Plural Subjects and Verbs

Read each sentence. Then, write the subject and verb in each sentence, and label them *plural* or *singular*.

EXAMPLE   My dog never eats food from the table.

ANSWER   subject: *dog*; verb: *eats* — singular

11. Air conditioning makes the room cool and inviting.
12. I reject the idea of passing up the challenge.
13. These luxurious rugs never go out of style.
14. Despite advances in technology, tornadoes are still difficult to predict.
15. The student body president is running for re-election.
16. Our science fair project is on volcanic activity in Hawaii.
17. The teams in this year's competition are very talented.
18. The sisters join the choir every year.
19. I am making a four-course meal for my family reunion.
20. The pages of this book are beginning to fade.

SPEAKING APPLICATION

Take turns with a partner. Tell about what you want to do after graduating from high school. Your partner should listen for and name the plural and singular nouns and verbs that you use.

WRITING APPLICATION

Use sentences 12, 16, and 18 as a model to write three similar sentences. Exchange papers with a partner. Your partner should change the subject from singular to plural or plural to singular, making sure that the verbs agree with the new subjects.

Intervening Phrases and Clauses

When you check for agreement, mentally cross out any words that separate the subject and verb.

> **A phrase or clause that separates a subject and its verb does not affect subject–verb agreement.**

In the first example below, the singular subject *discovery* agrees with the singular verb *interests* despite the intervening prepositional phrase *of the clay pots*, which contains a plural noun.

EXAMPLES   The **discovery** of the clay pots **interests** many people.

The **scientists**, whose testing is nearly finished, **require** more funding.

Intervening parenthetical expressions—such as those beginning with *as well as, in addition to, in spite of,* or *including*—also have no effect on the agreement of the subject and verb.

EXAMPLES   Your **information**, in addition to your eyewitness testimony, **is helping** to solve the crimes.

Angelina's **trip**, including visits to Italy and Greece, **is lasting** twelve months.

See Practice 19.1C
See Practice 19.1D

Relative Pronouns as Subjects

When *who, which,* or *that* acts as a subject of a subordinate clause, its verb will be singular or plural depending on the number of the antecedent.

> **The antecedent of a relative pronoun determines its agreement with a verb.**

EXAMPLES She is the only **one** of the doctors **who has** experience working in pediatrics.

(The antecedent of *who* is *one*.)

She is one of several **doctors who have** experience working in pediatrics.

(The antecedent of *who* is *doctors*.)

Compound Subjects

A **compound subject** has two or more simple subjects, which are usually joined by *or* or *and*. Use the following rules when making compound subjects agree with verbs.

Subjects Joined by *And*
Only one rule applies to compound subjects connected by *and:* The verb is usually plural, whether the parts of the compound subject are all singular, all plural, or mixed.

> **A compound subject joined by *and* is generally plural and must have a plural verb.**

19.1.5 RULE

TWO SINGULAR SUBJECTS — A **hurricane** and a **tornado make** news.

TWO PLURAL SUBJECTS — **Tomatoes** and **carrots cover** the top of the salad.

A SINGULAR SUBJECT AND A PLURAL SUBJECT — A **slice** of tomato and several **slices** of onion **go** on each sandwich.

There are two exceptions to this rule. The verb is singular if the parts of a compound subject are thought of as one item or if the word *every* or *each* precedes the compound subject.

EXAMPLES **Macaroni and cheese was** all he could cook.

Every weather center and emergency network in the United States issues warnings for severe weather.

Singular Subjects Joined by *Or* or *Nor*
When both parts of a compound subject connected by *or* or *nor* are singular, a singular verb is required.

RULE 19.1.6

Two or more singular subjects joined by *or* or *nor* must have a singular verb.

EXAMPLE A **banana** or a **carrot is** a healthy snack.

Plural Subjects Joined by *Or* or *Nor*
When both parts of a compound subject connected by *or* or *nor* are plural, a plural verb is required.

RULE 19.1.7

Two or more plural subjects joined by *or* or *nor* must have a plural verb.

EXAMPLE Neither **apples** nor **bananas are** as delicious as pears.

Subjects of Mixed Number Joined by *Or* or *Nor*
If one part of a compound subject is singular and the other is plural, the verb agrees with the subject that is closer to it.

RULE 19.1.8

If one or more singular subjects are joined to one or more plural subjects by *or* or *nor*, the subject closest to the verb determines agreement.

EXAMPLES Neither **Bridgette** nor my **friends are ready**.

Neither my **friends** nor **Bridgette is ready**.

See Practice 19.1E
See Practice 19.1F

PRACTICE 19.1C Identifying Intervening Phrases and Clauses

Read each sentence. Then, write the intervening phrase or clause between the subject and the verb.

EXAMPLE   Winter, my favorite of all seasons, is finally here.

ANSWER   *my favorite of all seasons*

1. Allan, along with his sisters, enjoys going to the movies.
2. These magazines in the doctor's office are outdated.
3. A pharmacist, a person who dispenses medicine, lives in our neighborhood.
4. This watch, unlike that one, is not expensive.
5. Lakes formed from craters in the earth are not very common around here.
6. Jane, accompanied by Lisa, has gone to see her first foreign film.
7. Tomorrow, the first student who answers a question correctly will receive extra credit.
8. The clock, which is digital, is brand new.
9. The coach of the team will soon retire.
10. A bicyclist, by law, must wear a helmet.

PRACTICE 19.1D Correcting Errors in Agreement With Intervening Phrases

Read each sentence. If there is an error in subject-verb agreement, write the subject and the correct verb form. If a sentence has no error, write *correct*.

EXAMPLE   The plains of North Dakota gets very cold in the winter.

ANSWER   *plains get*

11. The food, except for the desserts, were good.
12. Lisa's project, including drawings of trees, is almost finished.
13. Sometimes a book admired by many readers receive bad reviews.
14. Animals, such as deer and bears, live in the forest.
15. The grape vines has been growing near our house for years.
16. That graphic novel, which was co-written by two authors, have some great characters.
17. Often, new technology that baffles adults are understandable to kids.
18. One of our gardening specialists recommends putting fragrant plants near your house.
19. The clothes in that box is what I am donating to the shelter.
20. Melanie, whose costumes always turn out great, have been designing dresses, too.

SPEAKING APPLICATION

Take turns with a partner. Tell about a time when you were very happy about something. Use sentences with intervening clauses. Your partner should identify the intervening clauses in your sentences.

WRITING APPLICATION

Write a persuasive paragraph about an issue that matters to you. Use at least three sentences that have phrases or clauses between the subject and the verb.

PRACTICE 19.1E > **Making Verbs Agree With Relative Pronouns**

Read each sentence. Then, write the correct verb to agree with the relative pronoun based on the number of its antecedent.

EXAMPLE   An author who (write, writes) both literary and mystery stories is unusual.

ANSWER   *writes*

1. The tree that (bear, bears) so many pears needs pruning.
2. The tools that (work, works) best are expensive.
3. The cooks, who (were, was) efficient, prepared dinner for 100 people.
4. Abby, who (play, plays) both piano and drums, has talent.
5. Texas, which (is, are) the second largest of the states, is my home.
6. An animal that (appeal, appeals) to most people is the panda.
7. A singer who (were, was) popular 50 years ago is performing again.
8. My laptop, which (crash, crashes) at the worst times, is down again.
9. Students who (forget, forgets) their permission slips will not be allowed to go.
10. The book that my younger brother and sister (like, likes) is missing.

PRACTICE 19.1F > **Making Verbs Agree With Singular and Compound Subjects**

Read each sentence. Then, for each sentence, choose the form of the verb given in parentheses that agrees with the subject.

EXAMPLE   Some water or juice (is, are) what you need to feel hydrated.

ANSWER   *is*

11. Carrots and peas (go, goes) well together.
12. School and state office buildings (shut, shuts) down when there is a snowstorm.
13. Neither he nor they (are, is) busy.
14. Two sandwiches and two drinks (is, are) needed for the field trip.
15. Spaghetti and meatballs (were, was) my favorite homemade dish.
16. My sister and her family (live, lives) in South Carolina.
17. Mom or Dad (picks, pick) me up after school.
18. Neither the bus nor the train (travels, travel) near our house.
19. Cotton and silk (are, is) the most comfortable fabrics.
20. Keeping a notepad and pencil by the phone (make, makes) a lot of sense.

SPEAKING APPLICATION

Take turns with a partner. Tell about the last sporting event you attended. Your partner should identify the relative clauses that you use and correct any errors in subject-verb agreement.

WRITING APPLICATION

Write a short article about a recent school event. Use at least four sentences with compound subjects. Exchange papers with a partner and correct each other's errors.

Test Warm-Up

DIRECTIONS

Read the introduction and the passage that follows. Then, answer the questions to show that you understand and can correct errors in agreement in reading and writing.

Terrance wrote this paragraph about animals that do things people thought animals could not do. Read the paragraph and think about the changes you would suggest as a peer editor. When you finish reading, answer the questions that follow.

Animal Abilities

(1) For centuries, people believed that animals did not have certain abilities. (2) Now, however, there are scientists who has performed studies and think otherwise. (3) New evidence about animals' abilities have been accumulated by scientists who have researched the subject, and some of them make amazing claims. (4) For example, in his book *When Elephants Weep*, psychologist Jeffrey Masson documents unusual abilities in many species. (5) He describes elephants that seem to enjoy painting pictures as well as gorillas and gray parrots that knows 200 words in sign language. (6) He also says that certain bears, which apparently appreciate beauty, walk up a hill to watch the sunset.

---

1 What change, if any, should be made in sentence 2?

  A Change *are* to **is**

  B Change *has performed* to **have performed**

  C Change *think* to **thinks**

  D Make no change

2 What change, if any, should be made in sentence 3?

  F Change *have been accumulated* to **has been accumulated**

  G Change *have researched* to **has researched**

  H Change *make* to **makes**

  J Make no change

3 What change, if any, should be made in sentence 5?

  A Change *describes* to **describe**

  B Change *seem* to **seems**

  C Change *knows* to **know**

  D Make no change

4 What change, if any, should be made in sentence 6?

  F Change *says* to **say**

  G Change *appreciate* to **appreciates**

  H Change *walk* to **walks**

  J Make no change

Confusing Subjects

Some kinds of subjects have special agreement problems.

Hard-to-Find Subjects and Inverted Sentences
Subjects that appear after verbs are said to be **inverted.**
Subject–verb order is usually inverted in questions. To find out
whether to use a singular or plural verb, mentally rearrange the
sentence into subject–verb order.

> **A verb must still agree in number with a subject that comes after it.**

EXAMPLE

On the deck **are** two lounge **chairs**.

REARRANGED IN
SUBJECT–VERB ORDER

Two lounge **chairs are** on the deck.

The words *there* and *here* often signal an inverted sentence.
These words never function as the subject of a sentence.

EXAMPLES

There **are** the group **photos**.

Here **is** the revised **itinerary**.

Note About *There's* and *Here's*: Both of these contractions
contain the singular verb *is: there is* and *here is*. They should be
used only with singular subjects.

CORRECT

There's only one **family** expected.

Here's a pink **T-shirt** to try on.

See Practice 19.1G

Subjects With Linking Verbs
Subjects with linking verbs may also cause agreement problems.

> **A linking verb must agree with its subject, regardless of the number of its predicate nominative.**

EXAMPLES   The **coaches are** all former athletes.

One **reason** we expect a heat wave **is** that the temperature is already 90!

In the first example, the plural verb *are* agrees with the plural subject *coaches*. In the next example, the singular subject *reason* takes the singular verb *is*.

Collective Nouns

Collective nouns name groups of people or things. Examples include *audience*, *class*, *club*, and *committee*.

> **A collective noun takes a singular verb when the group it names acts as a single unit. A collective noun takes a plural verb when the group acts as individuals.**

SINGULAR   The freshman **class graduates** in 2012.

       (The members act as a unit.)

PLURAL   The senior **class were going** to different colleges.

       (The members act individually.)

Nouns That Look Like Plurals

Some nouns that end in *-s* are actually singular. For example, nouns that name branches of knowledge, such as *civics*, and those that name illnesses, such as *mumps*, take singular verbs.

> **Use singular verbs to agree with nouns that are plural in form but singular in meaning.**

SINGULAR   **Gymnastics is** very difficult.

When words such as *ethics* and *politics* do not name branches of knowledge but indicate characteristics, their meanings are plural. Similarly, such words as *eyeglasses*, *pants*, and *scissors* generally take plural verbs.

PLURAL   Jack's **eyeglasses are** on the table.

Indefinite Pronouns

Some indefinite pronouns are always singular, some are always plural, and some may be either singular or plural. Prepositional phrases do not affect subject–verb agreement.

RULE 19.1.13

Singular indefinite pronouns take singular verbs. Plural indefinite pronouns take plural verbs.

SINGULAR   *anybody, anyone, anything, each, either, everybody, everyone, everything, neither, nobody, no one, nothing, somebody, someone, something*

PLURAL   *both, few, many, others, several*

SINGULAR   **Everyone** on the tour bus **has exited**.

PLURAL   **Many** of the houses **were painted** today.

RULE 19.1.14

The pronouns *all, any, more, most, none,* and *some* usually take a singular verb if the antecedent is singular, and a plural verb if it is plural.

SINGULAR   **Some** of the building **was painted** by Monday.

PLURAL   **Some** of the people **are** waiting in the conference room.

Titles of Creative Works and Names of Organizations

Plural words in the title of a creative work or in the name of an organization do not affect subject–verb agreement.

RULE 19.1.15

A title of a creative work or name of an organization is singular and must have a singular verb.

EXAMPLES **The Centers for Disease Control and Prevention is** a helpful organization.
(organization)

Haystacks by Claude Monet **is** a famous series of art.
(creative work)

Amounts and Measurements
Although they appear to be plural, most amounts and measurements actually express single units or ideas.

> **A noun expressing an amount or measurement is usually singular and requires a singular verb.**

 19.1.16 RULE

EXAMPLES **Ten thousand dollars is** the cost in property taxes for the house.

(*Ten thousand dollars is one sum of money.*)

Six miles was our distance from the nearest camping site.

(*Six miles is a single distance.*)

Three quarters of the town **attends** the Spring Planting Fair.

(*Three quarters is one part of the town.*)

Half of the branches **were broken**.

(*Half refers to a number of individual branches, and not part of an individual branch, so it is plural.*)

See Practice 19.1H

PRACTICE 19.1G > Identifying Subjects and Verbs in Inverted Sentences

Read each sentence. Then, identify the subject and verb in each sentence.

EXAMPLE   Here are your books.

ANSWER   subject: *books*; verb: *are*

1. On the ground lie many colorful leaves.
2. There are no disagreements among the students.
3. Behind the fence grows a hodge podge of wild flowers.
4. Under our feet is the lush, thick lawn.
5. On the wall hangs the patchwork quilt.
6. There are three new students in our class.
7. At the end of the school year is our annual party.
8. Standing behind you were the principal and assistant principal.
9. Here is an updated version of that software.
10. At the top of the hill stood the lone oak tree.

PRACTICE 19.1H > Making Verbs Agree With Confusing Subjects

Read each sentence. Then, write the correct verb from the choices in parentheses to complete each sentence.

EXAMPLE   Two thirds of the movie (was, were) suspenseful.

ANSWER   *was*

11. The poetry series (end, ends) this week.
12. *The Lord of the Rings* (was, were) an outstanding trilogy.
13. The panel (deliberates, deliberate) on the proposal.
14. Half of my money (was, were) put into a savings account.
15. Civics (was, were) the class in which I got the highest grade.
16. Forty-four dollars (is, are) enough to pay for the train ticket.
17. The pair of gloves (is, are) too big for my hands.
18. The congressman's politics (help, helps) him get re-elected.
19. Everyone at the party (has, have) been dancing.
20. Most of the contestants (were, was) not familiar with the rules of the game.

SPEAKING APPLICATION

Take turns with a partner. Describe an interesting scene from a book that you've read, using some inverted sentences. Your partner should identify the subjects and verbs in your inverted sentences.

WRITING APPLICATION

Write three sentences that include confusing subjects. Then, underline the subject in each of your sentences and make sure the subjects and verbs in your sentences agree.

19.2 Pronoun–Antecedent Agreement

Like a subject and its verb, a pronoun and its antecedent must agree. An **antecedent** is the word or group of words for which the pronoun stands.

Find It/ FIX IT

17

Grammar Game Plan

WRITING COACH

Online

www.phwritingcoach.com

Grammar Tutorials

Brush up on your Grammar skills with these animated videos.

Grammar Practice

Practice your grammar skills with Writing Coach Online.

Grammar Games

Test your knowledge of grammar in this fast-paced interactive video game.

Agreement Between Personal Pronouns and Antecedents

While a subject and verb must agree only in number, a personal pronoun and its antecedent must agree in three ways.

> **A personal pronoun must agree with its antecedent in number, person, and gender.**

19.2.1

RULE

The **number** of a pronoun indicates whether it is singular or plural. **Person** refers to a pronoun's ability to indicate either the person speaking (first person), the person spoken to (second person), or the person, place, or thing spoken about (third person). **Gender** is the characteristic of nouns and pronouns that indicates whether the word is *masculine* (referring to males), *feminine* (referring to females), or *neuter* (referring to neither males nor females).

The only pronouns that indicate gender are third-person singular personal pronouns.

GENDER OF THIRD-PERSON SINGULAR PRONOUNS	
Masculine	*he, him, his*
Feminine	*she, her, hers*
Neuter	*it, its*

In the example below, the pronoun *his* agrees with the antecedent *Prince of Wales* in number (both are singular), in person (both are third person), and in gender (both are masculine).

EXAMPLE   The Prince of Wales has shared **his** memories with the reporter.

Pronoun–Antecedent Agreement   **491**

Agreement in Number

There are three rules to keep in mind to determine the number of compound antecedents.

> **Use a singular personal pronoun when two or more singular antecedents are joined by *or* or *nor*.**

EXAMPLES   Either Blane **or** Ben will bring **his** outline of a proposal to the meeting.

Neither Chase **nor** Kevin will eat **his** new power bar.

> **Use a plural personal pronoun when two or more antecedents are joined by *and*.**

EXAMPLE   Kate **and** I are baking for **our** fundraiser.

An exception occurs when a distinction must be made between individual and joint ownership. If individual ownership is intended, use a singular pronoun to refer to a compound antecedent. If joint ownership is intended, use a plural pronoun.

SINGULAR   **Benjamin and Carrie** played **his** drum set.

PLURAL   **Benjamin and Carrie** paid for **their** drum set.

SINGULAR   Neither **Amy nor Beth** let me ride **her** bike.

PLURAL   Neither **Amy nor Beth** let me ride **their** bike.

The third rule applies to compound antecedents whose parts are mixed in number.

> **Use a plural personal pronoun if any part of a compound antecedent joined by *or* or *nor* is plural.**

EXAMPLE If either the **congressman** or the **reporters** arrive, take **them** to the office.

See Practice 19.2A

Agreement in Person and Gender Avoid shifts in person or gender of pronouns.

> As part of pronoun–antecedent agreement, take care not to shift either person or gender.

19.2.5 RULE

SHIFT IN PERSON **Katherine** is planning to visit Paris, France, because **you** can see how the French live.

CORRECT **Katherine** is planning to visit Paris, France, because **she** wants to see how the French live.

SHIFT IN GENDER The **cat** threw **its** head up in the air and jumped in **his** spot.

CORRECT The **cat** threw **its** head up in the air and jumped in **its** spot.

Generic Masculine Pronouns Traditionally, a masculine pronoun has been used to refer to a singular antecedent whose gender is unknown. Such use is called *generic* because it applies to both masculine and feminine genders. Many writers now prefer to use *his or her, he or she, him or her,* or to rephrase a sentence to eliminate the situation.

> When gender is not specified, either use *his or her* or rewrite the sentence.

19.2.6 RULE

EXAMPLES Each **student** chose a famous author about which to write **his or her report**.

Students chose famous authors about which to write **their reports**.

See Practice 19.2B

Pronoun–Antecedent Agreement

PRACTICE 19.2A Making Personal Pronouns Agree With Their Antecedents

Read each sentence. Then, for each sentence, choose the personal pronoun in parentheses that agrees with the antecedent.

EXAMPLE   Dawn and I started a newsletter in (her, our) school.

ANSWER   *our*

1. Cecil was proud of (his, their) dogs' tricks.

2. Neither Karen nor her brothers like (her, their) soup too hot.

3. Andy or Donald will wait by (their, his) car.

4. Sandra let the hamsters out of (their, her) cages.

5. Neither Edith nor Sally brought (her, their) book to read on the bus.

6. The dog or the cat left (their, its) toy under the chair.

7. Mark hangs up his shirts and pants because (they, he) doesn't want them to get wrinkled.

8. Amy or Laura will lend you (her, their) notes.

9. The audience clapped (their, its) hands.

10. Each of the lions circled (its, their) prey.

PRACTICE 19.2B Revising for Agreement in Person and Gender

Read each sentence. Then, revise each sentence so that the pronoun agrees with the antecedent.

EXAMPLE   The dog is chasing his tail.

ANSWER   *The dog is chasing its tail.*

11. All citizens must pay her taxes.

12. The captain wears a band around their arm.

13. Kramer reads in bed because he believes that it helps you to sleep.

14. Both of my brothers gave his gently used clothes to the shelter.

15. Each person placed their ballot into the box.

16. The male part of the flower will fertilize the plant with his pollen.

17. The mailbox has flowers on her.

18. The children read his or her books.

19. Each manager has her own office.

20. The famous actress responds to all of her e-mails because she believes that you should keep in touch with your fans.

SPEAKING APPLICATION

Take turns with a partner. Tell about members of your family. Use several different pronouns in your sentences. Your partner should name the pronouns that you use and tell whether they agree with their antecedents.

WRITING APPLICATION

Use Sentences 14, 15, and 19 as models to write similar sentences. Then, exchange papers with a partner. Your partner should revise each sentence to make the personal pronoun agree with the antecedent.

Agreement With Indefinite Pronouns

When an indefinite pronoun, such as *each, all,* or *most,* is used
with a personal pronoun, the pronouns must agree.

> **Use a plural personal pronoun when the antecedent is a plural
> indefinite pronoun.**

EXAMPLES   **Many** of the children were excited about **their**
camping trip.

All the students forgot to bring **their** homework.

When the indefinite pronoun is singular, a similar rule applies.

> **Use a singular personal pronoun when the antecedent is a
> singular indefinite pronoun.**

In the first example, the personal pronoun *her* agrees in number
with the singular indefinite pronoun *one.* The gender (feminine) is
determined by the word *girls.*

EXAMPLES   Only **one** of the girls practiced **her** clarinet.

One of the girls remembered to bring **her**
clarinet.

If other words in the sentence do not indicate a gender, you may
use *him or her, he or she, his or her,* or rephrase the sentence.

EXAMPLES   **Each** of the playwrights read **his or her** lines.

The **playwrights** practiced **their** lines.

For indefinite pronouns that can be either singular or plural, such
as *all, any, more, most, none,* and *some,* agreement depends on
the antecedent of the indefinite pronoun.

EXAMPLES

Most of the park had lost **its** enjoyment.
(The antecedent of *most* is *park,* which is singular.)

Most of the students wanted **their** scores posted.
(The antecedent of *most* is *students,* which is plural.)

Some of the milk **was** too sour to drink.
(The antecedent of *some* is *milk,* which is singular.)

All of the plates **were** on the kitchen table.
(The antecedent of *all* is *plates,* which is plural.)

In some situations, strict grammatical agreement may be illogical.
In these situations, either let the meaning of the sentence
determine the number of the personal pronoun, or reword the
sentence.

ILLOGICAL   When **each of the cellphones buzzed** ,
I answered **it** as quickly as possible.

MORE
LOGICAL   When **each of the cellphones buzzed** ,
I answered **them** as quickly as possible.

MORE
LOGICAL   When **all of the cellphones buzzed** ,
I answered **them** as quickly as possible.   See Practice 19.2C

Agreement With Reflexive Pronouns

Reflexive pronouns, which end in *-self* or *-selves,* should only refer
to a word earlier in the same sentence.

RULE 19.2.9

A reflexive pronoun must agree with an antecedent that is
clearly stated.

EXAMPLES   **Katherine** made breakfast for **herself** .

You should tell **yourself** to be happy.

Professional **comedians** enjoy making fun
of **themselves** .

See Practice 19.2D
See Practice 19.2E
See Practice 19.2F

PRACTICE 19.2C Supplying Indefinite Pronouns

Read each sentence. Then, fill in the blank with an appropriate indefinite pronoun that agrees with the antecedent.

EXAMPLE   _____ of the boys could deliver his lines.

ANSWER   *None*

1. Only _Some_ of the girls remembered their locker numbers.

2. _All_ of the yard has weeds covering it.

3. _Some_ of my friends take their younger siblings with them to the park.

4. _Each_ of the houses has its own backyard.

5. _Many_ of the shirts already had tags on them.

6. _All_ of the students have finished choosing their research topic.

7. I liked the food, but _Some_ of it had too much garlic.

8. I think _One_ of these books have landscape pictures in them.

9. _Most_ of the pasta was eaten.

10. _All_ of the players on the girls' soccer team provide their own uniform.

PRACTICE 19.2D Supplying Reflexive Pronouns

Read each sentence. Then, rewrite each sentence, filling in the blank with the correct reflexive pronoun that agrees with the antecedent.

EXAMPLE   Can you imagine _____ in a meadow full of colorful flowers?

ANSWER   *Can you Imagine yourself in a meadow full of colorful flowers?*

11. I made _myself_ scrambled eggs for breakfast.

12. What are you planning to do with _yourself_ on a day off from school?

13. I think I will treat _myself_ to frozen yogurt today.

14. Perhaps we'll buy _ourselves_ new boots.

15. Rosie will go to the game by _herself_.

16. I think we can finish the job by _ourselves_.

17. You owe _yourself_ some alone time.

18. That silly dog is chasing _itself_ around in a circle.

19. Fortunately, Jessica did not injure _herself_ when she fell off the chair.

20. They told _themselves_ they would never do that again.

SPEAKING APPLICATION

Take turns with a partner. Say sentences with indefinite pronouns that agree with their antecedents. Your partner should repeat each of your sentences, substituting another indefinite pronoun that makes sense in the sentence.

WRITING APPLICATION

Use sentences 11, 12, and 16 as models to write similar sentences. Then, exchange papers with a partner. Your partner should rewrite each of your sentences, using the correct reflexive pronoun that agrees with the antecedent.

PRACTICE 19.2E
Correcting Problems in Pronoun-Antecedent Agreement

Read each sentence. If a sentence has an error in pronoun-antecedent agreement, rewrite it to correct the error. If a sentence has no error, write **correct**.

EXAMPLE   Each student should bring their own ticket.

ANSWER   *Each student should bring his or her own ticket.*

1. All artists should bring your materials to class.
   their

2. Most of the lettuce has lost its crispness.

3. Some of the guests is not hungry.
   are

4. The horse hurt his hoof and had to stay in its stable.
   his

5. Neither the cat nor the dogs enjoy their bath.

6. One of the cheerleaders forgot their coat.
   her

7. Every one of the football players has their uniform.

8. All of the corporations published their annual reports.

9. A visitor must carry their hall pass at all times.

10. All of the team members did his or her stretches.
    their

PRACTICE 19.2F
Using Pronouns Correctly

Write new sentences that include pronouns that agree in number, gender, and person with the antecedents provided.

EXAMPLE   most (plural)

ANSWER   *Most trees lose their leaves in the fall.*

11. team (singular)   *the team worked hard and won their game*

12. players

13. each

14. musicians

15. alligator

16. several

17. all (plural)

18. many (plural)

19. everyone   *Everyone here is*

20. one   *One of you is the murderer.*

SPEAKING APPLICATION

Take turns with a partner. Be the announcer for an imaginary race or game. Discuss the pronouns you each used and how the correct antecedents made the action easier to follow.

WRITING APPLICATION

Exchange the sentences you wrote for questions 12 and 19 in Practice 19.2F with a partner. Rewrite each other's sentences using the correct pronouns for the antecedents given.

Test Warm-Up

DIRECTIONS

Read the introduction and the passage that follows. Then, answer the questions to show that you know how to correct errors in pronoun-antecedent agreement in reading and writing.

Yvette wrote this paragraph as the start of a short story about two teens. Read the paragraph and think about the changes you would suggest as a peer editor. When you finish reading, answer the questions that follow.

Marching Orders

(1) Neither Cal nor Bob had sold their energy bars for the fundraiser, yet both needed to sell them soon, because they had agreed that every marching band member should do his or her part to raise money for new uniforms. (2) "Where can we sell our energy bars?" Bob asked. (3) "Most of the band members sold their energy bars at the last game," Cal answered, "and they said the bars sold well." (4) "Well, since football season is over, it's too late for us to do that," Bob sighed. (5) Each of the boys looked inside his box of energy bars and began counting them to see how many bars they had left to sell. (6) Suddenly, Cal said, "Hey! Let's ask permission to sell the energy bars in the cafeteria during lunch!" (7) "That's a good idea," Bob agreed. (8) "All of our friends eat his or her lunch the same time we do, and I'll bet many of them will buy our bars if they have extra money with them." (9) "Great! Let's go get permission to sell in the cafeteria!" Cal said.

---

1 What change, if any, should be made in sentence 1?

   A Change *their* to **his**

   B Change *them* to **it**

   C Change *his or her* to **their**

   D Make no change

2 What change, if any, should be made in sentence 3?

   F Change *their* to **his or her**

   G Change *they* to **he or she**

   H Change *the bars* to **it**

   J Make no change

3 What change, if any, should be made in sentence 5?

   A Change *his* to **their**

   B Change *them* to **it**

   C Change *they* to **he**

   D Make no change

4 What change, if any, should be made in sentence 8?

   F Change *his or her* to **their**

   G Change *our* to **their**

   H Change *they* to **he or she**

   J Make no change

19.3 Special Problems With Pronoun Agreement

This section will show you how to avoid some common errors that can obscure the meaning of your sentences.

Vague Pronoun References

One basic rule governs all of the rules for pronoun reference.

RULE 19.3.1

> **To avoid confusion, a pronoun requires an antecedent that is either stated or clearly understood.**

The pronouns *which*, *this*, *that*, and *these* should not be used to refer to a vague or overly general idea.

In the following example, it is impossible to determine exactly what the pronoun *these* stands for because it may refer to three different groups of words.

VAGUE REFERENCE
Chris was exhausted, the children were hungry, and the heater was broken. **These** made our trip to the ski lodge unbearable.

This vague reference can be corrected in two ways. One way is to change the pronoun to an adjective that modifies a specific noun. The second way is to revise the sentence so that the pronoun *these* is eliminated.

CORRECT
Chris was exhausted, the children were hungry, and the heater was broken. **These misfortunes** made our trip to the ski lodge unbearable.

CORRECT
Chris's exhaustion, the children's hunger, and the broken heater made our trip to the ski lodge unbearable.

> **The personal pronouns *it, they,* and *you* should always have a clear antecedent.**

In the next example, the pronoun *it* has no clearly stated antecedent.

VAGUE REFERENCE	Halley is planning to travel next year. **It** should be very eye-opening.

Again, there are two methods of correction. The first method is to replace the personal pronoun with a specific noun. The second method is to revise the sentence entirely in order to make the whole idea clear.

CORRECT	Halley is planning to travel next year. **The experience** should be very eye-opening.
CORRECT	**Halley's plan** to travel next year should be very eye-opening.

In the next example, the pronoun *they* is used without an accurate antecedent.

VAGUE REFERENCE	I enjoyed directing the show, but **they** never indicated which scenes were the best.
CORRECT	I enjoyed directing the show, but **the audience** never indicated which scenes were the best.
VAGUE REFERENCE	When we arrived at the theater, **they** told us which actors and actresses were running late.
CORRECT	When we arrived at the theater, **the usher** told us which actors and actresses were running late.

RULE

19.3.3

Use *you* only when the reference is truly to the reader or listener.

VAGUE REFERENCE	**You** couldn't understand a word the officer said.
CORRECT	**We** couldn't understand a word the officer said.

VAGUE REFERENCE	In the company my father worked for, **you** were expected to work long hours every day.
CORRECT	In the company my father worked for, **employees** were expected to work long hours every day.

Note About *It*: In many idiomatic expressions, the personal pronoun *it* has no specific antecedent. In statements such as "It is late," *it* is an idiom that is accepted as standard English.

See Practice 19.3A

Ambiguous Pronoun References

A pronoun is **ambiguous** if it can refer to more than one antecedent.

RULE

19.3.4

A pronoun should never refer to more than one antecedent.

In the following sentence, *she* is confusing because it can refer to either *Sally* or *Jane*. Revise such a sentence by changing the pronoun to a noun or rephrasing the sentence entirely.

AMBIGUOUS REFERENCE	Sally told Jane about the play **she** wanted to be in.
CORRECT	Sally told Jane about the play **Jane** wanted to be in.
	(Sally knew about the play.)

RULE

19.3.5

Do not repeat a personal pronoun in a sentence if it can refer to a different antecedent each time.

AMBIGUOUS REPETITION	When Brent asked his father if **he** could borrow the truck, **he** said that **he** needed it.
CLEAR	When Brent asked his father if **he** could borrow the truck, **Brent** said that **he** needed it.
CLEAR	When Brent asked his father if **he** could borrow the truck, his **father** said that **he** needed it **himself**.

Notice that in the first sentence above, it is unclear whether *he* is referring to Brent or to his father. To eliminate the confusion, Brent's name was used in the second sentence. In the third sentence, the reflexive pronoun *himself* helps to clarify the meaning.

Avoiding Distant Pronoun References

A pronoun should be placed close to its antecedent.

> **A personal pronoun should always be close enough to its antecedent to prevent confusion.**

19.3.6 RULE

A distant pronoun reference can be corrected by moving the pronoun closer to its antecedent or by changing the pronoun to a noun. In the example below, *it* is too far from the antecedent *ankle.*

DISTANT REFERENCE	Anne shifted her weight from her injured ankle. A week ago, she had fallen in ballet class, hurting herself on the wood floor. Now **it** was wrapped with bandages.
CORRECT	Anne shifted her weight from her injured ankle. A week ago, she had fallen in ballet class, hurting herself on the wood floor. Now her **ankle** was wrapped with bandages.

See Practice 19.3B

(*Ankle* replaces the pronoun *it*.)

PRACTICE 19.3A Correcting Vague Pronouns

Read each sentence. Then, rewrite each sentence to correct the use of vague pronouns.

EXAMPLE They said that it was going to be sunny today.

ANSWER *The weather person said that it was going to be sunny today.*

1. The gate is held closed with a latch, but it has rusted.

2. In Mexico, you must be a citizen to own beachside property.

3. Katrina saw the dress in the picture window and thought it was very nice.

4. The good news spread throughout the town, and it was well-received.

5. You can't buy tickets until the gate opens.

6. Jason has a great imagination, and this makes me eager to hear his stories.

7. The movie was confusing because they cut too many important scenes.

8. Many poets use vague references, and this confuses readers.

9. There were too many twists in the movie's plot and this upset the audience.

10. From where my cousin lives, you can see the ocean.

PRACTICE 19.3B Recognizing Ambiguous Pronouns

Read each sentence. Then, rewrite each sentence to avoid the use of ambiguous pronouns.

EXAMPLE Steve told Jesse that he might lose his job.

ANSWER *Steve told Jesse that Jesse might lose his job.*

11. Tim asked his father if he could go to a movie, but he said no.

12. When my uncle takes my cousin to the park, he is very happy.

13. Audrey told Marni that she was being given a raise.

14. When Tyra looked into the microscope to see the specimen, it seemed hazy.

15. I gave David a shirt and tie for his birthday, but it did not please him.

16. Before leaving Tatiana with Grandma, we should tell her where we're going.

17. Donna explained to Jane the story she just read.

18. After Nick told his father about the new job, he wished him luck.

19. Betsy told Nancy that her cat's health was improving.

20. When Kendra told Alexa that she was moving to Texas, she said she would miss her.

SPEAKING APPLICATION

Take turns with a partner. Say sentences that contain vague pronouns. Your partner should correct your sentences.

WRITING APPLICATION

Use sentences 11, 13, and 15 as models to write similar sentences. Then, exchange papers with a partner. Your partner should rewrite each sentence, correcting the ambiguous pronoun references.

CHAPTER 20

USING MODIFIERS

Understanding the degrees of adjectives and adverbs will help you make effective comparisons.

WRITE GUY *Jeff Anderson, M.Ed.*

WHAT DO YOU NOTICE?

Find the modifier that is used to compare as you zoom in on this sentence from the story "The Fall of the House of Usher" by Edgar Allan Poe.

MENTOR TEXT

> I shudder at the thought of any, even the most trivial, incident, which may operate upon this intolerable agitation of soul.

Now, ask yourself the following questions:

- Which degree of comparison is the adjective that modifies *incident*?
- Why did the author use this degree of comparison?

The phrase *most trivial* that modifies the noun *incident* is in the superlative degree. *Most* is used because the word *trivial* has three syllables, and adding the ending *-est* would sound awkward. The author used the superlative degree to show that even an incident that is more trivial than any other possible incident has a terrible effect on the narrator.

Grammar for Writers By using degrees of comparison, writers can help readers better understand ideas and visualize images. To craft clear comparisons, check whether you should use the endings *-er* or *-est* or the words *more* or *most*.

Why can't I say beautifuler *instead of* more beautiful?

Because beautifuler *is awkward. You wouldn't want to be* more awkward *than others, right?*

20.1 Degrees of Comparison

In the English language, there are three degrees, or forms, of most adjectives and adverbs that are used in comparisons.

Recognizing Degrees of Comparison

In order to write effective comparisons, you first need to know the three degrees.

RULE 20.1.1

The three degrees of comparison are the **positive,** the **comparative,** and the **superlative.**

The following chart shows adjectives and adverbs in each of the three degrees. Notice the three different ways that modifiers are changed to show degree: (1) by adding *-er* or *-est*, (2) by adding *more* or *most*, and (3) by using entirely different words.

DEGREES OF ADJECTIVES		
POSITIVE	COMPARATIVE	SUPERLATIVE
simple	simpler	simplest
impressive	more impressive	most impressive
good	better	best
DEGREES OF ADVERBS		
soon	sooner	soonest
impressively	more impressively	most impressively
well	better	best

See Practice 20.1A

Regular Forms

Adjectives and adverbs can be either **regular** or **irregular,** depending on how their comparative and superlative degrees are formed. The degrees of most adjectives and adverbs are formed regularly. The number of syllables in regular modifiers determines how their degrees are formed.

RULE 20.1.2

Use *-er* or *more* to form the comparative degree and *-est* or *most* to form the superlative degree of most one- and two-syllable modifiers.

| EXAMPLES | loud | louder | loudest |
| | spiteful | more spiteful | most spiteful |

All adverbs that end in *-ly* form their comparative and superlative degrees with *more* and *most*.

20.1.3 RULE

| EXAMPLES | importantly | more importantly | most importantly |
| | hopefully | more hopefully | most hopefully |

Use *more* and *most* to form the comparative and superlative degrees of all modifiers with three or more syllables.

20.1.4 RULE

| EXAMPLES | difficult | more difficult | most difficult |
| | ambitious | more ambitious | most ambitious |

Note About Comparisons With *Less* and *Least*: *Less* and *least* can be used to form another version of the comparative and superlative degrees of most modifiers.

| EXAMPLES | difficult | less difficult | least difficult |
| | ambitious | less ambitious | least ambitious |

See Practice 20.1B

Irregular Forms

The comparative and superlative degrees of a few commonly used adjectives and adverbs are formed in unpredictable ways.

The irregular comparative and superlative forms of certain adjectives and adverbs must be memorized.

20.1.5 RULE

In the chart on the following page, the form of some irregular modifiers differs only in the positive degree. The modifiers *bad*, *badly*, and *ill*, for example, all have the same comparative and superlative degrees (*worse*, *worst*).

IRREGULAR MODIFIERS		
POSITIVE	COMPARATIVE	SUPERLATIVE
bad, badly, ill	worse	worst
far (distance)	farther	farthest
far (extent)	further	furthest
good, well	better	best
late	later	last or latest
little (amount)	less	least
many, much	more	most

RULE

20.1.6

Bad is an adjective. Do not use it to modify an action verb. *Badly* is an adverb. Use it after an action verb but not after a linking verb.

INCORRECT Some seniors treated the younger students **bad**.

CORRECT Some seniors treated the younger students **badly**.

INCORRECT Jennifer feels **badly** about losing the election.

CORRECT Jennifer feels **bad** about losing the election.

Note About *Good* and *Well*: *Good* is always an adjective and cannot be used as an adverb after an action verb. It can, however, be used as a predicate adjective after a linking verb.

INCORRECT The band played their instruments **good** today.

CORRECT The band sounded **good** today.

Well is generally an adverb. However, when *well* means "healthy," it is an adjective and can be used after a linking verb.

CORRECT Marta kicks a soccer ball **well**.

CORRECT Marta should be **well** soon.

See Practice 20.1C
See Practice 20.1D

PRACTICE 20.1A Recognizing Positive, Comparative, and Superlative Degrees of Comparison

Read each sentence. Then, identify the degree of comparison of the underlined word or words as *positive*, *comparative*, or *superlative*.

EXAMPLE   Harrison might find it <u>harder</u> to see than Jesse.

ANSWER   *comparative*

1. Larry has the <u>fastest</u> horse on the team.

2. There have been <u>fewer</u> cases of chickenpox this year than last.

3. Mickey brought home an <u>excellent</u> report card today.

4. Last night I had the <u>weirdest</u> dream.

5. Leo began his speech <u>nervously</u>.

6. This is the <u>warmest</u> February I can remember.

7. Goldman will surely be named <u>most valuable</u> player this year.

8. Jenny will be <u>more cautious</u> on her next camping trip.

9. Jose ate his meal <u>hungrily</u>.

10. The patient seemed <u>more alert</u> after the medicine had worn off.

PRACTICE 20.1B Forming Regular Comparative and Superlative Degrees of Comparison

Read each sentence. Then, rewrite each sentence with the correct comparative or superlative degree of the modifier indicated in parentheses.

EXAMPLE   The problem was _____ than I expected. (difficult)

ANSWER   *The problem was more difficult than I expected.*

11. The _____ thing to do is to wait until we know all our options. (wise)

12. Their furniture is _____ than mine. (dark)

13. This pillow is _____ than that one. (soft)

14. Melanie is the _____ person in her family. (artistic)

15. She responded to the treatment _____ than he did. (quickly)

16. His opinion is _____ to understand than hers. (difficult)

17. That hard rock is the _____ place to sit. (comfortable)

18. The marathon will be _____ to complete if you train for it. (easy)

19. She is the candidate's _____ supporter. (eager)

20. The music was _____ than I expected. (loud)

SPEAKING APPLICATION

Take turns with a partner. Describe items found in your classroom. Use comparative, superlative, and positive degrees of comparison. Your partner should listen for and identify which degree of comparison you are using in each of your descriptions.

WRITING APPLICATION

Rewrite sentences 14, 15, and 17, changing the modifiers in parentheses. Then, exchange papers with a partner. Your partner should write the correct degree of the modifiers in your sentences.

PRACTICE 20.1C ▷ **Supplying Irregular Comparative and Superlative Forms**

Read each modifier. Then, write its irregular comparative and superlative forms.

EXAMPLE   good

ANSWER   *better, best*

1. far (distance)
2. far (extent)
3. little (amount)
4. bad
5. late
6. ill
7. well
8. badly
9. much
10. many

PRACTICE 20.1D ▷ **Supplying Irregular Modifiers**

Read each sentence. Then, fill in the blank with the form of the modifier indicated in parentheses that best completes each sentence.

EXAMPLE   I was the ____ person to vote. (late)

ANSWER   *last*

11. Despite taking the medicine, I still felt ____ than before. (ill)
12. The moderator would not allow any ____ debate on the subject. (far)
13. Even the ____ change in temperature can affect plant growth. (little)
14. Because of the cliffhanger, ____ people tuned in to the show than ever before. (many)
15. How much ____ do we have to go before we can rest? (far)
16. Global warming can have the ____ impact in the polar regions. (much)
17. In my opinion, the ____ cotton comes from Texas. (good)
18. Our team played much ____ during the second half of the game. (well)
19. Hervé was the ____ person to leave the show. (late)
20. I had the ____ grade in the entire class. (good)

SPEAKING APPLICATION

Take turns with a partner. Say sentences with irregular comparative and superlative forms. Your partner should indicate if incorrect forms have been used and suggest corrections.

WRITING APPLICATION

Write pairs of sentences using each of these modifiers correctly: *less* and *least*, *more* and *most*, *farthest* and *furthest*, *bad* and *badly*.

20.2 Making Clear Comparisons

The comparative and superlative degrees help you make comparisons that are clear and logical.

WRITING COACH

Online
www.phwritingcoach.com

Grammar Tutorials
Brush up on your Grammar skills with these animated videos.

Grammar Practice
Practice your grammar skills with Writing Coach Online.

Grammar Games
Test your knowledge of grammar in this fast-paced interactive video game.

Using Comparative and Superlative Degrees

One basic rule that has two parts covers the correct use of comparative and superlative forms.

> Use the **comparative degree** to compare two persons, places, or things. Use the **superlative degree** to compare three or more persons, places, or things.

RULE 20.2.1

The context of a sentence should indicate whether two items or more than two items are being compared.

COMPARATIVE His part is **harder** to learn than mine.

My costume is **more colorful** than hers.

Sandy has **less** time on stage than Marco.

SUPERLATIVE His part is the **hardest** one to learn.

My costume is the **most colorful** one in the cast.

Sandy has the **least** time on stage of anyone.

In informal writing, the superlative degree is sometimes used just for emphasis, without any specific comparison.

EXAMPLE Emily sang **most beautifully**!

Note About Double Comparisons: A double comparison is caused by using both -er and more or both -est and most to form a regular modifier or by adding an extra comparison form to an irregular modifier.

See Practice 20.2A

See Practice 20.2B

INCORRECT His sailboat is **more faster** than mine.

CORRECT His sailboat is **faster** than mine.

PRACTICE 20.2A Supplying the Comparative and Superlative Degrees of Modifiers

Read each sentence. Then, fill in the blank with the correct form of the underlined modifier.

EXAMPLE   This restaurant is good, but that one is even _____.

ANSWER   *better*

1. Candyce played badly on the soccer field, but Susan played even _____.

2. All of the salespeople are successful, but Jeanine is _____.

3. I still feel ill, but yesterday I felt _____.

4. George looks good in blue, but he looks _____ in green.

5. Randolph lives farther from school than Rick, but Cece lives the _____.

6. I have little interest in movies and even _____ in plays.

7. I have homework in English, more homework in science, and the _____ in French.

8. We drove quite far today, but we must drive _____ tomorrow.

9. There was much commotion in the hall, but inside the room there was even _____ commotion.

10. Gwen has a better record than Louis, but Kate has the _____ record of the three.

PRACTICE 20.2B Revising Sentences to Correct Errors in Modifier Usage

Read each sentence. Then, rewrite each sentence, correcting any errors in the usage of modifiers to make comparisons. If a sentence contains no errors, write *correct*.

EXAMPLE   Delia's recent babysitting experience was far best than the one before.

ANSWER   *Delia's recent babysitting experience was far better than the one before.*

11. Kenny is the more interesting person at the party.

12. Gary is funniest than his brother David.

13. She is the younger person to win the prize.

14. Which of the two towns is farthest from here?

15. The book is least suspenseful now that I've figured out what happens.

16. Marta is best at acting than her twin sister.

17. I was more impressed than you were.

18. Were you the stronger member of the wrestling team?

19. Which of the twins dances best?

20. Linda is the fastest runner on the track team.

SPEAKING APPLICATION

Take turns with a partner. Compare three books, using comparative and superlative degrees of modifiers. Your partner should listen for and identify your comparisons.

WRITING APPLICATION

Write three sentences with errors in modifier usage. Then, exchange papers with a partner. Your partner should correct your sentences.

Using Logical Comparisons

Two common usage problems are the comparison of unrelated items and the comparison of something with itself.

Balanced Comparisons
Be certain that things being compared in a sentence are similar.

> **Your sentences should only compare items of a similar kind.**

The following unbalanced sentences illogically compare dissimilar things.

UNBALANCED **Mike's statue** is taller than **Gina**.

CORRECT **Mike's statue** is taller than **Gina's**.

UNBALANCED The **height of the fence** is greater than the **dog can jump**.

CORRECT The **height of the fence** is greater than the **height the dog can jump**.

Note About *Other* and *Else* in Comparisons
Another illogical comparison results when something is inadvertently compared with itself.

> **When comparing one of a group with the rest of the group, make sure that your sentence contains the word *other* or the word *else*.**

20.2.3 RULE

Adding *other* or *else* when comparing one person or thing with a group will make the comparison clear and logical.

ILLOGICAL His paintings are more beautiful than any paintings.
(His paintings cannot be more beautiful than themselves.)

See Practice 20.2C
See Practice 20.2D

LOGICAL His paintings are more beautiful than any **other** paintings.

PRACTICE 20.2C ▸ Revising to Make Comparisons Balanced and Logical

Read each sentence. Then, rewrite each sentence, correcting the unbalanced or illogical comparison.

EXAMPLE   This year's team looks stronger than last year.

ANSWER   *This year's team looks stronger than last year's.*

1. Rita's den is larger than Mike.
2. Our school has a better team than any school in town.
3. Al's bike is newer than Levi.
4. Amiri's artistic ability is greater than Andy.
5. My sister handles pressure better than any member of our family.
6. Today's temperature is colder than yesterday.
7. Jane worked harder than any person on the nominating committee.
8. The instructions for baking a pie are easier than cake.
9. Leslie's SAT scores were higher than her sister.
10. Frannie's project had fewer diagrams than Donna.

PRACTICE 20.2D ▸ Writing Clear Comparisons

Read each sentence. Then, rewrite each sentence, filling in the blanks to make a comparison that is clear and logical.

EXAMPLE   Your sculpture was better than _____.

ANSWER   *Your sculpture was better than any other sculpture in the class.*

11. Mary's speech was more interesting than _____.
12. The tail of a beaver is broader and flatter than _____.
13. Aunt Winnie's homemade jelly is sweeter than _____.
14. The mileage we get in this car is better than _____.
15. A stroll in the garden is less invigorating than _____.
16. The grade on Kemau's paper is better than _____.
17. The egg of an ostrich is bigger than _____.
18. Replacing all four tires on a car will be more expensive than _____.
19. Today's weather is warmer than _____.
20. These directions for assembling a bicycle are less complicated than _____.

SPEAKING APPLICATION

Take turns with a partner. Say sentences that have unbalanced or illogical comparisons. Your partner should restate the sentences, using balanced and logical comparisons.

WRITING APPLICATION

Use sentences 11, 13, and 15 as models to write similar sentences. Then, exchange papers with a partner. Your partner should fill in the blanks to make the comparison in each sentence clear and logical.

Avoiding Comparisons With Absolute Modifiers

Some modifiers cannot be used logically to make comparisons because their meanings are *absolute*—that is, their meanings are entirely contained in the positive degree. For example, if a line is *vertical*, another line cannot be *more* vertical. Some other common absolute modifiers are *dead, entirely, fatal, final, identical, infinite, opposite, perfect,* and *unique*.

> **Avoid using absolute modifiers illogically in comparisons.**

20.2.4
RULE

| INCORRECT | The exam is the **most final** one before vacation. |
| CORRECT | The exam is the **final** one before vacation. |

Often, it is not only the word *more* or *most* that makes an absolute modifier illogical; sometimes it is best to replace the absolute modifier with one that expresses the intended meaning more precisely.

| ILLOGICAL | Your thesis is **more unique** than anyone else's. |
| CORRECT | Your thesis is **more original** than anyone else's. |

Sometimes an absolute modifier may overstate the meaning that you want.

| ILLOGICAL | That research paper caused the **most fatal** damage to my average this year. |
| CORRECT | That research paper caused the **most severe** damage to my average this year. |

See Practice 20.2E
See Practice 20.2F
See Practice 20.2G
See Practice 20.2H

In the preceding example, *most fatal* is illogical because something is either fatal or it is not. However, even *fatal* is an overstatement. *Most severe* better conveys the intended meaning.

PRACTICE 20.2E > **Revising Sentences to Correct Comparisons Using Absolute Modifiers**

Read each sentence. Then, correct each illogical comparison by replacing the absolute modifier with more precise words.

EXAMPLE   That painter has the most unique style of any other artist.

ANSWER   *That painter's style is unique among artists.*

1. His answer was more final than we expected.

2. Of all the children, Joanne looks most identical to her mother.

3. Carlo's answers are more right than Frank's.

4. Now that he is in the second grade, Jamison draws rounder circles than he once did.

5. He threw the ball straighter than an arrow.

6. I have never seen a deader plant than that fern.

7. The challenger's position is more opposite of mine than the incumbent's.

8. After the hike, he was more entirely exhausted than I was.

9. Her second novel was more perfect than her first.

10. The names of the most final contestants were announced.

PRACTICE 20.2F > **Revising Overstated Absolute Modifiers**

Read each sentence. Then, rewrite each sentence, revising the overstated absolute modifier.

EXAMPLE   His love for her is extremely everlasting.

ANSWER   *His love for her is everlasting.*

11. Joe's diagram is more perfect than Maura's.

12. A decision passed by the Supreme Court is the most absolute.

13. The plants in the garden are completely dead.

14. A fish is more mortal than a whale.

15. Funding for sports should be given more equally.

16. Of the pups in the litter, the black one is the most alive.

17. The captain's orders are more final than the first mate's.

18. Winning a gold medal is Tristan's most ultimate goal.

19. The trees by the river were slightly destroyed.

20. A red rose as a symbol for love is very eternal.

SPEAKING APPLICATION

Take turns with a partner. Say sentences that incorrectly use absolute modifiers. Your partner should restate your sentences correctly.

WRITING APPLICATION

Write three sentences with overstated absolute modifiers. Then, exchange papers with a partner. Your partner should revise the overstated absolute modifiers in your sentences.

PRACTICE 20.2G > Correcting Problems in Comparisons

Read each sentence. Then, correct each sentence that has a comparison error by rewriting it. If a sentence has no error, write *correct*.

EXAMPLE We stayed at the car wash longer than anybody.

ANSWER *We stayed at the car wash longer than anybody else.*

1. I like pears more better than peaches.

2. Luis hit more pitches in today's game than yesterday's.

3. That's the fascinatingest book I have ever read.

4. Bud is least talented as a singer than Mary Ann.

5. Apple pie is my most favoritest.

6. Mike's guitar picking is as good as Eric.

7. That car drives more smoothly than any other car I have driven.

8. It was the worse night ever.

9. The fish was more hard to catch than I expected.

10. That is the most unique costume I have ever seen.

PRACTICE 20.2H > Making Correct Comparisons

Write new sentences with comparisons. Use the topics and degrees of comparison specified.

EXAMPLE compare his paintings to all other paintings (superlative)

ANSWER *His paintings have the brightest colors of all the paintings.*

11. compare her voice to another's (comparative)

12. compare their mileage to other cars' (comparative)

13. compare her talents as a gymnast to others' (superlative)

14. compare his health today to his health yesterday (comparative)

15. compare their football team's record to that of a rival school (comparative)

16. compare the length of her hair to that of others (superlative)

17. compare his nervousness to that of others (superlative)

18. compare his skill at video games to that of one other (comparative)

19. compare one city's mass transit system to another's (comparative)

20. compare his music collection to his friend's (comparative)

SPEAKING APPLICATION

Take turns with a partner. Compare two movies or TV shows, one that you like and one that you don't. Your partner should identify any errors in your comparisons and suggest corrections.

WRITING APPLICATION

Write five sentences using the comparative. Then, trade papers with a partner. Each of you will turn your partner's comparative sentences into sentences with superlative comparisons.

Test Warm-Up

DIRECTIONS

Read the introduction and the passage that follows. Then, answer the questions to show that you understand how to revise to correct errors of comparison in reading and writing.

Albert wrote this paragraph about a friend's experience. Read the paragraph and think about the changes you would suggest as a peer editor. When you finish reading, answer the questions that follow.

World's Greatest Cat?

(1) Kayla entered her cat, Max, in the World's Greatest Cat competition. (2) Before the competition, she said, "Max has the best coat ever, and he has the sweetest temperament of any cat." (3) When Kayla entered the arena the day of the competition, she saw a man carrying a cat with such shiny fur that the cat looked like the star of a cat food commercial. (4) "This is Estrella," the man said. (5) When the judges compared Max's coat to Estrella's, they agreed Estrella's was prettier than Max. (6) In fact, the judges agreed that Estrella was the most best in all categories, and she triumphed over Max and all the other cats to be judged the greatest cat of all. (7) At first, Kayla felt more disappointed than she had anticipated, but she felt better when she realized that Max was the most wonderful cat in the world because he was hers.

---

1 What change, if any, should be made in sentence 2?

  A Change *best* to **better**

  B Change *sweetest* to **most sweet**

  C Add the word **other** after the word *any*

  D Make no change

3 What change, if any, should be made in sentence 6?

  A Change *most best* to **best**

  B Omit the word *other* before the word *cats*

  C Change *greatest* to **most greatest**

  D Make no change

2 What change, if any, should be made in sentence 5?

  F Change *Max's* to **Max**

  G Change *prettier* to **more pretty**

  H Change *Max* to **Max's**

  J Make no change

4 What change, if any, should be made in sentence 7?

  F Change *more disappointed* to **disappointeder**

  G Change *better* to **more better**

  H Change *most wonderful* to **wonderfulest**

  J Make no change

CHAPTER 21

MISCELLANEOUS PROBLEMS *in* USAGE

Knowing how to avoid common word usage problems will help you to write clearly and precisely.

WRITE GUY *Jeff Anderson, M.Ed.*

WHAT DO YOU NOTICE?

Think about how words are used as you zoom in on sentences from the Modoc myth "When Grizzlies Walked Upright" as retold by Richard Erdoes and Alfonso Ortiz.

MENTOR TEXT

> The mountains of snow and ice became their lodge. He made a big fire in the center of the mountain and a hole in the top so that the smoke and sparks could fly out.

Now, ask yourself the following questions:

- How do writers sometimes confuse the word *their*?
- Why is the word *that* used with *so* in the second sentence?

The possessive pronoun *their* is often confused with the adverb *there* and the contraction *they're* because they sound the same even though the spellings and meanings are different. Used alone, *so* is a coordinating conjunction like *and* or *but*. When used to mean "in order to," *so* should be paired with *that* or *as*.

Grammar for Writers Writers should check how they have used words that may be easily confused to ensure their writing is clear. A little extra time spent reviewing and editing text will polish your writing.

Their books have been there for a while.

You're right there, but they're going to pick them up soon.

21.1 Negative Sentences

In English, only one *no* is needed in a sentence to deny or refuse something. You can express a negative idea with words such as *not* or *never* or with contractions such as *can't, couldn't,* and *wasn't.* (The ending *-n't* in a contraction is an abbreviation of *not.*)

WRITING COACH

Online

www.phwritingcoach.com

Grammar Practice
Practice your grammar skills with Writing Coach Online.

Grammar Games
Test your knowledge of grammar in this fast-paced interactive video game.

Recognizing Double Negatives

Using two negative words in a sentence when one is sufficient is called a **double negative.** While double negatives may sometimes be used in informal speech, they should be avoided in formal English speech and writing.

RULE 21.1.1

> Do not use **double negatives** in formal writing.

The following chart provides examples of double negatives and two ways each can be corrected.

DOUBLE NEGATIVE	CORRECTIONS
Dave couldn't fix nothing.	Dave could fix nothing. Dave couldn't fix anything.
He didn't have no training in repairs.	He had no training in repairs. He didn't have any training in repairs.
He never asked no one for help.	He never asked anyone for help. He asked no one for help.

Sentences that contain more than one clause can correctly contain more than one negative word. Each clause, however, should contain only one negative word.

EXAMPLES The band **didn't** make the final round, but the musicians **weren't** discouraged.

They knew they **hadn't** practiced enough; they **wouldn't** do that again.

Forming Negative Sentences Correctly

There are three common ways to form negative sentences.

Using One Negative Word The most common ways to make a statement negative are to use one **negative word,** such as *never, no,* or *none,* or to add the contraction *-n't* to a helping verb.

> **Use only one negative word in each clause.**

21.1.2 RULE

DOUBLE NEGATIVE	She **wouldn't never** learn that by herself.
PREFERRED	She **would never** learn that by herself.
	She **wouldn't ever** learn that by herself.

Using *But* in a Negative Sense When *but* means "only," it usually acts as a negative. Do not use it with another negative word.

DOUBLE NEGATIVE	There **wasn't but** one part in the play left to cast.
PREFERRED	There was **but** one part in the play left to cast.
	There was **only** one part in the play left to cast.

Using *Barely, Hardly,* and *Scarcely* Each of these words is negative. If you use one of these words with another negative word, you create a double negative.

> **Do not use *barely, hardly,* or *scarcely* with another negative word.**

21.1.3 RULE

DOUBLE NEGATIVE	They **didn't barely** make minimum wage.
PREFERRED	They **barely** made minimum wage.
DOUBLE NEGATIVE	My family **doesn't hardly** celebrate birthdays.
PREFERRED	My family **hardly** celebrates birthdays.
DOUBLE NEGATIVE	I **hadn't scarcely** seen your car coming.
PREFERRED	I **had scarcely** seen your car coming.

See Practice 21.1A

Using Negatives to Create Understatement

Sometimes a writer wants to express an idea indirectly, either to minimize the importance of the idea or to draw attention to it. One such technique is called **understatement.**

> Understatement can be achieved by using a negative word and a word with a negative prefix, such as *un-, in-, im-, dis-,* and *under-.*

EXAMPLES   Mark did **not attend** practice **infrequently** .

He is **hardly unaware** of the time needed to master the jump shot.

He's **not inexperienced** at basketball.

These examples show that the writer is praising the people or things he or she is discussing. In the first example, the writer states that Mark actually attends practice frequently. In the second example, the writer states that he is aware of amount of time needed to master the jump shot. In the third example, the writer states that he is experienced at basketball.

If you choose to use understatement, be sure to use it carefully so that you do not sound critical when you wish to praise.

EXAMPLES   It seemed familiar, but the new movie about pirates **wasn't unexciting** .

Some of the stars **weren't untalented** , although I might have cast different people.

In both examples above, the writer is actually making a negative statement. In the first example, although the writer feels that while the movie was familiar, it was still somewhat exciting. In the second example, the writer seems to think that, while the stars were talented, other people could have been better cast.

See Practice 21.1B

PRACTICE 21.1A ▷ Revising Sentences to Avoid Double Negatives

Read each sentence. Then, rewrite each sentence to correct the double negative.

EXAMPLE   Eric can't have no dairy foods.

ANSWER   *Eric can't have any dairy foods.*

1. Miguel will never let nobody help him.

2. You won't never find a more loyal friend than Jasmine.

3. After tomorrow, we won't have no more classes.

4. There wasn't nobody there when we arrived.

5. You shouldn't have no more trouble with the car.

6. Neither of those boys don't know the way to the library.

7. We can never ask no questions during a test.

8. I can't find none of the game pieces for this board game.

9. I couldn't hardly believe it when I heard the news.

10. There weren't any seats nowhere in the auditorium.

PRACTICE 21.1B ▷ Using Negatives to Create Understatement

Read each item. Then, use each item to create understatement.

EXAMPLE   undercooked

ANSWER   *The meat wasn't undercooked, even though it was chewy.*

11. underestimated

12. impassive

13. unmoved

14. inaccurate

15. undeveloped

16. immovable

17. dissatisfied

18. insincere

19. immature

20. underfed

SPEAKING APPLICATION

Take turns with a partner. Say sentences that contain double negatives. Your partner should listen to and correct your sentences to avoid the double negatives.

WRITING APPLICATION

Use items 13, 16, and 19 to write other sentences that contain double negatives. Then, exchange papers with a partner. Your partner should correct your sentences.

Grammar Game Plan

Grammar Game Plan

(1) a, an The use of the article *a* or *an* is determined by the sound of the word that follows it. *A* is used before consonant sounds, while *an* is used before vowel sounds. Words beginning with *hon-, o-,* or *u-* may have either a consonant or a vowel sound.

EXAMPLES
a hero (*h* sound)

a one-hour lecture (*w* sound)

an honest opinion (no *h* sound)

an omen (*o* sound)

an underwater expedition (*u* sound)

(2) accept, except *Accept,* a verb, means "to receive." *Except,* a preposition, means "to leave out" or "other than."

VERB   I **accept** your offer to go to the store.

PREPOSITION   I'd be happy to shop for anything **except** shoes.

(3) adapt, adopt *Adapt* means "to change." *Adopt* means "to take as one's own."

EXAMPLES   Farmers **adapt** others' techniques to their soil.

They often **adopt** new techniques, too.

(4) affect, effect *Affect* is almost always a verb meaning "to influence." *Effect,* usually a noun, means "a result." Sometimes, *effect* is a verb meaning "to bring about" or "to cause."

VERB   Natural disasters **affect** farmers' success.

NOUN   Farmers know the **effects** of drought.

VERB   Hot summers also **effect** changes in the harvest.

(5) aggravate *Aggravate* means "to make worse." Avoid using this word to mean "annoy."

INCORRECT   The noise of the lawnmower **aggravated** me.

PREFERRED   The drought is **aggravating** the water quality.

(6) ain't   *Ain't,* which was originally a contraction for
am not, is no longer considered acceptable in standard English.
Always use *is not, are not,* or *am not,* and never use *ain't.* The
exception is in certain instances of dialogue.

(7) all ready, already   *All ready,* which consists of two separate
words used as an adjective, means "ready." *Already,* which is an
adverb, means "by or before this time" or "even now."

ADJECTIVE   Is everyone **all ready** to begin practicing?

ADVERB   We've started **already** .

(8) all right, alright   *Alright* is a nonstandard spelling. Make
sure you use the two-word form.

INCORRECT   Business in the downtown stores was **alright** during the
                 sale.

PREFERRED   Business in the downtown stores was **all right** during
                 the sale.

(9) all together, altogether   *All together* means "together as a
single group." *Altogether* means "completely" or "in all."

EXAMPLES   My family went to the park **all together** .

                 The flowers made an **altogether** beautiful display.

(10) among, between   Both of these words are prepositions.
Among shows a connection between three or more items.
Between generally shows a connection between two items.

EXAMPLES   Schools of brightly colored fish swam **among** the coral
                 reefs.

See Practice 21.2A   They swam **between** the rocks and the higher
                 formations, trying to avoid the sharks.

(11) anxious   This adjective implies uneasiness, worry, or fear.
Do not use it as a substitute for *eager.*

INCORRECT   The environmentalists were **anxious** for change.

PREFERRED   They were **anxious** about the effects of pollution.

(12) anyone, any one, everyone, every one *Anyone* and *everyone* mean "any person" or "every person." *Any one* means "any single person (or thing)"; *every one* means "every single person (or thing)."

EXAMPLES

Anyone can be an environmentalist.

Any one person can make a difference in helping to protect our planet.

Everyone has a responsibility to keep the planet safe.

Every one of us can recycle and live responsibly.

(13) anyway, anywhere, everywhere, nowhere, somewhere These adverbs should never end in *-s*.

INCORRECT

Before the fence was set up, my dog could wander **anywheres** in the neighborhood.

PREFERRED

Before the fence was set up, my dog could wander **anywhere** in the neighborhood.

(14) as Do not use the conjunction *as* to mean "because" or "since."

INCORRECT

Our recycling drive was not successful **as** we couldn't get enough people to work.

PREFERRED

Our recycling drive was not successful **because** we couldn't get enough people to work.

(15) as to *As to* is awkward. Replace it with *about*.

INCORRECT

There is some doubt **as to** whether I'll be able to complete my project on time.

PREFERRED

There is some doubt **about** whether I'll be able to complete my project on time.

(16) at Do not use *at* after *where*. Simply eliminate *at*.

INCORRECT

Where is my homework **at**?

PREFERRED

Where is my homework?

(17) at, about   Avoid using *at* with *about*. Simply eliminate *at* or *about*.

INCORRECT	My favorite television show is on **at about** 9:00.
PREFERRED	My favorite television show is on **at** 9:00.

(18) awful, awfully   *Awful* is used informally to mean that something is "extremely bad." *Awfully* is used informally to mean "very." Both words are overused and should be replaced with more descriptive words. In standard English speech and writing, *awful* should only be used to mean "inspiring fear or awe in someone."

OVERUSED	I'd made an **awful** mess of my report.
PREFERRED	I'd made a **terrible** mess of my report.
OVERUSED	Marcia was **awfully** angry with Denise.
PREFERRED	Marcia was **extremely** angry with Denise.
OVERUSED	The weather report was **awful**.
PREFERRED	The weather report was **dreadful**.

(19) awhile, a while   *Awhile* is an adverb that means "for a short time." *A while,* a noun, means "a period of time." It is usually used after the preposition *for* or *after.*

ADVERB	Some plants can grow **awhile** without sun.
	We waited **awhile** until our number was called.
NOUN	They may grow for **a while** in the shade, but most plants need sunlight.
	In **a while**, our waiting will be over.

(20) beat, win   When you *win*, you "achieve a victory in something." When you *beat* someone or something, you "overcome an opponent."

INCORRECT	The runner in lane 2 **won** the other runners.
PREFERRED	The runner in lane 2 **beat** the other runners.
	The runner in lane 2 wants to **win** the race.

See Practice 21.2B

PRACTICE 21.2A Recognizing Usage Problems 1–10

Read each sentence. Then, choose the correct item to complete each sentence.

EXAMPLE   Can we (adopt, adapt) that city's plan to benefit our small town?

ANSWER   *adapt*

1. I (ain't, am not) going to the baseball game today.

2. Human population growth can (affect, effect) endangered species.

3. Amanda has (already, all ready) finished the test.

4. I sat (among, between) two of my teammates on the bench.

5. He will (accept, except) the award.

6. Tree pollen (aggravates, annoys) my allergy symptoms.

7. We traveled (all together, altogether) to the beach.

8. Sue said it was (alright, all right) for me to borrow her book.

9. It would be (a, an) honor to serve in your administration.

10. The town recently (adopted, adapted) a new policy for meetings.

PRACTICE 21.2B Recognizing Usage Problems 11–20

Read each sentence. Then, choose the correct expression to complete each sentence.

EXAMPLE   The answer is (somewheres, somewhere) in this book.

ANSWER   *somewhere*

11. I was (awfully, extremely) tired after the race.

12. (As, Because) the park is close by, we decided to walk there.

13. I didn't have time to go to the mall (anyway, anyways).

14. Jamal (beat, won) all of his opponents in the tournament.

15. Tom and Raymond have known each other for quite (a while, awhile).

16. The party will begin (at about, at) 6:00 P.M.

17. Please share your suggestions (as to, about) how to organize the room.

18. Do you know where the softball field (is at, is located)?

19. (Every one, everyone) of the players attended the game.

20. Some of the students were so (eager, anxious) about the exam that they stayed up late studying.

SPEAKING APPLICATION

Take turns with a partner. Choose the pair of words in parentheses from sentence 2, 5, or 10, and tell your partner your choice. Your partner should say two sentences, using both words correctly.

WRITING APPLICATION

Use sentences 12, 13, 14, and 15 as models to write four similar sentences. Exchange papers with a partner. Your partner should choose the correct word that completes each of your sentences.

(21) because   Do not use *because* after the phrase *the reason*. Say "The reason is that" or reword the sentence.

INCORRECT	The **reason** I'm going to the library **is because** I have to do some research.
PREFERRED	The **reason** I'm going to the library **is** to do some research.

(22) being as, being that   Avoid using either of these expressions. Use *because* instead.

INCORRECT	**Being as** I was going past the store, I bought some lunch.
PREFERRED	**Because** I was going past the store, I bought some lunch.

(23) beside, besides   *Beside* means "at the side of" or "close to." *Besides* means "in addition to."

EXAMPLES	The equipment was lying **beside** the bleachers.
	No one **besides** the team could use it.

(24) bring, take   *Bring* means "to carry from a distant place to a nearer one." *Take* means "to carry from a near place to a far one."

EXAMPLES	Mike will **bring** my homework home while I'm sick.
	I'll **take** it back to school when I return.

(25) can, may   Use *can* to mean "have the ability to." Use *may* to mean "have permission to" or "to be likely to."

ABILITY	You **can** go to the library to find a book.
PERMISSION	You **may** also borrow my book.
POSSIBILITY	You **may** find a better book in the school library.

(26) clipped words   Avoid using clipped or shortened words, such as *gym* and *photo* in formal writing.

INFORMAL	I have many **photos** of my favorite singers.
FORMAL	I have many **photographs** of my favorite singers.

(27) different from, different than *Different from* is preferred in standard English.

INCORRECT New York's rainfall is **different than** Miami's.

PREFERRED New York's rainfall is **different from** Miami's.

(28) doesn't, don't Do not use *don't* with third-person singular subjects. Instead, use *doesn't*.

INCORRECT He **don't** want to leave until the game is over.

PREFERRED He **doesn't** want to leave until the game is over.

(29) done *Done* is the past participle of the verb *do*. It should always take a helping verb.

INCORRECT Jack **done** his homework in complete silence.

PREFERRED Jack **has done** his homework in complete silence.

(30) due to *Due to* means "caused by" and should be used only when the words *caused by* can be logically substituted.

INCORRECT **Due to** hunting, wolves almost became extinct.

PREFERRED The wolves' near extinction was **due to** hunting.

See Practice 21.2C

(31) each other, one another These expressions usually are interchangeable. At times, however, *each other* is more logically used in reference to only two and *one another* in reference to more than two.

EXAMPLES Students working in groups rely on **one another** when they assign tasks.

A pair of students often benefit from **each other's** knowledge and suggestions.

(32) farther, further *Farther* refers to distance. *Further* means "additional" or "to a greater degree or extent."

EXAMPLES The **farther** I swam, the more my muscles ached.

Clearly, I needed to **further** develop my strength.

(33) fewer, less Use *fewer* with things that can be counted. Use *less* with qualities and quantities that cannot be counted.

EXAMPLES **fewer** telephones, **less** communication

(34) get, got, gotten These forms of the verb *get* are acceptable in standard English, but a more specific word is preferable.

INCORRECT **get** nominated, **got** elected, **have gotten** laws passed

PREFERRED **was** nominated, **won** the election, **passed** laws

(35) gone, went *Gone* is the past participle of the verb *go* and is used only with a helping verb. *Went* is the past tense of *go* and is never used with a helping verb.

INCORRECT The birds **gone** south for the winter.

They should **have went** before the cold weather.

PREFERRED The birds **went** south for the winter.

They should **have gone** before the cold weather.

(36) good, lovely, nice Replace these overused words with a more specific adjective.

WEAK **good** description, **lovely** room, **nice** painting

BETTER **vivid** description, **cozy** room, **realistic** painting

(37) in, into *In* refers to position. *Into* suggests motion.

EXAMPLES Broadway is **in** New York City.

We have to go **into** the subway to go uptown.

(38) irregardless Avoid this word in formal speech and writing. Instead, use *regardless*.

(39) just When you use *just* as an adverb to mean "no more than," place it immediately before the word it modifies.

INCORRECT Bob **just** went to the corner store.

PREFERRED Bob went **just** to the corner store.

(40) kind of, sort of Do not use these phrases in formal speech. Instead, use *rather* or *somewhat*.

See Practice 21.2D

PRACTICE 21.2C > Recognizing Usage Problems 21–30

Read each sentence. Then, choose the correct expression to complete each sentence.

EXAMPLE   The twins are quite different (from, than) each other.

ANSWER   *from*

1. If we (don't, doesn't) leave soon, we'll be late for the movie.

2. (Beside, Besides) the regular menu, the restaurant offers daily specials.

3. The teacher asked us to (bring, take) extra pencils to class tomorrow.

4. The problems with the laptop computer were (because of, due to) software errors.

5. Denise (done, has done) a lot of work for that charity.

6. We selected milk (being as, because) it provides calcium and other minerals.

7. The official class (photo, photograph) will be taken on Friday, April 4.

8. The caretaker said we (can, may) visit the mansion only on weekends.

9. I left my cellphone (beside, besides) my keys.

10. The reason we're late is (because, that) we got lost.

PRACTICE 21.2D > Revising Sentences to Correct Usage Problems 31–40

Read each sentence. Then, rewrite each sentence, correcting the errors in usage.

EXAMPLE   How much further from here is the lake?

ANSWER   *How much farther from here is the lake?*

11. We have less dollars in our bank account since we took a vacation.

12. Van is a good dancer.

13. I was kind of tired by the end of the trip.

14. We will have practice irregardless of the weather.

15. Please move the bikes from the porch in the garage.

16. Myra just had one test today.

17. My mom got a new shirt for me.

18. Without farther delay, I will begin my speech.

19. Luke had went upstairs to look for his backpack.

20. Molly and Tamara enjoy one another's company.

SPEAKING APPLICATION

Take turns with a partner. Say sentences with usage problems. Your partner should correct each of your sentences.

WRITING APPLICATION

Write a paragraph about a topic of your choice. Include sentences that contain usage problems. Exchange papers with a partner. Your partner should correct the usage problems in your paragraph.

(41) lay, lie   The verb *lay* means "to put or set (something) down." Its principal parts—*lay, laying, laid, laid*—are followed by a direct object. The verb *lie* means "to recline." Its principal parts—*lie, lying, lay, lain*—are not followed by a direct object.

LAY	Mike asked me to **lay** the camera down.
	His artistic training **is laying** a foundation for his career.
	He **laid** the equipment bag on the ground.
	He **has laid** his tripod on the ground, too.
LIE	I like to **lie** on the ground and watch the clouds.
	The root of that tree **is lying** above the ground.
	Up above, I could see that a snake **lay** on a branch.
	The acorns from the tree **have lain** on the ground all winter.

(42) learn, teach   *Learn* means "to receive knowledge." *Teach* means "to give knowledge."

EXAMPLES	That film can help you **learn** about the rain forest.
	Ecologists **teach** us how to conserve effectively.

(43) leave, let   *Leave* means "to allow to remain." *Let* means "to permit."

INCORRECT	Some people **leave** their dogs run loose.
PREFERRED	Some people **let** their dogs run loose.

(44) like, as   *Like* is a preposition meaning "similar to" or "such as." It should not be used in place of the conjunction *as*.

INCORRECT	That exhibit looks **like** a rain forest should look.
PREFERRED	That exhibit looks **as** a rain forest should look.
	That exhibit looks **like** a rain forest.

(45) loose, lose   *Loose* is usually an adjective or part of such idioms as *cut loose, turn loose,* or *break loose. Lose* is always a verb and usually means "to miss from one's possession."

EXAMPLES	The tire is **loose**, and the bicycle is wobbling.
	A wobbling bike could cause you to **lose** your balance.

(46) maybe, may be *Maybe* is an adverb meaning "perhaps." *May be* is a helping verb connected to a main verb.

ADVERB	**Maybe** we can begin our recycling project soon.
VERB	It **may be** this year's most successful project.

(47) of Do not use *of* after a helping verb such as *should, would, could,* or *must*. Use *have* instead. Do not use *of* after *outside, inside, off,* and *atop*. Simply eliminate *of*.

INCORRECT	The octopus **would of** avoided us if it had seen us.
PREFERRED	The octopus **would have** avoided us if it had seen us.

(48) OK, O.K., okay In informal writing, *OK, O.K.,* and *okay* are acceptably used to mean "all right." Do not use them in standard English speech or writing, however.

INFORMAL	The principal said the dress code was **okay**.
PREFERRED	The principal said the dress code was **acceptable**.

(49) only *Only* should be placed immediately before the word it modifies. Placing it elsewhere can lead to confusion.

EXAMPLES	**Only** one person went to the store.
	(No one else went to the store.)
	One person went **only** to the store.
	(One person went nowhere but the store.)

(50) ought Do not use *ought* with *have* or *had*.

INCORRECT	Simon **hadn't ought** to have told me a lie.
PREFERRED	Simon **ought not** to have told me a lie.

See Practice 21.2E

(51) outside of Do not use this expression to mean "besides" or "except."

INCORRECT	No one remembers that actor's name **outside of** me.
PREFERRED	No one remembers that actor's name **except** me.

(52) plurals that do not end in -*s* The English plurals of certain nouns from Greek and Latin are formed as they were in their original language. Words such as *criteria, media,* and *phenomena* are plural. Their singular forms are *criterion, medium,* and *phenomenon.*

INCORRECT	One **criteria** for success in schoolwork is paying attention in class.
PREFERRED	One **criterion** for success in schoolwork is paying attention in class.
	You should learn all of the **criteria** for success in schoolwork.

(53) precede, proceed *Precede* means "to go before." *Proceed* means "to move or go forward."

EXAMPLES	The darkening sky **preceded** the thunderstorm.
	After the storm was over, the townspeople **proceeded** to clean up the damage.

(54) principal, principle As an adjective, *principal* means "most important" or "chief." As a noun, it means "a person who has controlling authority," as in a school. *Principle* is always a noun that means "a fundamental law."

ADJECTIVE	The **principal** goal of a sailor is to sail safely.
NOUN	My dad is the **principal** on the marina's board.
NOUN	My dad's company follows the **principles** of good management by treating its employees well.

(55) real *Real* means "authentic." In formal writing, avoid using *real* to mean "very" or "really."

INCORRECT	That new action movie was **real** exciting.
PREFERRED	That new action movie was **extremely** exciting.

(56) says *Says* should not be used as a substitute for *said.*

INCORRECT	Yesterday, the teacher **says** to read the next chapter.
PREFERRED	Yesterday, the teacher **said** to read the next chapter.

(57) seen *Seen* is a past participle and must be used with a helping verb.

INCORRECT   We **seen** the bright colors in the coral reef.

PREFERRED   We **had seen** the bright colors in the coral reef.

(58) set, sit *Set* means "to put (something) in a certain place." Its principal parts—*set, setting, set, set*—are usually followed by a direct object. *Sit* means "to be seated." Its principal parts—*sit, sitting, sat, sat*—are never followed by a direct object.

SET   **Set** the tools on the lawn.

Tim **is setting** the shovel down by the garden.

He **will set** the rake there, too.

I **have** already **set** the seed packages by their rows.

SIT   Tim likes to **sit** in the rocking chair.

He **is sitting** in it right now.

He **will sit** in it when he stops work.

His dad **has sat** in that chair many times, too.

(59) so Avoid using *so* when you mean "so that."

INCORRECT   Hawks use their eyesight **so** they can find food.

PREFERRED   Hawks use their eyesight **so that** they can find food.

(60) than, then Use *than* in comparisons. Use *then* as an adverb to refer to time.

EXAMPLES   I'm driving better today **than** when I first started.

I learned to start slowly, **then** accelerate.

(61) that, which, who Use these relative pronouns in the following ways: *that* and *which* refer to things; *who* refers only to people.

EXAMPLES   The bus **that** we take stops at every corner.

Its route, **which** is very long, is also very popular.

The driver **who** drives in the morning and afternoon talks to everyone he picks up.

(62) their, there, they're   *Their,* a possessive pronoun, always modifies a noun. *There* can be used either as an expletive at the beginning of a sentence or as an adverb showing place or direction. *They're* is a contraction of *they are.*

PRONOUN	The musicians in the band were all improvising **their** own solos.
EXPLETIVE	**There** will be a lot of people in the audience, and everyone wants to hear each performer play.
ADVERB	The amplifiers will be placed over **there**, at the front and sides of the stage.
CONTRACTION	I'm sure **they're** going to put on a great show.

(63) them   Do not use *them* as a substitute for *those.*

INCORRECT	**Them** trees are taller than any others I've seen.
PREFERRED	**Those** trees are taller than any others I've seen.

(64) to, too, two   *To* begins a prepositional phrase or an infinitive. *Too,* an adverb, modifies adjectives and other adverbs and means "excessively" or "also." *Two* is a number.

PREPOSITION	**to** the Arctic, **to** the North Pole
INFINITIVE	**to** study the polar ice, **to** see arctic seals
ADVERB	**too** cold, **too** dangerous
NUMBER	**two** polar bears, **two** pairs of gloves

(65) when, where   Do not use *when* or *where* immediately after a linking verb. Do not use *where* in place of *that.*

INCORRECT	Spring floods are **when** rivers overflow their banks.
	Wheat fields are **where** the floodwater goes.
PREFERRED	Spring floods **happen when** rivers overflow their banks.
	Wheat fields are **the places** where the floodwater goes.

See Practice 21.2F
See Practice 21.2G
See Practice 21.2H

PRACTICE 21.2E ▷ Recognizing Usage Problems 41–50

Read each sentence. Then, choose the correct item to complete each sentence.

EXAMPLE   Grandma (learned, taught) me all she knew about cooking.

ANSWER   *taught*

1. (May be, Maybe) we will go to the movies tonight.

2. It is not (acceptable, okay) to cheat on a test.

3. If you had given me your phone number, I would (have, of) called you.

4. (Leave, Let) your shoes by the door before you come inside.

5. I (lain, laid) the blanket over him.

6. I was the (only one, one only) to raise my hand.

7. Greg acted (as if, like) he cared.

8. The cat is (laying, lying) in the sun.

9. We (hadn't ought, ought not) to have spent so much money.

10. Young Billy keeps wiggling his (lose, loose) tooth.

PRACTICE 21.2F ▷ Revising Sentences to Correct Usage Problems 51–65

Read each sentence. Then, rewrite each sentence, correcting the errors in usage.

EXAMPLE   Please, carefully sit that bowl in the sink.

ANSWER   *Please, carefully set that bowl in the sink.*

11. Two o'clock is when we will have the election for class president.

12. There bicycles are in the garage.

13. Them students are in my math class.

14. By the lake is where we always meet.

15. I like their first album better then their second album.

16. I met the author that wrote my favorite book.

17. My cousin plans too visit two colleges next weekend.

18. The teacher approved our topic and told us to precede with our research.

19. I took a nap so I wouldn't be tired.

20. The chairperson of the company is also the principle stockholder.

SPEAKING APPLICATION

Reread each sentence in Practice 21.2E. Discuss with a partner usage errors you've made in past writing assignments.

WRITING APPLICATION

Use sentences 13, 14, and 17 as models to write similar sentences. Exchange papers with a partner. Your partner should correct your usage problems.

PRACTICE 21.2G > **Additional Practice With Usage Problems 1–30**

Read each sentence. Then, rewrite each sentence to correct its usage error. If a sentence has no error, write *correct*.

EXAMPLE   My little sister begged me to dress up as an horse.

ANSWER   *My little sister begged me to dress up as a horse.*

1. Beside my homework, I still have my college essay to do.

2. The talk between all the chorus members is that we will perform in competition.

3. You can be excused from the dinner table.

4. Stu done a lot of crazy things in his time.

5. I haven't mowed the lawn being as it has rained every day.

6. I will be all right as soon as I get some sleep.

7. Don't forget to bring your backpack when you go.

8. The reason there is no lemonade is because I forgot to make it.

9. If I drill two holes there, I can put up these curtains.

10. Counting to ten had the desired affect.

PRACTICE 21.2H > **Additional Practice With Usage Problems 31–65**

Read each sentence. Then, rewrite each sentence to correct its usage error. If a sentence has no error, write *correct*.

EXAMPLE   The dancer that fell sprained his ankle.

ANSWER   *The dancer **who** fell sprained his ankle.*

11. You should study for tests irregardless of the amount of time it takes.

12. The hawk left its perch and soared.

13. Will you lay down and get some sleep?

14. My father always lives by his principals.

15. I run a little further every day I am in training.

16. When Vern tried to sit the glass in the sink, his hand slipped.

17. Kate is participating in less activities than she did last year.

18. James sounded like he had a cold.

19. You should of seen the look on Carmen's face.

20. I fed them dogs, but they are whining again.

SPEAKING APPLICATION

Take turns with a partner. Each of you should read aloud five sentences in Practice 21.2G. Discuss usage errors you have heard recently on TV or radio.

WRITING APPLICATION

Write a few paragraphs about a trip you took, whether it was a few blocks from home or a thousand miles away. Include sentences that contain usage errors. Exchange papers with a partner. Correct each other's errors.

Test Warm-Up

DIRECTIONS
Read the introduction and the passage that follows. Then, answer the questions to show that you can identify and correct common usage errors in reading and writing.

Rose wrote this paragraph about a famous woman. Read the paragraph and think about the changes you would suggest as a peer editor. When you finish reading, answer the questions that follow.

Incomparable Education

(1) Born in 1880 in Alabama, Helen Keller lost her sight and hearing at a young age. (2) She had a disability that made her different than most other children her age. (3) However, that did not stop her from becoming a well-educated woman. (4) Her teacher Anne Sullivan did not except that Keller could not learn to communicate and was eager to teach her. (5) Sullivan taught Keller how to spell words by signing letters in Keller's hands. (6) After a while, Keller made the connection among the words she was spelling and the objects the words represented. (7) With Sullivan's help, Keller was able to continue her education and go on to support causes for the deaf and the blind. (8) Keller and Sullivan were by one another's side until Sullivan's death in 1936.

---

1 What change, if any, should be made in sentence 2?

A Change *a* to **an**

B Change *different than* to **different from**

C Change *most* to **all**

D Make no change

2 What change, if any, should be made in sentence 4?

F Change *except* to **accept**

G Change *eager* to **anxious**

H Change *to* to **too**

J Make no change

3 What change, if any, should be made in sentence 6?

A Change *a while* to **awhile**

B Change *was* to **were**

C Change *among* to **between**

D Make no change

4 What change, if any, should be made in sentence 8?

F Change *were* to **was**

G Change *one another's* to **each other's**

H Change *until* to **due to**

J Make no change

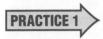

PRACTICE 1 Combining and Varying Sentences

Read the sentences. Then, rewrite each sentence according to the instructions in parentheses.

1. William ran around the track. (Invert the subject-verb order.)

2. Tiffany needed a flashlight. She also needed a sleeping bag to go camping. (Create a compound direct object, and start with an infinitive.)

3. The view is amazing at the top of the mountain. The weather is also amazing. (Create a compound subject, and start with a phrase.)

4. Kevin wore trunks. He also wore goggles when he went swimming. (Create a compound direct object, and start with a dependent clause.)

5. The sandpipers strutted toward the ocean. (Invert the subject-verb order.)

6. Clara wore a dress. She also wore high-heeled shoes to go dancing. (Create a compound direct object, and start with an infinitive.)

7. Jody fell asleep in class. Jody got caught falling asleep in class. (Create a compound verb, and start with a phrase.)

8. Crowds of people pushed and shoved through the mall. (Invert the subject-verb order.)

9. Carla raised her hand before time ran out. She also answered the question correctly. (Create a compound verb, and start with a phrase.)

10. I always eat a healthy breakfast in the morning. Sarah also eats a healthy breakfast. (Create a compound subject, and start with a phrase.)

PRACTICE 2 Revising Pronoun and Verb Usage

Read the sentences. Then, revise each sentence to eliminate problems in pronoun and verb usage. You may reorder, add, or eliminate words.

1. Tom and Hank usually take pride in his appearance.

2. Either Clarence or Jenna make the decisions regarding this project.

3. Mark and Julio becomes friends at the end of the movie.

4. Greg and Susie hope their test results is high.

5. A boy would have to be adventurous to enjoy their first camping experience.

6. Don't read scary stories to a little girl; it could give them nightmares.

7. Who do you see the most?

8. Both Cindy and Sara is taking advanced calculus.

9. We think it best if Pablo figures out the problem for themselves.

10. I'm worried about mine car because the mechanic overcharges us sometimes.

PRACTICE 3 Revising for Correct Use of Active and Passive Voice

Read the sentences. Then, revise each sentence to be in the active voice. You may reorder, add, or delete words.

1. The package was sent the next day by Alex.

2. Class was interrupted by the students in the hallway.

3. That problem was solved yesterday by Carlos.

4. The meeting was moved to four o'clock.

5. It was thought by many people, but it was said by Alia.

Continued on next page ▶

PRACTICE 4 ▷ Correcting Errors in Pronoun and Verb Usage

Read the sentences. Then, revise each sentence, correcting all errors in agreement, verb usage, and pronoun usage. If a sentence is already correct, write *correct*.

1. Joseph and Daryl runs the track tomorrow.
2. Either Lola or Matt have to do it.
3. Even though Lydia wanted to win prom queen, her thought Tammy deserves it.
4. Swimming and jogging is part of a healthy exercise regimen.
5. Her and me went hiking next week in the mountains.
6. If you don't stretch before exercising, I may injure yourself.
7. I answer the phone because she was responsible for taking messages.
8. Each of us have a responsibility for the success of our task.
9. Sally was generous to buy Karen's ticket.
10. If a person gets lost, they should stay put.

PRACTICE 5 ▷ Using Comparative and Superlative Forms Correctly

Read the sentences. Then, write the appropriate comparative or superlative degree of the modifier in parentheses.

1. Trevor is (old) than David.
2. Of the two cousins, I would say Jane is the (wise).
3. Yards are (long) than feet.
4. There are (few) cassette tapes in stores than there used to be.
5. Nick got the (high) score in the class on the geometry final exam.

PRACTICE 6 ▷ Avoiding Double Negatives

Read the sentences. Then, choose the word in parentheses that makes each sentence negative without forming a double negative.

1. I don't have (no, a) clue.
2. She (has, does not have) no response to the question.
3. Ben never (didn't take, took) any more than his share.
4. He didn't see (nothing, anything).
5. Jeanne (did, didn't) have anything to eat.

PRACTICE 7 ▷ Avoiding Usage Problems

Read the sentences. Then, choose the correct expression to complete each sentence.

1. We will (bring/take) a fruit salad to the barbecue.
2. Karla is concerned that the temperature will (affect/effect) the experiment.
3. The family will (accept/except) the award on William's behalf.
4. The school needs to (adapt/adopt) a new dress code policy.
5. She (all ready/already) fed the dog.
6. I (did/done) my chores in the morning.
7. Andrew was afraid the team would (loose/lose) the basketball game.
8. The fish swam (among/between) the coral.
9. Can (anyone/any one) of the members speak Spanish?
10. (Everyone/Every one) will come over after the ceremony.

CHAPTER 22

CAPITALIZATION

Correct use of the conventions of capitalization can guide your readers through your text and improve the clarity of your writing.

WRITE GUY *Jeff Anderson, M.Ed.*

WHAT DO YOU NOTICE?

Think about capitalization as you zoom in on sentences from the book *The Woman Warrior* by Maxine Hong Kingston.

MENTOR TEXT

> They should have been crying hysterically on their way to Vietnam. "If I see one that looks Chinese," she thought, "I'll go over and give him some advice."

Now, ask yourself the following questions:

- Why are the words *Vietnam* and *Chinese* capitalized?
- Why is the contraction *I'll* capitalized?

The word *Vietnam* is capitalized because it is a proper noun that names a specific place. Since the word *Chinese* is an adjective derived from the proper noun *China*, it is capitalized and classified as a proper adjective. The pronoun *I* is always capitalized no matter what its location in a sentence. The same rule applies when *I* is part of a contraction, such as in the case of *I'll*.

Grammar for Writers Writers can use capitalization to signal the beginning of a sentence or quotation or to highlight a specific name. Without correct capitalization, a text would be much more difficult to read and understand.

I'm planning a vacation. What is ideal?

Well, I know that Ideal is a nice town in South Dakota.

22.1 Capitalization in Sentences

Just as road signs help to guide people through a town, capital letters help to guide readers through sentences and paragraphs. Capitalization signals the start of a new sentence or points out certain words within a sentence to give readers visual clues that aid in their understanding.

WRITING COACH

Online

www.phwritingcoach.com

Grammar Practice
Practice your grammar skills with Writing Coach Online.

Grammar Games
Test your knowledge of grammar in this fast-paced interactive video game.

Using Capitals for First Words

Always capitalize the first word in a sentence.

RULE 22.1.1

Capitalize the first word in **declarative, interrogative, imperative,** and **exclamatory** sentences.

DECLARATIVE	**T**hey will be here in one hour.
INTERROGATIVE	**H**ow did you find it?
IMPERATIVE	**W**atch where you walk.
EXCLAMATORY	**H**e scored a home run!

RULE 22.1.2

Capitalize the first word in **interjections** and **incomplete questions.**

INTERJECTIONS	**T**errific!
INCOMPLETE QUESTIONS	**W**hy? **W**hat?

The word *I* is always capitalized, whether it is the first word in a sentence or not.

RULE 22.1.3

Always capitalize the pronoun *I.*

EXAMPLE	My brother and **I** went shopping.

RULE 22.1.4

Capitalize the first word after a colon only if the word begins a complete sentence. Do not capitalize the word if it begins a list of words or phrases.

SENTENCE FOLLOWING A COLON | He reached for the chair: **H**e was unable to continue standing.

LIST FOLLOWING A COLON | She put the following items in the trunk: **a** bedspread, a pillow, and a towel.

RULE 22.1.5

Capitalize the first word in each line of traditional poetry, even if the line does not start a new sentence.

EXAMPLE | **I** think that I shall never see

See Practice 22.1A

A poem lovely as a tree. – Joyce Kilmer

Using Capitals With Quotations

There are special rules for using capitalization with **quotations**.

RULE 22.1.6

Capitalize the first word of a **quotation**. However, do not capitalize the first word of a continuing sentence when a quotation is interrupted by identifying words or when the first word of a quotation is the continuation of a speaker's sentence.

EXAMPLES | Linda asked, "**W**ould you please pick me up at five?"

"**A**s I was typing," he said, "**t**he phone would not stop ringing."

Betsy mentioned that he is "**t**he smartest man she knows."

See Practice 22.1B

PRACTICE 22.1A > Capitalizing Words

Read each sentence. Then, write the word or words that should be capitalized in each sentence and correctly capitalize them.

EXAMPLE   oh, no! i forgot to mail the letter!

ANSWER   *Oh, I*

1. should we ask for directions?

2. the storm abated: the wind died down and the sun came out.

3. we learned about Columbus's three ships: *the Nina, the Pinta,* and *the Santa Maria.*

4. did you remember to bring the notes for today's meeting?

5. mom repeated her request: please clean your room.

6. did you buy a new sweater? what color is it?

7. we still need to buy these items for the party: balloons, juice, and napkins.

8. did you pass the driver's license test?

9. mrs. Jamadar gave me some tomatoes from her garden.

10. that was a remarkable story!

PRACTICE 22.1B > Using Capitals With Quotations

Read each sentence. Then, write the word or words in each sentence that should be capitalized and correctly capitalize them.

EXAMPLE   my mother asked, "do you have practice this afternoon?"

ANSWER   *My, Do*

11. the story began, "once upon a time, there was a girl named Anne."

12. Franklin D. Roosevelt said, "the only thing we have to fear is fear itself."

13. "that history test was really hard," Julia said.

14. "i think that she was right," Ron said, "when she told me to check my facts."

15. Ms. Smith replied, "yes, it is true. i have been to Spain three times."

16. Milly asked, "will you still be here when i get back?"

17. "foul ball!" yelled the umpire.

18. After learning that school was closed, Robert said, "let's go play outside in the snow!"

19. He replied, "of course you want to go to the game. your favorite team is playing."

20. "as it started to rain," Sam said, "i realized I had left my umbrella on the bus."

SPEAKING APPLICATION

Take turns with a partner. Say a variety of sentences about your favorite band. Your partner should indicate, with a nod of his or her head, each time you say a word that should be capitalized.

WRITING APPLICATION

Write a conversation between you and your teacher about an upcoming exam. Be sure to use correct capitalization in your quotations.

22.2 Proper Nouns

Capitalization makes important words stand out in your writing, such as the names of people, places, countries, book titles, and other proper names. Sometimes proper names are used as nouns and sometimes as adjectives modifying nouns or pronouns.

WRITING COACH

Online

www.phwritingcoach.com

Grammar Practice

Practice your grammar skills with Writing Coach Online.

Grammar Games

Test your knowledge of grammar in this fast-paced interactive video game.

Using Capitals for Proper Nouns

Nouns, as you may remember, are either **common** or **proper.**

Common nouns, such as *sailor, brother, city,* and *ocean,* identify classes of people, places, or things and are not capitalized.

Proper nouns name specific examples of people, places, or things and should be capitalized.

> **Capitalize all proper nouns.**

RULE **22.2.1**

EXAMPLES **M**elissa   **P**rofessor **D**oolittle   **G**overnor **P**erez

Second **S**treet   **H**ull **H**ouse   **A**lbany

Of **H**uman **B**ondage   **R.M.S. T**itanic

Names

Each part of a person's name—the given name, the middle name or initial standing for that name, and the surname—should be capitalized. If a surname begins with *Mc* or *O',* the letter following it is capitalized (McAdams, O'Reilly).

> **Capitalize each part of a person's name even when the full name is not used.**

RULE **22.2.2**

EXAMPLES **S**ally **F**ield   **Q. T. K**ettle   **H**arry **B. R**ichards

Capitalize the proper names that are given to animals.

EXAMPLES **F**licka   **S**pot   **C**uddles

Geographical and Place Names

If a place can be found on a map, it should generally be capitalized.

RULE

22.2.3

Capitalize geographical and place names.

Examples of different kinds of geographical and place names are listed in the following chart.

GEOGRAPHICAL AND PLACE NAMES	
Streets	Madison Avenue, First Street, Green Valley Road
Towns and Cities	Dallas, Oakdale, New York City
Counties, States, and Provinces	Champlain County, Texas, Quebec
Nations and Continents	Austria, Kenya, the United States of America, Asia, Mexico, Europe
Mountains	the Adirondack Mountains, Mount Washington
Valleys and Deserts	the San Fernando Valley, the Mojave Desert, the Gobi
Islands and Peninsulas	Aruba, the Faroe Islands, Cape York Peninsula
Sections of a Country	the Northeast, Siberia, the Great Plains
Scenic Spots	Gateway National Park, Carlsbad Caverns
Rivers and Falls	the Missouri River, Victoria Falls
Lakes and Bays	Lake Cayuga, Gulf of Mexico, the Bay of Biscayne
Seas and Oceans	the Sargasso Sea, the Indian Ocean
Celestial Bodies and Constellations	Mars, the Big Dipper, Venus
Monuments and Memorials	the Tomb of the Unknown Soldier, Kennedy Memorial Library, the Washington Monument
Buildings	Madison Square Garden, Fort Hood, the Astrodome, the White House
School and Meeting Rooms	Room 6, Laboratory 3B, the Red Room, Conference Room C

Capitalizing Directions

Words indicating direction are capitalized only when they refer to a section of a country.

EXAMPLES   I grew up in the **W**est.

Albany is **n**orth of New York City.

Capitalizing Names of Celestial Bodies

Capitalize the names of celestial bodies except *moon* and *sun*.

EXAMPLE   The **s**un is more than one hundred times larger than Earth.

Capitalizing Buildings and Places

Do not capitalize words such as *theater, hotel, university,* and *park,* unless the word is part of a proper name.

EXAMPLES   We are staying at the Waldorf Astoria **H**otel.

How far is the **h**otel from the airport?

Events and Times

Capitalize references to historic events, periods, and documents as well as dates and holidays. Use a dictionary to check capitalization.

> **Capitalize the names of specific events and periods in history.**

RULE 22.2.4

SPECIAL EVENTS AND TIMES	
Historic Events	the Battle of Waterloo, World War I
Historical Periods	the Manchu Dynasty, Reconstruction
Documents	the Bill of Rights, the Magna Carta
Days and Months	Monday, June 22, the third week in May
Holidays	Labor Day, Memorial Day, Veterans Day
Religious Holidays	Rosh Hashanah, Christmas, Easter
Special Events	the World Series, the Holiday Antiques Show

Capitalizing Seasons

Do not capitalize seasons unless the name of the season is being used as a proper noun or adjective.

EXAMPLES   My favorite place is New England in the **f**all.

We hope to go to the **S**ummer Olympics.

See Practice 22.2A

See Practice 22.2B

RULE 22.2.5

Capitalize the names of organizations, government bodies, political parties, races, nationalities, languages, and religions.

VARIOUS GROUPS	
Organizations	**R**otary, **K**nights of **C**olumbus, the **R**ed **C**ross
Institutions	the **M**useum of **F**ine **A**rts, the **M**ayo **C**linic
Schools	**K**ennedy **H**igh **S**chool, **U**niversity of **T**exas
Businesses	**G**eneral **M**otors, **P**rentice **H**all
Government Bodies	**D**epartment of **S**tate, **F**ederal **T**rade **C**ommission, **H**ouse of **R**epresentatives
Political Parties	**R**epublicans, the **D**emocratic party
Nationalities	**A**merican, **M**exican, **C**hinese, **I**sraeli, **C**anadian
Languages	**E**nglish, **I**talian, **P**olish, **S**wahili
Religions and Religious References	**C**hristianity: **G**od, the **H**oly **S**pirit, the **B**ible **J**udaism: the **L**ord, the **P**rophets, the **T**orah **I**slam: **A**llah, the **P**rophets, the Qur'an, **M**ohammed **H**induism: **B**rahma, the **B**hagavad **G**ita, the **V**edas **B**uddhism: the **B**uddha, **M**ahayana, **H**inayana

References to Mythological Gods When referring to mythology, do not capitalize the word *god* (the *gods* of Olympus).

RULE 22.2.6

Capitalize the names of awards; the names of specific types of air, sea, and spacecraft; and brand names.

EXAMPLES   the **F**reedom **A**ward   the **G**ood **C**onduct **M**edal

Raisin **N**ut cereal   **G**emini **V**

PRACTICE 22.2A ▷ **Identifying Proper Nouns**

Read each sentence. Then, underline the proper noun or nouns in each sentence.

EXAMPLE   Mr. Kennedy is my next-door neighbor.

ANSWER   <u>Mr. Kennedy</u> is my next-door neighbor.

1. On their trip to South Dakota, the Green family went to Mount Rushmore.

2. When they went to Aruba, Anna and Choi stayed on the western side of the island.

3. We studied World War I and World War II with Professor Smith.

4. Samuel Morse invented Morse code.

5. Alexis visited The Museum of Modern Art during her summer vacation.

6. The *Odyssey* was written by Homer.

7. Is Jupiter the largest planet in our solar system?

8. We saw the Washington Redskins play last Sunday.

9. My father has been a member of the Elks Club for many years.

10. My cousin Nicole is fluent in French.

PRACTICE 22.2B ▷ **Capitalizing Proper Nouns**

Read each sentence. Then, write the word or words that should be capitalized and capitalize them using conventions of capitalization correctly and consistently.

EXAMPLE   My friend elizabeth lives in new york.

ANSWER   *Elizabeth, New York*

11. The tudors ruled england from 1485 to 1603.

12. The walsh family visited the grand canyon.

13. My father is lithuanian, and my mother is hungarian.

14. Nick mcnulty was accepted to boston college and dartmouth.

15. On our summer vacation, we saw the st. louis arch, which is known as the gateway to the west.

16. The nobel prize was founded by alfred nobel.

17. st. patrick's day is a national holiday in ireland.

18. Sandra wished to speak to someone in the department of health and human services.

19. The *mayflower* brought the pilgrims to massachusetts from england.

20. Do the alps span both switzerland and france?

SPEAKING APPLICATION

Take turns with a partner. Tell about a historical event. Your partner should identify the proper nouns that you use.

WRITING APPLICATION

Use sentence 14 as a model to write three similar sentences. Replace the proper nouns in sentence 14 with other proper nouns, correctly and consistently using conventions of capitalization.

Using Capitals for Proper Adjectives

A **proper adjective** is either an adjective formed from a proper noun or a proper noun used as an adjective.

RULE 22.2.7

Capitalize most **proper adjectives**.

PROPER ADJECTIVES FORMED FROM PROPER NOUNS	**A**ustralian kangaroo	**C**haucerian play
	Canadian trip	**E**nglish settlers
	Spanish ambassador	**I**talian food
PROPER NOUNS USED AS ADJECTIVES	the **S**enate floor	the **R**iley speeches
	Chekhov festival	a **B**ible class
	the **G**reens' house	**N**ew **Y**ork pizza

Some proper adjectives have become so commonly used that they are no longer capitalized.

EXAMPLES	**h**erculean effort	**d**iesel engine
	pasteurized milk	**q**uixotic hope
	venetian blinds	**t**eddy bear

Brand names are often used as proper adjectives.

RULE 22.2.8

Capitalize a **brand name** when it is used as an adjective, but do not capitalize the common noun it modifies.

EXAMPLES	**T**imo **w**atches	**S**unset **c**ameras
	Super **C**ool **s**hirts	
	Longlasting **r**efrigerator	

Multiple Proper Adjectives

When you have two or more proper adjectives used together, do not capitalize the associated common nouns.

> **Do not capitalize a common noun used with two proper adjectives.**

ONE PROPER ADJECTIVE	TWO PROPER ADJECTIVES
Colorado River	Snake and Colorado rivers
William Street	William, Monroe, and Lemon streets
Gowanus Canal	Gowanus and Erie canals
Lacey Act	Lacey and Higher Education acts
Atlantic Ocean	Atlantic and Indian oceans
Sussex County	Sussex and Union counties
Cook Islands	Cook and Gilbert islands

Prefixes and Hyphenated Adjectives

Prefixes and hyphenated adjectives cause special problems. Prefixes used with proper adjectives should be capitalized only if they refer to a nationality.

> **Do not capitalize prefixes attached to proper adjectives unless the prefix refers to a nationality. In a hyphenated adjective, capitalize only the proper adjective.**

RULE 22.2.10

EXAMPLES	**a**ll-**A**merican **A**nglo-**A**merican
	English-**s**peaking **p**ro-**I**talian
	American **C**hinese-**l**anguage **n**ewspaper
	pre-**R**enaissance **S**ino-**R**ussian
	pre-**C**olumbian **a**rchitecture **I**ndo-**I**ranian

See Practice 22.2C
See Practice 22.2D

PRACTICE 22.2C ▷ **Capitalizing Proper Adjectives**

Read each sentence. Then, write the word or words in the sentence that should be capitalized and capitalize them correctly.

EXAMPLE   Have you been to that new japanese restaurant yet?

ANSWER   *Japanese*

1. Manuel's class is studying greek mythology.

2. My neighbor has two dogs: an irish setter and an italian greyhound.

3. Meet me in the library after spanish class.

4. Is your cousin of german descent?

5. Do you enjoy french food?

6. Our theater class will perform a shakespearean play.

7. We will visit the italian city of Rome during our trip.

8. I called Mom to tell her I was at the flynns' house.

9. We have an antique victorian chair in our living room.

10. Diana enjoys studying native american pottery styles.

PRACTICE 22.2D ▷ **Revising Sentences to Correct Capitalization Errors**

Read each sentence. Then, rewrite each sentence using conventions of capitalization correctly and consistently.

EXAMPLE   I'd like to visit the grand canyon during our trip to arizona.

ANSWER   *I'd like to visit the Grand Canyon during our trip to Arizona.*

11. At the entrance of the city, one can see the stadium where the baltimore ravens play.

12. A cold front came down from lake Ontario to cover new England.

13. The United States expanded its territory and settled the west.

14. Nelly ate dinner in little italy on sunday.

15. Many people confuse london bridge with tower bridge.

16. Lupe visited the national gallery of art in Washington, d.c.

17. There is a hotel, called hotel de glace, near Quebec city made entirely out of ice.

18. I'm not sure whether I will take spanish or french next semester.

19. The museum display included information about the pleistocene epoch.

20. The science club will meet in room 102 on wednesday afternoons.

SPEAKING APPLICATION

Discuss with a partner the importance of capitalization. Suggest three ways capitalization makes reading easier and helps with comprehension.

WRITING APPLICATION

Write 10 sentences. In each sentence, include a proper adjective. Be sure to use conventions of capitalization correctly and consistently.

22.3 Other Uses of Capitals

Find It/ FIX IT

8

Grammar
Game Plan

Even though the purpose of using capital letters is to make writing clearer, some rules for capitalization can be confusing. For example, it may be difficult to remember which words in a letter you write need to start with a capital, which words in a book title should be capitalized, or when a person's title—such as Senator or Reverend—needs to start with a capital. The rules and examples that follow should clear up the confusion.

Online

www.phwritingcoach.com

Grammar Practice

Practice your grammar skills with Writing Coach Online.

Grammar Games

Test your knowledge of grammar in this fast-paced interactive video game.

Using Capitals in Letters

Capitalization is required in parts of personal letters and business letters.

> **Capitalize the first word and all nouns in letter salutations and the first word in letter closings.**

22.3.1

RULE

SALUTATIONS	**D**ear **A**lice,
	Dear **G**entlemen:
	Dear **D**r. **D**err:
	My **d**ear **A**unt,
CLOSINGS	**W**ith **h**umble **a**pologies,
	Your **s**incere **f**riend,
	Always **y**ours,
	Best **w**ishes,

Using Capitals for Titles

Capitals are used for titles of people and titles of literary and artistic works. The charts and rules on the following pages will guide you in capitalizing titles correctly.

Capitalize a person's title only when it is used with the person's name or when it is used as a proper name by itself.

WITH A PROPER NAME	**C**ongressman **G**rover went to visit the troops.
AS A PROPER NAME	I'm glad you can join us, **U**ncle.
IN A GENERAL REFERENCE	The **s**enator decided not to run for another term.

The following chart illustrates the correct form for a variety of titles. Study the chart, paying particular attention to compound titles and titles with prefixes or suffixes.

SOCIAL, BUSINESS, RELIGIOUS, MILITARY, AND GOVERNMENT TITLES	
Commonly Used Titles	Sir, Madam, Miss, Professor, Doctor, Reverend, Bishop, Sister, Father, Rabbi, Corporal, Major, Admiral, Mayor, Governor, Ambassador
Abbreviated Titles	*Before names*: Mr., Mrs., Ms., Dr., Hon. *After names*: Jr., Sr., Ph.D., M.D., D.D.S., Esq.
Compound Titles	Vice President, Secretary of State, Lieutenant Governor, Commander in Chief
Titles With Prefixes or Suffixes	ex-Congressman Randolph, Governor-elect Loughman

Some honorary titles are capitalized. These include First Lady of the United States, Speaker of the House of Representatives, Queen Mother of England, and the Prince of Wales.

RULE 22.3.3

> **Capitalize certain honorary titles even when the titles are not followed by a proper name.**

EXAMPLE   The **p**resident and **F**irst **L**ady visited with the **q**ueen of England.

Occasionally, the titles of other government officials may be capitalized as a sign of respect when referring to a specific person whose name is not given. However, you usually do not capitalize titles when they stand alone.

EXAMPLES   We thank you, **G**overnor, for this very special gift.

Sixteen **s**enators voted for this bill.

RULE 22.3.4

> **Relatives are often referred to by titles. These references should be capitalized when used with or as the person's name.**

WITH THE PERSON'S NAME   In the winter, **A**unt **J**oyce used to take us skating.

AS A NAME   He says that **G**randfather enjoys bowling with his grandchildren.

RULE 22.3.5

> **Do not capitalize titles showing family relationships when they are preceded by a possessive noun or pronoun.**

EXAMPLES   their **a**unt   his **g**randfather   Barbara's **m**other

RULE 22.3.6

Capitalize the first word and all other key words in the titles of books, periodicals, poems, stories, plays, paintings, and other works of art.

The following chart lists examples to guide you in capitalizing titles and subtitles of various works. Note that the articles (*a, an,* and *the*) are not capitalized unless they are used as the first word of a title or subtitle. Conjunctions and prepositions are also left uncapitalized unless they are the first or last word in a title or subtitle or contain four letters or more. Note also that verbs, no matter how short, are always capitalized.

TITLES OF WORKS	
Books	*The Red Badge of Courage* *Profiles in Courage* *All Through the Night* *John Ford: The Man and His Films* *Heart of Darkness*
Periodicals	*International Wildlife, Allure,* *Better Homes and Gardens*
Poems	"The Raven" "The Rime of the Ancient Mariner" "Flower in the Crannied Wall"
Stories and Articles	"Editha" "The Fall of the House of Usher" "Here Is New York"
Plays and Musicals	*The Tragedy of Macbeth* *Our Town* *West Side Story*
Paintings	*Starry Night* *Mona Lisa* *The Artist's Daughter With a Cat*
Music	*The Unfinished Symphony* "Heartbreak Hotel" "This Land Is Your Land"

22.3.7
RULE

Capitalize titles of educational courses when they are language courses or when they are followed by a number or preceded by a proper noun or adjective. Do not capitalize school subjects discussed in a general manner.

WITH CAPITALS	Italian	Honors Algebra 1
	Psychology 105	Biology 4
	Geology 202	French

WITHOUT CAPITALS	geology	economics
	algebra	history
	biology	math

EXAMPLES

This year, I will be taking psychology, Russian, Honors Math 2, and world history.

Bill's favorite classes are art history, Italian, and algebra.

He does like physical education, but not as much as math.

See Practice 22.3A
See Practice 22.3B
See Practice 22.3C
See Practice 22.3D

After German class, I have to rush across the hallway to woodworking.

Read each phrase. Rewrite salutations and closings that contain capitalization errors. If a phrase does not have any errors, write *correct*.

EXAMPLE   To whom it may concern:

ANSWER   *To Whom It May Concern:*

1. Dear tyler,

2. My dear Esmerelda,

3. Very Truly Yours,

4. Cordially yours,

5. Your sincere Friend forever,

6. Dear gentlemen:

7. Dear dr. smith,

8. My dear Aunt Martha,

9. With Humble Apologies,

10. Best wishes,

Read each sentence. Then, write the word or words that should be capitalized, correctly capitalizing them.

EXAMPLE   Allie's favorite painting is *light at two lights* by Edward Hopper.

ANSWER   *Light at Two Lights*

11. uncle cory enjoys visiting museums.

12. "Theme for english b" was written by Langston Hughes.

13. I met delegate Simmons at the event.

14. My grandmother introduced me to her friend mrs. Addison.

15. Our class is reading *of Mice and Men.*

16. Did senator Smith attend the meeting?

17. My last two classes are honors biology 2 and math.

18. Have you read *the great gatsby?*

19. Last week dean Horvath lead the pledge of allegiance.

20. My sister enrolled in history 101 and spanish.

WRITING APPLICATION

In 30 seconds, list as many words as you can think of that should be capitalized in salutations and closings. Exchange lists with a partner, and check and correct each other's list.

SPEAKING APPLICATION

Discuss with a partner the importance of capitalizing titles. Answer the question *When is a title not capitalized?*

PRACTICE 22.3C Using All of the Rules of Capitalization

Read each sentence. Then, rewrite each sentence, using the conventions of capitalization correctly and consistently.

EXAMPLE   when it comes to generosity, mrs. cavanaugh has no equal.

ANSWER   *When it comes to generosity, Mrs. Cavanaugh has no equal.*

1. sophia thought that the spanish rice was delicious.

2. My academic advisor said biology 100 is a prerequisite for medicine 203.

3. Thank you for coming, mrs. lewis.

4. "when was the last time you saw lieutenant colonel alexander?" asked general fulton.

5. On our class trip, we will visit baltimore, maryland.

6. I met dean levits at a conference last june.

7. i couldn't see the english garden behind the tudor house.

8. The stars in orion's belt can clearly be seen tonight.

9. I sent the letter to my lawyer, Stella Notte, j.d.

10. We will attend a basketball game at madison square garden in new york city.

PRACTICE 22.3D Revising Using All the Rules of Capitalization

Read each sentence. Then, rewrite each sentence, adding or deleting capitalization to correct errors as necessary.

EXAMPLE   I went to visit my cousin in washington, d.c.

ANSWER   *I went to visit my cousin in Washington, D.C.*

11. My cousin carmen is a state Senator.

12. She's really my second Cousin; that's why she's so much older than i am.

13. We visited her at the State capital last Spring.

14. She introduced us to senator Ramirez.

15. He told us about how his Grandparents immigrated to the United States from nicaragua nearly 100 years ago.

16. Then the talk turned to some legislation that the senate was to vote on.

17. after a long day at the Office, we went out to dinner.

18. Carmen took us to a japanese restaurant.

19. I don't think my Dad liked it much, but my mom and I loved it.

20. After dinner, we went to see a revival of the play *The phantom of the opera*.

WRITING APPLICATION

Write a short story. In each sentence, include a title, proper noun, or proper adjective. Be sure to correctly use conventions of capitalization.

SPEAKING APPLICATION

Discuss with a partner when you should and shouldn't capitalize words like *senator, mom,* and *dad.* Discuss any patterns that you notice.

Test Warm-Up

DIRECTIONS
Read the introduction and the letter that follows. Then, answer the questions to show that you can use and understand the rules of capitalization in reading and writing.

Ross wrote this complaint letter. Read the letter and think about the changes you would suggest as a peer editor. When you finish reading, answer the questions that follow.

A Letter of Complaint

(1) Dear Customer Service manager:

(2) I am writing to complain about Cutting Edge Company's TV/DVD player, model #CE862, which I bought in march. (3) It has never worked properly, and the remote control has a terrible design. (4) The store refused to take it back. (5) I'm enclosing a copy of the receipt. (6) If you want my business ever again—or that of my numerous friends and relatives—you'll refund my money. (7) If you don't, I will file a complaint with the Better Business Bureau and forward this letter to *Consumer reports* magazine.

(8) Yours in Frustration,
(9) Ross Yablonsky

---

1 What change, if any, should be made in sentence 1?

A Change *Service* to **service**

B Change *Customer Service* to **customer service**

C Change *manager* to **Manager**

D Make no change

2 What change, if any, should be made in sentence 2?

F Change *Complain* to **complain**

G Change *Cutting Edge* to **cutting edge**

H Change *march* to **March**

J Make no change

3 What change, if any, should be made in sentence 7?

A Change *I* to **i**

B Change *reports* to **Reports**

C Change *Better Business Bureau* to **better business bureau**

D Make no change

4 How should the closing be revised?

F Change *Frustration* to **frustration**

G Change *in* to **In**

H Change *Yours* to **yours**

J Make no change

CHAPTER 23

PUNCTUATION

Understanding the conventions of punctuation will help you organize and connect ideas in your writing.

WRITE GUY *Jeff Anderson, M.Ed.*

WHAT DO YOU NOTICE?

Note examples of punctuation as you zoom in on this sentence from *The Autobiography* by Benjamin Franklin.

MENTOR TEXT

> While my care was employed in guarding against one fault, I was often surprised by another; habit took the advantage of inattention; inclination was sometimes too strong for reason.

Now, ask yourself the following questions:

- Why is a comma inserted after the word *fault*?
- Why are semicolons used to separate items in this sentence?

The comma inserted after *fault* serves to separate a subordinate clause, *while my care was employed in guarding against one fault,* from the main, or independent, clause, *I was often surprised by another.* The semicolons are used to separate related main clauses and take the place of coordinating conjunctions.

Grammar for Writers Writers who correctly use punctuation craft understandable text, whether a sentence is short or long. Before publishing your writing, check that your punctuation helps it flow smoothly.

What did the semicolon say to the comma?

Hmm . . . "What's the hurry? Slow down a little."

23.1 End Marks

End marks tell readers when to pause and for how long. They signal the end or conclusion of a sentence, word, or phrase. There are three end marks: the **period (.)**, the **question mark (?)**, and the **exclamation mark (!)**.

Using Periods

A **period** indicates the end of a declarative or imperative sentence, an indirect question, or an abbreviation. The period is the most common end mark.

RULE 23.1.1

> Use a **period** to end a declarative sentence, a mild imperative sentence, and an indirect question.

A **declarative sentence** is a statement of fact, idea, or opinion.

DECLARATIVE SENTENCE	This is a warm day.

An **imperative sentence** gives a direction or command. Often, the first word of an imperative sentence is a verb.

MILD IMPERATIVE SENTENCE	Complete the reading assignment.

An **indirect question** restates a question in a declarative sentence. It does not give the speaker's exact words.

INDIRECT QUESTION	Jane asked me if I should come along.

Other Uses of Periods

In addition to signaling the end of a statement, periods can also signal that words have been shortened, or abbreviated.

RULE 23.1.2

> Use a period after most abbreviations and after initials.

PERIODS IN ABBREVIATIONS	
Titles	Dr., Sr., Mrs., Mr., Gov., Maj., Rev., Prof.
Place Names	Ave., Bldg., Blvd., Mt., Dr., St., Ter., Rd.
Times and Dates	Sun., Dec., sec., min., hr., yr., A.M.
Initials	E. B. White, Robin F. Brancato, R. Brett

Some abbreviations do not end with periods. Metric measurements, state abbreviations used with ZIP Codes, and most standard measurements do not need periods. The abbreviation for inch, *in.,* is the exception.

EXAMPLES mm, cm, kg, L, C, CA, TX, ft, gal

The following chart lists some abbreviations with and without periods.

ABBREVIATIONS WITH AND WITHOUT END MARKS	
approx. = approximately	misc. = miscellaneous
COD = cash on delivery	mph = miles per hour
dept. = department	No. = number
doz. = dozen(s)	p. or pg. = page; pp. = pages
EST = Eastern Standard Time	POW = prisoner of war
FM = frequency modulation	pub. = published, publisher
gov. or govt. = government	pvt. = private
ht. = height	rpm = revolutions per minute
incl. = including	R.S.V.P. = please reply
ital = italics	sp. = spelling
kt. = karat or carat	SRO = standing room only
meas. = measure	vol. = volume
mfg. = manufacturing	wt. = weight

Sentences Ending With Abbreviations When a sentence ends with an abbreviation that uses a period, do not put a second period at the end. If an end mark other than a period is required, add the end mark.

EXAMPLES   Be sure to speak with Barrie Fine Jr**.**

Is that Mark Tanner Sr**.** **?**

See Practice 23.1A

RULE 23.1.3

Do not use periods with acronyms, words formed with the first or first few letters of a series of words.

ACRONYMS   USA (United States of America)

ECM (European Common Market)

RULE 23.1.4

Use a period after numbers and letters in outlines.

EXAMPLE

I**.** Maintaining your pet's health

     A**.** Diet

         1**.** For a puppy

         2**.** For a mature dog

     B**.** Exercise

Using Question Marks

A **question mark** follows a word, phrase, or sentence that asks a question. A question is often in inverted word order.

RULE 23.1.5

Use a **question mark** to end an interrogative sentence, an incomplete question, or a statement intended as a question.

INTERROGATIVE SENTENCE

Is the day over yet **?**

When are we going out tonight **?**

INCOMPLETE QUESTION

Many kinds of animals travel in packs. Why **?**

I will buy you dinner. Where **?**

Use care, however, in ending statements with question marks. It is better to rephrase the statement as a direct question.

STATEMENT WITH A QUESTION MARK	The sun hasn't risen yet **?**
	We are having vegetables with lunch **?**
REVISED INTO A DIRECT QUESTION	Hasn't the sun risen yet **?**
	Are we having vegetables with lunch **?**

Use a period instead of a question mark with an **indirect question**—a question that is restated as a declarative sentence.

EXAMPLE	Kate wanted to know when Tim was coming **.**
	She wondered if they would be on time **.**

Using Exclamation Marks

An **exclamation mark** signals an exclamatory sentence, an imperative sentence, or an interjection. It indicates strong emotion and should be used sparingly.

See Practice 23.1B

> **Use an exclamation mark to end an exclamatory sentence, a forceful imperative sentence, or an interjection expressing strong emotion.**

23.1.6 RULE

EXCLAMATORY SENTENCE	Look at the blue water **!**
FORCEFUL IMPERATIVE	Don't stop the water **!**

An interjection can be used with a comma or an exclamation mark. An exclamation mark increases the emphasis.

EXAMPLES	Wow **!** It was a great meal **.**
	Oh **!** It was a great show **.**
WITH A COMMA	Wow **,** it was a great meal **.**

PRACTICE 23.1A
Using Periods Correctly in Sentences

Read each sentence. Then, rewrite each sentence, adding periods where needed. If a sentence is correct, write *correct*.

EXAMPLE   F Scott Fitzgerald wrote <u>The Great Gatsby</u>

ANSWER   *F. Scott Fitzgerald wrote <u>The Great Gatsby</u>.*

1. Leo asked Kate if she heard the noise
2. The Washington Monument was finished on Dec. 6, 1884.
3. Her fiance gave Mimi a 2-kt diamond engagement ring.
4. Kent W. Burkes Sr led the parade
5. Dr. Benton's office is on Sixth St and Orange Ave
6. Leilani was born in Honolulu, Hawaii
7. You'll need 3 m of ribbon for your project.
8. Irvin told me about his trip to Mt McKinley.
9. Dinner is always at 6:00 PM on Tuesdays.
10. Ms Cabrera wants us to bring healthy snacks

PRACTICE 23.1B
Using Question Marks and Exclamation Marks Correctly in Sentences

Read each sentence. Then, write the correct end mark for each item.

EXAMPLE   Wow, what a performance

ANSWER   *!*

11. What is your favorite baseball team
12. How long will it take
13. Stop yelling
14. Mia, leave the room
15. What a pleasant surprise
16. How long is the play
17. When will the rain stop
18. Walk carefully
19. Where is Liechtenstein
20. Stop thief

SPEAKING APPLICATION

Take turns with a partner. Say sentences that contain abbreviations for titles, times and dates, and initials. Your partner should tell where periods would be used if the sentences were written.

WRITING APPLICATION

Write two sentences that use question marks correctly and two sentences that use exclamation marks correctly. Identify each sentence as *interrogative*, *exclamatory*, *forceful imperative*, or *sentence with an interjection*.

23.2 Commas

Find It/ FIX IT

13

Grammar
Game Plan

A **comma** tells the reader to pause briefly before continuing a sentence. Commas may be used to separate elements in a sentence or to set off part of a sentence.

Commas are used more than any other internal punctuation mark. To check for correct comma use, read a sentence aloud and note where a pause helps you to group your ideas. Commas signal to readers that they should take a short breath.

Using Commas With Compound Sentences

A **compound sentence** consists of two or more main or independent clauses that are joined by a coordinating conjunction, such as *and, but, for, nor, or, so,* or *yet.*

> Use a **comma** before a conjunction to separate two or more independent or main clauses in a **compound sentence.**

23.2.1

RULE

Use a comma before a conjunction when there are complete sentences on both sides of the conjunction.

EXAMPLE   John is practicing for his game, but I won't be

                          independent clause   independent clause

able to attend.

In some compound sentences, the main or independent clauses are very brief, and the meaning is clear. When this occurs, the comma before the conjunction may be omitted.

EXAMPLES   Jon typed carefully but he still had spelling errors.

                    Kate would like to visit Mom in May but she can't

                    get a ticket.

In other sentences, conjunctions are used to join compound subjects, objects, appositives, verbs, prepositional phrases, or subordinate clauses. When the conjunction joins only two elements, the sentence does not take a comma before the conjunction.

CONJUNCTIONS WITHOUT COMMAS	
Compound Subject	Bess and Sandra met for lunch on the beach.
Compound Verb	The group laughed and chatted as they danced at prom.
Two Prepositional Phrases	The bird flew through the room and out the door.
Two Subordinate Clauses	I enjoy shopping trips only if they are at the mall and I get what I want.

A **nominative absolute** is a noun or pronoun followed by a participle or participial phrase that functions independently of the rest of the sentence.

Use a comma after a nominative absolute.

EXAMPLE   Important symptoms having been missed**,**
            I decided to call the doctor.

Grammar Game Plan

Avoiding Comma Splices

Remember to use both a comma and a coordinating conjunction in a compound sentence. Using only a comma can result in a **run-on sentence** or a **comma splice**. A **comma splice** occurs when two or more complete sentences have been joined with only a comma. Either punctuate separate sentences with an end mark or a semicolon, or find a way to join the sentences. (See Section 23.3 for more information on semicolons.)

Avoid comma splices.

INCORRECT   The rain beat down on the flowers**,** many petals
              broke under the downpour.

CORRECT   The rain beat down on the flowers**.** Many petals
              broke under the downpour.

Using Commas in a Series

A **series** consists of three or more words, phrases, or subordinate clauses of a similar kind. A series can occur in any part of a sentence.

> **Use commas to separate three or more words, phrases, or clauses in a series.**

23.2.4 **RULE**

Notice that a comma follows each of the items except the last one in these series. The conjunction *and* or *or* is added after the last comma.

SERIES OF WORDS	The wildlife included birds, squirrels, deer, and snakes.
SERIES OF PREPOSITIONAL PHRASES	The directions led them through the streets, around the buildings, and through the center of town.
SUBORDINATE CLAUSES IN A SERIES	The radio reported that the election was over, that the turnout was good, and that the results were surprising.

If each item (except for the last one) in a series is followed by a conjunction, do not use commas.

EXAMPLE	I saw black bears and polar bears and brown bears.

A second exception to this rule concerns items such as *salt and pepper*, which are paired so often that they are considered a single item.

EXAMPLES	For my party, we had macaroni and cheese, franks and beans, and bacon and eggs.
	Ariel carried a big box with salt and pepper, plates and cups, and forks and knives.

Using Commas Between Adjectives

Sometimes, two or more adjectives are placed before the noun they describe.

23.2.5

> Use commas to separate **coordinate adjectives,** also called **independent modifiers,** or adjectives of equal rank.

EXAMPLES   a strong, tall man

a hopeful, productive, creative meeting

An adjective is equal in rank to another if the word *and* can be inserted between them without changing the meaning of the sentence. Another way to test whether or not adjectives are equal is to reverse their order. If the sentence still sounds correct, they are of equal rank. In the first example, *a tall, strong man* still makes sense.

If you cannot place the word *and* between adjectives or reverse their order without changing the meaning of the sentence, they are called **cumulative adjectives.**

23.2.6

> Do not use a comma between cumulative adjectives.

EXAMPLES   a new comforter cover
(*a comforter new cover* does not make sense)

many large animals
(*large many animals* does not make sense)

23.2.7

> Do not use a comma to separate the last adjective in a series from the noun it modifies.

INCORRECT   A large, powerful, truck picked up the soil.

CORRECT   A large, powerful truck picked up the soil.

See Practice 23.2A
See Practice 23.2B

PRACTICE 23.2A Using Commas Correctly in Sentences

Read each sentence. Then, rewrite each sentence, adding a comma or commas where needed. Write the reason(s) for the comma usage.

EXAMPLE   Laurence has a cavity so he is going to a dentist.

ANSWER   *Laurence has a cavity, so he is going to a dentist.* — compound sentence

1. Can you come now, or do you need more time?

2. We looked for the ball in the grass, in the shed, and under the car.

3. The phone suddenly shattering the silence, I dropped the dish.

4. I love to knit sweaters, but thick fluffy socks are my specialty.

5. I didn't pick up the dry cleaning, bread, or mail.

6. It was a small, bright, colorful footstool.

7. Her hair was tied with a red, curly ribbon.

8. I hoped to see Juan, but he wasn't at home.

9. Her kittens purring with contentment, the mother cat curled up and fell asleep.

10. Kit washed the car, and then she waxed it.

PRACTICE 23.2B Revising to Correct Errors in Comma Use

Read each sentence. Then, rewrite each sentence, adding or deleting commas as necessary.

EXAMPLE   Sitting on a bench I read my book.

ANSWER   *Sitting on a bench, I read my book.*

11. We painted pottery, and took skating lessons in the park on our day off from school.

12. Her pom poms waving, the cheerleader performed her routine.

13. Bob likes country music, yet he sets his radio to the rock station.

14. He's interested in cooking, and football.

15. The mouse squeaked, and ran to grab the piece of cheese.

16. I love to play tennis, and now I also enjoy ping-pong, badminton, and racquetball.

17. I thought Loren was a science major, but she just signed up for philosophy and economics.

18. May received a bouquet of beautiful, red roses.

19. The woman looked first, dashed across the street, and then ran down the block.

20. Marissa took Nahtali, Joachim, Peter, and Derek to the science museum.

SPEAKING APPLICATION

Take turns with a partner. Tell about what you have done this morning. List the activities in a series, and use adjectives of equal rank to describe them. Your partner should tell where commas would be inserted if your description were written.

WRITING APPLICATION

Write four sentences that use commas incorrectly. Exchange papers with a partner. Your partner should correct your sentences, adding or deleting commas as necessary.

Using Commas After Introductory Material

Most material that introduces a sentence should be set off with a comma.

> **Use a comma after an introductory word, phrase, or clause.**

KINDS OF INTRODUCTORY MATERIAL	
Introductory Words	Yes, we do expect to speak with them soon. No, there has been no phone call. Well, I was definitely surprised by her statement.
Nouns of Direct Address	Anthony, will you speak?
Introductory Adverbs	Hurriedly, they gathered up the camping gear. Patiently, the manager explained it to them again.
Participial Phrases	Acting quickly, she averted a potential traffic accident. Waiting for the start of the marathon, we introduced ourselves and started to chat.
Prepositional Phrases	In the shade of the leafy branches, the family picked several baskets of apples. After the lengthy seminar, we were all exhausted.
Infinitive Phrases	To choose the right foods, I consulted a nutrition book. To finish my paper on time, I will have to work all weekend.
Adverbial Clauses	When she asked for a permit for the store, she was sure it would be approved. If you compete in swim meets, you may be interested in this one.

Commas and Prepositional Phrases Only one comma should be used after two prepositional phrases or a compound participial or infinitive phrase.

EXAMPLES   In the pocket in his jacket, he found
his keys.

Wandering in the auditorium and scared, the fans
asked a security guard for directions.

It is not necessary to set off short prepositional phrases. However, a comma can help avoid confusion.

CONFUSING   In the rain water soaked my clothing.

CLEAR   In the rain, water soaked my clothing.

Using Commas With Parenthetical Expressions

A **parenthetical expression** is a word or phrase that interrupts the flow of the sentence.

> Use commas to set off parenthetical expressions from the rest of the sentence.

23.2.9 RULE

Parenthetical expressions may come in the middle or at the end of a sentence. A parenthetical expression in the middle of a sentence needs two commas—one on each side; it needs only one comma if it appears at the end of a sentence.

KINDS OF PARENTHETICAL EXPRESSIONS	
Nouns of Direct Address	Will you have brunch with us, April? I wonder, Ms. Bliss, where we'll go for brunch.
Adverbs	Someone had already bought them flatware, however. We could not, therefore, buy all of them.
Common Expressions	I listened to Athena's side as thoughtfully as anyone else did, I assume.
Contrasting Expressions	Arabella is ten, not eleven. Daphne's warmth, not her beauty, won Joshua's heart.

Find It/ FIX IT

7

Grammar
Game Plan

Find It/ FIX IT

11

Grammar
Game Plan

Using Commas With Nonessential Expressions

To determine when a phrase or clause should be set off with commas, decide whether the phrase or clause is *essential* or *nonessential* to the meaning of the sentence. The terms *restrictive* and *nonrestrictive* may also be used.

An **essential,** or **restrictive, phrase** or **clause** is necessary to the meaning of the sentence. **Nonessential,** or **nonrestrictive, expressions** can be left out without changing the meaning of the sentence. Although the nonessential material may be interesting, the sentence can be read without it and still make sense. Depending on their importance in a sentence, appositives, participial phrases, and adjectival clauses can be either essential or nonessential. Only nonessential expressions should be set off with commas.

NONESSENTIAL APPOSITIVE	The speech was given by Bill, the oldest member of the committee.
NONESSENTIAL PARTICIPIAL PHRASE	The long journey, traveled by many, crosses the entire continent.
NONESSENTIAL ADJECTIVAL CLAUSE	The mountain, which is covered with flowers in the summer, is popular with skiers.

Do not use commas to set off essential expressions.

ESSENTIAL APPOSITIVE	The part was played by the famous actress Meryl Streep.
ESSENTIAL PARTICIPIAL PHRASE	The woman baking the chicken is my mother.
ESSENTIAL ADJECTIVAL CLAUSE	The book that my teacher suggested would alter my conclusions.

See Practice 23.2C
See Practice 23.2D

PRACTICE 23.2C > Placing Commas Correctly in Sentences

Read each sentence. Then, rewrite each sentence, adding commas where they are needed.

EXAMPLE   Actually she hasn't finished her lunch yet I think.

ANSWER   *Actually, she hasn't finished her lunch yet, I think.*

1. After her mother gave her a reassuring nod, the child swam across the pool.

2. Looking slightly bemused, the professor applauded the student's satirical speech.

3. Although she liked the plan, she wasn't sure that the committee would approve it.

4. Luckily, no one was absent yesterday.

5. When Paige arrived at the campsite, she checked the cabin for broken windows.

6. The preface, "An Introduction to Physics," will help you understand the text.

7. Mary will win honors for her project, I am quite sure.

8. To pay for a new car stereo, Will got a job after school.

9. An estimated 200 people, almost all women, received an award from the council last year.

10. The most beautiful vistas, including the one where I took the picture, can be seen from Lauver's Lookout.

PRACTICE 23.2D > Revising Sentences for Proper Comma Use

Read each sentence. Then, rewrite each sentence, adding or deleting commas as necessary.

EXAMPLE   Absent-mindedly Jonna, poured orange juice not milk on her cereal.

ANSWER   *Absent-mindedly, Jonna poured orange juice, not milk, on her cereal.*

11. No, there aren't any blueberry muffins left.

12. Sleepily, Trent pulled on his pajamas and climbed into bed.

13. Seamounts, underwater mountains that do not break the surface of the water, are my favorite marine feature to study.

14. This Saturday Evening Post cover was created by the famous artist Norman Rockwell.

15. To win the game, you have to know your opponent's weaknesses.

16. China is the most densely populated country in the world.

17. Will you change the radio station, Jorge?

18. This river, the longest in the state, currently has over 60 beaver dams.

19. After their lengthy discussion, the men all shook hands.

20. In the dusky glow of the evening, Ryan looked relaxed, not at all impatient.

SPEAKING APPLICATION

With a partner, reread all of the sentences in Practice 23.2C. Discuss the purpose of each comma in all ten sentences.

WRITING APPLICATION

Write a story that includes at least five different ways to use commas, including introductory material, parenthetical expressions, and nonessential expressions.

Using Commas With Dates, Geographical Names, and Titles

Dates usually have several parts, including months, days, and years. Commas separate these elements for easier reading.

> **When a date is made up of two or more parts, use a comma after each item, except in the case of a month followed by a day.**

EXAMPLES   The journey began on June 6, 2010, and the preparations began on March 12, 2009.

The job began on January 1 and ended two weeks later.
(no comma needed after the day of the month)

Commas are also used when the month and the day are used as an appositive to rename a day of the week.

EXAMPLES   Monday, April 13, was the first day of the class.

Ben will arrive on Saturday, April 19, and will stay until Sunday.

When a date contains only a month and a year, commas are unnecessary.

EXAMPLES   I will leave in July 2011.

Ashley will visit Germany in May 2009.

If the parts of a date have already been joined by prepositions, no comma is needed.

EXAMPLE   The historic newspaper printed its first edition in June of 1890.

> **When a geographical name is made up of two or more parts, use a comma after each item.** **RULE** 23.2.11

See Practice 23.2E

EXAMPLES My sister who lives in Orlando, Florida, has a job working with the dolphins.

We're going to Montreal, Quebec, Canada, for our road trip.

> **When a name is followed by one or more titles, use a comma after the name and after each title.** **RULE** 23.2.12

EXAMPLE I see that Carlos Monegro, P.A., works there.

A similar rule applies with some business abbreviations.

EXAMPLE Eastern Smith, Inc., started publishing in 2001.

Using Commas in Numbers

Commas make large numbers easier to read by grouping them.

> **With large numbers of more than three digits, use a comma after every third digit starting from the right.** **RULE** 23.2.13

EXAMPLES 10,000 gallons, 1,600 miles, 1,246,314 pennies

> **Do not use a comma in ZIP Codes, telephone numbers, page numbers, years, serial numbers, or house numbers.** **RULE** 23.2.14

ZIP CODE	17458	YEAR NUMBER	1980
TELEPHONE NUMBER	(908) 962-2644	SERIAL NUMBER	105-256-815
PAGE NUMBER	Page 2651	HOUSE NUMBER	6494 Lake Street

See Practice 23.2F

PRACTICE 23.2E Using Commas With Dates and Geographical Names

Read each sentence. Then, rewrite each sentence to show where to correctly place commas in dates and geographical names.

EXAMPLE Galveston Texas is located on the Gulf of Mexico.

ANSWER *Galveston, Texas, is located on the Gulf of Mexico.*

1. Next Monday is January 2012.

2. The summer of 2008 was the last time Melanie went to Hartford Connecticut.

3. We will land in London England on Thursday March 5.

4. The package was sent to London Ontario Canada.

5. There was a flood in Annapolis Maryland on December 3 1993.

6. The ceremony will take place on Friday October 8.

7. The address on the envelope is for Canberra New South Wales Australia.

8. Penny went to Mexico City Mexico in June 2007.

9. The show opened on April 4 2010 and will close on May 10 2012.

10. I will vacation in Paris France from Monday December 1 to Friday December 5.

PRACTICE 23.2F Editing Sentences for Proper Comma Usage

Read each sentence. Then, rewrite each sentence, adding or deleting commas as necessary.

EXAMPLE I have lived in Valencia Spain and Okinawa Japan.

ANSWER *I have lived in Valencia, Spain, and Okinawa, Japan.*

11. This Wednesday November, 3 Janet is going to see her family in Topeka Kansas.

12. Mei was hired by Friendly Publishers, Inc.

13. On May 16, 2007, Professor Helen H. Fitzpatrick, Ph.D, received tenure from Colgate University.

14. Russell's car has 85672 miles on it, but it's still running well.

15. December 8, 1998 is the date, Natasha's family emigrated from St. Petersburg, Russia.

16. Exactly 2000 babies were born in that country in the year 2000.

17. Gianna, the girl next door, was Bargain City's 1000000th customer last Friday July 5.

18. This Tuesday, August 5 Kelly comes home from Montreal Quebec Canada.

19. There are 13485 residents in Smithtown, New York.

20. Dr. Moses Leverly M.D. will perform the operation next Thursday January 3.

SPEAKING APPLICATION

Discuss with a partner the reason for punctuation in writing. Then, discuss how commas help us when we read aloud.

WRITING APPLICATION

Write four sentences that show comma use with dates, geographical names, titles, and numbers.

Using Commas With Addresses and in Letters

Commas are also used in addresses, salutations of friendly letters, and closings of friendly or business letters.

> **Use a comma after each item in an address made up of two or more parts.**

RULE 23.2.15

Commas are placed after the name, street, and city. No comma separates the state from the ZIP Code. Instead, insert an extra space between them.

EXAMPLE   The package was delivered to Carlos Lopez**,** 25 Valley Road**,** Dallas**,** Texas 75201.

Fewer commas are needed when an address is written in a letter or on an envelope.

EXAMPLE   Mr. John Black

55 Highway Lane

Brooklyn**,** NY 11201

> **Use a comma after the salutation in a personal letter and after the closing in all letters.**

RULE 23.2.16

See Practice 23.2G

SALUTATIONS	Dear Uncle Teddy**,**	Dear Amanda**,**
CLOSINGS	Sincerely**,**	With love**,**

Using Commas in Elliptical Sentences

In **elliptical sentences,** words that are understood are left out. Commas make these sentences easier to read.

> **Use a comma to indicate the words left out of an elliptical sentence.**

RULE 23.2.17

EXAMPLE   Tia celebrates her anniversary formally; Bette **,** casually.

The words *celebrates her anniversary* have been omitted from the second clause of the sentence. The comma has been inserted in their place so the meaning is still clear. The sentence could be restated in this way: *Tia celebrates her anniversary formally; Bette celebrates her anniversary casually.*

Using Commas With Direct Quotations

Commas are also used to indicate where **direct quotations** begin and end. (See Section 23.4 for more information on punctuating quotations.)

> Use commas to set off a direct quotation from the rest of a sentence.

EXAMPLES   "You showed up late **,** " commented Beth's mother.

She said **,** "The committee meeting ran longer than I had hoped **.** "

"I hope **,** " Kyle's father said **,** "that his best friend doesn't forget to call **.** "

Using Commas for Clarity

Commas help you group words that belong together.

> Use a comma to prevent a sentence from being misunderstood.

UNCLEAR   Near the freeway developers were building a condo complex.

CLEAR   Near the freeway **,** developers were building a condo complex.

Misuses of Commas

Because commas appear so frequently in writing, some people are tempted to use them where they are not needed. Before you insert a comma, think about how your ideas relate to one another.

Find It/ FIX IT

7

Grammar
Game Plan

MISUSED WITH AN ADJECTIVE AND A NOUN	In the morning, I have a large, hot, cup of tea.
CORRECT	In the morning, I have a large, hot cup of tea.
MISUSED WITH A COMPOUND SUBJECT	Following the party, my sister Jane, and our cousin Rita, invited Bill to the barbeque.
CORRECT	Following the party, my sister Jane and our cousin Rita invited Bill to the barbeque.
MISUSED WITH A COMPOUND VERB	He watched as she spoke, and listened carefully.
CORRECT	He watched as she spoke and listened carefully.
MISUSED WITH A COMPOUND OBJECT	She chose a car with four doors, and a sunroof.
CORRECT	She chose a car with four doors and a sunroof.
MISUSED WITH PHRASES	Finding the skates, and hoping they were hers, Sally tried them on.
CORRECT	Finding the skates and hoping they were hers, Sally tried them on.
MISUSED WITH CLAUSES	He discussed what elements are crucial to winning, and which players are most valuable.
CORRECT	He discussed what elements are crucial to winning and which players are most valuable.

See Practice 23.2H
See Practice 23.2I
See Practice 23.2J

PRACTICE 23.2G ▶ Adding Commas in Addresses and Letters

Read each item. Then, add commas where needed.

EXAMPLE   Dear Aunt Edith

ANSWER   *Dear Aunt Edith,*

1. The Inn at the Lake Colorado Springs Colorado.

2. Hugs and kisses
Julianna

3. To my dear little brother

4. Donna Marie Dean 14 Kinnelon Street Jupiter Florida

5. Dear Aunt Lucy Cousin Maisy and Cousin Gracie

6. Mary's Igloo Alaska

7. Wishing you all the best
Robert Winston Jr.

8. Fulton on the Water Suite 10C

9. Lake Manitoba Winnipeg Canada

10. Daniel Chambers
144 Oak Avenue Apt. 4D
Winston-Salem NC 27101

PRACTICE 23.2H ▶ Revising Sentences With Misused Commas

Read each sentence. Then, if a sentence contains a misused comma, rewrite it to show correct comma usage. If the sentence is correct, write *correct*.

EXAMPLE   As she opened the package, with great care, Nia was excited.

ANSWER   *As she opened the package with great care, Nia was excited.*

11. If I cannot find anyone I'll just, go home.

12. Mother bought a computer, and a printer.

13. My chores include vacuuming the rug, and making the beds, and doing laundry.

14. Joe Novak Jr. put on his suit, knotted his tie and grabbed, his briefcase.

15. Jerry delivered the flowers, and then drove off in his van.

16. After school, I take a long, leisurely walk.

17. Gloria, and Leigh, are preparing for graduation.

18. Ravi can't pack his bowling ball, or his helmet.

19. In the room are Justine, and her parents.

20. Watching the movie, hoping that it would end soon, Jose was glad when the phone rang.

SPEAKING APPLICATION

After correcting the items above, read them aloud with a partner. Discuss why each comma is needed.

WRITING APPLICATION

Write ten sentences with misused commas. Exchange papers with a partner. Your partner should rewrite the sentences with the commas placed correctly.

PRACTICE 23.2I ▷ Revising Sentences for Missing Commas

Read each sentence. Then, rewrite each sentence, adding commas wherever they are needed. If there are no missing commas in a sentence, write *correct*.

EXAMPLE   At first I said yes but now I'm having second thoughts.

ANSWER   *At first I said yes, but now I'm having second thoughts.*

1. Zane, have you seen my guitar?

2. The fragrant, beautiful, crabapple blossoms clung to the branches.

3. The longest sentence in Joyce's *Ulysses* is 4,391 words; in Proust, 958 words.

4. My sister Susie, who has red hair, likes to wear green dresses.

5. Thinking quickly, she called 911.

6. To get the bookcase to look perfect, he sanded it three times.

7. According to the U.S. Consumer Products Safety Commission, toothpicks caused 9,000 injuries in 2008.

8. Warnings, having been ignored, people were surprised by the recession.

9. Dallas, Texas, has a modern transportation system.

10. I went to Galveston last spring and Austin last winter.   correct

PRACTICE 23.2J ▷ Identifying and Revising Comma Errors

Read each sentence. Then, rewrite each sentence to add any missing commas and delete any misused commas. If the sentence is correct, write *correct*.

EXAMPLE   It's been a long, hard, road to success for Lorenzo.

ANSWER   *It's been a long, hard road to success for Lorenzo.*

11. Spiders turn carbohydrates, and water into a fiber as strong as steel.

12. The day being hot, we decided to go swimming.

13. In the book, *The Wealth of Nations*, Adam Smith said emotions influence financial decisions.   Correct

14. In the depths of the ocean, scientists have found bizarre life forms.

15. It gets cold in January, yet that's when the sun is closest to Earth.

16. Wordsworth, who wrote nature poems, walked 180,000 miles in his life.

17. In India, during Gandhi's nonviolent protests, 300,000 people were jailed.   True

18. In all, Americans spent $25 billion on books in 2007.

19. No, I didn't feed Scamp yet.   True

20. The physicist, Marie Curie, was born November 7, 1867, in Poland.

SPEAKING APPLICATION

Take turns with a partner. Read aloud your corrected sentences from Practice 23.2I. Pause for each comma. Discuss how the pauses help listeners and readers make sense of the sentences.

WRITING APPLICATION

Write a brief biography of someone who interests you. Use several sentence structures. Exchange papers with a partner and review to correct comma usage. Discuss why you added or deleted commas.

Test Warm-Up

DIRECTIONS

Read the introduction and the passage that follows. Then, answer the questions to show that you can use and understand the function of commas in reading and writing.

Isaac wrote this paragraph about music education. Read the paragraph and think about the changes you would suggest as a peer editor. When you finish reading, answer the questions that follow.

Benefits of Music Education

(1) As budgets are cut school music programs are canceled. (2) But studies suggest that music is as important as reading, writing, and arithmetic. (3) For example, the Australian Music Association studied the effects of music lessons in schools. (4) After eight months of music lessons, students' spatial IQ increased by nearly 50 percent. (5) Spatial IQ is an important component of the higher brain functions people need to do complex tasks like higher math. (6) Music can calm people, and lower their blood pressure—or it can whip them into a frenzy. (7) It can reach children, who have been traumatized and help them heal.

---

1 How should sentence 1 be revised?

A As budgets are cut, school music programs are canceled.

B As budgets are cut, school music programs, are canceled.

C As budgets are cut school music programs, are canceled.

D As budgets are cut school, music programs are canceled.

2 What change, if any, should be made in sentence 3?

F Delete the comma after *example*

G Insert a comma after *Australian*

H Insert a comma after *Association*

J Make no change

3 What change, if any, should be made in sentence 6?

A Insert a comma after *calm*

B Delete the comma after *people*

C Insert a comma after *them*

D Make no change

4 How should sentence 7 be revised?

F It can reach children, who have been traumatized, and help them heal.

G It can reach children who have been traumatized, and help them heal.

H It can reach children who have been traumatized and help them heal.

J It can reach, children who have been traumatized, and help them heal.

23.3 Semicolons and Colons

The **semicolon (;)** is used to join related independent clauses. Semicolons can also help you avoid confusion in sentences with other internal punctuation. The **colon (:)** is used to introduce lists of items and in other special situations.

Using Semicolons to Join Independent Clauses

Semicolons establish relationships between two independent clauses that are closely connected in thought and structure. A semicolon can also be used to separate independent clauses or items in a series that already contains a number of commas.

> Use a semicolon to join related independent clauses that are not already joined by the conjunctions *and, but, for, nor, or, so,* or *yet.*

23.3.1 RULE

EXAMPLE   We explored the old house together; we were amazed at all the antiques we found inside.

Do not use a semicolon to join two unrelated independent clauses. If the clauses are not related, they should be written as separate sentences with a period or another end mark to separate them.

Note that when a sentence contains three or more related independent clauses, they may still be separated with semicolons.

EXAMPLE   The window shattered; the screen broke; the roof disappeared.

Semicolons Join Clauses Separated by Conjunctive Adverbs or Transitional Expressions

Conjunctive adverbs are adverbs that are used as conjunctions to join independent clauses. **Transitional expressions** are expressions that connect one independent clause with another one.

> Use a semicolon to join independent clauses separated by either a **conjunctive adverb** or a **transitional expression.**

23.3.2 RULE

CONJUNCTIVE ADVERBS	*also, besides, consequently, first, furthermore, however, indeed, instead, moreover, nevertheless, otherwise, second, then, therefore, thus*
TRANSITIONAL EXPRESSIONS	*as a result, at this time, for instance, in fact, on the other hand, that is*

Place a semicolon *before* a conjunctive adverb or a transitional expression, and place a comma *after* a conjunctive adverb or transitional expression. The comma sets off the conjunctive adverb or transitional expression, which introduces the second clause.

EXAMPLE   She never forgets her notes; in fact, she is the most prepared.

Because words used as conjunctive adverbs and transitions can also interrupt one continuous sentence, use a semicolon only when there is an independent clause on each side of the conjunctive adverb or transitional expression.

EXAMPLES   He visited a hundred restaurants and shops over two weeks; therefore, he had no time to write.

We were astounded, however, by Brett's painting of the blue sky.

Using Semicolons to Avoid Confusion

Sometimes, semicolons are used to separate items in a series.

RULE 23.3.3

Use semicolons to avoid confusion when independent clauses or items in a series already contain commas.

When the items in a series already contain several commas, semicolons can be used to group items that belong together. Semicolons are placed at the end of all but the last item.

INDEPENDENT CLAUSES
The canal, reportedly teeming with fish, was a legend; and the frustrated, tired fisherman would find it only in sea stories.

ITEMS IN A SERIES
On our trip to the city, my brother visited a friend, who works in the mall; our former neighbors, who live across town; and the Smiths, who own the town coffee shop.

Semicolons appear commonly in a series that contains nonessential appositives, participial phrases, or adjectival clauses. Commas should separate the nonessential material from the words it modifies; semicolons should separate the complete items in the series.

APPOSITIVES
I sent word to Mr. Lee, my language teacher; Mr. Will, my math teacher; and Mr. Dee, my soccer coach.

PARTICIPIAL PHRASES
I developed a passion for reading from my English teachers, learning about literature; from going to the library, reading British authors; and from bookstores, reading different novels.

ADJECTIVAL CLAUSES
The white yacht that I purchased has a sleeping compartment, which holds two people; a kitchen, which was just installed; and a greatroom, which is furnished.

Using Colons

The **colon (:)** is used to introduce lists of items and in certain special situations.

RULE 23.3.4

> **Use a colon after an independent clause to introduce a list of items. Use commas to separate three or more items.**

Independent clauses that appear before a colon often include the words *the following, as follows, these,* or *those.*

EXAMPLES   For our experiment, we had to interview the following experts: a biologist, a chemist, and a physiologist.

RULE 23.3.5

> **Do not use a colon after a verb or a preposition.**

INCORRECT   Cindy regularly orders: shoes, makeup, and purses online.

CORRECT   Cindy regularly orders shoes, makeup, and purses online.

RULE 23.3.6

> **Use a colon to introduce a quotation that is formal or lengthy or a quotation that does not contain a "he said/she said" expression.**

EXAMPLE   Oliver Wendell Holmes Jr. wrote this about freedom: "It is only through free debate and free exchange of ideas that government remains responsive to the will of the people and peaceful change is effected."

Even if it is lengthy, dialogue or a casual remark should be introduced by a comma. Use the colon if the quotation is formal or has no tagline.

A colon may also be used to introduce a sentence that explains the sentence that precedes it.

> **Use a colon to introduce a sentence that summarizes or explains the sentence before it.**

 RULE 23.3.7

EXAMPLE His explanation for being late was believable **:** He ran out of gas on the way.

Notice that the complete sentence introduced by the colon starts with a capital letter.

> **Use a colon to introduce a formal appositive that follows an independent clause.**

RULE 23.3.8

EXAMPLE I had finally decided where to move **:** Maine.

The colon is a stronger punctuation mark than a comma. Using the colon gives more emphasis to the appositive it introduces.

> **Use a colon in a number of special writing situations.**

 RULE 23.3.9

SPECIAL SITUATIONS REQUIRING COLONS	
Numerals Giving the Time	3**:**30 A.M. 5**:**15 P.M.
References to Periodicals (Volume Number: Page Number)	*People* 25**:**12 *National Geographic* 45**:**15
Biblical References (Chapter Number: Verse Number)	Proverbs 3**:**5
Subtitles for Books and Magazines	*A User's Guide for Cars***:** *Antique Cars and Their Parts*
Salutations in Business Letters	Dear Ms. Adams**:** Dear Sir**:**
Labels Used to Signal Important Ideas	**Danger:** Firing Range

See Practice 23.3A
See Practice 23.3B

PRACTICE 23.3A Adding Semicolons and Colons to Sentences

Read each item. Then, rewrite each item, adding semicolons and colons where they are needed.

EXAMPLE   The computer-generated voice said "The time is 427 P.M."

ANSWER   *The computer-generated voice said: "The time is 4:27 P.M."*

1. It is 215 P.M.

2. Ken will be our guide Mark will drive the car.

3. Dear Mr. Stark

4. Sydney is in New South Wales Perth is in Western Australia.

5. Let me reiterate my statement Keep this door locked at all times.

6. We wanted to start our vacation as soon as possible therefore, we left very early.

7. Diana wants to start working soon in fact, she has already had three interviews.

8. Manuel wants to apply to several schools Dartmouth, Harvard, Yale, and Brown.

9. Captain Ford demands one thing obedience.

10. For the hike, I will need a warm hat, strong, sturdy boots, and a bottle of water.

PRACTICE 23.3B Using Semicolons and Colons

Read each sentence. Then, rewrite each sentence, replacing the incorrect comma with a semicolon or a colon.

EXAMPLE   Which branch of the military is he in, Army, Air Force, Navy, or Marines?

ANSWER   *Which branch of the military is he in: Army, Air Force, Navy, or Marines?*

11. Peter has researched his report for two months, he will present it soon.

12. Thelma hurt her foot, therefore, she will not play basketball this season.

13. I like soccer, football, and baseball, however, they will never replace lacrosse.

14. Heather wants only healthy foods, carrots, celery, and apples.

15. The show starts at 4,15 P.M.

16. Mel ordered the following items, milk, eggs, bread.

17. Tiara wants to be like her big brother, he travels the world.

18. The wind died down, thus, we rowed to shore.

19. Warning, The floor is wet.

20. George's favorite animal is a tiger, his brother likes sharks.

SPEAKING APPLICATION

Take turns with a partner. Say sentences that would require colons or semicolons if they were written. Your partner should tell which punctuation would be needed for each of your sentences.

WRITING APPLICATION

Write two paragraphs about something that happened in English class last year. Use colons and semicolons to combine sentences in your paragraphs.

23.4 Quotation Marks, Underlining, and Italics

Quotation marks (" ") set off direct quotations, dialogue, and certain types of titles. Other titles are **underlined** or set in *italics*, a slanted type style.

Find It/FIX IT

6

Grammar Game Plan

Find It/FIX IT

18

Grammar Game Plan

Using Quotation Marks With Quotations

Quotation marks identify spoken or written words that you are including in your writing. A **direct quotation** represents a person's exact speech or thoughts. An **indirect quotation** reports the general meaning of what a person said or thought.

A **direct quotation** is enclosed in quotation marks.

RULE 23.4.1

DIRECT QUOTATION

"When I learn to paint," said the student, "I'll go to the studio every day."

An **indirect quotation** does not require quotation marks.

RULE 23.4.2

INDIRECT QUOTATION

The student said that when she learns to paint, she'll go to the studio every day.

Both types of quotations are acceptable when you write. Direct quotations, however, generally result in a livelier writing style.

Using Direct Quotations With Introductory, Concluding, and Interrupting Expressions

A writer will generally identify a speaker by using words such as *he asked* or *she said* with a quotation. These expressions, called **conversational taglines** or **tags,** can introduce, conclude, or interrupt a quotation.

Direct Quotations With Introductory Expressions

Commas help you set off introductory information so that your reader understands who is speaking.

> **Use a comma after short introductory expressions that precede direct quotations.**

EXAMPLE   My friend warned **,** **"**If you drive my car, you'll be responsible for it. **"**

If the introductory conversational tagline is very long or formal in tone, set it off with a colon instead of a comma.

EXAMPLE   At the end of the school year, Jane shared her desire **:** **"**I plan to become a teacher and help children read and think. **"**

Direct Quotations With Concluding Expressions

Conversational taglines may also act as concluding expressions.

> **Use a comma, question mark, or exclamation mark after a direct quotation followed by a concluding expression.**

EXAMPLE   **"**If you buy a new car, you'll be responsible for filling it with gas **,** **"** my father warned **.**

Concluding expressions are not complete sentences; therefore, they do not begin with capital letters. Closing quotation marks are always placed outside the punctuation at the end of direct quotations. Concluding expressions generally end with a period.

Divided Quotations With Interrupting Expressions

You may use a conversational tagline to interrupt the words of a direct quotation, which is also called a **divided quotation.**

> **Use a comma after the part of a quoted sentence followed by an interrupting conversational tagline. Use another comma after the tagline. Do not capitalize the first word of the rest of the sentence. Use quotation marks to enclose the quotation. End punctuation should be inside the last quotation mark.**
>
> **RULE 23.4.5**

EXAMPLE "If you buy a new car," my father warned, "you'll be responsible for filling it with gas."

> **Use a comma, question mark, or exclamation mark after a quoted sentence that comes before an interrupting conversational tagline. Use a period after the tagline.**
>
> **RULE 23.4.6**

EXAMPLE "You bought a new car," stated my father. "You are responsible for filling it with gas."

Quotation Marks With Other Punctuation Marks

Quotation marks are used with commas, semicolons, colons, and all of the end marks. However, the location of the quotation marks in relation to the punctuation marks varies.

> **Place a comma or a period *inside* the final quotation mark. Place a semicolon or colon *outside* the final quotation mark.**
>
> **RULE 23.4.7**

EXAMPLES "Sprinkles was a great kitten," sighed my sister.

We just learned about his "groundbreaking medical discovery"; we are very pleased.

> **Place a question mark or an exclamation mark inside the final quotation mark if the end mark is part of the quotation. Do not use an additional end mark.**
>
> **RULE 23.4.8**

EXAMPLE Ben wondered, "How could I lose the contest?"

Place a question mark or exclamation mark outside the final quotation mark if the end mark is part of the entire sentence, not part of the quotation.

EXAMPLE   Don't you dare say, "I forgot"!

Using Single Quotation Marks for Quotations Within Quotations

As you have learned, double quotation marks (" ") should enclose the main quotation in a sentence. The rules for using commas and end marks with double quotation marks also apply to **single quotation marks.**

RULE 23.4.10

Use **single quotation marks (' ')** to set off a quotation within a quotation.

EXAMPLES   "I recall Tiff quoting Macy, 'If it gets any busier, how will we find parking?'" John said.

"The surgeon said, 'It was successful!'" Ben explained.

Punctuating Explanatory Material Within Quotations

Explanatory material within quotations should be placed in brackets. (See Section 23.7 for more information on brackets.)

RULE 23.4.11

Use brackets to enclose an explanation located within a quotation. The brackets show that the explanation is not part of the original quotation.

EXAMPLE   The volunteer said, "This bridge is a link between two towns [Cane and Falls]."

See Practice 23.4A
See Practice 23.4B
See Practice 23.4C
See Practice 23.4D
See Practice 23.4E
See Practice 23.4F

PRACTICE 23.4A Using Quotation Marks

Read each sentence. Then, rewrite each sentence, inserting quotation marks where needed.

EXAMPLE   The professor said, Prepare to work hard this semester.

ANSWER   *The professor said, "Prepare to work hard this semester."*

1. Start running, said the coach, when you see my signal.

2. Are the final drafts due next week? Zeke inquired.

3. Donna cheered, Go team, go!

4. The actress must have said, 'Thank you' a dozen times, said the newscaster.

5. Did Aaron say, Lock all the doors?

6. I thought Raj said that he didn't want any juice, but he actually said, Yes, please.

7. Please leave your name and number, was the recorded message.

8. I can't see! wailed the child.

9. Maybe, Brenda suggested optimistically, I could finish the job.

10. Michael said that I said, Surprise! but I didn't.

PRACTICE 23.4B Revising for the Correct Use of Quotation Marks

Read each sentence. Then, rewrite each sentence, correcting the misuse of quotation marks.

EXAMPLE   "Howard said, No one has given me any instructions."

ANSWER   *Howard said, "No one has given me any instructions."*

11. "Yuen said," I think it's going to rain tomorrow.

12. "It is doubtful, said Mandy, that I will be home on time."

13. Yes! Tom exclaimed "as he rounded the bases."

14. "I heard Bethany yell, Home free! at the top of her lungs, said Greg."

15. Truth be told, said Ving, "I loved your performance tonight."

16. "Were you confused when I said, No?"

17. "Is your favorite painting a van Gogh? she asked."

18. "Don't forget to wear sunblock," said Mother. It's very sunny outside.

19. "Who would be crazy enough to pass up an opportunity like that? asked Nikki."

20. "Tom proclaimed, I passed!" when he received his grades.

SPEAKING APPLICATION

Take turns with a partner. Say sentences with direct quotations and indirect quotations. Your partner should tell which sentences would need quotation marks if they were written.

WRITING APPLICATION

Write a dialogue between two people at a bookstore. Include at least six lines of dialogue.

Read each sentence. Then, rewrite each sentence, punctuating the quotation properly.

EXAMPLE   Alana said Pecos Bill was a folk hero.

ANSWER   *Alana said, "Pecos Bill was a folk hero."*

1. The newscaster said There are storm warnings for our area.

2. Bret asked What's the score?

3. Benjamin Franklin said An investment in knowledge always pays the best interest.

4. My father always says The only constant is change.

5. Hope asked Do you really think I'd say Shut up?

6. Fran Lebowitz wrote the following Life is something to do when you can't get to sleep.

7. I love the poem Dust of Snow said Maria.

8. Thomas Jefferson proclaimed I cannot live without books.

9. Stacey asked Have you ever wondered why the sky is blue?

10. Al explained I thought Ron asked for more boots, but he actually said More soup.

Read each sentence. Then, rewrite each sentence, punctuating the quotation properly.

EXAMPLE   Don't forget Gloria said tomorrow is Election Day.

ANSWER   *"Don't forget," Gloria said, "tomorrow is Election Day."*

11. I was in the play Julie said I played a tree.

12. Sports are important to me Rob explained but not as important as music.

13. The only thing we have to fear said President Roosevelt is fear itself.

14. Guernica is a painting Jen said by Picasso.

15. Intelligence runs in my family Paul claimed but ambition walks with a limp.

16. If you give up on happiness Edith Wharton wrote you can have a fairly good time.

17. The only exercise I get Oscar joked is mood swings.

18. A house uncleaned Rebecca West pointed out is better than a life unlived.

19. You see George said it was all a mistake.

20. Humans are verbivores said Steven Pinker. We live on words.

SPEAKING APPLICATION

Take turns with a partner. Use one of the quotations in Practice 23.4C as a springboard to a conversation. Take notes on what you say. Write your dialogue with taglines and correct punctuation.

WRITING APPLICATION

Write five new quotations modeled on those in Practice 23.4D. Make sure you put the taglines in the middle of the quotations and use correct punctuation.

PRACTICE 23.4E ▶ **Properly Punctuating Quotations With Closing Taglines**

Read each sentence. Then, rewrite each sentence, punctuating the quotation properly.

EXAMPLE   Bring it Adrian challenged.

ANSWER   *"Bring it!" Adrian challenged.*

1. Carlos shouted I got it said Pete.

2. Jimi always wants exactly what he has Mom observed.

3. Love is the difficult realization that something other than oneself is real Iris Murdoch wrote.

4. Frank Lloyd Wright built a house over a waterfall Damian explained.

5. What's your favorite band Clive asked.

6. Never say never I say.

7. Traveling is the ruin of all happiness! Fanny Burney lamented.

8. Books do furnish a room Anthony commented.

9. Nature is a daily gift said John.

10. I just learned to play Stairway to Heaven Raoul bragged.

PRACTICE 23.4F ▶ **Revising to Correctly Punctuate Quotations**

Read each sentence. Then, rewrite each sentence to correct any errors in punctuation of quotations. If a sentence has no errors, write *correct*.

EXAMPLE   "Rosa"? Matt called.

ANSWER   *"Rosa?" Matt called.*

11. "Did you get Mom a birthday present"? Matt asked his sister.

12. "Not yet," Rosa admitted, "but I have some ideas."

13. "Me too," Matt said.

14. "You know how she's always complaining that 'our vacuum cleaner doesn't clean'?"

15. "Well, I wouldn't say 'always,'" Rosa shook her head.

16. "I guarantee that Mom would hate a vacuum cleaner for her birthday," she exclaimed!

17. Matt asked, "Why? It's thoughtful."

18. "Wouldn't it be more thoughtful if you'd vacuum occasionally?" Rosa suggested. correct

19. "Maybe I would," Matt said, "if we had a correct decent vacuum cleaner."

20. Rosa said, "How about a beautiful opal necklace instead?"

SPEAKING APPLICATION

Take turns with a partner to read aloud your correctly punctuated sentences from Practice 23.4E. Pause for each comma. For each sentence, use a tone of voice that fits its content. Try several different tones.

WRITING APPLICATION

Using Practice 23.4F as your model, write an imaginary conversation among at least three people. Double-check your punctuation.

Using Quotation Marks for Dialogue

A conversation between two or more people is called a **dialogue.**

RULE 23.4.12

When writing a dialogue, begin a new paragraph with each change of speaker.

The snow slowly fell over the top of the distant mountain, as the sun set in the west.

Dan sat by the fireplace and talked with his brother about his future.

"I'm going to the city," said Dan. "I think I'll like the atmosphere better; you know I don't like to be bored."

"Have you found a place yet?" asked Matt. "Can I have your couch?"

"It's all yours," said Dan. "It is fine with me if I never see it again."

RULE 23.4.13

For quotations longer than a paragraph, put quotation marks at the beginning of each paragraph and at the end of the final paragraph.

John McPhee wrote an essay about a canoe trip on the St. John River in northern Maine. He introduces his readers to the river in the following way:

"We have been out here four days now and rain has been falling three. The rain appears to be ending. Breaks of blue are opening in the sky. Sunlight is coming through, and a wind is rising.

"I was not prepared for the St. John River, did not anticipate its size. I saw it as a narrow trail flowing north, twisting through balsam and spruce—a small and intimate forest river, something like the Allagash. . . ."

Using Quotation Marks in Titles

Generally, quotation marks are used around the titles of shorter works.

> **Use quotation marks to enclose the titles of short written works.**

WRITTEN WORKS THAT USE QUOTATION MARKS	
Title of a Short Story	"The Black Cat" by Edgar Allan Poe "A Very Tight Place" by Stephen King
Chapter From a Book	"Of Alliances" in *War and Peace* "The Duty of Subjects" in *War and Peace*
Title of a Short Poem	"Fire and Ice" by Robert Frost
Essay Title	"The Over-Soul" by Ralph Waldo Emerson
Title of an Article	"Plugging the Gaps" by Katie Paul

> **Use quotation marks around the titles of episodes in a television or radio series, songs, and parts of a long musical composition.**

ARTISTIC WORK TITLES THAT USE QUOTATION MARKS	
Episode	"The Chairman" from *60 Minutes*
Song Title	"Hound Dog" by Elvis Presley
Part of a Long Musical Composition	"Spring" from *The Four Seasons* "E.T. Phone Home" from the *E.T. The Extra-Terrestrial* soundtrack

> **Use quotation marks around the title of a work that is mentioned as part of a collection.**

The title *Plato* would normally be underlined or italicized. In the example below, however, the title is placed in quotation marks because it is cited as part of a larger work.

EXAMPLE "Plato" from *Great Books of the Western World*

Using Underlining and Italics in Titles and Other Special Words

Underlining and **italics** help make titles and other special words and names stand out in your writing. Underlining is used only in handwritten or typewritten material. In printed material, italic (slanted) print is generally used instead of underlining.

 23.4.17 Underline or italicize the titles of long written works and the titles of publications that are published as a single work.

WRITTEN WORKS THAT ARE UNDERLINED OR ITALICIZED	
Title of a Book	*Great Expectations*
Title of a Newspaper	*The Chicago Tribune*
Title of a Play	*Les Misérables* *A Doll's House*
Title of a Long Poem	*To The Same*
Title of a Magazine	*Life*

The portion of a newspaper title that should be italicized or underlined will vary from newspaper to newspaper. *The New York Times* should always be fully capitalized and italicized or underlined. Other papers, however, can be treated in one of two ways: the *Los Angeles Times* or the Los Angeles *Times*. You may want to check the paper's Web site for correct formatting.

23.4.18 Underline or italicize the titles of movies, television and radio series, long works of music, and works of art.

ARTISTIC WORKS THAT ARE UNDERLINED OR ITALICIZED	
Title of a Movie	*Grease, Breakfast at Tiffany's*
Title of a Television Series	*The Honeymooners* *The Addams Family*
Title of a Long Work of Music	*Paris in D Major*
Title of an Album (on any media)	*Born in the USA*
Title of a Painting	*Starry Night, Café Terrace*
Title of a Sculpture	*Apollo and Daphne* *Aphrodite of Cindus*

Do not underline, italicize, or place in quotation marks the name of the Bible, its books and divisions, or other holy scriptures, such as the Torah and the Quran.

EXAMPLE   Blair read from John in the New Testament.

Government documents should also not be underlined or enclosed in quotation marks.

Do not underline, italicize, or place in quotation marks the titles of government charters, alliances, treaties, acts, statutes, speeches, or reports.

23.4.20

EXAMPLE   The Taft-Hartley Labor Act was passed in 1947.

Underline or italicize the names of air, sea, and space craft.

23.4.21

EXAMPLE   Were there dogs aboard the *Titanic*?

Underline or italicize words, letters, or numbers (figures) used as names for themselves.

23.4.22

EXAMPLES   Her *i*'s and her *I*'s look too much like *1*'s.

Avoid sprinkling your speech with *you know*.

Underline or italicize foreign words and phrases not yet accepted into English.

23.4.23

See Practice 23.4G
See Practice 23.4H

EXAMPLE   "*Bonne chance*," she said, meaning "good luck" in French.

PRACTICE 23.4G Using Punctuation in Titles and Dialogue

Read each sentence. Then, rewrite each sentence, adding correct punctuation where needed. If any words need to be italicized, underline those words.

EXAMPLE   I'd like to see the re-make of Hitchcock's Vertigo said Paul.

ANSWER   *"I'd like to see the re-make of Hitchcock's <u>Vertigo</u>," said Paul.*

1. The Venus de Milo is a famous statue.

2. The class is learning to sing the Star-Spangled Banner.

3. Stephen thought that he would go see An Inconvenient Truth at the movie theater.

4. My copy of Science Today was just delivered said Stephanie.

5. Laura is playing the part of Ophelia in our production of Hamlet.

6. Have you ever been aboard the USS Intrepid?

7. "Melanie complained, The assignment took me the whole weekend to complete."

8. Rich replied, Yeah, me, too."

9. I thought it was pretty interesting, said Miles.

10. Interesting but long, said Melanie.

PRACTICE 23.4H Revising Punctuation in Titles and Dialogue

Read each sentence. Then, rewrite the sentence, using correct punctuation. If any words need to be italicized, underline those words.

EXAMPLE   Sue will direct the play Waiting for Godot.

ANSWER   *Sue will direct the play <u>Waiting for Godot</u>.*

11. "The song Thin Fields" is based on an English famine.

12. Did Ming really say that his favorite poem is The Iliad?

13. "I plan on seeing The Phantom of the Opera in June, said Tiffany."

14. Sarah asked, "Did Hemingway write the short story Out of Season?"

15. The Fantastic Voyage is tied to the dock.

16. My favorite Star Trek episode is titled The Trouble With Tribbles.

17. Meghan asked John, Are you prepared for the algebra test today?

18. "John replied, I studied all weekend."

19. Liam chimed in, "So did I, but I'm still not sure about word problems.

20. Meghan answered, I bet we all do fine."

SPEAKING APPLICATION

Take turns with a partner. Say sentences that contain both dialogue and titles. For each sentence, your partner should indicate which words would be put in quotation marks and/or italicized if the sentences were written.

WRITING APPLICATION

Write a dialogue between two friends discussing their favorite songs and movies. Be sure to use correct punctuation.

23.5 Hyphens

The **hyphen (-)** is used to combine words, spell some numbers and words, and show a connection between the syllables of words that are broken at the ends of lines.

Find It / FIX IT

19

Grammar
Game Plan

Using Hyphens in Numbers

Hyphens are used to join compound numbers and fractions.

> **Use a hyphen when you spell out two-word numbers from twenty-one through ninety-nine.**

RULE **23.5.1**

EXAMPLES   forty - four inches   fifty - seven yards

> **Use a hyphen when you use a fraction as an adjective but not when you use a fraction as a noun.**

RULE **23.5.2**

ADJECTIVE   The recipe called for one - half cup of water.

NOUN   Three quarters of the report on India is complete.

> **Use a hyphen between a number and a word when they are combined as modifiers. Do not use a hyphen if the word in the modifier is possessive.**

RULE **23.5.3**

EXAMPLES   The staff took a 30 - minute break after lunch.

The team put 16 weeks' worth of training in before the game.

> **If a series of consecutive, hyphenated modifiers ends with the same word, do not repeat the modified word each time. Instead, use a suspended hyphen (also called a dangling hyphen) and the modified word only at the end of the series.**

RULE **23.5.4**

EXAMPLE   The sixth - and seventh - grade students came.

Hyphens   605

Using Hyphens With Prefixes and Suffixes

Hyphens help your reader easily see the parts of a long word.

RULE 23.5.5 Use a hyphen after a prefix that is followed by a proper noun or proper adjective.

The following prefixes are often used before proper nouns: *ante-*, *anti-*, *mid-*, *post-*, *pre-*, *pro-*, and *un-*.

EXAMPLES pre - Civil War   mid - December

RULE 23.5.6 Use a hyphen in words with the prefixes *all-*, *ex-*, and *self-* and words with the suffix *-elect*.

EXAMPLES all - knowing   governor - elect

Many words with common prefixes are no longer hyphenated. Check a dictionary if you are unsure whether to use a hyphen.

Using Hyphens With Compound Words

Hyphens help preserve the units of meaning in compound words.

RULE 23.5.7 Use a hyphen to connect two or more words that are used as one compound word, unless your dictionary gives a different spelling.

EXAMPLES master - at - arms   follow - up

mother - in - law   two - year - old

RULE 23.5.8 Use a hyphen to connect a compound modifier that appears before a noun. The exceptions to this rule include adverbs ending in *-ly* and compound proper adjectives or compound proper nouns that are acting as an adjective.

EXAMPLES WITH HYPHENS	EXAMPLES WITHOUT HYPHENS
a well-made raincoat	widely distributed products
the bright-eyed class	Labor Day event
an up-to-date list	the North American Continent

When compound modifiers follow a noun, they generally do not require the use of hyphens.

EXAMPLE   The trucks were **well made.**

However, if a dictionary spells a word with a hyphen, the word must always be hyphenated, even when it follows a noun.

EXAMPLE   The attendance list was up-to-date.

Using Hyphens for Clarity

Some words or group of words can be misread if a hyphen is not used.

See Practice 23.5A

See Practice 23.5B

> **Use a hyphen within a word when a combination of letters might otherwise be confusing.**

 23.5.9 RULE

EXAMPLES   weak-kneed, well-being, well-to-do

> **Use a hyphen between words to keep readers from combining them incorrectly.**

23.5.10 RULE

INCORRECT   the air conditioning-unit

CORRECT   the air-conditioning unit

PRACTICE 23.5A > **Using Hyphens Correctly**

Read each sentence. Then, write the words that need hyphenation, adding hyphens where necessary.

EXAMPLE   My brother in law sold me his car.

ANSWER   *brother-in-law*

1. Rose just met her four-year-old cousin for the first time.

2. Mr. Klein is a well-respected teacher at the high school.

3. Two thirds of the senior students plan on attending the last-minute study session.

4. One of the coowners sold his share of the business.   *Co-owners*

5. George is still interested in board games even though he is thirty-three years old.

6. I enjoyed the performance even though a reviewer deemed it second-rate.

7. The cruise we took to New Zealand was all-inclusive.

8. I will celebrate my twenty-first birthday on December 17.

9. Manuel works two part-time jobs to earn extra money.

10. The low-end model of the radio is inexpensive but may not operate very long.

PRACTICE 23.5B > **Revising Sentences With Hyphens**

Read each sentence. Then, rewrite each sentence, correcting any error in hyphenation. If the punctuation is correct, write *correct*.

EXAMPLE   That political party has ultra conservative ideas.

ANSWER   *That political party has ultra-conservative ideas.*

11. The governor-elect had close ties to the attorney-general.

12. My great-great-grandfather was a blacksmith in his day.   *dimly lit*

13. I walked into the dimly-lit room hoping to find the light switch.

14. The editor-in-chief of the local newspaper is an Ivy League graduate.   *self-educated*

15. The fact that he is selfeducated is a testament to his perseverance.

16. Max lost the race by only one-hundredth of a second.   *one hundredth*

17. Rhiannon told us that she aspires to be a singer-song writer.

18. It is a little-known fact that Monique is an accomplished-piano player.

19. The computers in the school all have up-to-date programs installed.

20. I didn't remember to add one-half cup of milk to the batter.

SPEAKING APPLICATION

Take turns with a partner. Describe the place where you grew up. Include hyphenated words in your sentences. Your partner should listen for and identify the hyphenated words.

WRITING APPLICATION

Write a paragraph describing someone you admire. Use at least four hyphenated words not used in Practice 23.5B in your paragraph.

Using Hyphens at the Ends of Lines

Hyphens help you keep the lines in your paragraphs more even, making your work easier to read.

Dividing Words at the End of a Line

Although you should try to avoid dividing a word at the end of a line, if a word must be broken, use a hyphen to show the division.

> **If a word must be divided at the end of a line, always divide it between syllables.**

23.5.11 RULE

EXAMPLE   Kate got up early the last day of June, hop-

ing to see everything that had been planned.

> **A hyphen used to divide a word should never be placed at the beginning of the second line. It must be placed at the end of the first line.**

23.5.12 RULE

INCORRECT   The boat sailed around the island and col

-lected passengers at each stop.

CORRECT   The boat sailed around the island and col-

lected passengers at each stop.

Using Hyphens Correctly to Divide Words

One-syllable words cannot be divided.

> **Do not divide one-syllable words even if they seem long or sound like words with two syllables.**

23.5.13 RULE

INCORRECT   tre-at   mou-se   fe-nce

CORRECT   treat   mouse   fence

RULE **23.5.14** Do not divide a word so that a single letter or the letters *-ed* stand alone.

INCORRECT	a-larm	stud-y	a-loud	abandon-ed
CORRECT	alarm	study	aloud	abandoned

RULE **23.5.15** Avoid dividing proper nouns and proper adjectives.

INCORRECT	Fe-lix	Af-rican
CORRECT	Felix	African

RULE **23.5.16** Divide a hyphenated word only after the hyphen.

INCORRECT We happily made plans to invite my moth-
er-in-law to see the children.

CORRECT We happily made plans to invite my mother-in-
law to see the children.

RULE **23.5.17** Avoid dividing a word so that part of the word is on one page and the remainder is on the next page.

Often, chopping up a word in this way will confuse your readers or cause them to lose their train of thought. If this happens, rewrite the sentence or move the entire word to the next page.

See Practice 23.5C
See Practice 23.5D

PRACTICE 23.5C > **Using Hyphens to Divide Words**

Read each word. If a word has been divided incorrectly, write the word, putting the hyphen in the correct place, or writing it as one word if it cannot be divided. If the word has been divided correctly, write *correct*.

EXAMPLE   dre-am

ANSWER   *dream*

1. African-American
2. ap-pear
3. a-bove
4. Ju-lia
5. em-pty-handed
6. sev-enteen
7. cor-rectly
8. guilt-y
9. Ital-ian
10. blue-berry

PRACTICE 23.5D > **Correcting Divided Words at the End of Lines**

Read each sentence. Then, for each sentence, rewrite the incorrectly divided word, putting the hyphen in the correct place, or writing it as one word if it cannot be divided.

EXAMPLE   A peacock has brighter-colored feat-hers than a peahen.

ANSWER   *fea-thers*

11. The new student in chemistry class answer-ed almost all the questions correctly.
12. Mr. Walters wants the exhibit to be a se-cret until the unveiling.
13. Collecting all the mail once a day is a timesa-ving procedure.
14. Drama, music, band, and other extracurr-icular activities are educational programs.
15. Mike can't leave until his older brother Jer-ry comes home.
16. Giorgio bought his grandmother a knitt-ed shawl.
17. The night was so hot, but the air-condit-ioned room was comfortable.
18. I can see spring flowers—tulips and daff-odils—poking up through the soil.
19. "During our next summer vacation," said Tim-othy, "I'll be working at the town pool."
20. Jenny spent her summer at a camp far a-way from the city.

SPEAKING APPLICATION

Take turns with a partner. Say five words not used in Practice 23.5C. Your partner should tell where each word can be divided.

WRITING APPLICATION

Write a paragraph about the importance of eating healthy foods. Be sure to include divided words at the ends of lines.

23.6 Apostrophes

The **apostrophe (')** is used to form possessives, contractions, and a few special plurals.

Using Apostrophes to Form Possessive Nouns

Apostrophes are used with nouns to show ownership or possession.

RULE **23.6.1**

Add an apostrophe and -s to show the possessive case of most singular nouns.

EXAMPLES
the shoes of the girl   the girl's shoes

the leash of the dog   the dog's leash

Even when a singular noun already ends in -s, you can usually add an apostrophe and -s to show possession. However, names that end in the *eez* sound get an apostrophe, but not an -s.

EXAMPLE
The Ganges' source is in the Himalayas.

For classical references that end in -s, only an apostrophe is used.

EXAMPLES
Confucius' writings   Zeus' crown

RULE **23.6.2**

Add an apostrophe to show the possessive case of plural nouns ending in -s or -es.

EXAMPLE
the branches of the trees   the trees' branches

RULE **23.6.3**

Add an apostrophe and an -s to show the possessive case of plural nouns that do not end in -s or -es.

EXAMPLE   the toys of the children

              the children**'s** toys

> Add an apostrophe and *-s* (or just an apostrophe if the word is a plural ending in *-s*) to the last word of a compound noun to form the possessive.

RULE 23.6.4

APOSTROPHES THAT SHOW POSSESSION	
Names of Businesses and Organizations	the Salvation Army**'**s office the National Park**'**s watch tower the Richardson & Associates**'** client list
Titles of Rulers or Leaders	Catherine the Great**'**s victories Louis XVI**'**s palace the head of the board**'**s decision
Hyphenated Compound Nouns Used to Describe People	my mother-in-law**'**s recipe the secretary-treasurer**'**s planner the nurse-practitioner**'**s files

> To form possessives involving time, amounts, or the word *sake,* use an apostrophe and an *-s* or just an apostrophe if the possessive is plural.

RULE 23.6.5

APOSTROPHES WITH POSSESSIVES	
Time	a week**'**s vacation three months**'** vacation an hour**'**s drive
Amount	one dollar**'**s worth twenty-five cents**'** worth
Sake	for Rebekah**'**s sake for the horses**'** sake

To show joint ownership, make the final noun possessive.
To show individual ownership, make each noun possessive.

JOINT OWNERSHIP	I enjoyed Bill and Deb's documentary.
INDIVIDUAL OWNERSHIP	Mike's and Alan's dry cleaning is hanging here.

Use the owner's complete name before the apostrophe to form the possessive case.

INCORRECT SINGULAR	Jame's car
CORRECT SINGULAR	James's car
INCORRECT PLURAL	four girl's bags
CORRECT PLURAL	four girls' bags

Using Apostrophes With Pronouns

Both indefinite and personal pronouns can show possession.

Use an apostrophe and -s with indefinite pronouns to show possession.

EXAMPLES	somebody's dress shoes
	each other's study guides

Do not use an apostrophe with possessive personal pronouns; their form already shows ownership.

EXAMPLES	his cards	our boat	his black convertible
	its mirrors	their yard	whose coat

Be careful not to confuse the contractions *who's*, *it's*, and *they're* with possessive pronouns. They are contractions for *who is*, *it is* or *it has*, and *they are*. Remember also that *whose*, *its*, and *their* show possession.

PRONOUNS	CONTRACTIONS
Whose homework is this?	*Who's* driving home tonight?
Its tires were all flat.	*It's* going to be sunny.
Their dinner is ready.	*They're going to the movies.*

Using Apostrophes to Form Contractions

Contractions are used in informal speech and writing. You can often find contractions in the dialogue of stories and plays; they often create the sound of real speech.

> **Use an apostrophe in a contraction to show the position of the missing letter or letters.**

23.6.9 RULE

COMMON CONTRACTIONS			
Verb + *not*	cannot	can't	are not	aren't
	could not	couldn't	will not	won't
Pronoun + *will*	he will	he'll	I will	I'll
	you will	you'll	we will	we'll
	she will	she'll	they will	they'll
Pronoun + *would*	she would	she'd	I would	I'd
	he would	he'd	we would	we'd
	you would	you'd	they would	they'd
Noun or Pronoun + *be*	you are	you're	I am	I'm
	she is	she's	Jane is	Jane's
	they are	they're	dog is	dog's

Still another type of contraction is found in poetry.

EXAMPLES   e'en *(even)*   o'er *(over)*

Other contractions represent the abbreviated form of *of the* and *the* as they are written in several different languages. These letters are most often combined with surnames.

EXAMPLES   O'Neil

d'Armiento

o'clock

l'Abbé

Using Contractions to Represent Speaking Styles
A final use of contractions is for representing individual speaking styles in dialogue. As noted previously, you will often want to use contractions with verbs in dialogue. You may also want to approximate a regional dialect or a foreign accent, which may include nonstandard pronunciations of words or omitted letters. However, you should avoid overusing contractions in dialogue. Overuse reduces the effectiveness of the apostrophe.

EXAMPLES   "Hey, ol' buddy. How you feelin'?"

"Don' you be foolin' me."

Using Apostrophes to Create Special Plurals

Apostrophes can help avoid confusion with special plurals.

> Use an apostrophe and *-s* to create the plural form of a letter, numeral, symbol, or a word that is used as a name for itself.

EXAMPLES   *A*'s and *an*'s cause confusion.

There are four *4*'s in that number.

I don't like to hear *if*'s or *maybe*'s.

Form groups of *4*'s or *5*'s.

I need four more *?*'s

See Practice 23.6A
See Practice 23.6B

PRACTICE 23.6A ▸ Identifying the Use of Apostrophes

Read each sentence. Then, tell if each apostrophe is used to form a *possessive*, a *contraction*, or a *special plural*.

EXAMPLE   Who's in charge of the fundraiser at school next week?

ANSWER   *contraction*

1. Ben and Sara's dog, Max, is a miniature poodle. *Possessive*

2. Steven received 3 A's and 2 B's on his report card. *S.P*

3. The Williamses' sailboat is docked at the Center Point marina. *Possessive*

4. Katrina's backpack can't hold many books. *Poss/Cont*

5. Matt's comic book is the latest issue. *Poss*

6. That New York ZIP Code has three 1's. *S.P*

7. The cat's hiding under my bed. *Contraction*

8. Somebody's computer was left on overnight. *Poss*

9. I can't believe it's Friday already. *Contraction*

10. When you revise your paper, try to take out any unnecessary and's. *S.P*

PRACTICE 23.6B ▸ Revising to Add Apostrophes

Read each sentence. Then, rewrite each sentence, adding apostrophes where they are needed.

EXAMPLE   Garret received all As on his reports and research papers.

ANSWER   *Garret received all A's on his reports and research papers.*

11. The way Rob writes his p's and q's is very similar.

12. That sweater is someone else's, not mine.

13. When you revise your paper, try to delete some of the that's.

14. I went to Eric's house after school yesterday.

15. Didn't Candace tell Ms. O'connor that she'd be back by eight o'clock?

16. Sometimes, Max mixes up his 6's and his 9's.

17. I think Z's are the most difficult letter to write in cursive.

18. Our new neighbor's pool is bigger than ours.

19. It's a beautiful day in Houston, Texas.

20. The child's outside, playing with her older siblings.

SPEAKING APPLICATION

Take turns with a partner. Say different sentences with words that indicate possession, contractions, and special plurals. Your partner should tell how each word uses an apostrophe.

WRITING APPLICATION

Write five sentences with words that require apostrophes. The words should show possession, contractions, and special plurals.

23.7 Parentheses and Brackets

Parentheses enclose explanations or other information that may be omitted from the rest of the sentence without changing its basic meaning or construction. Using parentheses is a stronger, more noticeable way to set off a parenthetical expression than using commas. **Brackets** are used to enclose a word or phrase added by a writer to the words of another.

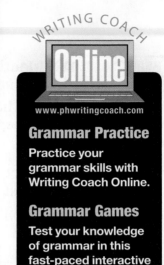

WRITING COACH

Online

www.phwritingcoach.com

Grammar Practice
Practice your grammar skills with Writing Coach Online.

Grammar Games
Test your knowledge of grammar in this fast-paced interactive video game.

Parentheses

Parentheses help you group material within a sentence.

RULE 23.7.1 > Use parentheses to set off information when the material is not essential or when it consists of one or more sentences.

EXAMPLE   End-of-the-month reports **(** on economics and trade **)** showed much improvement over last month.

RULE 23.7.2 > Use parentheses to set off numerical explanations such as dates of a person's birth and death and around numbers and letters marking a series.

EXAMPLES   Jill Collins invented many types of pie with the help of her husband, Rick **(**1946–2008**)**.

Go home and pack these items: **(**1**)** toothbrush, **(**2**)** pajamas, **(**3**)** sneakers.

Which is your favorite team: **(**a**)** Yankees, **(**b**)** Red Sox, or **(**c**)** Phillies?

Although material enclosed in parentheses is not essential to the meaning of the sentence, a writer indicates that the material is important and calls attention to it by using parentheses.

> When a phrase or declarative sentence interrupts another sentence, do not use an initial capital letter or end mark inside the parentheses.

RULE 23.7.3

EXAMPLE   Daryl finally completed his trip **(** the one we all planned together **)** and came home last night.

> When a question or exclamation interrupts another sentence, use both an initial capital letter and an end mark inside the parentheses.

RULE 23.7.4

EXAMPLE   Lucy **(** She is one funny lady **!** **)** continues to entertain us.

> When you place a sentence in parentheses between two other sentences, use both an initial capital letter and an end mark inside the parentheses.

RULE 23.7.5

EXAMPLE   America's parks are known to be breath-taking. **(** See the Grand Canyon as an example **.** **)** Excesses of nature are staggering to see.

> In a sentence that includes parentheses, place any punctuation belonging to the main sentence after the final parenthesis.

RULE 23.7.6

EXAMPLE   The town council approved the library **(** after some deliberations **)** **,** and they explained the new lending laws to the citizens **(** with some doubts about how the changes would be received **)** **.**

Special Uses of Parentheses

Parentheses are used to set off numerical explanations such as birth and death dates and numbers or letters marking a series.

EXAMPLES   Charles Dickens (1812–1870) was a popular English novelist.

Betty's phone number is (313) 515-8299.

Her group tour will take her to (1) Brazil, (2) Columbia, and (3) Argentina.

Brackets

Brackets are used to enclose a word or phrase added by a writer to the words of another writer.

> Use brackets to enclose words you insert in quotations when quoting someone else.

See Practice 23.7A
See Practice 23.7B

EXAMPLES   Cooper noted: "And with *[E.T.'s]* success, 'Phone home' is certain to become one of the most often repeated phrases of the year [1982]."

"The results of this vote [24–6] indicate overwhelming support for our building plan," she stated.

The Latin expression *sic* (meaning "thus") is sometimes enclosed in brackets to show that the author of the quoted material has misspelled or mispronounced a word or phrase.

EXAMPLE   Michaelson, citing Dorothy's signature line from *The Wizard of Oz,* wrote, "Theirs [sic] no place like home."

PRACTICE 23.7A > Using Parentheses and Brackets Correctly

Read each item. Then, write a sentence in which you enclose the item in either parentheses or brackets.

EXAMPLE   around 5 o'clock

ANSWER   *We will arrive at the reception a little late (around 5 o'clock).*

1. everyone could tell

2. I can't wait!

3. at Tillman Middle School

4. known as "Hotshot" to his teammates

5. Did you know?

6. 4:00 P.M. to 6:00 P.M.   *We're going to Jess's house at that time (4-6)*

7. the former state champion

8. the one in the red dress

9. sic   *(thus)*

10. my least favorite flavor

PRACTICE 23.7B > Revising to Add Parentheses or Brackets

Read each sentence. Then, add parentheses or brackets wherever they are appropriate.

EXAMPLE   The article stated, "Mr. Jones the superintendent is up for re-election."

ANSWER   *The article stated, "Mr. Jones [the superintendent] is up for re-election."*

11. My dog Jasper is a cocker spaniel.

12. The results of the vote 145–98 indicate that Jim will be the student-council president.

13. We my sister and I are donating canned goods to a soup kitchen.

14. Once I finally fell asleep sometime around 10:00 P.M., I had very vivid dreams.

15. This museum displays artifacts from an ancient civilization Mesopotamia.

16. They our high school lacrosse team are the best team in the state.

17. Could you help me dry the dishes, please?

18. The proverb states, "Luv sic is a puppy!"

19. Lucy and Alijah They're nice girls, aren't they? are the captains of the soccer team.

20. The article said, "He the president has left to pursue other opportunities."

SPEAKING APPLICATION

Take turns with a partner. Say three phrases. Your partner should put the phrases into sentences, indicating if the phrases would be appropriate in parentheses or brackets.

WRITING APPLICATION

Write three sentences about events in world history. Your sentences should correctly use either parentheses or brackets.

23.8 Ellipses, Dashes, and Slashes

An **ellipsis (. . .)** shows where words have been omitted from a quoted passage. It can also mark a pause or interruption in dialogue. A **dash (—)** shows a strong, sudden break in thought or speech. A **slash (/)** separates numbers in dates and fractions, shows line breaks in quoted poetry, and represents *or*. A slash is also used to separate the parts of a Web address.

Using the Ellipsis

An **ellipsis** is three evenly spaced periods, or ellipsis points, in a row. Always include a space before the first ellipsis point, between ellipsis points, and after the last ellipsis point. (The plural of *ellipsis* is *ellipses*.)

RULE 23.8.1

> Use an **ellipsis** to show where words have been omitted from a quoted passage.

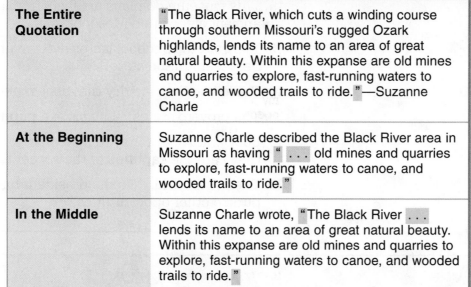

ELLIPSES IN QUOTATIONS	
The Entire Quotation	"The Black River, which cuts a winding course through southern Missouri's rugged Ozark highlands, lends its name to an area of great natural beauty. Within this expanse are old mines and quarries to explore, fast-running waters to canoe, and wooded trails to ride."—Suzanne Charle
At the Beginning	Suzanne Charle described the Black River area in Missouri as having " . . . old mines and quarries to explore, fast-running waters to canoe, and wooded trails to ride."
In the Middle	Suzanne Charle wrote, "The Black River . . . lends its name to an area of great natural beauty. Within this expanse are old mines and quarries to explore, fast-running waters to canoe, and wooded trails to ride."
At the End	Suzanne Charle wrote, "The Black River, which cuts a winding course through southern Missouri's rugged Ozark highlands, lends its name to an area of great natural beauty. . . . "

RULE 23.8.2

Use an ellipsis to mark a pause in a dialogue or speech.

EXAMPLE   The coach shouted, "On your mark . . . get set . . . go!"

Dashes

A **dash** signals a stronger, more sudden interruption in thought or speech than commas or parentheses. A dash may also take the place of certain words before an explanation. Overuse of the dash diminishes its effectiveness. Consider the proper use of the dash in the rule below.

RULE 23.8.3

Use dashes to indicate an abrupt change of thought, a dramatic interrupting idea, or a summary statement.

USING DASHES IN WRITING	
To indicate an abrupt change of thought	The magazine doesn't provide enough information on Italian cooking—by the way, where did you get the magazine?
	I cannot believe how many e-mails my mother hasn't answered—I need to talk to her about that.
To set off interrupting ideas dramatically	The school was built—you may find this hard to believe—in six months.
	The school was built—Where did they get the money and workers?—in six months.
To set off a summary statement	A solid sports background and strong writing skills—if you have these, you may be able to get a job as a sports reporter.
	To see his picture on the stage with the band—this was his dream.

Use dashes to set off a nonessential appositive or modifier when it is long, when it is already punctuated, or when you want to be dramatic.

APPOSITIVE | The cause of the damage to the bathroom tiles and the cabinets—a rare black mold—went undiscovered for months.

MODIFIER | The celebrity gossip columnist—bored with writing about spoiled movie stars—quit after the awards.

Dashes may be used to set off one other special type of sentence interrupter—the parenthetical expression.

Use dashes to set off a parenthetical expression when it is long, already punctuated, or especially dramatic.

EXAMPLE | Today, we visited a theater—what an entertaining place—in a small town.

Slashes

A **slash** is used to separate numbers in dates and fractions, lines of quoted poetry, or options. Slashes are also used to separate parts of a Web address.

Use slashes to separate the day, month, and year in dates and to separate the numerator and denominator in numerical fractions.

DATES | He listed his deployment date as 10/30/08.

My sister's first day of college was 9/2/09.

FRACTIONS | 5/7   3/4   1/3

RULE 23.8.7

Use slashes to indicate line breaks in up to three lines of quoted poetry in continuous text. Insert a space on each side of the slash.

EXAMPLE   I used a quote from William Blake, "Tyger! Tyger! burning bright. **/** In the forests if the night," to begin my paper.

RULE 23.8.8

Use slashes to separate choices or options and to represent the words *and* and *or.*

EXAMPLES   Choose your bun: sesame **/** seedless **/** rye.

Each hiker should bring a water bottle and gloves **/** rope.

You can e-mail and **/** or mail the last page of the article.

RULE 23.8.9

Use slashes to separate parts of a Web address.

EXAMPLES   http: **//** www.fafsa.ed.gov **/**
(for financial aid for students)

http: **//** www.whitehouse.gov **/**
(the White House)

http: **//** www.si.edu **/**
(the Smithsonian Institution)

See Practice 23.8A
See Practice 23.8B

PRACTICE 23.8A > Using Ellipses, Dashes, and Slashes Correctly

Read each sentence or phrase. Then, rewrite each sentence, adding dashes, ellipses, or slashes where appropriate.

EXAMPLE I can't answer right now could you come back later?

ANSWER *I can't answer right now—could you come back later?*

1. The home Web address for NASA is http://www.nasa.gov.

2. When I visit my grandmother she lives in Hawaii I spend a lot of time at the beach.

3. "Do you think I could uh join you?" he asked hesitantly.

4. The committee elected Eugene to be the next chairperson actually, it was a unanimous decision.

5. "Once upon a time"

6. Mr. Ramirez is the president/owner of the company.

7. Italian food chicken parmesan, meatballs, and pasta is my favorite cuisine.

8. Candidates must possess a degree in French and or have worked in a French-speaking country.

9. The meteor it's shooting across the sky!

10. The glass is 34 full of milk.

PRACTICE 23.8B > Revising Sentences With Ellipses, Dashes, and Slashes

Read each sentence. Then, use ellipses, dashes, or slashes to add or delete the information in parentheses to or from each sentence.

EXAMPLE The leader is Marie. (Add *captain*.)

ANSWER *The leader/captain is Marie.*

11. A colorful rainbow arched across the sky. (Add *and I do mean colorful*.)

12. "The team performed well and succeeded." (Delete *performed well and*.)

13. My sister is always there for me. (Add *my best friend*.)

14. Each student must have his permission slip signed by a parent. (Add *note*.)

15. I hope I get Professor Alexander next semester. (Add *the English professor*.)

16. "Despite the cold weather and the rain, the trip was a success." (Delete *and the rain*.)

17. The soccer team had the most people try out. (Add *the most popular sports team*.)

18. The show was a success. (add *it exceeded everyone's expectations*.)

19. The room will be painted blue and tan. (Add *or*.)

20. "My cousin who lives in Tampa picked me up from the airport." (Delete *who lives in Tampa*.)

SPEAKING APPLICATION

Take turns with a partner. Say different sentences that, if written, would contain dashes, ellipses, or slashes. Your partner should tell which punctuation is appropriate in each sentence.

WRITING APPLICATION

Write five sentences. Alter each sentence by using dashes or slashes to add information.

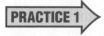 **PRACTICE 1** Using Periods, Question Marks, and Exclamation Marks

Read each sentence. Rewrite each sentence, adding question marks, periods, and exclamation marks where needed.

1. Oh, no I was supposed to be there by now

2. He didn't come home on time last night Why

3. Put your books away, and take out your pens

4. She wondered if tomorrow would be warmer

5. How coincidental it is that we should happen upon one another like this

6. That was such a dynamic interview

7. She eagerly anticipated the next performance

8. Martin Luther King Jr. was a very well-spoken individual

9. Did you have to take the earlier appointment

10. Pay attention to the instructions

PRACTICE 2 Using Commas Correctly

Read each sentence. Rewrite each sentence, adding commas where needed. If a sentence is correct as is, write *correct*.

1. Isaac said "I thought you attended that conference in April 2008."

2. "Katrina do you think you could loan me your dress for the dance?" Erica asked.

3. Expecting a crowd Sam arrived early.

4. The menu had appetizers salads entrees and desserts printed in an elegant font.

5. "Her birthday is May 2 1991" Kristen said.

6. Mike and Matt always got the best concert tickets because they waited in line for hours.

7. I usually bring my lunch to work but today I am going out to eat.

8. This dessert is a scrumptious, delicious end to a perfect meal.

9. "The store is over on Girard Avenue," Paul said. "The address is 616 Girard Avenue Plainville Kansas."

10. I wanted the red blouse not the green one.

PRACTICE 3 Using Colons, Semicolons, and Quotation Marks

Read each sentence. Rewrite each sentence, using colons, semicolons, and quotation marks where needed. If a sentence is correct as is, write *correct*.

1. Warning Dangerous curves ahead.

2. Samantha wrote her book review on *To Kill a Mockingbird* she thought the characters were well developed.

3. John said, We did a lot on our camping trip last summer swimming, fishing, hiking, and boating.

4. I usually try to get to bed by 1000 every night the alarm buzzing at 700 comes all too soon.

5. Melissa told us where the best gourmet restaurants were.

6. They each chose a topic for their science projects Fred volcanic activity Lyla erosion and Tim photosynthesis.

7. Mallory didn't want to be bothered with any more work however, she volunteered to help the team brainstorm new ideas.

8. The teacher read us O Captain! My Captain, by Walt Whitman it is a poem about Lincoln.

9. Resolved The cafeteria will no longer serve soft drinks.

10. Gus brought a list of his favorite foods hamburgers, fries, salad, and cookies.

Continued on next page ▶

Cumulative Review Chapters 22–23

PRACTICE 4 > **Using Apostrophes**

Read each sentence. Rewrite each sentence, using apostrophes where needed. If a sentence is correct as is, write *correct*.

1. I wouldnt bother Mom right now; shes busy.

2. Whos organizing this years fundraiser?

3. My brother-in-laws car is brand new.

4. Mr. Joness study had towers of books.

5. Henry brought two hundred dollars worth of supplies for the homecoming party.

6. Zeus thunderbolt is a symbol of his immense power over the other Greek gods.

7. Sabrina's project was better than theirs.

8. I dont know the answer to this problem; its too complicated.

9. Taras car needs work and is in the shop.

10. At 6 oclock, my family sits down to dinner.

PRACTICE 5 > **Using Underlining (or Italics), Hyphens, Dashes, Slashes, Parentheses, Brackets, and Ellipses**

Read each sentence. Rewrite each sentence, adding underlining (or italics), hyphens, dashes, slashes, brackets, parentheses, or ellipses. If a sentence is correct as is, write *correct*.

1. My brother and I often disagree about whether Star Wars is a better film than The Empire Strikes Back.

2. Simon he sits behind me in math always seems to know the answer.

3. My grandmother a well known essayist and poet is celebrating her ninety fifth birthday next week.

4. Tommy's dad he works for an advertising agency came to school on Career Day.

5. The USS Constitution a giant ship in the U.S. Navy was nicknamed Old Ironsides.

6. Before proceeding with the lecture, the professor gave the students a five minute break.

7. In his speech, the congressman said, "They taxes will not be raised during my term."

8. The play was set during the presidential term of Theodore Roosevelt 1901–1909.

9. The Gettysburg Address states that this nation ". . . is dedicated to the proposition that all men are created equal."

10. His baby sister was born on 12 22 2005.

PRACTICE 6 > **Using Capital Letters Correctly**

Read each sentence. Rewrite each sentence, using capital letters where they are needed.

1. mr. and mrs. o'callahan took a trip to dublin.

2. charles dickens, an english writer, wrote many works, including a christmas carol.

3. "i haven't been to the new american museum of art downtown yet," david said. "is it on main street or center street?"

4. the academy award for best picture went to a film that many people had not seen.

5. tina said, "today, i learned the names of many constellations, like aries and aquarius."

RESOURCES FOR
Writing
COACH

Writing in the content areas—math, social studies, science, the arts, and various career and technical studies—is an important tool for learning. The following pages give examples of content area writing along with strategies.

FORMS OF MATH WRITING

Written Estimate An estimate, or informed idea, of the size, cost, time, or other measure of a thing, based on given information.

Analysis of a Problem A description of a problem, such as figuring out how long a trip will take, along with an explanation of the mathematical formulas or equations you can use to solve the problem.

Response to an Open-Ended Math Prompt A response to a question or writing assignment involving math, such as a word problem or a question about a graph or a mathematical concept.

Writing in Math

Prewriting

- **Choosing a Topic** If you have a choice of topics, review your textbook and class notes for ideas, and choose one that interests you.

- **Responding to a Prompt** If you are responding to a prompt, read and then reread the instructions, ensuring that you understand all of the requirements of the assignment.

Drafting

- **State Problems Clearly** Be clear, complete, and accurate in your description of the problem you are analyzing or reporting on. Make sure that you have used technical terms, such as *ratio*, *area*, and *factor*, accurately.

- **Explain Your Solution** Tell readers exactly which mathematical rules or formulas you use in your analysis and why they apply. Clearly spell out each step you take in your reasoning.

- **Use Graphics** By presenting quantitative information in a graph, table, or chart, you make it easier for readers to absorb information. Choose the format appropriate to the material, as follows:

  ✓ **Line Graphs** Use a line graph to show the relationship between two variables, such as time and speed in a problem about a moving object. Clearly label the x- and y-axis with the variable each represents and with the units you are using. Choose units appropriately to make the graph manageable. For example, do not try to represent time in years if you are plotting changes for an entire century; instead, use units of ten years each.

  ✓ **Other Graphs** Use a pie chart to analyze facts about a group, such as the percentage of students who walk to school, the percentage who drive, and the percentage who take the bus. Use a bar graph to compare two or more things at different times or in different categories. Assign a single color to each thing, and use that color consistently for all the bars representing data about that thing.

  ✓ **Tables** Use a table to help readers look up specific values quickly, such as the time the sun sets in each month of the year. Label each column and row with terms that clearly identify the data you are presenting, including the units you are using.

Revising

- **Ensure Accuracy** For accuracy, double-check the formulas you use and the calculations you make.

- **Revise for Traits of Good Writing** Ask yourself the following questions: *How well have I applied mathematical ideas? Does my organizational plan help readers follow my reasoning? Is my voice suitable to my audience and purpose? Have I chosen precise words and used mathematical terms accurately? Are my sentences well constructed and varied? Have I made any errors in grammar, usage, mechanics, and spelling?* Use your answers to help you revise and edit your work.

Writing in Science

Prewriting

- **Choosing a Topic** If you have a choice of topics, look through class notes and your textbook, or conduct a "media flip-through," browsing online articles, or watching television news and documentaries to find a science-related topic.

- **Responding to a Prompt** If you are responding to a prompt, read the instructions carefully, analyzing the requirements and parts of the assignment. Identify key direction words in the prompt or assignment, such as *explain* and *predict*.

- **Gathering Details**
  - ✔ If your assignment requires you to conduct research, search for credible and current sources. Examples of strong sources may include articles in recent issues of science magazines or recently published books. Confirm key facts in more than one source.
  - ✔ If your assignment requires you to conduct an experiment, make sure you follow the guidelines for the experiment accurately. Carefully record the steps you take and the observations you make, and date your notes. Repeat the experiment to confirm results.

Drafting

- **Focus and Elaborate** In your introduction, clearly state your topic. Make sure you tell readers why your topic matters. As you draft, give sufficient details, including background, facts, and examples, to help your readers understand your topic. Summarize your findings and insights in your conclusion.

- **Organize** As you draft, follow a suitable organizational pattern. If you are telling the story of an important scientific breakthrough, consider telling events in chronological order. If you are explaining a natural process, consider discussing causes and the effects that follow from them. If you are defending a solution to a problem, you might give pros and cons, answering each counterargument in turn.

- **Present Data Visually** Consider presenting quantitative information, such as statistics or measurements, in a graph, table, or chart. Choose the format appropriate to the material. (Consult the guidance on visual displays of data under "Use Graphics" on page R2.)

Revising

- **Meet Your Audience's Needs** Identify places in your draft where your audience may need more information, such as additional background, more explanation, or the definition of a technical term. Add the information required.

- **Revise for Traits of Good Writing** Ask yourself the following questions: *How clearly have I presented scientific ideas? Will my organization help a reader see the connections I am making? Is my voice suitable to my audience and purpose? Have I chosen precise words and used technical terms accurately? Are my sentences well constructed and varied? Have I made any errors in grammar, usage, mechanics, and spelling?* Use your answers to revise and edit your work.

FORMS OF SCIENCE WRITING

Lab Report A firsthand report of a scientific experiment, following an appropriate format. A standard lab report includes a statement of the hypothesis, or prediction, that the experiment is designed to test; a list of the materials used; an account of the steps performed; a report of the results observed; and the experimenter's conclusions.

Cause-and-Effect Essay A scientific explanation of the causes and effects involved in natural or technical phenomena, such as solar flares, the digestion of food, or the response of metal to stress.

Technical Procedure Document A step-by-step guide to performing a scientific experiment or performing a technical task involving science. A well-written technical procedure document presents the steps of the procedure in clear order. It breaks steps into substeps and prepares readers by explaining what materials they will need and the time they can expect each step to take.

Response to an Open-Ended Science Prompt A response to a question or writing assignment about science.

Summary of a Science-Related Article A retelling of the main ideas in an article that concerns science or technology, such as an article on a new medical procedure.

Writing in Social Studies

FORMS OF SOCIAL STUDIES WRITING

Social Studies Research Report
An informative paper, based on research, about a historical period or event or about a specific place or culture. A well-written research report draws on a variety of sources to develop and support a thoughtful point of view on the topic. It cites those sources accurately, following an accepted format.

Biographical Essay An overview of the life of a historically important person. A well-written biographical essay reports the life of its subject accurately and clearly explains the importance of his or her contributions.

Historical Overview A survey, or general picture, of a historical period or development, such as the struggle for women's right to vote. A successful historical overview presents the "big picture," covering major events and important aspects of the topic without getting lost in details.

Historical Cause-and-Effect Essay An analysis of the causes and effects of a historical event. A well-written historical explanation makes clear connections between events to help readers follow the explanation.

Prewriting

- **Choosing a Topic** If you have a choice of topics, find a suitable topic by looking through class notes and your textbook. Make a quick list of topics in history, politics, or geography that interest you and choose a topic based on your list.

- **Responding to a Prompt** If you are responding to a prompt, read the instructions carefully, analyzing the requirements and parts of the assignment. Identify key direction words in the prompt or assignment, such as *compare*, *describe*, and *argue*.

- **Gathering Details** If your assignment requires you to conduct research, consult a variety of credible sources. For in-depth research, review both primary sources (documents from the time you are investigating) and secondary sources (accounts by those who analyze or report on the information). If you find contradictions, evaluate the likely reasons for the differences.

Drafting

- **Establish a Thesis or Theme** If you are writing a research report or other informative piece, state your main point about your topic in a thesis statement. Include your thesis statement in your introduction. If you are writing a creative piece, such as a historical skit or short story, identify the theme, or main message, you wish to convey.

- **Support Your Thesis or Theme** Organize your work around your main idea.

  ✔ In a research report, support and develop your thesis with well-chosen, relevant details. First, provide background information your readers will need, and then discuss different subtopics in different sections of the body of your report. Clearly connect each subtopic to your main thesis.

  ✔ In a creative work, develop your theme through the conflict between characters. For example, a conflict between two brothers during the Civil War over which side to fight on might dramatize the theme of divided loyalties. Organize events to build to a climax, or point of greatest excitement, that clearly conveys your message.

Revising

- **Sharpen Your Focus** Review your draft for sections that do not clearly support your thesis or theme, and consider eliminating them. Revise unnecessary repetition of ideas. Ensure that the sequence of ideas or events will help reader comprehension.

- **Revise for Traits of Good Writing** Ask yourself the following questions: *How clearly have I developed my thesis or my theme? Will my organization help a reader follow my development of my thesis or theme? Is my voice suitable to my audience and purpose? Have I chosen precise and vivid words, accurately using terms from the period or place about which I am writing? Are my sentences well constructed and varied? Have I made any errors in grammar, usage, mechanics, and spelling?* Use your answers to revise and edit your work.

Writing About the Arts

Prewriting

Experience the Work Take notes on the subject of each work you will discuss. Consider its mood, or general feeling, and its theme, or insight into life.

- ✔ For visual arts, consider the use of color, light, line (sharp or smooth, smudged or definite), mass (heavy or light), and composition (the arrangement and balance of forms).
- ✔ For music, consider the use of melody, rhythm, harmony, and instrumentation. Also, consider the performers' interpretation of the work.

Drafting

Develop Your Ideas As you draft, support your main ideas, including your insights into or feelings about a work, with relevant details.

Revising

Revise for Traits of Good Writing Ask yourself the following questions: *How clearly do I present my ideas? Will my organization help a reader follow my points? Is my voice suitable to my audience and purpose? Have I chosen precise and vivid words, to describe the works? Are my sentences varied? Have I made any errors in grammar, usage, and mechanics?* Use your answers to revise and edit your work.

Writing in Career and Technical Studies

Prewriting

Choosing a Topic If you have a choice of topics, find a suitable one by looking through class notes and your textbook or by listing your own related projects or experiences.

Drafting

Organize Information As you draft, follow a logical organization. If you are explaining a procedure, list steps in the order that your readers should follow. If they need information about the materials and preparation required, provide that information first. Use formatting (such as headings, numbered steps, and bullet points), graphics (such as diagrams), and transitional words and phrases (such as *first*, *next*, and *if… then*).

Revising

Revise for Traits of Good Writing Ask yourself the following questions: *Have I given readers all the information they will need? Will my organization help a reader follow my points? Is my voice suitable to my audience and purpose? Have I chosen precise words, using technical terms accurately? Are my sentences well constructed? Have I made errors in grammar, usage, and mechanics?* Use your answers to revise and edit your work.

FORMS OF WRITING ABOUT THE ARTS

Research Report on a Trend or Style in Art An informative paper, based on research, about a specific group of artists or trend in the arts.

Biographical Essay An overview of the life of an artist or performer.

Analysis of a Work A detailed description of a work offering insights into its meaning and importance.

Review of a Performance or Exhibit An evaluation of an artistic performance or exhibit.

FORMS OF CAREER AND TECHNICAL WRITING

Technical Procedure Document A step-by-step guide to performing a specialized task, such as wiring a circuit or providing first aid.

Response to an Open-Ended Practical Studies Prompt A response to a question or writing assignment about a task or concept in a specialized field.

Technical Research Report An informative paper, based on research, about a specific topic in a practical field, such as a report on balanced diet in the field of health.

Analysis of a Career An informative paper explaining the requirements for a particular job, along with the responsibilities, salary, benefits, and job opportunities.

WRITING FOR
Media

New technology has created many new ways to communicate. Today, it is easy to contribute information to the Internet and send a variety of messages to friends far and near. You can also share your ideas through photos, illustrations, video, and sound recordings.

Writing for Media gives you an overview of some ways you can use today's technology to create, share, and find information. **Here are the topics you will find in this section:**

- Blogs
- Social Networking
- Widgets and Feeds
- Multimedia Elements
- Podcasts
- Wikis

Blogs

A **blog** is a common form of online writing. The word *blog* is a contraction of *Web log*. Most blogs include a series of entries known as posts. The posts appear in a single column and are displayed in reverse chronological order. That means that the most recent post is at the top of the page. As you scroll down, you will find earlier posts.

Blogs have become increasingly popular. Researchers estimate that 75,000 new blogs are launched every day. Blog authors are often called bloggers. They can use their personal sites to share ideas, songs, videos, photos, and other media. People who read blogs can often post their responses with a comments feature found in each new post.

Because blogs are designed so that they are easy to update, bloggers can post new messages as often as they like, often daily. For some people blogs become a public journal or diary in which they share their thoughts about daily events.

Types of Blogs

Not all blogs are the same. Many blogs have a single author, but others are group projects. These are some common types of blog:

- **Personal blogs** often have a general focus. Bloggers post their thoughts on any topic they find interesting in their daily lives.

- **Topical blogs** focus on a specific theme, such as movie reviews, political news, class assignments, or health-care opportunities.

WEB SAFETY Using the Internet safely means keeping personal information personal. Never include your address (e-mail or physical), last name, or telephone numbers. Avoid mentioning places you go to often.

Never give out passwords you use to access other Web sites and do not respond to e-mails from people you do not know.

Anatomy of a Blog

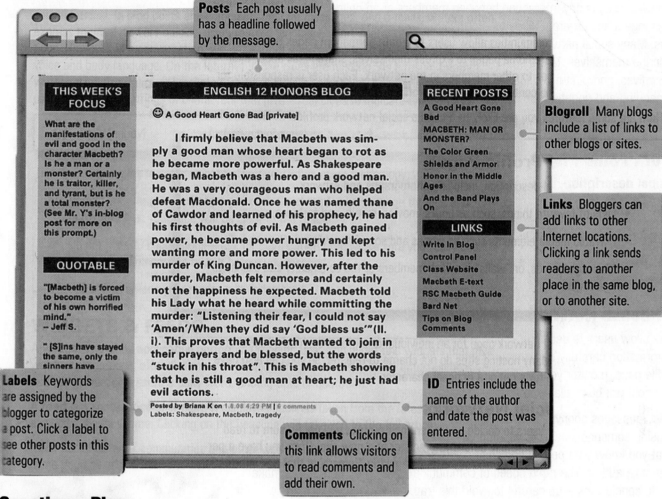

Posts Each post usually has a headline followed by the message.

THIS WEEK'S FOCUS

What are the manifestations of evil and good in the character Macbeth? Is he a man or a monster? Certainly he is traitor, killer, and tyrant, but is he a total monster? (See Mr. Y's in-blog post for more on this prompt.)

QUOTABLE

"[Macbeth] is forced to become a victim of his own horrified mind."
– Jeff S.

"[S]ins have stayed the same, only the sinners have

ENGLISH 12 HONORS BLOG

☺ A Good Heart Gone Bad [private]

    I firmly believe that Macbeth was simply a good man whose heart began to rot as he became more powerful. As Shakespeare began, Macbeth was a hero and a good man. He was a very courageous man who helped defeat Macdonald. Once he was named thane of Cawdor and learned of his prophecy, he had his first thoughts of evil. As Macbeth gained power, he became power hungry and kept wanting more and more power. This led to his murder of King Duncan. However, after the murder, Macbeth felt remorse and certainly not the happiness he expected. Macbeth told his Lady what he heard while committing the murder: "Listening their fear, I could not say 'Amen'/When they did say 'God bless us'"(II. i). This proves that Macbeth wanted to join in their prayers and be blessed, but the words "stuck in his throat". This is Macbeth showing that he is still a good man at heart; he just had evil actions.

Posted by Briana K on 1.8.08 4:29 PM | 6 comments
Labels: Shakespeare, Macbeth, tragedy

RECENT POSTS

A Good Heart Gone Bad
MACBETH: MAN OR MONSTER?
The Color Green
Shields and Armor
Honor in the Middle Ages
And the Band Plays On

LINKS

Write In Blog
Control Panel
Class Website
Macbeth E-text
RSC Macbeth Guide
Bard Net
Tips on Blog Comments

Blogroll Many blogs include a list of links to other blogs or sites.

Links Bloggers can add links to other Internet locations. Clicking a link sends readers to another place in the same blog, or to another site.

Labels Keywords are assigned by the blogger to categorize a post. Click a label to see other posts in this category.

Comments Clicking on this link allows visitors to read comments and add their own.

ID Entries include the name of the author and date the post was entered.

Creating a Blog

Keep these hints and strategies in mind to help you create an interesting and fair blog:

- Focus each blog entry on a single topic.

- Vary the length of your posts. Sometimes, all you need is a line or two to share a quick thought. Other posts will be much longer.

- Choose font colors and styles that can be read easily.

- Many people scan blogs rather than read them closely. You can make your main ideas pop out by using clear or clever headlines and boldfacing key terms.

- Give credit to other people's work and ideas. State the names of people whose ideas you are quoting or add a link to take readers to that person's blog or site.

- If you post comments, try to make them brief and polite.

Social Networking

Social networking means any interaction between members of an online community. People can exchange many different kinds of information, from text and voice messages to video images. Many social network communities allow users to create permanent pages that describe themselves. Users create home pages to express themselves, share ideas about their lives, and post messages to other members in the network. Each user is responsible for adding and updating the content on his or her profile page.

Here are some features you are likely to find on a social network profile:

Features of Profile Pages

- A **biographical description**, including photographs and artwork
- **Lists of favorite things**, such as books, movies, music, and fashions
- **Playable media** elements such as videos and sound recordings
- **Message boards**, or "walls," on which members of the community can exchange messages

Privacy in Social Networks

Social networks allow users to decide how open their profiles will be. Be sure to read introductory information carefully before you register at a new site. Once you have a personal profile page, monitor your privacy settings regularly. Remember that any information you post will be available to anyone in your network.

Users often post messages anonymously or using false names, or pseudonyms. People can also post using someone else's name. Judge all information on the Net critically. Do not assume that you know who posted some information simply because you recognize the name of the post author. The rapid speed of communication on the Internet can make it easy to jump to conclusions—be careful to avoid this trap.

You can create a social network page for an individual or a group, such as a school or special interest club. Many hosting sites do not charge to register, so you can also have fun by creating a page for a pet or a fictional character.

Tips for Sending Effective Messages

Technology makes it easy to share ideas quickly, but writing for the Internet poses some special challenges. The writing style for blogs and social networks is often very conversational. In blog posts and comments, instant messages, and e-mails, writers often express themselves very quickly, using relaxed language, short sentences, and abbreviations. However in a face-to-face conversation, we get a lot of information from a speaker's tone of voice and body language. On the Internet, those clues are missing. As a result, Internet writers often use italics or bracketed labels to indicate emotions. Another alternative is using emoticons—strings of characters that give visual clues to indicate emotion.

:-) **smile** *(happy)*   **:-(** **frown** *(unhappy)*   **;-)** **wink** *(light sarcasm)*

Use these strategies to communicate effectively when using technology:

✔ *Before you click Send,* **reread your message** *to make sure that your tone is clear.*

✔ **Do not jump to conclusions**—*ask for clarification first. Make sure you really understand what someone is saying before you respond.*

✔ **Use abbreviations** *your reader will understand.*

Widgets and Feeds

A **widget** is a small application that performs a specific task. You might find widgets that give weather predictions, offer dictionary definitions or translations, provide entertainment such as games, or present a daily word, photograph, or quotation.

A **feed** is a special kind of widget. It displays headlines taken from the latest content on a specific media source. Clicking on the headline will take you to the full article. Many social network communities and other Web sites allow you to personalize your home page by adding widgets and feeds.

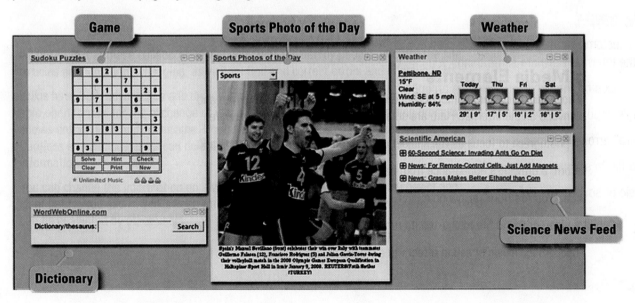

Game   **Sports Photo of the Day**   **Weather**

Science News Feed

Dictionary

Multimedia Elements

One of the great advantages of communicating on the Internet is that you are not limited to using text only. When you create a Web profile or blog, you can share your ideas using a wide variety of media. In addition to widgets and feeds (see page R9), these media elements can make your Internet communication more entertaining and useful.

GRAPHICS	
Photographs	You can post photographs taken by digital cameras or scanned as files.
Illustrations	Artwork can be created using computer software. You can also use a scanner to post a digital image of a drawing or sketch.
Charts, Graphs, and Maps	Charts and graphs can make statistical information clear. Use spreadsheet software to create these elements. Use Internet sites to find maps of specific places.

VIDEO	
Live Action	Digital video can be recorded by a camera or recorded from another media source.
Animation	Animated videos can also be created using software.

AUDIO	
Music	Many social network communities make it easy to share your favorite music with people who visit your page.
Voice	Use a microphone to add your own voice to your Web page.

Editing Media Elements

You can use software to customize media elements. Open source software is free and available to anyone on the Internet. Here are some things you can do with software:

- **Crop** a photograph to focus on the subject or brighten an image that is too dark.
- **Transform** a drawing's appearance from flat to three-dimensional.
- **Insert** a "You Are Here" arrow on a map.
- **Edit** a video or sound file to shorten its running time.
- **Add** background music or sound effects to a video.

Podcasts

A **podcast** is a digital audio or video recording of a program that is made available on the Internet. Users can replay the podcast on a computer, or download it and replay it on a personal audio player. You might think of podcasts as radio or television programs that you create yourself. They can be embedded on a Web site or fed to a Web page through a podcast widget.

Creating an Effective Podcast

To make a podcast, you will need a recording device, such as a microphone or digital video camera, as well as editing software. Open source editing software is widely available and free of charge. Most audio podcasts are converted into the MP3 format. Here are some tips for creating a podcast that is clear and entertaining:

- **Listen to several podcasts by different authors** to get a feeling for the medium.

- **Make a list** of features and styles you like and also those you want to avoid.

- **Test your microphone** to find the best recording distance. Stand close enough to the microphone so that your voice sounds full, but not so close that you create an echo.

- **Create an outline** that shows your estimated timing for each element.

- **Be prepared** before you record. Rehearse, but do not create a script. Podcasts are best when they have a natural, easy flow.

- **Talk directly to your listeners**. Slow down enough so they can understand you.

- Use software to **edit your podcast before publishing it**. You can edit out mistakes or add additional elements.

Wikis

A **wiki** is a collaborative Web site that lets visitors create, add, remove, and edit content. The term comes from the Hawaiian phrase *wikiwiki*, which means "quick." Web users of a wiki are both the readers and the writers of the site. Some wikis are open to contributions from anyone. Others require visitors to register before they can edit the content. All of the text in these collaborative Web sites was written by people who use the site. Articles are constantly changing, as visitors find and correct errors and improve texts.

Wikis have both advantages and disadvantages as sources of information. They are valuable open forums for the exchange of ideas. The unique collaborative writing process allows entries to change over time. However, entries can also be modified incorrectly. Careless or malicious users can delete good content and add inappropriate or inaccurate information. Wikis may be useful for gathering background information, but should not be used as research resources.

You can change the information on a wiki, but be sure your information is correct and clear before you add it. Wikis keep track of all changes, so your work will be recorded and can be evaluated by other users.

Writing is something many people do every day at work, school, or home. They write letters and reports, do research, plan meetings, and keep track of information in notes.

Writing for the Workplace shows you some models of the following forms of writing:

- **Note Cards**
- **Meeting Agenda**
- **Business Letter**
- **Friendly Letter**

Creating Note Cards

Whether you are working on a research report or gathering information for another purpose, it is helpful to keep your notes on individual cards or in note files on a computer. You will need to make sure that you note your sources on your cards. You can organize information many different ways, but it is most helpful to keep notes of one kind together.

> You can name the **source**, as shown here, or refer to the source by number (e.g., Source 3) if you are using source cards.

> The **topic** is the main focus of the notes.

Topic: Octopus

Source: PBS Web site Accessed 10/15/2010
http://www.pbs.org/wnet/nature/episodes/ the-octopus-show/
a-legend-of-the-deep/2014/

- Acrobatic and shy animals
- Can squeeze into very small spaces to hide or catch food
- Talented swimmers
- Can change color
- Live in all kinds of environments

> *In the notes section focus on the ideas that are most important to your research. Note that these ideas may not always be the main ideas of the selection you are reading. You do not need to write in full sentences. However, you may want to use bullets to make your notes easier to read.*

Writing a Meeting Agenda

When you have a meeting, it is helpful to use an agenda. An agenda tells what will be discussed in the meeting. It tells who is responsible for which topic. It also provides a guide for the amount of time to be spent on each topic.

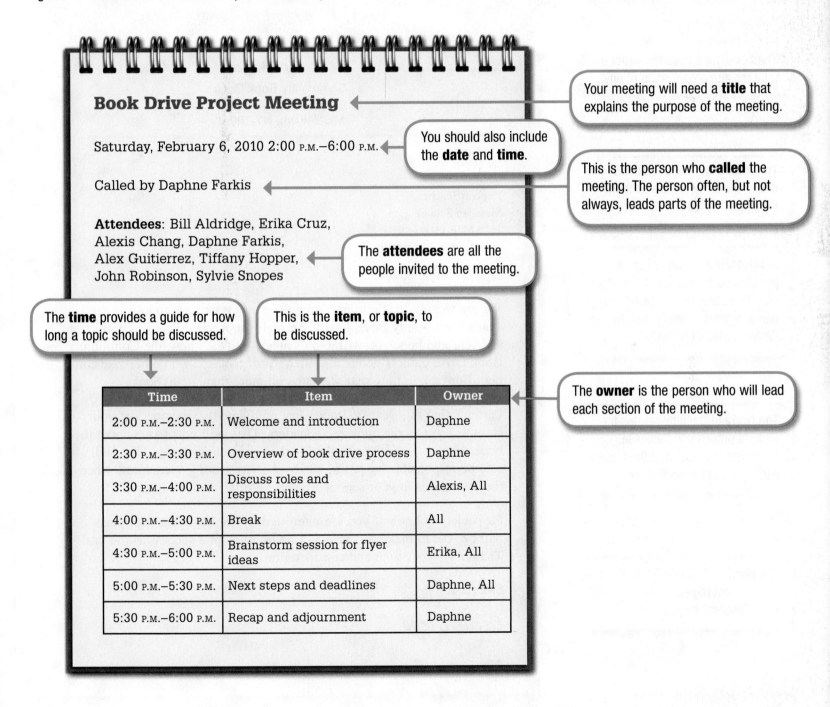

Book Drive Project Meeting

Saturday, February 6, 2010 2:00 P.M.–6:00 P.M.

Called by Daphne Farkis

Attendees: Bill Aldridge, Erika Cruz, Alexis Chang, Daphne Farkis, Alex Guitierrez, Tiffany Hopper, John Robinson, Sylvie Snopes

Time	Item	Owner
2:00 P.M.–2:30 P.M.	Welcome and introduction	Daphne
2:30 P.M.–3:30 P.M.	Overview of book drive process	Daphne
3:30 P.M.–4:00 P.M.	Discuss roles and responsibilities	Alexis, All
4:00 P.M.–4:30 P.M.	Break	All
4:30 P.M.–5:00 P.M.	Brainstorm session for flyer ideas	Erika, All
5:00 P.M.–5:30 P.M.	Next steps and deadlines	Daphne, All
5:30 P.M.–6:00 P.M.	Recap and adjournment	Daphne

Your meeting will need a **title** that explains the purpose of the meeting.

You should also include the **date** and **time**.

This is the person who **called** the meeting. The person often, but not always, leads parts of the meeting.

The **attendees** are all the people invited to the meeting.

The **time** provides a guide for how long a topic should be discussed.

This is the **item**, or **topic**, to be discussed.

The **owner** is the person who will lead each section of the meeting.

Writing Business Letters

Business letters are often formal in tone and written for a specific business purpose. They generally follow one of several acceptable formats. In block format, all parts of the letter are at the left margin. All business letters, however, have the same parts: heading, inside address, salutation, body, closing, and signature.

The **heading** shows the writer's address and organization (if any).

The **inside address** indicates where the letter will be sent and the date.

A **salutation**, or **greeting,** is punctuated by a colon. When the specific addressee is not known, use a general greeting such as "To Whom It May Concern."

The **body** of the letter states the writer's purpose. In this case, the writer requests that the class participate in the book drive.

The **closing**, "Sincerely," is common, as are "Best regards," "Yours truly," and "Respectfully yours."

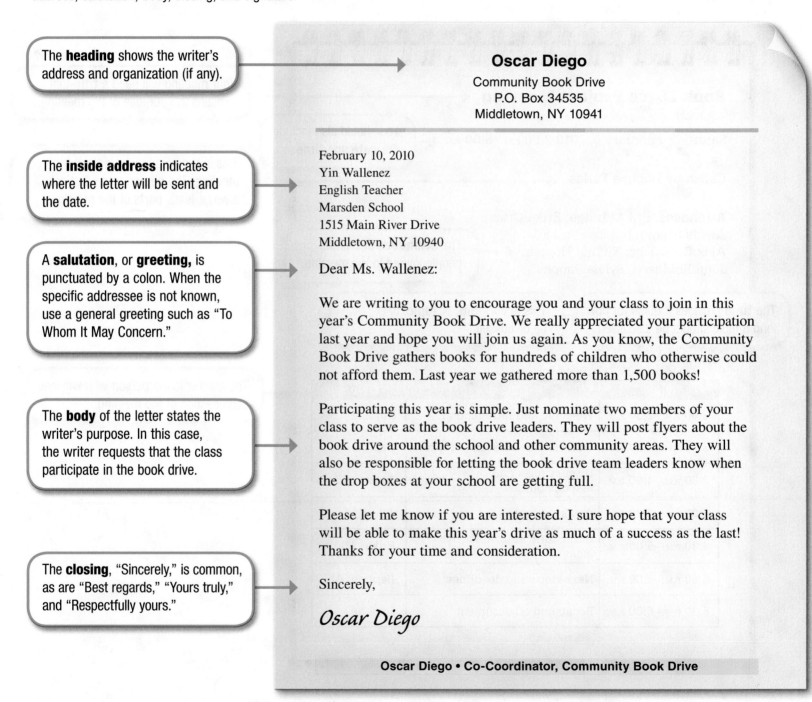

Oscar Diego
Community Book Drive
P.O. Box 34535
Middletown, NY 10941

February 10, 2010
Yin Wallenez
English Teacher
Marsden School
1515 Main River Drive
Middletown, NY 10940

Dear Ms. Wallenez:

We are writing to you to encourage you and your class to join in this year's Community Book Drive. We really appreciated your participation last year and hope you will join us again. As you know, the Community Book Drive gathers books for hundreds of children who otherwise could not afford them. Last year we gathered more than 1,500 books!

Participating this year is simple. Just nominate two members of your class to serve as the book drive leaders. They will post flyers about the book drive around the school and other community areas. They will also be responsible for letting the book drive team leaders know when the drop boxes at your school are getting full.

Please let me know if you are interested. I sure hope that your class will be able to make this year's drive as much of a success as the last! Thanks for your time and consideration.

Sincerely,

Oscar Diego

Oscar Diego • Co-Coordinator, Community Book Drive

Writing Friendly Letters

Friendly letters are less formal than business letters. You can use this form to write to a friend, a family member, or anyone with whom you'd like to communicate in a personal, friendly way. Like business letters, friendly letters have the following parts: heading, inside address, salutation, body, closing, and signature. The purpose of a friendly letter might be:

- to share news and feelings
- to send or answer an invitation
- to express thanks

The **heading** includes the writer's address and the date on which he or she wrote the letter. In some very casual letters, the writer may not include his or her address.

The **body** of the letter is the main section and contains the message of the letter.

Some common **closings** for friendly letters include "Best wishes," "Love," and "Take care."

345 Whitehall Dr.
Beaverton, OR 97005
July 20, 2010

Dear Grandma and Grandpa,

Thank you so much for the journal you sent me. I can't wait to write in it. The cover is gorgeous. Did you know that red is my favorite color? I also love the pen—I can't believe that it is erasable. How cool!

I am having a great summer. I've played soccer a lot and read a lot of books. It sure is hot here, though. Yesterday it was 90 degrees! I know that is nothing compared to summers in Texas, but it is sure hot for us.

Mom says that you are planning a visit for the early fall. I'm really looking forward to it. Maybe you can come watch me play soccer.

Thanks again for the terrific journal.

Love,

Rhonda

MLA Style for Listing Sources

Book with one author	London, Jack. *White Fang.* Clayton: Prestwick, 2007. Print.
Book with two or three authors	Veit, Richard, and Christopher Gould. *Writing, Reading, and Research.* 8th ed. Boston: Wadsworth-Cengage Learning, 2009. Print.
Book prepared by an editor	Twain, Mark. *The Complete Essays of Mark Twain.* Ed. Charles Neider. New York: Da Capo, 2000. Print.
Book with more than three authors or editors	Donald, Robert B., et al. *Writing Clear Essays.* 3rd ed. Upper Saddle River: Prentice, 1996. Print.
A single work from an anthology	Poe, Edgar Allan. "The Fall of the House of Usher." *American Literature: A Chronological Approach.* Ed. Edgar H. Schuster, Anthony Tovatt, and Patricia O. Tovatt. New York: McGraw, 1985. 233–247. Print. [Indicate pages for the entire selection.]
Introduction, foreword, preface, or afterword in a book	Vidal, Gore. Introduction. *Abraham Lincoln: Selected Speeches and Writings.* By Abraham Lincoln. New York: Vintage, 1992. xxi–xxvii. Print.
Signed article in a weekly magazine	Walsh, Brian. "Greening This Old House." *Time* 4 May 2009: 45–47. Print. [For a multipage article that does not appear on consecutive pages, write only the first page number on which it appears, followed by a plus sign.]
Signed article in a monthly magazine	Fischman, Josh. "A Better Life with Bionics." *National Geographic* Jan. 2010: 34–53. Print.
Unsigned editorial or story	"Wind Power." Editorial. *New York Times* 9 Jan. 2010: A18. Print. [If the editorial or story is signed, begin with the author's name.]
Signed pamphlet	[Treat the pamphlet as though it were a book.]
Audiovisual media, such as films, slide programs, videocassettes, DVDs	*Where the Red Fern Grows.* Dir. Norman Toker. Perf. James Whitmore, Beverly Garland, and Stewart Peterson. 1974. Sterling Entertainment, 1997. DVD.
Radio or TV broadcast transcript	"Texas High School Football Titans Ready for Clash." *Weekend Edition Sunday.* Host Melissa Block. Guests Mike Pesca and Tom Goldman. Natl. Public Radio. KUHF, Houston, 18 Dec. 2009. Print. Transcript.
A single page on a Web site	U.S. Census Bureau: Customer Liaison and Marketing Services Office. "State Facts for Students: Texas." *U.S. Census Bureau.* U.S. Census Bureau, 15 Oct. 2009. Web. 1 Nov. 2009. [Indicate the date of last update if known or use "n.d." if not known. After the medium of publication, include the date you accessed the information. You do not need the URL unless it is the only way to find the page. If needed, include it in angled brackets at the end, i.e. <http://www.census.gov/schools/facts/texas.html >.]
Newspaper	Yardley, Jim. "Hurricane Sweeps into Rural Texas; Cities Are Spared." *New York Times* 23 Aug. 1999: A1. Print. [For a multipage article that does not appear on consecutive pages, write only the first page number on which it appears, followed by a plus sign.]
Personal interview	Jones, Robert. Personal interview. 4 Sept. 2006.
Audio with multiple publishers	Simms, James, ed. *Romeo and Juliet.* By William Shakespeare. Oxford: Attica Cybernetics; London: BBC Education; London: Harper, 1995. CD-ROM.
Signed article from an encyclopedia	Askeland, Donald R. "Welding." *World Book Encyclopedia.* 1991 ed. Print. [For a well-known reference, you do not need to include the publisher information, only the edition and year, followed by the medium used.]

Commonly Misspelled Words

The list on this page presents words that cause problems for many people. Some of these words are spelled according to set rules, but others follow no specific rules. As you review this list, check to see how many of the words give you trouble in your own writing.

absence	benefit	conscience	excellent	library	prejudice
absolutely	bicycle	conscientious	exercise	license	previous
accidentally	bought	conscious	experience	lightning	probably
accurate	brief	continuous	explanation	likable	procedure
achievement	brilliant	convenience	extension	literature	proceed
affect	bulletin	coolly	extraordinary	mathematics	pronunciation
agreeable	bury	cooperate	familiar	maximum	realize
aisle	buses	correspondence	fascinating	minimum	really
all right	business	courageous	February	misspell	receipt
allowance	cafeteria	courteous	fiery	naturally	receive
analysis	calendar	criticism	financial	necessary	recognize
analyze	campaign	curiosity	foreign	neighbor	recommend
ancient	canceled	deceive	fourth	niece	rehearse
anniversary	candidate	decision	generally	ninety	repetition
answer	capital	defendant	genuine	noticeable	restaurant
anticipate	capitol	definitely	government	occasion	rhythm
anxiety	career	dependent	grammar	occasionally	sandwich
apologize	cashier	description	guidance	occur	schedule
appearance	category	desert	height	occurred	scissors
appreciate	ceiling	dessert	humorous	occurrence	theater
appropriate	certain	dining	immediately	opinion	truly
argument	changeable	disappointed	immigrant	opportunity	usage
athletic	characteristic	distinguish	independence	parallel	valuable
attendance	clothes	effect	independent	particularly	various
awkward	colonel	eighth	individual	personally	vegetable
bargain	column	embarrass	intelligence	persuade	weight
battery	commercial	enthusiastic	judgment	physician	weird
beautiful	commitment	envelope	knowledge	possibility	whale
beginning	condemn	environment	lawyer	precede	yield
believe	congratulate	especially	legible	preferable	

A

accurate (ak´yər it) *adj.* without errors; true

advantage (ad vant´ij) *n.* something that puts a person in a better position than others; a way in which one thing is better than another

aesthetic (es thet´ik) *adj.* relating to beauty; artistic; pleasing to the senses

analysis (ə nal´ə sis) *n.* the process of looking at something closely in order to understand its meaning, structure, or parts

analytical (an´ə lit´ik əl) *adj.* relating to, or using, logical reasoning

assertion (ə sʉr´shən) *n.* a strong statement of fact or belief about a subject

assumption (ə sump´shən) *n.* a fact or statement which is taken as true, without proof, sometimes incorrectly

B

ballad (bal´əd) *n.* a song-like poem that tells a story, often of love and adventure

beliefs (bə lēfs´) *n.* firm opinions or ideas on a subject; religious convictions

C

character (kar´ik tər) *n.* a person (or animal) who plays a part in the action of a story, play, or movie

characterization (kar´ik tər i zā´shən) *n.* the act of creating and developing a character in a story

citation (sī tā´shən) *n.* a reference to a source of information

climax (klī´maks´) *n.* the high point of interest, drama, or suspense in a story or other literary work

commentary (käm´ən ter´ē) *n.* a set of notes which explains, interprets, or comments on a text; opinions or explanations about an event or situation

compelling (kəm pel´ing) *adj.* (of an argument) very convincing; demanding attention; drawing interest, admiration, or attention in a powerful way; forceful

complex (käm pleks´) *adj.* having many parts or details; difficult to understand

concluding paragraph (kən klüd´ing par´ə graf´) *n.* the closing paragraph at the end of a piece of writing; the paragraph that sums up and puts forward a conclusion

conflict (kän´flikt´) *n.* the struggle between people or opposing forces which creates the dramatic action in a play or story

consider (kən sid´ər) *v.* to take into account; to think about with care

context (kän´tekst´) *n.* the part of a sentence which surrounds a word and which can be used to shed light on the word's meaning; the situation in which something occurs which can help that thing to be fully understood; the setting or environment

convention (kən ven´shən) *n.* a standard way of doing something; a method or practice

convey (kən vā´) *v.* to make something (for example, an idea or a feeling) known to someone; to communicate

convincing (kən vins´ing) *adj.* (of an argument) strong enough to be able to make someone agree or believe something is true; believable, powerful

counter-argument (kount´ər är´gyü mənt) *n.* a reason against the original argument

couplet (kup´let) *n.* a two-line stanza in a poem; two lines of verse, often with a rhythmic pattern and a rhyme

D

debate (dē bāt´) *v.* to argue in a formal way; to discuss the pros and cons, ins and outs of an issue; *n.* a formal discussion at a public meeting on a topic; an argument about a topic

determine (dē tʉr´mən) *v.* to discover or figure out the facts about something, often by looking at it closely, or doing research or calculations; to decide

device (di vīs´) *n.* the use of words to gain a particular effect in a piece of writing

dialogue (dī´ə lôg´) *n.* a conversation between two or more people in a book, play, or movie

E

embedded (em bed´əd) *adj.* placed firmly in the middle of something; (of a quotation) placed inside a sentence, not set apart from the rest of the text

emotion (ē mō′shən) *n.* a feeling, such as love or joy; feelings and automatic response, as opposed to logical thoughts and conclusions

engaging (en gāj′ing) *adj.* something which draws in and interests (engages) the reader; charming, interesting

essay (es′ā) *n.* a short piece of non-fiction writing on a particular subject

ethics (eth′iks) *n.* a set of moral principles or beliefs about what is right and wrong which guide how a person or group lives

evaluate (ē val′yü āt′) *v.* to look into something carefully so as to assess and judge it

evidence (ev′ə dəns) *n.* anything that gives proof or shows something to be true

F

figurative (fig′yər ə tiv′) *adj.* (of language) writing that is full of metaphors and images, where the words are very descriptive but not meant to be taken literally

formal (fôr′məl) *adj.* reflecting language that is traditional and correct, not casual

formatting (fôr′mat′ing) *adj.* related to the arrangement of text, images, and graphics on a page

I

imagery (im′ij rē) *n.* descriptive language that paints pictures in the mind or appeals to the senses

introductory paragraph (in′trə duk′tə rē par′ə graf′) *n.* in a piece of writing, the beginning or opening paragraph which often gives both the topic and thesis

issue (ish′ü) *n.* an important subject that is being argued about, investigated, or discussed; the most important part of a situation or discussion; a personal problem

L

literary (lit′ar er′ē) *adj.* of or relating to books or other written material

logical (läj′i kəl) *adj.* clear and reasonable; based on logic

M

metaphor (met′ə fôr′) *n.* a figure of speech in which something is described as if it were another thing

mood (müd) *n.* the atmosphere or overall feeling of a piece of writing as created by the author

N

narrative (nar′ə tiv) *n.* a story, either fiction or non-fiction

non-stereotypical (nän ster′ē ə tip′i kəl) *adj.* not conforming to a pre-existing, simple idea of how something should be or how someone should act; unusual, unconventional

O

oppose (ə pōz′) *v.* to go against, disagree

organization (ôr′gə ni zā′shən) *n.* a way something (such as a poem or essay) is structured or arranged

P

perspective (pər spek′tiv) *n.* a particular way of seeing or thinking about something; a viewpoint, point of view, or opinion

phase (fāz) *n.* a stage in a process

poetic (pō et′ik) *adj.* beautiful, expressive, sensitive, or imaginative; like a poem

point of view (point uv vyü) *n.* the perspective from which a story is told; an attitude, position, standpoint, or way of looking at a situation; an opinion

position (pə zish′ən) *n.* a point of view or attitude toward something

precise (prē cīs′) *adj.* exact, accurate; careful about details

primary (prī′mer′ē) *adj.* (of sources, documents, or information) firsthand (such as newspapers, diaries) or direct; first in order or importance; basic

project (prä′jekt′) *n.* a planned task for a specific purpose

proposal (prə pōz′əl) *n.* a plan under consideration for approval

Q

quote (kwōt) *v.* to write or say a group of words copied exactly from a piece of writing or someone's spoken words

R

reader-friendly (rēd′ər frend′lē) *adj.* easy for an audience to read and understand

refrain (ri frān´) *n.* a line or group of lines which is regularly repeated in a song or poem, usually at the end of each verse

relevant (rel´ə vənt) *adj.* closely connected, important, or significant to the matter at hand

reliability (ri lī´ə bil´i tē) *n.* the degree to which something or someone can be trusted and counted on to be consistent

request (ri kwest´) *n.* something asked for

resolution (rez´ə lü´shən) *n.* what happens to resolve the conflict in the plot of a story

rhetorical devices (ri tôr´i kəl di vī´səz) *n.* strategies and techniques—for example, metaphor and hyperbole—used by writers to draw in or persuade readers

S

schema (skēm´ə) *n.* a diagram representing an organizational plan or outline

secondary (sek´ən der´ē) *adj.* (of sources, documents, or information) not direct but secondhand, derived from primary sources; less important, of second rank or value

sensory (sen´sər ē) *adj.* relating to the senses

sonnet (sän´it) *n.* a poem of fourteen lines, often with a set pattern of rhymes

source (sôrs) *n.* (in research) a book or document that can be used as evidence in research, or when making an argument and trying to prove a point; a place, person, or thing which supplies information or other things; the place something begins, the origin

statement (stāt´mənt) *n.* something written or said which presents information in a clear and definite way

statistics (stə tis´tiks) *n.* facts and data that come from analyzing information expressed in numbers

strategy (strat´ə jē) *n.* in a piece of writing, a literary tactic or method (such as flashback or foreshadowing) used by the writer to achieve a certain goal or effect

stylistic (stī lis´tik) *adj.* of, or relating to, artistic or literary style

substantial (səb stan´shəl) *adj.* important, large or weighty; real and not imaginary; well-constructed

sufficient (sə fish´ənt) *adj.* as much as is needed; enough

suitable (süt´ə bəl) *adj.* appropriate, right for a particular purpose

summary (sum´ə rē) *n.* a short statement giving the main points without the details; *adj.* (as in summary paragraph) short, summing up (at the end)

suspense (sə spens´) *n.* a feeling of anxiety and uncertainty about what will happen in a story or other piece of writing **T**

technique (tek nēk´) *n.* a method of doing an activity or carrying out a task, often involving skill

thesis (thē´sis) *n.* an idea or theory that is stated and then discussed in a logical way

tone (tōn) *n.* a writer's attitude toward his or her subject

transition (tran zish´ən) *n.* the change from one part, place, or idea to another

V

valid (val´id) *adj.* reasonable and logical, and therefore worth taking seriously; acceptable as true and correct

validity (və lid´ə tē) *n.* the quality of being reasonable, logical, or acceptable as true

Spanish Glossary

A

accurate / correcto *adj.* sin errores; verdadero

advantage / ventaja *s.* algo que le pone a alguien en una mejor posición que a otros; la forma en la que una cosa es mejor que otra

aesthetic / estético *adj.* perteneciente a la belleza; artístico; agradable a los sentidos

analysis / análisis *s.* el proceso de examinar algo detenidamente para entender su significado, su estructura o sus partes

analytical / analítico *adj.* perteneciente a, o utilizando el razonamiento lógico

assertion / aseveración *s.* una declaración fuerte de un hecho o creencia sobre un tema

assumption / suposición *s.* un hecho o declaración que se interpreta como la verdad, sin pruebas, y a veces equivocadamente

B

ballad / balada *s.* una canción poética que cuenta una historia, muchas veces del amor y la aventura

beliefs / creencias *s.* opiniones o ideas firmes de un tema; convicciones religiosas

C

character / personaje *s.* un individuo (humano o animal) que tiene un papel en la acción de un cuento, una obra de teatro o una película

characterization / caracterización *s.* el acto de crear y desarrollar un personaje en un cuento

citation / cita *s.* una referencia a una fuente de información

climax / clímax *s.* el punto de máximo interés, drama, o suspenso de un cuento u otra obra literaria

commentary / comentario *s.* una serie de notas que explican, interpretan, o comentan un texto; opiniones o explicaciones de un evento o situación

compelling / convincente *adj.* (de un argumento) muy persuasivo; que exige atención; que atrae interés, admiración, o atención de un modo poderoso; contundente

complex / complejo *adj.* que tiene muchas partes o muchos detalles; difícil de entender

concluding paragraph / párrafo conclusivo *s.* el párrafo final de una obra escrita; el párrafo que resume y concluye

conflict / conflicto *s.* la lucha entre personas o fuerzas opuestas que crea la acción dramática en una obra de teatro o un cuento

consider / considerar *v.* tomar en cuenta; meditar sobre algo

context / contexto *s.* la parte de una oración que rodea una palabra y que se puede usar para sacar el significado de la palabra; la situación en la que algo ocurre que puede facilitar la comprensión de la cosa; el escenario o el entorno

convention / convención *s.* un modo estándar de hacer algo; un método o práctica

convey / expresar *v.* darse a entender algo a alguien (por ejemplo, una idea o sentimiento); comunicar

convincing / convincente *adj.* (de un argumento) suficientemente persuasivo para que alguien se ponga de acuerdo o crea que algo es verdadero; creíble

counter-argument / contraargumento *s.* una razón contra el argumento original

couplet / pareado *s.* una estrofa de dos versos en un poema; dos versos, muchas veces con un patrón rítmico y una rima

D

debate / debatir *v.* discutir formalmente; hablar sobre las ventajas y las desventajas y los detalles de un asunto; debate *s.* una discusión formal sobre un tema en un foro público; una discusión sobre un tema

determine / determinar *v.* descubrir o descifrar los hechos de algo, muchas veces por examinar detenidamente, investigar o hacer cálculos; decidir

device / técnica (literaria) *s.* el uso de palabras para tener un efecto específico en una obra escrita

dialogue / diálogo *s.* una conversación entre dos personajes o más en un libro, obra de teatro o película

E

embedded / colocado *adj.* metido firmemente en medio de algo; (de una cita) insertada dentro de una oración, no separada del resto del texto

emotion / sentimiento *s.* una sensación emotiva como el amor o la alegría; sensaciones y respuestas automáticas, en contraste a los pensamientos y conclusiones lógicos

engaging / interesante *adj.* algo que le atrae y le interesa al lector; encantador, interesante

essay / ensayo *s.* una obra escrita breve de no ficción sobre un tema particular

ethics / ética *s.* principios morales o creencias sobre lo que es correcto e incorrecto que guían cómo vive una persona o grupo

evaluate / evaluar *v.* investigar algo cuidadosamente para analizarlo y valorarlo

evidence / pruebas *s.* cualquier cosa que demuestre o indique que algo es cierto

F

figurative / figurado *adj.* (de lenguaje) escritura que está repleta de metáforas e imágenes, donde las palabras son muy descriptivas pero su significado no debe ser interpretado literalmente

formal / formal *adj.* que refleja el lenguaje tradicional y correcto, no informal

formatting / formateo *s.* la colocación de texto, imágenes y gráficos en una página

I

imagery / imaginario *s.* lenguaje descriptivo que crea dibujos en la mente o atrae los sentidos

introductory paragraph / párrafo introductorio *s.* en una obra escrita, el párrafo al principio que muchas veces expone tanto el tema como la tesis

issue / asunto *s.* un tema importante que se discute, se investiga o se habla; la parte más importante de una situación o discusión; un problema personal

L

literary / literario *adj.* perteneciente o relativo a los libros u otros materiales escritos

logical / lógico *adj.* claro y razonable; basado en la lógica

M

metaphor / metáfora *s.* una figura retórica que describe algo como si fuera otra cosa

mood / ambiente, tono *s.* el ambiente o sentimiento general de una obra escrita creado por el autor

N

narrative / narrativa *s.* un cuento de ficción o no ficción

non-stereotypical / no estereotípico *adj.* que no se ajusta a una idea preexistente y simple de cómo debe ser algo o cómo debe comportarse alguien; poco común o convencional

O

oppose / oponer *v.* estar en contra de; no estar de acuerdo

organization / organización *s.* la manera en la que algo (por ejemplo un poema o ensayo) se estructura o se arregla

P

perspective / perspectiva *s.* una manera particular de interpretar o pensar algo; un punto de vista u opinión

phase / fase *s.* una etapa en un proceso

poetic / poético *adj.* bonito, expresivo, sensible o imaginativo; como un poema

point of view / punto de vista *s.* la perspectiva de la cual se cuenta una historia; una actitud, postura, o manera de interpretar una situación; una opinión

position / postura *s.* el punto de vista o la actitud hacia algo

precise / preciso *adj.* exacto, certero; cuidadoso con detalles

primary / primario, primordial adj. (de fuentes, documentos o información) de primera mano (por ejemplo periódicos, diarios) o directo; primero en orden de importancia; básico

project / proyecto *s.* una tarea planeada para un propósito específico

proposal / propuesta *s.* plan propuesto a consideración para ser aprobado

Q

quote / citar *v.* escribir o decir un grupo de palabras copiadas exactamente de un texto o de las palabras habladas de alguien.

R

reader-friendly / fácil de leer *adj.* no complicado, fácil de entender y leer

refrain / refrán *s.* un verso o grupo de versos que se repite regularmente en una canción o poema, normalmente al final de cada estrofa

relevant / relevante *adj.* conectado estrechamente, importante o significante al asunto en cuestión

reliability / fiabilidad, consistencia *s.* el grado al que se puede fiar de algo o alguien o que se puede contar con su consistencia

request / petición, pedido *s.* algo pedido por alguien

resolution / resolución *s.* lo que ocurre para resolver el conflicto en el argumento de una historia

rhetorical devices / técnicas retóricas *s.* estrategias y técnicas (por ejemplo la metáfora e hipérbole) utilizadas por los escritores para atraer o persuadir a los lectores

S

schema / esquema *s.* un diagrama que representa un plan de organización o un borrador

secondary / secundario, de segunda mano *adj.* (de fuentes, documentos o información) no directo, que no viene de primera mano, derivado de fuentes primarias; de menos importancia, rango o valor

sensory / sensorial *adj.* perteneciente o relativo a los sentidos

sonnet / soneto *s.* un poema de catorce versos, muchas veces con un patrón determinado de rima

source / fuente *s.* (en la investigación) un libro o documento que se puede usar como pruebas en una investigación o cuando se expone un argumento para demostrar un argumento; un lugar, una persona o una cosa que da información u otras cosas; el lugar en el que empieza algo, el origen

statement / declaración *s.* algo escrito o dicho que presenta información de una manera clara y definitiva

statistics / estadísticas *s.* hechos y datos que vienen de analizar información expresada en números

strategy / estrategia *s.* en un texto, una táctica o método literario (como el *flashback* o el presagio) empleado por el autor para lograr un objetivo o efecto específico

stylistic / estilístico *adj.* perteneciente o relativo al estilo artístico o literario

substantial / considerable *adj.* importante, grande o pesado; real y no imaginario; bien construido

sufficient / suficiente *adj.* tanto como sea necesario; bastante

suitable / apropiado *adj.* adecuado, acertado para un propósito particular

summary / resumen *s.* una declaración breve que expone los puntos centrales sin los detalles; de resumen *adj.* (como en "summary paragraph" o párrafo de resumen) breve, recapitulando (al final)

suspense / suspenso *s.* una sensación de ansiedad e incertidumbre sobre lo que va a pasar en una historia u otra obra escrita

T

technique / técnica *s.* una manera de hacer una actividad o llevar a cabo una tarea, muchas veces con destrezas específicas

thesis / tesis *s.* una idea o teoría que se expone y se discute de una manera lógica

tone / tono *s.* la actitud de un escritor hacia su tema o materia

transition / transición *s.* el cambio entre partes, lugares y conceptos

V

valid / válido *adj.* razonable y lógico y por lo tanto vale la pena tomarlo en serio; aceptable como verdadero y correcto

validity / validez *s.* la cualidad de ser razonable, lógico o aceptable como verdadero

Meeting Agenda

Meeting Title: _____

Date: _____

Time: _____

Called by: _____

Attendees: _____

_____

Time	Item	Owner

Cause and Effect Chart

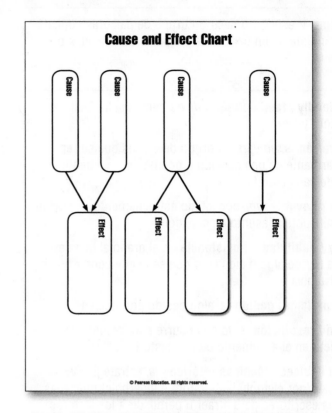

Cluster Diagram

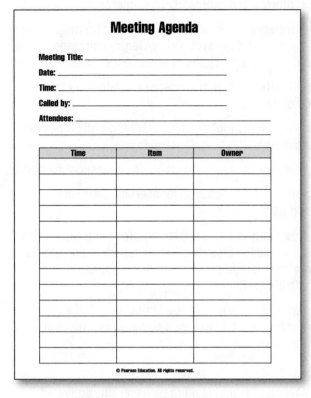

Five Ws Chart

Use these questions as you read, and write important details. Remember, you may not need to answer every question.

Who?
What?
When?
Where?
Why?

Writing Coach Online

Resource Go online for printable versions of these graphic organizers.

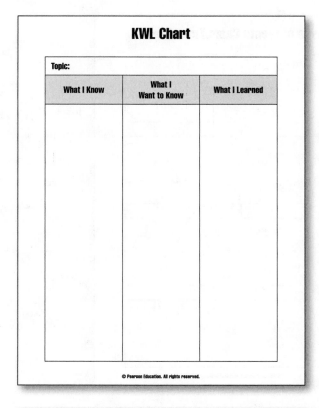

KWL Chart

Topic:

What I Know	What I Want to Know	What I Learned

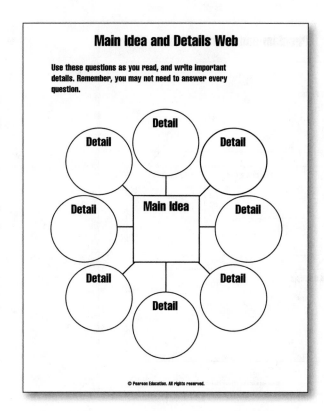

Main Idea and Details Web

Use these questions as you read, and write important details. Remember, you may not need to answer every question.

Detail · Detail · Detail · Detail · Main Idea · Detail · Detail · Detail · Detail

Meeting Notes

Topic

Decisions

Next Steps

Note Card

Topic:

Source:
-
-
-

Topic:

Source:
-
-
-

Graphic Organizer Handbook   R25

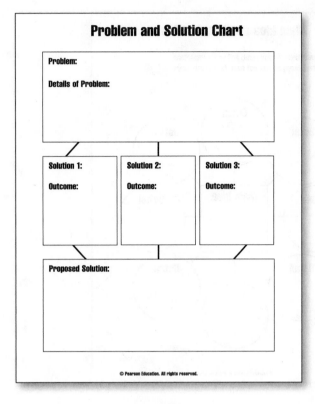

Problem and Solution Chart

Problem:

Details of Problem:

Solution 1:

Outcome:

Solution 2:

Outcome:

Solution 3:

Outcome:

Proposed Solution:

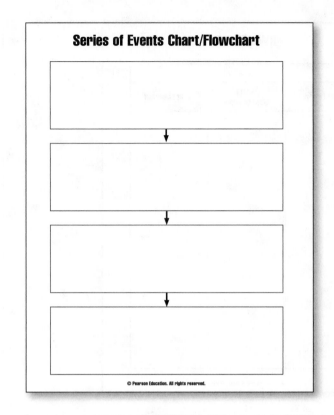

Series of Events Chart/Flowchart

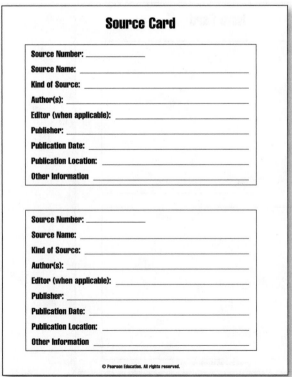

Source Card

Source Number: _____

Source Name: _____

Kind of Source: _____

Author(s): _____

Editor (when applicable): _____

Publisher: _____

Publication Date: _____

Publication Location: _____

Other Information _____

Source Number: _____

Source Name: _____

Kind of Source: _____

Author(s): _____

Editor (when applicable): _____

Publisher: _____

Publication Date: _____

Publication Location: _____

Other Information _____

Outline

Topic   I. _____

    Subtopic   A. _____

        Supporting details
1. _____
2. _____
3. _____
4. _____

    Subtopic   B. _____

        Supporting details
1. _____
2. _____
3. _____
4. _____

Topic   II. _____

    Subtopic   A. _____

        Supporting details
1. _____
2. _____
3. _____
4. _____

    Subtopic   B. _____

        Supporting details
1. _____
2. _____
3. _____
4. _____

Steps in a Process Chart

Steps	Details
Step 1:	
Step 2:	
Step 3:	
Step 4:	
Step 5:	

Storyboard

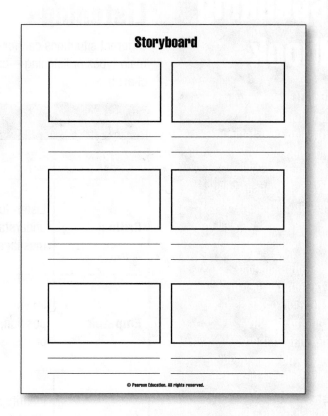

Timeline

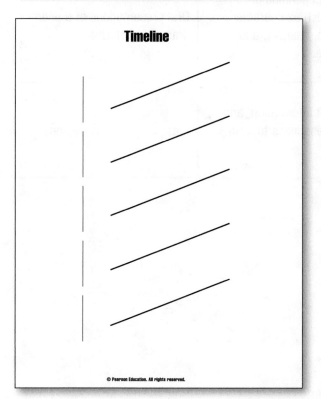

Venn Diagram

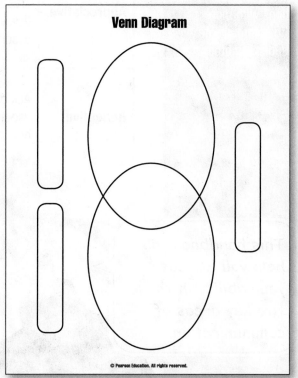

Graphic Organizer Handbook   R27

Listening and Speaking Handbook

Communication travels between people in many forms. You receive information by listening to others, and you convey information through speaking. The more developed these skills are, the more you will be able to communicate your ideas, as well as to comprehend the ideas of others.

If you improve your listening skills, it will become easier to focus your attention on classroom discussions and to identify important information more accurately. If you develop good speaking skills, you will be better prepared to contribute effectively in group discussions, to give formal presentations with more confidence, and to communicate your feelings and ideas to others more easily.

This handbook will help you increase your ability in these two key areas of communication.

Listening

Different situations call for different types of listening. Learn more about the four main types of listening—critical, empathic, appreciative, and reflective—in the chart below.

Types of Listening		
Type	**How to Listen**	**Situations**
Critical	Listen for facts and supporting details to understand and evaluate the speaker's message.	Informative or persuasive speeches, class discussions, announcements
Empathic	Imagine yourself in the other person's position, and try to understand what he or she is thinking.	Conversations with friends or family
Appreciative	Identify and analyze aesthetic or artistic elements, such as character development, rhyme, imagery, and descriptive language.	Oral presentations of a poem, dramatic performances
Reflective	Ask questions to get information, and use the speaker's responses to form new questions.	Class or group discussions

Using Different Types of Questions

A speaker's ideas may not always be clear to you. You may need to ask questions to clarify your understanding. If you understand the different types of questions, you will be able to get the information you need.

- An **open-ended question** does not lead to a single, specific response. Use this question to open up a discussion: "What did you think of the piano recital?"

- A **closed question** leads to a specific response and must be answered with a yes or no: "Did you play a piece by Chopin at your recital?"

- A **factual question** is aimed at getting a particular piece of information and must be answered with facts: "How many years have you been playing the piano?"

Participating in a Group Discussion

In a group discussion, you openly discuss ideas and topics in an informal setting. The group discussions in which you participate will involve, for the most part, your classmates and focus on the subjects you are studying. To get the most out of a group discussion, you need to participate in it.

Use group discussions to express and to listen to ideas in an informal setting.

Communicate Effectively Think about the points you want to make, the order in which you want to make them, the words you will use to express them, and the examples that will support these points before you speak.

Ask Questions Asking questions can help you improve your comprehension of another speaker's ideas. It may also call attention to possible errors in another speaker's points.

Make Relevant Contributions Stay focused on the topic being discussed. Relate comments to your own experience and knowledge, and clearly connect them to your topic. It is important to listen to the points others make so you can build off their ideas. Work to share the connections you see. For example, say whether you agree or disagree, or tell the group how your ideas connect.

Speaking

Giving a presentation or speech before an audience is generally recognized as public speaking. Effective speakers are well prepared and deliver speeches smoothly and with confidence.

Recognizing Different Kinds of Speeches

There are four main kinds of speeches: informative speeches, persuasive speeches, entertaining speeches, and extemporaneous speeches.

Consider the purpose and audience of your speech before deciding what kind of speech you will give.

- Give an **informative speech** to explain an idea, a process, an object, or an event.

- Give a **persuasive speech** to get your listeners to agree with your position or to take some action. Use formal English when speaking.

- Give an **entertaining speech** to offer your listeners something to enjoy or to amuse them. Use both informal and formal language.

- Give an **extemporaneous speech** when an impromptu occasion arises. It is an informal speech because you do not have a prepared manuscript.

Preparing and Presenting a Speech

If you are asked to deliver a speech, begin by choosing a topic that you like or know well. Then, prepare your speech for your audience.

To prepare your speech, research your topic. Make an outline, and use numbered note cards.

Gather Information Use the library and other resources to gather reliable information and to find examples to support your ideas.

Organizing Information Organize your information by writing an outline of main ideas and major details. Then, when you deliver your speech, write the main ideas, major details, quotations, and facts on note cards.

When presenting your speech, use rhetorical forms of language and verbal and nonverbal strategies.

Use Rhetorical Language Repeat key words and phrases to identify your key points. Use active verbs and colorful adjectives to keep your speech interesting. Use parallel phrases to insert a sense of rhythm.

Use Verbal and Nonverbal Strategies Vary the pitch and tone of your voice, and the rate at which you speak. Speak loudly and emphasize key words or phrases. Avoid consistently reading your speech from your notes. Work to maintain eye contact with the audience. As you speak, connect with the audience by using gestures and facial expressions to emphasize key points.

Evaluating a Speech

Evaluating a speech gives you the chance to judge another speaker's skills. It also gives you the opportunity to review and improve your own methods for preparing and presenting a speech.

When you evaluate a speech, you help the speaker and yourself to learn from experience. Listed below are some questions you might ask yourself while evaluating another person's speech or one of your own speeches.

- Did the speaker introduce the topic clearly, develop it well, and conclude it effectively?

- Did the speaker support each main idea with appropriate details?

- Did the speaker approach the platform confidently and establish eye contact with the audience?

- Did the speaker's facial expressions, gestures, and movements appropriately reinforce the words spoken?

- Did the speaker vary the pitch of his or her voice and the rate of his or her speaking?

- Did the speaker enunciate all words clearly?

Listening Critically to a Speech

Hearing happens naturally as sounds reach your ears. Listening, or critical listening, requires that you understand and interpret these sounds.

Critical listening requires preparation, active involvement, and self-evaluation from the listener.

Learning the Listening Process Listening is interactive; the more you involve yourself in the listening process, the more you will understand.

Focus Your Attention Focus your attention on the speaker and block out all distractions—people, noises, and objects. Find out more about the subject that will be discussed beforehand.

Interpret the Information To interpret a speaker's message successfully, you need to identify and understand important information. You might consider listening for repeated words or phrases, pausing momentarily to memorize and/or write key statements, watching non-verbal signals, and combining this new information with what you already know.

Respond to the Speaker's Message Respond to the information you have heard by identifying the larger message of the speech, its most useful points, and your position on the topic.

Note: Page numbers in **boldface** refer to pages where terms are defined; *italicized* page numbers refer to writing applications.

Direct quotation, 582, **593–595**

Discrepancies, 239, 252

Divided quotations, 594–595

Dividing words, 609–610, *611*

Docudrama, 249

Documentaries, 86, 225

Documentary script, 86, *87*

Documentation, 228, 236, 240, 244, 246

Documented essays, 21

Double comparisons, 511, *512, 517*

Double negatives, 520, 521, *523*

Doubt, subjunctive mood to express, 453

Drafting, 35
    analytical essays, 167
    argumentative essays, 182–183, 193
    fiction narratives, 104–105, 115
    interpretative responses, 219
    nonfiction narratives, 76–77, 87
    poetry and description, 141
    research writing, 238–241, 252
    workplace writing, 250, 261, 263, 267

E

Editing, 42–45
    analytical essays, 167
    argumentative essays, 188–189, 193
    fiction narratives, 110–111, 115
    interpretative responses, 219
    media elements, R10
    nonfiction narratives, 82–83, 87
    poetry and description, 141
    research writing, 246–247, 253
    workplace writing, 250, 261, 263, 267

Editorials, 18, 173

Educational courses, titles of, 559

Ellipses, 622–623, *626*

Elliptical clauses
    adverbial, **383,** *387*
    dangling, 413, *414*
    pronouns in, 473, *474*

Elliptical sentence, 339, 581–582

E-mails, 22

Emotional appeals, 175

Emotions, in script adaptations, 218

Emphatic tenses, 423, *424*
    past, 439, 440
    present, 436, 437

End, 76, 80, 104, 105, 108

End marks, 564–567, *568*
    correcting run-ons with, 410
    inside parentheses, 619
    quotation marks with, 594–596
    in sentences, 396, *397*
    See also specific marks

Engaging story, 66, *75, 89,* 92, 103, *117*

Essay, 140–141

Essential phrases or clauses. *See*
    Restrictive phrases or clauses

Event names, 549

Evidence, 194
    in analytical essays, 146, 148, *155,*
    160, *169*
    in argumentative essays, 172, 174,
    180, *181,* 183, *184,* 186, *195, 221*
    in expositions, *195*
    in interpretative response essays,
    206, *207,* 208, *255*
    in proposals, *192*

in research writing, 224, 227, 233,
238–240
in responses to literature, 20

Examples, 16, 186, 210, 240

Exclamation marks, 564, **567,** *568*
    with quotation marks, 594–596
    sentences with, 396, *397*

Exclamatory sentences, 396, *397*
    capitalizing, 544
    in parentheses, 619 punctuating,
    567
    subjects/verbs in, 345, *346*

Experiment journals, 21

Expert opinions
    for analytical essays, 155
    for argumentative essays, 181, 186
    for research writing, 232, 234
    for workplace writing, *265*

Explanatory material, punctuating, 596,
    618

Exposition (expository essays), 15,
    15–17, *195*
    analytical essays, 145–169
    publishing, 47
    summary of a feature article, 166,
    167

Eyewitness accounts, 10

F

Facts
    in analytical essays, 155
    in argumentative essays, 181, 186
    ideas contrary to, 453–454
    in research writing, 240, 251
    in workplace writing, 250, 260–263,
    265, 267, *269*

Family feedback, *245*

parallel structures, 189
punctuation, 247
quotation capitalization, 215

Graphic elements, 129

Graphic organizers, R24–R27
for analytical essays, 153, *154*
for argumentative essays, 179, *180*
for fiction narratives, 101, *102*
for interpretative responses, 205, *206*
for narrative nonfiction, 73, *74*
for narrowing topics, 33
for poetry and description, 127, *128*
for research writing, 231

Graphics, 241, 251, 252, *269*

Graphs, 241

Group discussions, speaking in, R30

Group names, 550, *551*

H

Haiku, 14, 121

Handwriting, 84, 138, 190

Headings, 234, 241

Health reports, 225

Helping verbs, 311
conjugation with, 433
passive voice and, 457
subjunctive mood and, 454, *455*

Historical events, 92

Historical fiction, 11, 92, 94–115
drafting, 104–105
editing, 110–111
prewriting, 100–103
publishing, 112
revising, 106–109
script based on, *113,* 114, *115*

Historical present tense, 437

Historical reports, 225

Hyperbole, 55

Hyphenated words
apostrophes with, 613
capitalizing, 553
dividing, 610

Hyphens, 605, *608, 611*
for clarity, 607
with compound words, 295, 315, 606–607
to divide words, 609–610
at ends of lines, 609
in numbers, 605
with prefixes and suffixes, 606
suspended, **605**

I

Idea notebook, 4

Ideas, 3, 4
contrary to fact, 453–454
for poetry and description, 128, 130
for research writing, 251
as writing trait, 26, 27, 28, 56, 63, 83, 111, 137, 163, 189, 215, 247
See also Controlling idea; Strategies to generate ideas

Idioms, 502

Illustrations, 241

Imagery, 120, 131

Images, in research writing, 252

Imperative mood, 453, *455,* 457

Imperative sentences, 396, *397*
capitalizing, 544
punctuating, 564, 567
subjects/verbs in, 345, *346*

Indefinite articles, 314, *317*

Indefinite pronouns, 304, *305*
as adjectives, **315–316**
antecedent agreement with, 495–496, *497*
apostrophes with, 614
verb agreement with, 488

Independent clauses, 373–374, *376*
adjectival clauses and, 374–375
colon after, 590
commas separating, 569
faulty coordination between, 418–419
joining, 388, 398, 587–589
nonparallel, 416
in types of sentences, 388–389, *391*
See also Main clauses

Independent modifiers, 572

Indicative mood, 453, 454, *455,* 457

Indirect objects, 347, 349, *352–354*
adjectival phrases modifying, 357, *359*
appositive phrases and, 361
compound, 349, *352*
gerund phrases with, 369
gerunds as, 368
infinitive phrases with, 371
noun clauses as, 384, 385
objective pronouns as, 466

Indirect questions, 564, 567

Indirect quotations, 593

Inferences, 234, 251, *265*

Infinitive fragments, 408

Infinitive phrases, 136, 356, **371,** *372*
commas after introductory, 574
dangling, 413, *414*
nonparallel, 416
starting a sentence with, 405

Infinitives, 370–371, *372*
adverbial clauses modifying, 378

Word order, inverted
direct objects in, 348
in direct questions, 472
subjects in, 343–345, *346*
subject-verb agreement in, 486–487, *490*
varying sentences using, 405, *406*
who, whom and, 472

Words, transitional, 161

Workplace writing, 22–23, 256–269, *268–269*
business letters, R14
college application essays, 258–259
cover letters, 257, 260–261
forms of, 257
friendly letters, R15
meeting agendas, R13
note cards, R12
proposals, 262–263
request for letter of recommendation, 266–267
research reports, 264–265

Writer's Eye, *71, 99, 125, 151, 177, 203, 229*

Writer's Response Symbols, 71

Writing, 2–7
See also specific topics

Writing for media, 24, *25*
definition essay, **140,** *141*
movie pitch, 114, *115*
proposal, 192–193
request for letter of recommendation, 266–267
summary of a feature article, 166–167
television interview script, 250, *251–252, 253*
See also New media

Writing process, 26–47
drafting, 35
editing, 42–45
prewriting (planning), 32–34
publishing, 46–47
reasons for using, 31
revising, 36–41
rubrics, 28–29
steps in, 30
writing traits, 26–27

Writing to a Prompt
exposition, *168, 195*
fiction narration, *116*
narrative nonfiction, *88, 117, 143*
persuasion, *194, 221*
poetry, *169*
poetry and description, *142*
research writing, *254–255*
response to literature, *220*
workplace writing, *268–269*

Writing traits, 26–28, 56–59, 63
rubrics based on, 83, 111, 137, 163, 189, 215, 247

Written works, titles of. *See* Titles

Index of Authors and Titles

Acknowledgments

Grateful acknowledgment is made to the following for copyrighted material:

Alfred A. Knopf, Inc., A Division of Random House, Inc.

"The Song of Stones River" by Jennifer Armstrong from *What a Song Can Do: 12 Riffs On the Power of Music.* Copyright © 2004 by Jennifer Armstrong. "The Negro Speaks of Rivers" from *The Collected Poems of Langston Hughes* by Langston Hughes. Copyright © 1994 by the Estate of Langston Hughes. Used by permission of Alfred A. Knopf, a division of Random House, Inc.

National Council of Teachers of English (NCTE)

"Mistakes are a fact of Life: A National Comparative Study" by Andrea A. Lunsford and Karen J. Lunsford translated from *bcs. bedfordstmartins.com/lunsford/PDF/Lunsford_article_Mistakes. pdf.* Copyright © NCTE. Used by permission of National Council of Teachers of English (NCTE).

The New York Times

"Sleep is One Thing Missing in Busy Teenage Lives" by Denise Grady from *The New York Times, Health & Fitness Section, 11/5/02 Issue, Section F, Page 5.* All rights reserved. Used by permission of The New York Times www.nytimes.com and protected by the Copyright Laws of United States. The printing, copying, redistribution, or retransmission of the material without express written permission is prohibited.

Harold Ober Associates Incorporated

"The Negro Speaks of Rivers" from *The Collected Poems of Langston Hughes* by Langston Hughes, copyright © 1994 by The Estate of Langston Hughes. Used by permission of Harold Ober Associates Incorporated.

Oxford University Press, UK

"Introduction" by Bette Bao Lord from The Chinese-American Family Album by Dorothy & Thomas Hoobler, copyright © 1994, 1998 by Oxford University Press, Inc.

University of Oklahoma Press

"The Bailiff's Daughter of Islington" as sung by Mrs. Joan Taylor Wood from *Ballads and Folk Songs of the Southwest,* by Ethel and Chauncey O. Moore. Copyright © University of Oklahoma Press. Used by permission.

Writer's House, LLC

"The Song of Stones River" by Jennifer Armstrong from *What a Song Can Do: 12 Riffs On the Power of Music.* Copyright © 2004 by Jennifer Armstrong.

Note: Every effort has been made to locate the copyright owner of material reproduced in this component. Omissions brought to our attention will be corrected in subsequent editions.

Image Credits

Illustrations
   Dan Hubig

All interior photos provided by Jupiter Images. Except 64: © Pete Saloutos/age fotostock; 90: © GoodShoot/age fotostock; 118: © Corbis/age fotostock; 170: © Hill Street Studios/age fotostock; 196: © Jose Luis Pelaez Inc/age fotostock; 203: Courtesy of The Library of Congress; 226: © NASA.